Securities & Investment Institute Diploma

STUDY BOOK
Financial Derivatives
For examinations up to and including Winter 2007

2007

In this 2007 edition

- A user-friendly format for easy navigation
- Exam tips to put you on the right track
- A Test your knowledge quiz at the end of each chapter
- A full index

APPROVED WORKBOOK

BPP LEARNING MEDIA

Published March 2007

ISBN 9780 7517 4353 1

British Library Cataloguing-in-Publication Data
A catalogue record for this book
is available from the British Library

Published by

BPP Learning Media Ltd
Aldine House, Aldine Place
London W12 8AW

www.bpp.com/learningmedia

Printed in Great Britain by
Ashford Colour Press

Your learning materials, published by BPP Learning Media Ltd, are printed on paper sourced from sustainable, managed forests.

© BPP Learning Media Ltd, 2007

All our rights reserved. No part of this publication may be reproduced, stored in a retrieval system or transmitted, in any form or by any means, electronic, mechanical, photocopying, recording or otherwise, without the prior written permission of BPP Learning Media Ltd. The descriptions, examples and calculations shown in this publication are for educational purposes only. No liability can be accepted by BPP Learning Media Ltd for their use in any circumstances connected with actual trading activity or otherwise. Readers should seek specific advice for specific situations.

Contents

Chapter 1 Introduction to Futures and Options	**Page 1**
Chapter 2 Trading Practice	**Page 23**
Chapter 3 Clearing and Settlement	**Page 37**
Chapter 4 Financial Mathematics	**Page 59**
Chapter 5 Probability	**Page 95**
Chapter 6 Basic Pricing of Futures and Options	**Page 121**
Chapter 7 Strategies	**Page 151**
Chapter 8 Options Pricing – Binomial and Black Scholes	**Page 193**
Chapter 9 Equity Derivatives	**Page 253**
Chapter 10 Bond Derivatives	**Page 275**
Chapter 11 Interest Rate Derivatives	**Page 333**

Chapter 12 Currency Derivatives	**Page 369**
Chapter 13 Swaps	**Page 391**
Chapter 14 Other OTC Derivative Products	**Page 443**
Chapter 15 Hybrid Securities	**Page 473**
Chapter 16 Risk Management	**Page 499**
Chapter 17 The Regulatory Environment	**Page 527**
Index	**Page 569**

1 Introduction to Futures and Options

INTRODUCTION

The purpose of this section is to introduce the basic characteristics of futures and options and how they may be used by speculators and hedgers. We also introduce here the markets in traded futures and options and the OTC market.

Though we will ultimately be looking at a variety of products they all have these basic characteristics and uses in common.

CHAPTER CONTENTS

	Page
1 Overview	2
2 Futures	3
3 Options	10
4 Options on Futures	17
5 Gearing	17
6 Summary of Risk	18
7 Over-the-Counter Products	19
Chapter Roundup	19
Test Your Knowledge	21

1: INTRODUCTION TO FUTURES AND OPTIONS

Chapter Learning Objectives

They syllabus areas covered by this section are

- **General principles of registration, clearing margining, settlement, exercise, assignment and prices.**

   Prices summary

   Constituents and definitions of options/futures prices, including: tick values, strike prices and futures price.

   Settlement

   Premium/margin settlement terms and times.

- **Uses of futures**

   Characteristics of futures

   General
   - Obligation to buy or sell at future date(s), cash settlement and delivery.

   Specific characteristics
   - Notional contracts for bonds
   - Index pricing
   - Gearing (leverage)

- **Uses of options**

   Characteristics of options contracts

   General: right for the holder to buy/sell, contingent obligation for the writer. Exchange traded or over the counter/traditional options, Set Expiration. European/American exercise. Specific delivery standards. Ownership of interest dividends and entitlements. Gearing.

1 Overview

In the minds of the general public, and indeed those of many people involved in the financial services industry, futures and options are thought of as very complicated. They are also thought of as having little to do with the real world. Television coverage showing pictures of young traders in brightly coloured jackets shouting at each other in an apparent frenzy makes it difficult to imagine that what they are engaged in may be of enormous value to the smooth functioning of the economy.

At the heart of futures and options is the concept of deferred delivery. Both instruments allow you, albeit in slightly different ways, to agree **today** the price at which you will buy or sell an asset at sometime in the future. This is unlike normal, everyday transactions. When we go to a supermarket, we pay our money and take immediate delivery of our goods. Why would someone wish to agree today a price for delivery at some time in the future? The answer is **certainty**.

Imagine a farmer growing a crop of wheat. To grow such a crop costs money – money for seed, labour, fertiliser, etc. All this expenditure takes place with no certainty that when the crop is eventually harvested, the price at which the wheat is sold will cover these costs. This is obviously risky and many farmers will be unwilling to take on this burden. How can this uncertainty be avoided?

By using futures or options, the farmer will be able to agree **today** a price at which the crop will ultimately be sold, in maybe four or six months' time. This enables the farmer to achieve a minimum sale price for his crop. He is no longer subject to fluctuations in wheat prices. He knows what price his wheat will bring and can therefore plan his business accordingly.

From their origins in the agricultural world, futures and options have become available on a wide range of other assets, from metals and crude oil, to bonds and equities. To understand futures and options properly requires considerable application. There is much terminology to master, and many definitions to be understood, but essentially, they are really quite simple. They are products that allow you to fix today the price at which assets may be bought or sold at a future date.

In this chapter, futures and options are discussed separately. Let us start with futures.

2 FUTURES

2.1 Definition of a future

'A future is an agreement to buy or sell a standard quantity of a specified asset on a fixed future date at a price agreed today.'

There are two parties to a futures contract, a buyer and a seller.

- The buyer of a future enters into an **obligation** to buy on a specified date.
- The seller of a future is under an **obligation** to sell on a future date.

These obligations relate to a 'standard quantity' of a 'specified' asset on a 'fixed future date' at a 'price agreed today'.

2.1.1 Standard quantity

Exchange-traded futures are traded in standardised parcels known as **contracts**.

For example, a futures contract on lead might be for 25 tonnes of the metal, or a currency future might be for 125,000 Swiss francs. The purpose of this standardisation is so that buyers and sellers are clear about the quantity that will be delivered. If you sold one lead future, you would know that you were obligated to sell 25 tonnes of lead.

Futures are only traded in whole numbers of contracts. So, if you wished to buy 50 tonnes of lead, you would buy two lead futures.

2.1.2 Specified asset

Imagine that you entered into a futures contract on a car. Let us say you buy one car futures contract that gives you the obligation to buy a car at a fixed price of £15,000, with delivery taking place in December.

It is obvious that something very important is missing from the contract, namely any detail about what type of car you are to buy. Most of us would be happy to pay £15,000 for a Porsche, but rather less happy if all our £15,000 bought was a Reliant Robin.

All futures contracts are governed by their contract specifications, and these legal documents set out in great detail the size of each contract, when delivery is to take place, and what exactly is to be delivered. It is not enough to know that a lead futures contract is for 25 tonnes of the metal. Users will want to know what purity and shape of metal they are dealing in.

2.1.3 Fixed futures date

The delivery of futures contracts takes place on a specified date(s) known as **Delivery Day(s)**. This is when buyers exchange money for goods with sellers. Futures have finite lifespans so that once the **last trading day** is past, it is impossible to trade the futures for that date.

At any one time, a range of delivery months may be traded and as one delivery day passes, a new date is introduced.

2.1.4 Price agreed today

The final phrase in the definition is the most important of all. The reason why so many people – from farmers to fund managers – like using futures is that they introduce certainty.

Imagine a farmer growing a crop of wheat. In the absence of a futures market, he has no idea whether he will make a profit or loss when he plants the seeds in the ground. By the time he harvests his crop, the price of wheat may be so low that he will not be able to cover his costs. However, with a futures contract, he can fix a price for his wheat many months before harvest. If he sells a wheat future six months before the harvest, he enters into an obligation to sell wheat at that price on the stipulated delivery day. In other words, he knows what price his goods will fetch.

You might think that this is all well and good, but what happens if there is a drought or a frost that makes it impossible for the farmer to deliver his wheat?

Futures are tradable so, although the contract obligates the buyer to buy and the seller to sell, these obligations can be **offset** by undertaking an equal and opposite trade in the market.

For example, let us suppose a farmer has sold one September wheat future at £120 per tonne. If, subsequently, the farmer decides he does not wish to sell his wheat, but would prefer to use the grain to feed his cattle, he simply buys one September future at the then prevailing price. His original sold position is now offset by a bought position, leaving him with no outstanding delivery obligations.

This offsetting is common in future markets; very few contracts run through to delivery.

2.2 Other futures terms

A **tick** is the smallest permitted price movement in a futures contract and is found in a legal document known as the contract specification.

For the wheat future traded on Euronext.liffe, the tick is 5 pence per metric tonne. If the current quote were £120.00, the quote must change by at least 5 pence to £120.05 or £119.95. It could not change to £120.01, as this would be a movement of less than a tick. The reason for exchanges limiting the minimum amount by which prices may change is purely administrative – it avoids potentially huge numbers of trading prices.

Following on from tick size is the concept of **tick value**. Since each futures contract has a fixed size (for wheat this is 100 tonnes), the smallest price movement can be given a monetary value. In the case of the wheat future, this is 100 × 5p or £5.

Each tick will mean a difference of £5 in the cost of buying or selling 100 tonnes of wheat. By knowing the tick size and tick value, it becomes easy to calculate the resultant profits and losses from futures trades as we will see in the next section on futures usage.

2.3 Using futures

All sorts of people use futures. Some, like the wheat farmer, may use them to reduce risk. Others, to seek high returns, for which they are willing to take high risks. Futures markets are, in fact, wholesale markets in risk – markets in which risks are transferred from the cautious to those with more adventurous (or reckless) spirits. The users of futures fall into one of three categories; the **hedger**, the **speculator** and the **arbitrageur**.

1: INTRODUCTION TO FUTURES AND OPTIONS

- The hedger is someone seeking to reduce risk.
- The speculator is a risk-taker seeking large profits.
- The arbitrageur seeks riskless profits from exploiting market inefficiencies.

In this section, we will look at the first two types of user, starting with the speculator.

2.3.1 The speculator – Buying a future

Introduction

A transaction in which a future is purchased to open a position is known as a long futures position. The purchase of an oil future would be described as going **long the future** or simply **long**.

The purpose of undertaking such a transaction is to open the investor to the risks and rewards of ownership of the underlying asset by an alternative route.

Let us imagine a speculator thinks that the situation in the Middle East is becoming more dangerous and that war is imminent. If war takes place, he would expect oil supplies to become restricted and the price of oil to rise.

He therefore buys one July oil future at $20.50 per barrel. The cash price of oil is $19.00.

The contract size is 1,000 barrels, the tick size 1 cent. The tick value is $10, i.e. 1,000 × $0.01.

May 1 – Action: Buy one July oil future at $20.50

Regrettably, the speculator's fears prove correct and the Middle East goes to war with oil prices rising accordingly. The cash price (that is, the price of oil for immediate delivery) rises to $29.

May 21 – Action: Sell one July oil future at $30

To calculate the profit from this trade, we must first find out how many ticks the contract has moved, then multiply this by the tick value and further multiply it by the number of contracts involved.

Formula to learn

> Profit/loss = Ticks × Tick value × Contracts

How many ticks?

The contract has moved from $20.50 to $30. This is $9.50 or 950 ticks (a tick, remember, is one cent).

The tick value, we are told, is $10.

The number of contracts is one.

Therefore

Ticks × Tick value × Contracts
950 × $10 × 1
= $9,500 profit

The reason the speculator has made a profit is that the futures market has risen in response to a rise in the cash market price of oil. Generally, futures prices can be expected to move at the same rate and to the same extent as cash market prices. This is a far from trivial observation. The cash market and the futures market in this example have both risen. The cash market from $19 to $35 – an increase of $16 per barrel; and the futures market from $20.50 to $30.00 – a rise of $9.50. The reasons why the movement has not been the same in both markets are explained later in this workbook, but for the moment, remember that the futures and cash markets, whilst related, are separate markets each subject to their own supply and demand pressures.

1: INTRODUCTION TO FUTURES AND OPTIONS

In the oil example above, the speculator bought a futures contract in anticipation of a rise in oil prices. A transaction in which a future is purchased to open a position is known as a **long position**. Thus, the purchase of the oil future would be described as 'going long of the future' or simply **long**.

Conversely, when a future is sold to open a position, this is described as 'going short' or simply, **short**.

Before going on to consider a short futures position, let us summarise the risk of being long a future.

Summary of long futures position

Risk	Almost unlimited. The maximum loss would occur if the future fell to zero. For our oil speculator, this would be if the July future fell from $20.50 to $0, i.e. a loss of $20.50.
Reward	Unlimited. As the futures price could rise to infinity, the profit is potentially unlimited.

2.3.2 The speculator – Selling a future

Introduction

A transaction in which a future is sold to open a position is known as a short futures position. The sale of an oil future would be described as **going short the future** or simply **short**.

The purpose of shorting a future is to open the investor to the opposite risks and rewards to those of the ownership of the asset i.e. gain if the asset price falls.

Let us take another example. If a speculator thinks that an asset price will fall, he will seek to make a profit by selling the future at the currently high price and subsequently buying it back at a low price. This is not an activity commonly undertaken in the cash markets and therefore needs a little explanation.

There are two ways of making profits. The first is to buy at a low price and sell at a high price. For example, we may buy a house at £80,000 and sell it at £100,000, making a £20,000 profit. In futures markets, it is equally possible to sell something at a high price and buy it back at a low price. If you thought the property market was going to fall, you could sell a house at £100,000 and buy it back at £80,000, realising a £20,000 profit. In the actual property market, it is not easy to go 'short' of a house. But in the futures market, in which deliveries are at some future date, it is straightforward.

Let us imagine that a speculator feels that the oil market is becoming oversupplied and that oil prices will fall.

July 1 – Action: Sell one September oil future at $22

July 14 – Action: Buy one September oil future at $20

By July 14, the future price has fallen and the speculator 'buys back' his short futures position, thus extinguishing any delivery obligations. The profit can be calculated by again multiplying

$$\text{Tick movement} = \frac{22.00 - 20.00}{0.01^*} = 200$$

Ticks × Tick value × Contracts
200 × $10 × 1
= $2,000 profit

*1 cent or 1/100 of a dollar is the tick size.

Let us summarise the risk of being short the future.

Summary of short futures position

Risk	Unlimited.
Reward	Limited, but large. The future can only fall to zero, giving in this example a maximum gain of $22 per barrel.

2.3.3 The hedger – Protecting against a fall

Speculators use futures to take on risks in the hope of large profits. Hedgers use futures to reduce the risk of existing cash market positions. They are motivated by a need for certainty and security.

Let us think about the position of an oil producer. The producer's profitability will be determined largely by the price of crude oil. When times are good, and demand for oil is high, he will make good profits. However, if oil prices fall, he may find that the market price for oil is so low that the price does not cover the costs of extracting the oil from the ground. It is in helping such people that futures have their most important application.

The following graph shows the oil producer's exposure to the price of oil.

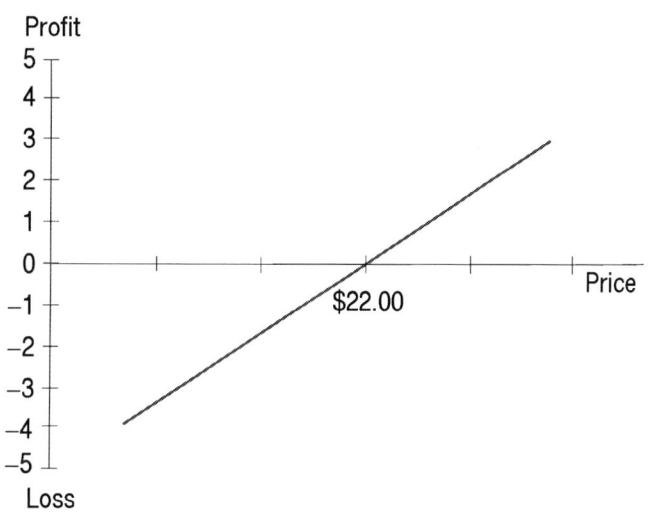

This shows that if prices go up, so do profits. If the price falls below a certain level, losses will emerge. This position is described as a **long position**.

How can the risk of losses from a fall in price be reduced?

This can be done by selling futures and thereby entering into a contract that will obligate the futures seller to deliver oil at some time in the future at a price agreed today. Through this mechanism, the oil producer can establish a sale price for his, say, July production of oil some time in advance, without having to wait until July, when the price may be much lower. When futures are sold to hedge a long cash market position, it is known as a **short hedge**.

The theory of futures hedging is based on the future's position producing profits or losses to offset the profits or losses in the cash market.

For example, an oil producer will have 100,000 barrels of crude oil available for delivery in July. He is nervous about the price of oil and expects it to fall sharply. On 1 May, the cash market price of oil is $22 a barrel, and the July future is trading at $23.

May 1 – Action: Sell 100* July oil futures at $23

The oil producer is now long in the physical market (that is, he has 100,000 barrels for July delivery). He is also short 100,000 barrels in the futures market.

By the middle of June, the oil price has fallen to $18 a barrel and the July future has fallen to $19 a barrel. The oil producer has managed to find a buyer for his July production at $18 and therefore buys back his futures contracts at $19.

* 100 because each contract represents 1,000 barrels, and the producer is hedging 100,000 barrels.

June 15 – Action: Buy 100 July oil futures at $19

The profit from the futures trade should, if we have constructed the hedge properly, compensate the producer for the fall in oil prices. Let us see if this is true by first calculating the futures profit and then calculating the oil market loss.

Futures profit

Ticks × Tick value × Contracts

$$\frac{23.00 - 19.00}{0.01} \times \$10 \times 100$$

= $400,000 profit

Cash market loss

18.00 − 22.00 × 100,000
= $400,000 loss

As can be seen, the profit and loss net each other out, demonstrating that the fall in oil prices did not hurt the producer.

Graphically, this can be shown as

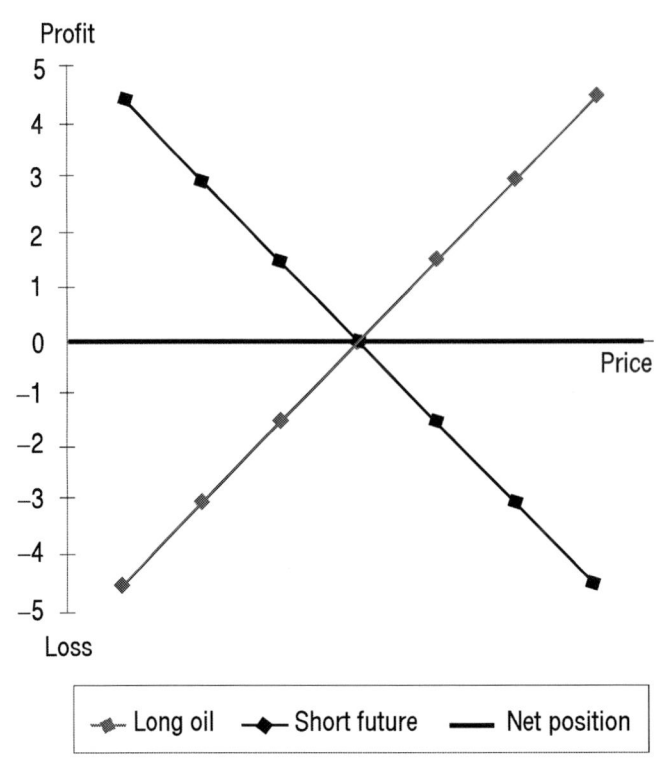

[Graph: Profit/Loss vs Price showing Long oil (upward line), Short future (downward line), and Net position (horizontal line at 0)]

Legend: Long oil — Short future — Net position

Whether the price of oil goes up or down, the producer need not worry since, by selling futures, he is 'locked in' a sale price for his oil.

The numbers in this example are slightly unrealistic. They assume a perfect offset between cash and futures markets. In the real world, however, futures do not always move precisely in line with the cash market. This point will be more fully examined in later chapters.

In the above example, we have seen how futures can be used to protect the oil producer against a price fall with a short hedge.

Short Hedge: Protects Against Price Fall

2.3.4 The hedger – Protecting against a rise

Let us now look at another type of futures hedge that can be used to protect against a price rise, a long hedge.

Imagine a chemical company, whose principal raw material is crude oil, is becoming nervous about a rise in oil prices.

The current cash price of crude oil is $18.00 and the November future trades at $18.50 per barrel.

To protect itself against the possibility of a rise, the company could agree today the price it will pay for oil to be delivered in November. To guarantee the purchase price, all the company need do is buy (or go long in) the futures contract.

September 20 – Action: Buy 10* November oil futures at $18.50

As feared, the price of oil rises steeply so that by 10 October, the cash price of oil has risen to $24.00 and the November future has also risen to $24.50.

* To hedge its requirement for 10,000 barrels.

October 10 – Action: Sell 10 November oil futures at $24.50

Has the hedge worked? To find out, let us see how the price rise would have affected the cost of purchasing the physical oil.

Cash price on 10 October	= $24.00
Cash price on 20 September	= $18.00
Difference	= $ 6.00

For the quantity required by the chemical manufacturer (10,000 barrels), this movement would have increased its costs by $60,000 ($6 × 10,000).

This increased cost should, in whole or in part, be offset by the futures profit.

Futures profit

$$\frac{24.50 - 18.50}{0.01} \times \$10 \times 10$$

= $60,000 profit

Thus, whilst the physical oil will now cost more to acquire, the cost of purchase will in fact be reduced by the futures profit.

		$
Cash price of 10,000 barrels of oil 10 October	=	240,000
Less futures profit	=	(60,000)
Effective cost	=	180,000

or $18 per barrel

1: INTRODUCTION TO FUTURES AND OPTIONS

This is an example of a long hedge that protects against a rise.

Long Hedge: Protects Against a Rise

3 OPTIONS

3.1 Definition

> 'An option is a contract that confers the right, but not the obligation, to buy or sell an asset at a given price on or before a given date.'

This lengthy sentence needs to be understood before moving on. One of the best methods of gaining such an understanding is to contemplate the way in which a speculator hoping for a rise in the price of, say, cocoa, would use the instrument.

Conventionally, a speculator anticipating a rise in the price of cocoa would straightforwardly buy cocoa for immediate delivery and then store the goods, hoping to sell them for a profit once the price rose. If we imagine that the price of cocoa is £600 per tonne and that the speculator buys just one tonne, then the expenditure would be

Cost × Quantity
= £600 × 1
= £600

Another way of representing the hope of a rise in cocoa prices would be to buy a cocoa option – specifically, an option that would give the right, but not the obligation, to buy cocoa at a price of £600 per tonne for a period of three months. The purchase of this option would cost, say, £5 a tonne. Remember that an option is a contract for a future delivery, so it would not be necessary to pay £600 in the first instance – the only money to be invested at this point is the £5. If an option on one tonne of cocoa was bought, it would cost

Cost × Quantity
= £5 × 1
= £5.00

One advantage is immediately apparent. Options are cheaper than purchasing the underlying asset.

3.1.1 Three Months Later...

As expected, the price of cocoa has risen from £600 to £700 per tonne.

This is good news for both the conventional cocoa buyer and the cocoa options buyer.

First, let us look at the position of the speculator who bought physical cocoa.

Purchase price	£600
Sale price	£700
Profit	£100

On an investment of £600, the investor has made a profit of £100 in just three months.

Let us now look at the profit for the options buyer. Three months ago, he entered into a contract that gave him the right, but not the obligation, to buy cocoa at £600. When purchased, that right cost just £5 per tonne. With cocoa now trading at £700, the right to buy at £600 must be worth at least £100 – the difference between the current price and the stated price in the contract.

This point needs some further explanation. Imagine that, given a market price of £700, the option to buy at £600 costs just £40. Any sensible investor would take up his right to buy at £600 and then immediately sell cocoa in the market at £700. The profit and loss calculation would look like this

Buy option	£40
Buy cocoa	£600
Total cost	£640
Sell cocoa at market price	£700

The investor would have spent £640 and received £700 for no risk. Markets rarely, if ever, give money away without requiring people to take some risk. In an efficient market, the right to buy at £600 with a market price of £700, must be worth £100.

Returning to our original options transaction, you will remember that the right to buy at £600 was purchased for £5. With the market price at £700 at the end of the option's life, the option will now be worth £100.

Purchase price	£5
Current value	£100
Unrealised profit	£95

On an investment of £5, a £95 profit has been achieved. In percentage terms, this profit is spectacularly greater than on the conventional purchase and sale of physical cocoa.

One important thing to note is that options are tradable instruments. It is not necessary for the underlying asset to be bought or sold. What more commonly occurs is that **options** are bought and sold. Thus, an option bought at £5 could be sold to the market at £100, realising a £95 profit with the investor never having any intention of buying the underlying asset.

At this stage, it is necessary to introduce some of the vocabulary used in the options market.

3.2 Terminology

In the definition of an option given earlier, an option was described as being the right, but not the obligation, to **buy** or **sell**. The right to buy and the right to sell are given different names.

- The right to buy is known as a **call option**.

- The right to sell is known as a **put option**.

- The rights to buy (call) or sell (put) are held by the person buying the option, who is known as the **holder**.

- The person selling an option is known as a **writer**.

It is important to understand the relationship between holders and writers. The following diagram shows this.

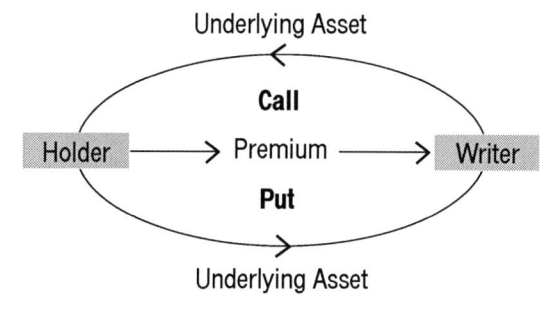

The first thing to understand is the flow of **premium**. Premium is the cost of an option. In our cocoa example, the premium was £5 and this is paid by the holder and received by the writer.

In return for receiving premium, the writer agrees to fulfil the terms of the contract, which are, of course, different for calls and puts.

Call writers agree to deliver the asset underlying the contract if 'called' upon to do so. When options holders wish to take up their rights under the contract, they are said to **exercise** the contract. For a call, this means that the writer must deliver the underlying asset for which he will receive the fixed amount of cash stipulated in the original contract.

Therefore, for a cocoa call option that gives the holder the right, but not the obligation, to buy at £600. This would mean that the writer would be required to deliver cocoa to the holder at £600. The option's holder will only want to buy at £600 when it would be advantageous for him to do so, i.e. only when the real or market price is somewhat higher than £600. If the market price were less than £600, there would be no sense in paying more than the market price for the goods.

Call options writers run very considerable risks. In return for receiving the option's premium, they are committed to delivering the underlying asset at a fixed price. As the price of the asset could rise infinitely in theory, they could be forced to buy the underlying asset at a high price and then deliver it to the option's holder at a much lower value. The price at which an options contract gives the right to buy (call) or sell (put) is known as the **exercise price** or **strike price**.

The dangers for put options writers are also substantial. The writer of a put is obligated to pay the exercise price for assets that are delivered to him. Put options are only exercised when it is advantageous for the holders to do so. This will be when they can use the option to sell their assets at a higher price than would be otherwise available in the market.

To summarise, in return for receiving premium, options writers run very large risks. This is similar to the role undertaken by insurance companies. For a relatively modest premium, they are willing to insure your house against fire. However, if your house burns down, they will be faced with a claim for many thousands of pounds. The reason why insurers and options writers enter into such contracts is that houses don't often burn down, and markets don't often rise or fall substantially. If writers price options properly, they hope to make money in most instances. Options writing is not for the faint-hearted, nor for those without substantial resources. That said, many conservative users do write options as part of strategies involving the holding of the underlying asset. Such uses that are **covered** are much less risky and are discussed later.

When investors buy or hold options, the risk is limited to the option's premium. If the market moves against them, they can simply decide not to exercise their options and sacrifice the premium. Remember, options holders have the right, **but not the obligation**, to buy (call) or sell (put). If it does not make sense to buy or sell at the exercise price, the holder can decide to **abandon** the option.

3.3 Describing options

So far, we have learnt so far that options come in two forms: calls and puts.

We have also learnt that the price paid for an option is known as the premium and that the price at which the option gives the right to buy or sell is known as the exercise price or strike price.

Another way in which options are described relates to their maturity. Options are instruments with limited life spans. The date on which an option comes to the end of its life is known as its **expiry date**. The expiry date is the last day on which the option may be exercised or traded. After this date, the option disappears and cannot be traded or exercised.

Options are available with different **exercise styles**, which are specified when the options are traded. They may be

- **American style options**, which can be exercised by the holder at any time after the option has been purchased.
- **European style options** can only be exercised on their expiry date.

1: INTRODUCTION TO FUTURES AND OPTIONS

There are many variations on the basic options described so far. These are commonly called exotics and are described in Chapter 14, Other OTC Derivative Products.

A person describing an option will specify its

- Underlying asset (e.g. cocoa)
- Expiry date (e.g. May)
- Exercise price (e.g. 600)
- Call/Put (e.g. call)

Below is laid out a display of call options prices on the shares of a fictitious company, XYZ plc. The options give an entitlement to buy (call) the company's shares. The underlying price is 76.

XYZ calls

Exercise Price	January Premium	April Premium	July Premium
60	23	28	33
70	12	18	23
80	5	8	12

You will notice that there are a range of exercise prices and expiry dates available. Normally, you would expect there to be exercise prices available both below and above the underlying price. As the underlying price fluctuates, new exercise prices are introduced.

There is also a range of expiry dates available – this allows investors a choice as to the maturity of their options. As one expiry date passes, a new expiry date is introduced, thus maintaining the choice of dates.

A similar range of exercise prices and expiry dates would be available in XYZ puts. The premiums quoted for calls and puts would, however, be different.

3.4 How much would you pay?

In our table, the premium quoted for the April 60 call is 28. To find out how much the actual money amount would be, we must know two things. Firstly, how the product is quoted and secondly, the contract size.

Options are traded on a wide variety of assets from currencies, bonds and shares to metals, oils and commodities. Each market has different conventions. For example, crude oil prices are normally quoted in US dollars per barrel, whilst share prices for UK companies are quoted in pence per share. Governing the operation of options contracts are contract specifications that set out, amongst other things, rules specifying how they are quoted, expiry dates and when exercise prices are introduced. These documents are important because they enable everyone to understand the details of the contract. Exchange-traded options, like futures contracts, are 'standardised', with the method of quotation and contract size being fixed. The only variable is the option's premium.

So, what does a quote of 28 for the April 60 call mean?

From the contract specification, we find out that the premium is quoted in pence per share. Thus, '28' means 28 pence per XYZ share.

To determine how much the option costs, we must consult the contract specification again to find out the contract size. This is given as 1,000 shares per contract.

1: INTRODUCTION TO FUTURES AND OPTIONS

All options, like futures, are traded in standardised lots or contracts. It is only possible to trade in whole numbers of contracts. You could not, for example, buy one and a half April 60 calls.

We know that the quote for XYZ options is in pence per share and that the contract size is 1,000 shares. Therefore, one XYZ April 60 call would cost

28p × 1,000 = 28,000 pence

or

£280.00

3.5 The simple uses of options

This section covers four basic strategies and uses of options.

The common perception of options is that they are invariably high risk investments. This is not the case. Some positions may be high risk, whilst others may be considerably less risky than a holding in the underlying asset. It is vital that everyone involved in trading, administering or settling options understands the differences between high and low risk strategies.

3.5.1 Buying a call

Buying a call is motivated by a view that an asset's price will rise.

Risk	The investor's risks are limited to the premium he pays for the options. So, if the 80 call could be bought for a premium of 5, the 5 is all he risks. The premium of the call option will only be a fraction of the cost of the underlying asset, so the option can be considered less risky than buying the asset itself.
	Whilst this is true, remember that the whole premium is at risk and it is easy to lose 100% of your investment, albeit a relatively small amount of money.
Reward	The rewards from buying a call are unlimited. As the contract gives the holder the right to buy at a fixed price, this right will become increasingly valuable as the asset price rises above the exercise price.

Imagine an investor who buys one XYZ call option, which gives him the right, but not the obligation, to buy the XYZ asset at a fixed price of 80 between now and the option's expiry date in January. The cost of this option is 5.

If the asset price rises to 120, the right to buy at 80, i.e. the premium of the 80 call, must now be worth at least 40. The net profit for the call would be 40 − 5 (the original cost of the option) = 35. Of course, if the price of XYZ falls below 80 at the option's expiry date, the 80 call will be worthless and 100% of the initial 5 invested will be lost. This loss occurs because no sensible person would want the right to buy at 80 if they could buy the asset more cheaply elsewhere.

By using graphs, we can show how much an option will be worth at expiry.

On the vertical axis of the graph is profit/loss and on the horizontal axis is the asset price.

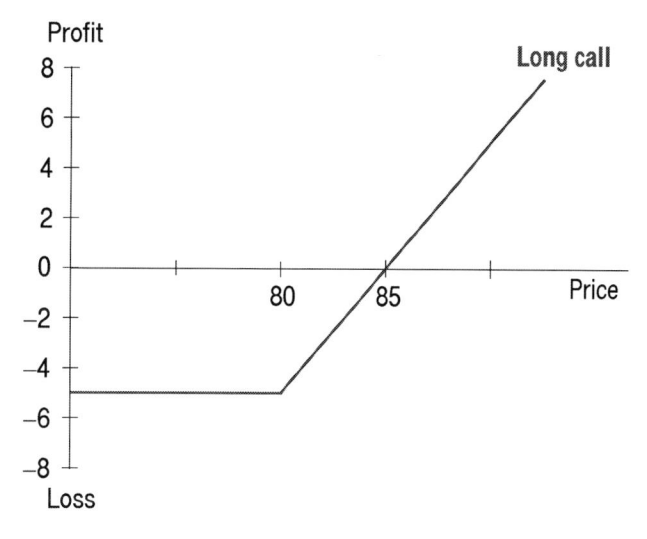

1: INTRODUCTION TO FUTURES AND OPTIONS

Holder of one XYZ January 80 call – Premium 5

What the graph shows is that losses of 5 are made anywhere below 80, whilst profits emerge above 85. 85 represents the **breakeven** point. This is the point at which the original investment is recouped and it is calculated by simply adding the premium to the exercise price, e.g. 80 + 5 = 85. The buying of a call to open a position is known as a 'long call'.

3.5.2 Selling a call

Risk	Selling a call, or writing a call, without being in possession of the underlying asset at the same time is extremely risky. The risk is unlimited because the writer has a duty to deliver the asset at a fixed price regardless of the prevailing asset price. As the share price could, in theory, rise to infinity, the call writer assumes an unlimited risk. This strategy is sometimes called **naked** call writing and as it suggests, can leave you feeling very exposed.
Reward	You might ask why someone would assume such an unlimited risk. The answer, of course, is the hope of a profit. The maximum profit the writer can make is the premium he receives. Let us look again at an 80 call with a premium of 5. The seller of this call will receive the 5 premium, and as long as the asset price at expiry is less than 80, no-one will rationally want to exercise the right to buy. The graph for selling a call is set out below. You will see that it is the equal and opposite of buying a call.

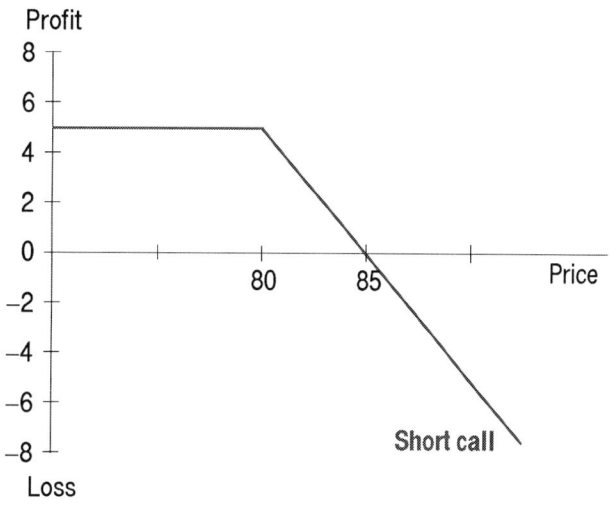

Writer of one XYZ January 80 call – Premium 5

As the graph demonstrates, the call writer believes that the asset price is likely to either stay the same or fall. If this happens, the writer simply pockets the premium received and will not have to deliver the asset. The selling of a call to open a position is known as a 'short call'.

3.5.3 Buying a put

Risk	As when buying a call, the risk of buying a put is limited to the premium paid. The motivation behind buying a put will be to profit from a fall in the asset's price. The holder of a put obtains the right, but not the obligation, to sell at a fixed price. The value of this right will become increasingly valuable as the asset price falls.
Reward	The greatest profit that will arise from buying a put will be achieved if the asset price falls to zero.

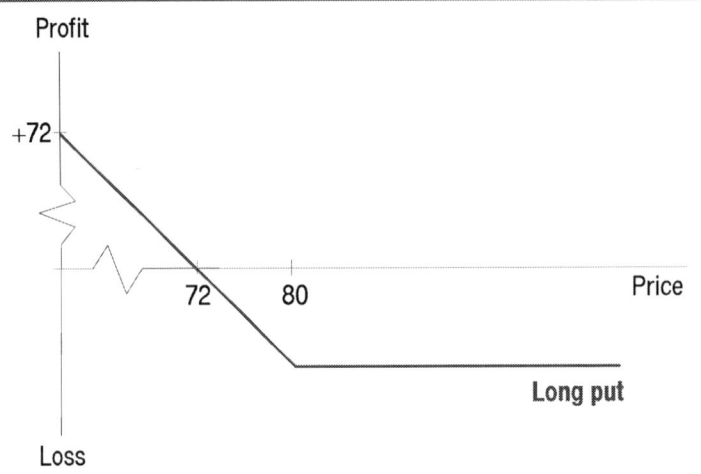

Holder of one XYZ July 80 put – Premium 8

The breakeven point, and maximum profit, is calculated by deducting the premium from the exercise price, e.g. 80 – 8 = 72. Like the purchase of a call, the premium needs to be recovered before profits are made. The buying of a put to open a position is known as a 'long put'.

3.5.4 Selling a put

Risk	Selling or writing a put is dangerous, as the writer enters into an obligation to purchase an asset at a fixed price. If the market price of that asset falls, the put writer will end up paying a large amount of money for what could be a valueless asset. The worst case will arise when the asset price falls to zero. If this happens, the loss will be the exercise price less the premium received.
Reward	What the put option writer hopes for is that the put will not be exercised. This will occur if the asset has a price above the exercise price at expiry. The maximum reward is the premium received. The selling of a put to open a position is known as a 'short put'.

Profit

Short put

72   80   *Price*

−72

Loss

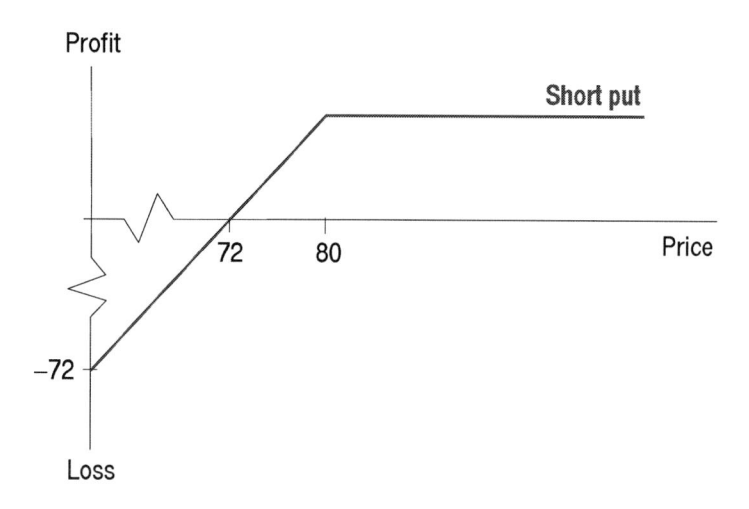

Writer of one XYZ July 80 put – Premium 8

The four basic strategies outlined above form the building blocks of all the more complicated option techniques. You should reread the material so that you are clear about three things.

- What is the motivation behind each trade?
- What are the risks associated with them?
- What are the rewards?

4 OPTIONS ON FUTURES

The options so far discussed have been options which, upon exercise, result in the purchase or sale of a tangible underlying security such as a share.

More common than these types of options are options on futures. This apparently complex term merely describes options which result in a long or short futures position when exercised.

Thus, the exercise of a **long call** results in the holder establishing a **long futures** position.

The exercise of a **long put** results in the holder establishing a **short futures** position.

Clearly, the attributes of futures products and tangible assets are quite different. Two characteristics are worth highlighting – gearing and risk.

5 GEARING

One of the most attractive, but also dangerous attributes of futures and options, is that they can be used in a geared (or leveraged) way.

Gearing describes the power of such products to control, for a low or nil cost, a much more expensive asset. This has the effect of magnifying profits and losses.

To demonstrate how options gearing works, let us look at an example using options.

Example

An investor buys one XYZ January 70 call for 12.

The XYZ share price is 76.

XYZ's share price at expiry is 100 and the call is worth 30. From an investment of 12, a profit of 18 is made. In percentage terms, this is

$$\frac{\text{Profit}}{\text{Initial investment}} = \frac{18}{12} \times 100$$

= 150% profit

If the XYZ share had been bought at 76 and subsequently sold at 100, the figure would be

$$\frac{\text{Profit}}{\text{Initial investment}} = \frac{24}{76} \times 100$$

= 31.6% profit

As can be seen, the profit from the options trade is very much larger. However, if we imagine a fall in the shares to 70 at expiry, we will see that gearing works both ways.

Buy call	12	
Call at expiry	0	
Loss	12	or 100%

If instead the stock had been bought at 76 and subsequently sold at 70 for a loss of 6, the percentage loss would be

$$\frac{6}{76} \times 100 = 7.9\% \text{ Loss}$$

Gearing should therefore be treated with great respect and only investors who understand this attribute should speculate with futures and options. It is very easy to lose your entire investment, or worse.

6 SUMMARY OF RISK

Set out below is a table that summarises the risks and rewards from the basic speculative futures and options positions described in this chapter.

Position	Risk	Reward
Long Call	Limited to Premium	Unlimited
Long Put	Limited to Premium	Limited, but large*
Short Call	Unlimited	Limited
Short Put	Limited, but large *	Limited
Long Future	Limited, but large**	Unlimited
Short Future	Unlimited	Limited, but large**

*   Asset cannot fall below zero
**   Future cannot fall below zero

7 OVER-THE-COUNTER PRODUCTS

The focus of the examination is on exchange-traded futures and options. However, it is important to recognise that other types of derivative products are traded off exchange.

Derivative products such as forwards and swaps, as well as exotic options, are traded on the Over-the-Counter (OTC) market. This is not a formal market centred on an exchange, but rather a telephone and screen-based market with no administrative centre. Contracts are made on a bilateral basis with the terms negotiated separately for each transaction.

The table set out below seeks to summarise the differences between the OTC and exchange-traded market. Some of the terms used will be explained in greater depth in subsequent chapters.

7.1 Comparison of exchange-traded and OTC products

	Exchange-Traded	OTC
Quantity	The quantity covered by each contract is determined by the exchange. Only whole contracts may be traded.	Can be tailored to meet the need of the investor exactly.
Quality	Defined by the contract specification.	Can be varied according to need.
Delivery/Expiry Dates	Only allowed on dates fixed by the exchange.	Can be tailored to meet the customer's needs.
Liquidity	Generally good, but dependent upon the product.	May be limited; market may be made by just one firm.
Counter-Party Risk	No counterparty risk to the clearing member once contract registered.	Risk exists of default, credit rating of counterparty is very important.
Margin	Margin will normally be required.	Normally, no margin.
Regulation	Subject to significant regulation as RIEs/DIEs.	Less actively regulated. May not be suitable for certain categories of customer.

CHAPTER ROUNDUP

- You need to be familiar with the
  - Definition of a future or option
  - The characteristics and terminology of futures and options
  - The use of futures by speculators and hedges
  - The use of options by speculators

TEST YOUR KNOWLEDGE

Check your knowledge of the Chapter here, without referring back to the text.

1. Define a future and an option.

2. What are the risks and rewards of a long future position and of a short futures position.

3. Describe the two main exercise styles for options.

4. What are the risks and rewards of selling a put.

1: INTRODUCTION TO FUTURES AND OPTIONS

TEST YOUR KNOWLEDGE: ANSWERS

1. A future is an agreement to buy or sell a standard quantity of a specified asset on a fixed future date at a price agreed today.

    An option is a contract that confers the right, but not the obligation, to buy or sell an asset at a given price on or before a given date.'

2. Summary of long futures position

Risk	Almost unlimited. The maximum loss would occur if the future fell to zero.
Reward	Unlimited. As the futures price could rise to infinity, the profit is potentially unlimited.

    Summary of short futures position

Risk	Unlimited.
Reward	Limited, but large. The future can only fall to zero.

3. - **American style options**, which can be exercised by the holder at any time after the option has been purchased.
   - **European style options** can only be exercised on their expiry date.

4.
Risk	Selling a put is dangerous, as the writer enters into an obligation to purchase an asset at a fixed price. If the market price of that asset falls, the put writer will end up paying a large amount of money for what could be a valueless asset. The worst case will arise when the asset price falls to zero. If this happens, the loss will be the exercise price less the premium received.
Reward	What the put option writer hopes for is that the put will not be exercised. This will occur if the asset has a price above the exercise price at expiry. The maximum reward is the premium received. The selling of a put to open a position is known as a 'short put'.

2 Trading Practice

INTRODUCTION

If we wish to trade in a particular tradable security we need to know the market that it is traded on, the rules and regulations of that market, any membership requirements and how to undertake trades. These are all examined in this section.

CHAPTER CONTENTS

		Page
1	Overview	24
2	Euronext.liffe Membership and Trading Rules	24
3	FSA Guidance	25
4	Trading Rules	28
5	Client Order	28
6	Other Trading Issues	30
	Chapter Roundup	33
	Test Your Knowledge	35

2: TRADING PRACTICE

CHAPTER LEARNING OBJECTIVES

The syllabus areas covered by this section are

- **Exchange regulations, dealing practice, customer accounts and legislation**

  Exchange structure

  Requirements for membership of various markets and exchanges. Ownership of the Exchange, management and committee structures. Revenue sources and costs. A knowledge of the roles and responsibilities of market participants and the distinction between them.

  Client documentation

  Risk disclosure
  Use of margin
  Discretionary Accounts

  Contracts

  Standardisation
  Introduction of new contracts

  Market characteristics

  Open outcry markets and electronic markets
  Recording and display of bargains
  Disputes procedures
  Declaration of in house orders
  Types of orders including GFD, GTC, use of board limits, contingent and stop loss
  Kerb trading
  Limit up – Limit down
  Orderly markets and rotations
  Position limits

Exam tip | Though clearly in the syllabus, the subject matter in this section is rarely examined, the exam concentrating on an application of knowledge rather than definitional items.

1 OVERVIEW

In this section, the basics of trading futures and options on the Euronext.liffe (the London International Financial Futures and Options Exchange) market are examined.

2 EURONEXT.LIFFE MEMBERSHIP AND TRADING RULES

2.1 Euronext.liffe – An introduction

LIFFE was established in 1982, and is today one of the world's largest derivatives exchanges. In November 2001, it was acquired by Euronext becoming Euronext.LIFFE.

The Euronext.liffe market provides a market place for the trading of financial derivatives in three distinct types of product: government bonds, short-term interest rates and equities. All these products trade on Euronext.liffe's electronic screen-based system, called CONNECT.

3 FSA Guidance

During 1993, the FSA issued guidance on what constitutes proper markets and trades. The guidance lays down general criteria by which recognised investment exchanges and their participants should abide.

3.1 What Constitutes a Proper Market?

The FSA lists the following criteria for a proper market.

Market	There must be a distinct market in each product whose operation is governed by rules
Participation	There must be sufficient participants to represent forces of supply/demand
Trading System and Access	The market should allow equitable access to all members (subject to membership categorisation)
Relationship with Underlying	The derivative product must have links with the underlying market and achieve convergence
Market Values	Each market should determine a fair and authoritative value at least once each day
Liquidity	Liquidity is defined as the ability to accommodate transactions of reasonable size at acceptable price spreads in a short space of time

3.2 What constitutes a proper trade?

The FSA's guidance on proper trades offers some insight into the interpretation of FSA Principle 3 (Market Conduct) and also lists a number of improper trades.

Proper trades are those entered into for legitimate reasons, such as speculation, hedging and arbitrage, and which are exposed to the pricing mechanism of the market, e.g. not undertaken secretively off-floor.

In addition, trades (with the exception of cross-trades and closing trades) should expose counterparties to market risk. The guidance specifies five improper trades.

3.2.1 Improper trades

Trade	Explanation
Pre-Arranged Trades	Trades secretly agreed in advance
Wash Trades	Trades with no economic basis, undertaken simply to give the illusion of activity
Accommodation Trades	Trades dealt at uncompetitive prices
Indemnified Trades	Trades in which a party agrees to pay the counterparty for any resultant losses
Crosses	Whilst most types of cross are acceptable, those done to create a false impression of volume are considered improper

2: TRADING PRACTICE

3.2.2 Incentive schemes

The FSA guidance permits exchanges to promote their products in a number of ways, such as by fee rebates and fee holidays for their members. Certain incentive schemes would not be allowable, specifically schemes that might lead members to make improper trades (as defined above).

3.3 Membership rules

The Euronext.liffe market, in common with most derivative markets, was established as a mutual 'seat-based' market.

However, running alongside Euronext.liffe's move to screen-based trading has been another project to reform its membership structure.

The exchange has altered its ownership structure, demutualised and separated trading rights from ownership.

3.3.1 Membership criteria

Notwithstanding the above, the exchange sets criteria for trading/clearing membership. Euronext.LIFFE membership criteria are

- Be fit and proper (including relevant qualifications).
- Have good financial and business standing.
- Be authorised, licensed or permitted by an appropriate regulatory body.
- Have adequate internal controls and procedures.
- Comply with Euronext.liffe financial resources rules.

3.3.2 Clearing arrangements

Both Euronext.liffe and the London Clearing House (LCH.Clearnet) set the rules for eligibility to clearing membership. Whilst LCH.Clearnet rules deal generally and unsurprisingly with financial resources, Euronext.liffe rules concentrate on the relationship between shares and clearing capacity.

To be a clearing member of Euronext.liffe, and thus LCH.Clearnet, you must have a membership appropriate to the contracts that you seek to clear.

Clearing members may be either individual or general clearing members. General Clearing Members (GCMs) are entitled to clear their own proprietary and client business as well as that of other members.

Clearing arrangements between members are formalised using standard forms.

Form	Purpose
Clearing Services Agreement	Agreement between an Individual Clearing Member (ICM) and a GCM to provide clearing for products in which the ICM does not hold the relevant membership
Clearing Agreement	Agreement between a non-clearing member and a GCM
Clearing Arrangements Registration Certificate	Issued to a member, evidencing its clearing arrangements in a particular product group
Clearing Arrangements Exemption Certificate	Issued to members who have no need for clearing arrangements, e.g. members who have leased out their permits

3.3.3 Public Order Membership

Certain Euronext.liffe members may handle both client and other member business subject to the level of their financial resources. Such members are described as Public Order Members (POMs).

Membership Type	Capital Requirement
General Clearing Members	£2,000,000
Individual Public Order Clearing Member	£1,000,000
Individual Non-Public Order Clearing Member	£500,000
Non-Clearing Public Order Member	£250,000
Non-Clearing, Non-Public Order Members	£25,000

3.3.4 Records, returns and visits

Members are required to maintain records explaining trading activity, margin, requirements and payments.

Members must, when required, supply information to the Market Supervision Department (MSD) and allow the MSD access to their records and offices without prior notice.

Members are required to supply the exchange with quarterly financial returns. These returns may be in a similar format to FSA returns. In addition, members must also supply annual audited accounts.

3.3.5 Margin calculations

Members must calculate margin requirements daily and, in doing so, must apply at least the clearing house requirements.

Margins should be called immediately and fully from all clients. No credit should be extended for financial derivative positions. Credit lines are, however, allowed for commodity positions.

(Margin calls are made to cover losses on open positions as well as to cover the worst probable one-day loss that might be sustained.)

The no-credit rule for financial derivatives exceeds FSA requirements, which allow for temporary extensions of credit as well as long-term credit arrangements agreed as part of an FSA-approved credit management policy.

3.3.6 Opening of client accounts

When client accounts are opened and where FSA rules require two-way agreements to be exchanged (private customers engaged in contingent liability transactions/discretionary customers), Euronext.liffe imposes additional requirements.

These additional clauses, *inter alia*, include a statement to the effect that a similar contract to that which exists between the customer and member has been undertaken on the Euronext.liffe floor.

2: TRADING PRACTICE

4 TRADING RULES

The Euronext.LIFFE trading rules, in common with those of other RIEs, seek to 'allow for business to be conducted in an orderly manner, so as to afford proper protection to investors'.

The rules themselves are relatively brief, with the trading procedures issued by General Notice, providing the detail as to how trading should take place. These procedures have the same status with regard to enforceability as the rules.

4.1 Trading hours

The Euronext.liffe market sets specific trading times for each of its contracts. Within these times, trading is continuous. After hours, trading other than to transfer certain positions is strictly prohibited.

The purpose of these rules is to concentrate liquidity, aid price discovery and consequently promote compliance with best execution rules. In addition, such rules promote the value of membership.

4.2 Basis trading facility for bonds

These allow for the futures leg of a basis trade (when the cash instrument is bought and the future sold or vice versa) to be traded at an off-market price. As these trades might be large, it is quite possible that if the order had traded in the normal way, then this could impact on the price, perhaps sufficiently to render the basis trade unprofitable. The purpose behind this facility is to remove the execution risk associated with trading the futures leg.

4.3 Standardisation

Only contracts that conform to Euronext.liffe standard contract specifications may be executed on the market place.

4.4 Parallel contracts

Whilst contracts may be undertaken by non-clearing members, contracts registered at the clearing house must be in the names of clearing members. The rules state that parallel contracts, that is contracts of a similar nature, may emerge between clearing and non-clearing members.

5 CLIENT ORDER

5.1 Priority

Orders without special conditions (e.g. limits) should be dealt in time stamp order regardless of whether they are clients orders or for the proprietary account.

5.2 Cross transactions

Cross transactions are those in which a firm has simultaneous buy and sell orders in the same contract.

Whilst the rules for the trading of such orders are complex, they are designed to achieve two ends. First, they force the orders to be executed in the normal market, thus exposing the orders to the price-making mechanism of the market. This prevents the orders being matched at some arbitrary price that might benefit one side of the trade and disadvantage the other.

Secondly, cross trades may have the appearance of being pre-arranged. The rules require that all traders should be given an opportunity to participate in the trade if they so wish. To achieve this, the orders must be separately and deliberately bid and offered.

5.3 Fast market

The exchange may declare a fast market when trading gets particularly hectic. The significance of this is that trade reports may be less accurate or timely than in normal market conditions.

5.4 Closing prices

The determination of authoritative and fair closing/settlement prices is of tremendous importance in derivative markets. This is because margin calculations, profit/loss accounts and delivery values are influenced by them. Consequently, the Market Supervision Department (MSD) seek to ensure that such values are fair and are not manipulated by participants (a practice known as high or low ticking).

The exchange is responsible for determining a closing price that is a fair reflection of the market. In doing this, the official considers not just the last traded price, but activity during the two minutes prior to the close.

5.5 Prohibited trading practices

The Euronext.liffe rules, in large part, replicate the FSA Guidance on Improper Trades in prohibiting prearranged trades, wash trades and accommodation transactions. In addition, the rules also prohibit half trades.

Half trades are trades by which a trader, by the arrangement of quotations with another trader, achieves a preferred aggregate execution price. Whilst the averaging of trades is not outlawed, the prearrangement clearly is.

5.6 Disputes

If a contract is the subject of a dispute and the matter cannot be resolved, one or more parties to the dispute shall notify the dispute to an exchange official, who may require one or both of such parties to take any step to limit any loss. If the contract under dispute has already been reported for clearing, the reported buyer and the reported seller shall complete a document for the purposes of clearing to stipulate any amendment required.

5.7 Records

The rules require the retention of **trading cards, TRS slips and order slips for a minimum of six months**, and Euronext.liffe requires members to keep records of all trades done for five years.

2: TRADING PRACTICE

6 OTHER TRADING ISSUES

6.1 Position limits

In order that no one firm, individual or connected group of individuals establish a dominant and potentially destabilising position in a market, some exchanges establish **position limits**.

These limits prevent the creation of a position in which manipulation of the market can take place. Position limits are particularly useful in markets where liquidity is limited.

In 1980, the Texan billionaires, the Hunt family, set about buying as much physical silver as possible; they also bought as many silver futures as possible. This left those who had sold silver futures without already owning silver, in considerable difficulties. As the Hunt family controlled almost all freely available metal, they were in a position to ask whatever price they wished from shorts looking to make delivery.

Such manipulation does little to enhance the reputation of futures markets. It also undermines their roles in price discovery. Although position limits are commonplace in the US, **no position limits exist on UK markets**.

6.2 Price limits

Futures and options markets are sometimes blamed for making market movements larger than they would otherwise be.

Some derivative exchanges impose price limits to prevent prices moving too far or too fast within a trading session. If the market moves too far, a temporary suspension of trading is announced. This, it is hoped, will give traders time to settle and calm any panic.

If the price goes up to a price limit and trading is suspended, the market is said to be **limit up**. If the market is suspended after a price fall, the market goes **limit down**.

Price limits have potentially serious consequences for investors, as they may be prevented from trading when they wish. Few UK exchanges impose price limits; below is a list of UK exchanges/products on which price limits do operate.

UK Price Limits:	Euronext.liffe	– Japanese Government Bond
	LME	– Occasional

6.3 Order types

Customers in futures and options markets are able to submit a complicated range of dealing instructions or order types to their brokers. This allows them to give precise instructions as to how their orders will be treated.

6.3.1 Market order

The market order simplest of all order types – it requires the dealer to buy or sell at the prevailing market price. Such orders should be executed immediately.

6.3.2 Limit order

In the limit order, the dealer is restricted as to the price at which he can buy or sell, e.g. buy five contracts at 98.50.

With this type of order, the dealer must trade at 98.50 or better. In terms of a buy order, better means below the limit price; for a sell order, it means above the limit price.

The problem with this order type is that execution is not guaranteed. If the market moves significantly, the order may not be executed.

6.3.3 Stop order

A stop order, sometimes called a stop loss order or stop, is an instruction to buy or sell once a particular market level is reached.

Often, but not always, these orders are used to prevent further losses occurring and thus are motivated by a desire to close an existing position.

Imagine a speculator who opens a short futures position in crude oil at $18. The short futures position will make money if the oil price declines, but may make unlimited losses if the market rises. To protect himself, the speculator could put in a stop order to buy at $19. This order will be kept by the dealer, who will be required to buy a future once the trigger price of $19 is touched. In this way, the speculator seeks to limit his loss to $1 a barrel.

There are two points worth remembering.

First, markets sometimes 'jump' or move discontinuously. For example, if the Gulf states were to go to war, oil prices would increase dramatically. In such a case, the buy stop at $19 may prove impossible to execute. The next trading level might be $40 and it would be at this price that the dealer would execute the order.

Secondly, the price stipulated in the order is the price at which the order becomes activated. Once this price is reached, the order is dealt as a market order.

6.3.4 Guaranteed stops

Guarantee stops are a special type of stop which, as the name implies, guarantee an execution at the stop price. As such, these orders represent potentially large risks for the brokers willing to accept them and consequently incur large charges.

6.3.5 Market-if-touched orders (MITs)

Market-if-touched orders are very similar to stop orders, in that they become market orders if a certain price is reached.

Generally, MITs are used to open positions, being particularly popular with technical analysts who like to enter positions at significant support or resistance levels.

The difference between MITs and stops is in their relationships to the market price.

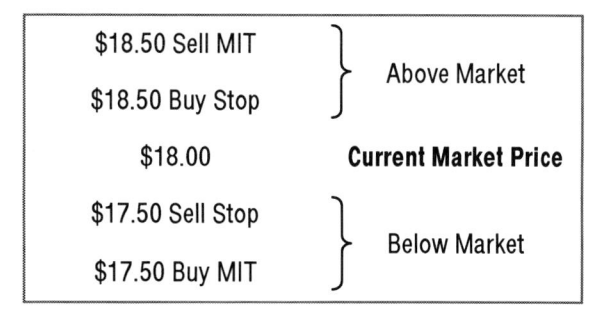

$18.50 Sell MIT	Above Market
$18.50 Buy Stop	
$18.00	**Current Market Price**
$17.50 Sell Stop	Below Market
$17.50 Buy MIT	

This becomes simpler to understand if you remember that stops are typically used to close positions and MITs are used to open. Thus, if you bought a future to open a position and then wished to protect yourself, you would enter a sell stop below the market. MITs work in an opposite fashion.

6.3.6 Spread orders

Sometimes, customers wish to simultaneously buy a future in one delivery month and sell another with a different delivery month – these are known as spread orders.

These are more fully explained in the strategy section.

6.3.7 Scale order

Scale orders are orders in which the customer wishes to make a gradual entry or exit from the market rather than execute the trade at just one price.

Example

A customer may wish to buy ten Crude futures at $18, with a further ten contracts being bought for each 20 cent rise in price.

6.3.8 Opening order

An opening order has to be executed within the opening range, but not necessarily at the opening price. If the broker is unable to fill the order within the range, it is cancelled.

Example

Buy ten at $18 opening.

6.3.9 Closing order

A closing order works like an opening order, except that execution is attempted at the close.

6.3.10 Limit or market on close order

This is an order that combines a limit and a further stipulation for the order to be treated as a market order on the close. This type of order is used by a client who is willing to hold out during the trading day for a particular price, but must receive an execution on the close.

The order is treated as a limit order during the day, but as a market order on the close.

6.3.11 Stop limit order

A stop limit order like a normal stop, except that the customer stipulates the parameters within which the dealer must operate. A stop limit order normally contains two prices: the stop price at which the order is activated and a limit price that prevents the trader paying more or receiving less than a particular price.

6.3.12 Good till cancelled (GTC)

A further stipulation added to certain orders, which relates to the validity of the order. Good till cancelled (GTC) orders are, as the name suggests, valid until explicitly cancelled by the client. Good for the Day (GD) orders are an alternative to GTC orders and are only valid for one trading day.

6.3.13 Public Limit Orders (PLOs)

Public limit orders are limit orders that are passed on to exchange officials for execution. A feature of the public limit order is that it takes priority over other business at the same price.

PLOs are not available on all London markets. Only Euronext.liffe provides this service for certain of their option products.

6.4 Crossing

Crossing is when an investment firm has both the buy side and the sell side of an order. For example, a customer may ring his broker and ask to sell five futures at $18. On receipt of this order, either the firm itself or another client may wish to buy five futures at the same price. In these circumstances, a cross trade may be executed.

Open outcry markets have strict rules governing the crossing of orders. Generally, the rules require that the cross is brought into the relevant pit for execution and that the dealing slips from the resultant trade are scrutinised by exchange officials.

Crossing is sometimes known as **self-trading** or **matching**.

6.5 Time and sales

A time and sales report is the exchange's authoritative record of the market's quotations and trades shown by time.

Chapter Roundup

- You need to be familiar with and able to describe
    - FSA guidance on proper markets and trades.
    - Euronext.LIFFE membership rules and trading rules
    - Client orders
    - Position and price limits
    - Order types

TEST YOUR KNOWLEDGE

Check your knowledge of the Chapter here, without referring back to the text.

1. What are the FSA criteria for a proper market?

2. What are the Euronext.LIFFE criteria for membership?

3. What is a basis trade?

4. What is a cross transaction?

5. What is a position limit?

6. Describe a guarantee stop.

7. What is a scale order?

TEST YOUR KNOWLEDGE: ANSWERS

1.

Market	There must be a distinct market in each product whose operation is governed by rules
Participation	There must be sufficient participants to represent forces of supply/demand
Trading System and Access	The market should allow equitable access to all members (subject to membership categorisation)
Relationship with Underlying	The derivative product must have links with the underlying market and achieve convergence
Market Values	Each market should determine a fair and authoritative value at least once each day
Liquidity	Liquidity is defined as the ability to accommodate transactions of reasonable size at acceptable price spreads in a short space of time

2.
- Be fit and proper (including relevant qualifications).
- Have good financial and business standing.
- Be authorised, licensed or permitted by an appropriate regulatory body.
- Have adequate internal controls and procedures.
- Comply with Euronext.liffe financial resources rules.

3. Where a cash investment is bought and a future sold (or vice versa).

4. Where a firm has simultaneous buy and sell orders in the same contract.

5. A position limit prevents the creation of a position in which manipulation of the market can take place.

6. Guarantee stops are a special type of stop which, as the name implies, guarantee an execution at the stop price. As such, these orders represent potentially large risks for the brokers willing to accept them and consequently incur large charges.

7. Scale orders are orders in which the customer wishes to make a gradual entry or exit from the market rather than execute the trade at just one price.

3 Clearing and Settlement

INTRODUCTION

When trading in any market it is clearly essential that we are familiar with how trades are cleared and settles and the costs and procedures involved. This section examines these details in the context of futures and options traded on Euronext.LIFFE.

CHAPTER CONTENTS

		Page
1	Overview	38
2	Clearing Structure	39
3	Margin	41
4	Collateral	46
5	Credit Lines	47
6	Delivery and Settlement – Futures	47
7	Delivery and Settlement – Options	49
8	Contracts for Differences	53
	Chapter Roundup	53
	Test Your Knowledge	55

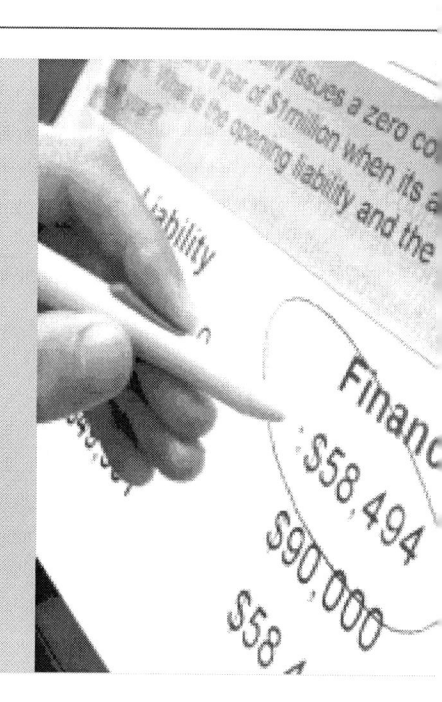

3: CLEARING AND SETTLEMENT

CHAPTER LEARNING OBJECTIVES

The syllabus areas covered by this section are

- **General principles of registration, clearing margining, settlement, exercise, assignment and prices**

    Registration of trades

    Principles and purposes of registration. Outline of the mechanics of registration.

    Clearing

    Definition and purpose of clearing traded options and futures: in particular leveraged contract risks, separation of counterparties, matching off, open positions, margining, offsetting and clearing guarantees. Independent vs subsidiary clearing systems.

    Premiums and margins

    Option premiums: receipt and payment terms, writers' collateral against exercise, margin requirements, scales of collateral value, pledging terms.

    Futures margins: Initial and variation, netting off, acceptable collateral, scale of value of collateral.

    Margins on options and options on futures: marginable premiums, futures/options offset.

    Understanding Span Margining Systems

    Option exercise

    Times of exercise and expiry, exercise and assignment, allocation, delivery of underlying, cash settlement.

    Futures delivery and settlement

    Delivery, cash settlement, exchange delivery settlement price, exchange for physical.

    Guarantees

    Default by member, broker or client. Guarantees/restitution of loss.

> **Exam tip** As with the Trading Practice section, though areas covered here are clearly in the syllabus they are rarely examined, the exam tending to concentrate on applied knowledge rather than definitional terms.

1 OVERVIEW

In this section, the general principles of registration, clearing, margining and settlement are discussed. Whilst rarely anyone's favourite subject, it is important that everyone from front office, back office and boardroom has an appreciation of the principles outlined. Futures and options are potentially very risky instruments if inadequately understood. If positions are mismanaged, not only do clients suffer, but the survival of the firm itself can be brought into question.

2 CLEARING STRUCTURE

The clearing and settlement of exchange-traded futures and options is highly centralised. Unlike other markets, such as securities, in which organisations such as Euroclear, Clearstream or CREST play a part in co-ordinating banking and delivery, the 'clearing houses' in futures and options fulfil two much more important roles.

- Clearing houses become legal counterparties to the original transaction.
- Clearing houses guarantee the performance of contracts.

To understand these roles, it is necessary to understand the hierarchical structure of derivative settlement.

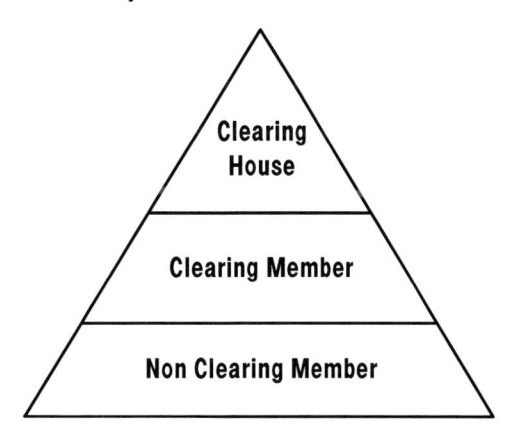

```
        Clearing
         House
        ─────────
      Clearing Member
        ─────────
    Non Clearing Member
```

At the top of the structure comes the clearing house – the administrative centre that co-ordinates delivery and settlement. Most futures and options exchanges have their own clearing houses.

Below the clearing house come the clearing members. These are members of the relevant derivative exchange who are authorised to clear business. To gain such authorisation requires that the clearing member has substantial capital resources. Most of the largest brokers and investment banks are clearing members.

Clearing members come in two forms. Either the clearing member can be described as a General Clearing Member (GCM) and is authorised to clear business for the firm, its clients and other investment businesses, or it can be described as an individual Clearing Member (ICM) authorised to clear solely its own business and that of its clients.

Beneath the clearing members are the Non-Clearing Members (NCM). These will be the smaller exchange members who do not satisfy the strict capital requirements for clearing membership. Consequently, they only gain indirect access to the clearing system by using the services of GCMs.

Where are the clients in this structure?

Potentially, customers can be clients of ICMs, GCMs or NCMs. The diagram below outlines the possibilities.

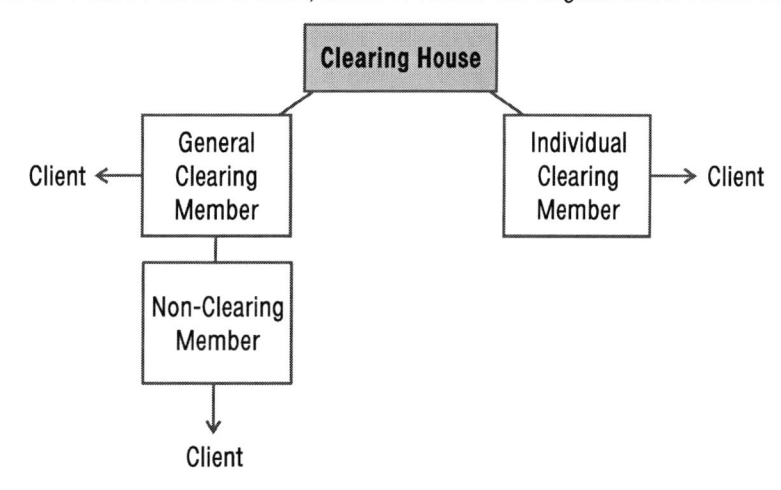

```
                    Clearing House
                    /            \
        General Clearing      Individual Clearing
Client ← Member                Member → Client
              |
        Non-Clearing
          Member
              ↓
           Client
```

2.1 Recognised Clearing Houses

In order to provide the services of a clearing house in the UK, it is necessary to become recognised by the Financial Services Authority.

For derivatives, only one clearing house has Recognised Clearing House (RCH) status, namely the **London Clearing House (LCH.Clearnet)**, which provides clearing services to Euronext.liffe, IPE and LME.

The OM London Exchange market clears its own trades and is entitled to do this by virtue of its wider recognition as a recognised investment exchange (RIE).

LCH.Clearnet, as the most important clearing house in London, is considered in detail in this chapter.

2.2 Registration and guarantee

Amongst the roles fulfilled by the clearing house are those of registrar and guarantor.

Clearing houses act as registrars or bookkeepers to the market place by recording details of all matched trades.

Details of all matched trades are electronically passed to the clearing house each day. Registration typically takes place shortly after the market closes.

At the moment of registration, an important change in the legal character of all derivative contracts takes place. Prior to registration, the contracts are bilateral undertakings between the buyer and seller, with the attendant risk of counterparty default. However, from the instant of registration, the clearing house becomes the buyer to every seller and the seller to every buyer and thus, the counterparty to every contract. This legal change is known as **novation** and eliminates counterparty risk for clearing members.

Aside from acting as registrar, the clearing house also acts as guarantor. This is a natural follow-on from novation and simply means that even if the original counterparty were to go into liquidation or default, the clearing house will honour all contractual obligations. The existence of the guarantee is fundamental to maintaining confidence in the markets.

It is important to recognise that only clearing members (at least in the UK) benefit from the clearing house guarantee. This type of guarantee structure is known as **principal to principal**.

The clearing member in turn extends a guarantee to the customer. Whilst the credibility of the clearing house is beyond doubt, the strength of a clearing member's guarantee rests ultimately on its own balance sheet, which is likely to be less strong than that of the clearing house.

2.3 Mutual and independent guarantees

A common type of structure is the mutual guarantee. Mutual guarantees involve not only the clearing house, but also the clearing members. If default occurs, the clearing member who has responsibility for the account of the defaulter will use all its resources. If necessary, the other clearing members will use their **guarantee fund contributions** (fixed sums of money). It is only if all these contributions are exhausted that the clearing house's own resources are used. This, in essence, is what LCH offers, as it is owned by its members.

Alternatively, some clearing houses offer what is known as an independent guarantee, which means that the guarantee is backed by the resources of the clearing house alone once the resources of the clearing member responsible for the default have been exhausted.

2.4 LCH ownership and guarantee

The London Clearing House (LCH.Clearnet) is owned by its Members (45.1%) and Exchanges (45.1%), with the balance held by Euroclear.

The Members have contributed a total of £150m into a Members Default Fund. This fund would represent cash collateral for indemnities to fund possible member default losses. This financial backing is further supplemented by insurance cover of £100m.

2.5 Net Clearer

LCH serves Euronext.liffe, IPE and LME. The daily settlement amounts called from members by LCH represent their net requirements across all the markets. This is a considerable advantage over other markets, where typically there is a separate clearing house for each exchange.

For example, if a clearing member is **owed** £1m for its IPE business, but is due **to pay** £2m for its Euronext.liffe business, LCH simply calls the net amount of £1m.

2.6 Other LCH functions

Aside from undertaking the role of guarantor and registrar, LCH is also involved in vetting applications for clearing membership and in the treasury management of margin monies.

Of central importance to the resilience of the clearing house structure is the quality of LCH clearing members. To ensure such quality, LCH sets out minimum criteria on capital adequacy, banking arrangements and systems with which all clearing members must comply on a continuing basis.

LCH is also responsible for the treasury management of cash and collateral deposited for margining purposes by clearing members. LCH pays clearing members interest on cash deposited, although clearing members are not themselves obligated under client money rules to pass this interest on to their customers.

A further function undertaken by LCH is that of monitoring the positions held by clearing members in order to avoid the development of too large an exposure to a single clearing member. Although no position limits are operated, LCH retains powers to instruct clearing members to reduce their exposures.

3 MARGIN

Exam tip

> Margin and how it is paid impacts on derivatives pricing as we will see later. You are unlikely to be directly asked about margin but you need to fully understand it in order to appreciate the pricing implications.

The greatest fear of clearing houses, clearing members, non-clearing members and indeed customers, is that of default, i.e. the inability of a party to a trade to perform the contract. Each day, many hundreds of billions of dollars of exposure change hands in the derivatives market, and an elaborate system of margining has been developed to protect against default.

Margin comes in a variety of forms.

3.1 Initial margin

Initial margin is a returnable good faith deposit paid in cash or collateral required from all those entering 'risky' positions. The amount called is usually linked to the worst probable one-day loss that a position could sustain. The amount of initial margin will vary subject to market volatility. If the market suddenly becomes highly volatile, additional margins may be called at short notice. This is known as **intraday** margining.

For example, the LCH currently estimates that the worst probable movement in the UK equity market each day is 300 FTSE 100 index points. As each point has a tick value of £10, the initial margin becomes £10 × 300 = £3,000 per futures contract.

3: CLEARING AND SETTLEMENT

Thus, should an investor open either a long or short futures position, he will be required to pay an initial margin. It is important to recognise that this sum of money/collateral will be returned as long as the investor honours his contractual obligations. However, should the investor default, this initial margin will be used by the clearing member/clearing house to offset the effect of default – 'a returnable good faith deposit.'

Initial margins are due to the clearing house immediately after a risky position is established – normally, no later than the business day following the day of trade. To enable clearing members to meet this timetable, customers are often required to give their clearing members initial margin before such a position is opened.

3.1.1 Who pays initial margin?

Initial margin is required from all those entering into 'risky' positions. As we know from our earlier examination of basic futures and options positions, some trades have limited risk whilst others have unlimited risk. If we remember that the purpose of margin is to prevent or, at least, manage default, we would expect that both long and short futures positions are always margined.

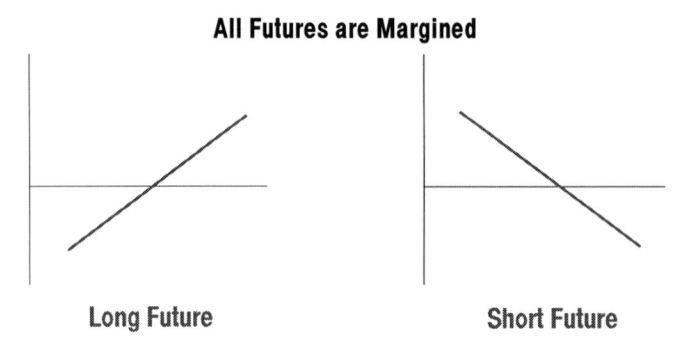

All Futures are Margined

Long Future   Short Future

In addition, all short or written options positions will also be margined.

Written Positions are Always Margined

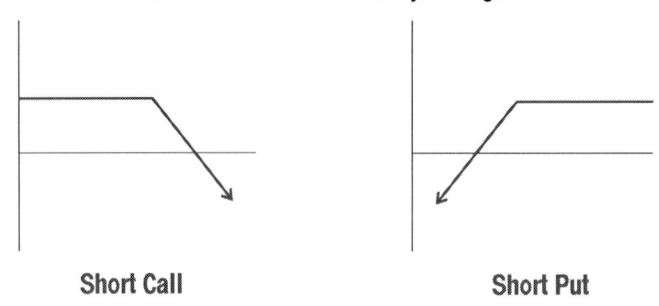

Short Call   Short Put

When investors buy options, the risk is always limited to the premium paid. If this premium is paid immediately after the trade is executed, no margin is payable. On certain exchanges, however, premiums are not paid immediately and consequently, a small margin will be payable.

Purchased or Long Options Positions are Not Normally Margined*

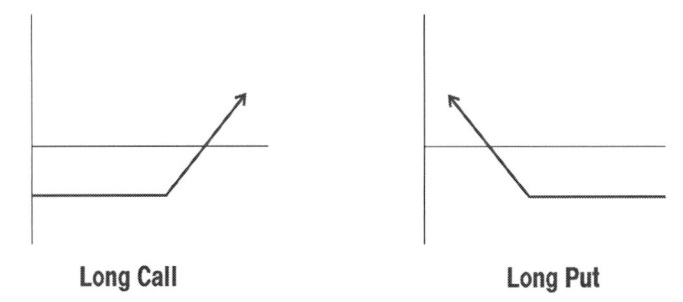

Long Call   Long Put

* Will be margined when premiums are not paid in full when options bought.

3.1.2 Initial margin for options and portfolios

Initial margin is related to the worst probable loss that could be sustained in a day. Whilst this is easily visualised for a straightforward futures position, it is more difficult to calculate for a more complex position involving a number of futures and options positions.

To illustrate this, imagine an investor has the following positions in FTSE 100 futures and options.

Position	View
Long 10 Sept 5200 Calls	Bullish
Long 10 Nov 5000 Puts	Bearish
Long 15 Sept Futures	Bullish
Short 15 Dec Futures	Bearish

At first sight, the position looks both complicated and confused: some trades are bullish whilst others are bearish. The challenge is to work out how much the position might lose in one day. Although we will find it difficult to calculate precisely what might be lost, we can see that the position is, to some extent, hedged. For example, if the market goes down, our long position will lose whilst our short position will gain.

3.2 Variation margin

In addition to initial margin, variation margin is called on all futures and certain options positions. Variation margin represents the profit/loss in a position each day.

At the close of each trading day, a settlement value is announced for each contract traded on the exchange. Equipped with this information, the clearing house and its members calculate the profits/losses sustained on each position during the day.

Example

> At 09:30 5/2/01, investor **sells to open** one FTSE 100 June Future at 5600.
> At 16:10 5/2/01, FTSE 100 Settlement Value = 5618

As can be seen, over the course of the day the short position moves against the investor by 18 index points. Although the investor has not closed the position by offset, i.e. by buying back the future, the loss to date will be calculated.

> **Ticks × Tick value × No. of contracts**
> 18 × £10 × 1
> = £180

This loss must now be paid by the client to the clearing member. Normally, such variation margin calls should be with the clearing member no later than **10:00** on the following business day. The calculation of variation margin is much more than a simple bookkeeping exercise. Its effect is to realise profits or losses on a daily basis so that those customers with loss-making positions pay money and those with profit-making positions receive money.

This process, sometimes called **'marking-to-market'** takes place each and every day that the position is open. (**NB:** On certain exchanges, such as LME and OM London Exchange, variation margin is not paid daily in cash, but may be covered using collateral.)

3: CLEARING AND SETTLEMENT

To avoid the need for constant cash movements between customers and their brokers, it is conventional for customers to leave cash on deposit with the broker and for variation margins to be credited/debited from this account.

LCH clearing members pay/receive variation margin payments via the automated protected payments system (PPS).

The Variation Margin Process

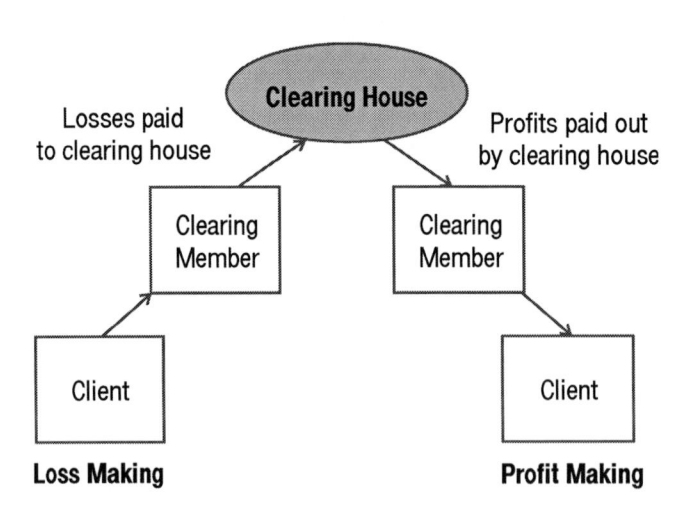

3.3 Maintenance margin

A number of exchanges, particularly those in the US, operate a system of maintenance margin.

On opening a position, initial margin is called in the normal way. However, variation margin calls are not made until the losses bring the margin account down to what is described as the maintenance margin level. The maintenance margin level is normally set at two-thirds of the initial margin rate. When the balance in the margin account falls below the maintenance level, the client is required to replenish the account up to the initial margin level.

Operation of Maintenance Margin

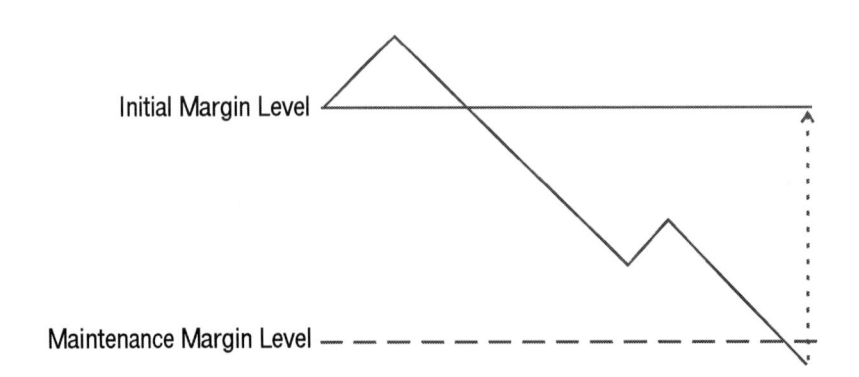

3.4 Span margining

Exam tip | SPAN is a practical example of Value at Risk (VaR) which we examine in detail in the risk management section.

To calculate **initial** margins for portfolios of positions that may include options and futures, LCH – like many other exchanges and clearing houses throughout the world – uses SPAN.

SPAN stands for the **Standard Portfolio Analysis of Risk**.

SPAN takes the entire open position and treats it as a single portfolio of positions. It is known that various factors will change the risk in the portfolio – some positions may directly offset each other or a combination of positions may reduce liability and therefore, the costs of closing out the position. With options, there are several factors that affect the price or premium at which it can be bought or sold, including

- The price of the underlying stock or future.
- The time to expiry.
- Volatility.

LCH takes all these factors into account in determining the right level of initial margin (in SPAN terminology, the **scanning loss**). To calculate volatility (the likelihood and size of future changes in price), historic data is used to evaluate the largest probable one-day changes in price. Having set these parameters, LCH then calculates what impact a variety of changes in volatility and price would have on the portfolio.

LCH will calculate the potential worst-case risk in the portfolio across a number of changes in price and volatility. As this involves a recalculation of each position in the portfolio using an options pricing model, it can only be done with the aid of a computer.

The SPAN 'scanning loss' can be adjusted to take account of special market rules or allowable offsets between highly correlated products. Examples of these are **inter-month spread charges, spot-month charges** and **inter-commodity spread credits**.

3.5 Inter-month spread charges

The initial SPAN calculation will assume that the risk of a long position in one month will be cancelled by a short position in another. But, as the prices of different months do not move exactly together, there remains a residual risk, i.e. inter-month basis risk. SPAN will call an inter-month spread charge to cover this risk.

3.6 Spot month charges

Volatility can increase as a contract approaches delivery. To cover this risk, LCH will call a spot-month charge, thereby increasing the initial margin.

3.7 Inter-commodity spread credit

In certain cases, it is possible to reduce the overall risk by considering opposing positions in different, but correlated, contracts, e.g. Bund/Gilt, FTSE 100/FTSE 250. This reduction in risk is reflected as an inter-commodity spread credit that reduces the overall initial margin.

3.8 Clearing house vs Broker margins

The margin amounts calculated by SPAN relate to the amounts that must be paid by the clearing members to the clearing house. The clearing house thus quantifies the risk that each clearing member represents. In turn, the clearing members calculate the risk that their own clients represent to themselves.

The amount of margin that clearing members call from their clients must at least equal the clearing house minimum. Clearing members and non-clearing members are perfectly entitled to call more margin from customers than is required by clearing house systems. To avoid the need to constantly call customers for small amounts of money, and to provide an additional buffer against the possibility of default, many brokers will require customers to maintain a large balance in cash whilst holding an open position.

4 COLLATERAL

Although margin is calculated as a cash sum, initial margin calls can in fact be satisfied by supplying assets other than cash, i.e. providing collateral.

Below are listed the types of collateral accepted by the LCH; similar types of high-quality collateral are accepted by most clearing houses.

Cash (in approved currencies)
UK Bank Guarantees Issued by an Approved Bank
UK Treasury Bills
UK Gilts
US Treasury Bills/Notes/Bonds
£/$ Certificates of Deposit
Spanish Government Bills/Bonds
Italian Government Bills/Bonds
French Government Bills/Bonds
Dutch Government Bills/Bonds
German Government Bonds
Canadian Government Bills/Bonds
Swedish Government Bills/Bonds
Australian Government Bills/Bonds
Belgium Government Bills/Bonds
FTSE 100 Equities and Stocks Underlying Equity Options

The collateral is either delivered to the clearing house (as in the case of guarantees) or posted to them through the relevant settlement system. Shares are deposited with a nominee and re-registered.

It should be noted that equities can only be used to cover equity margin requirements.

Except for bank guarantees (which are taken at their face value), all collateral is subject to some form of **discount** (known as a **haircut**). This is done to ensure that the clearing house only takes the collateral into account at a value that it can reasonably expect to realise, should it be forced to sell the collateral to meet losses. The discount varies depending on the nature of the collateral from 5% in the case of currencies (to cover exchange risks) to 20% in the case of certain UK shares.

5 CREDIT LINES

Subject to FSA and exchange rules, it is sometimes permissible for investment businesses to extend credit to customers in order to finance their derivatives trading.

On markets such as LME, the provision of credit facilities is commonplace, whilst for Euronext.liffe financial products, members are prohibited from doing so.

The FSA rules relating to credit arrangements are discussed in the chapter on special regulations.

6 DELIVERY AND SETTLEMENT – FUTURES

Exam tip

> You are unlikely to asked about these areas in general, though you are expected to be fully familiar with the delivery and settlement of the specific contracts examined in later sections and how these impact on pricing.

6.1 Introduction

The vast majority of futures contracts never go to delivery (or **tender**). They are normally closed by the holder of the position entering into an offsetting contract and the position being closed out.

Those positions that remain open on the maturity of the contract will be fulfilled by cash settlement or physical delivery. The method of delivery varies from market to market and depends to a large extent on the commodity or other asset underlying the future.

6.2 The physical delivery process

Most futures contracts tend to expire (reach maturity) from the middle of each month onwards. The contract will normally be quoted by the exchange or market as being for a specific delivery month, and the exchange will produce a timetable showing the expiry date for each contract.

6.3 Seller's options

It is a feature of all futures markets that delivery is at the option of the seller (the **short**). This means that the short may decide at any time during the delivery period that he will issue a notice of intention to deliver. If the exchange rules permit, the seller will also have some flexibility regarding what he will deliver and where he will deliver it. This has been done to make the contracts more flexible and to avoid the possibility of a 'squeeze' developing. Exchanges may also allow delivery at a number of delivery points. In the case of many physical commodities, e.g. wheat and metals, delivery may be made at any approved warehouse by passing over a store holder's warrant. For other contracts, physical goods change hands.

The Seller's Choices
What?
Where?
When?

6.4 The timetable

The timings within the delivery process will be affected by whether or not it is permitted to give notice of delivery before expiry. With markets in which expiry and the date on which the notice may be submitted are different, the first day that notices may be given is known as the **first notice day**.

The delivery process begins when the short informs his brokerage firm of his intention to deliver. If the firm is a clearing member, it will handle the delivery procedure directly with the clearing house. If not, it will work through a clearing member. The clearing member sends the delivery notice to the clearing house where the position of a long (buyer) is selected at random and matched with the short position to accept delivery.

The method of delivery varies according to the market and the contract. Usually, the short delivers the appropriate storekeepers warrant or certificates to the clearing house via the clearing member, and the clearing house passes it onto the long via their clearing member. The long pays for the underlying commodity via the clearing member and clearing house who, in turn, pay the clearing member for the short.

6.5 Invoice amounts

The amount of money to be paid by the long to the short for delivery of the underlying commodity is fixed by the exchange on the delivery day. This is known as the **EDSP** (the exchange delivery settlement price).

The EDSP is a figure determined by the exchange and is often an average figure for prices over a set period. The averaging process reduces the possibility of manipulation taking place. The EDSP is set by the exchange to become the basis for all **invoice amount** calculations. The EDSP is then multiplied by the **scaling factor**, which converts the quotation into the price of one contract. This is finally multiplied by the number of contracts involved. It is important to note that the EDSP is not the figure that the long necessarily bought his contracts at.

Example

A metal trader buys one lead futures contract, with a delivery date of 26 June, at $805.

On the delivery date, the EDSP is at $830 and the invoice amount equals the price in dollars per tonne, times the number of contracts, multiplied by the number of tonnes per contract, i.e.

Invoice amount = EDSP × Scaling factor × Contracts
= $830 × 25 × 1
= $20,750

This is the amount that will be paid by the long to the short.

The invoice amount therefore represents the price of the delivery month as it expired. What must be remembered, however, is that the profits/losses accruing to the long and short since the opening of their position will have already been accounted for through the variation margin debits and credits. Thus, although the amount paid by the long in this example is $830 per tonne, the real price will in fact be $830 less variation margin credits.

The invoice amount calculated may need to be adjusted to take account of accrued interest (on bond futures), storage (most physical commodities) and delivery of non-standard grades. The principle remains the same across all futures contracts.

6.6 Cash-settled futures

Many futures contracts, such as stock-index products, short-term interest rate contracts and some physical futures contracts, are cash settled. This means that at delivery, no physical exchange of goods takes place. Rather, cash changes hands. The amount of cash that changes hands is simply the final variation margin credit or debit. Let us illustrate this with an example.

Example

1 February

A customer sells one June FTSE 100 futures contract at 5380.

June Delivery Date

On the June delivery date, the FTSE 100 EDSP = 5375

The amount of money that will change hands will be calculated with reference to the difference between the EDSP and the settlement price of the business day prior to delivery. This is because earlier movements will have already been accounted for by way of variation margin credits or debits. In our example, the downwards move of the market from 5380 to 5375 will, in large part, have already been received by the future's seller.

If the settlement price on the day before delivery was 5377 and the EDSP 5375, the seller would receive two index points of variation margin credit. The monetary amount this represents can be found by multiplying points moved by the value of each point stipulated in the contract specification. For a FTSE 100 future, this is £10 a point and consequently, a variation margin credit of £20 would be paid.

7 DELIVERY AND SETTLEMENT – OPTIONS

Exam tip | You are unlikely to asked about these areas in general, though you are expected to be fully familiar with the delivery and settlement of the specific contracts examined in later sections and how these impact on pricing.

7.1 Introduction

Like futures, the majority of options contracts are never exercised. Instead, profits and losses are realised by trading in the options market itself. There are two aspects of option settlement that need to be understood: how the premium is accounted for and how the delivery process works.

7.2 Payment of premium

There are two methods of paying premium. **Either** (as in the case of Euronext.liffe equity options) it is paid immediately and in full after the trade is undertaken, i.e. T + 1 settlement **or** (as is the case with Euronext.liffe financial and commodity options) it is paid when the option expires so that the premium will only be paid if the buyer has incurred losses on entering into the option contract. Under this regime, to guard against the possible default of the options buyer, the holder pays a very small initial margin upfront. It is a fundamental principle of options that the holder of the option can never lose more than the premium.

The immediate or upfront payment of options premium is the method used by most options markets internationally. This requires the buyer to pay the full premium price for their options on the business day following the day of trade. The premium payment is received by the broker who makes payment to the clearing house who, in turn, pays the seller (writer) through their broker. It should be remembered that brokers and clearing members are obliged to make prompt payments to the clearing house whether or not they have funds from their customer.

When premiums are paid on the closing of the contract, the buyer will be margined. The amount of margin called is determined by the margining system for the particular exchange, but it will never exceed the amount of the options premium. Profits and losses in the positions are paid daily through variation margin that is calculated in the same way as for futures. Strictly speaking, when the option premium is paid on the expiry of the option ('futures style' premium settlement), the premium actually accrues to the seller of the option over the term of the option, at the rate of the option's time decay or daily theta (see Section 8.2.3 for discussion of theta). Thus, the premium is in fact paid by the buyer to the seller, via the daily variation margin payment, at the rate of the option's time decay.

The following table summarises the methods of premium settlement used in London.

Market	Premium Paid Upfront	Premium Paid on Closing and Margin
Euronext.liffe (financial and commodity)	No	Yes
Euronext.liffe (equity)	Yes	No
OM London Exchange	Yes	No
ICE Futures	No	Yes
LME	Yes	No

7.3 Early exercise

With American style options it is possible for the holder to exercise options before expiry. This, however, is not usually the optimal thing to do.

The reason for this is that, in exercising early, the holder will lose any remaining time value in an option and merely realise its intrinsic value.

Example

In December

An investor buys one June 100 call at 7, when the underlying is 100.

In March

By March, the underlying trades at 120 and the 100 call trades at 21.5.

If the investor were to sell the option he would realise

Sale price	21.5
Less purchase price	(7.0)
	14.5

If he were to exercise the option, he would be able to buy at 100, subsequently sell at 120, and thus realise a gain of 20 which, net of the premium originally paid (7), would leave 13 profit.

The difference of 1½ in the outcome relates to the residual time value in the June calls. As a consequence of this, it is **normally irrational to exercise early**.

It was stated above that it is not usually optimal to exercise early. There are, however, certain occasions when it is the best thing to do. Clearly, to justify early exercise, the advantage of exercising early must outweigh the time value that is being discarded.

7.3.1 Early exercise of options on dividend paying stock

Dividends are not paid to option holders, they are paid to the owners of the shares. There may be an advantage in exercising a call option early, just before the stock goes ex-dividend (thus capturing the dividend), if the advantage of this is greater than any remaining time value.

A call option price will reflect a reduction equal to the present value of any future expected dividend due before expiry. Therefore, the value of the option will not fall by the dividend amount when the stock goes ex-dividend.

Example

Date	Friday 15/09
Call Option	Strike 150p
Stock price (cum div)	175p
Dividend to be paid	10p
Share to go ex-div	Monday 18/09
Time value of option	6p

Friday	Monday
Value of option	**Value of option**
= Intrinsic + Time – PV of div	= 15 + 6 – 0
= 25 + 6 – 10	= 21
= 21	
Value if exercised	**Value if exercised**
= Value of share – Strike price	= 165 – 150
= 175 – 150	= 15
= 25	
Early exercise is optimal	Early exercise no longer optimal

From the above, it is clear that early exercise may be optimal just before a stock goes ex-dividend. Early exercise will never be appropriate if a stock does not pay a dividend.

Other options which may be candidates for early exercise would include

- Deep in-the-money (ITM) put option on a low interest yielding currency, where there is an advantage to selling the low yielding currency in exchange for a high yielding currency.

- Deep ITM call option on a high yielding currency in exchange for a low yielding currency. These are less likely to be candidates for early exercise due to the unlimited upside potential of a call (as distinct to the limited upside potential of a put).

- Options on futures that pay their premium upfront, i.e. are stock-type settled. It is possible if interest rates are sufficiently high and volatility sufficiently low for there to be an advantage in exercising a deep ITM option, thereby crystallising the profit and earning interest on it.

When the conditions exist to make early exercise optimal, an American option will be exercised. But what of a European option that cannot be exercised? For these options, there is a **disadvantage** to having to hold it to maturity until it can be exercised, therefore they will have **negative time value**, i.e. will trade below their intrinsic value.

7.4 Options delivery

The **holder** of an options contract has several choices open to him when closing a long position.

The alternatives available to the holder of the options contract are as follows.

7.4.1 Closing sale

The holder of the option can go into the market and enter into an offsetting transaction which will close the open position.

7.4.2 Exercise

The holder exercises the option to buy (call) or sell (put) the underlying by giving notice of exercise to the clearing house (through his broker). Exercise takes place in accordance with the terms of the contract and may be in American, European or Asian style.

7.4.3 Abandonment

If an option position is worthless, the holder can simply leave the option to expire and all he will have lost is his premium. Some investors, rather than abandon options prefer to undertake a **cabinet trade**, which is a trade where a worthless option position is closed for a notional consideration to facilitate crystallisation of profits and losses, for taxation and accounting purposes.

7.5 Writers

The **writer** of an option has the converse choices to the holder. Like the holder, he can enter the market and enter into an offsetting contract to close his open position. Unlike the holder, he has the obligation to perform the option if the holder exercises it.

The writer of the option is subject to two eventual outcomes, should the position remain open.

7.5.1 Assignment

A European or Asian style option can only be exercised at expiry, whereas the American style option may be exercised by the holder at any time up to expiry. Should the holder of an American style option exercise their option before expiry, the clearing house will **randomly** choose a short position and inform that writer (short option position) that their option has been exercised against them.

When the holder of an option exercises, the clearing house matches the exercise notice with an open short position in a process known as **assignment**. On being assigned, the writer will be required to buy (put) or sell (call) the underlying.

7.5.2 Abandonment

If the holder decides to abandon the option, it will simply remain open until the expiry. If this happens, the writer will not be required to fulfil his contractual obligations.

7.6 Automatic exercise

As mentioned above, the holder of an option will normally exercise by giving an 'exercise notice' to the clearing house. To avoid the unnecessary generation of exercise notices on an expiry, it has become common practice for clearing houses to operate an automatic exercise facility for the benefit of members.

The automatic exercise facility will normally have the effect of exercising all in-the-money options without the need for the holder or their broker to submit an exercise notice. The terms on which the automatic exercise procedure will operate are normally set by the clearing house, for example, LCH will usually automatically exercise all positions that are in the money by one tick.

If the clearing house operates an automatic exercise routine, the brokers can normally prevent its application on a particular position by filing a suppression notice with the clearing house.

8 CONTRACTS FOR DIFFERENCES

Contracts for differences is a rather complicated term used to describe cash-settled derivatives.

In such contracts, cash passes between buyer and seller at expiry rather than a physical asset or future. The reason why some contracts are cash settled is largely for administrative ease. Whilst it might be possible to design an equity index product, e.g. FTSE 100, that leads to the physical delivery of each of its hundred constituents (in FTSE's case), this would be both cumbersome and expensive. Rather than do this, a cash value changes hands.

For instance, an investor buys and subsequently exercises one call option on the FTSE index. The exercise price is 5350 and the EDSP 5390.

At expiry, this option has 40 points of intrinsic value and, in accordance with the contract specification, each point has a value of £10.

Following exercise, £400 (40 × £10) will be paid by the call option writer to the holder.

The contract is thus cash settled for the difference between the exercise price and the settlement price.

CHAPTER ROUNDUP

You need to be familiar with and able to describe

- The clearing structure, the function of clearing houses, registration and guarantees.
- The purpose and form of margin and how it is assessed.
- Delivery and settlement requirements for both futures and options.
- Contracts for differences.

3: CLEARING AND SETTLEMENT

Test Your Knowledge

Check your knowledge of the Chapter here, without referring back to the text.

1. Describe the role of Recognised Clearing Houses in the trading of derivatives in the UK.
2. Describe mutual and independent guarantees.
3. Describe initial margin.
4. Describe SPAN margin.
5. Describe the sellers options with respect to futures delivery.
6. When may the holder of an American style option choose to exercise it before expiry.
7. What is a contract for difference.

3: CLEARING AND SETTLEMENT

Test Your Knowledge: Answers

1. In order to provide the services of a clearing house in the UK, it is necessary to become recognised by the Financial Services Authority.

    For derivatives, only one clearing house has Recognised Clearing House (RCH) status, namely the **London Clearing House (LCH.Clearnet)**, which provides clearing services to Euronext.liffe, IPE and LME.

    The OM London Exchange market clears its own trades and is entitled to do this by virtue of its wider recognition as a recognised investment exchange (RIE).

    LCH.Clearnet, as the most important clearing house in London, is considered in detail in this chapter.

2. A common type of structure is the mutual guarantee. Mutual guarantees involve not only the clearing house, but also the clearing members. If default occurs, the clearing member who has responsibility for the account of the defaulter will use all its resources. If necessary, the other clearing members will use their **guarantee fund contributions** (fixed sums of money). It is only if all these contributions are exhausted that the clearing house's own resources are used. This, in essence, is what LCH offers, as it is owned by its members.

    Alternatively, some clearing houses offer what is known as an independent guarantee, which means that the guarantee is backed by the resources of the clearing house alone once the resources of the clearing member responsible for the default have been exhausted.

3. Initial margin is a returnable good faith deposit paid in cash or collateral required from all those entering 'risky' positions. The amount called is usually linked to the worst probable one-day loss that a position could sustain. The amount of initial margin will vary subject to market volatility. If the market suddenly becomes highly volatile, additional margins may be called at short notice. This is known as **intraday** margining.

    Initial margins are due to the clearing house immediately after a risky position is established – normally, no later than the business day following the day of trade. To enable clearing members to meet this timetable, customers are often required to give their clearing members initial margin before such a position is opened.

4. To calculate **initial** margins for portfolios of positions that may include options and futures, LCH – like many other exchanges and clearing houses throughout the world – uses SPAN.

    SPAN stands for the **Standard Portfolio Analysis of Risk**.

    SPAN takes the entire open position and treats it as a single portfolio of positions. It is known that various factors will change the risk in the portfolio – some positions may directly offset each other or a combination of positions may reduce liability and therefore, the costs of closing out the position. With options, there are several factors that affect the price or premium at which it can be bought or sold, including

    - The price of the underlying stock or future.
    - The time to expiry.
    - Volatility.

    LCH takes all these factors into account in determining the right level of initial margin (in SPAN terminology, the **scanning loss**). To calculate volatility (the likelihood and size of future changes in price), historic data is used to evaluate the largest probable one-day changes in price. Having set these parameters, LCH then calculates what impact a variety of changes in volatility and price would have on the portfolio.

LCH will calculate the potential worst-case risk in the portfolio across a number of changes in price and volatility. As this involves a recalculation of each position in the portfolio using an options pricing model, it can only be done with the aid of a computer.

The SPAN 'scanning loss' can be adjusted to take account of special market rules or allowable offsets between highly correlated products. Examples of these are **inter-month spread charges, spot-month charges** and **inter-commodity spread credits**.

5. It is a feature of all futures markets that delivery is at the option of the seller (the **short**). This means that the short may decide at any time during the delivery period that he will issue a notice of intention to deliver. If the exchange rules permit, the seller will also have some flexibility regarding what he will deliver and where he will deliver it. This has been done to make the contracts more flexible and to avoid the possibility of a 'squeeze' developing. Exchanges may also allow delivery at a number of delivery points. In the case of many physical commodities, e.g. wheat and metals, delivery may be made at any approved warehouse by passing over a store holder's warrant. For other contracts, physical goods change hands.

The Seller's Choices
What?
Where?
When?

6. Dividends are not paid to option holders, they are paid to the owners of the shares. There may be an advantage in exercising a call option early, just before the stock goes ex-dividend (thus capturing the dividend), if the advantage of this is greater than any remaining time value.

    A call option price will reflect a reduction equal to the present value of any future expected dividend due before expiry. Therefore, the value of the option will not fall by the dividend amount when the stock goes ex-dividend.

7. A contract for difference is a cash settled contract. When entering the position the contract would have a value, on exiting that value is liable to be different. This difference in value will represent a gain to one counterparty and a loss to the other and is paid as cash from the loser to the winner.

3: CLEARING AND SETTLEMENT

4 Financial Mathematics

INTRODUCTION

The areas covered in this section are discounted cash flow (DCF) and volatility. DCF is a basic, but very important, evaluative technique that we will be utilising when we investigate the valuation of futures and options later. Similarly, risk measurement is essential to these evaluation ideas for options as it is uncertain whether it will be worth exercising or not and any price volatility may have a significant impact.

You should not expect to see pure DCF or pure volatility questions in the exam but an understanding of these ideas is central to understanding options pricing.

CHAPTER CONTENTS

		Page
1	Introduction	60
2	The Time Value of Money and Interest Rates	60
3	Terminal/Future Values and Present Values	67
4	Present Values and Net Present Values	70
5	Internal Rate of Return/Yield	76
6	Securities Evaluation and DCF	79
7	Assumptions Underlying DCF	80
8	Risk Measurement	81
	Chapter Roundup	87
	Test Your Knowledge	89

4: FINANCIAL MATHEMATICS

CHAPTER LEARNING OBJECTIVES

The syllabus areas covered by this section are

- **Uses of futures**
    - Value in futures contracts
    - Value in options contracts

Exam tip

> These areas are unlikely to be examined in isolation but are key to understanding pricing ideas covered in later sections. As such you should not move on to these later pricing sections until you have mastered the content of this section.

1 INTRODUCTION

Central to all our theories regarding the valuation of securities and derivatives is discounted cash flow (DCF) and the time value of money. It is therefore essential that we thoroughly understand this topic and the relevance of the measures that we derive.

The various valuation ideas are based on the **Dividend Valuation Model (DVM)**, which states that

The market value of a security is the present value of the future expected receipts discounted at the investors' required rate of return.

We will see this idea time and time again, hence the importance placed on the basics.

2 THE TIME VALUE OF MONEY AND INTEREST RATES

2.1 Introduction

A starting point is the realisation and appreciation of the time value of money. We will all be aware of this fact as a result of the payment (or possibly the receipt) of bank interest.

Bank interest can take one of two forms

- Simple interest, or
- Compound interest.

Each of which are illustrated below with the aid of the following example.

Example

£100 is deposited in an account paying interest at 10% p.a. (simple or compound as applicable). How much interest will be earned during, and what will be the value of the deposit at the end of

- The first year?
- The nth year (say 5th)?

2.2 Simple interest

If a bank account were to offer a **simple interest** rate, then the interest received each year would be based on the **original capital invested only**. Hence, in relation to the above example, we would have the following.

Solution

First year

The interest earned in this year would be based on the capital originally invested (£100) and the simple rate of interest (10%). The interest could be calculated using the following formula

Formula to learn

$$i_1 = D_0 \times r$$

where

i_1 = interest earned in the first year (year 1)
r = interest rate stated as a decimal, e.g. 10% = 0.10
D_0 = original capital invested at the outset (Time = 0)

giving

$$i_1 = £100 \times 0.10 = £10$$

At that date the deposit will be worth £110, which we could have calculated directly using the formula

Formula to learn

$$D_1 = D_0(1+r)$$

where

D_1 = the value of the deposit at Time 1

Nth year

With simple interest, the interest generated each subsequent year will be exactly the same, since it is only based on the original capital invested. Hence, we can apply the same formula to calculate this year's interest as

$$i_n = D_0 \times r$$

Again giving, for the fifth year

$$i_5 = £100 \times 0.10 = £10$$

Hence, the value of our deposit is growing by £10 each year.

Thus, with simple interest, we earn the same amount of interest each year. Hence, at the end of n years, the total interest we will have earned will be

n × Annual interest

or

$$i_{total} = n \times D_0 \times r = D_0 \times (n \times r)$$

Which, when added to our starting capital of D_0, gives the value of our deposit as

$$D_n = D_0(1 + n \times r)$$

Applying this to the above example gives

4: FINANCIAL MATHEMATICS

$$D_5 = D_0(1 + n \times r) = £100(1 + 5 \times 0.10) = £150$$

Which is perhaps the result we expected. Five years' interest at 10% p.a. should add a total of 50% to the value of the deposit with flat interest.

2.3 Compound interest

2.3.1 Annual compounding

Interest rates are described as **compound interest** if, in each year, interest is earned on the **total value of the deposit at the start of the year**, i.e. original capital plus any interest previously earned. Thus, with compound interest, we receive interest on our previous interest.

Solution

First year

The interest earned in this year would be based on the value of the deposit at the start of the year, i.e. the capital originally invested of £100, and the compound rate of interest (10%). The interest could again be calculated using the formula

$$i_1 = D_0 \times r$$

where

i_1 = interest earned in the first year (year 1)
r = interest rate stated as a decimal, e.g. 10% = 0.10
D_0 = original capital invested at the outset (Time = 0)

giving

$$i_1 = £100 \times 0.10 = £10$$

At that date, the deposit will be worth £110, which we could have calculated directly using the formula

Formula to learn

$$D_1 = D_0(1+r)$$

Where D_1 = the value of the deposit at Time 1. We can see that so far this is identical to the simple interest example above. However, this is only true for the very first year.

N^{th} year

With compound interest, the interest generated each subsequent year will be based on the value of the deposit at the start of each year. We could state this in a formula as

Formula to learn

$$i_n = D_{n-1}$$

Thus, to calculate the interest for the fifth year, we would need to know the value of the deposit at the start of the fifth year. From our Year 1 illustration above, we noted that the value of the deposit at the end of the first year/start of the second was given by

$$D_1 = D_0(1 + r)$$

This amount would then grow by the end of the second year/start of the third year to

$$D_2 = D_1(1 + r) = D_0(1 + r)^2$$

In a similar way, we could calculate the value of the deposit at the end of each subsequent year as

$$D_3 = D_2(1 + r) = D_0 (1 + r)^3 - \text{end of third/start of fourth}$$
$$D_4 = D_3(1 + r) = D_0 (1 + r)^4 - \text{end of fourth/start of fifth}$$
$$D_5 = D_4(1 + r) = D_0 (1 + r)^5 - \text{end of fifth/start of sixth}$$

Which could be described generally as

Formula to learn

$$D_n = D_0(1+r)^n - \text{end of nth/start of } (n+1)^{th}$$

Thus, at the end of the fourth year/start of the fifth, the value of the deposit would be

$$D_4 = D_0(1 + r)^4 = £100 (1 + 0.10)^4 = £100 \times 1.1^4 = £146.41$$

And hence, the interest generated in the fifth year would be

$$i_5 = D_4 \times r = £146.41 \times 0.10 = £14.641$$

Taking the value of the total deposit up to £161.051 (£146.41 + £14.641) by the end of the year, which we can confirm with the formula

$$D_5 = D_0 (1 + r)^5 = £100 (1 + 0.10)^5 = £100 \times 1.1^5 = £161.051$$

Clearly, this is a larger sum than under simple interest, since we are getting interest on our previously earned interest.

2.3.2 Non-annual compounding

Generally, bank and building society accounts quote an annual interest rate that is liable to be compounded, though the compounding may be more regular than once per annum. There is no standard in relation to the frequency of compounding. Bank accounts regularly compound monthly, instant access building society accounts are frequently compounded quarterly, though many are six monthly or annually.

Generally, two rates are quoted

- A flat rate.
- An Annual Percentage Rate (APR).

What are these quotes and what difference does this make to our deposit?

Flat rate

Example

Based on the above example, but now assuming that the interest quoted is a flat rate
of 10% that compounds quarterly, calculate the interest earned and value of the deposit by the end of the

- First year.
- n^{th} year (say 5th).

Solution

First year

A flat rate r, which compounds m times a year would generate interest of r/m each period, i.e. with a flat rate of 10% compounding quarterly (four times p.a.), the interest generated each period would be $10\%/4 = 2.5\%$.

We are generating an interest rate of 2.5% per period, hence at the end of four periods (one year), the value of our deposit will have grown to

$$£100 (1 + 0.025)^4 = £100 \times 1.025^4 = £110.38$$

Which is slightly more than when interest is compounded annually.

N^{th} year

We could give a general expression for this relationship as

$$D_n = D_0\left(1+\frac{r}{m}\right)^{n \times m}$$

Applying this expression to the first year gives

$$D_1 = £100\left(1+\frac{0.10}{4}\right)^{1 \times 4} = £100 \times 1.025^4 = £110.38$$

And applying this expression to the fifth year gives

$$D_5 = £100\left(1+\frac{0.10}{4}\right)^{5 \times 4} = £100 \times 1.025^{20} = £163.86$$

If we compare either of these to the equivalent figures using annual compounding, we find that they are both higher, especially the five-year figure. This highlights the benefit of more frequent compounding, which can be further reinforced by the following example.

Example

Same example as above, but with interest compounding monthly. What is the value of the deposit at the end of five years?

Solution

Using

$$D_n = D_0\left(1+\frac{r}{m}\right)^{n \times m}$$

gives

$$D_5 = £100\left(1+\frac{0.10}{12}\right)^{5 \times 12} = £100 \times 1.0083333^{60} = £164.53, \text{ i.e. higher still.}$$

What we can show mathematically is

- The more frequent the compounding, the better.
- The higher the interest rate, the greater the benefit of frequent compounding.

Annual Percentage Rate

We can see from the above that we have generated interest of £10.38 over the first year based on our initial £100 deposit – an effective rate of 10.38%. This effective rate is the APR. It tells you exactly how much you will earn over a year (or pay if you are borrowing) based on the flat rate and the frequency of compounding. Providing an expression for this, we could say

$$1 + APR = \left(1 + \frac{r}{m}\right)^m$$

or

Formula to learn

$$APR = \left(1 + \frac{r}{m}\right)^m - 1$$

Applying this to the above example gives

$$APR = \left(1 + \frac{0.10}{4}\right)^4 - 1$$
$$= 1.025^4 - 1$$
$$= 1.1038 - 1$$
$$= 0.1038 \text{ or } 10.38\%$$

2.4 Continuous compounding and exponential growth

Exam tip

Pricing models may utilise discrete discounting (above) but most models utilise the ideas of continuous compounding/discounting and log normal returns covered below. You must be able to deal with these ideas and calculations.

Interest rates tend to be quoted in annual terms, i.e. the interest rate is p.a. regardless of the frequency of the payments. If we are quoted such a rate of interest, then the actual annual return that we receive will depend on how frequently it is compounded.

Example

We are quoted a rate of 32% p.a., this may be 16% each half year or 8% per quarter or 2.667% per month or 0.0877% per day. If we compound these up to get the actual annual rate that we will earn we get

Compound Period	Calculation	Actual Rate%
Annual	$1.32^1 - 1$	32.00
Half yearly	$1.16^2 - 1$	34.56
Quarterly	$1.08^4 - 1$	36.05
Monthly	$1.02667^{12} - 1$	37.14
Daily	$1.000877^{365} - 1$	37.69

4: FINANCIAL MATHEMATICS

As we can see, the actual rate is increasing, but tending towards a limit. This limit is given by

Formula to learn

$$R = e^{rt} - 1$$

where

e = exponential constant (2.7182818)
r = quoted annual rate as a decimal
t = time period being considered as a proportion of a year

Thus, over one year, if the 32% is continuously compounded, the effective APR is

$e^{rt} - 1$

$2.7182818^{0.32 \times 1} - 1$

$1.3771 - 1$

0.3771 or 37.71%

A slightly higher rate than the daily one, as it compounds continuously.

2.5 Natural log (Log normal) returns

Above we saw how if you had a quoted annual rate and wanted to see what the actual annual return was if the annual rate was continuously compounded, we applied

Formula to learn

$$R = e^{rt} - 1$$

What happens if we know the actual annual return from an investment that was continuously compounded but we wanted to know the quoted annual rate?

Example

A security rises from 100 to 110 over half a year. What is the annual continuously compounded rate of return?

Solution

$R = e^{rt} - 1$

Or

$1 + R = e^{rt}$

Now

$1 + R = \dfrac{110}{100} = 1.10$

giving

$e^{rt} = 1.10$

Now for a half a year, t = 0.5, and so to get the annual return r, we need to solve

$e^{r \times 0.5} = 1.10$

We can do this by taking the natural log of both sides, i.e.

$\ln(e^{r \times 0.5}) = \ln(1.10) = 0.0953$

Now by definition, $\ln(e^x) = x$, and so we have

$r \times 0.5 = 0.09531$

$r = 0.1906$ or 19.06% p.a.

This method of establishing a discount rate is used in option valuation models. The observed market rates are converted into the equivalent continuous rates, and the model can set aside questions of payment timings.

Benefits of natural log returns

Natural log returns more accurately model the continuous/exponential growth exhibited by companies (market value movements) and economies (GDP growth).

Natural log (continuously compounded) returns have the advantage of being additive, i.e. in order to calculate the annual return from, say, quarterly returns, the four quarters figures simply need to be added (instead of compounded). A natural log measurement is, therefore more convenient when assessing returns over several time periods.

Natural log returns will be lower that their equivalent arithmetic returns, though there is little benefit in this as such. Risk and return information is useless in isolation, its relevance becomes clear when methodology has been applied to the calculation of all alternatives (i.e. all returns have been calculated on a natural log basis or all on an arithmetic basis.

A log-normal distribution of prices has the advantage that share volatility in absolute terms varies with the underlying price (e.g. a share that has 10× the value than another is likely to exhibit price variations that are 10× larger than the other). It also has the advantage share prices can never be negative.

Example

The one-year money market rate is 8%. What continuously compounded rate gives the same return?

Solution

$e^{rt} - 1 = 0.08$

$e^{rt} = 1.08$

$rt = \ln(1.08)$

$r = \dfrac{\ln(1.08)}{t} = \dfrac{0.076961}{1} = 0.076961$ or 7.6961%

---

3 TERMINAL/FUTURE VALUES AND PRESENT VALUES

3.1 Introduction

A **terminal value** or **future value** is the value of a deposit at the end of a period of time, having received interest over that period, i.e. D_n is the terminal value in the above examples.

A **present value** is the equivalent value of the same deposit before the effects of interest, i.e. D_0 is the present value in the above examples.

4: FINANCIAL MATHEMATICS

Calculating terminal or present values for investment opportunities provides a means of appraising them. Indeed, as we noted at the outset, the calculation of a present value provides a method for evaluating a security, i.e. determines its market value.

All calculations with regard to these ideas utilise the concept of **compound interest**.

3.2 Terminal/Future values

Exam tip

> Terminal value ideas aim to provide a mechanism to allow us to determine the value of an asset at some future date. This is a key requirement for understanding and assessing many derivatives.

3.2.1 Introduction

Terminal/Future value calculations consider

- Each cash flow generated by an investment; and
- The timing of the cash flow;

and calculates how much cash could be generated to the end of the investment period if the returns were banked each year to generate interest.

If the returns plus the interest that they can generate exceed the total that would be generated, had we simply banked the cash at the outset rather than investing it, then we accept the investment. The decision criteria can be stated as

An investment should be accepted if it produces a surplus in cash terms after accounting for interest.

Example

Two alternatives to banking the £100 are investments A and B, both of which will terminate in three years.

Investment A will return £41.00 p.a. for the next three years, Investment B will return £134.00 at the end of the third year.

Which investment opportunity is superior and which, if either, should be accepted?

Solution

Since we can receive 10% p.a. on any cash generated, then the effects of selecting A or B would be as follows.

Investment A

Time	Balance b/f £	Interest for Year £	Receipt at Year End £	Balance c/f £
1	–	–	41.00	41.00
2	41.00	4.10	41.00	86.10
3	86.10	8.61	41.00	135.71

Thus, undertaking Investment A will result in cash in the bank of £135.71 at the end of the three years – this is its terminal value.

Investment B

Investment B will result in a receipt of £134.00 at the same time, hence this is its terminal value.

Bank account

Time	Balance b/f £	Interest for Year £	Receipt at Year End £	Balance c/f £
1	100.00	10.00	–	110.00
2	110.00	11.00	–	121.00
3	121.00	12.10	–	133.10

Conclusion

Both investments produce a better end position than the simple investment in the bank. Investment A will result in £2.61 more cash (£135.71 – £133.10) and Investment B, £0.90 more (£134.00 – £133.10). Comparing the two, Investment A now appears preferable to Investment B.

It would certainly seem that it is in the investor's interest to pay more attention to the cash flows expected from an investment and the timing of these cash flows, than to solely consider the level of profit.

Alternative Solution

An alternative way of dealing with the example would be by compounding the interest on each flow individually.

Investment A

Time	Cash Flow (£)	Compound Factor	Terminal Value (£)
1	41.00	1.1^2	49.61
2	41.00	1.1	45.10
3	41.00	1	41.00
Terminal value			135.71

Investment B

Time	Cash Flow (£)	Compound Factor	Terminal Value (£)
1	0.00	1.1^2	0.00
2	0.00	1.1	0.00
3	134.00	1	134.00
Terminal value			134.00

Here, we have compounded each flow by adding on interest at 10% p.a. for the number of years remaining until the end of the lives of the investments. To achieve this, we have multiplied in each case by the compound factor which, in general terms, may be written as

Formula to learn

Compound factor with n years to run = $(1+r)^n$

Where r is the rate of interest expressed as a decimal (here, r = 0.1) and n is the number of years compounding required.

Clearly the calculations have produced the same result, but the method used is somewhat neater. We have compounded the flows to produce what is termed the terminal value of each flow.

Again this can be compared to the £133.10 terminal value from the bank account to show that the investments are worthwhile.

3.2.2 Net terminal value

The net surplus or deficit from the investment (£2.61 for Investment A, £0.90 for Investment B as calculated above) is known as the net terminal value (NTV), and since it is positive, indicating a surplus, the investments are worthwhile and should be accepted. Had it been negative, indicating a deficit, we would have rejected both investments.

Rather than calculating the terminal values of the investment and the bank account separately, we can combine them in one net terminal value calculation as follows.

Investment A

Time	Cash Flow (£)	Compound Factor	Terminal Value (£)
0	(100.00)	1.1^3	(133.10)
1	41.00	1.1^2	49.61
2	41.00	1.1	45.10
3	41.00	1	41.00
Terminal value			2.61

Here, we are considering the £100 invested initially as a cash outflow from the business on which we will lose interest. In turn, we get the investment inflows, which generate interest, but it is the net difference we are interested in.

Investment B

Time	Cash Flow (£)	Compound Factor	Terminal Value (£)
0	(100.00)	1.1^3	(133.10)
1	0.00	1.1^2	0.00
2	0.00	1.1	0.00
3	134.00	1	134.00
Terminal value			0.90

4 PRESENT VALUES AND NET PRESENT VALUES

Exam tip

> Present value ideas allow us to place a value on an asset today, i.e. determine its current price. When we look at the pricing of derivatives we will be applying the ideas below, hence a full understanding of this area is essential.

4.1 Introduction

One way of accounting for the interest is, as we have just seen, by compounding the flows and calculating the terminal values. However, as we stated, if we are to compare investments, we will have to calculate to a common date, say the end of the longest investment period. An alternative approach is to use present values where we take the common date as the present.

4.2 Present values

4.2.1 Introduction

For any investment, **present value** calculations consider

- Each relevant cash flow; and
- The timing of the cash flow

and calculate how much cash would need to be invested now to generate these same amounts of cash at these same dates.

If we can get the same cash at the same dates by investing less upfront now, then we should accept the investment.

Solution

Investment A

Investment A generates the following cash flows

Time	Cash Flow £
1	41.00
2	41.00
3	41.00

Looking at each of these in turn, how much cash would we need to invest now at a 10% rate of return to have £41.00 in each year?

Year 1

If we invest x now, then in one year, it will grow to $x \times 1.1 = 1.1x$. Since we know that this is £41.00, then we can calculate x as

$$1.1x = £41.00$$

or

$$x = \frac{1}{1.1} \times £41.00$$

$$x = £37.27$$

Year 2

Similarly, x invested now will grow to $x \times 1.1^2 = 1.21x$ after two years, hence

$$1.21x = £41.00$$

or

$$x = \frac{1}{1.21} \times £41.00$$

$$x = £33.89$$

Year 3

x invested now will grow to $x \times 1.1^3 = 1.331x$ after three years, hence

$$1.331x = £41.00$$

4: FINANCIAL MATHEMATICS

or

$$x = \frac{1}{1.331} \times £41.00$$

$$x = £30.80$$

Conclusion

Putting all these together, we have

Time	Cash Flow (£)	Discount Factor	Present Value (£)
1	41.00	$\frac{1}{1.1}$	37.27
2	41.00	$\frac{1}{1.1^2}$	33.89
3	41.00	$\frac{1}{1.1^3}$	30.80
Present value			101.96

Thus, the present value of these receipts in total is £101.96. What this means is that given this rate of return, we would be indifferent between £41.00 each year for three years and £101.96 now.

Rather than compounding up the cash values for interest generated to the end of the investment, we are **discounting down**, i.e. making future cash receipts look less valuable since they are further in the future.

This discounting is effectively the reverse of our compounding process and, in a similar way, we could apply a general formula for any year of

Formula to learn

$$\text{Discount factor at Time n} = \frac{1}{(1+r)^n}$$

Where r is the **discount rate**, i.e. rate of interest expressed as a decimal (here r = 0.10) and n is the number of years discounting required.

Investment B

Calculating the present value for Investment B gives

Time	Cash Flow (£)	Discount Factor	Present Value (£)
3	134.00	$\frac{1}{1.1^3}$	100.68
Present value			100.68

What this means is that we would be indifferent, given the 10% rate of return, between £134.00 in three years and £100.68 now.

Bank

What is the present value of our option of banking the cash? Under this option, we left the cash in the bank until Year 3, by which time it had grown to £133.10.

Time	Cash Flow (£)	Discount Factor	Present Value (£)
3	133.10	$\dfrac{1}{1.1^3}$	100.00
Present value			100.00

This case really proves the idea. It shows that we are indifferent between £133.10 in three years and £100.00 now, which stands to reason as to get £133.10 in three years will require us to deposit £100.00 now.

4.2.2 Net present value

The present value of Investment A is £1.96 higher than could be expected from the bank. Investment B has a present value that is £0.68 higher than that from the bank. These represent the **net present values** of these investments.

In a similar way to terminal values, we can calculate a net present value in one go rather than separately calculating the present value of the investment and the banking options.

Solution

Investment A

Time	Cash Flow (£)	Discount Factor	Present Value (£)
0	(100.00)	1	(100.00)
1	41.00	$\dfrac{1}{1.1}$	37.27
2	41.00	$\dfrac{1}{1.1^2}$	33.89
3	41.00	$\dfrac{1}{1.1^3}$	30.80
Net present value			1.96

You will note that the cash flow at Time 0 (now) is not discounted. £100 now is worth £100 now. What discounting takes account of is the Time Value of money.

Investment B

Time	Cash Flow (£)	Discount Factor	Present Value (£)
0	(100.00)	1	(100.00)
3	134.00	$\dfrac{1}{1.1^3}$	100.68
Net present value			0.68

4: FINANCIAL MATHEMATICS

4.2.3 Conclusion

For an accept or reject decision, the criterion is as before – **a positive net present value (NPV) indicates a cash surplus after accounting for interest and therefore, we should accept**. A negative NPV indicates a cash deficit and therefore, we should reject.

To choose between various investments, we would simply select the investment with the highest NPV.

4.3 Discount factors

4.3.1 Basic discount factor

We established above that the general term for a discount factor to be applied to cash flows at Time n is

$$\text{Discount factor at Time n} = \frac{1}{(1+r)^n}$$

There are some alternatives that may enable us to reduce our workload, specifically in the situations of

- Level annuities.
- Level perpetuities.

4.3.2 Level annuities

This is the situation when there is the same cash flow for a number of years. To calculate the present value of the annuity, the following formula may be used.

Formula to learn

Annuity discount factor for a flow from Time 1 to Time n $\dfrac{1}{r}\left(1-\dfrac{1}{(1+r)^n}\right)$

Reworking Investment A from the previous example.

Time	Cash Flow (£)	Discount Factor	Present Value (£)
0	(100.00)	1	(100.00)
1-3	41.00	$\dfrac{1}{0.1}\left(1-\dfrac{1}{1.1^3}\right)$	101.96
Net present value			1.96

4.3.3 Level perpetuity

This is a cash flow that is the same every year into perpetuity (infinity). The formula is

Formula to learn

Perpetuity discount factor for a flow from Time 1 into perpetuity = $\dfrac{1}{r}$

4.3.4 Continuous discounting

Just as it is possible to have continuous compounding, so it is possible to have continuous discounting.

Discrete Compounding	Continuous Compounding

$(1 + r)^n$
where: r = annual rate
        n = compounding period in years
	e^{rt}
	where: r = annual rate
	        t = compounding period in years

Discrete Discounting	**Continuous Discounting**
$\dfrac{1}{(1+r)^n}$	$\dfrac{1}{e^{rt}} = e^{-rt}$

It is the continuous method of discounting that is used in most option-pricing models.

4.3.5 Discount factor tables

As an alternative to being given a rate and needing to calculate the discount factor for use in evaluation, you may be given a discount factor directly, probably in a small discount factor table. Based on the 10% rate we have been using so far, the discount factor table would be

Time	Discount factor	
1	0.909090	$= \dfrac{1}{1.10}$
2	0.826446	$= \dfrac{1}{1.10^2}$
3	0.751315	$= \dfrac{1}{1.10^3}$

Example

Calculate the present value of three annual payments of £100

Solution

Time	Cash Flow	Discount Factor	Present Value
1	100.00	0.909090	90.91
2	100.00	0.826446	82.65
3	100.00	0.751315	75.13
Net present value			248.69

5 Internal Rate of Return/Yield

5.1 Introduction

Internal rate of return (IRR) calculations are another way of employing the DCF technique that can be extremely useful in certain circumstances.

Since the net present values of all our investments so far have been positive, we have determined that we should accept them. However, since our calculations are based on forecasts, it could easily be the case that there will be some mis-estimates and that we should have rejected the investments. One element that could obviously be incorrect is the 10% cost of capital that we have used. This could affect our decision for two reasons.

- It may not stay at 10% throughout the life of the investment.
- The calculation of the current rate being 10% may be incorrect.

On the basis of the above, we may be in a position where all we can say is that the cost of capital is about 10%.

At exactly 10% the NPV is positive and we accept, but what if the cost were actually a little higher, would the NPV still be positive and would we still be correct in accepting? One approach to deal with this problem would be to calculate the NPV at various rates of interest and investigate the results.

For our example, the NPVs at various rates of interest are as follows.

Rate %	Investment A NPV £	Investment B NPV £
5.0	11.65	15.75
7.5	6.62	7.86
10.0	1.96	0.68
12.5	(2.36)	(5.88)
15.0	(6.39)	(11.89)
17.5	(10.14)	(17.40)
20.0	(13.63)	(22.45)

As expected, the investments become less worthwhile as the cost of money increases. Logically, as interest rates rise, fewer and fewer investments will generate a return sufficient to service that interest. Hence, fewer will be worthwhile.

On a graph, we can see a fairly standard illustration of how NPVs vary, with changes in the cost of capital for normal investments where we make an initial investment and then receive future returns.

4: FINANCIAL MATHEMATICS

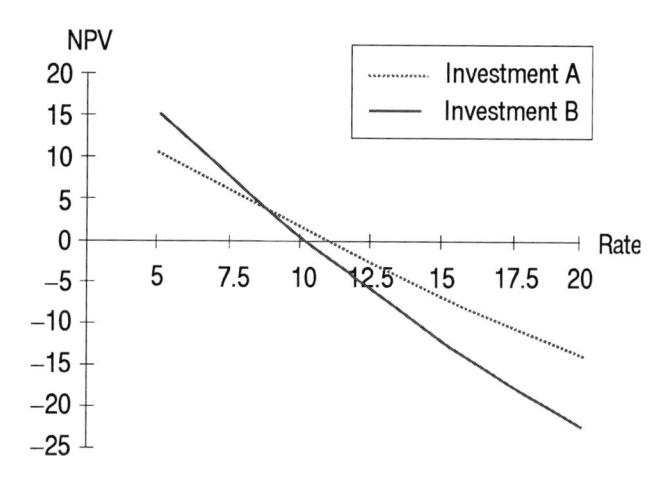

Graph showing NPV vs Rate for Investment A (dotted) and Investment B (solid). NPV axis ranges from -25 to 20; Rate axis from 5 to 20.

As we can see, the NPV of Investment A will be zero for a cost of capital of roughly 11%. We can say that for a cost of capital of up to 11%, we should accept Investment A, whereas if the cost of capital exceeds 11%, we should reject it.

Similarly, it appears that the NPV of Investment B becomes zero at roughly 10.3%, and therefore, though it shows a positive NPV at our estimated cost of capital of 10%, we do not have a very big margin of error in these calculations.

These are, however, estimates from the graph. To get the true figure, we would need to undertake a process of trial and error – try a rate and see if it gives a zero NPV.

5.2 Definition

This breakeven rate is known as the **internal rate of return** (IRR), which we can define as

IRR = the rate of interest that discounts the investment flows to a net present value of zero

Calculating the IRR of an investment gives two things

- The breakeven cost of capital.
- The margin of safety we have regarding the estimated cost of capital.

Although the above trial and error approach is really the only way of finding the exact internal rate of return, it is obviously time consuming. The exact IRR for Investment A calculated by using this approach turns out to be 11.11% to two decimal places.

As an alternative, we have a quick approximation that we can use. We would very rarely need a precise figure for the IRR and this approach is therefore quite adequate.

5.3 Calculation

The method we use is called **interpolation** whereby we evaluate the NPV at two different costs of capital and then, by assuming a straight-line relationship, estimate where it becomes zero. The formula for this is

Formula to learn

$$IRR = R_1 + \left(\frac{N_1}{N_1 - N_2} \times (R_2 - R_1) \right)$$

where

- R_1 = first selected cost of capital
- R_2 = second selected cost of capital
- N_1 = NPV of the investment when discounted at R_1
- N_2 = NPV of the investment when discounted at R_2

4: FINANCIAL MATHEMATICS

Interpolation means finding a result between the two figures that we have chosen, i.e. selecting R_1 and R_2 such that the IRR falls in between.

Extrapolation means estimating a figure outside of that range, i.e. selecting values for R_1 and R_2 such that the IRR does not fall in between.

Interpolation will give the more accurate solution, hence we should always try to achieve this if possible.

Continuing with Our Example

Investment A

At 10%, the net present value is £1.96, and therefore 10% is clearly not the IRR. It must be a higher rate than 10%, since we know that the NPV decreases with increases in the cost of capital.

We therefore make a second guess at a higher rate, say 15%, at which we find the NPV is (£6.39).

We now know that the IRR lies somewhere between 10% and 15%. We need to estimate the rate that will yield zero, but how?

Over a range of 5%, i.e. from 10% to 15%, the net present value has fallen by £8.35, i.e. from £1.96 to (£6.39). We therefore assume that the £8.35 fall in the NPV equates to the 5% increase in the cost of capital linearly.

If we take 10% as our starting point (for which the NPV is £1.96), we need a change of (£1.96) to get the NPV down to zero. This will require a change in the rate of interest of

$$\text{Change in rate} = £1.96 \times \frac{5\%}{£8.35} = 1.17\%$$

The internal rate of return is therefore

$$\text{IRR} = 10\% + \left(\frac{£1.96}{£1.96 - (-£6.39)} \times (15\% - 10\%) \right)$$

$$\text{IRR} = 11.17\%$$

As we can see, this corresponds fairly closely to the true IRR of 11.11%. However, it is important to appreciate that this is only an approximation to the IRR, since we have assumed that the NPV changes linearly with the rate of interest, which we already know from the earlier graph is not the case.

In addition, a different pair of rates would yield a different IRR. The closer the rates to the actual IRR, the more accurate the result.

If we had used rates of 5% and 20%, we would estimate the IRR as

$$\text{IRR} = 5\% + \left(\frac{£11.16}{£11.16 - (-£13.63)} \times (20\% - 5\%) \right)$$

$$\text{IRR} = 11.75\%$$

6 Securities Evaluation and DCF

6.1 Introduction

The dividend valuation model (DVM) is the basis for all our calculations relating to the market value of any investment.

In order to raise finance, a company must attract investors, i.e. the investors must believe that they will receive a return sufficient to match their requirements. If they do not believe this, then they will not invest.

As a result, the market value of a security at any point in time is determined by two factors.

- The returns (dividends/interest/capital growth) that the investors expect.
- The rate of return that the investors require.

The dividend valuation model states that the

> Market value = Present value of the future expected receipts discounted at the investors' required rate of return

In other words, we assume that investors evaluate rationally the returns in order to determine what they are willing to pay. Though we may be cynical about particular investors, in the UK we can be fairly sure that the majority of dealing is rationally assessed.

Alternatively the investors' required rate of return can be calculated as the IRR of the current market value and subsequent repayments (dividends, interest, capital, etc.).

NB: These comments relate equally to **all** investments.

6.2 Equity valuation

Assume a company pays a constant dividend of £1 into perpetuity. The value of the share will be the present value of the dividends that are paid into perpetuity, discounted at the shareholders' required return, e.g. 10%.

$$MV = \frac{£1}{0.1} = £10$$

6.3 Bond valuation

6.3.1 Irredeemable bonds

These can be valued in the same way as equity. The coupon, paid into perpetuity, will be discounted at the bondholders' required rate of return.

6.3.2 Redeemable bonds

The way to value these is to discount the future flows at the required rate. The required rate can either be the yield or the appropriate spot rate.

Example

A bond pays an annual coupon of 9% and is to be redeemed at par in three years. The required return on these bonds is 8%. What will be their market value?

Solution

Their market value can be established by calculating the present value of the associated cash flows at the required rate of 8%. The cash flows from the bond will be £9 coupon at the end of each year and £100 capital redemption at the end of the third year, i.e. £109 is received in total at that time. The market value can, therefore, be calculated as

Time	Cash Flow (£)	Discount Factor	Present Value (£)
1	9.00	$\dfrac{1}{1.08}$	8.33
2	9.00	$\dfrac{1}{1.08^2}$	7.72
3	109.00	$\dfrac{1}{1.08^3}$	86.53
Market value			102.58

6.3.3 Floating Rate Notes

A short-cut method of valuing a FRN is to use the following formula.

Formula to learn

$$MV = \frac{C + 100}{1 + r}$$

where

C = next coupon
r = appropriate spot rate to receipt of next coupon

7 ASSUMPTIONS UNDERLYING DCF

7.1 Introduction

At this stage it is worthwhile to consider the assumptions of DCF we have implicitly been making in all of the NPV and IRR calculations made to date.

7.1.1 The basic assumptions

- The cash flows expected to accrue from any investment can be considered in isolation, and are independent of decisions relating to any other investment.
- The cash flows are known with certainty.
- No firm or individual has sufficient funds to affect the price of funds.
- Investors have a time preference for money and make rational decisions accordingly.

7.1.2 The assumptions as to reinvestment rates

The fundamental difference between NPV and IRR is the assumption made about reinvestment rates. Under NPV, we are implicitly assuming that any surplus funds generated can be reinvested to earn a return equal to the discount rate.

However, the IRR calculation assumes that surplus funds will be reinvested to earn a return equal to the IRR and that the time value placed on money is this rate.

Conceptually NPV is better because, regardless of the actual investment that is generating the cash flows, we always assume the flows can be reinvested at the same rate. There is no real justification for saying that returns from one investment can be reinvested to earn a return in excess of the returns earned from any other investment.

8 RISK MEASUREMENT

Exam tip

You are unlikely to be asked to calculate the risk or volatility of an asset but it is essential that you understand what these measures show as they are key inputs to derivatives pricing models.

8.1 Introduction

In the subsequent pricing chapters, a vital input into an option-pricing model is volatility. Volatility is a measure of variability (in, for example, share price). How is this mathematically calculated?

Variability, or volatility, is measured as the standard deviation (σ) of returns. This can be calculated using historic data or anticipated future price movements.

The formula to calculate the standard deviation of historic returns is

Formula to learn

$$\sigma = \sqrt{\frac{\sum f(r - \bar{r})^2}{n}}$$

Or

Formula to learn

$$\sigma = \sqrt{\frac{\sum fr^2 - n\bar{r}^2}{n}}$$

If using a **sample** of past returns (rather than the whole universe of data) it is more accurate to use n – 1 as the denominator. This adjustment is known as Bessel's correction.

Example

Quarterly returns for two securities, A and B, over the last two years are as follows.

Year	Quarter	A (%)	B (%)
1	1	16	14
	2	18	15
	3	12	12
	4	15	14
2	1	14	13
	2	15	15
	3	17	17
	4	13	12
		120	112

4: FINANCIAL MATHEMATICS

Mean returns, $\bar{r}$, can be calculated as follows.

Security A: $\bar{r} = \dfrac{120}{8} = 15\%$

Security B: $\bar{r} = \dfrac{112}{8} = 14\%$

Standard deviation – Security A

Year	Quarter	r (%)	$(r-\bar{r})$ (%)	$(r-\bar{r})^2$ (%)	r^2 (%)
1	1	16	1	1	256
	2	18	3	9	324
	3	12	−3	9	144
	4	15	0	0	225
2	1	14	−1	1	196
	2	15	0	0	225
	3	17	2	4	289
	4	13	−2	4	169
		120		28	1,828

The final column is only shown so that the use of the second formula can be demonstrated.

$$\sigma = \sqrt{\dfrac{28}{8-1}} = 2\%$$

or

$$\sigma = \sqrt{\dfrac{1{,}828 - 8 \times 15^2}{8-1}} = 2\%$$

Standard deviation – Security B

Year	Quarter	r (%)	$(r-\bar{r})$ (%)	$(r-\bar{r})^2$ (%)
1	1	14	0	0
	2	15	1	1
	3	12	−2	4
	4	14	0	0
2	1	13	−1	1
	2	15	1	1
	3	17	3	9
	4	12	−2	4
		112		20

$$\sigma = \sqrt{\dfrac{20}{8-1}} = 1.69\%$$

8.2 Comments

In the examination, it has never been a requirement to calculate the volatility from raw data as just demonstrated. What has occurred in the exam – in the context of equity basket options – is the need to combine securities and calculate the combined volatility covered next.

Before moving on, however, it is important to emphasise what the standard deviation is actually giving us, which may have been lost in the calculation. The standard deviation is the average of the deviations (either up or down) of the observed values away from the mean. As such it represents the average amount by which we believe prices will rise if we expect them to rise, or by which we believe prices will fall if we expect them to fall. It is the average or expected movement either up or down and we will see the relevance of this under options pricing later.

8.3 Calculating the risk of a combination of securities

To do this, one additional piece of information is required, namely the correlation between the returns of the two securities.

The following formula can then be used.

Formula to learn

$$\sigma_{a+b} = \sqrt{p_a^2 \sigma_a^2 + p_b^2 \sigma_b^2 + 2 p_a p_b \sigma_a \sigma_b \text{cor}_{ab}}$$

where

- p = proportion of funds invested in each security
- σ = standard deviation (risk) of each security's returns
- cor = correlation between the returns on two securities

Example

Calculate the volatility of an evenly weighted portfolio consisting of Security A and Security B if the correlation coefficient between the returns of A and the returns of B is 0.60.

$$\sigma_{a+b} = \sqrt{0.5^2 \times 2^2 + 0.5^2 \times 1.69^2 + 2 \times 0.5 \times 0.5 \times 2 \times 1.69 \times 0.6}$$

$\sigma_{a+b} = 1.65\%$

From the above, it can be noted that there are three factors that influence the resulting risk.

- Volatilities of the individual securities.
- Proportion of each security within the portfolio.
- Correlations between the returns of the individual securities.

If any one of these changes, then the resulting risk will change.

What if the correlation between the two securities was zero, i.e. no correlation?

$$\sigma_{a+b} = \sqrt{0.5^2 \times 2^2 + 0.5^2 \times 1.69^2}$$

$\sigma_{a+b} = 1.2946\%$

What if the proportions become 70% Security A and 30% Security B?

$$\sigma_{a+b} = \sqrt{0.7^2 \times 2^2 + 0.3^2 \times 1.69^2 + 2 \times 0.7 \times 0.3 \times 2 \times 1.69 \times 0.6}$$

$\sigma_{a+b} = 1.7518\%$

4: FINANCIAL MATHEMATICS

The above examples have all looked at combining two securities. What if there was a need to combine more than two? The answer is to extend the previously used formula by including the proportion of funds invested in the additional securities and also by including a function relating to all the possible correlations that exist between the various securities. For example, if three securities are included, the formula becomes

Formula to learn

$$\sigma_{a+b+c} = \sqrt{p_a^2\sigma_a^2 + p_b^2\sigma_b^2 + p_c^2\sigma_c^2 + 2p_ap_b\sigma_a\sigma_b cor_{ab} + 2p_ap_c\sigma_a\sigma_c cor_{ac} + 2p_bp_c\sigma_b\sigma_c cor_{bc}}$$

If four securities are involved the formula becomes

Formula to learn

$$\sigma_{a+b+c+d} = \sqrt{\begin{array}{l} p_a^2\sigma_a^2 + p_b^2\sigma_b^2 + p_c^2\sigma_c^2 + p_d^2\sigma_d^2 + 2p_ap_b\sigma_a\sigma_b cor_{ab} + 2p_ap_c\sigma_a\sigma_c cor_{ac} \\ + 2p_bp_c\sigma_b\sigma_c cor_{bc} + 2p_ap_d\sigma_a\sigma_d cor_{ad} + 2p_bp_d\sigma_b\sigma_d cor_{bd} + 2p_cp_d\sigma_c\sigma_d cor_{cd} \end{array}}$$

As formulae, these are starting to get out of hand, however ignoring the square root sign the right hand side can be split into two components.

- Combined weighted variances for each security i.e.

$$p_a^2\sigma_a^2 + p_b^2\sigma_b^2 + \ldots$$

- Correlation terms between each pair at securities, i.e.

$$2p_ap_b\sigma_a\sigma_b cor_{ab}$$
$$2p_ap_c\sigma_a\sigma_c cor_{ac}$$
$$\vdots$$

Calculations for more than two securities are probably best dealt with in a tabular form.

Example

You are given the following information about a portfolio of three securities

Security	Weighting	Volatility %
A	0.4	25
B	0.3	30
C	0.3	20

Correlation matrix

	A	B	C
A	1.00	0.50	0.40
B		1.00	0.60
C			1.00

Calculate the volatility of the portfolio.

Solution

Security	Weighting p	Volatility σ	Portfolio
A	0.4	25	100.0
B	0.3	30	81.0
C	0.3	20	36.0
$p_a^2\sigma_a^2 + p_b^2\sigma_b^2 + p_c^2\sigma_c^2$			217.0

Correlation terms

$2p_a p_b \sigma_a \sigma_b \text{cor}_{ab} = 2 \times 0.4 \times 0.3 \times 25 \times 30 \times 0.5 =$ 90.0

$2p_a p_c \sigma_a \sigma_c \text{cor}_{ac} = 2 \times 0.4 \times 0.3 \times 25 \times 20 \times 0.4 =$ 48.0

$2p_b p_c \sigma_b \sigma_c \text{cor}_{bc} = 2 \times 0.3 \times 0.3 \times 30 \times 20 \times 0.6 =$ 64.8

σ_{a+b+c}^2 419.8

$\sigma_{a+b+c} = \sqrt{419.8} = 20.49\%$

CHAPTER ROUNDUP

- To calculate a present or terminal value there are three relevant factors.
  - Cash flow – value to be multiplied by the relevant compound or discount factor.
  - Timing – determines which factor to use, basic, annuity, perpetuity.
  - Rate – determines the rate r for that factor.
- Fisher equation

  $$(1+r) = (1+i)(1+R)$$

- Discount factors
  - Basic

    $$\frac{1}{(1+r)^n}$$

  - Basic continuous

    $$\frac{1}{e^{rt}}$$

  - Annuity

    $$\frac{1}{r}\left(1 - \frac{1}{(1+r)^n}\right)$$

  - Perpetuity

    $$\frac{1}{r}$$

  - IRR

    Calculated by guessing two rates then interpolating using

    $$IRR = R_1 + \left(\frac{N_1}{N_1 - N_2} \times (R_2 - R_1)\right)$$

- You need to be aware what the standard deviation means.
- You need to be able to calculate a portfolio's risk.

Test Your Knowledge

Check your knowledge of the Chapter here, without referring back to the text.

1. What is the terminal value of £1,000 invested now for six years at 8% p.a.?

2. What does £475 become if invested at a compound interest rate of 11% for eight years?

3. What is the terminal value of £1,000 invested now for three years at 8% followed by three years at 9%?

4. You invest £500 at 8% for five years, then withdraw the funds and invest this at 9% for four years. What is the value of the account at the end of nine years?

5. You invest £7,000 at 7% for four years and 8% thereafter. What is the terminal value at the end of nine years?

6. An asset is purchased for £50. Over the next four quarters, it has returns of 4%, 5%, 2% and –3%. what will be the value of the asset at the end of the year?

7. An investment rises in value from £5,000 to £6,742 over four years. What is its constant annual rate of appreciation?

8. What is the present value of £1,000 received in eight years' time at 10% p.a.?

9. What is the present value of £7,000 to be received eight years from now if the annual interest rate is 9%?

10. Before pressing ahead with a major investment project costing £12 million, the managing director of a large engineering firm examines detailed cash flow projections. She believes that the project will yield returns of £3 million at the end of each of the first three years, at which point it will still be worth £9 million. What is the net present value of this project, with a discount rate of 10%?

11. What is the present value of receiving £1,000 p.a. for six years starting in one year's time at 8% p.a.?

12. The rate of interest for a repayment mortgage of £75,000 over 25 years is 9%. What is the annual repayment required at the end of each year?

13. A repayment mortgage of £75,000 is taken out over 20 years at a rate of interest of 11.1%. What is the annual repayment required at the end of each year?

14. What is the value of a bond with an infinite life that pays £100 per annum when the required rate of return is 8%?

15. What is the present value of receiving £1,000 p.a. in perpetuity at 8% p.a. starting now?

16. What is the continuously compounded rate of interest for 100 days given an annual rate of 8%?

17. What is the terminal value of £10,000 invested at 8% for 150 days continuously compounded?

18. If an investment grows from £240 to £260 over a period of 267 days in a normal 365 day year, what is the annual rate of return calculated on a continuously compounded basis?

19. What is the present value of £10,000 received in 200 days at 9% p.a. continuously compounded?

4: FINANCIAL MATHEMATICS

20. An investor bought 1,000 shares in Megagrowth plc at 74 pence each, received net dividends of 3 pence per share and 6 pence per share at the end of each of the first two years respectively, and then sold them at the end of the second year for 80 pence each. What is the internal rate of return on this investment?

21. If an investor buys 1,000 shares at £3.55 each and receives dividends of 20 pence, 30 pence, and 32 pence at the end of each of the next three years respectively, before selling them at £3.98 each, what is the internal rate of return on this investment

22. If an investor buys 750 shares at 104 pence each and receives a dividend of 5 pence at the end of the first year, 6 pence at the end of the second year, and 6.5 pence at the end of the third year, at which point he sells them for 120 pence each, what is the internal rate of return on this investment?

23. A three security portfolio contains the following shares

Security	Weighting	Volatility	Correlations x	y	z
x	0.25	10%	1.00	0.40	0.30
y	0.50	12%		1.00	0.50
z	0.25	16%			1.00

Calculate the portfolio risk.

TEST YOUR KNOWLEDGE: ANSWERS

1.

Time	Cash flow (£)	Compound factor	Terminal value (£)
0	1,000	1.08^6	1,587

2. £475 × 1.11^8 = £1,095

3.

Time	Cash Flow	Compound Factor	Terminal Value
	£		£
0	1,000	$1.08^3 \times 1.09^3$	1,631

4. £500 × 1.08^5 × 1.09^4 = £1,037.04

5.

Time	Cash (£)	CF	PV (£)
0	7,000	$1.07^4 \times 1.08^5$	13,482

6. £50 × 1.04 × 1.05 × 1.02 × 0.97 = £54.02

7. $1 + r = \sqrt[4]{\dfrac{6,742}{5,000}} = 1.0776$

   r = 0.0776 or 7.76%

8.

Time	Cash flow (£)	Discount factor	Present Value (£)
8	1,000	$\dfrac{1}{1.1^8}$	467

9. PV = £7,000 × $\dfrac{1}{1.09^8}$ = £3,513

10.

Time	Cash Flow	DF (10%)	PV
0	(12)	1.0000	(12.00)
1	3	0.9091	2.73
2	3	0.8264	2.48
3	12	0.7513	9.02
			2.23

4: FINANCIAL MATHEMATICS

11.

Time	Cash Flow (£)	Discount Factor	Present Value (£)
1	1,000	$\dfrac{1}{1.08}$	926
2	1,000	$\dfrac{1}{1.08^2}$	857
3	1,000	$\dfrac{1}{1.08^3}$	794
4	1,000	$\dfrac{1}{1.08^4}$	735
5	1,000	$\dfrac{1}{1.08^5}$	681
6	1,000	$\dfrac{1}{1.08^6}$	630
Present value			4,623

Alternative

Using the annuity formula gives

$$1,000 \times \frac{1}{0.08}\left(1-\frac{1}{1.08^6}\right) = 4,623$$

12. £75,000 = Annual payment × AF(1-25)

$$AF(1\text{-}25) = \frac{1}{0.09}\left(1-\frac{1}{1.09^{25}}\right) = 9.823$$

Annual payment = = £7,635

13. PV of 20 year annuity = £75,000, i.e. annual payment × AF(1-20) = 75,000

$$AF(1\text{-}20@11.1\%) = \frac{1}{0.111}\left(1-\frac{1}{1.111^{20}}\right) = 7.9115$$

Annual payment = $\dfrac{£75,000}{7.9115}$ = £9,480

14. $£100 \times \dfrac{1}{1.08} = £1,250$

15. $PV = 1,000 + 1,000 \times \dfrac{1}{0.08} = £13,500$

16. r = 0.08   t = 100/365 = 0.274

Continously compounded rate equals

$e^{rt} - 1 = e^{0.08 \times 0.274} - 1 = 0.02216 = 2.216\%$

17. r = 0.08   t = 150/365 = 0.411

The terminal value

$£10,000 \times e^{rt} = £10,000 \times e^{0.08 \times 0.411} = £10,000 \times 1.0334 = £10,334$

18. £240 × e^{rt} = £260

    or

    $e^{rt} = \dfrac{260}{240} = 1.083333$

    Now t = 267/365 = 0.7315

    Therefore

    $e^{r \times 0.7315} = 1.083333$

    Taking the natural log of each side of this equation gives

    $\ln(e^{0.7315r}) = \ln(1.083333)$

    0.7315r = 0.08004

    r = 0.08004/0.7315 = 0.1094 or 10.94% p.a.

19. r = 0.09   t = 200/365 = 0.548

    The present value equals

    £10,000 × e^{-rt} = £10,000 × $e^{-0.09 \times 0.548}$ = £10,000 × 0.9519 = £9,519

20. Using the interpolation approach

    Amount invested = 74p

    Total return = 89p (3p + 6p + 80p)

    Approx total return = 89/74 = 1.20 or 20% over 2 years or 10% p.a.

    Trying 5% and 10% gives

Time	Cash flow	DF (5%)	PV	DF (10%)	PV
0	(74)	1	(74.00)	1	(74.00)
1	3	$\dfrac{1}{1.05}$	2.86	$\dfrac{1}{1.10}$	2.73
2	6	$\dfrac{1}{1.05^2}$	5.44	$\dfrac{1}{1.10^2}$	4.96
2	80	$\dfrac{1}{1.05^2}$	72.56	$\dfrac{1}{1.10^2}$	66.12
			6.86		(0.19)

    IRR = 5% + $\dfrac{6.86}{6.86 - (0.19)}$ × (10% − 5%) = 9.87%

21. Using the interpolation approach

    Amount invested = 355p
    Total return = 480p (20p + 30p + 32p + 398p)
    Approx total return = 480/355 = 1.35 or 35% over 3 years or about 11% p.a.
    Trying 10% and 15% gives

4: FINANCIAL MATHEMATICS

Time	Cash Flow	DF (10%)	PV	DF (15%)	PV
0	(355)	1	(355.00)	1	(355.00)
1	20	$\dfrac{1}{1.10}$	18.18	$\dfrac{1}{1.15}$	17.39
2	30	$\dfrac{1}{1.10^2}$	24.79	$\dfrac{1}{1.15^2}$	22.68
3	430	$\dfrac{1}{1.10^3}$	323.07	$\dfrac{1}{1.15^3}$	282.73
			11.04		(32.20)

$$IRR = 10\% + \frac{11.04}{11.04(32.20)} \times (15\% - 10\%) = 11.28\%$$

22. Using the interpolation approach

Amount invested = 104p
Total return = 137.5p (5p + 6p + 6.5p + 120p)
Approx total return = 137.5/104 = 1.32 or 32% over 3 years or about 10% p.a.
Trying 10% and 15% gives

Time	Cash Flow	DF (10%)	PV	DF (15%)	PV
0	(104.00)	1	(104.00)	1	(104.00)
1	5.0	$\dfrac{1}{1.10}$	4.55	$\dfrac{1}{1.15}$	4.35
2	6.0	$\dfrac{1}{1.10^2}$	4.96	$\dfrac{1}{1.15^2}$	4.54
3	6.5	$\dfrac{1}{1.10^3}$	4.88	$\dfrac{1}{1.15^3}$	4.27
3	120.0	$\dfrac{1}{1.10^3}$	90.16	$\dfrac{1}{1.15^3}$	78.90
			0.55		(11.94)

$$IRR = 10\% + \frac{0.55}{0.55(11.94)} \times (15\% - 10\%) = 10.22\%.$$

23.

Security	Weighting	Volatility	$p^2\sigma^2$
x	0.25	10	6.25
y	0.50	12	36.00
z	0.25	16	16.00
$p_a^2\sigma_a^2 + p_b^2\sigma_b^2 + p_c^2\sigma_c^2$			58.25

Correlation terms

– x with y	$2 \times 0.25 \times 0.5 \times 10 \times 12 \times 0.4 =$	12.00
– x with z	$2 \times 0.25 \times 0.25 \times 10 \times 16 \times 0.3 =$	6.00
– y with z	$2 \times 0.5 \times 0.25 \times 12 \times 16 \times 0.5 =$	24.00
σ_{x+y+z}^2		100.25

$\sigma_{x+y+z} = \sqrt{100.25} = 10.01\%$

5

Probability

INTRODUCTION

At any time before expiry it is uncertain whether an option may be exercised or not, and the chances of exercise may be expressed in terms of a likelihood or probability. As such an understanding of the ideas contained in this section are central to understand the valuation of options.

It is unlikely that pure probability questions will be asked in the exam but they will by utilised in pricing models later.

CHAPTER CONTENTS

		Page
1	Introduction	96
2	Definition	96
3	More Complex Applications	100
4	Probability Distributions	102
5	Binomial Distribution	103
6	Standard Normal Distribution	106
7	Lognormal Distribution	111
	Chapter Roundup	115
	Test Your Knowledge	117

Chapter Learning Objectives

The syllabus areas covered by this section are

- **Uses of futures**
    - Value in futures contracts
    - Value in options contracts

Exam tip | In this chapter, some introductory material on probability theory is discussed. It should be understood before dealing with its more directed application in the chapter on options-pricing.

1 Introduction

Very few things in life are absolutely certain, which frequently makes it impossible to determine exactly what will happen. For example, when you set off for work, you never know exactly (to the second) how long it will take to get in, or when you toss an unbiased coin, you will never know which way it will fall.

Investment returns clearly fall into this same category, i.e. they are subject to uncertainty. It is unlikely that we will know for sure what return a particular share will provide over the next year. This may make it somewhat difficult to decide which share should be selected for a portfolio whose performance is assessed annually.

Probability theory aims to provide a means of assessing the various possible outcomes or **events** in order to facilitate decision-making under such circumstances. Probability theory provides a basis for the assessment of risk in many contexts, such as the insurance industry, though our primary concern here is in the assessment of risk and expected return in investment appraisal.

Probability theory was first developed in relation to gambling and many of our examples are based on the use of coins, dice, cards, etc. because of their familiarity to people. Our ultimate aim is, however, to apply the ideas to the more practical business of options pricing.

2 Definition

2.1 Basic definition

The probability of an **event**, E, occurring as a result of undertaking a **test** or **trial** could be defined as

Formula to learn

$$P(E) = \frac{\text{The number of ways E can occur}}{\text{Total number of equally likely outcomes}}$$

This definition is relatively easy to appreciate with some fairly simple and logical examples.

Example 1

An unbiased coin is tossed, what is the probability of it coming up heads?

Solution 1

Applying the above relationship, there are a total of two equally likely possible outcomes (heads or tails) of which only one (heads) would be considered a success, hence

$$P(Heads) = \frac{1}{2} = 0.5 \text{ or } 50\%$$

Example 2

An unbiased dice is rolled, what is the probability of throwing a six?

Solution 2

Applying the above relationship once more, there are a total of six equally likely possible outcomes (1, 2, 3, 4, 5, 6) of which only one (6) would be considered a success, hence

$$P(Six) = \frac{1}{6} = 0.1667 \text{ or } 16.67\%$$

Example 3

A card is selected at random from a pack, what is the probability of it being a spade?

Solution 3

Once again applying the above relationship, there are a total of four equally likely possible outcomes (hearts, diamonds, clubs, spades) of which only one (spades) would be considered a success, hence

$$P(Spade) = \frac{1}{4} = 0.25 \text{ or } 25\%$$

2.2 Extending the definition

One problem with the above definition is that it requires complete knowledge of all possible outcomes in particular circumstances. Clearly, this is not always going to be the case. For example, what is the probability that a particular individual will crash his car this year?

The only approach that can be adopted here is to ascertain the frequency of occurrence in the past and assume that the same frequency will continue into the future, i.e.

Formula to learn

$$P(E) = \frac{\text{The number of observed occurrences of E}}{\text{Total number of observed occurrences}}$$

It can be seen that this is not dissimilar to the initial definition above, and all insurance policies are based upon this type of probability calculation as are investment projections.

Example

A share price has fallen on seven days out of ten, what is the probability that the share price will rise on any day?

Solution

Applying the above relationship, in a ten-day period the price will rise on three days, hence

$$P(\text{Rise on one day}) = \frac{3}{10} = 0.30 \text{ or } 30\%$$

2.3 Probability values

2.3.1 Basic Values

Probabilities are generally expressed as a fraction, decimal or a percentage as above, though throughout this session, we utilise fractions and decimals.

From the above definition, it is evident that the probability of a particular event occurring lies between 0 and 1 (or 100%) and these two extremes can be viewed as follows.

- If it is certain that the event (E) **will not** occur, then the number of occurrences will always be zero, hence probability of it occurring is zero, $P(E) = 0$.
- If it is certain that the event (E) **will** definitely occur, then the number of occurrences will always equal the number of trials, hence the probability of it occurring is one, $P(E) = 1$.

Clearly, all events lie somewhere between absolutely no chance and a dead certainty, hence the probabilities lie between 0 and 1 as we noted above.

2.3.2 Sum of probabilities

Extending this idea, the sum of the probabilities of all possible outcomes must equal one, since it is certain that one of them will occur.

Example 1

Earlier we established that when we toss an unbiased coin

$$P(\text{Heads}) = \frac{1}{2}$$

similarly

$$P(\text{Tails}) = \frac{1}{2}$$

and, since these represent all the possibilities, we can see

$$P(\text{Heads}) + P(\text{Tails}) = \frac{1}{2} + \frac{1}{2} = 1$$

Example 2

Earlier we also established that when we select a card from a pack

$$P(\text{Spades}) = \frac{1}{4}$$

similarly

$$P(\text{Hearts}) = P(\text{Diamonds}) = P(\text{Clubs}) = \frac{1}{4}$$

and since these represent all the possibilities, we can see

$$P(\text{Spades}) + P(\text{Hearts}) + P(\text{Diamonds}) + P(\text{Clubs})$$
$$= \frac{1}{4} + \frac{1}{4} + \frac{1}{4} + \frac{1}{4} = 1$$

2.3.3 The Concept of NOT

Continuing this last example enables us to illustrate the concept of NOT. Clearly, if we do not select a spade, then we select a heart, diamond or club, hence

$$P(\text{NOT Spades}) = P(\text{Hearts}) + P(\text{Diamonds}) + P(\text{Clubs}) = \frac{3}{4}$$

Now

$$P(\text{Spades}) + P(\text{Hearts}) + P(\text{Diamonds}) + P(\text{Clubs}) = 1$$

from which it follows that

$$P(\text{Spades}) + P(\text{NOT Spades}) = 1$$

and hence

$$P(\text{Spades}) = 1 - P(\text{NOT Spades})$$

In this context, this seems obvious but superfluous. The idea can be seen to have some attractions. However, let us consider the following example.

Example

What is the probability of finding two or more misprinted pages in 500?

Solution

We do not have the information to actually evaluate this problem, though we can, at least, consider the approach. There are two possible approaches we could adopt to the calculation, as follows.

Alternative 1

$$P(2 \text{ or more}) = P(2) + P(3) + P(4) + \cdots + P(500)$$

Alternative 2

$$P(2 \text{ or more}) = 1 - P(\text{NOT 2 or more})$$
$$= 1 - [P(0) + P(1)]$$

which will be a lot easier to evaluate.

3 More Complex Applications

3.1 Introduction

So far, we have considered relatively easy examples looking at just one test (one toss of the coin, one throw of the dice, one day's observation) and determining the probability of just one event or outcome (a head, a six, a price rise). The problems that arise in relation to probabilities are

- The ways that events are related and the implications of this on the performance of the trials.
- The ways that events may be combined when more than one is considered.

3.2 Relationships between events

When we undertake a test or series of tests, we will find that the possible outcomes may either be

- **Independent**, i.e. the outcome of one has no effect on the outcome of the others.
- **Dependent**, i.e. the outcome of one test **does** have an effect on the subsequent ones.

When we consider the possible outcomes from any one test, they may be either

- **Mutually exclusive**, i.e. they may **not** occur simultaneously.
- **Not mutually exclusive**, i.e. they may occur together.

The impact of these relationships is considered below.

3.3 Combining events

3.3.1 Introduction

In certain types of tests, there are several ways of viewing the events. In our example above, involving the selection of a card from a pack, we ascertained the probability of selecting a spade. We could equally have calculated the probability of selecting a card with a specific value.

Example

A card is selected at random from a pack, what is the probability of it being an ace?

Solution

There are a total of 52 possible outcomes (Ace, 2, 3, 4, 5, 6, 7, 8, 9, 10, J, Q, K), of which only four (Ace) we would consider a success, hence

$$P(Ace) = \frac{4}{52}$$

What we are seeing are different ways of viewing the outcomes, i.e. two different **events** arising from the same test, and there are two ways that we could consider combining these events.

- What is the probability of a particular suit AND a particular value?
- What is the probability of a particular suit OR a particular value?

3.3.2 AND – The multiplication law

Independent events

What if, in our cards example, we wanted to establish the probability of selecting a card that is both a particular suit **AND** a particular value, e.g. the ace of spades. Clearly, the suit and the value of the card are independent of each other, since all four suits have all 13 values, hence we are combining independent events. The relationship that can be used to establish this probability is

$$P(A \text{ AND } B) = P(A) \times P(B)$$

Example

A card is selected at random from a pack, what is the probability of it being both a spade and an ace, i.e. the ace of spades?

Solution

There are two possible approaches to this question, use

- First principles.
- The multiplication law.

The purpose of this example is clearly to illustrate the latter, though in this situation, the former is more obvious. The former can be seen as a proof of the multiplication law.

First principles

There are a total of 52 possible outcomes (52 different cards in a pack), of which only one (the ace of spades) would be considered a success, hence

$$P(\text{Ace of Spades}) = \frac{1}{52}$$

Multiplication law

We established above that

$$P(\text{Ace}) = \frac{1}{13}$$

$$P(\text{Spade}) = \frac{1}{4}$$

The probability of both occurring, i.e. the probability of selecting the ace of spades, in this situation can be found by using

$$P(A \text{ AND } B) = P(A) \times P(B)$$

giving

$$P(\text{Ace AND Spade}) = P(\text{Ace}) \times P(\text{Spade})$$
$$= \frac{1}{13} \times \frac{1}{4} = \frac{1}{52}$$

3.3.3 OR – The addition law

Mutually exclusive events

What if, returning to our cards example, we wished to establish the probability of selecting a card that is either a spade **or** a heart. These are two mututally exclusive events since a card cannot be both a spade and a heart simultaneously. The relationship that can be used to establish the probability in this situation is

$$P(A \text{ OR } B) = P(A) + P(B)$$

Example

A card is selected at random from a pack, what is the probability of it being either a spade or a heart?

Solution

Again, there are two possible approaches to this question, use either

- First principles; or
- The addition law.

Once more the purpose of this example is to illustrate the latter, though the former is used as a proof of the addition law.

First principles

There are a totally of 52 possible outcomes (52 different cards in a pack) of which 26 (thirteen spades and thirteen hearts) would be considered a success, hence

$$P(\text{Spade OR Heart}) = \frac{26}{52} = 0.50$$

Addition law

We established above that

$$P(\text{Spade}) = P(\text{Hearts}) = \frac{1}{4}$$

The probability of either occurring in this situation may be found by using

$$P(A \text{ OR } B) = P(A) + P(B)$$

giving

$$P(\text{Spade or Heart}) = P(\text{Spade}) + P(\text{Heart})$$

$$= \frac{1}{4} + \frac{1}{4} = \frac{1}{2}$$

4 PROBABILITY DISTRIBUTIONS

Probability distributions provide an alternative way of considering the full set of possibilities and of calculating the related probabilities.

There are two different types of distribution that we shall consider.

- The binomial distribution.
- The Normal distribution.

It is important that you are aware under what circumstances these distributions may be useful.

5 Binomial Distribution

5.1 Introduction

The binomial distribution extends our basic probability ideas to aid calculations that involve large samples of independent trials with **two** possible outcomes. We will illustrate this idea with the following example.

Example

If three cards are chosen at random from a normal pack one at a time, the previously selected card having been replaced and the pack shuffled between selections to ensure independence, what is the probability that two are hearts?

We will firstly solve this question from first principles and then introduce the binomial expression and show how it could have been solved much more quickly.

Solution

In this situation, there are only two possible outcomes for any selection, specifically

- We have selected a heart (H) – probability 0.25.
- We have not selected a heart (N) – probability 0.75.

If we now consider all the possible outcomes from selecting three cards, we get the following.

	Outcomes	Probability Calculation	Probability
All Hearts	H AND H AND H	$0.25 \times 0.25 \times 0.25 = 0.015625$	0.015625
Two Hearts	H AND H AND N H AND N AND H N AND H AND H	$0.25 \times 0.25 \times 0.75 = 0.046875$ $0.25 \times 0.75 \times 0.25 = 0.046875$ $0.75 \times 0.25 \times 0.25 = 0.046875$	0.140625
One Heart	H AND N AND N N AND H AND N N AND N AND H	$0.25 \times 0.75 \times 0.75 = 0.140625$ $0.75 \times 0.25 \times 0.75 = 0.140625$ $0.75 \times 0.75 \times 0.25 = 0.140625$	0.421875
No Hearts	N AND N AND N	$0.75 \times 0.75 \times 0.75 = 0.421875$	0.421875 1.000000

What we can see from this example is that there are a number of different ways of achieving any one result, e.g. three ways of selecting two hearts, though each way has an equal probability.

Thus, the probability of selecting two hearts in three cards is 0.140625.

5.2 Binomial expression

The binomial expression gives us a means to calculate any of these probabilities directly without listing all of the alternatives.

Given two possible outcomes, one of which is considered a success (with probability p) and one of which is considered a failure (with probability 1 – p), then the probability of r successes in n trials is given by

Formula to learn

$$P(r) = \frac{n!}{r!(n-r)!} \times p^r \times (1-p)^{n-r}$$

where

$$\frac{n!}{r!(n-r)!}$$ = the number of possible combinations of r successes in n trials

$p^r \times (1-p)^{n-r}$ = the probability of r successes and n failures in one trial

Solution

Applying this binomial expression to the above example, we can calculate that the probability of two hearts (a success) in three cards is given by

$$P(2) = \frac{3!}{2!1!} \times 0.25^2 \times 0.75^1$$
$$= 3 \times 0.0625 \times 0.75$$
$$= 0.140625$$

5.3 Use of the expression

The real use of the binomial expression comes when we consider more complex problems such as the following one.

Example

The probability of passing a driving test is 0.3. If ten people take the driving test, what is the probability that at least two will pass?

Solution

P(At least two) = P(Two or more)

and

P(Two or more) = 1 − P(0 OR 1)
= 1 − [P(0) + P(1)]

Now

$$P(0) = \frac{10!}{0!10!} \times 0.3^0 \times 0.7^{10} = 1 \times 1 \times 0.0282 = 0.0282$$

and

$$P(1) = \frac{10!}{1!9!} \times 0.3^1 \times 0.7^9 = 10 \times 0.3 \times 0.0404 = 0.1211$$

Hence

P(At least two) = 1 − [P(0) + P(1)]
= 1 − [0.0282 + 0.1211]
= 1 − 0.1493
= 0.8507

5.4 Binomial distribution

If we were to plot a histogram of probability against number of possible successes, we would be constructing the binomial distribution. Whether this distribution is symmetrical or skewed is dependent upon the probability of achieving a success.

In general, the binomial distribution is a histogram, which shows

- All the possible outcomes along the x axis.
- The probabilities of the y axis, the height of each histogram bar being calculated using the above binomial expression.

As a result, the area of the histogram will be proportional to the frequency of the occurrences of the various events and the total area underneath the histogram must be 1, since the sum of all probabilities is 1.

5.4.1 Symmetrical

If, in the above driving test example, the probability of passing the driving test was 0.5, then in considering the probabilities of all possible number of successes between 0 and 10, the binomial distribution would appear symmetrical as follows.

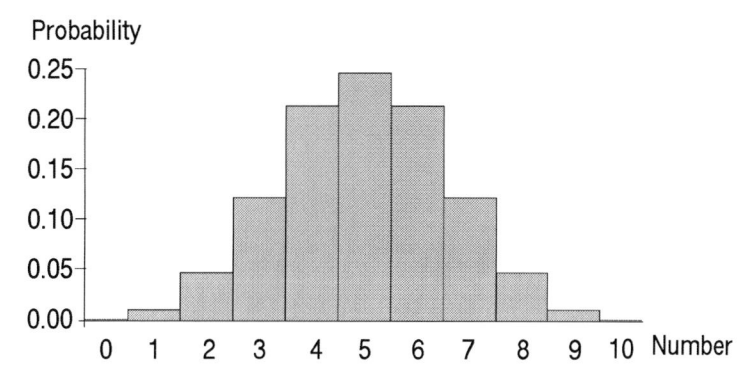

5.4.2 Skewed

Positively skewed

If we use the probability of passing the driving test of 0.3, as in the example above, calculated the probability of all possible numbers of successes between 0 and 10 and plotted these on a histogram, we would obtain a positively skewed distribution as illustrated below. A positively skewed distribution is one where more items lie above the most frequently occurring event than lie below it. In this example, we can see that the most frequently occurring event is three, which we could have expected since, on average, three in ten pass.

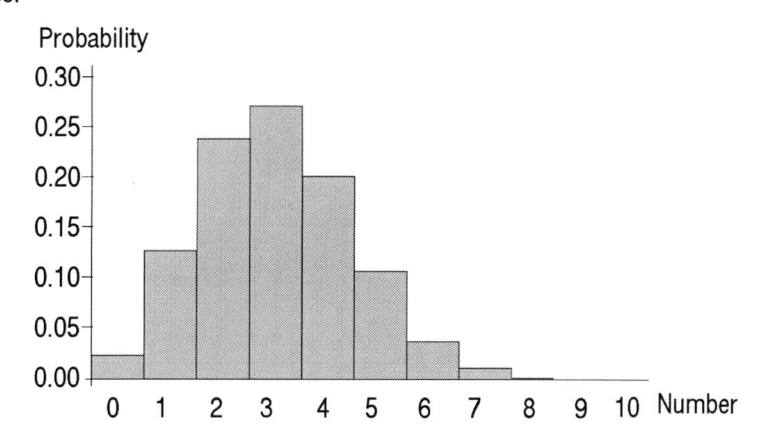

Negatively skewed

Similarly if the probability of a success in the driving test was 0.7, then the most likely number of successes in 10 trials would be 7 and we would have a negatively skewed distribution as illustrated below.

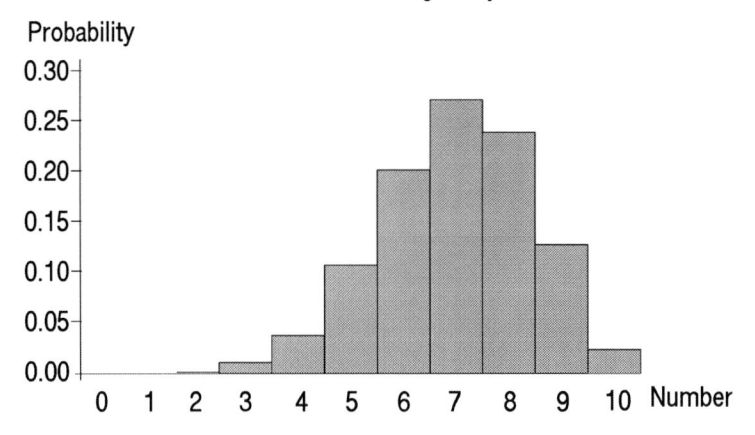

6 STANDARD NORMAL DISTRIBUTION

6.1 Introduction

The binomial distribution deals with **discrete data**, e.g. whole numbers of people passing a driving test, and enables us to calculate the probability of certain outcomes.

The Normal distribution enables us to perform similar calculations on **continuous data**, i.e. data that does not just take whole values, e.g. heights, weights, growth rates.

The Normal distribution appears very similar to the symmetrical binomial distribution and, indeed, may be used as an approximation to the binomial distribution where there are a very large number of items as we outline below.

As for the binomial distribution, the area under the curve between any two points represents the probability of observing a value between those two points, and the total area under the curve is 1 (the total of all probabilities of all possible outcomes). The area under the curve between two points could be established mathematically, though it is much more convenient to utilise the Normal distribution tables that are included as an appendix to this session.

6.2 Characteristics of the distribution

6.2.1 Graphically

Graphically, the Normal distribution appears as follows.

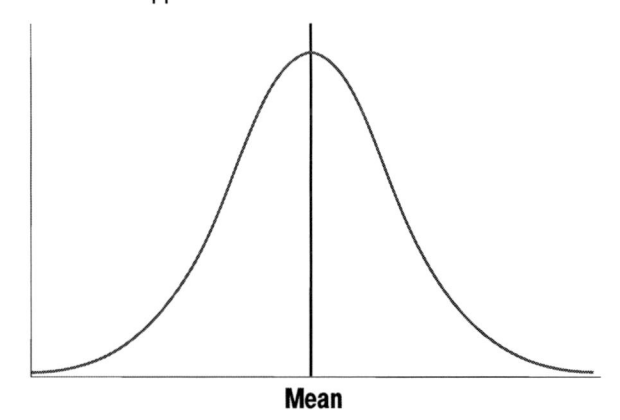

6.2.2 Characteristics

characteristics of this distribution are

- It is bell-shaped.
- It is symmetrical, i.e. there is an equal probability of being either above or below the central point and as a result, the Normal distribution tables can be used on both sides of the mean as we will illustrate below.
- The mean equals the highest central point, i.e. the mode (since it is symmetrical).
- It is asymptotic, i.e. neither tail ever reaches the x axis.
- The total area under the curve equals 1.
- The area under the curve between two points gives the probability of observing an item lying within that range.
- There is a measure of spread, the standard deviation of the distribution, which determines how wide the distribution is.

All normal distributions are defined by two measures.

- The **mean**, the central and most frequently occurring value.
- The **standard deviation**, an indication of the spread of values about that mean or central point.

6.3 Uses of the normal distribution

6.3.1 Introduction

Where a population is Normally distributed, we can calculate the probability of observing a value in a particular range using just two things.

- **Z value**

Formula to learn

$$Z = \frac{x - \mu}{\sigma}$$

That is, the distance of the observed value x from the mean μ expressed as a multiple of the standard deviation σ. **NB:** The sign of the Z value may be ignored when looking it up in the normal distribution tables as we illustrate below.

- **Normal Distribution Tables** – provide the area of the curve beyond a point, hence the probability of observing a value beyond that point when moving away from the mean, i.e. above that value if the value lies above the mean, or below it if the value lies below the mean.

6.3.2 Calculating probabilities given values

Approach

What we must do to calculate probabilities associated with particular ranges of values is

- Draw up the curve and establish the area that we are interested in. A quick sketch to highlight the relevant points is essential.
- Determine how we can construct just this area by either
    - Adding together non-overlapping areas that make it up; or
    - Deducting the areas that are not wanted from the others.

i.e. at the end of the day, it is a simple problem of addition and/or subtraction.

5: PROBABILITY

Relating the approach to probability theory

In adding areas together, we are saying that the value lies in one area or the other. The justification for this, in terms of probability theory, is that as long as they are not overlapping, then they will be mutually exclusive and hence

Formula to learn

$$P(A \text{ OR } B) = P(A) + P(B)$$

In deducting areas, we are saying that the value falls in a particular area, excluding a certain part – simply the reverse idea of the addition law.

Important considerations

The most important characteristics to bear in mind when undertaking this are

- The area under the curve between any two points corresponds to the probability of observing an item between those two points.
- The total area under the curve = 1, i.e. the sum of all the probabilities of all possibilities is 1.
- The area above the mean = the area below = 0.5, i.e. the probability of a value falling above the mean = probability of falling below = 0.5.
- The Normal distribution tables give the area beyond the selected point when moving away from the mean, i.e. the probability of being that far from the mean or more.

This all sounds a little complicated when expressed in words and may best be illustrated with a series of examples.

Example

The mean daily UK temperature has been measured as 12.5° and the standard deviation measured as 7.5°.

What is the probability of

- A freeze on any one day?
- A below average temperature on any one day that does not result in a freeze?
- A temperature above 20° on any one day?

Solution

Probability of a freeze

Drawing up the Normal distribution curve and plotting the relevant points (a freeze corresponding to the temperature falling to $\leq 0°$) reveals the following.

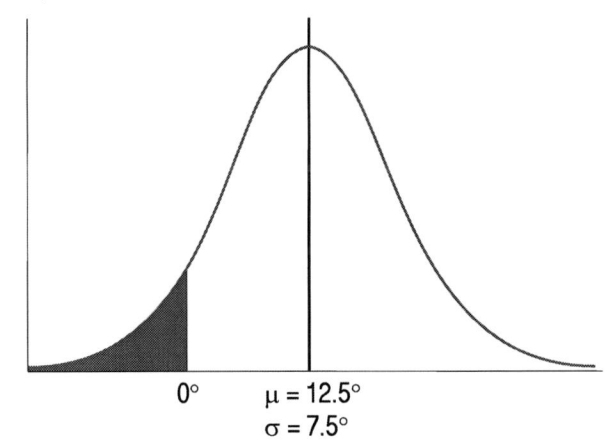

0° $\mu = 12.5°$
    $\sigma = 7.5°$

The area of this curve that we are interested in is the shaded area below 0°, the probability of which we can directly calculate if we can ascertain its Z value by using

$$Z = \frac{x - \mu}{\sigma}$$

which gives

$$Z = \frac{0 - 12.5}{7.5} = -1.67$$

There are two factors relevant in this Z value, the

- **Sign** – i.e. + or –, a positive sign indicates that the relevant point lies above the mean, a negative sign indicates that it lies below.
- **Value** – this is the factor looked up in the Normal distribution tables to give the probability of being **beyond** the selected point. In using the Normal distribution tables, the sign can be ignored.

Looking up a Z value of 1.67 in the Normal distribution tables gives

$$P(\leq 0°) = 0.04746$$

Probability of below average temperature not resulting in a freeze

This requires the consideration of a temperature between 0° and 12.5° which, using the above diagram, corresponds to the area below the mean which is **not** shaded.

Now, we know that the total area below the mean is 0.5000 and hence

$$\begin{aligned} P(0° \text{ to } 12.5°) &= 0.50000 - P(\leq 0°) \\ &= 0.50000 - 0.04746 = 0.45254 \end{aligned}$$

In terms of probability theory, this corresponds to

$$\begin{aligned} P(0° \text{ to } 12.5°) &= P(\leq 12.5° \text{ NOT} \leq 0°) \\ &= P(\leq 12.5°) - P(\leq 0°) \\ &= 0.50000 - 0.04746 = 0.45254 \end{aligned}$$

Probability of temperature $\geq 20°$

Quickly drawing up the Normal distribution curve reveals the following.

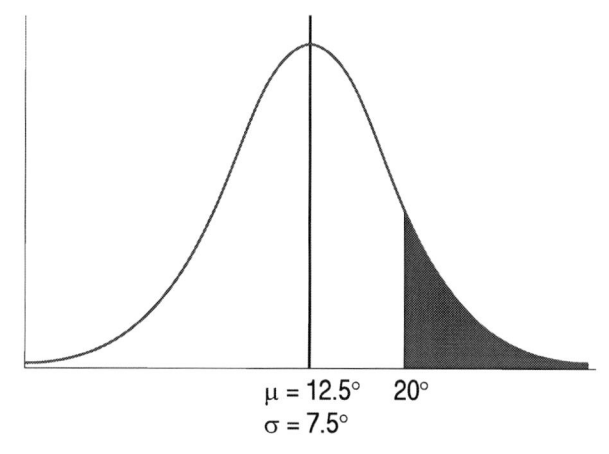

$\mu = 12.5°$ $20°$
$\sigma = 7.5°$

The area of the curve that we are interested in is the shaded area lying above 20°. Calculating the Z value for 20° and looking this up in the tables will, therefore, give the desired result.

$$Z = \frac{x - \mu}{\sigma} = \frac{20 - 12.5}{7.5} = 1.00$$

5: PROBABILITY

Looking this Z value of 1.00 up in the tables gives

P (≥ 20°) = 0.15866

6.3.3 Application to option pricing

In the above examples, we have used the characteristics of a Normal distribution to calculate the probability of a certain temperature occurring. In option pricing, we will use the characteristics of the Normal distribution to calculate the probability of an option expiring in-the-money and the probable value of the underlying asset at the expiry date of the option.

6.3.4 Approximation to the binomial distribution

Introduction

The binomial distribution is used for discrete data, whereas the Normal distribution is used for continuous data. However, where there are a large number of discrete items in a binomial distribution, it becomes almost continuous and the Normal distribution may be used as an approximation to it.

To illustrate this point, we have plotted below the binomial distribution for a variety of different sample sizes (n = 4 to 1,024) where p = 0.2.

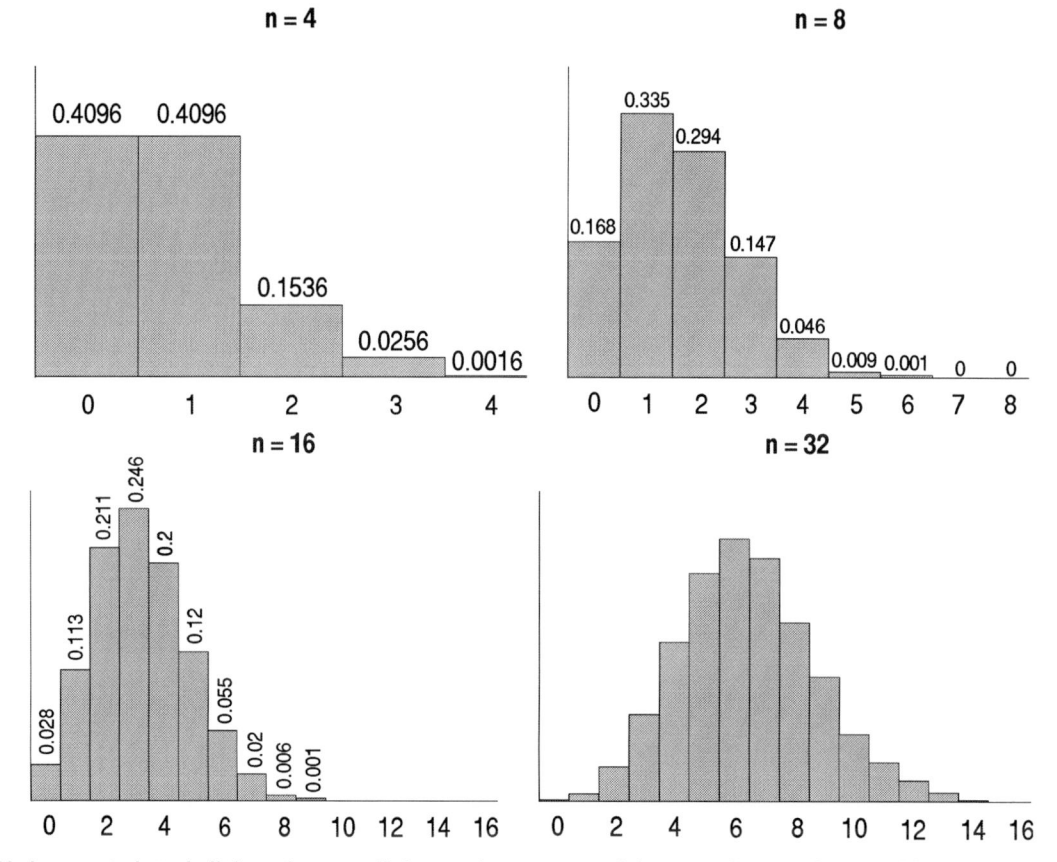

We have not plotted all the values on all the graphs as many of them are 0, e.g. when n = 32, we have only plotted up to 16. What we can see is that by the time n has reached 32, the outline of the distribution bears a striking resemblance to that of a Normal distribution and that resemblance becomes stronger as n is increased.

It should be noted that this relationship does not seem to hold so well for values of p below 0.1 or above 0.9.

The conclusion is that for large quantities (n ≥ 30), and values of p between 0.1 and 0.9, the Normal distribution may be used as a reasonable approximation to the binomial distribution.

7 LOGNORMAL DISTRIBUTION

In the standard Normal distribution, the horizontal scale is linear. This means that the probability of an outcome lying a given number of units above the mean is that of it lying the same number of units below the mean. If, for example, the mean were 100, the probability of an outcome lying above 120 would be equal to the probability of it lying below 80.

In a lognormal distribution, the distribution appears symmetrical when the horizontal axis plots the logarithm of the values. The consequence of this is that it is as probable to see a value double as it is to see the value halve, or to see a price quadruple as it is to see a price reduced to one-quarter of its original value.

For example, if share price movements are lognormally distributed and the current share price is £1, then the probability of the share price falling to 50p (halving in value) is equal to the probability of it rising £2 (doubling in value), and the probability of the share price falling to 25p (one-quarter of the original price) is equivalent to that of the share price rising to £4 (four times the original price).

The Black Scholes model of options pricing assumes that share price movements are lognormally distributed. This certainly seems more reasonable than a standard Normal distribution, which would suggest that if a company has a share price of £1, then it is as likely to go into liquidation (share price fall to £0) as it is to see the share price rise to £2. This idea appears completely unrealistic and the idea of the lognormally distributed price movement intuitively feels much more sensible.

There is, however, little evidence to support this theory. In fact, given human nature and the herding instinct (following the leader) witnessed in the markets, it is quite frequently the case that if a share starts to move a little bit, it moves a long way, as everybody frantically buys or sells it. This is certainly not what is predicted by a lognormal distribution. Perhaps in a perfect capital market, where people did their own securities evaluation rather than following others, this would not be the case and a lognormal distribution would be a realistic idea.

A lognormal distribution looks as follows.

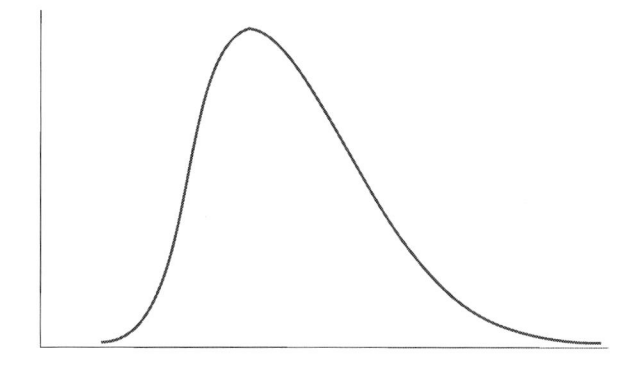

APPENDIX – NORMAL DISTRIBUTION TABLES

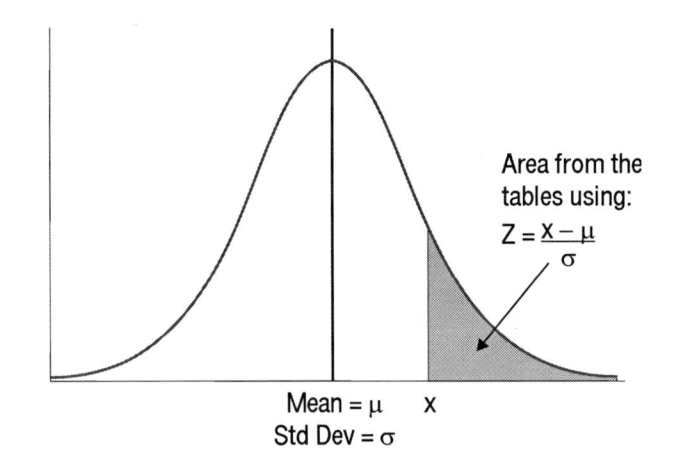

Area from the tables using:
$$Z = \frac{x - \mu}{\sigma}$$

Mean = μ
Std Dev = σ

Z	0.00	0.01	0.02	0.03	0.04	0.05	0.06	0.07	0.08	0.09
0.00	0.50000	0.49601	0.49202	0.48803	0.48405	0.48006	0.47608	0.47210	0.46812	0.46414
0.10	0.46017	0.45620	0.45224	0.44828	0.44433	0.44038	0.43644	0.43251	0.42858	0.42465
0.20	0.42074	0.41683	0.41294	0.40905	0.40517	0.40129	0.39743	0.39358	0.38974	0.38591
0.30	0.38209	0.37828	0.37448	0.37070	0.36693	0.36317	0.35942	0.35569	0.35197	0.34827
0.40	0.34458	0.34090	0.33724	0.33360	0.32997	0.32636	0.32276	0.31918	0.31561	0.31207
0.50	0.30854	0.30503	0.30153	0.29806	0.29460	0.29116	0.28774	0.28434	0.28096	0.27760
0.60	0.27425	0.27093	0.26763	0.26435	0.26109	0.25785	0.25463	0.25143	0.24825	0.24510
0.70	0.24196	0.23885	0.23576	0.23270	0.22965	0.22663	0.22363	0.22065	0.21770	0.21476
0.80	0.21186	0.20897	0.20611	0.20327	0.20045	0.19766	0.19489	0.19215	0.18943	0.18673
0.90	0.18406	0.18141	0.17879	0.17619	0.17361	0.17106	0.16853	0.16602	0.16354	0.16109
1.00	0.15866	0.15625	0.15386	0.15151	0.14917	0.14686	0.14457	0.14231	0.14007	0.13786
1.10	0.13567	0.13350	0.13136	0.12924	0.12714	0.12507	0.12302	0.12100	0.11900	0.11702
1.20	0.11507	0.11314	0.11123	0.10935	0.10749	0.10565	0.10383	0.10204	0.10027	0.09853
1.30	0.09680	0.09510	0.09342	0.09176	0.09012	0.08851	0.08692	0.08534	0.08379	0.08226
1.40	0.08076	0.07927	0.07780	0.07636	0.07493	0.07353	0.07215	0.07078	0.06944	0.06811
1.50	0.06681	0.06552	0.06426	0.06301	0.06178	0.06057	0.05938	0.05821	0.05705	0.05592
1.60	0.05480	0.05370	0.05262	0.05155	0.05050	0.04947	0.04846	0.04746	0.04648	0.04551
1.70	0.04457	0.04363	0.04272	0.04182	0.04093	0.04006	0.03920	0.03836	0.03754	0.03673
1.80	0.03593	0.03515	0.03438	0.03362	0.03288	0.03216	0.03144	0.03074	0.03005	0.02938
1.90	0.02872	0.02807	0.02743	0.02680	0.02619	0.02559	0.02500	0.02442	0.02385	0.02330
2.00	0.02275	0.02222	0.02169	0.02118	0.02068	0.02018	0.01970	0.01923	0.01876	0.01831
2.10	0.01786	0.01743	0.01700	0.01659	0.01618	0.01578	0.01539	0.01500	0.01463	0.01426
2.20	0.01390	0.01355	0.01321	0.01287	0.01255	0.01222	0.01191	0.01160	0.01130	0.01101
2.30	0.01072	0.01044	0.01017	0.00990	0.00964	0.00939	0.00914	0.00889	0.00866	0.00842
2.40	0.00820	0.00798	0.00776	0.00755	0.00734	0.00714	0.00695	0.00676	0.00657	0.00639

Z	0.00	0.01	0.02	0.03	0.04	0.05	0.06	0.07	0.08	0.09
2.50	0.00621	0.00604	0.00587	0.00570	0.00554	0.00539	0.00523	0.00508	0.00494	0.00480
2.60	0.00466	0.00453	0.00440	0.00427	0.00415	0.00402	0.00391	0.00379	0.00368	0.00357
2.70	0.00347	0.00336	0.00326	0.00317	0.00307	0.00298	0.00289	0.00280	0.00272	0.00264
2.80	0.00256	0.00248	0.00240	0.00233	0.00226	0.00219	0.00212	0.00205	0.00199	0.00193
2.90	0.00187	0.00181	0.00175	0.00169	0.00164	0.00159	0.00154	0.00149	0.00144	0.00139
3.00	0.00135	0.00131	0.00126	0.00122	0.00118	0.00114	0.00111	0.00107	0.00104	0.00100
3.10	0.00097	0.00094	0.00090	0.00087	0.00084	0.00082	0.00079	0.00076	0.00074	0.00071
3.20	0.00069	0.00066	0.00064	0.00062	0.00060	0.00058	0.00056	0.00054	0.00052	0.00050
3.30	0.00048	0.00047	0.00045	0.00043	0.00042	0.00040	0.00039	0.00038	0.00036	0.00035
3.40	0.00034	0.00032	0.00031	0.00030	0.00029	0.00028	0.00027	0.00026	0.00025	0.00024
3.50	0.00023	0.00022	0.00022	0.00021	0.00020	0.00019	0.00019	0.00018	0.00017	0.00017
3.60	0.00016	0.00015	0.00015	0.00014	0.00014	0.00013	0.00013	0.00012	0.00012	0.00011
3.70	0.00011	0.00010	0.00010	0.00010	0.00009	0.00009	0.00008	0.00008	0.00008	0.00008
3.80	0.00007	0.00007	0.00007	0.00006	0.00006	0.00006	0.00006	0.00005	0.00005	0.00005
3.90	0.00005	0.00005	0.00004	0.00004	0.00004	0.00004	0.00004	0.00004	0.00003	0.00003
4.00	0.00003	0.00003	0.00003	0.00003	0.00003	0.00003	0.00002	0.00002	0.00002	0.00002

Note: Normal distribution tables may be presented in a number of different ways and care needs to be taken to determine which tables are given, hence how to use them.

The tables above show the probability of having a value greater than x. With these, the higher the Z value, the lower the probability.

Tables may alternatively show the probability of being below x. With these, the higher the Z value the higher the probability, these tables are most useful for options pricing.

Exam tip

It is common to be given an extract from Normal distribution tables in the exam for use in options pricing questions.

Chapter Roundup

- You should be aware of how basic probabilities are assessed

    - $P(E) = \dfrac{\text{The number of ways E can occur}}{\text{Total number of equally likely outcomes}}$

    - $P(E) = \dfrac{\text{The number of observed occurrences of E}}{\text{Total number of observed occurrences}}$

    and that the sum of all the probabilities of all possible outcomes equals 1.

- P(NOT E) = 1 − P(E)
- P(A AND B) = P(A) × P(B)
- P(A OR B) = P(A) + P(B)
- You should be aware of the ideas of binomial and Normal distributions.
- You should be able to describe a Normal and a lognormal distribution.
- You should be able to determine a probability from Normal distribution tables.

5: PROBABILITY

TEST YOUR KNOWLEDGE

Check your knowledge of the Chapter here, without referring back to the text.

1. Describe the usefulness of the binomial distribution.
2. Contrast the usefulness of the binomial and Normal distributions.
3. Describe the characteristics of the Normal distribution.
4. Contrast a Normal and a lognormal distribution.
5. If a distribution has a mean of 10 and a standard deviation of 4, calculate the probability of a value
   (a) Greater than 12
   (b) Less than 12
   (c) Less than 6
   (d) Between 6 and 12

   based on the Normal distribution tables in the appendix.

5: PROBABILITY

TEST YOUR KNOWLEDGE: ANSWERS

1. The binomial distribution extends the basic probability ideas to aid calculations that involve large samples of independent trials with **two** possible outcomes.

2. The binomial distribution deals with **discrete data**, e.g. whole numbers of people passing a driving test, and enables us to calculate the probability of certain outcomes.

   The Normal distribution enables us to perform similar calculations on **continuous data**, i.e. data that does not just take whole values, e.g. heights, weights, growth rates.

3. The characteristics of this distribution are

   - It is bell-shaped.
   - It is symmetrical, i.e. there is an equal probability of being either above or below the central point and as a result, the Normal distribution tables can be used on both sides of the mean as we will illustrate below.
   - The mean equals the highest central point, i.e. the mode (since it is symmetrical).
   - It is asymptotic, i.e. neither tail ever reaches the x axis.
   - The total area under the curve equals 1.
   - The area under the curve between two points gives the probability of observing an item lying within that range.
   - There is a measure of spread, the standard deviation of the distribution, which determines how wide the distribution is.

   All normal distributions are defined by two measures.

   - The **mean**, the central and most frequently occurring value.
   - The **standard deviation**, an indication of the spread of values about that mean or central point.

4. In the standard Normal distribution, the horizontal scale is linear. This means that the probability of an outcome lying a given number of units above the mean is that of it lying the same number of units below the mean. If, for example, the mean were 100, the probability of an outcome lying above 120 would be equal to the probability of it lying below 80.

   In a lognormal distribution, the distribution appears symmetrical when the horizontal axis plots the logarithm of the values. The consequence of this is that it is as probable to see a value double as it is to see the value halve, or to see a price quadruple as it is to see a price reduced to one-quarter of its original value.

5. (a) P(>12)

   $$z = \frac{12-10}{4} = 0.5$$

   giving

   P(>12) = 0.30854

   (b) P(<12)

   P(<12) = 1 − P(>12)

   = 1 − 0.30854 = 0.69146

(c) *P(<6)*

$$z = \frac{6-10}{4} = -1.0$$

minus sign simply shows that we are below the mean, looking up the value (1) in the Normal tables gives

P(<6) = 0.15866

(d) *P(Between 6 and 12)*

$$\begin{aligned} P(6\text{-}12) &= P(\text{NOT }(<6 \text{ OR } >12)) \\ &= 1 - P(<6 \text{ OR } >12) \\ &= 1 - P(<6) - P(>12) \\ &= 1 - 0.15866 - 0.30854 = 0.53280 \end{aligned}$$

6 Basic Pricing of Futures and Options

INTRODUCTION

This section covers the ideas of futures pricing which are expanded on and illustrated for specific contracts in later sections.

With respect to options, this section introduces the basic price drivers that impact on the price of an option, boundry limits on those prices and the link between option values through both put-call parity and a consideration of convexity.

These areas are regularly examined on their own, but also lead in to detailed option pricing covered in a later section.

CHAPTER CONTENTS

	Page
1 Futures	122
2 Options	128
Chapter Roundup	145
Test Your Knowledge	147

6: BASIC PRICING OF FUTURES AND OPTIONS

CHAPTER LEARNING OBJECTIVES

The syllabus areas covered by this section are

- **Uses of futures**

    Value in futures contracts

    Basis and cost of carry. Forward pricing. Implied (including specific examples) financing rates. Convergence, Embedded Options in Bond Basis, Basis Trading and Arbitrage.

- **Uses of options**

    Value in options contracts

    Price of the underlying asset. Strike price of the option. Time to expiry. Role of Volatility. Cost of carry.

1 FUTURES

1.1 Cash/Futures relationship

One of the most important steps towards understanding futures is to study how they are priced.

If we were to compare the cash market price of lead with the futures price for delivery in three months, we might observe the following prices.

    Cash price of lead $480 per tonne
    3-month future $500 per tonne

Why should the futures price be higher than the cash price? Intuitively, we might think that the futures price is higher because it indicates that the price of lead is due to rise. This explanation of futures pricing is only part of the story. Futures prices are in fact the product of the interplay between a number of factors, including supply and demand in the cash markets, interest rates, sentiment, and practical issues such as dividend yields and transportation costs.

1.2 Simple basis

Simple basis or crude basis is the term used to describe the numerical difference between a cash price and a futures price. Basis is normally quoted as the cash price minus the futures price.

Formula to learn

> Basis = Cash price − Futures price

Let us look at the following example.

    Cash price of wheat = £120 per tonne
    Price of July future = £125

Therefore

    Basis = 120 − 125   = −5

In this case, the basis is 'negative'; in some markets, this would be described as '£5 under futures'.

If the calculation gave rise to a positive number, the basis would be described as positive or 'over futures'.

Although cash and futures prices generally move broadly in line with one another, the basis is not constant. During some periods, cash prices move faster than futures. At other times, futures outpace the cash market.

This movement in basis is brought about by a variety of factors. Most important is the relationship between supply and demand. Under normal conditions, futures prices of physical commodities are higher than cash prices. The reasons for this are discussed later in this chapter, but where futures prices are higher than cash prices, the market is said to be in **contango**.

However, this normal or contango situation in which futures prices are higher than cash prices can be radically altered if there is some short-term lack of supply. If, for example, there is very little zinc available for delivery, the price demanded for what little is available can be very high indeed. Markets in which futures prices are lower than cash prices are said to be in **backwardation**. The terms contango and backwardation are not typically used in financial futures markets. More normally, when futures are higher than cash prices, the market is said to be at a **premium** or a **negative carry** market; when futures are lower than cash, it is said to be at a **discount**, or a **positive carry** market. The terms negative or positive carry relate to the difference between finance costs and yield on a financial asset. When the yield is greater than the finance costs, it is a positive carry market and vice versa. The concept of carry is more fully developed below.

Contango Market

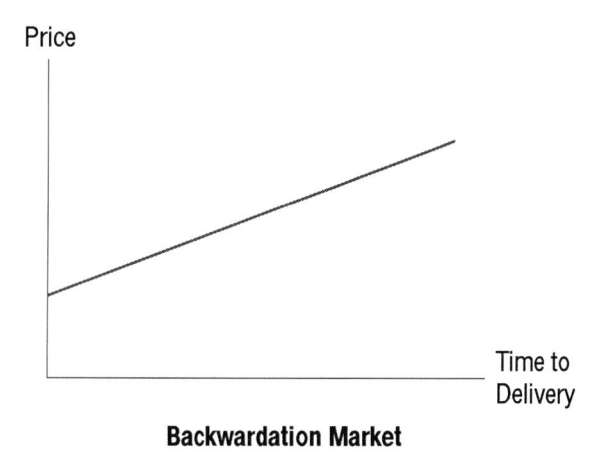

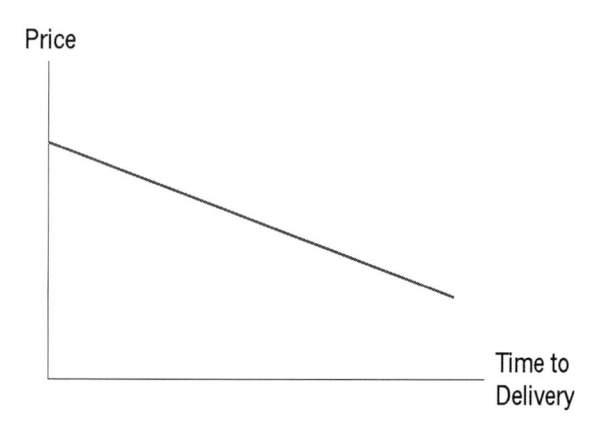

Backwardation Market

1.2.1 Theoretical basis and value basis

Aside from simple or crude basis, practitioners also talk of theoretical basis and value basis.

Theoretical basis is the difference between the cash market price and the fair value of the future.

Formula to learn

Cash price – Fair value

6: BASIC PRICING OF FUTURES AND OPTIONS

Value basis is the difference between the market price of a future and its fair value.

Formula to learn

Fair value – Future = Value basis

Very confusingly, there is no authoritative method of calculating any of the 'basis' numbers outlined above. Some practitioners will calculate simple basis as futures minus cash, rather than cash minus futures. Similarly, the terms in the theoretical and value basis formula can also be reversed. Notwithstanding these complications, the basis calculations outline the differential.

1.3 Basis risk

Changes in basis represent a threat and an opportunity to futurexs users, i.e. they face basis risk. To illustrate this, let us consider a farmer who undertook a short hedge by selling an August wheat future on 10 February to protect himself against a price fall. It is now 10 July – time to lift the hedge.

	Cash Price		Futures Price		Basis
10 February	140	–	150	=	–10
10 July	120	–	135	=	–15
	(20) Loss		15 Profit		

As can be seen, the hedge has not been entirely effective. A £20 fall in the price of cash wheat has only been partially offset by a £15 gain in the futures market. This difference emerges because the cash price has moved further than the futures price. In other words, there has been a change in basis. The hedger faces basis risk.

When the basis becomes more negative or less positive, as above, it is said to **weaken**.

When the basis becomes more positive or less negative, it is said to **strengthen**.

If the basis moves nearer to zero, there is said to be a **narrowing** of the basis. Narrowing could therefore imply either a strengthening or a weakening.

If the basis moves away from zero, this is said to be a **widening** of the basis. This could also be either a strengthening or a weakening.

Basis changes do occur and thus represent potential profits or losses to investors. Notwithstanding the fact that the relationship between cash and futures may vary, the risk this represents is very much smaller than the risk of remaining unhedged. In short, basis risk is smaller than outright risk.

1.4 Fair value

Exam tip

You may well be asked to establish the fair value of a given futures contract and critically appraise the figure established.

For markets where there is an adequate supply of the assets subject to delivery, it is possible to calculate a 'fair' or theoretical price of a future.

The **fair value** of a future is the price at which investors are indifferent as to whether they buy the underlying asset or the future.

Imagine a jeweller who knows that he will need to buy 5oz of gold to make wedding rings in three months' time. He has two ways in which he can guarantee the price of gold – either he can buy the physical metal now or, alternatively, buy the gold future that will deliver in three months' time.

If he buys physical gold, he will pay for it immediately. The money to finance this purchase will come either from borrowing it or withdrawing it from his bank account. However he finances the purchase, there will be an interest rate penalty in the form of paying off his loan, or a loss of interest on his credit balances. In addition, the gold will need to be insured and safely stored between the date of purchase and use.

If instead he buys the future, he will only pay for the gold in three months' time. In addition, he will also save on storage and insurance costs. Altogether, it would seem that using the future is preferable to buying the gold. However, in futures markets, as in life, money is not given away. The futures, if fairly priced, will incorporate the costs of finance, storage and insurance. The reasons these costs are included are best explained if we look at the future from the seller's rather than the buyer's perspective. If you were a prudent futures seller, you would not simply sell the future at some arbitrary price. You would calculate how much it would cost you to get the gold to delivery at no risk. This would require that the moment you sold the gold future, you would prepare to meet the delivery obligation by buying cash gold and hold and insure it through to delivery day. As the seller will incur these costs, known collectively as the **cost of carry**, he will add these to the cash price of gold to find the minimum acceptable selling price of the future.

1.5 Calculating fair values

If cash gold is $355 per oz, interest rates 5% per annum and insurance and storage charges a further 0.5% per annum, we can calculate the fair value of the three-month future.

1.5.1 Method

Calculate the cost of carry by working out how much the cost of finance and other charges will be for a three-month period (90 days). (When dealing in US dollars, it is conventional to use a 360-day year.)

$$\text{Cash} \times (\text{Interest} + \text{Storage/Insurance}) \times \frac{\text{Days}}{360}$$

$$\$355 \times 5.5\% \times \frac{90}{360}$$

$$= \$4.88 \text{ Cost of Carry}$$

To find the fair value, add the cost of carry to the cash price.

$$\$355 + \$4.88 = \$359.88$$

The fair value of the three-month future is $359.88.

In the example above, we have calculated the fair value of a gold future. We could just as easily calculate the fair value of other futures, as long as the market has adequate supply. For futures on bonds, equities and currencies, the mathematics become more complicated, as account has to be taken of the **yield** from the underlying asset, but the same principles apply.

These will be dealt with in more detail in subsequent chapters.

1.6 Arbitrage

Arbitrage is an activity in which traders (arbitrageurs) seek to make riskless profits from exploiting mispricings between markets.

We have established that for most futures it is possible to calculate a fair value. If the future is not trading at its fair value, this will mean that it is, in theoretical terms, either cheap or expensive. When this occurs, arbitrageurs will sell what is expensive and buy what is cheap whilst, at the same time, undertaking an offsetting trade in the cash market. For example, if the future is expensive relative to fair value, the arbitrageur will

Sell Futures and Buy Underlying Asset: A Cash and Carry Arbitrage

6: BASIC PRICING OF FUTURES AND OPTIONS

If the future is cheap, he will

Buy Futures and Sell Underlying Asset: A Reverse Cash and Carry Arbitrage

The activity of the arbitrageur in buying 'cheap' assets and selling 'expensive' ones will tend to bring the future back to its correct level. This is because sellers will appear if the future is expensive and drive the price down and vice versa.

Whilst most ordinary investors do not have the low costs necessary to make arbitrage economically viable, the fact that many professionals undertake this activity is highly important, as it maintains the linkage between cash and futures markets.

Although professional traders might theoretically be expected to undertake arbitrage as soon as the future trades at variance to its fair value, even professionals have some costs. Thus, in reality, the future must move some way above or below fair value before arbitrageurs will appear. Exchange fees, taxes and bid/offer spreads all mean that there is an area, known as the arbitrage **channel**, either side of fair value within which arbitrage will not take place. As costs vary between participants, so too does the width of the channel.

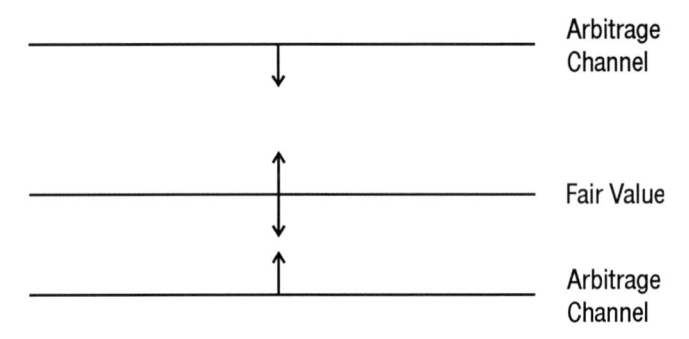

1.7 Convergence

Once a future reaches its last trading day, the cost of carry will be nil. At the moment of delivery, the futures market and the cash market will have the same price, since both quotes will be for the immediate delivery of the underlying asset. This coming together of the future and cash is known as **convergence** and it is the only time in a future's life when it necessarily has the same price as the cash market.

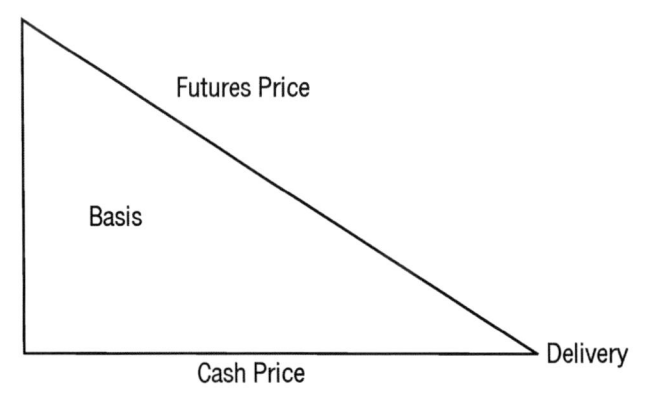

1.8 Estimating basis

Hedgers who intend to lift their hedges prior to the delivery date are subject to basis risk.

If it is assumed that basis converges to zero in a linear fashion, it becomes possible to estimate what the basis will be on a particular date.

To illustrate this, let us contemplate the following example using an interest rate future.

Date	= 14 July	
Three-month LIBOR	= 6.87%	
September Futures	= 93.05	(This reflects 100 – Future rate)
Basis	= +0.08	[(100 – 3M LIBOR) – 93.05]

A treasurer is contemplating using September futures to hedge a borrowing requirement that he needs on 1 September, and wishes to estimate the 1 September basis.

$$\text{Basis} = \text{Basis at start} \times \frac{\text{Basis period}}{\text{Hedge period} + \text{Basis period}}$$

Basis Period = Days from lifting of hedge until futures expiration

Hedge Period = Days from when hedge is established until it is lifted

Basis Period = 1/9-14/9 (third Wednesday) = 13 days

Hedge Period = 14/7-1/9 = 62 days

$$\text{Basis} = 0.08 \times \frac{13}{62}$$

$$= 0.02$$

As a consequence, the treasurer's expected borrowing rate would be the borrowing rate implied by future less the expected basis.

Expected borrowing rate = 6.95 – 0.02 = 6.93

1.9 Future price vs Forward price

Many authors talk at length about the difference between the forward price of an asset and the price of a future on that asset. The principal difference between the two prices is accounted for by the variation margin flows and the interest payments/receipts that occur on those flows. As interest rates can change, and these changes cannot be precisely forecast, there is a variable element in the pricing of futures that might not be present in the pricing of a forward. When calculating the price of a forward, it would be possible to lock into an interest rate, i.e. the cost of borrowing now. Therefore, the non-arbitrage price of a forward can be accurately determined. When pricing a future, the rates for reinvesting the future variation flows will be unknown and certain pricing assumptions will have to be made that would influence the price of a future so that it may not be the same as a forward.

One other factor that could create a difference between a forward and a future price is credit risk. With exchange-traded futures, there is no counterparty risk to factor into the price, whilst with a non-exchange traded forward agreement an element of credit risk will be present that may well affect the price of a forward.

Notwithstanding the above, for practical purposes, one can consider the price of a forward as being the same as the price of a future. If the difference became too great, then there could potentially be arbitrage. In conclusion, we may, rather simplistically, state that it is possible to calculate the price of a forward in the same way we would calculate the price of a future.

2 Options

2.1 Futures/Options compared

Options pricing has similarities to futures pricing. The cost of finance and the passage of time are important considerations. However, remember that the products have different attributes: delivery of futures is an obligation, but delivery of options only a possibility. It is in the evaluation of whether or not an option is likely to be exercised that some of the complexities emerge. Options are priced according to probability and it is in working out how to price probability that some complicated mathematics is used. Before reading this chapter, it is recommended that the chapter on probability is understood.

2.2 Factors affecting the price of an option

2.2.1 Introduction

Why are some options more expensive than others? The following lists the factors that affect the price of an option.

- Value of the underlying asset.
- Exercise price.
- Time to expiry.
- Volatility.
- Interest rates.
- Dividends (but only for options on dividend paying securities).

The prices for call options on a particular asset are below. The underlying price is 98.

Exercise Price	Expiry Date		
	Jan Premium	April Premium	July Premium
70	29	31	32
80	19	21	22
90	10	12	13
100	3	4	5
110	1	2	2.5
120	0	0.5	1

2.2.2 Value of underlying and exercise price

Compare the value of the January 70 call and the January 90 call from the table. The 70 call is priced at 29 whilst the 90 call is priced at 10. Why?

Remember that we are looking at call options, i.e. the right to buy. The value of the 70 call is greater than the 90 call because the right to buy at a low price (70) must be more attractive than the right to buy at a high price (90).

Why is the 70 call priced at 29?

We can readily explain at least part of the premium. If we bear in mind that the underlying stock is trading at 98, the right to buy at 70 must be worth at least 28. If the 70 call was worth less than 28, it would be possible to buy the call, exercise it to acquire stock and immediately sell the stock at the market price of 98, thereby realising a risk-free profit. However, markets do not give away money. The 70 call, with an underlying stock at 98, must be worth at least 28. This value of 28 is known as the option's **intrinsic value**.

The option is not just valued at 28, its price is 29, so where does the 1 come from?

This part of the premium is known as **time value**. The amount of time value in an option is a function of probability, i.e. the chance of further movements in the underlying asset.

The premium of the 70 is made up of two things: intrinsic value and time value.

> **Formula to learn**
>
> Premium = Intrinsic value + Time value

Premium = 28 + 1 = 29

Not all options have intrinsic value. If you look at the table, you will see the premium of the January 110 call is 1.

The 110 call has no intrinsic value because it gives the right to buy at a level above the current price of 98. It is therefore not immediately valuable. However, because things may change between now and expiry, the option has a time value of 1.

At expiry, no time is left, so an option is worth its intrinsic value or nothing. The table below gives the expiry values of call options with the underlying at 98.

Exercise Price of Call	Value
70	28
80	18
90	8
100	0
110	0
120	0

Options that have intrinsic value are described as being **in-the-money**.

Options that have only time value are described as being **out-of-the-money**.

Practitioners sometimes describe options as being **'at-the-money'**. This term has nothing to do with intrinsic value, it merely describes the option exercise price that is nearest to the current underlying price. Thus, the 100 call from our table, as the exercise price nearest the underlying (98), would be the 'at-the-money' option.

2.2.3 Time to expiry

From the previous table, we can see that the January 70 call is priced at 29, the April 70 at 31 and the July 70 at 32. You will notice from these, and from the other options, that the more life remaining in an option, the more expensive it is. This is very similar to the insurance market. If you asked an insurance company to give you two quotes, one for six months' cover on your car and one for 12 months, the quote for a year would be much more expensive. This is because the insurance company would be taking the risk over a longer period. Similarly, options writers will want larger rewards for taking larger risks.

Another point to note about time value is that it is not evenly distributed across all the different exercise prices for a particular expiry.

For the January calls with an underlying price at 98, time values are distributed as follows.

6: BASIC PRICING OF FUTURES AND OPTIONS

Exercise Price	Intrinsic Value	Time Value
70	28	1
80	18	1
90	8	2
100	0	3
110	0	1
120	0	0

You can note that time value is greatest for the 100 exercise price, i.e. the at-the-money option. This is always the case with options and is again related to the probability of whether an option will be exercised. The 70 call has a time value of only 1 because it is almost inevitable that the option will be exercised; the 110 call also has a time value of 1 because it is likely to expire unexercised. All the uncertainty, and thus all the time value, is concentrated in the 100 call. This is because there is an approximately 50/50 chance of the option being exercised. This uncertainty represents risk, and where there is risk, time value will always be higher.

The final point to note about time value relates to the pace of time decay as expiry draws near. We have already observed that time value erodes as expiry draws near, but it is important to understand that such erosion does not take place evenly. As expiry approaches, the pace of decay increases dramatically.

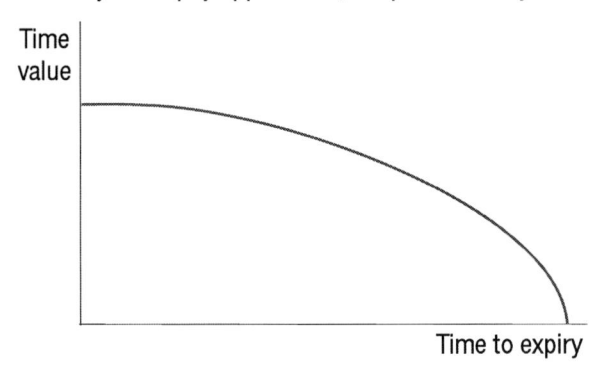

A rough and ready approximation of the **relative** amount of time value that options on the same underlying (with the same strike, but with different times to expiry) might have is given by considering the values of the square root of the time remaining to expiry, e.g.

No. of days to expiry	90	80	70	60	50	40	30	20	10	1
$\sqrt{\text{No. of days to expiry}}$	9.48	8.94	8.36	7.74	7.07	6.32	5.48	4.47	3.16	1

From the above, we might surmise that, all other things being equal, an option with approximately 22 days remaining will have half the time value of an option with 90 days to expiry. Alternatively, with 90 days remaining an option will lose only 29% of its time value when its time to expiry has fallen by 50% (to 45 days).

The erosion of time value has important consequences for investors.

For option holders, the passage of time is painful in that, all other things remaining equal, every day that passes means their options lose value.

Holders are hurt by time decay.

Conversely, option writers welcome the passage of time as, again, all other things remaining equal, the options they originally sold are worth less as each day passes and will be cheaper to repurchase.

Writers are helped by time decay.

Investors should be conscious of time decay, particularly if contemplating buying options with a short time left to expiry.

2.2.4 Volatility

Aside from time to expiry, the underlying security price and the exercise price, the most important other factor is **volatility**.

Volatility is a measure of how much an underlying price varies. If an underlying asset varies a great deal, the risk for the options writer becomes larger and the premiums they demand rise accordingly. If, however, an option is sold on an unvolatile asset, the premiums will be lower. At times of crisis or change, such as wars or elections, people become uncertain about the future. This uncertainty brings with it higher options premiums.

This is analogous to the insurance market. If you were an insurer and you were asked to quote a premium for an 18-year old and a 40-year old driving the same model of car, the premium you would demand from the 18-year old would invariably be much higher than that for the 40 year old. This would be reasonable, as the likelihood of the 18-year old crashing his car and making a claim is statistically much greater than that of the older driver doing so. Where risks are perceived to be higher, so too will be the premiums.

The challenge for all options traders is to know how risky or volatile an asset may be in the future so that they can calculate appropriate option prices. Regrettably, we cannot know what will happen in the future, so options traders analyse how variable an asset has been in the recent past and use this to estimate how variable it may be in the future.

The impact of changes in volatility is quite straightforward.

- If volatility rises, call and put premiums increase.
- If volatility falls, call and put premiums decrease.

In the same way that an actuary working for an insurance company needs to know something about the riskiness of the policyholder to quote a premium, so too does an options trader. For the actuary making a price for a life insurance policy, he will require details about dangerous hobbies, drinking, age, etc. to work out the probabilities of an early death. For the options trader, he will wish to know something about the likely price movements of the underlying asset so that he can estimate what the fair value should be. As we have already noted, if the likely variability of the asset is high, commensurately higher options premiums will need to be charged. In addition, the options trader will want to be able to attribute a particular probability to a particular outcome taking place.

To illustrate this, imagine a security is trading at 100. What values might this asset have at expiry? To start with, we can establish some boundaries – the price cannot be less than zero and cannot be higher than infinity. Beyond this we could, using our intuition, suggest that at expiry the likeliest values for the asset would be near 100, and we would attribute increasing lesser probabilities to the asset price being either substantially higher or lower than 100. The shape of the distribution might look something like this.

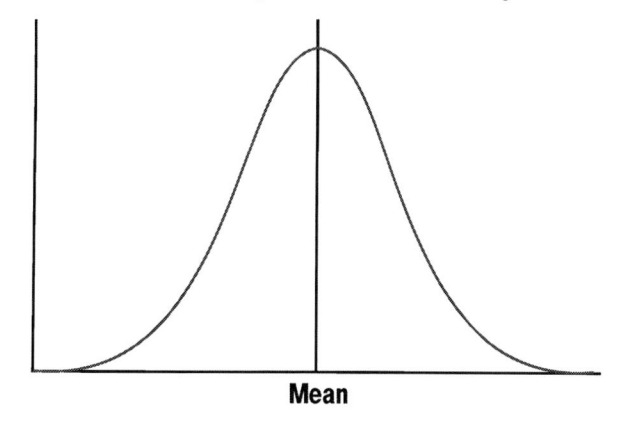

Mean

6: BASIC PRICING OF FUTURES AND OPTIONS

Many will immediately recognise this shape as a normal distribution curve. Such distributions are often found in nature, for example, if heights were measured amongst UK males, most would have a height at or around the average of 5'10" whilst fewer would be either substantially taller or shorter than the average.

Such curves can be described by two numbers: their mean and their standard deviation. The mean is the average outcome and locates the peak of the curve. The standard deviation describes how far the curve spreads out. By knowing the standard deviation of returns, it also becomes possible to attribute a probability to a particular outcome taking place.

What does this mean? The standard deviation describes how spread out the distribution curve will be, and what the probability is of a particular return being made. The volatility or standard deviation figure quoted is a one standard deviation price change (in %) at the end of one year. To illustrate this, imagine a commodity is trading at 1000 and has a volatility of 10%. Assuming that its price is Normally distributed, one year from now we would expect the commodity to be trading between 900 and 1100 about 68% of the time; between 800 and 1200 around 95% of the time and between 700 and 1300 about 99.7% of the time.

Most options do not have lifespans of a year, so it is useful to be able to compute daily, weekly or monthly volatilities. To change a yearly volatility to a volatility over a shorter time, we divide the annual volatility by square root of the number of trading periods in a year.

$$\text{Monthly volatility} = \frac{\text{Annual volatility}}{\sqrt{12}} \text{ or Annual volatility} \times \sqrt{1/12}$$

$$\text{Weekly volatility} = \frac{\text{Annual volatility}}{\sqrt{52}} \text{ or Annual volatility} \times \sqrt{1/52}$$

$$\text{Daily volatility} = \frac{\text{Annual volatility}}{\sqrt{256}^*} \text{ or Annual volatility} \times \sqrt{1/256}$$

* 256 is used, as it is the approximate number of trading days in a year and has an exact square root (16).

Exercise

What is the daily volatility of the FTSE 100 index, if the index level is 3000 and its annual volatility is 16%?

$$\frac{16}{\sqrt{256}^*} = 1\% \text{ or } 16 \times \sqrt{1/256} = 1\%$$

Thus, a one standard deviation move would be 3000 × 1% = 30 points up/down.

Two standard deviations = 60 points

Three standard deviations = 90 points

Lognormal distributions

Earlier, we suggested that asset prices are Normally distributed. Is this assertion reasonable?

Whilst the idea of a Normal distribution of prices meets most of our needs, there are two potential defects. First, a Normal distribution curve is symmetrical around its mean and allows for outcomes from minus to plus infinity. Obviously, an asset cannot have a negative value.

The other problem relates to the equal chance such a distribution gives to a down and an up move. For certain assets, commodities and equities, the existence of inflation makes an up move more likely. Certainly, over time, we would expect commodity and share prices to rise.

6: BASIC PRICING OF FUTURES AND OPTIONS

To overcome both of these two defects, options traders and most models think not about absolute money moves, but rather percentage moves. If a share trading at 100p can change by 5%, its value can change by 5p. However, should the price fall to 50p and the same 5% change takes place, its value can change by just 2.5p whilst if the price rises to 200p, a 5% change gives rise to a 10p change in price. Under this scenario, i.e. using percentage changes rather than absolute changes, negative prices would be impossible and the value of the shares would show an upwards bias – a so-called lognormal distribution.

Within options pricing models such as Black Scholes, a lognormal distribution of asset prices is assumed whilst the **percentage** changes are normally distributed.

Types of volatility

Options traders use the term volatility very widely. To avoid confusion, the various types of volatility are explained below.

Future volatility

Future volatility is the volatility that will exist in the future. Something everyone would like to know, but can't.

Historic volatility

Historic volatility is a measure of how historically variable an asset has been in the past can be calculated by finding the annualised standard deviation of a number of observations. As the purpose behind calculating historic volatility is to estimate future volatility, what sample period should be used? There is no obvious answer to this question but, conventionally, options traders normally examine a period that coincides with the lifespan of their options. Thus, for a one-year option, a year of historic data will be examined. In addition, most calculations examine daily price changes rather than weekly or monthly.

Forecast volatility

Forecast volatility is the expected future volatility of an asset.

Implied volatility

Implied volatility is a measure of volatility derived from current option prices.

2.2.5 Interest rates

The impact of changes in interest rates varies depending upon whether an option is physically settled, e.g. a stock option, or is an option on a futures contract. The way in which the premium is settled is also important.

For options on physicals

Interest Rate Rise: Call Premiums Rise
                      Put Premiums Fall

For options on futures (When the premium is paid immediately)

Interest Rate Rise: Call and Put Premiums Fall

For options on futures (When the premium is margined)

Interest Rate Rise: No Influence

For options on futures that settle their premiums upfront, the impact of a rise in rates will be to reduce the premiums. To understand this, it is useful to consider the premium as the present value of the expected return from an option. If interest rates rise, the discount factor will rise, thereby reducing the present value of the option. In short, investors will reduce the value of the bet to compensate them for the increased carrying costs. For options on futures on which the premium is settled on a margin, there is no effect. For options on physicals that settle their premiums upfront, the effect is most marked. To illustrate this, imagine a market maker who is short a call. To hedge himself, he will buy some of the underlying stock. If interest rates rise, the carrying cost of the position will also rise. The increased cost of hedging will manifest itself in a higher call premium. Now consider the position of a market maker who is short a put: to hedge his position, he will short sell some stock. If rates rise, the interest income on the short sale will increase, reducing the cost of hedging and consequently, the put premium.

2.2.6 Dividends

The dividend yields on physically settled stocks also influence stock option prices through their influence on the cost of carry as we saw with futures.

The writer of call options who has borrowed to hold shares as a hedge against their exercise will benefit from dividends received on those shares, reducing the cost of carry. The writer of puts, on the other hand, will have a short shares position as a hedge and any increase in dividend yields will be detrimental to his position increasing the cost of carry.

The dividends paid by stocks also influence stock option prices because when companies pay dividends to shareholders, the share price drops by the amount of the dividend paid.

Example

UKCO plc, whose current share price is 450p, announces that a 40p dividend will be paid on Monday, 8 November.

On Monday, 8 November, 40p is paid out as a dividend and the share price drops to 410p.

As this drop in price is predictable, option traders discount the impact of the fall well in advance, by **gradually** reducing call premiums and increasing put premiums. This reduction/increase in premium relates to the present value of the anticipated dividend.

2.2.7 Summary of factors

Exam tip You are expected to be comfortable with these factors and be able to explain the effects.

Increase in	Impact on	
	Call Option	**Put options**
Asset price (S)	Up	Down
Exercise price (X)	Down	Up
Volatility	Up	Up
Time to expiry	Up	Up
Interest rates – Options on physicals – Options on futures – Options on futures, premium margined	Up Down –	Down Down –
Asset yield	Down	Up

2.3 Boundary rules

Exam tip: Questions frequently arise requiring you to determine whether given options prices are reasonable. One of the factors to consider is these boundary rules.

Although option pricing is complex, there are certain pricing rules that must be obeyed. These rules create options price boundary conditions, i.e. they suggest the possible maximum and minimum prices that options can have. Another important rule is that options must be correctly priced against each other and the underlying asset. This will be explored in more detail when we look at put/call parity. But first, let us outline the boundary rules.

c = value of a European call
C = value of an American call
p = value of a European put
P = value of an American put
S = asset stock price
X = exercise price

2.3.1 Upper bounds, i.e. maximum value

The right to buy an asset cannot be worth more than the asset itself.

$c \leq S$
$C \leq S$

The right to sell an asset cannot be worth more than the sale proceeds.

$P \leq X$

For a European option with time t to expiry, the upper bound will be

$p \leq Xe^{-rt}$

2.3.2 Lower bound, i.e. minimum value

At expiry, an option's minimum value will be its intrinsic value or zero if it has no intrinsic value.

$c = \max(S - X, 0)$
$C = \max(S - X, 0)$
$p = \max(X - S, 0)$
$P = \max(X - S, 0)$

Before expiry, things are a little different. For European options, as the strike price cannot be paid until the expiry date, it is the PV of the strike price that is relevant.

$c \geq \max(S - Xe^{-rt}, 0)$
$p \geq \max(Xe^{-rt} - S, 0)$

As American options can be exercised immediately, this means the strike price does not need to be discounted.

$C \geq \max(S - X, 0)$
$P \geq \max(X - S, 0)$

For call options on a non-dividend paying stock, $S - Xe^{-rt}$ will always be greater than $S - X$. Therefore, it can be stated that prior to expiry, an American call option will also have a minimum value of

$C \geq \max(S - Xe^{-rt}, 0)$

This shows that early exercise of an American call option on non-dividend paying stock is not optimal.

If the option was on a dividend paying stock, then the lower boundary condition will be different. Assume the PV of the dividend anticipated to be paid before expiry is D.

For a European call, the holder will not receive the dividend, as it is paid before they can exercise. This reduces the value of the options by the PV of the dividend.

$$c \geq \max(S - D - Xe^{-rt}, 0)$$

The holder of an American call can exercise the option early by paying the strike price, thus ensuring they receive the dividend (which is of course factored into the current stock price). This gives the lower boundaries.

$$C \geq \max(S - X, 0)$$

As $S - X$ could be greater than $S - D - Xe^{-rt}$, this suggests that it may sometimes be optional to exercise an American option early if it is a dividend paying stock, depending on the relative size of the dividend (D) in relation to the interest rate effect on the strike price (Xe^{-rt}).

2.4 Put/Call parity theorem

2.4.1 Introduction

Exam tip | Put/call parity is a key pricing relationship and questions regularly arise from this area.

This rather intimidating phrase means simply that there is a relationship between put prices, call prices and the underlying asset. An understanding of this theory is vital as it provides the linkage between call prices and the corresponding put prices.

To illustrate this, let us compare two trades: the purchase of a future at 100 and the simultaneous purchase of a 100 call, and sale of a 100 put on the same future where options premiums are margined.

Diagrammatically, it looks as follows.

Outright Purchase of Future at 100

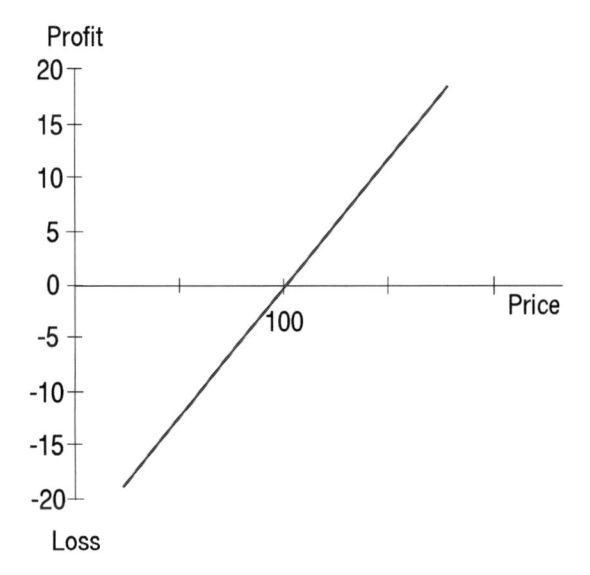

6: BASIC PRICING OF FUTURES AND OPTIONS

Or when tabulated

Futures Price	Profit/Loss
70	–30
80	–20
90	–10
100	0
110	+10
120	+20
130	+30

Another way of replicating the same profile would be to buy a call and sell a put with the same expiry and exercise price.

Buy one 100 call at 10, sell one 100 put at 10

Futures Price at Expiry	Intrinsic Value of 100 Call	Profit/Loss of 100 Call	Intrinsic Value of 100 Put	Profit/Loss of 100 Put	Net Profit/Loss
70	0	–10	30	–20	–30
80	0	–10	20	–10	–20
90	0	–10	10	0	–10
100	0	–10	0	+10	0
110	10	0	0	+10	+10
120	20	+10	0	+10	+20
130	30	+20	0	+10	+30

You will see the net profit and loss from this trade is exactly the same as that for the long future. In fact, the position established by buying a call and selling a put is known as a synthetic long position.

Following from this relationship, if we knew the price of the future and the price of the call, for example, it would be possible to find the price of the put.

The formula used is

Formula to learn

$$C - P = S - X$$

where

C = call price
P = put price
S = future price
X = exercise price

This can be reconfigured to find the value of the put.

$$P = C - S + X$$

Let us try an example using options on Bund futures.

C = 0.26
S = 96.31
X = 97.00

6: BASIC PRICING OF FUTURES AND OPTIONS

Therefore

P = 0.26 − 96.31 + 97.00
P = 0.95

The formula can be manipulated to find the value of the call.

C = P + S − X

Or the value of the future

S = C − P + X

2.4.2 Variations on put/Call parity

The formula outlined above only works for options on futures and, more specifically, only when the option premiums are margined – different formulae are used for other options.

Physically settled options

If we look at a physically settled option, for example a stock option, the underlying price is the price for immediate delivery, whilst the option's strike price will not be paid until the expiry date, perhaps several months in the future.

In efficient markets, the difference between these prices will be the cost of carry. The put/call parity formula for physically settled options needs to be adjusted to account for these costs. The formula becomes

Formula to learn

$$C - P = S - Xe^{-rt}$$

where

C = call price
P = put price
S = stock price
X = exercise price
e = exponential constant (approx. 2.7182818)
r = continuously compounded interest rate
t = time to expiry in days over 365 (£) or 360 ($)

Example

What would be the price of the call on a physically settled option, if

P = 5p
X = 100p
S = 100p
r = 6%
t = 60 days

$$C = P + S - Xe^{-rt}$$

therefore

$C = 5 + 100 \times -100 \times e^{-0.06 \times 60/365}$
$C = 5 + 100 - 99.02$
$C = 5.98$

6: BASIC PRICING OF FUTURES AND OPTIONS

The formula for physically settled options only differs from the formula for options on futures in that the exercise price is discounted to reflect carrying costs.

If the example above had been on a physically settled stock option that pays dividends, the cost of carry would need to be adjusted.

If a stock has an ex-dividend date before the option expiry date, then either the call price will be reduced by the present value of the dividends, or the put price will be correspondingly raised. So put/call parity may be amended from

$$C - P = S - Xe^{-rt}$$

to

$$C - P = S - Xe^{-rt} - D$$

where

D = the present value of the expected dividend

Example

What is the present value of a 5p dividend that will be paid in 90 days' time? Interest rates are 6%.

$$5 \times e^{-rt}$$
$$5 \times e^{-0.06 \times 0.247}$$
$$= \mathbf{4.926}$$

Stock index options

As with the previous example, consideration must be taken of the dividends paid on the underlying shares. Rather than consider discrete dividends, we can treat the dividend income as a continuous dividend yield at an annual rate of 'd'.

The put/call parity formula now becomes

Formula to learn

$$C - P = Se^{-dt} - Xe^{-rt}$$

where

S = cash price of index

Currency options

This builds on the above idea of the underlying asset generating a continuous yield. In this case, the underlying asset is foreign currency and the yield is the interest earned on that currency – 'f'.

The put/call parity formula now becomes

Formula to learn

$$C - P = Se^{-ft} - Xe^{-rt}$$

where

S = spot price of currency

Options on futures when premiums are paid upfront

The first example of put/call parity we saw, i.e.

$$C - P = S - X$$

is the appropriate formula when the option premiums are **not** paid upfront, but **are** collected via the margining system. When the premiums **are** paid upfront, allowance has to be taken of the fact that the initial net premium has to be financed to expiry.

The formula now becomes

Formula to learn
$$(C - P)(e^{rt}) = S - X$$

Or

Formula to learn
$$C - P = Se^{-rt} - Xe^{-rt}$$

where

S = the price of the future

A final point is that the put/call parity formula should theoretically only be applied to European style options. In fact, the formula works well for American style options as long as there is little or no chance of early exercise.

Using put/Call parity for arbitrage

Occasionally, options prices and underlying prices can get 'out of line' and therefore violate put/call parity. If this happens, arbitrage opportunities appear.

Example

The Gilt future for September trades at 103.78. The September 103 call trades at 1.29 and the September 103 put at 0.53. Both are options on the September future.

Compare the relative costs of buying the future and creating a synthetic long (long call/short put).

Cost of future	= 103.78
Cost of synthetic	= Premium call − Premium put + Exercise price
	= 1.29 − 0.53 + 103
	= 103.76

As can be seen, the synthetic long is cheaper than the future and an arbitrage opportunity exists.

What the arbitrageur would do is buy what is relatively cheap (the synthetic long) and sell what is relatively expensive (the future).

Buy at	103.76
Sell at	103.78
Profit	0.02

A two-tick profit is certain to be made at the September expiry.

When the future/underlying is sold and the synthetic long is purchased, the trade is known as a **reversal**.

Of course the violation may be the other way around. The synthetic is expensive and the future is cheap. In such a case, the future would be bought and a short synthetic (short call/long put) established. This trade is known as a **conversion**.

Example

The October Crude future trades at 16.90, the October 17.00 call at 0.47 and the October 17.00 put at 0.53. Both are options on the October future.

Cost of future = 16.90
Cost of synthetic = 0.47 − 0.53 + 17.00
= 16.94

Here, the future is cheap and would be bought, whilst the synthetic is expensive and would be sold (sell call, buy put). The arbitrage profit at expiry would be 4 ticks.

Further examples of conversions and reversals are given in the strategy section of the workbook.

2.4.3 Summary of put/Call parity

	Options on	Continuous Discounting	Discrete Discounting
1.	Non-dividend paying stock	$C - P = S - Xe^{-rt}$	$C - P = S - \dfrac{X}{(1+rt)}$
2.	Dividend paying stock	$C - P = S - D - Xe^{-rt}$	$C - P = S - D - \dfrac{X}{(1+rt)}$
3.	A stock index	$C - P = Se^{-yt} - Xe^{-rt}$	$C - P = \dfrac{S}{(1+yt)} - \dfrac{X}{(1+rt)}$
4.	Currency	$C - P = Se^{-yt} - Xe^{-rt}$	$C - P = \dfrac{S}{(1+yt)} - \dfrac{X}{(1+rt)}$
5.	Futures (premiums margined)	$C - P = S - X$	$C - P = S - X$
6.	Futures (premium paid upfront)	$C - P = Se^{-rt} - Xe^{-rt}$	$C - P = \dfrac{S}{(1+ft)} - \dfrac{X}{(1+rt)}$

2.5 Convexity arbitrage

As options move in- and out-of-the-money, their value changes. Both the intrinsic value and the time value will alter, with the effect that there is not a linear relationship between the value of the underlying asset and the option price. This is explored in greater detail in the option pricing chapter when option sensitivities (the greeks) are discussed.

For now, however, it is important to realise that there is a **convex** relationship, prior to expiry, between asset price and option price. This can convexity be shown diagrammatically from a call option.

6: BASIC PRICING OF FUTURES AND OPTIONS

[Graph: Value of option vs Value of asset. Shows two curves — "At expiry value, intrinsic value only" (kinked line) and "Value before expiry, intrinsic + time value" (smooth curve above it). Shaded area between represents time value.]

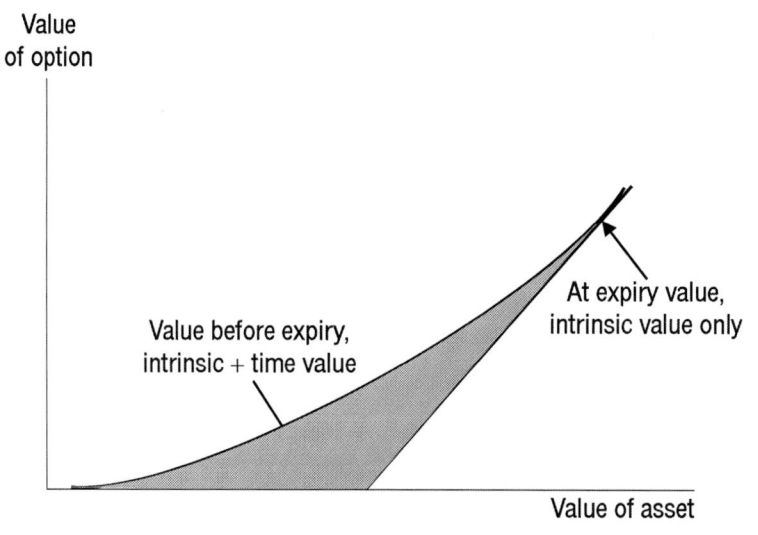

The shaded area represents time value, which is shown to be greatest for the at-the-money option, but getting smaller as options move to being in-the-money or out-of-the-money.

As explained in put/call parity, if options prices do not obey the 'rules', there are potentially arbitrage profits up for grabs.

One of these rules would suggest that options with different strikes, but on the same asset, should be priced along the curved line above. If they were not, i.e. one option with a certain strike was priced inappropriately to the others, this 'mispricing' could be exploited to make a profit.

This 'convexity arbitrage' can be demonstrated by considering the following options on the same stock, with a price of 200.

Strike Price	Call Premium
180	30
200	20
220	6

At first glance, the premiums look to be in order, i.e. premiums fall as the strike price increases, but have they fallen by the 'correct' amount? If they have not, an arbitrage profit is available.

How can we check that these three options are correctly priced with regards to each other?

One way of doing this is to construct a trade known as a long butterfly (see the strategies chapter). In this example, it would involve buying one low strike (180) call, selling two mid strike (200) calls and buying one high strike (220) call. The important thing to note with this strategy is that its initial cost is the maximum that can be lost. The initial cost in this example would be as follows.

Buy one 180 strike at	(30)
Sell two 200 strike at	40
Buy one 220 strike at	(6)
Initial cost	4

So the most you could lose is a **profit** of 4, i.e. you can only make money from this strategy. This suggests that at least one of these options is incorrectly priced relative to the others. In this case, either the 180 or 220 strikes are too cheap or the 200 strike is too expensive. The arbitrage was possible because the convex pricing relationship between options, with different strikes but on the same asset, has been broken.

The principle here is that if a strategy offers a no-lose position then something must be mispriced.

Note this long butterfly can be constructed either as

- All call options.
- All put options.
- A combination of calls and puts

but will always be

- Long one low strike option
- Short two mid strike options
- Long one high strike option

and if the sum of the premiums received/(paid) is positive (a net gain) then mispricing exists.

Chapter Roundup

- You should be familiar with the relevant factors in the pricing of futures including the ideas of
    - Basis and basis risk
    - Convergence
    - Arbitrage and the arbitrage value
    - Fair value = Cash price + Cost of Carry

- You should be familiar with the factors contributing to the value of an option, how they are related and how they affect options values, specifically
    - Premium = Intrinsic value + Time value
    - Intrinsic value (IV)
        - Call option   IV = Higher of (S – X, 0)
        - Put option   IV = Higher of (X – S, 0)
    - Other factors and how they impact on premiums
        - Volatility
        - Time
        - Interest rates
        - Asset yields

- You should be familiar with and able to apply put-call parity for various types of option.

	Options on	Continuous Discounting	Discrete Discounting
1.	Non-dividend paying stock	$C - P = S - Xe^{-rt}$	$C - P = S - \dfrac{X}{(1+rt)}$
2.	Dividend paying stock	$C - P = S - D - Xe^{-rt}$	$C - P = S - D - \dfrac{X}{(1+rt)}$
3.	A stock index	$C - P = Se^{-yt} - Xe^{-rt}$	$C - P = \dfrac{S}{(1+yt)} - \dfrac{X}{(1+rt)}$
4.	Currency	$C - P = Se^{-yt} - Xe^{-rt}$	$C - P = \dfrac{S}{(1+yt)} - \dfrac{X}{(1+rt)}$
5.	Futures (premiums margined)	$C - P = S - X$	$C - P = S - X$
6.	Futures (premium paid upfront)	$C - P = Se^{-rt} - Xe^{-rt}$	$C - P = \dfrac{S}{(1+ft)} - \dfrac{X}{(1+rt)}$

- You should be familiar with convexity arbitrage, specifically the net position from
    - Writing one low strike option
    - Buying two mid strike options
    - Writing one high strike option

    Should be a net cost. If it is a net gain them some mispricing exists.

Test Your Knowledge

Check your knowledge of the Chapter here, without referring back to the text.

1. The FTSE 100 index stands at 6,215 and has a dividend yield of 3.46%. Short term interest rates are 5.25%. Calculate the fair value of a futures contract maturing in 56 days and comment on two factors that could affect the accuracy of this calculation.

2. You are given the following for a non-dividend paying stock

    - Share price = £4.25
    - Call price = £0.40
    - Exercise price = £4.20
    - Time to expiry = 140 days
    - Interest rate (140 day) = 5.25%

    Determine the fair value of the corresponding put.

3. Explain when it may be beneficial to exercise an American style option before the expiry date.

4. A share is priced at 100 and will pay no dividend in the next three months. The price of three month (91 day) American options on this share are

Strike	Call	Put
90	14.0	2.9
100	6.7	5.5
110	3.2	11.8
120	1.0	19.0

    If interest rates are 5%, identify any arbitrage opportunities.

6: BASIC PRICING OF FUTURES AND OPTIONS

TEST YOUR KNOWLEDGE: ANSWERS

1.
Cash price	6,215
Cost of carry	
– Interest $6{,}215 \times 5.25\% \times 56/365 =$	50
– Yield $6{,}215 \times 3.46\% \times 56/365 =$	(33)
	6,232

    Two factors to consider

    - Through interest accrues evenly across a period, dividend yields are not paid evenly. We should be factoring in the dividend payments due in the next 56 days, not simply an average annual figure.

    - No account has been taken of dealing costs which would establish an arbitrage channel rather than simply a single price.

2. $C - P = S - Xe^{-rt}$

    $P = C - S + Xe^{-rt}$

    $= 40 - 425 + 420e^{-0.0525 \times 140/365}$

    $= 26.6p$

3. Whenever an option is exercised prior to expiry the value realised is the intrinsic value only, the time value is given up. Early exercise can, therefore, only be justified if some other benefit will be gained from this early exercise that more than covers this loss of time value.

    It would be beneficial to exercise a call if the dividend captured through early exercise was greater than the time value lost.

    It would be beneficial to exercise a put early if the interest that could be earned on the intrinsic value exceeded the time value, plus any asset yield lost.

4. Potential arbitrages may be highlighted by looking for violations of

    - Lower boundary limits, which for an American option are

        – $C \geq \max(S - X, 0)$
        – $P \geq \max(X - S, 0)$

    - Put/call parity, which for a non-dividend paying stock is

        – $C - P = S - Xe^{-rt}$

    - Convexity relationships – the net premium on a butterfly should be a net cost.

    Lower boundry limits

Strike	Call Max (S – X, 0)	Put Max (X – S, 0)
90	10	0
100	0	0
110	0	10
120	0	**20**

A potential arbitrage exists on the 120 put which could be bought for 19 and immediately exercised for a net benefit of 20.

Put/Call parity

X	C	P	C – P	S	Xe^{-rt}	$S - Xe^{-rt}$	Potential Profit	Action
90	14.0	2.9	11.1	100	88.9	11.1	0	–
100	6.7	5.5	1.2	100	98.8	1.2	0	–
110	3.2	11.8	–8.6	100	108.6	–8.6	0	–
120	1.0	19.0	–18.0	100	118.5	–18.5	0.5	Conversion

A potential arbitrage gain arises on the 120 options.

Convexity

	Call	Put	
Long one 90 option	(14.0)	(2.9)	
Short two 100 options	13.4	11.0	
Long one 110 option	(3.2)	(11.8)	
Net	(3.8)	(3.7)	No convexity violations
Long one 100 option	(6.7)	(5.5)	
Short two 110 options	6.4	23.6	
Long one 120 option	(1.0)	(19.0)	
Net	(1.3)	(0.9)	No convexity violations

6: BASIC PRICING OF FUTURES AND OPTIONS

7 Strategies

INTRODUCTION

There are many options strategies that may be undertaken beyond the four basics (long call, long put, short call, short put). We need to be familiar with the

- Contruction
- Attributes
- Motivation

of the major strategies.

CHAPTER CONTENTS

		Page
1	Options Strategies	152
2	Motivation	153
3	Terminology	153
4	Introduction to Strategies	154
5	Options Strategy Planner	157
6	Futures Strategies	186
	Chapter Roundup	189
	Test Your Knowledge	191

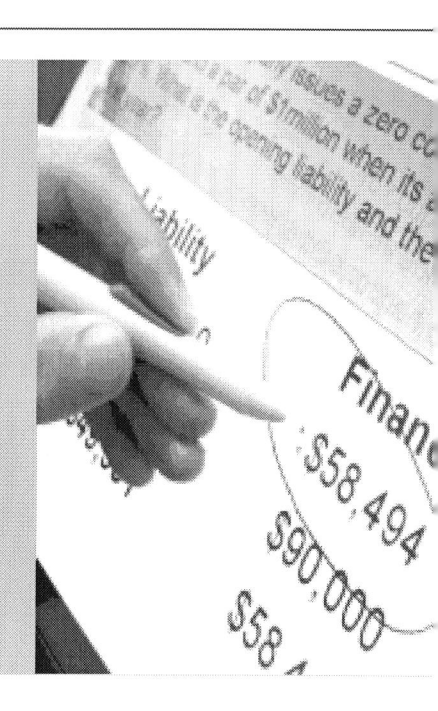

7: STRATEGIES

CHAPTER LEARNING OBJECTIVES

The syllabus areas covered by this section are

- **Uses of futures**

    Trading and arbitrage

    Students are required to display understanding of common trading strategies and arbitrage structures between futures contracts and their underlying instruments, including outright trading, intra-contract spreads, inter-contract spreads.

- **Uses of options**

    Applications

    Students are required to display understanding of a range of strategies from an investment and hedging perspective including potential risk and return for given combinations of options and/or underlying assets. In particular, the impact of volatility and time on option performance in different market conditions must be understood.

- **Derivatives risk management**

    Individual derivatives

    – Risk profiles

1 OPTIONS STRATEGIES

So far in this study book, we have looked at a number of ways in which we can use futures and options. These uses have fallen into three categories.

- Speculation
- Hedging
- Arbitrage

In this section we go further and examine some more sophisticated option strategies.

If you were to meet an options trader, it is likely that their conversation would be full of seemingly impenetrable jargon. There might be talk of straddles and strangles, bull spreads and synthetics. Despite its apparent complexity, this jargon describes options strategies and if you can understand the four simple options trades, it does become possible to understand these more sophisticated transactions.

Throughout the examples used in this chapter, a fictitious stock (ABC) is used and for the sake of simplicity, no allowances are made for commissions, taxes, interest or dividend payments. However, anyone contemplating the use of strategies in the 'real' world must consider what effects these additional costs would have on the viability of the transaction.

Some of the examples combine long or short positions in the underlying asset with options. In such examples, it should be recognised that the underlying asset might be either a futures contract or a position in a physical asset, such as crude oil.

2 MOTIVATION

Before embarking on a detailed discussion of the attributes of the various options trades, let us first think about the reasons why they are undertaken.

The first and most obvious reason for speculating in the markets is that investors have a view on their future direction, be it up or down. These are **directional** trades and may be either **bullish** (the investor feels the market is likely to go up) or **bearish** (the investor feels the market is likely to go down). Investors may also feel the market is likely to go up or down very markedly, or only slightly. There are option trades to accommodate all views.

People also trade because they feel the market is likely to be highly volatile or remain broadly static. These investors do not know in which direction the market may move, but have opinions as to its likely variability. These types of trades are known as **volatility** trades and options are unique in allowing investors to trade in this way.

The final category of strategies is called **arbitrage** trades.

Here, investors have no interest in market direction or volatility, but seek to make riskless or near riskless profits, by exploiting mis-pricings between options and the underlying assets.

All these different trades are discussed on the following pages.

3 TERMINOLOGY

In the strategy planner, you are introduced to the terminology that explains the various trades. The terms used are those most normally employed, but may not be those used by all practitioners. To avoid errors, it is always best to check with traders and customers exactly what they mean before executing a trade.

A differentiation is made between trades that involve positions **exclusively** in either calls or puts (**spreads**), and those trades in which calls and puts are used together (**combinations**).

An options spread is a transaction that involves the buying and selling of options of the same type (i.e. calls or puts) on the same underlying asset, e.g.

>Buy one April 220 call, sell one April 240 call

>or

>Sell one October 80 put, buy one December 80 put.

Within this broad definition, there are certain sub-categories: the vertical, horizontal and diagonal spreads.

To illustrate this, let us look at the call options on ABC.

7: STRATEGIES

Exercise Price	Expiry Date September	Expiry Date December
98.5	1.74	2.24
99.0	1.47	1.99
99.5	1.20	1.76
100.0	0.98	1.55
100.5	0.79	1.36
101.0	0.62	1.19
101.5	0.48	1.03

→ **Horizontal Spread** (same exercise price, different expiry)

↓ **Vertical Spread** (same expiry, different exercise price)

↘ **Diagonal Spread** (different expiry and exercise price)

The three different spreads are as follows.

Vertical Spreads	These involve the purchase and sale of options with the same expiry date but different exercise prices.
Horizontal Spreads	These involve the purchase and sale of options with the same exercise price but different expiry dates.
Diagonal Spreads	These involve the purchase and sale of options with different exercise prices and expiry dates.

A combination is a transaction that involves the buying/selling of both calls and puts on the same underlying asset, e.g.

Buy one April 200 call, buy one April 200 put.

In the pages that follow, the various strategies are examined. There is a lot of material to master. To consolidate your knowledge, it is worth practising using prices from the *Financial Times* or a screen.

4 INTRODUCTION TO STRATEGIES

In the pages that follow, the trades that you must master for the examination are detailed.

The Options Strategy Planner on the following pages shows which category (directional, volatility or arbitrage) each trade falls into.

Each strategy is allocated a separate page, listing the motivation, construction and key formulae involved.

At the foot of each page is a worked example depicted in both graph and table form.

To help you understand the make-up of the various trades, a rather fuller discussion of two simple spread and combination trades is laid out below.

4.1 Options spreads

As already discussed, an options spread is a transaction that involves the buying and selling of options of the same type (i.e. calls or puts) on the same underlying asset, e.g.

> Buy one April 220 call, sell one April 240 call

or

> Sell one October 80 put, buy one December 80 put.

Imagine an investor who believes that the price of ABC is likely to rise by 10 pence from 100 to 110 in the next month. This view is moderately bullish and to exploit it, he could buy a 100 call and, at the same time, sell a 110 call.

In doing this, the investor appears to be contradicting himself. By buying the 100 call, he is establishing a bullish position, whilst by selling the 110 call, he is being bearish. The key to the trade is in the different exercise prices that are bought and sold.

Remember the investor's view: he believes that ABC will rise from 100 to 110. If this is so, he will have no need of the 100 call above 110. He is, therefore, happy to give this exposure to someone else by selling the 110 call. If the investor is right and the stock at expiry is 110 or less, the right to buy at 110 will be worthless and he will keep the premium received from its sale.

The advantage of selling the 110 call is in making the profit from the trade more likely.

If he simply bought the 100 call for a premium of 6, his breakeven point would be the exercise price plus the premium, i.e. 106. However, by buying the 100 call at 6 and selling the 110 for 3, his breakeven point becomes 103 (100 + 6 − 3). Thus, the chances of profit become greater.

What happens if the price at expiry is above 110?

If this occurred, the 110 call would be exercised and it would become necessary for the investor to deliver the asset at a price of 110. Remember, however, that the investor has bought a 100 call, which gives him the right to buy at 100. Thus, the position is hedged.

The diagram of the position at expiry looks like this.

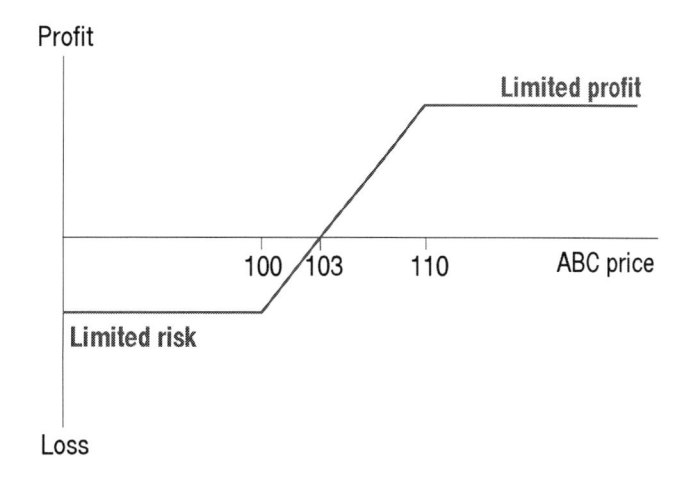

As you can see, the position has limited risk and limited reward. The limited nature of the risk and reward is characteristic of option spreads. When these positions are margined, you will see that the requirement is much lower than that required from simple written options transactions.

There are a wide variety of spreads and the example above is just an illustration of one of them.

4.2 Options combinations

A combination is a transaction that involves the buying/selling of both calls and puts on the same underlying asset.

e.g.   Buy one April 200 call, buy one April 200 put.

Thus far, we have concerned ourselves with using options to exploit views on direction. With options combinations, we are introduced to the idea of volatility trading.

Let us imagine that the situation in the Middle East is getting dangerous, with the threat of war growing daily. A United Nations' representative is engaged in talks, which if successful, will resolve the situation, but if they fail, will lead to war. If war breaks out, the price of oil will rise whilst if the talks succeed, oil prices will fall as calm returns.

How could an investor create an options position to profit from the potential volatility?

4.2.1 Action

Undertake the following crude oil options trade.

Buy one September $19.00 call for	0.50
Buy one September $19.00 put for	0.45
Total expenditure	0.95

In this trade, the investor is clearly unsure about direction. He buys a call to profit from a rise in oil prices and a put to make money from a fall. Whilst unsure about direction, the investor is certain about one thing – that volatility will increase.

Before securing a profit, the market must move by at least 0.95 either up or down. This is to cover the initial cost of both options. The breakeven points are therefore $18.05 and $19.95. Beyond these points, there is potential for unlimited or very large profits.

If the investor's view had been that volatility would decrease, he could sell both a call and a put. In this case, profits would emerge between $18.05 and $19.95. However, if the movement were greater than this, unlimited losses could result. This is just one of the trades from a range of combinations.

5 OPTIONS STRATEGY PLANNER

Exam tip | Familiarity with strategies is essential to the exam.

| Directional |||| Volatility |||| Arbitrage ||
Bull		Bear		More Volatile		Less Volatile				
Long Call	A	Long Put	B	Long Straddle	O	Short Straddle	P	Conversions	X
Short Put	C	Short Call	D	Long Strangle	Q	Short Strangle	R	Reversals	Y
Bull Spread	E	Bear Spread	F	Short Butterfly	S	Long Butterfly	T	Box	Z
Synthetic Long	G	Synthetic Short	H	Ratio Back Spread	U	Ratio Spread	V		
Synthetic Long Call	I	Synthetic Short Call/ Covered Put	J			Horizontal Spread	W		
Synthetic Short Put/ Covered Call	K	Synthetic Long Put	L						
Diagonal Spread (Bull)	M	Diagonal Spread (Bear)	M						
Cylinder	N								

7: STRATEGIES

Strategy A	Long Call
Motivation	Directional, very bullish
Construction	Opening purchase of a call. Choice of call depends on degree of bullishness; buy out-of-the-money options if very bullish, in-the-money options if less so.
Key Formulae	Maximum risk: Premium paid Maximum reward: Unlimited Breakeven at expiry: Exercise price + Premium
Comments	Position suffers from time decay.
Example **Graph**	Buy 100 Call @ 0.98
Table	

Stock Price at Expiry	Intrinsic Value of 100 Call	Profit/Loss
98	0	−0.98
100	0	−0.98
102	2	+1.02
104	4	+3.02
106	6	+5.02

Strategy B	Long Put
Motivation	Directional, very bearish
Construction	Opening purchase of a put. Choice of put depends on degree of bearishness. Buy out-of-the-money put if very bearish, in-the-money if less so.
Key Formulae	Maximum risk: Premium paid Maximum reward: Exercise price – Premium Breakeven at expiry: Exercise price – Premium
Comments	Position suffers from time decay.
Example Graph	Buy 100 Put @ 1.91

Stock Price at Expiry	Intrinsic Value of 100 Put	Profit/Loss
94	6	+4.09
96	4	+2.09
98	2	+0.09
100	0	−1.91
102	0	−1.91

7: STRATEGIES

Strategy C	Short Put
Motivation	Directional, bullish to neutral
Construction	Opening sale of a put. Choice of put depends on degree of bullishness. Sell in-the-money put if very bullish, out-of-the-money if less so.
Key Formulae	Maximum risk: Exercise price – Premium Maximum reward: Premium received Breakeven at expiry: Exercise price – Premium
Comments	Position helped by time decay.
Example Graph	Sell 100 Put @ 1.91 *(Profit/Loss graph showing profit line rising from -2 at price 96 through breakeven near 98 to maximum profit of +1.91 at prices 100 and above)*
Table	

Stock Price at Expiry	Intrinsic Value of 100 Put	Profit/Loss
94	6	–4.09
96	4	–2.09
98	2	–0.09
100	0	+1.91
102	0	+1.91

7: STRATEGIES

Strategy D	Short Call
Motivation	Directional, bearish to neutral
Construction	Opening sale of a call. Choice of call depends on degree of bearishness. Sell in-the-money call if very bearish, out-of-the-money if less so.
Key Formulae	Maximum risk: Unlimited Maximum reward: Premium received Breakeven at expiry: Exercise price + Premium
Comments	Position helped by time decay.
Example Graph	Sell 100 Call @ 0.98

Stock Price at Expiry	Intrinsic Value of 100 Call	Profit/Loss
98	0	+0.98
100	0	+0.98
102	2	−1.02
104	4	−3.02
106	6	−5.02

7: STRATEGIES

Strategy E	Bull Spread
Motivation	Directional, moderately bullish
Construction	Purchase of low-strike call (put) and sale of high-strike call (put).
Key Formulae	**When constructed with calls** Maximum risk: Net initial debit Maximum reward: Difference between strikes − Initial debit Breakeven at expiry: Lower strike + Initial debit **When constructed with puts** Maximum risk: Difference between strikes − Initial credit Maximum reward: Net initial credit Breakeven at expiry: Higher strike price − Initial credit
Comments	Only moderate exposure to time decay.
Example **Graph**	Buy 100 Call @ 0.98, Sell 101 Call @ 0.62
Table	See table below

Example: Buy 100 Call @ 0.98, Sell 101 Call @ 0.62

Profit/Loss graph showing flat loss of approximately −0.36 for prices below 100, rising to a profit of approximately +0.64 at price 101 and above.

Stock Price at Expiry	Intrinsic Value of 100 Call	Profit/ Loss of 100 Call	Intrinsic Value of 101 Call	Profit/ Loss of 101 Call	Net Profit/ Loss
98	0	−0.98	0	+0.62	−0.36
99	0	−0.98	0	+0.62	−0.36
100	0	−0.98	0	+0.62	−0.36
101	1	+0.02	0	+0.62	+0.64
102	2	+1.02	1	−0.38	+0.64

7: STRATEGIES

Strategy F	Bear Spread
Motivation	Directional, moderately bearish
Construction	Sale of low-strike call (put) and purchase of high-strike call (put).
Key Formulae	**When constructed with calls** Maximum risk: Difference between strikes – Initial credit Maximum reward: Net initial credit Breakeven at expiry: Lower strike + Initial credit **When constructed with puts** Maximum risk: Net initial debit Maximum reward: Difference between strikes – Initial debit Breakeven at expiry: Higher strike price – Initial debit
Comments	Only moderate exposure to time decay.
Example Graph	Sell 100 Put @ 1.91, Buy 101 Put @ 2.55

Stock Price at Expiry	Intrinsic Value of 100 Put	Profit/ Loss of 100 Put	Intrinsic Value of 101 Put	Profit/ Loss of 101 Put	Net Profit/ Loss
98	2	−0.09	3	+0.45	+0.36
99	1	+0.91	2	−0.55	+0.36
100	0	+1.91	1	−1.55	+0.36
101	0	+1.91	0	−2.55	−0.64
102	0	+1.91	0	−2.55	−0.64

7: STRATEGIES

Strategy G	Synthetic Long
Motivation	Directional, very bullish
Construction	Purchase of call and sale of put at same strike and with same expiry.
Key Formulae	Maximum risk: Exercise price +/– Net initial debit/credit Maximum reward: Unlimited Breakeven at expiry: Exercise price +/– Net initial debit/credit
Comments	Will behave like a long futures/physical position.
Example Graph	Buy 100 Call @ 0.98, Sell 100 Put @ 1.91
Table	See table below

Buy 100 Call @ 0.98, Sell 100 Put @ 1.91

Stock Price at Expiry	Intrinsic Value of 100 Call	Profit/Loss of 100 Call	Intrinsic Value of 100 Put	Profit/Loss of 100 Put	Net Profit/Loss
97	0	−0.98	3	−1.09	−2.07
98	0	−0.98	2	−0.09	−1.07
99	0	−0.98	1	+0.91	−0.07
100	0	−0.98	0	+1.91	+0.93
101	1	+0.02	0	+1.91	+1.93
102	2	+1.02	0	+1.91	+2.93
103	3	+2.02	0	+1.91	+3.93

7: STRATEGIES

Strategy H	Synthetic Short
Motivation	Directional, very bearish
Construction	Sale of call and purchase of put at same strike and with same expiry.
Key Formulae	Maximum risk: Unlimited Maximum reward: Exercise price –/+ Net initial debit/credit Breakeven at Expiry: Exercise price –/+ Net initial debit/credit
Comments	Will behave like a short futures/physical position.
Example Graph	Sell 100 Call @ 0.98, Buy 100 Put @ 1.91

Stock Price at Expiry	Intrinsic Value of 100 Call	Profit/ Loss of 100 Call	Intrinsic Value of 100 Put	Profit/ Loss of 100 Put	Net Profit/ Loss
97	0	+0.98	3	+1.09	+2.07
98	0	+0.98	2	+0.09	+1.07
99	0	+0.98	1	–0.91	+0.07
100	0	+0.98	0	–1.91	–0.93
101	1	–0.02	0	–1.91	–1.93
102	2	–1.02	0	–1.91	–2.93
103	3	–2.02	0	–1.91	–3.93

7: STRATEGIES

Strategy I	Synthetic Long Call
Motivation	Directional, bullish but with limited downside risk
Construction	Long position in stock/future and purchase of put.
Key Formulae	Maximum risk: Initial value of stock/future − Exercise price + Put premium Maximum reward: Unlimited Breakeven at expiry: Initial value of stock/future + Put premium
Comments	Classic options hedge of long position in underlying; protects downside but allows profit if market advances. More flexible and thus more expensive than short hedge with futures.
Example Graph	Long ABC Stock @ 99.07, Buy 100 Put @ 1.91

Stock Price at Expiry	Profit/ Loss of ABC	Intrinsic Value of 100 Put	Profit/ Loss of 100 Put	Net Profit/ Loss
97	−2.07	3	+1.09	−0.98
98	−1.07	2	+0.09	−0.98
99	−0.07	1	−0.91	−0.98
100	+0.93	0	−1.91	−0.98
101	+1.93	0	−1.91	+0.02
102	+2.93	0	−1.91	+1.02
103	+3.93	0	−1.91	+2.02

Strategy J	Synthetic Short Call/Covered Put
Motivation	Directional, bearish-neutral, subject to exercise price
Construction	Short position in stock/future and sale of put.
Key Formulae	Maximum risk: Unlimited Maximum reward: Initial value of stock/future − Exercise price + Put premium Breakeven at expiry: Initial value of stock/future + Put premium
Comments	Mirror image of synthetic long call; not a common investment strategy, but premium income can enhance returns in static market.
Example **Graph**	Short ABC Stock @ 99.07, Sell 100 Put @ 1.91

Stock Price at Expiry	Profit/Loss of ABC	Intrinsic Value of 100 Put	Profit/Loss of 100 Put	Net Profit/Loss
97	+2.07	3	−1.09	+0.98
98	+1.07	2	−0.09	+0.98
99	+0.07	1	+0.91	+0.98
100	−0.93	0	+1.91	+0.98
101	−1.93	0	+1.91	−0.02
102	−2.93	0	+1.91	−1.02
103	−3.93	0	+1.91	−2.02

7: STRATEGIES

Strategy K	Synthetic Short Put/Covered Call
Motivation	Directional, bullish-neutral, subject to strike
Construction	Long position in stock/future, and sale of call. If call sold is out-of-the-money, the trade is bullish; if at-the-money call is sold, trade is neutral.
Key Formulae	Maximum risk: Initial value of stock/future – Call premium Maximum reward: Exercise price – Initial value stock/future + Call premium Breakeven at expiry: Initial value of stock/future – Call premium
Comments	Very familiar investment strategy that can enhance returns in static markets, whilst also providing limited protection against falls. (Protection = Call premium)
Example Graph	Buy ABC Stock @ 99.07, Sell 100 Call @ 0.98
Table	

Stock Price at Expiry	Profit/ Loss of ABC	Intrinsic Value of 100 Call	Profit/ Loss of 100 Call	Net Profit/ Loss
97	–2.07	0	+0.98	–1.09
98	–1.07	0	+0.98	–0.09
99	–0.07	0	+0.98	+0.91
100	+0.93	0	+0.98	+1.91
101	+1.93	1	–0.02	+1.91
102	+2.93	2	–1.02	+1.91
103	+3.93	3	–2.02	+1.91

7: STRATEGIES

Strategy L	Synthetic Long Put
Motivation	Directional, bearish
Construction	Short position in stock/future and purchase of call.
Key Formulae	Maximum risk: Exercise price − Initial value of stock/future + Call premium Maximum reward: Initial value of stock/future − Call premium Breakeven at expiry: Initial value of stock/future − Call premium
Comments	Alternative to conventional purchase of put.
Example	Short ABC Stock @ 99.07, Buy 100 Call @ 0.98
Graph	
Table	

Stock Price at Expiry	Profit/Loss of ABC	Intrinsic Value of 100 Call	Profit/Loss of 100 Call	Net Profit/Loss
97	+2.07	0	−0.98	+1.09
98	+1.07	0	−0.98	+0.09
99	+0.07	0	−0.98	−0.91
100	−0.93	0	−0.98	−1.91
101	−1.93	1	+0.02	−1.91
102	−2.93	2	+1.02	−1.91
103	−3.93	3	+2.02	−1.91

7: STRATEGIES

Strategy M	Diagonal Spread
Motivation	Directional – bullish if constructed with calls, bearish if constructed with puts
Construction	Sale of short-dated call/put and purchase of longer dated and further out-of-the-money call/put.
Key Formulae American style physically settled options only	**Maximum risk:** Difference between strikes – Initial credit or initial debit **Maximum reward:** At short-dated expiry, limited **Breakeven at expiry:** Dependent on relative movements of premiums
Comments	Undertaken when short-term view is bearish (calls) or bullish (puts) and subsequently expected to move in opposite direction. As trade involves options with different expiries, it is difficult to estimate potential rewards and breakevens without computer assistance. Point of highest profit at short-term expiry (at exercise price).
Example **Graph** **Table**	Sell September 100 Call @ 0.98, Buy December 101 Call @ 1.19 *[Profit/Loss graph peaking at price 100 with profit ~1, declining on both sides]* <table><tr><th>Stock Price at Expiry</th><th>Intrinsic Value of 100 Call</th><th>Profit/ Loss of 100 Call</th><th>Market Value of 101 Call</th><th>Profit/ Loss of 100 Call</th><th>Net Profit/ Loss</th></tr><tr><td>98</td><td>0</td><td>+0.98</td><td>0.40</td><td>−0.79</td><td>+0.19</td></tr><tr><td>99</td><td>0</td><td>+0.98</td><td>0.66</td><td>−0.53</td><td>+0.45</td></tr><tr><td>100</td><td>0</td><td>+0.98</td><td>1.00</td><td>−0.19</td><td>+0.79</td></tr><tr><td>101</td><td>1</td><td>−0.02</td><td>1.46</td><td>+0.27</td><td>+0.25</td></tr><tr><td>102</td><td>2</td><td>−1.02</td><td>2.02</td><td>+0.83</td><td>−0.19</td></tr><tr><td>103</td><td>3</td><td>−2.02</td><td>2.68</td><td>+1.49</td><td>−0.53</td></tr></table>

7: STRATEGIES

Strategy N	Cylinder
Motivation	Directional – moderately bullish, but with desire for downside protection
Construction	Sale of call at a high strike and purchase of put at a lower strike, combined with a long position in the underlying.
Key Formulae	Maximum risk: Limited; cap set by put Maximum reward: Limited; floor set by call Breakeven at expiry: Stock price +/− Net initial debit/credit
Comments	This is simply a synthetic bull spread. Alternative terms are collar or fence. Can sometimes be done for zero cost: a costless collar.
Example	Sell 101 Call @ 0.62, Buy 99 Put @ 1.40 Long ABC @ 99.07

Graph

Profit/Loss graph with Profit axis from −3 to 3 and Price axis centred at 100. The payoff is flat at approximately −1 below price 99, rises linearly between 99 and 101, and is flat at approximately +1 above 101.

Table

Stock at Expiry	Profit/ Loss ABC	Intrinsic Value of 99 Put	Profit/ Loss of 99 Put	Intrinsic Value of 101 Call	Profit/ Loss of 101 Call	Net Profit/ Loss
97	−2.07	2	+0.60	0	+0.62	−0.85
98	−1.07	1	−0.40	0	+0.62	−0.85
99	−0.07	0	−1.40	0	+0.62	−0.85
100	+0.93	0	−1.40	0	+0.62	+0.15
101	+1.93	0	−1.40	0	+0.62	+1.15
102	+2.93	0	−1.40	1	−0.38	+1.15

7: STRATEGIES

Strategy 0	Long Straddle
Motivation	Volatility – undertaken to exploit increasing variability
Construction	Purchase of call and put with same exercise price and expiry.
Key Formulae	Maximum risk: Premiums paid Maximum reward: Unlimited Breakeven at expiry: Upside: Exercise price + Both premiums Downside: Exercise price – Both premiums
Comments	Prone to severe time decay if position held near to expiry.
Example Graph	Buy 100 Call @ 0.98, Buy 100 Put @ 1.91

Stock Price at Expiry	Intrinsic Value of 100 Call	Profit/Loss of 100 Call	Intrinsic Value of 100 Put	Profit/Loss of 100 Put	Net Profit/Loss
94	0	−0.98	6	+4.09	+3.11
96	0	−0.98	4	+2.09	+1.11
98	0	−0.98	2	+0.09	−0.89
100	0	−0.98	0	−1.91	−2.89
102	2	+1.02	0	−1.91	−0.89
104	4	+3.02	0	−1.91	+1.11
106	6	+5.02	0	−1.91	+3.11

7: STRATEGIES

Strategy P	Short Straddle
Motivation	Volatility – undertaken to exploit decreasing variability
Construction	Sale of call and put with same exercise price and expiry.
Key Formulae	**Maximum risk:** Unlimited **Maximum reward:** Limited to premiums **Breakeven at expiry:** Upside: Exercise price + Both premiums Downside: Exercise price – Both premiums
Comments	Benefits from time decay, but beware, unlimited risk.
Example Graph	Sell 100 Call @ 0.98, Sell 100 Put @ 1.91

Stock Price at Expiry	Intrinsic Value of 100 Call	Profit/ Loss of 100 Call	Intrinsic Value of 100 Put	Profit/ Loss of 100 Put	Net Profit/ Loss
94	0	+0.98	6	−4.09	−3.11
96	0	+0.98	4	−2.09	−1.11
98	0	+0.98	2	−0.09	+0.89
100	0	+0.98	0	+1.91	+2.89
102	2	−1.02	0	+1.91	+0.89
104	4	−3.02	0	+1.91	−1.11
106	6	−5.02	0	+1.91	−3.11

7: STRATEGIES

Strategy Q	Long Strangle
Motivation	Volatility – expect large increase in market variability
Construction	Purchase of call and put with same expiry, but different strike.
Key Formulae	**If call strike higher than put**
	Maximum risk: Limited to premiums
	Maximum reward: Unlimited
	Breakeven at expiry: Upside: Higher strike + Premiums
	Downside: Lower strike – Premiums
	If call strike lower than put
	Maximum risk: Limited to premium – Difference between strikes
	Maximum reward: Unlimited
	Breakeven at expiry: Upside: Lower strike + Premiums
	Downside: Higher strike – Premiums
Comments	Generally a lower cost alternative to a long straddle, which is less prone to time decay, but breakevens further apart.
Example Graph	Buy 101 Call @ 0.62, Buy 99 Put @ 1.40

Stock Price at Expiry	Intrinsic Value of 101 Call	Profit/ Loss of 101 Call	Intrinsic Value of 99 Put	Profit/ Loss of 99 Put	Net Profit/ Loss
94	0	–0.62	5	+3.6	+2.98
96	0	–0.62	3	+1.6	+0.98
98	0	–0.62	1	–0.4	–1.02
100	0	–0.62	0	–1.4	–2.02
102	1	+0.38	0	–1.4	–1.02
104	3	+2.38	0	–1.4	+0.98
106	5	+4.38	0	–1.4	+2.98

7: STRATEGIES

Strategy R	Short Strangle
Motivation	Volatility – expect large decrease in market variability
Construction	Sale of call and put with same expiry, but different strike.
Key Formulae	**If call strike higher than put**
	Maximum risk: Unlimited
	Maximum reward: Premiums received
	Breakeven at expiry: Upside: Higher strike + Premiums
	Downside: Lower strike – Premiums
	If call strike lower than put
	Maximum risk: Unlimited
	Maximum reward: Premiums received – Difference between strikes
	Breakeven at expiry: Upside: Lower strike + Premiums
	Downside: Higher strike – Premiums
Comments	Alternative to short straddle, generally breakevens more widely displaced and thus, position is less quickly loss making.
Example Graph	Sell 99 Call @ 1.47, Sell 101 Put @ 2.55

Stock Price at Expiry	Intrinsic Value of 99 Call	Profit/Loss of 99 Call	Intrinsic Value of 101 Put	Profit/Loss of 101 Put	Net Profit/Loss
94	0	+1.47	7	–4.45	–2.98
96	0	+1.47	5	–2.45	–0.98
98	0	+1.47	3	–0.45	+1.02
100	1	+0.47	1	+1.55	+2.02
102	3	–1.53	0	+2.55	+1.02
104	5	–3.53	0	+2.55	–0.98
106	7	–5.53	0	+2.55	–2.98

7: STRATEGIES

Strategy S	Short Butterfly
Motivation	Volatility – undertaken to exploit increasing variability
Construction	Sale of low-strike call/put. Purchase of two mid-strike calls/puts. Sale of high-strike call/put.
Key Formulae	Maximum risk: Difference between one set of strikes less initial credit Maximum reward: Net initial credit Breakeven at expiry: Lower strike + Credit Higher strike – Credit
Comments	Alternative to long straddle/strangle. Less prone to time decay, but at cost of very limited profit.
Example	Sell One 103 Put @ 0.62, Buy Two 104 Puts @ 1.04, Sell One 105 Put @ 1.63
Graph	*(Profit/Loss graph showing V-shaped loss region around price 104, with profit plateau of ~0.17 on either side and maximum loss of ~-0.83 at 104)*

Table

Stock at Expiry	Intrinsic Value 103 Put	Profit/Loss 103 Put	Intrinsic Value 104 Put	Profit/Loss 2 × 104 Put	Intrinsic Value 105 Put	Profit/Loss 105 Put	Net Profit/Loss
101	2	−1.38	3	+3.92	4	−2.37	+0.17
102	1	−0.38	2	+1.92	3	−1.37	+0.17
103	0	+0.62	1	−0.08	2	−0.37	+0.17
104	0	+0.62	0	−2.08	1	+0.63	−0.83
105	0	+0.62	0	−2.08	0	+1.63	−0.17
106	0	+0.62	0	−2.08	0	+1.63	−0.17
107	0	+0.62	0	−2.08	0	+1.63	−0.17

Strategy T	**Long Butterfly**
Motivation	Volatility – undertaken to exploit reducing variability
Construction	Purchase of low-strike call/put. Sale of two mid-strike calls/puts. Purchase of high-strike call/put.
Key Formulae	Maximum risk: Net initial debit Maximum reward: Difference between one set of strikes – Initial debit Breakeven at expiry: Lower strike + Debit Higher strike – Debit
Comments	Constructed to be delta neutral. Patently less risky than short straddle/strangle.
Example	Buy One 103 Call @ 1.52, Sell Two 104 Calls @ 0.94, Buy One 105 Call @ 0.53

Graph

(Profit/Loss graph showing peak at 104)

Table

Stock at Expiry	Intrinsic Value 103 Call	Profit/Loss 103 Call	Intrinsic Value 104 Call	Profit/Loss 2 × 104 Call	Intrinsic Value 105 Call	Profit/Loss 105 Call	Net Profit/Loss
101	0	–1.52	0	+1.86	0	–0.53	–0.19
102	0	–1.52	0	+1.86	0	–0.53	–0.19
103	0	–1.52	0	+1.86	0	–0.53	–0.19
104	1	–0.52	0	+1.86	0	–0.53	+0.81
105	2	+0.48	1	–0.14	0	–0.53	–0.19
106	3	+1.48	2	–2.14	1	+0.47	–0.19
107	4	+2.48	3	–4.14	2	+1.47	–0.19

7: STRATEGIES

Strategy U	Ratio Back Spread
Motivation	Volatility expected to rise, directional bias bullish when constructed with calls, bearish with puts
Construction	Call: Sale of low-strike call and purchase of two or more high-strike calls. Put: Sale of high-strike put and purchase of two or more low-strike puts.
Key Formulae	**When constructed with puts** Maximum risk: Difference between strikes and net initial debit Maximum reward: Breakeven value Breakeven at expiry: Lower strike – Initial debit – Difference between strikes
Comments	Expectation that volatility will rise and that up (call) or down (put) move is likely.
Example Graph	Buy Two 100 Puts @ 1.91, Sell One 101 Put @ 2.55

Stock Price at Expiry	Intrinsic Value of 100 Call	Profit/Loss of 100 Call	Intrinsic Value of 101 Call	Profit/Loss of 101 Call	Net Profit/Loss
97	3	+2.18	4	–1.45	+0.73
98	2	+0.18	3	–0.45	–0.27
99	1	–1.82	2	+0.55	–1.27
100	0	–3.82	1	+1.55	–2.27
101	0	–3.82	0	+2.55	–1.27
102	0	–3.82	0	+2.55	–1.27

Strategy V	**Ratio Spread**
Motivation	Volatility expected to fall; directional bias bearish when constructed with calls, bullish with puts
Construction	Call: Purchase of low-strike call and sale of two or more high-strike calls. Put: Purchase of high-strike put and sale of two or more low-strike puts.
Key Formulae	**When constructed with calls** Maximum risk: Unlimited Maximum reward: Difference between strikes + Initial credit Breakeven at expiry: Higher strike + Maximum profit
Comments	Expectation that volatility will decline and that up (call) or down (put) move is unlikely.
Example Graph	Buy One 100 Call @ 0.98, Sell Two 101 Calls @ 0.62

Stock Price at Expiry	Intrinsic Value of 100 Call	Profit/ Loss of 100 Call	Intrinsic Value of 101 Call	Profit/ Loss of 101 Call	Net Profit/ Loss
99	0	−0.98	0	+1.24	+0.26
100	0	−0.98	0	+1.24	+0.26
101	1	+0.02	0	+1.24	+1.26
102	2	+1.02	1	−0.76	+0.24
103	3	+2.02	2	−2.76	−0.74

7: STRATEGIES

Strategy W	Horizontal Spread
Motivation	Volatility, undertaken to take advantage of static market
Construction	Sale of short-dated call (put) and purchase of longer dated call (put) with the same strike.
Key Formulae American style physically settled options only	Maximum risk: Net initial debit Maximum reward: Indeterminate, subject to relative changes in premiums Breakeven at expiry: Indeterminate, subject to relative changes in premiums
Comments	Trade exploits the fact that short-dated options will lose time value more quickly than long-dated options. Ideal position is if stock expires at the exercise price by the shorter term expiry.
Example **Graph** **Table**	Sell September 100 Call @ 0.98, Buy December 100 Call @ 1.55

Stock Price at Sept. Expiry	Intrinsic Value of Sept. Call	Profit/Loss of Sept. Call	Theoretical Value of Dec. Call	Profit/Loss of Dec. Call	Net Profit/Loss
96	0	+0.98	+0.23	−1.32	−0.34
98	0	+0.98	+0.64	−0.91	+0.07
100	0	+0.98	+1.44	−0.11	+0.87
102	2	−1.02	+2.67	+1.12	+0.1
104	4	−3.02	+4.26	+2.71	−0.31

7: STRATEGIES

Strategy X	Conversions
Motivation	**Arbitrage** – Employed to exploit mis-pricing between options and futures/stock. Conversion used when synthetic short is expensive and the underlying is relatively cheap.
Construction	Sell call and buy put with same exercise price and expiry, simultaneously buy underlying stock/future.
Key Formulae	Maximum risk: None Maximum reward: Extent of pricing anomaly
Comments	Strategy rests on violation of put/call parity (see chapter on pricing). In efficient markets, synthetic long/short positions should be in line with the underlying.
Example	Sell 100 Call @ 0.98, Buy 100 Put @ 1.91, Buy ABC @ 99.05

Graph

Profit/Loss chart with a horizontal line at +0.02 across all prices, with price axis marked at 100.

Table

Stock at Expiry	Intrinsic Value 100 Call	Profit/ Loss 100 Call	Intrinsic Value 100 Put	Profit/ Loss 100 Put	Profit/ Loss ABC	Net Profit/ Loss
96	0	+0.98	4	+2.09	−3.05	0.02
98	0	+0.98	2	+0.09	−1.05	0.02
100	0	+0.98	0	−1.91	+0.95	0.02
102	2	−1.02	0	−1.91	+2.95	0.02
104	4	−3.02	0	−1.91	+4.95	0.02
106	6	−5.02	0	−1.91	+6.95	0.02

7: STRATEGIES

Strategy Y	Reversals
Motivation	Arbitrage – Employed to exploit mis-pricing between options and futures/stock. Reversal used when synthetic long is cheap and the underlying is relatively expensive.
Construction	Buy call and sell put with same exercise price and expiry, simultaneously sell underlying stock/future.
Key Formulae	Maximum risk: None Maximum reward: Extent of pricing anomaly
Comments	Strategy rests on violation of put/call parity (see chapter on pricing).
Example	Buy 100 Call @ 1.52, Sell 100 Put @ 2.72, Sell ABC @ 98.83

Graph

Stock at Expiry	Intrinsic Value 100 Call	Profit/Loss 100 Call	Intrinsic Value 100 Put	Profit/Loss 100 Put	Profit/Loss ABC	Net Profit/Loss
96	0	−1.52	4	−1.28	+2.83	0.03
98	0	−1.52	2	+0.72	+0.83	0.03
100	0	−1.52	0	+2.72	−1.17	0.03
102	2	+0.48	0	+2.72	−3.17	0.03
104	4	+2.48	0	+2.72	−5.17	0.03
106	6	+4.48	0	+2.72	−7.17	0.03

7: STRATEGIES

Strategy Z	Box
Motivation	Arbitrage – Employed to exploit mis-pricing between synthetic long position at one strike and a synthetic short at another. Similar to conversion/reversal but with lower risk, as no underlying position established.
Construction	Buy call and sell put with same exercise price and expiry; simultaneously sell call and buy put at different strike. You are long (short) the box if you are synthetically long (short) at the lower strike.
Key Formulae	Maximum risk: None Maximum reward: Extent of pricing anomaly
Comments	Strategy rests on violation of put/call parity. If present value of box differs from the present value of the difference between the strikes, then an arbitrage opportunity exists.
Example	Buy 100 Call @ 0.95, Sell 100 Put @ 1.91 Sell 99 Call @ 1.47, Buy 99 Put @ 1.40
Graph	Profit/Loss graph: flat line at 0.03 across all prices.
Table	*see below*

Stock at Expiry	Intrinsic Value 100 Call	Profit/Loss 100 Call	Intrinsic Value 100 Put	Profit/Loss 100 Put	Intrinsic Value 99 Call	Profit/Loss 99 Call	Intrinsic Value 99 Put	Profit/Loss 99 Put	Net Profit/Loss
97	0	−0.95	3	−1.09	0	+1.47	2	+0.60	0.03
98	0	−0.95	2	−0.09	0	+1.47	1	−0.40	0.03
99	0	−0.95	1	−0.91	0	+1.47	0	−1.40	0.03
100	0	−0.95	0	+1.91	1	+0.47	0	−1.40	0.03
101	1	+0.05	0	+1.91	2	−0.53	0	−1.40	0.03
102	2	+1.05	0	+1.91	3	−1.53	0	−1.40	0.03

5.1 Box Spread

Strategy Z notes that a long box is synthetically long at one strike and synthetically short at a higher strike, whilst a short box is synthetically short the lower strike and synthetically long the higher strike.

Another way of looking at this is to consider the long box as a call bull spread plus a put bear spread, and the short box as a put bull spread and a call bear spread.

An analysis of the payoffs will reveal the payoff at expiry will be the difference between the two strikes. With a long box, the difference will be received; with a short box, the difference will be paid out.

As the future cash flows are known with certainty at the outset of the trade, the fair price of the box should be the present value of the difference in the two strike prices. If the cost of the box is not at the present value of the difference in the strike price, then this gives rise to the arbitrage opportunity outlined.

Apart from potential arbitrage opportunities it should be appreciated that a box spread can be used to create synthetic risk-free funding or investment opportunities.

Consider a long box that is fairly priced, i.e. there is no arbitrage opportunity. The cost of this box is the present value of the certain payoff, the difference between the two strikes. Therefore, if you buy the box, it is the same as lending the cost of the box now and receiving that amount plus the risk-free rate back on the expiry date of the box. Thus, a long box creates a synthetic risk-free lending opportunity. It follows that a short box, where the present value of the payoff is received now and the difference in strike paid out on expiry, is effectively an opportunity to create a synthetic borrowing at the risk-free rate.

5.2 Covered calls

One of the most commonplace investment strategies undertaken by institutions is the covered call/synthetic short put. Constructed by holding stock and selling a call, it provides a method of enhancing returns in a generally flat market; it also provides the user with a little bit of protection against a market fall. The major disadvantage is the possibility of considerable opportunity loss, should the price of the underlying be considerably above the strike at expiry.

In analysing this strategy, a number of calculations are undertaken: return if exercised, return if unchanged and downside protection.

5.2.1 Return if exercised

A simple measure of the return on the investment if a call option is exercised and the stock is sold.

Example

A fund manager buys one XYZ share at 100 and sells one three-month 120 call at 7.

Initial investment = 100 Stock price
(7) Premium
93

If the call were exercised, he will sell at 120.

Therefore, over the three-month period, he will have a gain of 27 (120 − 93).

As a percentage of the original investment, this equals

$$\frac{27}{93} = 29\%$$

Annualised: $29\% \times \frac{365}{91} = 116\%$

(Whilst it is conventional to annualise returns for comparison, such annualisation is somewhat unrealistic, as it implies the ability to undertake similarly successful trades several times in the year.)

Return if unchanged

A measure of the standstill performance.

Example

A fund manager buys one XYZ share at 100 and sells one three-month 120 call at 7. At expiry, the shares remain at 100.

Initial investment: 93
Value at expiry: 100
Gain: 7

$$\text{Return} = \frac{\text{Gain}}{\text{Initial investment}}$$

$$= \frac{7}{93} \times \frac{365}{91}$$

$$= 0.30 \, (30\%)$$

5.2.2 Downside protection

A measure of the degree of protection that the strategy provides, should the underlying asset decline in price. As will be seen, the extent of the protection is a function of the premium that is received. Consequently, if one is neutral/bearish, in-the-money calls should be written. There is, however, a trade-off: if in-the-money options are written, the return, if exercised, will be very low. If you are neutral/bullish, out-of-the-money calls should be written.

Example

A fund manager holds one XYZ share at 100 and sells one three-month 110 call at 13.

The amount of protection is simply

$$\frac{\text{Premium}}{\text{Stock price}} = \frac{13}{100} = 13\%$$

6 FUTURES STRATEGIES

In this section we identify five types of futures strategy: the intramarket spread, the intermarket spread, basis trades, stacks and strips.

6.1 Intramarket spreads

Intramarket spreads are futures positions in which one delivery month is bought and another delivery month sold within the same product, e.g.

> Buy June gilt future
> Sell September gilt future

Such spreads are undertaken when profits are anticipated from relative movements between delivery months. This may happen when, owing to temporary supply and demand pressures, one delivery month trades expensively to its own fair value.

In an intramarket spread, there exist simultaneous obligations to buy and sell the underlying asset. As a result of this, the potential profit and loss are normally limited; a fact recognised by margining systems that calculate reduced margins for such spreads.

When the near dated future is bought and the longer dated future sold, this is described as **buying** the spread.

If the near dated is sold and the longer dated bought, this is described as **selling** the spread.

Example

1 February

An investor believes that the July cocoa market is likely to be oversupplied, but that by September, the market will revert to an equilibrium between supply and demand.

> July cocoa trades at £663 per ton
> September cocoa at £665 per ton

Action – Sell the July/September spread

End March

> July future   = £650
> September future = £660

Action – Buy the July/September Spread

Result

July		September	
Sold at	£663	Bought at	£665
Bought at	£650	Sold at	£660
Profit	£13	Loss	£5

£13 – £5 = **£8 Net profit**

6.2 Intermarket spreads

Intermarket spreads are trades in which futures positions are bought in one delivery month and sold in the delivery month of a related contract, e.g.

Buy June gilt future, sell June FTSE future

or

Buy March crude future, sell March gas oil future

As with intramarket spreads, the purpose is to benefit from a change in the relationship between the two products. Often such spreads are executed when an historic relationship between two highly correlated products has broken down, but is likely to be re-established, e.g. between gas oil and crude oil.

When such spreads are undertaken through the same clearinghouse, margining concessions are made available to take account of the reduced risk.

6.3 Basis trading

Whereas the futures spreads discussed above seek to make money from a change in the differential between futures contracts, basis trades look to profit from a change in the relationship between the cash price and the future.

Example

An oil trader expecting a strengthening basis executes the following trade. (Remember: **Basis = Cash price – Future**)

Physical Market	Futures Market	Basis
1 October Buy Brent cargo @ $25	1 October Sell Brent futures @ $26	–1
10 October Sell Brent cargo @ $28.50	10 October Buy Brent future @ $29	–0.5
Profit $3.50	Loss $3.00	Profit $0.50

If the trader had anticipated a weakening basis, the reverse trade could have been undertaken.

6.4 Strip vs Stack hedges

If a futures hedger wishes to lock in a price or yield over a long period of time, two strategies are available.

The strip hedge consists of trading the appropriate number of futures contracts in a range of delivery dates covering the exposure. For example, an institution wishing to protect its bond portfolio for a year may trade March, June, September and December contracts. For most futures contracts, with the exception of short-term interest rate contracts, such a strategy is often not feasible. This is because liquidity is poor beyond the spot month.

An alternative is the stack hedge, in which the full number of contracts required to hedge are traded in the spot month and then incrementally rolled into the next month as liquidity develops.

In an ideal world, the strip hedge is preferable as it minimises basis risk. However, liquidity constraints may often make the stack necessary.

Chapter Roundup

- You need to be fully familiar with, able to identify and able to discuss the construction, attributes and motivation of options strategies, including

| Directional ||| Volatility |||| Arbitrage ||
Bull		Bear		More Volatile		Less Volatile			
Long Call	A	Long Put	B	Long Straddle	O	Short Straddle	P	Conversions	X
Short Put	C	Short Call	D	Long Strangle	Q	Short Strangle	R	Reversals	Y
Bull Spread	E	Bear Spread	F	Short Butterfly	S	Long Butterfly	T	Box	Z
Synthetic Long	G	Synthetic Short	H	Ratio Back Spread	U	Ratio Spread	V		
Synthetic Long Call	I	Synthetic Short Call/ Covered Put	J			Horizontal Spread	W		
Synthetic Short Put/ Covered Call	K	Synthetic Long Put	L						
Diagonal Spread (Bull)	M	Diagonal Spread (Bear)	M						
Cylinder	N								

And various futures strategies

- Intermarket spread
- Intramarket spread
- Basis trades
- Strip hedge
- Stack hedge

7: STRATEGIES

Test Your Knowledge

Check your knowledge of the Chapter here, without referring back to the text.

1. If you buy one June 100 call and sell one June 110 call what strategy have you created and what is the motivation?

2. If you are long a future and short a call what position have you synthesised?

3. If you sell a June 100 call and buy a September 100 call what strategy have you undertaken and why?

4. If you buy a 100 call at 7 and a 100 put at 6
   (a) What strategy have you created?
   (b) What is the maximum potential loss?
   (c) What is the maximum potential profit?
   (d) When does the strategy break even?
   (e) What is the motivation for the trade?

5. What would be the dangers of buying a future and buying a put.

7: STRATEGIES

TEST YOUR KNOWLEDGE: ANSWERS

1. Vertical bull call spread – moderately bullish

2. Synthetic short put

3. Horizontal spread – benefit from more rapid time decay in a short option when markets are static (low and steady volatility).

4.
    (a) Long straddle
    (b) Maximum potential loss = 13p (Sum of premiums)
    (c) Unlimited on the upside, 87p on the downside
    (d) 87p, 113p
    (e) Believe volatility will increase

5. The net position is a synthetic long call. The danger would be that the price would not rise above the synthetic breakeven point.

8 Options Pricing – Binomial and Black Scholes

INTRODUCTION

We introduced the factors that influence the prices of options in an ealier section. We now need to see how these factors can be mathematically combined within various full pricing models.

The ideas in this section also draw on the knowledge we have gained from the earlier sections on financial mathematics and probability and this section should not be attempted before these three earlier sections have been mastered.

CHAPTER CONTENTS

		Page
1	Fair Value of Options	194
2	Sensitivity of Option Values	221
3	Hedging	232
	Chapter Roundup	237
	Test Your Knowledge	241

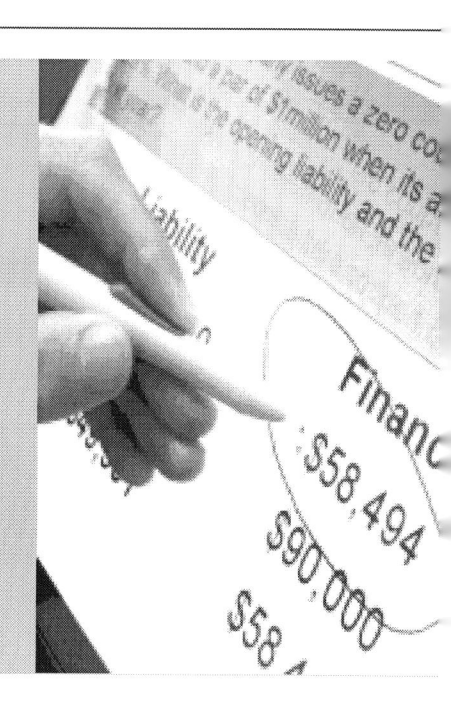

8: OPTIONS PRICING – BINOMIAL AND BLACK SCHOLES

CHAPTER LEARNING OBJECTIVES

The syllabus areas covered by this section are

- **Uses of options**

    Types of options contracts

    – Black Scholes, binomial models and other option models. Assumptions behind different option models.

    – Common price sensitivities and how to use them.

- **Derivative risk management**

    Individual derivatives

    – Dynamic hedging
    – Delta, gamma and vega hedging

    Derivatives portfolios

    – Aggregating derivatives risk

Exam tip | Questions involving the application of options pricing models and the consideration of price sensitivities (the Greeks) arise in almost every exam.

1 FAIR VALUE OF OPTIONS

It is possible to calculate the fair value of an option by using complex mathematical formulae. The best known of these are

- The Cox-Ross-Rubenstein or Binomial model.
- The Black Scholes model.

1.1 Binomial model

The binomial model starts from the assumption that the share price can only be one of two values at the end of a period based on its value at the start. This may seem a little unrealistic, since share prices may move over a considerable range in a period. However, by shortening the length of each period from years to weeks to days to seconds, etc. and correspondingly increasing the number of periods, we may be able to get a useful model.

1.1.1 Single-period illustration

Exam tip | Single period binomial questions are regularly examined.

Example

Imagine that a stock has a current price of 100p and it is known that at the end of one month, it will be either 120p or 90p. The risk-free rate is 8% p.a. with continuous compounding. What is the value of a one-month European 95p call?

8: OPTIONS PRICING – BINOMIAL AND BLACK SCHOLES

Solution

Diagrammatically

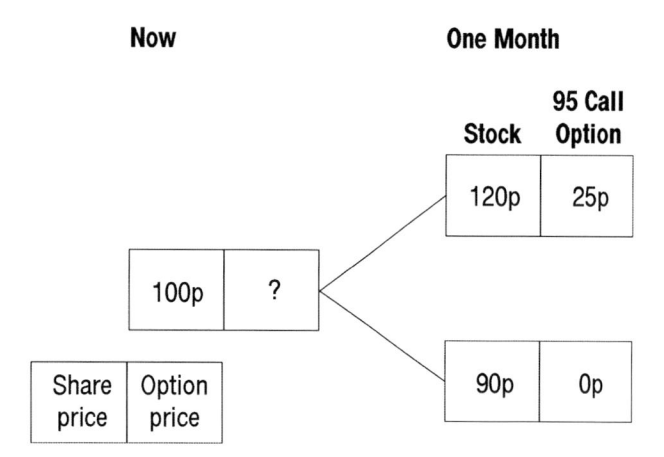

```
              Now                    One Month

                                              95 Call
                                     Stock    Option

                                     120p     25p
              100p    ?

              Share  Option          90p      0p
              price  price
```

We can see that the value of the call at its expiry in one month's time will be either 25p (the intrinsic value of the 95 call if the stock is 120) or 0p. What we need to do is attribute a weighting to the particular outcomes by determining the probability of an upmove and a downmove.

To do this, we use the following formula for the probability of an upmove.

Formula to learn

$$p = \frac{R - d}{u - d}$$

where

p = the probability of an upmove

R = the risk-free rate of interest for the period

u = the expected percentage upmove, e.g. 1.1 for a 10% upmove, or for our example $\left(\frac{120}{100}\right) = 1.20$

d = the expected percentage downmove, e.g. 0.91 for a 9% downmove, or for our example $\left(\frac{90}{100}\right) = 0.90$

(For a derivation of this formula, see Appendix 1 at the end of this chapter.)

Using continuous compounding

Using continuous compounding, the risk free compound factor for the period is e^{rt}

Formula to learn

Compound factor (R) = e^{rt}

and hence

$$p = \frac{e^{rt} - d}{u - d}$$

where

r = annual interest rate

t = period as a fraction of a year

giving

$R = e^{0.08 \times 1/12} = 1.0067$

Inserting into formula, the probability of an upmove is

8: OPTIONS PRICING – BINOMIAL AND BLACK SCHOLES

$$p = \frac{1.0067 - 0.90}{1.20 - 0.90}$$

$$p = \frac{0.1067}{0.30}$$

$$p = 0.3557$$

Consequently, the probability of a downmove is $1 - p$, i.e. 0.6443.

Now we have the probabilities to weight the potential outcomes giving the expected expiry (terminal) value of the call option as

$$C_1 = (0.3557 \times 25) + (0.6443 \times 0)$$

This future value can be brought back to present value by discounting at the continuously discounted rate for the period, R.

$$C = \frac{(0.3557 \times 25) + (0.6443 \times 0)}{1.0067} = 8.83p$$

This may be expressed as

Formula to learn

$$C = \frac{pC_u + (1-p)C_d}{e^{rt}}$$

where

- p = Probability of an upmove in price
- C_u = Call value if asset price rises
- C_d = Call value if asset price falls
- r = Annualised risk free rate of interest for the period
- t = Time to expiry in years

Using discrete compounding

The above example used continuous compounding. If not specifically stated, it would have been possible to use discrete compounding where the compound factor is

Formula to learn

$$R = (1 + r)^t$$

and hence

$$p = \frac{(1+r)^t - d}{u - d}$$

This would give

$$p = \frac{1.08^{1/12} - 0.90}{1.20 - 0.90}$$

$$p = 0.3547$$

$$C = \frac{(0.3547 \times 25) + (0.6453 \times 0)}{1.08^{1/12}}$$

$$C = 8.81 \text{ pence}$$

A similar process may be used for a put.

Example

The current price of a stock is 50p, and at the end of a six-month period it will be either 45p or 55p. The risk-free rate is 10% p.a. continuously compounded. What is the value of a European style six-month put?

Solution

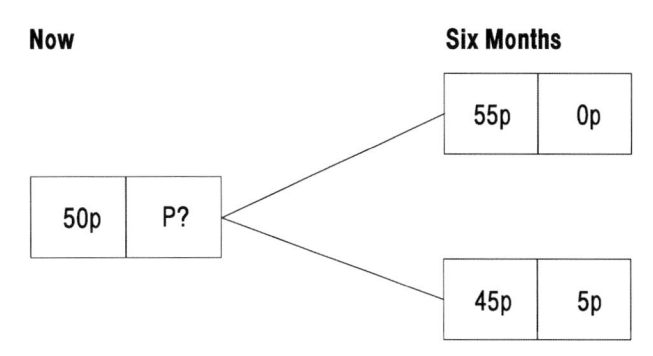

Now			Six Months	
			55p	0p
50p	P?			
			45p	5p

Using continuous compounding

$$p = \frac{e^{rt} - d}{u - d}$$

$$p = \frac{e^{0.10 \times 0.5} - 0.9}{1.1 - 0.9}$$

$$p = \frac{0.1513}{0.20}$$

$$p = 0.7565$$

Hence the probability of a down move is

$$1 - p = 0.2435$$

Giving the terminal value of the put as

$$P_1 = (0.7565 \times 0) + (0.2435 \times 5)$$

and hence the present value (current price) is

$$P = \frac{(0.7565 \times 0) + (0.2435 \times 5)}{1.0513}$$

$$P = 1.16$$

1.1.2 Multi-period illustration

Exam tip | Multi-period binomial questions are regularly examined numerically.

The two examples above have been for a single period only. We can extend the idea to a two-period model as follows.

Example

The continuously compounded rate of interest is 8% p.a. A stock is priced at 100, pays no dividends and has an annual volatility of 25%. What is the current value of a European style 95 call two months before expiry, taking a period as being one month?

8: OPTIONS PRICING – BINOMIAL AND BLACK SCHOLES

Solution

In this example, the expected value of the stock is provided obliquely through the volatility figure. Remember that the standard deviation represents the average or expected movement, either up or down. So if we are considering a price rise, then the expected percentage upmove across a full year will be

$$u = e^{\sigma}$$

or over a fraction of a year t, this will be

Formula to learn

$$u = e^{\sigma\sqrt{t}}$$

where

σ = annualised standard deviation of returns expressed as a decimal
t = time in each period expressed as a fraction of a year

Thus for a one month options, where $t = \frac{1}{12} = 0.08333$, $\sqrt{t} = 0.2887$

$$u = e^{0.25 \times 0.2887}$$
$$u = 1.0748, \text{ i.e. it is expected to move up by 7.48\% each month}$$

Similarly the expected percentage downmove will be give by

$$d = e^{-\sigma\sqrt{t}}$$

where the standard deviation, once again, represents the average or expected annual movement.

This can, however, be more conveniently calculated as

$$d = \frac{1}{u}$$

$$d = \frac{1}{1.0748}$$

$$d = 0.9304$$

(**NB:** This is the same as saying $d = e^{-\sigma\sqrt{t}}$)

Now we can solve for p.

$$p = \frac{e^{rt} - d}{u - d}$$

$$p = \frac{e^{(0.08 \times \frac{1}{12})} - 0.9304}{1.0748 - 0.9304}$$

$$p = \frac{0.0763}{0.1444}$$

$$p = 0.528$$

Hence the probability of a down move is

$$1 - p = 0.472$$

Having now found u, d, p and 1 – p, let us consider the two-period lattice.

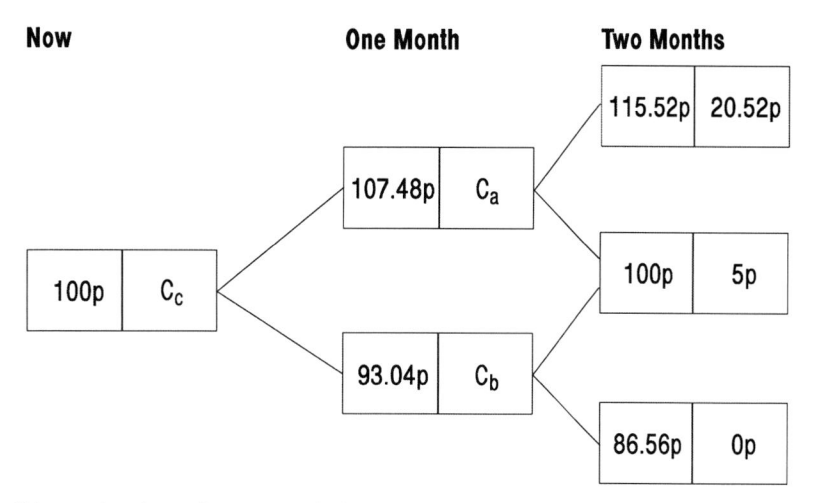

```
    Now              One Month         Two Months
                                       ┌─────────┬───────┐
                                       │ 115.52p │ 20.52p│
                                       └─────────┴───────┘
                     ┌────────┬────┐  ╱
                     │ 107.48p│ Cₐ │◄
                     └────────┴────┘  ╲
                    ╱                  ┌──────┬────┐
 ┌──────┬────┐     ╱                   │ 100p │ 5p │
 │ 100p │ Cc │◄                        └──────┴────┘
 └──────┴────┘     ╲                  ╱
                    ╲ ┌────────┬────┐╱
                      │ 93.04p │ Cᵦ │
                      └────────┴────┘╲
                                       ┌─────────┬────┐
                                       │ 86.56p  │ 0p │
                                       └─────────┴────┘
```

The three possible stock prices after two periods are found as follows.

(i) Upmove followed by upmove
$100 \times 1.0748 \times 1.0748 = 115.52p$

(ii) Upmove followed by downmove
$100 \times 1.0748 \times 0.9304 = 100p$
(This value could be reached by a downmove followed by an upmove.)

(iii) Downmove followed by downmove
$100 \times 0.9304 \times 0.9304 = 86.56p$

The intrinsic value of the 95 call at expiry would be 20.52p if the stock is 115.52p, 5p if the stock is at 100p, and 0 if the stock is at 86.56p.

Value of the 95 call after an upmove in the first period (C_a) is

$$C_a = \frac{(0.528 \times 20.52) + (0.472 \times 5)}{1.0067} = 13.11p$$

Value of the 95 call after a downmove in the first period (C_b) is

$$C_b = \frac{(0.528 \times 5) + (0.472 \times 0)}{1.0067} = 2.62p$$

Value of the 95 call now at (C_c) is

$$C_c = \frac{(0.528 \times 13.11) + (0.472 \times 2.62)}{1.0067} = 8.10$$

It is worth noting that when calculating a **non-annual interest rate** from an annual rate, it is simply time apportioned.

Example

Annual rate = r = 12%
Rate for six months = $r \times \frac{1}{2}$
Rate for three months = $r \times \frac{1}{4}$
Rate for one month = $r \times \frac{1}{12}$

8: OPTIONS PRICING – BINOMIAL AND BLACK SCHOLES

This has been seen above where the continuous compounded rate for one month based on an annual rate of 8% = $e^{rt} = e^{0.08 \times 1/12}$ = 1.006688 (rounded to 1.0067 in above example).

However, when calculating **non-annual volatility** from annual volatility, it is **not** simply time apportioned. The correct relationship is given by

$$\sigma_{6 \text{ months}} = \sigma_{annual} \sqrt{1/2}$$

$$\sigma_{3 \text{ months}} = \sigma_{annual} \sqrt{1/4}$$

$$\sigma_{month} = \sigma_{annual} \sqrt{1/12}$$

The reason for the square root is that risks combine by adding variances (σ^2) rather than adding standard deviations (σ).

To understand the above we can state that

$$\sigma^2_{annual} = 12 \times \sigma^2_{monthly}, \text{ i.e. the variances are added}$$

$$\sigma^2_{monthly} = \sigma^2_{annual} \times 1/12$$

$$\sigma_{monthly} = \sigma_{annual} \sqrt{1/12}$$

The above idea can be extended as follows.

e.g.

$$\sigma_{Sept} = 0.8\%$$
$$\sigma_{Oct} = 0.9\%$$

What is the volatility for September and October, i.e. for a two-month period, assuming no correlation between the months (no serial correlation)?

$$\sigma^2_{Sept} + \sigma^2_{Oct} = \sigma^2_{2 \text{ months}}$$

Therefore, $\sigma_{2 \text{ months}} = \sqrt{\sigma^2_{Sept} + \sigma^2_{Oct}}$

1.1.3 An alternative approach to the binomial model

Exam tip

> You only need to know one method for the exam and the method we have already outlined is probably the easiest. This alternative is included her only for completeness and for those who are already familiar with it.

Example

Consider the following single-period (one month) illustration showing the value of a share and a 95p call option. The risk-free rate is 8% p.a. Assume continuous compounding. Calculate the value of a 100p call.

Solution

We could show this diagrammatically as follows.

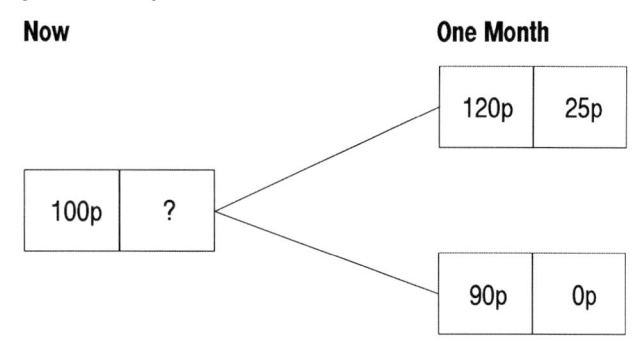

Now   **One Month**

```
                    ┌─────┬─────┐
                    │120p │ 25p │
                    └─────┴─────┘
                   ╱
   ┌─────┬───┐ ───
   │100p │ ? │
   └─────┴───┘ ───
                   ╲
                    ┌─────┬─────┐
                    │ 90p │ 0p  │
                    └─────┴─────┘
```

We can see that these two investment returns are perfectly positively correlated, i.e. they move up and down together, though not by the same amount. If we therefore buy some shares and sell some calls, we will have a portfolio of two perfectly **negatively** correlated securities (when we gain from the shares, we will lose from the calls and vice versa).

Hedge ratio

We must, therefore, be able to construct a portfolio that offers a risk-free return such that the gains on the shares exactly cancel the losses on the calls if the share price rises (or vice versa if the share price falls).

The possible difference in prices of the call options is £0.25 and the possible difference in share prices is £0.30. Hence, to achieve an exact hedge (exactly cancelling gains and losses), we would need $\frac{25}{30}$ shares for each call option sold. This fraction is called the **hedge ratio** and could be written as

Formula to learn

$$h = \frac{C_u - C_d}{S_u - S_d}$$

where

C_u = call value if the share price goes up
C_d = call value if the share price goes down
S_u = share price if it goes up
S_d = share price if it goes down

Hence, to achieve a perfect hedge on the writing (sale) of 30 call options, we would need to buy 25 shares. Our position would then be

Portfolio	Cost Now	Value at Expiry Either	
	S = £1.00	S = £1.20	S = £0.90
	C = C	C = £0.25	C = £0.00
Buy 25 shares	£25.00	£30.00	£22.50
Write 30 calls	(30C)	(£7.50)	£0.00
	£25 – 30C	£22.50	£22.50

That is, we have a return at expiry of £22.50 regardless of how the share price moves – a risk-free return.

Since the risk-free rate over this period is 8%, we would have expected to have made a net investment of £22.35 (£22.50 × $e^{-0.08 \times 1/12}$), hence the net value of our investment now must amount to this.

Thus

         £25.00 – 30C = £22.35

8: OPTIONS PRICING – BINOMIAL AND BLACK SCHOLES

hence

$$30C = £2.65$$

giving

$$C = 8.83p$$

Note: the probabilities of how the share prices may move has not entered our evaluation. The factors that we have considered are

- The current share price.
- The possible future share prices based on the volatility of the share.
- The exercise price.
- The time to exercise.
- The risk-free rate.

We could write the above calculations mathematically as

$$(hS - C)e^{rt} = hS_u - C_u \; (= hS_d - C_d)$$

where the last two terms are the expiry values we calculated above (for one option), and the first term ties the current position to this end position on the basis that it generates the risk-free return. Hence, applying these formulae

$$\left(\frac{25}{30} \times £1.00 - C\right) \times e^{0.08 \times 1/12} = \frac{25}{30} \times £1.20 - £0.25 \left(= \frac{25}{30} \times £0.90 - £0.00\right)$$

$$\left(\frac{25}{30} \times £1.00 - C\right) \times e^{0.08 \times 1/12} = £0.75$$

$$£0.8333 - C = £0.75 \times e^{-0.08 \times 1/12}$$

$$C = 8.83p \text{ (this is the same rate obtained earlier)}$$

Again, it should be noted that although we have used continuous discounting here it is possible to use discrete discounting.

Multi-period illustration

The illustration above only covered a single time period. However, as we have noted before, we can extend these ideas to cover more periods. The following example is done using **discrete** discounting.

If we base our illustration on the same volatilities and assume a two-period model, we get the following.

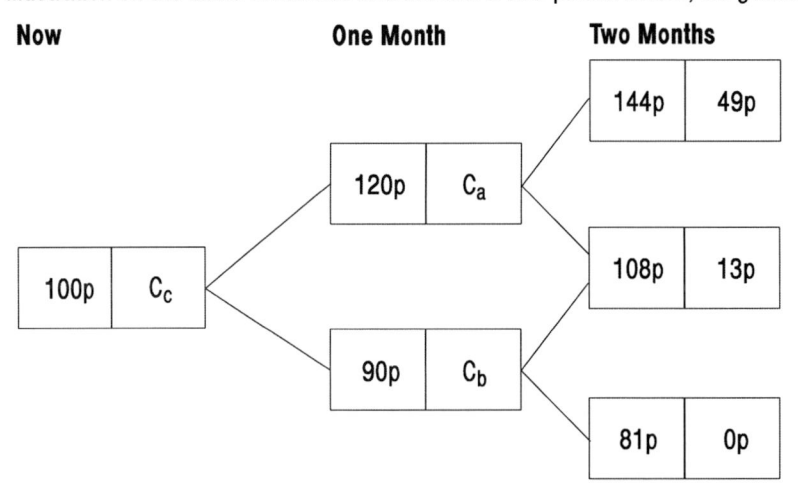

Now	One Month	Two Months
		144p | 49p
	120p | C_a	
100p | C_c		108p | 13p
	90p | C_b	
		81p | 0p

Using our above ideas, we can calculate (in this order)

- The value of the call option (a?) at Time 1 from the Time 2 values that could follow from it.
- The value of the call option (b?) at Time 1 from the Time 2 values that could follow from it.
- The value of the call option (c?) now from the Time 1 values that could follow from it (a? and b?).

As follows by applying the formulae

$$h = \frac{C_u - C_d}{S_u - S_d}$$

and $(hS - C)(1 + r) = hS_u - C_u \ (= hS_d - C_d)$

Call option C_a

$$h = \frac{C_u - C_d}{S_u - S_d}$$

gives

$$h = \frac{49p - 13p}{144p - 108p} = 1$$

Hence

$$[hS - C_a](1 + r) = hS_u - C_u$$

gives (using discrete discounting)

$$[£1.20 - C_a] \times 1.08^{1/12} = £1.44 - £0.49 = £0.95$$

$$£1.20 - C_a = \frac{£0.95}{1.08^{1/12}} = £0.9439$$

$$C_a = £1.20 - £0.9439 = £0.2561$$

Call option C_b

$$h = \frac{C_u - C_d}{S_u - S_d}$$

gives

$$h = \frac{13p - 0p}{108p - 81p} = \frac{13}{27}$$

Hence

$$[hS - C_b](1 + r) = hS_u - C_u$$

gives

$$[\frac{13}{27} \times £0.90 - C_b] \times 1.08^{1/12} = \frac{13}{27} \times £1.08 - £0.13 = £0.39$$

$$£0.4333 - C_b = \frac{£0.39}{1.08^{1/12}} = £0.3875$$

$$C_b = £0.4333 - £0.3875 = £0.0458$$

Call option c?

$$h = \frac{C_u - C_d}{S_u - S_d}$$

gives

$$h = \frac{25.61 - 4.58}{120p - 90p} = \frac{21.03}{30}$$

Hence

$$[hS - C_c](1 + r) = hS_u - C_u$$

gives

$$[\frac{21.03}{30} \times £1.00 - C_c] \times 1.08^{1/12} = £1.20 \times \frac{21.03}{30} - £0.2561 = £0.5851$$

$$£0.701 - C_c = \frac{£0.5851}{1.08^{1/12}} = £0.5814$$

$$C_c = £0.701 - £0.5814 = £0.1196$$

We can see that this is a higher value than the single-period estimate reflecting the increased time value.

Note: The hedge is not static; our hedge ratio changes each period depending on how the share price has moved. Also, once again, the probabilities ascribed to the possible movements are not incorporated into our calculations, it is only dependent on the factors noted above.

If we calculated the option value in this way for various levels of share price and various periods to expiry, we would get the following.

Call Option Value

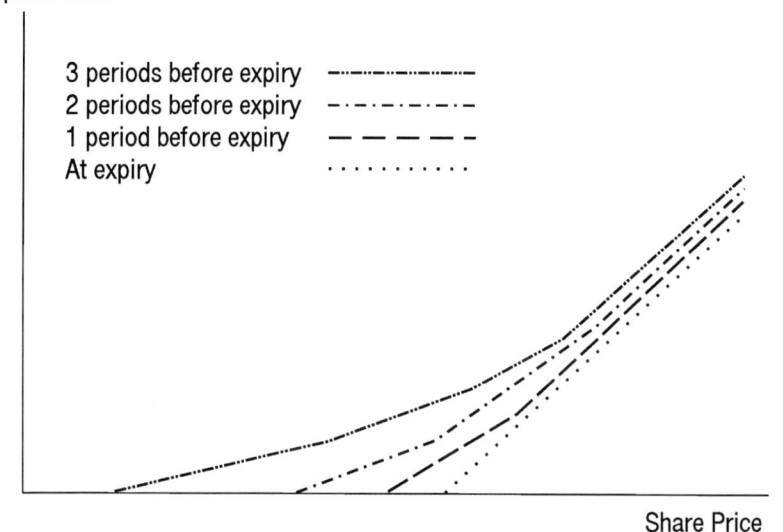

3 periods before expiry
2 periods before expiry
1 period before expiry
At expiry

Share Price

What this demonstrates is the time value adding to the intrinsic value (value at expiry) as we move further from the exercise date.

In the examples used so far, both continuous and discrete discounting/compounding have been used. This has been done to illustrate both methods. As pricing models tend to use continuous compounding, this will be the method adopted from now on.

1.2 American style options and early exercise

All the previous examples have been with European style options, however, the majority of exchange-traded options are American.

8: OPTIONS PRICING – BINOMIAL AND BLACK SCHOLES

In applying the binomial model to American style options, the calculated value at each node should be compared with its intrinsic. If the intrinsic is higher, it is that value that should be used in computing the values at the earlier nodes. This idea is best illustrated with an example.

Example

The continuously compounded rate of interest is 12% p.a., and the volatility of a stock that is priced at 100 and pays no dividends is 33%.

(a) Show that in a binomial lattice based on monthly intervals, the stock price rises by 10% or falls by 9% each month.

(b) Using this lattice, show that an at-the-money two-month put may be exercised prematurely and calculate the value of this put.

Solution

First, let us determine u and d from the annual volatility figure

$$u = e^{\sigma\sqrt{t}}$$
$$u = e^{0.33 \times 0.2887}$$
$$u = 1.0999$$

Assuming a Lognormal distribution

$$d = \frac{1}{u}$$
$$d = \frac{1}{1.0999}$$
$$d = 0.909$$

Thus $u \approx 10\%$
$d \approx 9\%$

Let us now construct the two monthly lattice using u = 1.1 and d = 0.91.

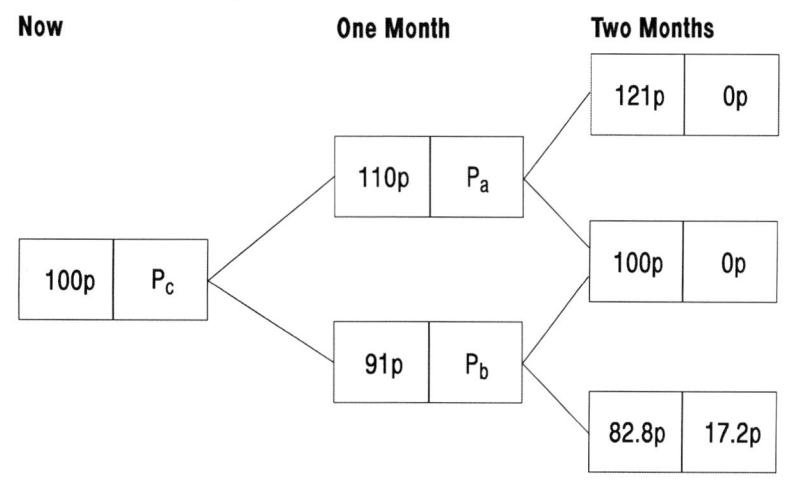

	Now	One Month	Two Months
			121p / 0p
		110p / P_a	
	100p / P_c		100p / 0p
		91p / P_b	
			82.8p / 17.2p

The question asks us to find the value of the 100 put 'now'. To do this we must work out the value of the put at both 110 and 91 at the one-month node and from these values, determine the current value.

To do this requires p and 1 – p, therefore

8: OPTIONS PRICING – BINOMIAL AND BLACK SCHOLES

$$p = \frac{e^{rt} - d}{u - d}$$

$$p = \frac{e^{(0.12 \times 1/12)} - 0.91}{1.1 - 0.91}$$

$$p = \frac{0.1}{0.19}$$

$$p = 0.526$$

Hence the probability of a downmove is

$$1 - p = 0.4736$$

The discount factor for each period is

$$e^{rt} = e^{0.12 \times 1/12} = 1.01$$

Hence, the value of the 100 put after one period if the stock is at 91 (p_b) is

$$P_b = \frac{(0.526 \times 0) + (0.4736 \times 17.2)}{1.01} = 8.07$$

As this value is less than the intrinsic value of 9 (100 – 91), we put the higher intrinsic value into the lattice.

The value of the 100 put at the end of one period if the stock is 110 is

$$P_a = \frac{(0.526 \times 0) + (0.4736 \times 0)}{1.01} = 0$$

Now, we must derive the initial value of the 100 put using the values at Period 1.

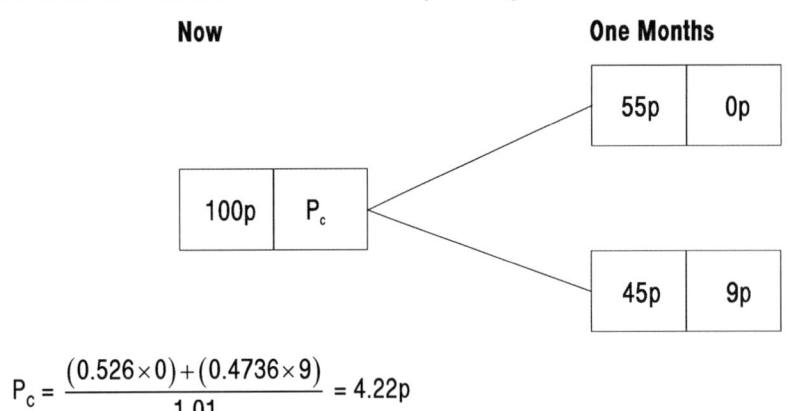

Now   **One Months**

		→	55p	0p
100p	P_c
		→	45p	9p

$$P_c = \frac{(0.526 \times 0) + (0.4736 \times 9)}{1.01} = 4.22p$$

In this question, the calculated value for the 100p put after one period with the stock price at 91p was 8.07p. This would have given rise to an early exercise opportunity: buy put at 8.07p, buy stock at 91p and then sell via exercise at 100p: a net profit of 0.93p.

1.3 Binomial model – Variations

All the examples outlined so far have focused on valuing an option where the underlying asset has been a share. What has not been included in these calculations is any dividend paid on the underlying shares. This idea of including the yield from the underlying asset can be extended to cover equity index options, currency options and options on futures.

1.3.1 Equity index options

When calculating the probability of an upmove for an equity index option, we need to reflect the fact that we are receiving the yield from the underlying asset. To do this, the following formula is used.

Formula to learn

$$p = \frac{e^{(rt-yt)} - d}{u - d} = \frac{e^{(r-y)t} - d}{u - d}$$

where

y = dividend yield

Example

r = 8% p.a.
y = 5% p.a.
t = 1 month
s = 100
u = 1.05
d = 0.90

What is the value of a 95 call?

Solution

$$p = \frac{e^{(0.08 \times 1/12 - 0.05 \times 1/12)} - 0.90}{1.05 - 0.90}$$

p = 0.6834

1 − p = 0.3166

$$C = \frac{(0.6834 \times 10) + (0.3166 \times 0)}{e^{0.08 \times 1/12}} = 6.788p$$

If the alternative approach is used, the hedge ratio will need to reflect the dividend yield.

$$h = \frac{C_u - C_d}{S_u - S_d} \times e^{-yt}$$

$$h = \frac{10 - 0}{105 - 90} \times e^{-0.05 \times 1/12}$$

h = 0.6639

The value of the call would then be

$$(hS - C)e^{rt} = hS_u e^{yt} - C_u$$

The extra e^{yt} term in here representing the value of any yield over the period.

$$[(0.6639 \times 100) - C] e^{0.08 \times 1/12} = (0.6639 \times 105) - 10 + [0.6639 \times 105 \times (e^{0.056 \times 1/12} - 1)]$$

C = 6.788

8: OPTIONS PRICING – BINOMIAL AND BLACK SCHOLES

1.3.2 Currency option

The above example looked at a stock option index where the yield was the dividend yield. The logic would be exactly the same for currency options where the underlying is a currency. The yield then would be the interest rate of the currency, i.e.

$$p = \frac{e^{(r_1 t - r_2 t)} - d}{u - d}$$

where

r_1 and r_2 are the interest rates in the traders base currency and the currency being traded respectively.

1.3.3 Summary

The binomial model has a number of advantages over the Black Scholes model discussed below. It can allow for early exercise, and also allows for different interest rates and volatility levels in each period. A major disadvantage is the formula's reliance on repetitive numerical calculations rather than just a single formula.

As the number of periods increases, the answers derived from the binomial model get close to the Black Scholes model, which uses the properties of a Normal distribution to calculate the fair values of options.

Perhaps the best generalised formula is as we had for equity index options,

Formula to learn

$$p = \frac{e^{(r-y)t} - d}{u - d}$$

where

r = interest rate on cash/traders base currency.
y = yield on underlying asset/underlying currency being traded

1.4 Black Scholes

1.4.1 Value of a call option

As we increase the number of stages in the binomial expansion, it tends towards the Normal distribution. Similarly, as we increase n by taking smaller and smaller time intervals, the Cox-Ross-Rubenstein model tends to converge to the Black Scholes model.

The Black Scholes model (and its variants) is highly popular as it enables us to replicate the results of the binomial model, but at a fraction of the effort, and all in one formula.

However, to the non-mathematician, the Black Scholes formula appears exceedingly complex. But for our purposes, all we need to be able to do is apply it. Such an application need not be unthinking and indeed, within the model, we will see many of the things we have already considered albeit at a more intuitive level.

The most basic Black Scholes model relates to European options on non-dividend paying stocks and can be expressed as follows.

Formula to learn

$$C = SN(d1) - Xe^{-rt} N(d2)$$

where

$$d_1 = \frac{\ln\left(\frac{S}{X}\right) + (r + 0.5\sigma^2)t}{\sigma\sqrt{t}}$$

$$d_2 = \frac{\ln\left(\frac{S}{X}\right) + (r - 0.5\sigma^2)t}{\sigma\sqrt{t}} \text{ or } d_2 = d_1 - \sigma\sqrt{t}$$

S = underlying share price
X = exercise price
r = continuously compounded risk-free rate expressed on an annual basis
t = time to expiry in years
σ = risk of the underlying stock, measured as the annual volatility
N(d) = cumulative probabilities that deviations less than d will occur in a normal distribution with a mean of 0 and a standard deviation of 1

Alternatively, d_1 and d_2 can be written as follows.

$$d_1 = \frac{\ln\left(\frac{S}{X}\right) + rt}{\sigma\sqrt{t}} + 0.5\sigma\sqrt{t}$$

$$d_2 = \frac{\ln\left(\frac{S}{X}\right) + rt}{\sigma\sqrt{t}} - 0.5\sigma\sqrt{t} \text{ or } d_2 = d_1 - \sigma\sqrt{t}$$

Into this formula, we enter details of underlying price, strike price, interest rate, time to expiry and volatility and we achieve a fair or theoretical value.

Whilst many of these symbols are ones we have already come across, some require a little explanation.

ln(S/X): This is the natural inverse of the log normal return on the stock that is required for it to exceed the strike price of X. Natural log returns were considered in the Financial Mathematics section alongside the ideas of continuous compounding. The 'ln' function is found on most calculators.

N(d): This is the cumulative normal distribution function. The application of this function is very similar to our use of Normal distribution tables in our earlier discussion of probabilities. More specifically

$N(d_2)$ = Risk neutral probability that the option will expire in the money and hence the exercise price will be paid.

$N(d_1)$ = Expected value of the return on the share in the event that the option expires in the money.

1.4.2 Volatility

We can see that one of the inputs we require is a figure for the annualised volatility (σ). How do we obtain this figure? The first thing to notice is that we will need to know the future volatility. We should be pricing options based on the volatility that is expected over the future life of the option. How do we determine this? A good starting point for predicting future volatility is to consider past, or historic, volatility. If we are pricing a two-month option, we need to consider what volatility will be over the next two months using as a basis volatility from a historic two month period.

But what period should be used? There is no single correct answer to this question. The volatility of the most recent two months might well be different from a two-month period, three or six months ago. What the investor must do is to identify a period from the past that he/she believes best reflects the future conditions they are expecting. Having selected an appropriate period in the past, it is then necessary to decide whether to calculate volatility based on daily, weekly or even monthly price change observations. In practice, investors usually use daily price data to calculate volatility. This is then converted into annual volatility and that figure is input into the pricing model.

8: OPTIONS PRICING – BINOMIAL AND BLACK SCHOLES

Example

A call option with an exercise price of 40p expires in three months. The current price and risk of the underlying share are 36p and 50% respectively. The annual continuously compounded risk-free rate is 5%. What is the fair price of the call option?

Solution

$$d_1 = \frac{\ln\left(\frac{S}{X}\right) + (r + 0.5\sigma^2)t}{\sigma\sqrt{t}}$$

$$d_1 = \frac{\ln\left(\frac{36}{40}\right) + \left[0.05 + 0.5 \times 0.50^2\right]0.25}{0.50\sqrt{0.25}}$$

$$d_1 = \frac{-0.10536 + (0.175)0.25}{0.25}$$

$$d_1 = \frac{-0.10536 + 0.04375}{0.25}$$

$$d_1 = \frac{-0.06161}{0.25}$$

$$d_1 = -0.246 \text{ (round to } -0.25\text{)}$$

Hence

$$d_2 = -0.246 - 0.5\sqrt{0.25}$$

$$d_2 = -0.496 \text{ (round to } -0.50\text{)}$$

We now need to look up these values for d_1 and d_2 in a cumulative Normal distribution table. This table will be slightly different to the one previously seen, as it will provide us with the **cumulative** probability. If we look up any particular value in these tables, it will simply give us the probability of that event occurring. The mean in this distribution is zero. Therefore, a negative value (e.g. –0.25) simply implies the value is to the left of the mean and a positive value implies it is to the right of the mean.

An extract from a cumulative Normal distribution table (typical of that given in the examination) is shown below.

X	N(x)	X	N(x)
0.0	0.5000	0.5	0.6915
0.1	0.5398	0.6	0.7257
0.2	0.5793	0.7	0.7580
0.3	0.6179	0.8	0.7881
0.4	0.6554	0.9	0.8159

The values given in the N(x) column represent the area to the left of the x value and hence, the probability of it occurring.

8: OPTIONS PRICING – BINOMIAL AND BLACK SCHOLES

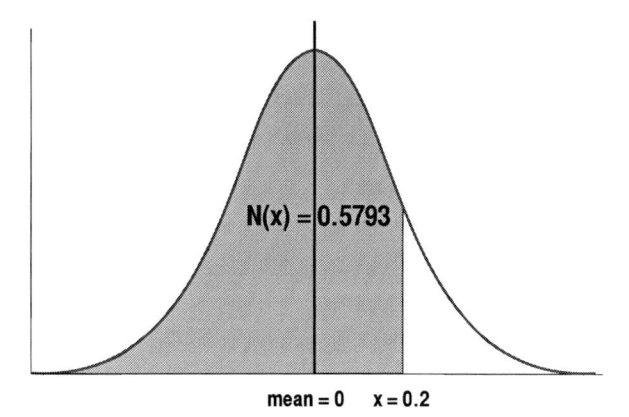

N(x) = 0.5793

mean = 0   x = 0.2

Note that negative values for x are not given in the table. This poses no problem. As the distribution is symmetrical about the mean, a negative value can be interpreted as 1 − N (x). If we had an x value of −0.2, the probability of that event occurring is 1 − 0.5793 or 0.4207.

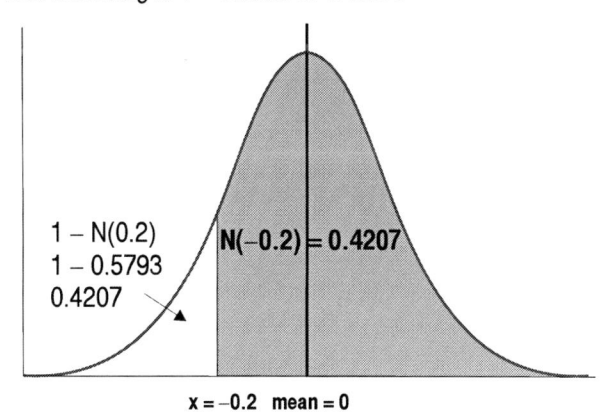

1 − N(0.2)
1 − 0.5793
0.4207

N(−0.2) = 0.4207

x = −0.2   mean = 0

Using the limited data that the table provides, it will be necessary to interpolate between two values. It is easiest to do this in a linear fashion.

$d_1 = -0.25$

$N(d_1) = N(-0.25)$
$= 1 - N(0.25)$
$= 1 - 0.5986$
$= 0.4014$

Here we have averaged N(0.2) and N(0.3) to get N(0.25)

$d_2 = -0.50$

$N(d_2) = N(-0.50)$
$= 1 - N(0.50)$
$= 1 - 0.6915$
$= 0.3085$

Hence

$$C = SN(d_1) - Xe^{-rt}N(d_2)$$

gives

$$C = 36 \times 0.4014 - 40 \times e^{-0.05 \times 0.25} \times 0.3085$$

$$C = 2.26p$$

8: OPTIONS PRICING – BINOMIAL AND BLACK SCHOLES

Table alternative 1

The above example calculated $N(d_1)$ and $N(d_2)$ from a **cumulative** probability table. As stated before, a cumulative probability table gives the area to the left of the x value, which is what $N(d_1)$ and $N(d_2)$ represent.

It is possible that the values for $N(d_1)$ and $N(d_2)$ will have to be calculated from a standard (i.e. non-cumulative) Normal distribution table – like that shown in Appendix 1 at the end of the chapter on probability.

Appendix 1 gives the area under the curve beyond the x value into the tail of the distribution. Using this table to calculate $N(d_1)$ and $N(d_2)$ for the above example, we get the following.

$d_1 = -0.25$
$d_2 = -0.50$

Looking these up in the table and remembering that negative numbers are to the left of the area, we get

$N(d_1) = 0.40129$
$N(d_2) = 0.30854$

These are the same as before.

Table alternative 2

It is further possible that the distribution table might give the area under the curve **between** the mean and the x value – an extract of this type of table is shown below.

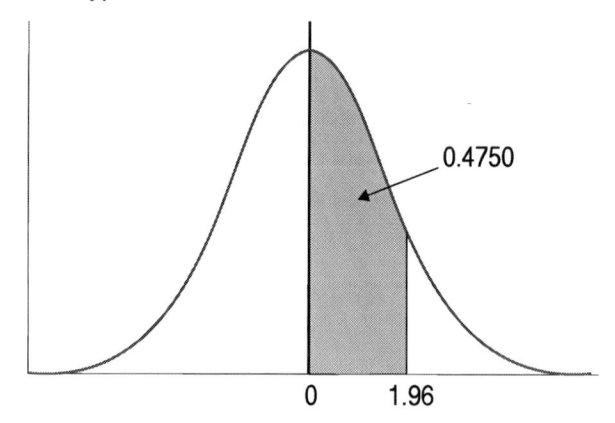

Example

$Pr(0 \leq x \leq 1.96) = 0.4750$
$Pr(x \geq 1.96) = 0.5 - 0.4750 = 0.025$

x	0.00	0.01	0.02	0.03	0.04	0.05	0.06	0.07	0.08	0.09
0.0	0.0000	0.0040	0.0080	0.0120	0.0160	0.0199	0.0239	0.0279	0.0319	0.0359
0.1	0.0398	0.0438	0.0478	0.0517	0.0557	0.0596	0.0636	0.0675	0.0714	0.0753
0.2	0.0793	0.0832	0.0871	0.0910	0.0948	0.0987	0.1026	0.1064	0.1103	0.1141
0.3	0.1179	0.1217	0.1255	0.1293	0.1331	0.1368	0.1406	0.1443	0.1480	0.1517
0.4	0.1554	0.1591	0.1628	0.1664	0.1700	0.1736	0.1772	0.1808	0.1844	0.1879
0.5	0.1915	0.1950	0.1985	0.2019	0.2054	0.2088	0.2123	0.2157	0.2190	0.2224

Using this table

$d_1 = -0.25$, value from table = 0.0987
$d_2 = -0.50$, value from table = 0.1915

As the above values for d_1 and d_2 are negative and we want the area under the curve to the left of these values.

$N(d_1) = 0.5 - 0.0987 = 0.4013$
$N(d_2) = 0.5 - 0.1915 = 0.3085$

Again, these are the same values as before.

1.4.3 Call summary

If we plot the call values derived from this model against the value of the underlying share, we get the following, which is very similar to the binomial situation above.

Diagrammatically

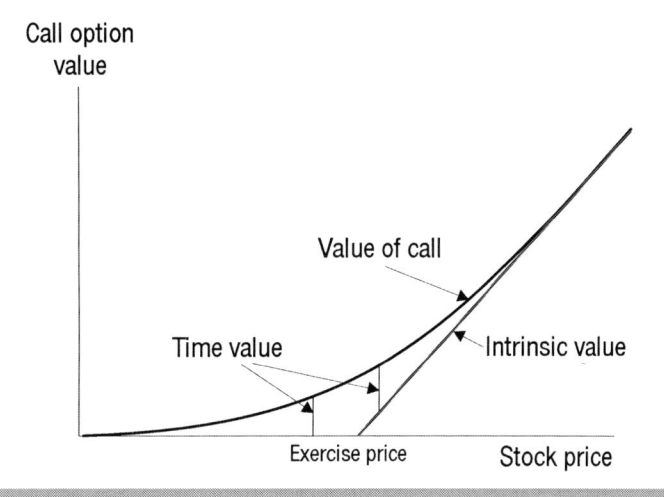

To consolidate our understanding of the model, let us try another example.

Example

Calculate the value of a European style call with a strike of 95, given the following information.

S = 92
X = 95
t = 50 days (0.137 of a year)
r = 7.12%
σ = 35%

Solution

$$d_1 = \frac{\ln\left(\frac{S}{X}\right) + \left(r + 0.5\sigma^2\right)t}{\sigma\sqrt{t}}$$

$$= \frac{\ln\left(\frac{92}{95}\right) + \left[0.0712 + 0.5(0.35)^2\right] \times 0.137}{0.35\sqrt{0.137}}$$

8: OPTIONS PRICING – BINOMIAL AND BLACK SCHOLES

$$= \frac{-0.0321 + 0.0181456}{0.129}$$

$$= \frac{-0.0139544}{0.129}$$

$$= -0.1082$$

$$d_2 = d_1 - \sigma\sqrt{t}$$

$$= -0.1082 - 0.129$$

$$= -0.2372$$

By interpolation from the tables

$$N(d_1) = 0.4570$$

$$N(d_2) = 0.4063$$

And so using

$$C = SN(d_1) - Xe^{-rt}N(d_2)$$

gives

$$C = 92 \times 0.4570 - 95 \times e^{-0.0712 \times 0.137} \times 0.4063$$

$$C = 42.04 - 38.22$$

$$C = 3.82$$

1.4.4 The valuation of a put option.

The examples done so far have been to calculate the value of a call. It is possible to rearrange the basic Black Scholes formula to allow for the valuation of a put as follows.

Formula to learn

$$P = Xe^{-rt}N(-d_2) - SN(-d_1)$$

Example

A put option with an exercise price of 50p expires in three months. The current price of the underlying share is 48p and annual volatility is 20%. The risk-free rate is 5%. What is the fair price of the put option?

$$d_1 = \frac{\ln\left(\frac{S}{X}\right) + \left(r + 0.5\sigma^2\right)t}{\sigma\sqrt{t}}$$

$$= \frac{\ln\left(\frac{48}{50}\right) + \left[0.05 + 0.5 \times 0.2^2\right] \times 0.25}{0.2\sqrt{0.25}}$$

$$= \frac{-0.040822 + 0.0175}{0.1}$$

$$= -0.23322$$

$$d_2 = -0.23322 - 0.1$$

$$= -0.33322$$

$$N(-d_1) = N(0.23322)$$
$$= 0.5921$$

$$N(-d_2) = N(0.33322)$$
$$= 0.6304$$

$$P = 50 \times e^{-0.05 \times 0.25} \times 0.6304 - 48 \times 0.5921$$
$$= 2.71p$$

Alternative approach

Exam tip | This is the preferred approach as no new formulae are needed.

(i) Calculate the value of a call.

$$C = SN(d_1) - Xe^{-rt}N(d_2)$$
$$d_1 = -0.23322$$
$$d_2 = -0.33322$$
$$N(d_1) = 1 - 0.5921$$
$$= 0.4079$$
$$N(d_2) = 1 - 0.6304$$
$$= 0.3696$$
$$C = 48 \times 0.4079 - 50 \times e^{-0.05 \times 0.25} \times 0.3696$$
$$C = 1.33$$

(ii) Use put/call parity to calculate the value of the put.

$$C - P = S - Xe^{-rt}$$
$$P = C - S + Xe^{-rt}$$
$$P = 1.33 - 48 + 50 \times e^{-0.05 \times 0.25}$$
$$P = 2.71p \text{ (as before)}$$

Exam tip | As it is necessary to know the put/call parity formula for the examination, using the alternative approach means that you only have to remember the Black Scholes formula for calls.

1.5 Problems with Black Scholes

There are a number of restrictive assumptions underlying the Black Scholes option pricing model.

1. The underlying asset does not pay dividends or accrue interest payments.
2. The option being valued is European style i.e. cannot be exercised before expiry.
3. The risk-free interest rate is constant over the life of the option.
4. Volatility is constant over the life of the option.
5. The underlying asset price is Lognormally distributed.
6. Perfect markets with continuous trading and no costs/taxes.
7. Short selling of securities with no restrictions is permitted.

1.5.1 Assumptions

Assumption 1

This can be overcome by reducing the stock price by the present value of the dividends. More broadly, the original model designed for stock options has been modified to deal with options on futures (Black model) and other variants.

Assumption 2

Generally, this assumption is not restrictive, as early exercise is not normally optimal. Where early exercise may be rational, other models may be more appropriate.

Assumption 3

It is an obvious weakness to assume interest rates are constant and this has the following two consequences. Firstly, on the premiums, and secondly, on certain underlying assets, such as currencies and bonds.

With respect to premiums, a rise in interest rates will have various effects dependent on the option being examined.

Aside from the influence that changes in interest rates have on premiums, it will also have an effect on most underlying assets. This, however, is a risk associated with trying to evaluate the underlying asset rather than an option on that contract.

Assumption 4

A necessary simplification perhaps, but not one borne out in reality. Most assets will have periods of movement, followed by periods of inactivity during an option's life. As an option's sensitivity to volatility varies over time (long-dated options are most sensitive), a period of high volatility in the first part of its life would have an effect on its value, whilst a change in volatility late in its life may not. By assuming constant volatility, options may, for a given period, be either over or undervalued.

Assumption 5

There may be assets such as bonds that do not 'fit' the Lognormal distribution. This is for two reasons. Firstly, in the real world, interest rates tend to a long-term average. For example, if bond yields in the UK were 25%, the most logical next move in yields would normally be for them to go lower. Conversely, if bond yields were 1%, one might reasonably suggest that the next move would be upwards. This attribute of interest rate products is known as mean reversion. The other bond-specific problem that arises from using a Lognormal distribution is that it takes no account of the pull to par as redemption gets nearer.

Assumption 6

Perfect or efficient markets are a device used in many elegant theories, but do not fully exist in practice. Implicit in this idea is a belief that markets move randomly, that trading is continuous and that there are no 'jumps' in an asset's price. Events in the UK over the last decade, such as the stock market crash, ERM exit, and the February 1994 bond market sell-off prove such things do happen. Jumps are problematic in the context of the Black Scholes model in that they assume one is able to constantly readjust a position to maintain delta neutrality – this may be impossible in practice.

Assumption 7

Short selling is not available to all participants. In the UK, the ability to go short is limited in stock markets to registered market makers.

1.5.2 Overcoming the restrictions

Exam tip: All of the variations on the Black Scholes model covered on the next few pages are regularly numerically examined.

European style calls on dividend paying stocks

The Black Scholes model can be adjusted to take account of dividends by reducing the stock price throughout the formula by the present value of the dividends paid before expiry. The discounting should be from the anticipated payment date and not the ex-dividend date. This variation is sometimes described as the Known Dividend Model. It does not allow for early exercise.

The rationale behind this is that the shares expected value at expiry (after the ex-date) will be lower to the extent of dividends whose ex-date is already past.

American style calls on dividend paying stocks

These can be evaluated using Black's approximation. This is indeed an approximation and should be seen as a relatively crude method. American style calls on dividend paying stocks should rationally be exercised just prior to the ex-dividend date, if the present value of the dividends is greater than the time value that would be lost.

In this method, two calculations are done: the price of a European style call that expires on the expiry date is calculated as well as the price of a European style call that expires just before the stock goes ex-dividend (in this case no adjustment for dividends is made). The higher of these two values is the price of the American call. This is sometimes known as the Pseudo-American Model.

European style call on a stock index

The normal method for dealing with the dividend flows on an index is to subtract the dividend yield from the continuously compounded risk-free rate. This is analogous to the procedure involved in pricing a stock index future.

The formula therefore becomes

Formula to learn: $C = Se^{-yt}N(d_1) - Xe^{-rt}N(d_2)$

$$d_1 = \frac{\ln\left(\frac{S}{X}\right) + (r - y + 0.5\sigma^2)t}{\sigma\sqrt{t}}$$

$$d_2 = d_1 - \sigma\sqrt{t}$$

where

y = expected annual dividend yield, expressed as a decimal

European style call on a currency

Very much the same adjustment is made for currency options. Account is taken of the interest rates in both the domestic and the foreign currency. The result is the Garman-Kohlhagen model.

Formula to learn: $C = Se^{-yt}N(d_1) - Xe^{-rt}N(d_2)$

where

S = the spot exchange rate
r = the continuously compounded interest rate in the domestic currency
y = the continuously compounded interest rate in the foreign currency

and $d_1 = \dfrac{\ln\left(\dfrac{S}{X}\right)+\left(r-y+0.5\sigma^2\right)t}{\sigma\sqrt{t}}$

$d_2 = d_1 - \sigma\sqrt{t}$

European style call on futures/forwards

In the formulae used for stocks, indices and currency options, interest rates and dividend yields have been used to calculate the forward price of the asset on the expiry date. When dealing with options on futures, none of these complications exist. The formula for options with up front premiums becomes

$c = Fe^{-rt}N(d_1) - Xe^{-rt}N(d_2)$

or

Formula to learn

$C = (FN(d_1) - XN(d_2))e^{-rt}$

$d_1 = \dfrac{\ln\left(\dfrac{F}{X}\right)+0.5\sigma^2 t}{\sigma\sqrt{t}}$

$d_2 = d_1 - \sigma\sqrt{t}$

where

F = the future/forward price

This variation on Black Scholes is known as the Black Model.

The formula above is appropriate for options on futures that settle their premiums upfront. Where options premiums are settled futures style, no discounting takes place at all.

Formula to learn

$C = FN(d_1) - XN(d_2)$

Example 1

What is the price of the one-year at-the-money call on the CBOT T-bond future (up-front premium) where the future is 100, volatility 10% and interest rates 5%.

$C = (FN(d_1) - XN(d_2))e^{-rt}$

$d_1 = \dfrac{\ln\left(\dfrac{100}{100}\right)+0.50\times 0.1^2 \times 1}{0.1\sqrt{1}}$

$= \dfrac{0.005}{0.1}$

$= 0.05$

$d_2 = 0.05 - 0.1$

$= -0.05$

$N(d_1) = 0.5199$

$N(d_2) = 0.48006$

$C = (100 \times 0.5199 - 100 \times 0.48006)e^{-0.05} = 3.79$

Example 2

What is the value of an at-the-money six-month Euribor call (margined premium) traded on Euronext.liffe where the future trades at 92.00, volatility is 3%.

$$C = FN(d_1) - XN(d_1)$$

$$d_1 = \frac{\ln\left(\frac{92.00}{92.00}\right) + 0.50 \times 0.03^2 \times 0.5}{0.03\sqrt{0.5}}$$

$$= \frac{0.000225}{0.021213}$$

$$= 0.0106$$

$$d_2 = 0.0106 - 0.021213$$

$$= -0.0106$$

$N(d_1) = 0.5042$

$N(d_2) = 0.4958$

$C = 92 \times 0.5042 - 92 \times 0.4958$

$C = 46.38 - 45.61$

$C = 0.77$ (or 77 ticks)

1.6 Other models

So far in this text, we have mentioned the following models.

- Binomial model or Cox-Ross-Rubenstein model.
- Black Scholes model – basic model for non-dividend paying stock.
- Known Dividend Model – extension of basic Black Scholes to allow for a known dividend paid on a discrete date before expiry. The possibility of early exercise is ignored.
- Pseudo-American model – allows for payments of dividends on stock options that are American-style.
- Black Model (1976) – options on future.
- Garman-Kohlhagen model (1983) – options on currency.

In addition, there are other models that attempt to overcome some of the assumptions previously mentioned or evaluate more exotic options. Detailed knowledge of these is not required as, mathematically, they get increasingly complex and demand an increasing number of inputs, although an awareness of their names and applications should be noted.

- **Roll-Geshe-Whaley model** – this calculates the value of an American call option when one known dividend is paid over the life of the option. It can be generalised to take account of more than one dividend payment.
- **Heath-Jarrow-Morton model** (1992) – an alternative interest rate pricing model that takes the initial term structure of interest rates and models the evolution of forward rates rather than modelling the evolution of the spot interest rates.

1.7 Implied volatility

Implied volatilities are calculated by using a pricing model, but instead of using it to compute a theoretical premium based on the inputs discussed above, the formula is used to find volatility. When used in this form, users input time to expiry, exercise price, underlying price, interest rates and the actual market price of the option. The model then determines the unknown, namely volatility. In this way, users can find out what the market's perception is of future volatility – sometimes this may be better than relying on historic volatilities, which may not fully incorporate the impact of information recently released to the market.

One would assume that in an efficient market, the implied volatilities of all options on the same asset would be the same. However, empirically, this is not the case. In some cases, deeply in or deeply out-of-the-money options show much higher implied volatilities than at-the-money options.

This phenomenon, known as kurtosis, springs from a suggested defect in the Black Scholes model: namely, its assumption of Lognormally distributed price changes. Whilst this model of distributions is reasonably accurate in theory, option traders, from their own experience, recognise that the chance of either a big up or big downmove is more likely than the Normal distribution would suggest.

Also, demand for deep OTM options is often high due to the 'lottery effect', where investors may achieve high returns for a small investment. This demand also boosts implied volatility.

This phenomenon gives rise to something often referred to as the volatility smile. It has been stated that the market puts a higher value on deep in and deep out-of-the-money options than the Black Scholes model would suggest.

When calculating the implied volatility from the market prices, Black Scholes will therefore produce lower figures for the at-the-money options and higher implied volatilities for in and out-of-the-money options. Graphically, this can be shown as follows.

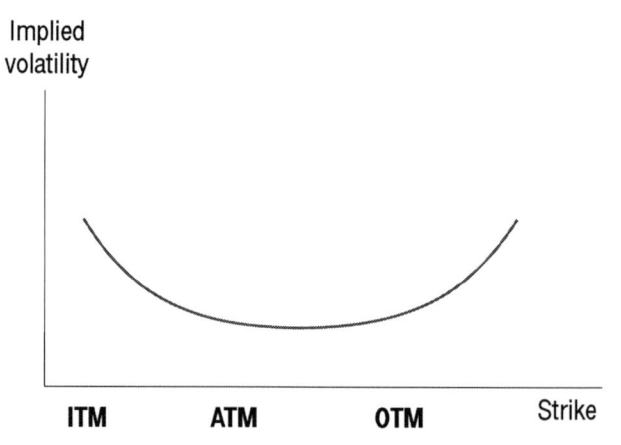

It may be that the implied volatility produces a **skew** rather than a smile. A glance at a Bloomberg screen will typically show higher implied volatility for lower strike options, i.e. out-of-the-money puts and in-the-money calls. Graphically, this can be shown as

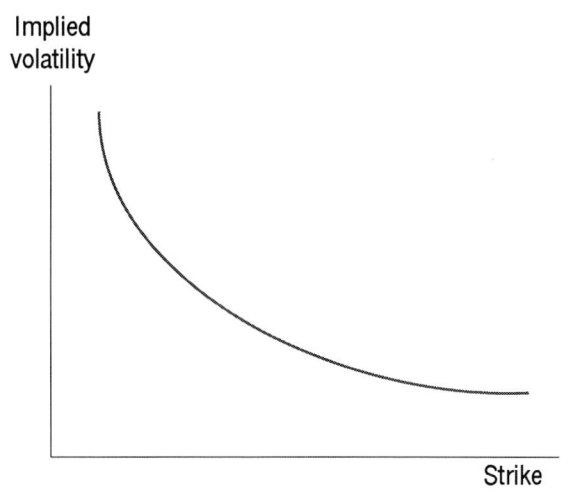

A possible reason for this is that hedgers looking for downside protection bid up the price of out-of-the-money puts. The higher price is interpreted by the Black Scholes model as higher implied volatility. If we can accept that out-of-the-money puts will exhibit higher implied volatility, why would in-the-money calls exhibit the higher implied volatility? The answer to this is put/call parity. If a put and a call with the same strike were priced off different volatility there will be an arbitrage possibility, at least in theory.

Also, note that the volatility smile/skew is usually less pronounced for longer dated options, supporting the idea that there is a term structure to volatility.

The propensity of implied volatility distributions to show higher volatilities for deeply in or out-of-the-money options is known as 'kurtosis' or more colloquially as 'fat tails'. The distribution would look as follows.

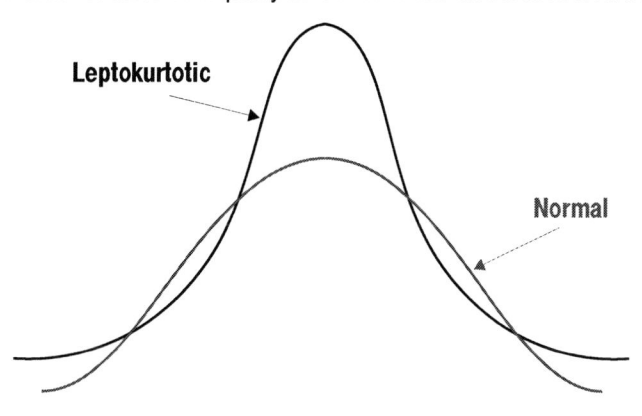

2 Sensitivity of Option Values

Exam tip

Questions regularly arise asking for the definitions and characteristics of the various sensitivity measures along with numerical applications, especially involving delta and gamma.

It has already been noted that there are five factors that influence the fair value of all options. They are

- Value of underlying.
- Exercise price.
- Time to expiry.
- Volatility.
- Interest rates.

NB: Dividend payments will also influence the fair value of options on dividend-paying stock.

A change in any one of these factors will impact on the price of an option. A holder of an option will want to know what the exact impact is likely to be, i.e. they will wish to know how sensitive their options are to changes in these factors.

Option sensitivities are named after Greek letters, as follows.

Sensitivity to	Known as
Underlying	Delta
Changes in Delta	Gamma
Time Decay	Theta
Volatility	Kappa or Vega*
Interest Rates	Rho

* Vega is not a Greek letter but, for alliterative purposes, it is often used as an alternative to Kappa.

2.1 Delta (δ)

2.1.1 Definition

Delta is the rate of change of an option's premium with respect to the underlying security.

It is one of the terms of the Black Scholes pricing model, specifically

Delta = $N(d_1)$

It can be viewed in the following three ways.

- Delta is the rate of change of an option's premium with respect to the underlying security. For example, an option with a delta of 0.25 can theoretically be expected to move at one quarter of the amount of the underlying. If the underlying goes up or down by 4, the option could be expected to go up or down by 1, all other factors remaining constant.

- It follows from this that delta is also the riskless hedge ratio that arises from the Black Scholes model. You will recall that we introduced hedge ratios in this context under the binomial pricing model above. It can be thought of as the theoretical number of shares which the holder of the call is long, or of which the holder of a put option is short if he wishes to achieve a risk-free hedge. For example, if the delta of a call (put) is 0.25, the holder of a call (put) is theoretically long (short) a quarter of a share, and needs to sell (buy) 0.25 shares to achieve the hedge. In this example, the call holder's position at this instant is equivalent to a long position in a quarter of a share, i.e. the holder will make or lose money at a quarter of the rate of a share.

- Delta can also be viewed as representative of the probability that an option will expire in-the-money. Thus, a delta of 0.25 or 25% means that there is only a small chance of being in-the-money; a delta of 0.9 or 90% gives an obviously higher chance.

2.1.2 Use of delta

Delta (δ) may be used to provide a first estimate of the change in the price of an option that will result from a given change in the price of the underlying asset.

Example

A share is priced at 90, and a corresponding 100 call has a premium of 6 and a delta of 0.4. Calculate the change in premium, and the new resulting premium, if the share price

Falls 3p

Rises 5p

Solution

Share Falls 3p

This relationship may be expressed mathematically as

Formula to learn

Change in premium = $\delta \times \Delta S$

where

δ = option Delta

ΔS = change in the share price

Applying this relationship gives

Change in premium = $\delta \times \Delta S = 0.4 \times (-3) = -1.2$

Giving a new premium of 4.8p (6.0p – 1.2p)

Share rises 5p

Change in premium = $\delta \times \Delta S = 0.4 \times 5 = +2.0$

Giving a new premium of 8.0p (6.0p + 2.0p)

Comments

Note that these are just first estimates since the delta changes as the share price changes. This is dealt with under gamma below.

2.1.3 Positive and negative deltas

If you are long of a call, you have a positive delta, i.e. if the underlying asset goes up, so does the call option premium, a move to the benefit of the holder.

Conversely, if you are short of a call and the market moves up, such a move is to your disadvantage, as the option becomes more expensive – you have a negative delta.

Put holders benefit from downwards price movements in the underlying asset, but are hurt by upwards moves. They are negatively correlated with the underlying asset.

Finally, short puts are helped by up moves, but are hurt by down moves; they have positive deltas.

Long Calls	Positive Delta
Short Puts	Positive Delta
Long Puts	Negative Delta
Short Calls	Negative Delta

2.1.4 How deltas change

An option's sensitivity to price changes does not stay constant – it changes as the underlying price moves and time to expiry shortens.

Deep in-the-money options normally have deltas near to 1, indicating that premiums change at nearly the same rate as the underlying price. A delta of 1 or 100% indicates that it is almost certain that the option will expire in-the-money.

At-the-money options have deltas of approximately 0.5 or 50%. They move at half the rate of the underlying asset and there is a 50:50 chance of expiring in-the-money.

Deep out-of-the-money options have deltas near to zero. This means they are almost insensitive to movements in the underlying and have a negligible chance of expiring in-the-money.

As options move in and out-of-the-money, their deltas change. It should be noted that the delta of the underlying asset or futures contract is **always** 1. If you are long of a future, you have a positive delta; if short, a negative delta of 1.

The change in delta can be seen from the following diagram, relating to the value of a call option compared to the price of the underlying stock.

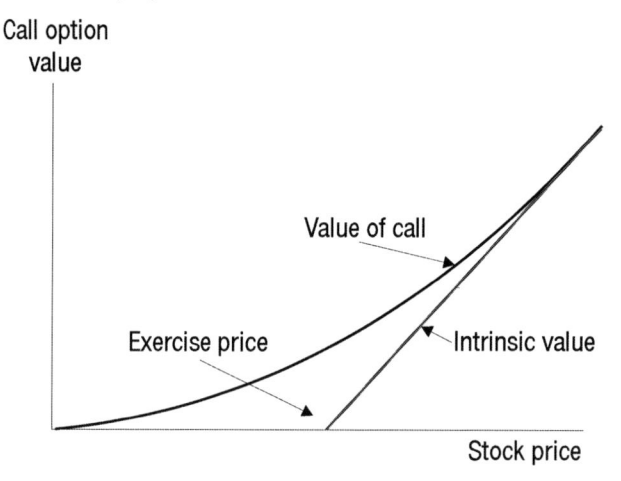

Delta is the **slope** of the option value line. This ranges from 0 (when deeply out-of-the-money) through 0.5 (when at-the-money) to 1 (when deeply in-the-money).

2.1.5 Portfolio deltas

The delta of a portfolio can be assessed as the weighted combination of the asset deltas.

Example

You have a position that includes the following trades. Calculate your overall exposure to changes in the price of the underlying.

Short 2 calls	Delta 0.5
Long 1 put	Delta 0.3
Long 5 calls	Delta 0.2

Solution

The first thing to work out is which positions have positive or negative deltas.

From the table above, we can see that short calls are negative, long puts are negative and long calls are positive. The positive and negative symbols are now attributed to the relevant delta.

Having done this, we simply multiply the number of contracts by the delta.

$2 \times (-0.5) = -1$

$1 \times (-0.3) = -0.3$

$5 \times (+0.2) = +1$

Net delta $= -0.3$

Our net delta is -0.3, or equivalent to short 0.3 futures contracts.

2.1.6 Delta hedging – Delta neutral positions

Whilst the delta of a futures/underlying position remains constant, option deltas are dynamic. This presents problems to hedgers who often like to have a delta position of zero (sometimes called a delta neutral position), which gives them no exposure to movements in the underlying asset price.

Example

A share has a price of 36. Call options written on that share have a premium of 2.26 and a delta of 0.4.

- Construct a delta neutral position.
- Determine how this position will change as the underlying share price moves.

Solution

Delta neutral position

Since we have a delta of 0.4, we will need to be long four shares and short ten options (or long 0.4 of a share and short one option). Then, a change in the price of the options position would counterbalance the change in price of the shares.

Movements in the underlying

Such neutrality is only real for as long as the delta of the option remains the same. This means that the position is only technically delta neutral for infinitesimally small changes in stock price. Should the option move further in or out-of-the-money, the neutrality will be lost, necessitating a readjustment of the position when the delta changes significantly.

The problem with not adjusting a delta neutral position is that the value of the portfolio will decline as the stock price moves in either direction. This is because as the stock price rises, the delta of the call option will increase and the loss on the short call position will accelerate. We therefore lose out on the relative price movements.

As the value of the stock falls, the delta of the option reduces. This means that its price falls at a slower rate compared to the stock. Thus, the gains we make on the short call are less than the losses we suffer on the long stock position.

This could be represented on a graph as follows, based on an original stock price of 36 and a position consisting of four shares and ten short options.

**Value of a Portfolio Delta Neutral
at a Stock Price of 36**

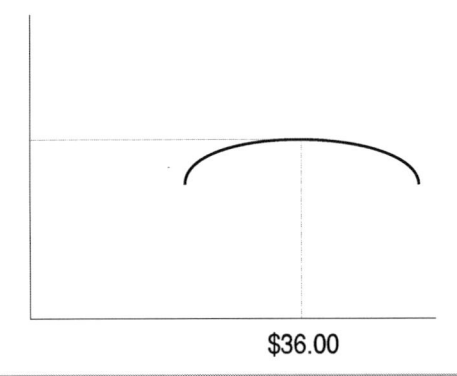

$36.00

2.2 Gamma (γ)

2.2.1 Definition

> Gamma is the rate of change of delta with respect to the underlying security.

As noted earlier, the delta of the underlying asset or futures contract is **always** 1. If you are long a future, you have a positive delta; if short, a negative delta of 1.

Whilst the delta of a futures/underlying asset position is static, option deltas are dynamic. An option's sensitivity to price changes does **not** stay constant, rather it changes as the underlying asset price moves and time to expiry shortens. Deep in-the-money options normally have deltas near 1; at-the-money options have deltas of approximately 0.5; deep out-of-the-money options have deltas near to zero. As options move in-to and out-of-the-money, their deltas change and the gamma reflects the rate of this change.

These dynamics presents problems to hedgers who often like to have a delta position of zero (sometimes called a delta neutral position), which gives them no exposure to movements in the underlying as long as the deltas of the options remain the same. Should any of the options move further in or out-of-the-money, the neutrality will be lost, necessitating a readjustment of the position. Traders can achieve a delta neutral position, but if this is done by using options with high gammas, the comfort of the hedge can be illusory.

Options that are at-the-money and close to expiry have the highest gammas, thus particular care needs to be taken if such options are used in a hedge. Out-of-the-money options have low or zero gammas, as the options will have deltas of zero. Similarly, in-the-money options which will already have deltas of 1 will have zero gammas, as these options are bound, subject to an extraordinary move, to expire in-the-money.

Referring back to the earlier delta diagram

- Delta is **the slope** of the value line ranging from 0 (when deeply out-of-the-money) though 0.5 (when at-the-money) to 1 (when deeply in-the-money).

- Gamma is **the curve** of the value line, indicating how the slope, i.e. delta changes. The curve is greatest for at-the-money and gradually reduces (as the line becomes increasingly straight) as the option is more in or out-of-the-money.

One final initial aspect is the sign of the gamma.

- Long options postions have a positive gamma since as the underlying price increases the delta becomes less negative/more positive.

- Short options positions have a negative gamma.

2.2.2 Use of gamma

Gamma can be used to give a more accurate assessment of the change in the premium of an option that will result from a given change in the share price.

Example

Extending our earlier example, a share is priced at 90, and a corresponding 100 call has a premium of 6, a delta of 0.4, and a gamma of 0.007. Calculate the change in premium, and the new resulting premium, if the share price

- Falls 3p.
- Rises 5p.

Solution

Share falls 3p

Alternative 1 – Using an average delta

As we noted above, delta changes as the share price changes, hence using it to forecast price movements will lead to inaccuracies. To overcome this, we could use the gamma to calculate the average delta over the given range of share prices and use this to more accurately assess the change in premiums as follows.

Delta at share price of 90p		0.4000
Change due to gamma if shares fall 3p	$0.007 \times (-3)$	−0.0210
Delta at share price of 87p		0.3790
Average delta	$(0.4000 + 0.3790) \div 2$	0.3895

Hence

$$\text{Change in premium} = \text{Average } \delta \times \Delta s = 0.3895 \times (-3) = -1.1685$$

Giving a new premium of 4.8315 (6.0000p − 1.1685p)

Alternative 2 – Mathematical relationship

Note, we could calculate the above average delta from the original delta (δ) and gamma (γ) as

$$\text{Average } \delta = \delta + \tfrac{1}{2}\gamma \times \Delta S$$

$$= 0.4000 + \tfrac{1}{2} \times 0.0070 \times (-3)$$

$$= 0.3895$$

and substituting this equation in the above premium change formula gives

$$\text{Change in premium} = \text{Average } \delta \times \Delta S$$

$$= (\delta + \tfrac{1}{2}\gamma \times \Delta S) \times \Delta S$$

$$= \delta \times \Delta S + \tfrac{1}{2}\gamma \times \Delta S^2$$

That is, this whole average delta approach may be combined into a single formula to speed the calculation and expressed mathematically as

Formula to learn

$$\text{Change in premium} = \delta \times \Delta S + \tfrac{1}{2}\gamma \times \Delta S^2$$

where

- δ = option delta at the original share price
- γ = options gamma at the original share price
- ΔS = change in the share price

Applying this relationship gives

$$\text{Change in premium} = \delta \times \Delta S + \tfrac{1}{2}\gamma \times \Delta S^2$$
$$= 0.400 \times (-3) + \tfrac{1}{2} \times 0.007 \times (-3)^2$$
$$= -1.1685$$

This is a negative figure, hence the premium will fall by 1.1685p to 4.8315p (6.000 – 1.1685p) as calculated above in Alternative 1.

Share rises 5p

Applying the formula gives

$$\text{Change in premium} = \delta \times \Delta S + \tfrac{1}{2}\gamma \times \Delta S^2$$
$$= 0.400 \times 5 + \tfrac{1}{2} \times 0.007 \times 5^2$$
$$= 2.0875\text{p}$$

This is positive, hence the premium will rise by 2.0875p to 8.0875p.

2.2.3 Gamma hedging

As was discussed above regarding delta hedging, it is also appropriate to hedge a position's gamma. As the gamma is the sensitivity of the delta to the underlying, it is also a reflection of how frequently a portfolio would have to be rehedged to maintain its delta. One thing to note with gamma hedging is that unlike delta hedging, it cannot be done by adjusting the amount of underlying in the portfolio. This is because the gamma of the underlying asset is zero. Therefore, gamma hedging will necessitate adjusting the gamma via options, which will make it more expensive. Typically therefore, it will be done less frequently.

2.3 Theta (θ)

> The theta of an option reflects the rate of change of the option price with respect to time.

As we are aware, the price or premium of an option is a combination of intrinsic and time value. If all other factors remain constant, by how much will the time value, hence the premium, move over a period of, say, one day?

Theta is an absolute measure, hence if an option has a premium of 1.50 and a theta of 0.05, the next day, all other things remaining equal, the option will have a value of 1.45.

The relationship here (all other factors being equal) is

Formula to learn

> Change in premium = $\theta \times \Delta T$

where

θ = option theta at the original date
ΔT = number of days that have elapsed

For buyers of options, theta is negative, buyers suffer from time decay. For sellers of options, theta is positive, sellers benefit from time decay.

The buyer of an option may be concerned by this, as the value of his investment (the price of his option) falls as time moves towards expiry. He will therefore require a return from other factors, such as the movement in the underlying asset price, that will more than offset the loss due to time decay over any specified period. The theta provides a means for assessing this time decay.

As we indicated earlier, the rate of time decay is non-constant, i.e. the theta of an option also varies with time. As options move towards expiry, the rate of time decay increases, hence theta attracts a larger value.

2.4 Vega (or kappa) (κ)

2.4.1 Definition

> The vega (or kappa) of an option reflects the rate of change of the option price with respect to volatility.

As an asset becomes more/less volatile, option premiums rise/fall. Vega assesses this rate of change.

The relationship here (all other factors being equal) is

Formula to learn
> Change in premium = $\kappa \times \Delta\sigma$

where

κ = option vega (kappa) at the original volatility

$\Delta\sigma$ = change in the volatility

The higher the vega, the greater the impact on an option premium for a given change in volatility. This may be of use to speculators in assessing volatility trades such as straddles and strangles.

At-the-money options have the greatest sensitivity to volatility, i.e. have the greatest vega. Options that are deeply in-the-money or out-of-the-money have little sensitivity to volatility and hence, very low vegas.

Although an at-the-money option has the highest vega, this vega is relatively insensitive to changes in volatility itself. However, the vega of options which are deeply in or out-of-the-money are more sensitive to changes in volatility.

Vega acts rather like time decay, i.e. the effect of time passing (less time) is the same as a reduction in volatility (less volatility), however, the vega of all options decline as expiry approaches.

Long-option positions are vega positive.

Short-option positions are vega negative.

2.4.2 Vega hedging

As with gamma hedging, vega hedging can be done to reduce a position's exposure to volatility. One thing to note is that the measurement, and indeed use of vega, is only really suitable for options that have a single-sign gamma. For options whose gamma can be positive or negative, e.g. binary options, a vega measure could be calculated as zero. This is inappropriate, as these options are very exposed to volatility risk. Once more, vega hedging can only be done by rebalancing a portfolio using options.

2.5 Rho

> The rho of an option measures the rate of change of an option price with respect to interest rates.

It is usually expressed as the price change for a 1% change in interest rates. If an increase in interest rates increases the value of an option, it will be rho positive. If it reduces the value, it will be rho negative.

We are aware that interest rates influence option premiums, though the impact on calls and puts differs. Rho measures the sensitivity to this change and can be used to assess risk in an option in times of interest rate volatility.

8: OPTIONS PRICING – BINOMIAL AND BLACK SCHOLES

The impact of interest rate changes – as already noted – varies according to what type of option it is. What is true is that, of the factors discussed so far, interest rate changes and rho will be the least significant.

Options on Physicals	Call options will have positive rhos
	Put options will have negative rhos
Options on Futures (premiums paid upfront)	Call and put options will have negative rhos
Options on Futures (premiums margined)	Call and put options have a zero rho

With currency options, there are two interest rates that need to be considered – the domestic rate (r) and the foreign currency rate (f).

Sensitivity to the domestic rate is rho (or rho_1) whilst sensitivity to the foreign currency rate is phi (or rho_2).

A summary of the impact of interest rate changes on foreign currency options is

	Domestic Rate Rises	Domestic Rate Falls	Foreign Rate Rises	Foreign Rate Falls
Call	Rise	Fall	Fall	Rise
Put	Fall	Rise	Rise	Fall

The relationship here (all other factors being equal) is

Formula to learn

Change in premium = $\rho \times \Delta r$

where

- ρ = option rho at the original rate of interest
- Δr = change in the interest rate

2.6 Combined

Combining all of the above individual factors gives

Formula to learn

Change in premium = $\delta \times \Delta S + \frac{1}{2}\gamma \times \Delta S^2 + \theta \times \Delta T + \kappa \times \Delta\sigma + \rho \times \Delta r$

2.7 Summary

To help put these interrelationships in context, the following tables may be useful.

If your delta position is	You want underlying to
Positive	Rise
Negative	Fall
If your gamma position is	**You want underlying to**
Positive	Make big change
Negative	Stand still

If your theta position is	Passage of time
Positive	Helps
Negative	Hurts
If your vega position is	**You want volatility to**
Positive	Rise
Negative	Fall

Position	Delta	Gamma	Theta	Vega
Long Future	+	0	0	0
Short Future	−	0	0	0
Long Call	+	+	−	+
Short Call	−	−	+	−
Long Put	−	+	−	+
Short Put	+	−	+	−

2.8 Derivation of the Greeks

All the sensitivity measures just discussed can be derived from the various pricing models. An appreciation of which element of the pricing model is **delta** is sufficient for our needs.

Option		Delta of a Call	Delta of a Put
1.	Non-dividend paying stock	$N(d_1)$	$-N(-d_1)$
2.	Dividend paying stock#	$N(d_1)$	$-N(-d_1)$
3.	Stock index	$e^{-yt}N(d_1)$	$-e^{-yt}N(-d_1)$
4.	Currency	$e^{-yt}N(d_1)$	$-e^{-yt}N(-d_1)$
5.	Future (premiums margined)	$N(d_1)$	$-N(-d_1)$
6.	Futures (premiums paid up front)	$e^{-rt}N(d_1)$	$-e^{-rt}N(-d_1)$

Where 'S' in the calculation of d is S − PV(D)

Generalising we have that the call delta

$$\delta_{Call} = N(d_1)e^{-xt}$$

and put deltas

$$\delta_{Put} = -N(d_1)e^{-xt}$$

where x=

- Zero for non-yielding stocks and futures whose premiums are margined, in which case $e^{-xt} = 1$ and can be ignored.
- Yield (y) on an index.
- Yield (y) on a currency.
- Interest rate (r) on futures with up front premiums.

Now $N(-d_1) = 1 - N(d_1)$

So the put delta becomes

$$\delta_{Put} = -(1-N(d_1))e^{-xt}$$
$$\delta_{Put} = N(d_1)e^{-xt} - e^{-xt}$$

or

$$\delta_{Put} = \delta_{Call} - e^{-xt}$$

3 HEDGING

If a trader sells an option, they are clearly exposed to potential loss, which they will need to hedge. For example, if a call option on a share is sold, the trader will wish to protect themselves against an increase in the value of the share. This can be done by ensuring that they hold an appropriate amount of the underlying share, the basic idea being that as they lose on the option, they gain on the share.

The question is therefore "how many shares should be held?". The initial response to this will be given by looking at the delta of the option. As previously discussed, the delta can be defined as

Formula to learn

$$\text{Delta} = \frac{\text{Change in value of option}}{\text{Change in value of underlying security}}$$

e.g. a call option written on ABC plc has a delta of 0.5. The option value changes by 50% of the change in value of the ABC share, and each contract represents 1,000 shares, thus we will need to buy $1,000 \times 0.5 = 500$ shares.

If the share price then rises by one pence.

Loss on option = $1,000 \times (0.5 \times 1p) = 500p$
Gain on share = $500 \times 1p = 500p$

The delta is, therefore, the appropriate hedge ratio.

We must remember that the delta of an option is not constant: it changes due to changes in the value of the underlying, volatility or time to expiry. We have also examined gamma, a second derivative greek, that represents how sensitive an option's delta is to changes in the underlying asset price. To complicate the matter further, the gamma is itself sensitive to volatility, time to expiry and interest rates. It is possible to calculate a gamma that factors in the effect of volatility. This would be more accurate and is sometimes called the shadow gamma.

For dynamic hedging, it is therefore necessary not just to hedge the option's delta, but also to take into account the option's gamma – remembering at all times that the hedge will have to be adjusted as frequently as possible.

What about the sensitivities? It might be considered appropriate to consider hedging a position against changes in volatility – this would necessitate knowledge of an option's vega and its sensitivities as already discussed.

Appendix 1

Derivation of formula for calculating the probability of an upmove = 'p'.

Consider the following.

Current price of a share = 100p

This could increase to 110p, or fall to 90p, by the end of one period.

Risk-free interest rate for the period = 1% (assume continuous compounding).

It follows that the current value of the share (100p) is the present value of the share's expected value in one period's time.

$$100 = \frac{(p \times 110) + (1-p) \times 90}{e^{0.01}}$$

when p = probability of an upmove
      1 − p = probability of a downmove

Which can be rearranged as

$$100 \times e^{0.01} = 110p + 90 - 90p$$

$$p = \frac{100 \times e^{0.01} - 90}{110 - 90}$$

Or generally, dividing by 100, we get

$$p = \frac{e^{0.01} - 0.9}{1.1 - 0.9}$$

Or more generally

$$p = \frac{e^{rt} - d}{u - d}$$

Derivation of formula for calculating the probability of an upmove 'p' when the underlying asset yields 'y'

Current price of underlying = 100p
Yield = 4% p.a.
Risk-free interest rate = 7% p.a.

Value of underlying in one year − if it increases = 110p
                                 − if it falls = 90p

It is still the case that the current value of the underlying is the present value of the shares' expected return in one year, but we must now also consider the yield we will have received. Therefore

$$100 = \frac{(p \times 110) + [(1-p) \times 90]}{e^{0.07}} \times e^y$$

$$\frac{100 \times e^{0.07}}{e^{0.04}} = 110p + 90 - 90p$$

Divide by 100 and rearrange to solve p

$$p = \frac{e^{(0.07 - 0.04)} - 0.9}{1.1 - 0.9}$$

Or more generally

$$p = \frac{e^{(rt - yt)} - d}{u - d}$$

8: OPTIONS PRICING – BINOMIAL AND BLACK SCHOLES

Appendix 2

Derivation of the Black Scholes Model.

Fair price = Present value of expected returns.

Expected value of call options at expiry – $E(C_t) = E[\max(S_t - X), 0]$

where

S_t = value of underlying at expiry

X = exercise price

$S_t - X$ = intrinsic value at expiry

i.e. if at expiry $S_t > X$, then $E[\max(S_t - X), 0] = S_t - X$

if at expiry $S_t < X$, then $E[\max(S_t - X), 0] = 0$

Let p = probability that option expires in-the-money so that $S_t > X$

$$E(C_t) = p \times \underbrace{(E[S_t \mid S_t > X] - X)}_{\text{expected value of } S_t \text{ given that } S_t > X} + (1-p) \times 0$$

$$\underbrace{}_{\text{expected value of call at expiry}}$$

Discounting back to get present value on a risk-neutral basis

$$C = p \times e^{-rt} \times (E[S_t \mid S_t > X] - X)$$

Calculate the probability of S_t being greater than X. To do this, we use the properties of a Normal distribution where the expected annual return on a stock is μ and the annual variation in the return is σ. It can be shown that given a stock price today of S, its expected value in time $t(S_t)$ will be given by

$$= Se^{\left(\mu t + \frac{\sigma^2 t}{2}\right)}$$

and that the expected return if there is an upmove will be

$$= e^{\left(\mu t + \sigma\sqrt{t}\right)}$$

For example, suppose S = 100p
μ = 10%
σ = 15%
t = 0.5
probability of upmove = 0.5
probability of downmove = 0.5

$$S_t = 100e^{\left(0.1 \times 0.5 + \frac{0.15^2 \times 0.5}{2}\right)}$$

S_t = 105.72p

Expected return if upmove

$$= e^{\left(0.1 \times 0.5 + 0.15\sqrt{0.5}\right)}$$
$$= 1.1689$$

Expected return if downmove

$$= e^{(0.1 \times 0.5 - 0.15\sqrt{0.5})}$$
$$= 0.9455$$

Expected value of S_t

$$S_t = (100 \times 1.1689 \times 0.5) + (100 \times 0.9455 \times 0.5)$$
$$S_t = 105.72p \text{ (as already calculated)}$$

Using the risk-neutral ideas already discussed, we can see that the future expected value of a share when discounted back by the risk-free rate will be the current value of the share

That is, $\quad Se\left(\mu t + \dfrac{\sigma^2 t}{2}\right) \times e^{-rt} = S$

$$e\left(\mu t + \dfrac{\sigma^2 t}{2}\right) = e^{-rt}$$

$$\mu t + \dfrac{\sigma^2 t}{2} = rt$$

$$\mu + \dfrac{\sigma^2}{2} = r$$

or $\quad \mu = r - \dfrac{\sigma^2}{2}$

We have now established that the return will be Normally distributed around a mean of $r - \dfrac{\sigma^2}{2}$ and a standard deviation of σ.

For a call option to expire in-the-money, the return on the share must be at least $\ln\left(\dfrac{X}{S}\right)$ – this is the change from the current price to the exercise price measured as the log of the price relative.

Back to the Normal distribution of returns.

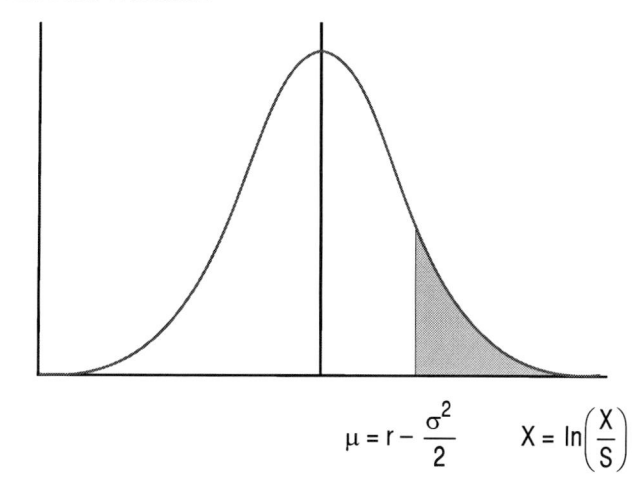

$$\mu = r - \dfrac{\sigma^2}{2} \qquad X = \ln\left(\dfrac{X}{S}\right)$$

The shaded area is the probability of the option expiring in-the-money and hence, the probability of paying the exercise price.

8: OPTIONS PRICING – BINOMIAL AND BLACK SCHOLES

Probability of $S_t > X$ over time period t = probability of $\left[\text{returns} > \ln\left(\dfrac{X}{S}\right)\right]$

$$= 1 - N\left(\dfrac{X - \mu t}{\sigma\sqrt{t}}\right)$$

where

N = cumulative Normal distribution, i.e. the area to the left of critical value X

Therefore, probability of $S_t > X = 1 - N\left[\dfrac{\ln\left(\dfrac{X}{S}\right) - \left(r - \dfrac{\sigma^2}{2}\right)t}{\sigma\sqrt{t}}\right]$

as $1 - N(d) = N(-d)$

Probability of $S_t > X = N\left[\dfrac{\ln\left(\dfrac{S}{X}\right) + \left(r - \dfrac{\sigma^2}{2}\right)t}{\sigma\sqrt{t}}\right]$

Probability of $S_t > X = N(d_2)$

The formula for pricing a call is now

$$C = N(d_2) \times e^{-rt} \times (E[S_t \mid S_t > X] - X)$$

To calculate a value for $E[S_t \mid S_t > X]$, we need to integrate the Normal distribution curve over the range X $\to \infty$. The result is

$$E[S_t \mid S_t > X] = Se^{rt}\dfrac{N(d_1)}{N(d_2)}$$

where

S = current price and Se^{rt} = the mean price at Time t

$$C = N(d_2) \times e^{-rt} \times \left[Se^{rt}\dfrac{N(d_1)}{N(d_2)} - X\right]$$

$$C = N(d_2)e^{-rt}Se^{rt}\dfrac{N(d_1)}{N(d_2)} - N(d_2)e^{-rt}X$$

$C = SN(d_1) - Xe^{-rt}N(d_2)$ (the basic Black Scholes model).

Chapter Roundup

- Binomial model – Alternative 1

$$C = \frac{pC_u + (1-p)C_d}{e^{rt}}$$

where

C_u = Value of call at end of period if price rises to S_u

C_d = Value of call at end of period if asset price falls to S_d

Risk free compound factor for the period

Continuous Discounting	Discrete Discounting
$R = e^{rt}$	$R = (1 + r)^t$

r = Annual interest rate

t = Time to expiry in years

p = Probability of an upmove

$$p = \frac{e^{(r-y)t} - d}{u - d}$$

y = Yield on asset/currency acquired per period

u = Expected percentage upmove, $u = e^{\sigma\sqrt{t}}$

d = Expected percentage downmove, $d = \frac{1}{u}$

Note

- The same formula is used for puts.
- For American style options, the option value at each node must never be below instrinsic value, hence at each node the option value is

American node value = Max(C, Intrinsic value)

- Binomial model – Alternative 2

Option	Continuous Compounding	Discrete Compounding
Call	$(hS - C)e^{rt} = hS_u - C_u$	$(hS - C)(1 + r)^t = hS_u - C_u$
Put	$(hS + p)e^{rt} = hS_d + P_d$	$(hS + p)(1 + r)^t = hS_d + P_d$

where

h = hedge ratio (= option delta)

$$h = \frac{C_u - C_d}{S_u - S_d}$$

C_u = call value if the share price goes up
C_d = call value if the share price goes down
S_u = share price if it goes up

8: OPTIONS PRICING – BINOMIAL AND BLACK SCHOLES

S_d = share price if it goes down

- Binomial model – yielding asset/currency

$$p = \frac{e^{(r-y)t} - d}{u - d}$$

where

r = interest rate on cash/traders base currency.
y = yield on underlying asset/underlying currency being traded

- Black Scholes Model

$$C = SN(d_1) - Xe^{-rt}N(d_2)$$

where

$$d_1 = \frac{\ln\left(\frac{S}{X}\right) + \left(r + 0.5\sigma^2\right)t}{\sigma\sqrt{t}}$$

$$d_2 = \frac{\ln\left(\frac{S}{X}\right) + \left(r - 0.5\sigma^2\right)t}{\sigma\sqrt{t}} \text{ or } d_2 = d_1 - \sigma\sqrt{t}$$

- Black Scholes limitations
    1. The underlying asset does not pay dividends or accrue interest payments.
    2. The option being valued is European style.
    3. The risk-free interest rate is constant over the life of the option.
    4. Volatility is constant over the life of the option.
    5. The underlying asset price is Lognormally distributed.
    6. Perfect markets with continuous trading and no costs/taxes.
    7. Short selling of securities with no restrictions is permitted.

- Black Scholes variants

Option	Call Value	d_1	d_2
European, no dividends	$C = SN(d_1) - Xe^{-rt}N(d_2)$	$d_1 = \dfrac{\ln\left(\frac{S}{X}\right) + \left(r + 0.5\sigma^2\right)t}{\sigma\sqrt{t}}$	$d_2 = d_1 - \sigma\sqrt{t}$
European, stock index	$C = Se^{-yt}N(d_1) - Xe^{-rt}N(d_2)$	$d_1 = \dfrac{\ln\left(\frac{S}{X}\right) + \left(r - y + 0.5\sigma^2\right)t}{\sigma\sqrt{t}}$	$d_2 = d_1 - \sigma\sqrt{t}$
European, currency	$C = Se^{-yt}N(d_1) - Xe^{-rt}N(d_2)$	$d_1 = \dfrac{\ln\left(\frac{S}{X}\right) + \left(r - y + 0.5\sigma^2\right)t}{\sigma\sqrt{t}}$	$d_2 = d_1 - \sigma\sqrt{t}$
European on future with up front premium	$C = (FN(d_1) - XN(d_2))e^{-rt}$	$d_1 = \dfrac{\ln\left(\frac{F}{X}\right) + 0.5\sigma^2 t}{\sigma\sqrt{t}}$	$d_2 = d_1 - \sigma\sqrt{t}$
European on future premium margined	$C = FN(d_1) - XN(d_2)$	$d_1 = \dfrac{\ln\left(\frac{F}{X}\right) + 0.5\sigma^2 t}{\sigma\sqrt{t}}$	$d_2 = d_1 - \sigma\sqrt{t}$

Option	δ_{Call}	δ_{Put}
European, no dividends	$N(d_1)$	$\delta_{Call} - 1$
European, stock index	$N(d_1)e^{-yt}$	$\delta_{Call} - e^{-yt}$
European, currency	$N(d_1)e^{-yt}$	$\delta_{Call} - e^{-yt}$
European on future with up front premium	$N(d_1)e^{-rt}$	$\delta_{Call} - e^{-rt}$
European on future premium margined	$N(d_1)$	$\delta_{Call} - 1$

- Greeks
    - Delta is the rate of change of an option's premium with respect to the underlying security.

      Change in premium = $\delta \times \Delta S$
    - Gamma is the rate of change of delta with respect to the underlying security.

      Change in premium = $\delta \times \Delta S + \frac{1}{2}\gamma \times \Delta S^2$
    - The theta of an option reflects the rate of change of the option price with respect to time.

      Change in premium = $\theta \times \Delta T$
    - The vega (or kappa) of an option reflects the rate of change of the option price with respect to volatility.

      Change in premium = $\kappa \times \Delta\sigma$
    - The rho of an option measures the rate of change of an option price with respect to interest rates.

      Change in premium = $\rho \times \Delta r$
    - Combined change in premium = $\delta \times \Delta S + \frac{1}{2}\gamma \times \Delta S^2 + \theta \times \Delta T + \kappa \times \Delta\sigma + \rho \times \Delta r$

Test Your Knowledge

Check your knowledge of the Chapter here, without referring back to the text.

1. Identify the profits and losses from the following transactions.

    (a) You write a call option at an exercise price of £5.00 for a premium of £0.50 per share. The price goes to £5.30 at the time of maturity.

    (b) You buy a put option at an exercise price of £1.20 for 10p per share and the share price goes to £0.90.

    (c) You write a put option at an exercise price of £1.20 for 10p per share and the share price goes to £1.70.

    (d) You write the put in part (c) above, and buy the share at its current market price of £1.30. Subsequently, the share price rises to £1.70.

2. A share is currently priced at £5.00 and there are only two possible prices at the maturity of one year options written on it, either £7.00 or £4.00. If the exercise price of a call option written on this share is X = £6.00, and the risk-free interest rate is 5%

    (a) Calculate the hedge ratio h in this specific case.
    (b) Use the one-period binomial model to determine the value of the call.

3. A share is currently priced at £2.40. An investor holds 30 shares and determines that they will either rise to £4.00 or fall to £2.00 within 4 months. The risk-free rate over this period is 6%. Calculate the number of call options he should write with an exercise price of £2.50 to perfectly hedge his shares and the value of the call using a single period binomial model.

4. The current share price is S = £10. The share price may rise in each future quarter by 40% or drop in each quarter by 20%. The risk-free interest rate is 16%.

    (a) Assume that a call is written on this share with exercise price X = £11. Illustrate graphically the profile of the share and the call at the end of the first and second quarters.

    (b) Calculate the equilibrium price now for a six month call option.

5. You are given the following information.

    Dollar/Euro exchange rate is $1.27:€1
    Annual volatility   16%

    The yield curves in the US and Europe are flat with interest rates at 5% and 3.5% respectively

    Calculate the fair price and option delta for a two month 1.25 call option on Euros using a two period binomial.

8: OPTIONS PRICING – BINOMIAL AND BLACK SCHOLES

6. An asset is priced at 1,136 and has a volatility at 18% p.a. UK Interst rates are 5% p.a. You are given the following cumulative Normal probabilities N(x)

x	N(x)	x	N(x)
0.0	0.5000	0.5	0.6915
0.1	0.5398	0.6	0.7257
0.2	0.5793	0.7	0.7580
0.3	0.6179	0.8	0.7881
0.4	0.6554	0.9	0.8159

Calculate the value and delta of a three month 1,150 call and a three month 1,150 put if

(a) The asset is a non-yielding stock.
(b) The asset is an index with an annual yield of 3%.
(c) The asset is a currency subject to annual interest of 3%
(d) The asset is a future and the option premium is paid up front.
(e) The asset is a future and the option premium is margined.

7. A share is currently priced at 430p. A 440 put option on the share currently has a premium of 38, a delta of –0.54, and a gamma of 0.004. Calculate the new premium if the share price

(a) Rises to 440.
(b) Falls to 425.

Test Your Knowledge: Answers

1. (a)

Proceeds:	Option premium	0.50
	Exercise price	5.00
		5.50
Cost:	Purchase price	5.30
Profit		**£0.20**

(b)

Proceeds:	Exercise price		1.20
Cost:	Option premium	0.10	
	Purchase price	0.90	
			1.00
Profit			**£0.20**

(c)

Proceeds:	Option premium **Profit**	**£0.10**

Share price rises so option not exercised and expires worthless.

(d)

Proceeds:	Option premium (options not exercised)	0.10
	Profit on shares owned 1.70 – 1.30	0.40
Profit		**£0.50**

2. (a) *Diagrammatically*

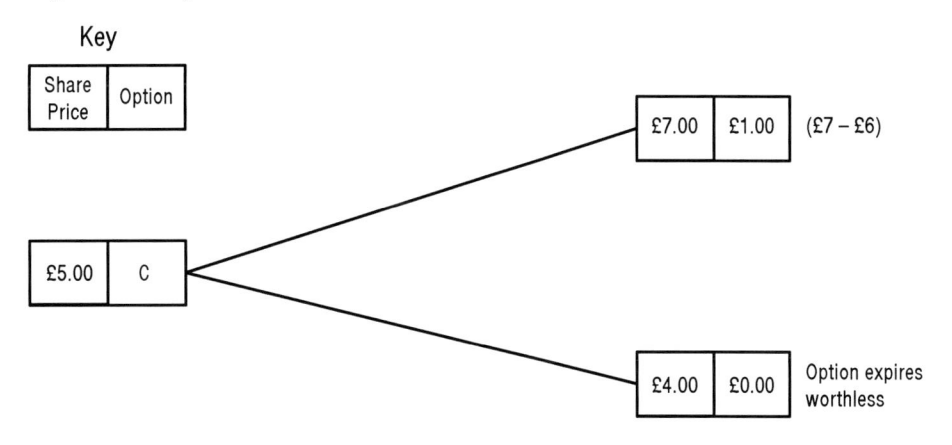

Key: Share Price | Option

£5.00 | C

£7.00 | £1.00   (£7 – £6)

£4.00 | £0.00   Option expires worthless

C_u = call value if the share price goes up = £1.00 (£7.00 – £6.00).
C_d = call value if the share price goes down = £0.00 as the option expires worthless.
S_u = share price if it goes up = £7.00.
S_d = share price if it goes down = £4.00.

To achieve a perfect hedge we would need to apply the hedge ratio

$$h = \frac{C_u - C_d}{S_u - S_d} = \frac{£1.00 - £0.00}{£7.00 - £4.00} = \frac{1}{3}$$

The hedge ratio h is 1 share for every 3 written options.

(b) *Alternative approach 1*

$$u = \frac{7.00}{5.00} = 1.40$$

$$d = \frac{4.00}{5.00} = 0.80$$

Probability of a call upmove

$$p = \frac{e^{rt} - d}{u - d} = \frac{e^{0.5} - 0.80}{1.40 - 0.80} = 0.418785$$

Call value

$$C = \frac{pC_u + (1-p)C_d}{e^{rt}} = \frac{0.418785 \times 1.00 + 0.581215 \times 0}{e^{0.5}} = 0.398 \text{ or } 39.8p$$

Alternative approach 2

	Now	At Expiry Either	
	S = £5	S = £7	S = £4
	C = ?	C = £1	C = £0
	(£)	(£)	(£)
Write 3 calls	3C	(3.00)	0.00
Buy 1 shares	(5.00)	7.00	4.00
		4.00	4.00

Thus, the net present value of investing in one share and writing three calls now must be equivalent to receiving a risk-free £4 at the end of the period when risk-free rates of return are 5%. Hence using

$$(hS - C)e^{rt} = hS_u - C_u \;(= hS_d - C_d)$$

gives

$$(\tfrac{1}{3} \times £5.00 - C) \times e^{0.05} = \tfrac{1}{3} \times £7.00 - £1.00 = £1.33\tfrac{1}{3}$$

or: $(£5 - 3C) \times e^{0.05} = £4$

$$£5.00 - 3C = \frac{£4.00}{e^{0.05}} = £3.81$$

$3C = £1.195$

$C = 39.8p$

3. (a) *Diagrammatically*

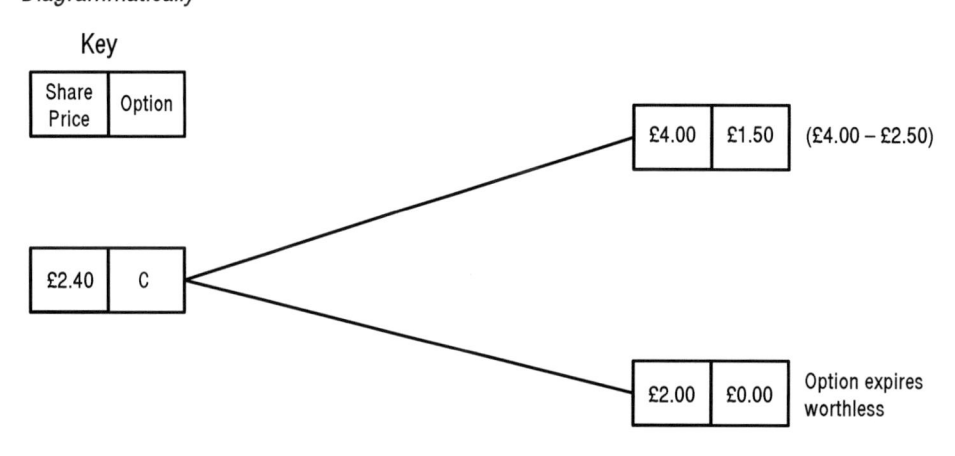

Key

| Share Price | Option |

£2.40 — C

— £4.00 | £1.50 (£4.00 – £2.50)

— £2.00 | £0.00 Option expires worthless

C_u = call value if the share price goes up = £1.50 (£4.00 – £2.50).
C_d = call value if the share price goes down = £0.00 as the option expires worthless.
S_u = share price if it goes up = £4.00.
S_d = share price if it goes down = £2.00.

To achieve a perfect hedge we would need to apply the hedge ratio

$$h = \frac{C_u - C_d}{S_u - S_d} = \frac{£1.50 - £0.00}{£4.00 - £2.00} = \frac{3}{4} = 0.75$$

Alternative approach 1

$$u = \frac{400}{240} = 1.666667$$

$$d = \frac{200}{240} = 0.833333$$

Probability of an upmove

$$p = \frac{e^{rt} - d}{u - d} = \frac{e^{0.06 \times 4/12} - 0.833333}{1.666667 - 0.833333} = 0.224242$$

Call value

$$C = \frac{pC_u + (1-p)C_d}{e^{rt}} = \frac{0.224242 \times 1.50 + 0.775758 \times 0}{e^{0.06 \times 4/12}} = 0.3297 \text{ or } 33.0p$$

Alternative approach 2

Hence to create the perfect hedge on the 30 shares held he should write 40 calls.

	Now	At Expiry Either	
	S = £2.40 C = ?	S = £4.00 C = £1.50	S = £2.00 C = £0.00
	(£)	(£)	(£)
Write 40 calls	40C	(60.00)	0.00
Buy 30 shares	(72.00)	120.00	60.00
		60.00	60.00

Thus, the net present value of holding 30 shares and writing 40 calls now must be equivalent to receiving a risk free £60 at the end of the period when risk free rates of return are 2%. Hence using

$$(hS - C)e^{rt} = hS_u - C_u \; (= hS_d - C_d)$$

gives

$$(0.75 \times £2.40 - C) \times e^{0.06 \times 4/12} = 0.75 \times £4.00 - £1.50 = £1.50$$

$$£1.80 - C = \frac{£1.50}{e^{0.06 \times 4/12}} = £1.470$$

$$C = 33.0p$$

8: OPTIONS PRICING – BINOMIAL AND BLACK SCHOLES

4. (a) *Diagrammatically*

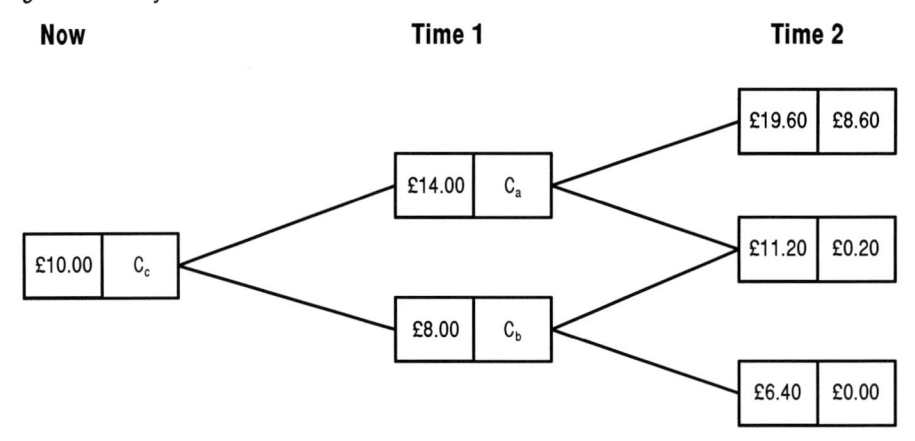

	Now	Time 1	Time 2

£10.00 | C_c

£14.00 | C_a
£8.00 | C_b

£19.60 | £8.60
£11.20 | £0.20
£6.40 | £0.00

(b) *Alternative Approach 1*

u = 1.40

d = 0.80

$R = e^{rt} = e^{0.6 \times 3/12} = e^{0.04}$

Probability of a call upmove

$P = \dfrac{e^{rt} - d}{u - d} = \dfrac{e^{0.04} - 0.80}{1.40 - 0.80} = 0.401351$

Call Values

$C = \dfrac{pC_u + (1-p)C_d}{e^{rt}}$

giving

$C_a = \dfrac{(0.401351 \times 8.60) + (0.598649 \times 0.20)}{e^{0.04}} = 3.431314$

$C_b = \dfrac{(0.401351 \times 0.20) + (0.598649 \times 0)}{e^{0.04}} = 0.077123$

$C_c = \dfrac{(0.401351 \times 3.431314) + (0.598649 \times 0.077123)}{e^{0.04}} = 1.367521$

Call value = £1.3675

Alternative Approach 2

Call Option a?

$h = \dfrac{C_u - C_d}{S_u - S_d} = \dfrac{860p - 20p}{1,960p - 1,120p} = 1$

Hence

$(hS - C_a)e^{rt} = hS_u - C_u$

gives

$(£14.00 - C_a) \times e^{0.04} = £19.60 - £8.60 = £11.00$

$£14.00 - C_a = \dfrac{£11.00}{e^{0.04}} = £10.568784$

$$C_a = £14.00 - £10.5769 = £3.431316$$

Call Option b?

$$h = \frac{C_u - C_d}{S_u - S_d} = \frac{20p - 0p}{1{,}120p - 640p} = \frac{20}{480}$$

Hence

$$(hS - C_b)e^{rt} = hS_u - C_u$$

gives

$$\left(\frac{20}{480} \times £8.00 - C_b\right) \times e^{0.04} = \frac{20}{480} \times £11.20 - £0.20 = £0.266667$$

$$£0.333333 - C_b = \frac{£0.2667}{e^{0.04}} = £0.256211$$

$$C_b = £0.333333 - 0.256211 = 0.077122$$

Call Option c?

$$h = \frac{C_u - C_d}{S_u - S_d} = \frac{343.132p - 7.712p}{1{,}400p - 800p} = \frac{335.42}{600} = 0.559033$$

Hence

$$(hS - C_c)e^{rt} = hS_u - C_u$$

gives

$$\left(\frac{335.42}{600} \times £10.00 - C_c\right) \times e^{0.04} = \frac{335.42}{600} \times £14.00 - £3.431316 = 4.39515$$

$$£5.59033 - C_c = \frac{4.39514}{e^{0.04}} = £4.2228$$

$$C_c = £5.5903 - £4.2228 = £1.3675$$

5. We are looking to byt Euros (Euro call) with dollars, hence the traders base currency is dollars and we are looking for the option price in dollars. Based on this we have

   $\sigma = 0.16$ (16%)
   $r = 0.05$ (5% – traders base currency)
   $y = 0.035$ (3.5% – traded asset/currency yield)

Expected percentage monthly moves

$$u = e^{\sigma\sqrt{t}} = e^{0.16\sqrt{1/12}} = 1.047271$$

$$d = \frac{1}{u} = 0.954862$$

Probability of a call upmove

$$p = \frac{e^{(r-y)t} - d}{u - d} = \frac{e^{(0.05-0.035)1/12} - 0.954862}{1.047271 - 0.954862} = 0.501994$$

Binomial tree – Call prices in brackets

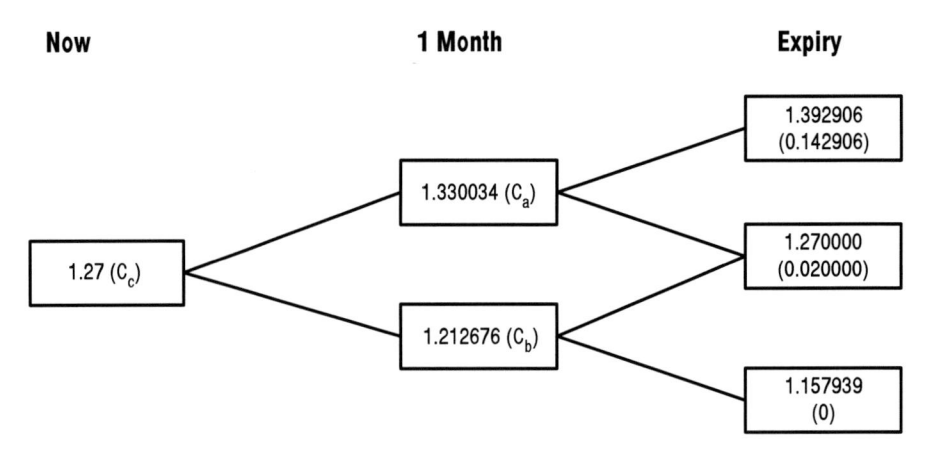

```
            Now              1 Month              Expiry

                                              ┌─────────┐
                                              │ 1.392906│
                                              │(0.142906)│
                                              └─────────┘
                         ┌──────────────┐   ╱
                         │1.330034 (Cₐ) │──
                         └──────────────┘   ╲
                        ╱                    ┌─────────┐
        ┌──────────┐  ╱                      │ 1.270000│
        │1.27 (C_c)│                         │(0.020000)│
        └──────────┘  ╲                      └─────────┘
                        ╲                   ╱
                         ┌──────────────┐ ──
                         │1.212676 (C_b)│   ╲
                         └──────────────┘    ┌─────────┐
                                              │ 1.157939│
                                              │   (0)   │
                                              └─────────┘
```

Call values

Using

$$C = \frac{pC_u + (1-p)C_d}{e^{rt}}$$

gives

$$C_a = \frac{0.501994 \times 0.142906 + 0.498006 \times 0.02}{e^{0.05 \times 1/12}} = 0.081358$$

$$C_b = \frac{0.501994 \times 0.02 + 0.498006 \times 0}{e^{0.05 \times 1/12}} = 0.009998$$

$$C_c = \frac{0.501994 \times 0.081358 + 0.498006 \times 0.009998}{e^{0.05 \times 1/12}} = 0.045630$$

Call price = $0.045630

$$\text{Call delta} = \frac{C_u - C_d}{S_u - S_d} \times e^{-yt} = \frac{0.081358 - 0.009998}{1.330034 - 1.212676} \times e^{-0.035 \times 1/12} = 0.0606283$$

6. We are given

    s = 1,136
    σ = 18% or 0.18
    r = 5% or 0.05
    X = 1,150

   (a) *Non-yielding stock*

    $$d_1 = \frac{\ln\left(\frac{S}{X}\right) + \left(r + 0.5\sigma^2\right)t}{\sigma\sqrt{t}}$$

    $$d_1 = \frac{\ln\left(\frac{1,136}{1,150}\right) + \left(0.05 + 0.5 \times 0.18^2\right) \times \frac{3}{12}}{0.18 \times \sqrt{3/12}}$$

    $$d_1 = \frac{-0.01225 + 0.01655}{0.09} = 0.047793$$

    $d_2 = d_1 - \sigma\sqrt{t} = 0.047793 - 0.18 \times \sqrt{3/12} = -0.042207$

    $N(d_1) = N(0.047793)$

Now N(0.0) = 0.5000

N(0.1) = 0.5398

So by interpolation

$N(d_1) = N(0.047793) = 0.5000 + \dfrac{0.047793}{0.100000} \times (0.5398 - 0.5000) = 0.519022$

$N(d_2) = N(-0.042207) = 1 - N(0.042207)$

By interpolation

$N(0.042207) = 0.5000 + \dfrac{0.042207}{0.100000} \times (0.5398 - 0.5000) = 0.516798$

$N(d_2) = 1 - 0.516798 = 0.483202$

So the call value is

$C = SN(d_1) - Xe^{-rt}N(d_2)$

$C = 1{,}136 \times 0.519022 - 1{,}150 \times e^{-0.035 \times 3/12} \times 0.483202$

$C = 589.608 - 548.779$

$C = 40.829$

By put-call parity, the put value is

$P = C + Xe^{-rt} - S$

$P = 40.829 + 1150 \times e^{-0.05 \times 3/12} - 1136$

$P = 40.544$

Call delta (δ_{call}) = $N(d_1)$ = 0.519022

Put delta (δ_{Put}) = $\delta_{call} - 1$ = 0.519022 − 1 = −0.480978

(b) *Index with 3% yield*

$d_1 = \dfrac{\ln\left(\dfrac{S}{X}\right) + (r - y + 0.5\sigma^2)t}{\sigma\sqrt{t}}$

$d_1 = \dfrac{\ln\left(\dfrac{1{,}136}{1{,}150}\right) + (0.05 - 0.03 + 0.5 \times 0.18^2) \times \dfrac{3}{12}}{0.18 \times \sqrt{3/12}}$

$d_1 = \dfrac{-0.0122486 + 0.00905}{0.09}$

$d_1 = -0.03554$

$d_2 = d_1 - \sigma\sqrt{t} = -0.03554 - 0.18 \times \sqrt{3/12} = -0.12554$

$N(d_1) = N(-0.03554) = 1 - N(0.03554)$

By interpolation

$N(0.03554) = 0.5000 + \dfrac{0.03554}{0.10000} \times (0.5398 - 0.5000) = 0.5141$

$N(d_1) = 1 - 0.5141 = 0.4859$

$N(d_2) = N(-0.12554) = 1 - N(0.12554)$

By interpolation

$$N(0.12554) = 0.5398 + \frac{0.02554}{0.10000} \times (0.5797 - 0.5398) = 0.5499$$

$N(d_2) = 1 - 0.5499 = 0.4501$

So the call value is

$C = Se^{-yt}N(d_1) - Xe^{-rt}N(d_2)$

$C = 1{,}136 \times e^{-0.03 \times 3/12} \times 0.4859 - 1{,}150 \times e^{-0.05 \times 3/12} \times 0.4501$

$C = 547.807 - 511.198$

$C = 36.609$

By put call parity the put value is

$P = C + Xe^{-rt} - Se^{-yt}$

$P = 36.609 + 1{,}150 \times e^{-0.05 \times 3/12} - 1{,}136 \times e^{-0.03 \times 3/12}$

$P = 44.812$

Call delta $(\delta_{Call}) = N(d_1) = 0.4859$

Put delta $(\delta_{Put}) = \delta_{Call} - e^{-yt} = 0.4859 - 0.9925 = -0.5103$

(c) *Currency with 3% interest rate*

Whether the underlying asset is an index with a 3% yield or a currency with a 3% yield makes no difference – it is an asset with a 3% yield. Hence the value would be exactly the same, i.e.

Call value	36.609
Put value	44.812
Call delta	0.4859
Put delta	–0.5103

(d) *Future with up-front premium*

$$d_1 = \frac{\ln\left(\frac{S}{X}\right) + 0.5\sigma^2 t}{\sigma\sqrt{t}}$$

$$d_1 = \frac{\ln\left(\frac{1{,}136}{1{,}150}\right) + 0.5 \times 0.18^2 \times \frac{3}{12}}{0.18 \times \sqrt{3/12}}$$

$$d_1 = \frac{-0.012249 + 0.00405}{0.09} = -0.091096$$

$d_2 = d_1 - \sigma\sqrt{t} = -0.091096 - 0.18 \times \sqrt{3/12} = -0.181096$

$N(d_1) = N(-0.091096) = 1 - N(0.091096)$

By interpolation

$$N(0.091096) = 0.5000 + \frac{0.091096}{0.100000} \times (0.5398 - 0.5000) = 0.536256$$

$N(d_1) = 1 - 0.536256 = 0.463744$

$N(d_2) = N(-0.181096) = 1 - N(0.181096)$

By interpolation

$N(0.181096) = 0.5398 + \dfrac{0.081096}{0.100000} \times (0.5793 - 0.5398) = 0.571833$

$N(d_2) = 1 - 0.571833 = 0.428167$

So the call value is

$C = (SN(d_1) - XN(d_2))e^{-rt}$

$C = (1{,}136 \times 0.463744 - 1{,}150 \times 0.428167)\,e^{-0.05 \times 3/12}$

$C = (526.813 - 492.392) \div 1.012578$

$C = 33.993$

By put-call parity

$P = C + Xe^{-rt} - Se^{-rt}$

$P = 33.998 + 1{,}150 \times e^{-0.05 \times 3/12} - 1{,}136 \times e^{-0.05 \times 3/12}$

$P = 33.993 + 1{,}135.714 - 121.888$

$P = 47.819$

Call delta $(\delta_{Call}) = N(d_1) = 0.463744 \times e^{-0.05 \times 3/12} = 0.45798$

Put delta $(\delta_{Put}) = \delta_{Call} - e^{-rt} = 0.45798 - e^{-0.05 \times 3/12} = -0.52960$

(e) *Futures with margined premium*

d_1, d_2, $N(d_1)$, $N(d_2)$ are as part (d)

So the call value is

$C = SN(d_1) - XN(d_2)$

$C = 1{,}136 \times 0.463744 - 1{,}150 \times 0.428167$

$C = 526.813 - 492.392$

$C = 34.421$

By put-call parity

$P = C + X - S$

$P = 34.421 + 1{,}150 - 1{,}136$

$P = 48.421$

Call delta $(\delta_{Call}) = N(d_1) = 0.463744$

Put delta $(\delta_{Put}) = \delta_{Call} - 1 = 0.463744 - 1 = -0.536256$

7. (a) **Share Price 440**

Change in premium $= \delta \times \Delta S + \tfrac{1}{2}\gamma \times \Delta S^2$

$= -0.54 \times 10 + \tfrac{1}{2} \times 0.004 \times 10^2$

$= -5.2$

This is negative, hence the premium will fall by 5.2p to 32.8p (38.0p – 5.2p).

(b) **Share Price 425**

Change in premium $= \delta \times \Delta S + \frac{1}{2}\gamma \times \Delta S^2$

$= -0.54 \times -5 + \frac{1}{2} \times 0.004 \times (-5)^2$

$= +2.75$

This is positive, hence the premium will rise by 2.75p to 40.75p (38.0p + 2.75p).

9 Equity Derivatives

INTRODUCTION

Equities represent one of the primary investment asset class that a fund manager may hold and one of the primary sources of finance for a business. How we can gain or hedge exposure to equities will be of great importance to these individuals. The specific products available and how they may be used are examined in this section.

CHAPTER CONTENTS

	Page
1 The Cash Market	254
2 Equity Derivatives	254
Chapter Roundup	269
Test Your Knowledge	271

9: EQUITY DERIVATIVES

CHAPTER LEARNING OBJECTIVES

The syllabus areas cover by this section are

- **Uses of futures**

  Types of futures contracts

  Money market, bond, currencies and stock indices

  Hedging

  Students are required to display understanding of the methodology of creating a hedge including:

  – Evaluation of exposure and the setting of objectives – choice of vehicle construction of a hedge ratio.

  – Management of the hedge programme.

- **Uses of options**

  Types of options contracts

  – Stocks
  – Indices

  Primary international exchanges where options are traded.

1 THE CASH MARKET

The cash market for equities needs little introduction. In the UK the focus for trading is the London Stock Exchange, which uses market makers to quote bid/offer prices throughout the day.

2 EQUITY DERIVATIVES

The most important London market for equity futures and options is Euronext.LIFFE. There is, however, another market (OM London Exchange) that trades equity products which, although traded in London, predominantly relates to the Swedish market. OM London Exchange also trades volatility futures.

All Euronext.liffe equity products are cleared by LCH and use SPAN margining systems. Option premiums are paid upfront on equity options.

More details on OM London Exchange are given at the end of the chapter.

2.1 Summary of Euronext.liffe equity products

Futures	
	FTSE 100 (£10 per point)
	FTSE 250 (£10 per point)
	FTSE Eurotop 100 (€20 per point)
	FTSE Eurofirst 80/100 (€10 per point)
	FTSE Eurofirst 300 (€20 per point)
	MSCI Euro/PanEuro (€20 per point)
	Universal stock futures
Options	
	FTSE 100 – Flex Style (£10 per point)
	FTSE 100 – European Style (£10 per point)
	FTSE Eurofirst 80/100 (€10 per point)
	Options on over 90 of the largest UK companies

Contract information correct at December 2006.

2.1.1 Other Exchange-Traded Equity Index Futures

Exchange	Product	Size
Eurex	DAX® future	€25 per point
CME	S&P 500 future	$250 per point

Contract information correct at December 2006.

2.2 Quotation

2.2.1 Index products

The FTSE 100 future is quoted in index and half index points. The size of the contract is a monetary amount determined by a multiplier of £10.

If you bought one future at 5800.0, this would give a contract exposure of £58,000 (5800 × £10). The contract, although it relates to share values, is cash settled and is what is known as a contract for a difference.

Below is the contract specification of Euronext.liffe's FTSE 100 Index Future.

Contract Size	Valued at £10 per index point (e.g. value £65,000 at 6500.0)
Delivery Months	March, June, September, December (nearest four available for trading)
Last Trading Day	10:15 (London time) Third Friday in delivery month
Delivery Day	First business day after the Last Trading Day
Quotation	Index points (e.g. 6500.0)
Minimum Price Movement (Tick Size & Value)	0.05 (£5.00)
Trading Hours	08:00-17:30

Details correct at December 2006.

9: EQUITY DERIVATIVES

Contract standard – Cash settlement based on the Exchange Delivery Settlement Price (EDSP).

EDSP – The value of the FTSE 100 index is calculated by FTSE International by reference to the outcome of the EDSP intra-day auction at the LSE carried out on the last Trading Day.

FTSE options premiums are also quoted in index and half index points although the multiplier here is £10 per index point.

If an investor bought one option with a premium of 35, this would cost £350 (35 × £10).

Below is the contract specification of Euronext.liffe's FTSE 100 Index Option (European Style Exercise).

Contract Size	Valued at £10 per index point (e.g. value £65,000 at 6500.0)
Delivery Months	Nearest eight of Mar, June, Sept, Dec plus such additional months that the nearest four calender months are always available for trading
Exercise Day	Exercise by 18:00 on last trading day
Last Trading Day	10:15 (London time) Third Friday in delivery month
Quotation	Index points (e.g. 6500.0)
Minimum Price Movement (Tick Size & Value)	0.5 (£5.00)
Trading Hours	08:00-16:30

Details correct at December 2006.

Contract standard – Cash settlement based on a Daily Settlement Price for non-expiring series or the Exchange Delivery Settlement Price for expiring series.

Daily Settlement Price – The daily settlement price is based on the 16:30 price of the FTSE 100 Index.

EDSP – The value of the FTSE 100 index is calculated by FTSE International by reference to the outcome of the EDSP intra-day auction at the LSE carried out on the last Trading Day.

Option premium – Payable in full by the buyer on the business day following a transaction.

Exercise price and exercise price intervals – The interval between exercise prices is determined by the time to maturity of a particular expiry month and is either 50 or 100 Index points. The exchange reserves the right to introduce tighter strike intervals (e.g. 25 points) where necessary.

Introduction of new exercise prices – Additional exercise prices will be introduced after the underlying index level has exceeded the second highest, or fallen below the second lowest, available exercise price.

2.2.2 Equity products

Equity options are quoted in pence per share. The consideration for one contract can be calculated by multiplying the premium by the number of shares in the contract (normally 1,000 shares), e.g.

Premium 18p × 1,000 = £180

Below is the contract specification of Euronext.liffe's equity options.

9: EQUITY DERIVATIVES

Unit of Trading	One option normally equals rights over 1,000 shares
Expiry Months	March Cycle (M); means the three nearest expiry months from Mar, June, Sept, Dec cycle
Exercise	Exercise by 17:20 on any business day, extended to 18:00 for all series on a last trading day
Last Trading Day	16:30 (London time) Third Friday in expiry month
Settlement Day	Settlement Day is four business days following the day of exercise/last trading day
Quotation	Pence/share
Minimum Price Movement (Tick Size & Value)	0.5 pence/share (£5.00) or 0.25 pence/share (£2.50) depending on underlying equity
Trading Hours	08:00-16:30

Details correct at December 2006.

Option premium – Payable in full by the buyer on the business day following a transaction.

Exercise price and exercise price intervals – The interval between the exercise prices is set according to a fixed scale determined by the exchange.

Introduction of new exercise prices – Additional exercise prices will be introduced after the underlying index level has exceeded the second highest, or fallen below the second lowest, available exercise price.

2.2.3 Delivery – Index futures

For a FTSE future, whose tick size is 0.5 and tick value is £5.

On 1 June, buy five FTSE futures at 5710

30 June futures settle at EDSP of 5740

To calculate tick movement: $\dfrac{(5740 - 5710)}{0.5} = 60$

Ticks	×	Tick value	×	Contracts
60	×	£5.00	×	5

= £1,500 Cash profit

2.2.4 Delivery – Index options

For a FTSE 100 option, whose tick size is 0.5 and tick value is £5.

Investor A buys one July 4900 call

The expiry value of the index = 4950

Tick movement = $\dfrac{4950 - 4900}{0.5} = 100$

9: EQUITY DERIVATIVES

$$\text{Ticks} \times \text{Tick value} \times \text{Contracts}$$
$$100 \times £5 \times 1$$
$$= £500 \text{ Cash settlement}$$

2.2.5 Delivery – Stock options

Equity options are physically settled by the delivery of shares. Delivery takes place four business days after exercise.

2.3 Special features of Euronext.liffe equity products

2.3.1 Contract size/Exercise price

Companies sometimes announce 'rights issues' and 'scrip issues', and as a result of them, contract size and exercise prices may temporarily change.

2.3.2 Dividends

The ownership of an option or future gives no entitlement to dividends or any other company benefit. If an investor wishes to receive a dividend or benefit, he must own the shares.

2.3.3 Suspension

Dealings in the shares themselves are occasionally suspended by the London Stock Exchange. If this happens, trading in the relevant options is also suspended.

2.4 Pricing stock index futures

2.4.1 Fair value

Exam tip | Pricing is regularly examined.

For a stock index future, such as the FTSE 100, a cash and carry calculation is undertaken. However, as the cash asset here is a basket of equities, the carrying charges are different.

If you own a share, you will receive (at least in times of profit) dividends. These are distributions of unretained profits made by the company. Shares pay income, therefore, the cost of carry equals the finance cost less the dividends.

Let us consider pricing the FTSE 100 future, given the following information.

Date: 25 June
Cash FTSE: 5780
Interest rate: 6% per annum
Dividend yield: 4% per annum
Days till expiry: 91

Cash price	+	**Cost of carry**	=	**Fair value**
5780	+	$\left(5780 \times \dfrac{6-4}{100} \times \dfrac{91}{365}\right)$		
5780	+	28.82	=	5809

The calculation above is naive and we might refine it as follows.

9: EQUITY DERIVATIVES

In the real world, the carrying period of the stock may be slightly different from the financing period, as UK stocks bought today will settle in three business days' time which, depending on bank holiday and weekends, may be between three and seven days. More important than this will be the uncertainty over the flow of dividends.

Traditionally, dividend payments do not occur smoothly over the course of the year, as companies have different year-ends. A large number of companies have a year-end of December or March. This will create an unevenness as to when dividends are paid. Furthermore, the size of such cash flows is unpredictable; companies need only announce their dividends some ten days prior to going ex-dividend. Such uncertainty makes the accurate evaluation of fair value quite difficult.

A more refined method of calculating fair value would be

Formula to learn

> Fair value = Cash price + Cost of carry

where

$$\text{Cost of carry} = \text{Cash price} \times \left(\frac{r}{100} \times \frac{t}{365} - \frac{d}{100} \times \frac{p1}{p2} \right)$$

where

- r = interbank rate for period of t days
- t = number of days three business days from today until three business days after the futures delivery day
- d = percentage annual dividend yield on index
- $p1$ = dividend payments expected between now and futures delivery
- $p2$ = total dividend payments expected in the full year ending on the expiry of the futures contract

A further level of sophistication could be added by compounding the interest at the appropriate intervals and by discounting the dividends to present value (to take account of the fact that dividends may not be paid until perhaps a month or even three months after the ex-dividend date).

Example

Assume an index level of 5800 on 3 January, no increase in dividends from constituent companies over the coming quarter, a 4% yield on the index, a three-month interbank rate of 6.5% with a quarter of the annual dividends being paid in the period to March. What is the fair value of the March future with a delivery date of 17 March?

$$\text{Fair value} = 5800 + \left[5800 \times \left(\frac{6.5}{100} \times \frac{73}{365} - \frac{4}{100} \times \frac{1}{4} \right) \right]$$

$$= 5817.58 \text{ (to nearest tick)}$$

2.4.2 Arbitrage channel

Whilst this is the future's fair price, there is a range within which the future could realistically trade – this is known as the arbitrage channel and comprises transaction costs such as stamp duty, equity dealing spreads and commissions. The width of this channel will vary from user to user. Below are listed some of the key round trip costs for proprietary traders and institutions. (Round trip cost is the cost of opening and closing a position.)

	Percentage	Index Points (@ FTSE 5800)
Equity bid/offer spread*	0.80%	46.40
Stamp duty (purchases only)	0.50%	29.00
Equity commission	0.40%	23.20
FTSE 100 futures spread	0.03%	1.74
FTSE 100 futures commission	0.03%	1.74
Total institutional	1.76%	102.08
Total equity trader (only *)	0.80%	46.40

Example

Calculate the no-arbitrage bid/offer prices for the December FTSE 100 futures for both market makers and non-market makers, given the following information.

Forecast dividend yield	= 4.5% (assume smooth flow)
Funding cost	= 5.75%
Average FTSE equity bid/offer spread	= 0.90%
Stamp duty	= 0.50%
Stock commission (round trip)	= 0.40%
Future commission (round trip)	= 0.30%
FTSE today (mean price)	= 5,800
December expiry	= 15/12/99
Today's date	= 22/09/99

Method

Futures Offer Price, i.e. buy stocks and sell futures.

	(%)
Stock bid/offer spread (Half the spread from the mean price)	0.45
Stock commission	0.40
Future commission	0.30
Stamp duty	0.50
Transaction costs	1.65

Buy stock	5800
+ Transaction costs (5,800 × 1.65%)	95
	5896
+ Finance cost (5896 × 0.0575 × 84/365)	78
− Dividend yield (5800 × 0.045 × 84/365)	(60)
Fair value future offer price	5914

Futures Bid Price, i.e. sell stocks and buy futures.

	(%)
Stock bid/offer spread (half the spread from the mean price)	0.45
Stock commission	0.40
Future commission	0.30
Stamp duty	0.50
Transaction costs	1.65

9: EQUITY DERIVATIVES

Sell stock	5,800
Less costs (5,800 × 1.65%)	(95)
	5705
+ Finance cost (5705 × 0.0575 × 84/365)	75
− Dividend yield (as above)	(60)
Fair value future offer price	5720

If the market maker was to add on a spread of four ticks on the future price, the result would be

Bid: 5720 − 1 = 5719
Offer: 5914 + 1 = 5915

The above calculations indicate the arbitrage channel for an investor who faces all the costs. For a market, the arbitrage channel would be a lot less, due to reduced costs.

For a market maker, the bid/offer prices would be

Futures Offer Price

Stock bid/offer spread   0.9%

Buy stocks	5800
+ Transaction costs (5800 × 0.45%) – half the spread	26
	5826
+ Finance cost (5826 × 0.0575 × 84/365)	77
− Dividend yield	(60)
Fair value future offer price	5843

Futures Bid Price

Sell stock	5,800
Less costs (5800 × 0.45%) – half the spread	(26)
	5774
+ Finance cost (5774 × 0.0575 × 86/365)	76
− Dividend yield	(60)
Fair value future offer price	5790

There is no need to consider the future bid/offer spread. Therefore, the result is

Bid: 5790
Offer: 5843

2.5 Using equity derivatives

Exam tip | The approaches to and results of hedging equity portfolios is regularly examined.

2.5.1 Hedging with futures

What risk will the hedge eliminate?

We have already discussed risk in the context of shares in earlier chapters. It is important at this stage to emphasise that risk is the variability in future returns as measured by the standard deviation (σ).

What causes returns to vary? What risk is there in holding a share? At this point, we need to break risk into two components. The total risk of a security (σ_{total}) is made up of unsystematic risk (σ_u) and systematic risk (σ_s). Mathematically these combine as follows.

9: EQUITY DERIVATIVES

Formula to learn

$$\sigma_{total}^2 = \sigma_u^2 + \sigma_s^2$$

Unsystematic risk, or **specific risk** as it is also called, relates to risk factors specific to a particular company. These would be factors such as management, products, location, etc. These factors will influence a company's returns to some extent. These specific risk factors can be eliminated by holding a diversified portfolio. This is a concept known as modern portfolio theory that we do not need to discuss in any more detail here.

Having eliminated unsystematic (specific) risk of investments through holding a diversified portfolio, for example a portfolio of the FTSE 100 Index stocks, we are still left with the systematic risk of the shares in the portfolio. It is clear that if an investor holds the market portfolio, i.e. FTSE 100 stocks, there is still variability in returns, as evidenced by the movement in the FTSE 100 Index from one day to the next. This variability, or risk, is a function of the market (rather than being a function of things specific to a particular company). It cannot be eliminated by diversification. It is this risk that is eliminated by equities hedging with a suitable derivative, such as the FTSE 100 Index future. What we are saying is that the risk or variability associated with the market (FTSE 100 Index) is eliminated by using a future based on the price movement, or variability, of that index.

Let us first consider the approach of a fund manager holding a portfolio of equities consistent with the make-up of the FTSE 100 Index.

In the UK, to achieve an equities hedge with index futures the fund manager will look to sell FTSE Futures. If the equity market were to fall, the short futures position should generate profits to offset the loss on the equity position, e.g.

Fund manager with £30m portfolio

1 September

FTSE Index 5700. FTSE Future 5720, so at £10 per index point the future can gain/hedge £57,200 of exposure to the index.

How many futures should be sold?

$$\text{Number of contracts} = \frac{\text{Value of portfolio}}{\text{Futures value}} = \frac{£30,000,000}{£57,200}$$

= 524.48, if 524 contracts (nearest whole number)

The example above is somewhat simplistic in that it assumes perfect correlation between the FTSE future and the portfolio being hedged, i.e. the portfolio moves precisely in line with the FTSE 100 index. Of course, this is only likely to be true of an index-tracking fund.

2.5.2 Beta

If we wish to hedge a portfolio that does not match the market we need to consider the beta of the portfolio. The beta of a stock or portfolio is defined as the ratio of the expected change in the price of the stock/portfolio to changes in the market itself. It is obtained by regressing stock prices against the overall market over time. A beta of 1.2, for example suggests, at least historically, that the stock has moved at 1.2 times the rate of the market. If the market were to move by 10%, the stock would be expected to move by 10% × 1.2 or 12%. As the stock in this example is more volatile than the market, more futures would be required to hedge it.

The beta of a portfolio is simply the arithmetic weighted average of the individual stock betas making up the portfolio. The weighting factor is the market value of the stocks. This idea of applying a ratio reflecting relative volatility when calculating the correct hedge ratio is simply an extension of using BPVs when hedging bonds with bond futures.

Example 1

A fund holds the following stocks.

Stock	Holding	Price	Beta
Alpha plc	100,000	£3	1.1
November plc	500,000	£1	0.8
Romeo plc	200,000	£4	1.25

The weighted average beta is

$$\beta_p = \frac{(100,000 \times £3 \times 1.1) + (500,000 \times £1 \times 0.8) + (200,000 \times £4 \times 1.25)}{1,600,000} = \frac{1,730,000}{1,600,000} = 1.08125$$

To calculate the number of futures contracts

$$\text{Number of contracts} = \frac{\text{Value of portfolio}}{\text{Futures value}} \times \text{Portfolio Beta}$$

If the future is 5,700, this becomes

$$\text{Number of contracts} = \frac{£1.6m}{5,700 \times £10} \times 1.08125 = 30 \text{ futures (rounded)}$$

Example 2

On 1 January, a portfolio contains the following stocks.

Value (£m)	Beta
2	0.8
4	1.2
3	1.3
1	0.7
10	

Current FTSE is 5760 and the March futures price is 5800.

How many futures would you use to hedge this portfolio?

1. Calculate the portfolio beta.

$$\beta_p = \frac{(2 \times 0.8) + (4 \times 1.2) + (3 \times 1.3) + (1 \times 0.7)}{10}$$

Beta = 1.1

2. Calculate the number of futures contracts.

$$\text{Number of contracts} = \frac{£10m}{5800 \times £10} \times 1.1$$

= 190 futures

2.5.3 Period of hedge and locked in value

In these foregoing examples, the denominator used to calculate the number of contracts was based on the price of the future. This would certainly be the correct approach if the hedge was for a short time but varies depending on the period of the hedge. If the hedge is going to be held until maturity, then it would be more appropriate to base the denomination on the underlying cash index, **not** the price of the future.

Example

Cash Index = 5800
FTSE 100 Future (trading at a 5% premium to cash) = 6090
Value to be hedged = £6,090,000
Portfolio beta = 1.2

Solution

Scenario 1 – Immediate 2% change

If the index immediately rises by 2% to 5916 then the future should also rise by 2% to 6211.8 a gain of 121.8 points.

Conversely, if the index immediately falls by 2% to 5684 then the future should also fall by 2% to 5968.2, a loss of 121.8 points.

Calculating the number of contracts to hedge the portfolio based on the price of the future we would have

$$\text{Number of contracts} = \frac{£6,090,000}{6,090 \times £10} \times 1.2 = 120 \text{ contracts}$$

The resulting position would be

	2% Increase (£)	2% Decrease (£)
Original portfolio value	6,090,000	6,090,000
Portfolio gain/loss 6,090,000 × 2% × 1.2	146,160	(146,160)
Futures loss/gain 121.8pts × 10 × 120	(146,160)	(146,160)
Locked in value	£6,090,000	£6,090,000

Here the value is the same irrespective of how the index has moved. We have locked in to the current portfolio value of £6,090,000 through this strategy.

Hence, if we are anticipating an immediate change in the index then we can lock in to the current portfolio value if we base the number of contracts on the futures price.

Scenario 2 – 2% change by expiry

At maturity, the futures price will be equal to the cash price. If the index has risen 2% to 5916 the future will be priced at 5916. If the index has fallen 2% to 5684 then the future will be priced at 5684.

Calculating the number of contracts to hedge the portfolio based on the **cash price** we have

$$\text{Number of contracts} = \frac{£6,090,000}{5800 \times £10} \times 1.2 = 126$$

The resulting expiry position would be

	2% Increase (£)	2% Decrease (£)
Original portfolio value	6,090,000	6,090,000
Portfolio gain/loss 6,090,000 × 2% × 1.2	146,160	(146,160)
Futures gain (6090 – 5916) × £10 × 126	(146,160)	
(6090 – 5684) × £10 × 126		511,560
Locked in value	£6,455,400	£6,455,400

Here the value is the same irrespective of how the index has moved. Though it may not be obvious, we have locked in to the value the portfolio would have at an index level equal to the futures price of 6090 as illustrated below.

If the index rises from 5800 to 6090 it has risen 5%. A portfolio with a beta of 1.2 will therefore rise 6% (5% × 1.2)

	(£)
Original portfolio value (index at 5800)	6,090,000
Gain £6,090,000 × 6%	(146,160)
Portfolio value at index level of 6090	£6,455,400

Conclusion

If we are hedging against an immediate price movement we should calculate the number of contracts based on the futures price.

If we are hedging against a price movement and maintaining the hedge until maturity of the contract we should calculate the number of contracts based on the cash price.

It follows that if the hedge were to be lifted part way through the period to maturity we should interpolate between these two numbers of contracts.

Example

Based on the above example, how many contracts are needed to hedge the position for just one third of the period to maturity.

Solution

Since we are closer to the present than to maturity the number of contracts should be nearer to 120 than 126.

$$\text{Number of contracts} = 120 \times \frac{2}{3} + 126 \times \frac{1}{3} = 122 \text{ contracts}$$

Exam tip

For the examination, simply use cash index or the price of the future and state any assumption you feel necessary.

9: EQUITY DERIVATIVES

2.5.4 Protecting and hedging with stock options

Protecting

Protecting equities with options can be achieved in a number of ways. The classic protection strategy for an existing position is achieved by buying puts (a protective put or synthetic long call). This will have the effect of limiting any loss potential if prices fall, whilst leaving profits available if prices rises.

The number of puts to be purchased equals

Formula to learn

$$\text{Number of puts} = \frac{\text{Number of shares held}}{\text{Number of shares per contract}}$$

Thus, for a holding of 100,000 ICI, with ICI options representing 1,000 shares for each contract

$$\frac{100,000}{1,000} = 100 \text{ contracts}$$

Buy **100** put option contracts.

Hedging

Hedging and protection differ in that protection seeks to limit losses whilst retaining the opportunity to make profits. Hedging seeks to eliminate loss potential but, as a consequence, must give up the profit potential. Could we use this above formula to calculate the number of options to hedge a position? The answer is no.

This basic calculation does not take into account the delta of the option – or it assumes the option has a delta of one. From our knowledge of deltas, it is apparent that the number of options required to provide a hedge will have to take into account the price change in the option relevant to the underlying stock. If an option has a delta of 0.5, it will be necessary to double the number of options to correctly hedge any change in the value of the underlying.

The basic calculation will then become

Formula to learn

$$\text{Number of puts} = \frac{\text{Number of shares held}}{\text{Contract size}} \times \frac{1}{\text{Option delta}}$$

We must also remember that the delta of an option constantly changes. Therefore, if a fund manager wishes to actively maintain a delta neutral position, he will have to monitor the deltas constantly and continually adjust the number of options. Any fund manager will have to balance the cost of continually adjusting the hedge ratio against the directional exposure that a non-delta-neutral position will have. Also, as options become more out-of-the-money, the number required to hedge effectively will increase – it will therefore become more effective to use at or in-the-money options. Any hedger using at-the-money options will also have to bear in mind the gamma of the options.

2.5.5 Protecting and hedging with stock index options

Protecting

For a portfolio position we could use the idea we established for futures when looking to protect a portfolio, i.e.

$$\text{Number of puts} = \frac{\text{Value of portfolio}}{\text{Value of put}} \times \text{Portfolio beta}$$

Example 1

The FTSE is at 4710, its yield is 4% and the rate of interest is 10%. You hold a portfolio with a value of £10m and a beta of 2.

How many puts would you buy to protect the portfolio?

Solution 1

$$\text{Number of puts} = \frac{£10m}{4710 \times £10} \times 2$$

$$= 425 \text{ puts (rounded)}$$

Hedging

The previous arguments relating to the delta of the option should, however, also be applied when hedging, giving

$$\text{Number of puts} = \frac{\text{Value of portfolio}}{\text{Value of put}} \times \text{Portfolio beta} \times \frac{1}{\text{Option Delta}}$$

Example 2

The FTSE is at 4840. You intend hedging a £10m portfolio, which has a beta of 1.6, with at-the-money equity index options.

How many puts would you buy?

Solution 2

An at-the-money option has a delta of 0.5, giving

$$\text{Number of puts} = \frac{£10m}{4840 \times £10} \times 1.6 \times \frac{1}{0.5}$$

$$= 661 \text{ (rounded)}$$

2.5.6 Equity derivatives in fund management

Many funds may be designed to track a particular index or to guarantee a certain return relative to a particular index or indices. It is possible that these futures may use equity derivatives to achieve these objectives.

Index tracker funds

This type of fund may offer investors the chance to enjoy the same return as a particular equity index, e.g. FTSE 100.

This could be achieved by a synthetic tracker fund investing in a suitable number of futures contracts, thus gaining the required exposure. This would typically be a non-geared fund. The value of the fund not being used to cover margin requirement would be invested in risk-free assets whose income, together with the change in basis, should equal the total return on the index.

9: EQUITY DERIVATIVES

Guarantee funds

Typically, a guarantee fund will offer a certain return, usually the initial investment, after a particular length of time plus an exposure to an index. These are a couple of ways this can be achieved.

- **Fiduciary calls (or 90/10 fund)**

    The fund manager will invest in risk-free assets to provide the guaranteed sum and then purchase call options to give upside exposure of

    The guaranteed minimum sum will be the terminal value of the risk free investment, i.e.

    $$M = X(1+r)^t$$

    where

    M = guaranteed minimum fund value
    X = investment in risk-free assets
    r = risk-free return
    t = maturity of the fund

    And the number of call options acquired to provide upside exposure will be

    $$N = \frac{V - X}{C}$$

    where

    N = number of options
    V = initial value of the fund
    C = price of a call option

- **Protective Put**

    This will involve the fund manager investing in equities to provide the upside exposure and the purchase of a suitable number of puts plus an investment in risk-free assets to produce the guaranteed sum.

    Here the guaranteed sum will be the terminal value of the risk-free investment plus the strike price (minimum value) of the put option investment, i.e.

    $$M = X(I+r)^t + NK$$

    where

    K = strike price

    And the number of put options acquired will be

    $$N = \frac{(V-X)}{S+P}$$

    Where

    P = where price of a put option
    S = value of stock relating to one option

9: EQUITY DERIVATIVES

Chapter Roundup

- You need to be familiar with the various
    - Equity products available (especially the FTSE index futures and options).
    - Exchanges they are traded on.

- Futures pricing

	Assuming dividends accrue evenly	Based on actual dividend payments
Cash price	C	C
Cost of carry		
– Interest	$C \times t \times \dfrac{t}{365}$	$C \times r \times \dfrac{t}{365}$
– Dividends	$\left(C \times d \times \dfrac{t}{365}\right)$	$\left(C \times d \times \dfrac{P_1}{P_2}\right)$
Futures price	F	F

where

C = Cash price
r = Interbank rate for the period to delivery
t = Time to delivery (in days) – 3 business days from today until 3 business days after delivery
d = Annual dividend yield on the index
P_1 = Dividend payments expected between now and the futures delivery
P_2 = Total dividend payments expected in a full year ending on the expiry of the futures contract

- Hedging with futures/Protecting with options

    Number of contracts = $\dfrac{\text{Portfolio value}}{\text{Futures value}} \times$ Portfolio beta

    where

    - Portfolio beta is the weighted average of the stock betas.
    - Futures value = Future quote × Futures value per point
      (n.b. use cash price quote if hedge is to be held to maturity)

- Hedging with options

    Number of puts = $\dfrac{\text{Portfolio value}}{\text{Options value}} \times$ Portfolio beta $\times \dfrac{1}{\text{Option delta}}$

    where

    Options value = Options quote × Options value per point

9: EQUITY DERIVATIVES

9: EQUITY DERIVATIVES

TEST YOUR KNOWLEDGE

Check your knowledge of the Chapter here, without referring back to the text.

1. The FTSE 100 index stands at 5874 and is yielding 3.36%. If interest rates are 5.25% calculate the price of a FTSE 100 futures contract maturing in 86 days assuming

    (a) Dividends accrue evenly across the year.

    (b) That 37% of the annual dividend will be paid in that period.

    (c) Determine the arbitrage channel to a market maker for scenario (b) if the average equity bid/offer spread on the index is 0.8%.

2. A £26m portfolio contains the following stocks.

Stock	Value (£m)	Beta
A	12	0.8
B	5	1.0
C	4	1.1
D	5	1.2
	26	

If the FTSE 100 index is standing at 6060 and the six month FTSE 100 index future is standing at 6100

    (a) How many FTSE 100 futures contracts are needed to hedge the portfolio against an immediate index movement.

    (b) Calculate the equity value you expect to lock in if you decide to hedge the portfolio to the maturity of the futures contract.

    (c) How many 6100 FTSE 100 index put option contracts would be needed assuming a delta of 0.45.

9: EQUITY DERIVATIVES

TEST YOUR KNOWLEDGE: ANSWERS

1. (a)

	Pts
Cash price	5874.0
Cost of carry	
– Interest $5874 \times 5.25\% \times 86/365 =$	72.5
– Dividends $5874 \times 3.36\% \times 86/365 =$	(46.5)
Futures price	5900.0

(b)

	Pts
Cash price	5874.0
Cost of carry	
– Interest $5874 \times 5.25\% \times 86/365 =$	72.5
– Dividends $5874 \times 3.36\% \times 37\% =$	(73.0)
Futures price	5873.5

(c)

	Bid	Offer
Cash price (Mid)	5874.0	5874.0
Cost of carry		
– Spread $5874 \times 0.4\% =$ (Half the spread each way)	(23.5)	23.5
Cash price (Bid/Offer)	5850.5	5897.5
– Interest $5850.5 \times 5.25\% \times 86/365 =$	72.5	
$5897.5 \times 5.25\% \times 86/365 =$		73.0
– Dividends (as for (b) above)	(46.5)	(46.5)
Futures price (Bid/Offer)	5876.5	5924.0

2. (a) Number of contracts = $\dfrac{\text{Portfolio value}}{\text{Futures value}} \times$ Portfolio beta

Portfolio beta

Stock	Value (£m)	Beta	Value × Beta (£m)
A	12	0.8	9.6
B	5	1.0	5.0
C	4	1.1	4.4
D	5	1.2	6.0
	26		25.0

Portfolio beta = $\dfrac{25}{26}$

Hence

Number of contracts = $\dfrac{26{,}000{,}000}{6100 \times 10} \times \dfrac{25}{26}$ = 409.8 or 410 (rounded)

(b) If we hedge to maturity we would use the cash price rather than the futures price to calculate the number of contracts. By doing this we are locking in the portfolio value corresponding to an index level of 6100 when the current index is 6060, a gain of 40 points in 6060 or 0.66%.

A portfolio with a beta of 1 will therefore rise by 0.66%. A portfolio with a beta of $25/26$ will rise by 0.6345% $(0.6 \times 25/26)$.

Pulling this together

	(£m)
Current portfolio value	26.000
Portfolio gain £26m × 0.6345%	0.165
Locked in value	26.165

(c) Number of puts = $\dfrac{\text{Portfolio value}}{\text{Option value}} \times \text{Portfolio beta} \times \dfrac{1}{\text{Option delta}}$

$= \dfrac{26{,}000{,}000}{6100 \times 10} \times \dfrac{25}{26} \times \dfrac{1}{0.45}$ = 910.7 or 911 (rounded)

10 Bond Derivatives

INTRODUCTION

Alongside equities, bonds represent one of the primary investment asset classes that a fund manager may hold and one of the primary sources of finance for a business. How we gain or hedge exposure to bonds will be of great importance to these individuals. The specific products available and how they may be used are examined in this section.

CHAPTER CONTENTS

	Page
1 What is a Bond?	276
2 Pricing Bonds	280
3 Returns Measures – The Yield	288
4 The Risks of Holding a Bond	294
5 Bond Derivatives	305
Chapter Roundup	327
Test Your Knowledge	329

10: BOND DERIVATIVES

CHAPTER LEARNING OBJECTIVES

The syllabus areas covered by this section are

- **Uses of futures**

    Types of futures contracts

    – Money market, bond, currencies and stock indices.

    Hedging

    Students are required to display understanding of the methodology of creating a hedge including.

    – Evaluation of exposure and the setting of objectives – choice of vehicle contruction of a hedge ratio.

    – Management of the hedge programme.

- **Uses of options**

    Types of options contracts

    – Bonds

    Primary international exchanges where options are traded.

1 WHAT IS A BOND?

1.1 Definition and development

A bond may be defined as a negotiable debt instrument for a fixed principal amount issued by a borrower for a specific period of time, making a regular payment of interest/coupon to the holder until it is redeemed at maturity, when the principal amount is repaid.

Historically, bonds began as very simple negotiable debt instruments, paying a fixed coupon for a specified period, then being redeemed at face value – a 'straight bond'. In the 1960s and 1970s, bond markets were seen as being investment vehicles for 'widows and orphans'. They were thought to be dull markets with predictable returns and very little in the way of gains to be made from trading.

The bond markets emerged from this shadow during the mid-1970s when both interest rates and currencies became substantially more volatile. Bonds have emerged over the past few decades to be much more complex investments, and there are now a significant number of variations on the basic theme.

Whilst it is perhaps easy to be confused by the variety of 'bells and whistles' that have been introduced into the market in recent years, one should always bear in mind that the vast majority of issues are still straight bonds. The reason for this is that investors are wary of buying investments that they do not fully understand. If an issue is too complex, it will be difficult to market.

1.2 Who issues bonds and why

Bonds are used by a number of issuers as a means of raising finance. Major bond issuers include the following.

- **Sovereign governments** – who need to raise finance to help them cover any national debt or budget shortfall.

- **Local authorities** – who need to raise finance to help them cover any local budget shortfall.
- **Companies** – who need to raise cash to help them finance business requirements.

Regardless of who the issuer is, there are a number of general characteristics that any bond is likely to have which we will examine next.

1.3 General characteristics

Examining the above definition in a little more detail reveals the general characteristics that a bond may have.

1.3.1 Negotiable instrument

Negotiability means that it is a piece of paper that can be bought and sold. For certain types of bonds, this is easier than for others. Government bonds tend to be highly liquid, i.e. very easy to buy or sell, whereas certain corporate bonds are almost illiquid and are usually held to maturity by the initial buyer.

1.3.2 Nominal value

As we noted above, all bonds are issued for a fixed principal amount or nominal value, which historically represented the amount invested. On UK bonds, it is normal to have a bond nominal value of £100, and bond prices are quoted on this basis. This nominal value serves two important purposes.

- Determining the scale of the coupon payments.
- Determining the value of the redemption proceeds.

We will discuss both purposes below.

1.3.3 Maturity

Initially, all bonds were redeemable after a specific maturity date, which determines when the principal is due for repayment. However, there are now a number of variations we will need to consider. We can subcategorise bonds between

- Redeemable bonds.
- Irredeemable/perpetual bonds.

Redeemable bonds

The majority of bonds fall into this category, though there are some subsets which we will need to consider, as follows.

- **Single-dated bonds** – bonds which mature at a pre-set date only.
- **Double-dated bonds** – bonds that can be redeemed by the issuer between specified dates. On a double-dated bond, the earlier date specifies when the issuer may redeem, the later date specifies when the bond must be redeemed.
- **Callable bonds** – where the issuer of the bond is able to redeem the bond at an earlier date, should they wish to do so. Double-dated bonds may be considered as a subset of callable bonds, though callable bonds may have many other features (e.g. call premiums) and may be callable throughout their lives.
- **Putable bonds** – a more recent innovation, which gives the holder the ability to sell the bond back to the issuer at a premium over the face value.

Irredeemable bonds

On irredeemable or perpetual or undated bonds, there is no maturity date and the issuer is under no obligation to redeem the principal sum, though he may have the right to do so if he wishes. On these bonds, the coupon will be paid into perpetuity.

1.3.4 Coupon

The basis for the determination of the bond coupon is set before issue, though this does not mean that the value is known at that date. Whilst the vast majority of bonds issued are straights (i.e. a fixed coupon), there are a number of variants on this theme. In addition, there are bonds whose coupons vary with economic factors. We may, therefore, categorise bond coupons between

- Pre-determined.
- Variable.

However the amount is calculated, the full coupon for the period will be paid to the holder of the bond on the ex-div date.

Pre-determined coupons

This category would include, as we have already stated, the vast majority of bonds. On these bonds, the gross annual coupon (i.e. the amount due to be paid in a one-year period, irrespective of the frequency of payment) is specified as a percentage of the nominal value of the bond. Sub-classes here would include

- **Straight/fixed coupon bonds** – where the coupon is at a set level for the entire life of the bond.
- **Stepped coupon bonds** – where the coupon increases in steps to pre-specified amounts as the bond moves through its life.
- **Zero-coupon bonds** – bonds that carry no coupon and simply redeem at face value at maturity. On such bonds, the investors realise a return by paying only a fraction of the face value.

Variable coupons

This category would include

- **Floating rate bonds** – where the coupon varies as interest rates vary.
- **Index-linked bonds** – where the coupon and redemption proceeds figures get scaled for the effects of inflation.

1.3.5 Coupon frequency

The frequency of the payment of the coupons is predetermined before issue, normally following the local market conventions. As a result, all investors will (or should) be aware of those dates.

Conventions regarding the frequency of payment differ between the various bond markets. Some markets have a convention of paying semi-annual coupons, as is the case in the UK and the US, whereas other markets, in particular the Eurobond market, France and Germany, pay coupons on an annual basis.

1.3.6 Recipient

The norm is that the holder of the bond receives all of the asset flows from that bond throughout its life to the maturity date. There are, however, some markets where it is possible to strip the coupons and the bond apart so that the holder of the underlying bond may receive the redemption proceeds, whilst the coupons (the 'tint') are paid to another party.

1.3.7 Redemption at maturity

As we noted above, it is possible for bonds to be issued that will not redeem at maturity, namely irredeemables. Most bonds are, however, redeemed though (once again) there are a few variations to be aware of. The primary consideration here is the form that the redemption proceeds takes, which may be either

- Cash.
- Other assets.

Cash redemption proceeds

Once more, the vast majority of bonds fall into this category whereby the bonds are redeemed in cash at maturity. This redemption may be

- **At par value** – redeemed at the nominal value of the bond at the redemption date.
- **At a premium** – redeemed at a specified premium above the nominal value of the bond at the redemption date.

Other assets

Instead of obliging the issuer to repay cash at maturity, the bond may offer the holder the choice between normal cash redemption proceeds and some other asset, such as

- An alternative bond of a later maturity.
- Shares issued by a corporation.

1.4 UK Government bonds – gilts

1.4.1 Characteristics

Governments, as a rule, spend more money in a year than they raise in revenue. Consequently, they are obliged to borrow money to cover the deficit. Due to their high credit rating, they are able to borrow substantial sums with a wide range of maturities. The combination of this high credit rating and the size of the issues attracts investors. Government debt markets are the largest markets in the world in terms of activity.

1.4.2 Gilts

Gilts are UK government bonds. Historically, they were issued and managed by the Bank of England on behalf of the government; however, this role is now undertaken by the Debt Management Office (DMO).

Let us take a typical issue and examine the key features.

Treasury	12½%	2007-9	@	126.56
|	|	|		|
Name	**Coupon**	**Maturity**		**Price**

Name

Each stock bears a title. Treasury, Exchequer, Funding, Conversion, Consolidated (Consols), and War Loan are names used to indicate the government department that issued the debt. The names are irrelevant, since all debt is the government's debt and ranks equally.

Coupon

This is the rate of interest that will be paid each year based on the nominal value of the stock. In the UK, the convention is for this coupon to be paid on a semi-annual basis, in equal instalments. However, the 2½% consolidated stock pays on a quarterly basis.

Maturity

This is the date on which the government has agreed to repay the debt. In this case, the government has issued debt with two dates. The government has reserved its right to redeem the debt from 2007, but must redeem the stock by 2009. The decision on redemption will be taken with reference to the coupon. If the government is able to replace the borrowing at a cheaper rate, then it will redeem the stock on the earlier of the two dates. Gilt-edged stocks are classified with respect to their maturity dates. The official Debt Management Office definitions are as follows.

- **Shorts** – gilts with **7 years or less** to run.
- **Mediums** – gilts with **between 7 and 15 years** until redemption.
- **Longs** – gilts with **over 15 years** until redemption.

Double-dated stocks are normally classified using the later of the two dates, since this is the point on which redemption has to take place.

In the past, the government has been able to issue some bonds without specifying a date on which redemption will take place. These **undated stocks** are all redeemable from a certain date. For example, the Treasury 3% 66 **Aft** has been redeemable since (**or after**) 1966, however, unlike double-dated stocks, there is no date by which the issue must be redeemed.

Price

This is quoted in terms of the amount that an investor would have to pay in order to buy £100 nominal of the stock. Technically, an investor can buy as much as they want of a gilt. The market simply adopts this as a convention for the quote. The price is quoted in pounds and pence (decimal terms).

Yield

In the *Financial Times*, both the Flat and Gross Redemption Yield (GRY) are published. By convention, the yield figures shown for gilts is twice the six-monthly yield, **not** the six-monthly yield compounded.

2 PRICING BONDS

Exam tip | You may be required to undertake basic bond pricing.

2.1 Introduction

Since the cash flow values and timings from a bond are known with such certainty, at least for a straight bond, the application of DCF evaluation techniques is clearly appropriate.

There are, however, two bond pricing aspects to consider.

- DCF evaluation.
- Clean and dirty bond pricing.

The first of these ideas is the method that we will primarily use to evaluate a bond, the second of these is relevant for determining the correct tax treatment.

2.2 Discounted cash flow evaluation

2.2.1 Fixed coupon bonds

Annual coupon redeemables

A straight redeemable bond pays a coupon to the maturity date, then pays the redemption proceeds at that date. If we know the required return to the bondholders, we can, evaluate this bond using DCF. If the bond is of a fairly short maturity, we may consider each cash flow separately. If, however, the bond is longer dated, it would be more convenient to apply the idea and calculation of an annuity.

Example

A bond pays an annual coupon of 9% and is redeemable at par in three years. Evaluate this bond if interest rates are

- 8%
- 9%
- 10%

Solution

Interest rate at 8%

Time	Cash Flow (£)	DF (8%)	Present Value (£)
1	9.00	$\dfrac{1}{1.08}$	8.33
2	9.00	$\dfrac{1}{1.08^2}$	7.72
3	109.00 (100.00 + 9.00)	$\dfrac{1}{1.08^3}$	86.53
			102.58

Interest rate at 9%

Time	Cash Flow (£)	DF (9%)	Present Value (£)
1	9.00	$\dfrac{1}{1.09}$	8.26
2	9.00	$\dfrac{1}{1.09^2}$	7.57
3	109.00	$\dfrac{1}{1.09^3}$	89.17
			100.00

10: BOND DERIVATIVES

Interest rate at 10%

Time	Cash Flow (£)	DF (9%)	Present Value (£)
1	9.00	$\dfrac{1}{1.10}$	8.18
2	9.00	$\dfrac{1}{1.10^2}$	7.44
3	109.00	$\dfrac{1}{1.10^3}$	89.89
			97.51

Conclusion

This example illustrates two important features about bonds, specifically

- There is an **inverse relationship between bond prices and interest rates**, i.e. as interest rates rise, market values fall (and vice versa).
- When the **coupon rate on the bond is equal to the prevailing interest rate, the bond will be valued at par**, as illustrated above when interest rates are 9%.

It is vital that you are aware of, and comfortable with, these two conclusions. Their appreciation is essential for the effective appraisal of a bond investment or the management of a bond portfolio.

This calculation may be expressed mathematically as follows.

Formula to learn

$$\text{Straight bond price} = \frac{C_1}{(1+r)} + \frac{C_2}{(1+r)^2} + \frac{C_3}{(1+r)^3} + \cdots + \frac{C_n + R}{(1+r)^n}$$

where

r = investor's required return

We shall refer to this formula from time to time, however, the above tabular approach to the calculation is probably most convenient.

Example

Calculate the value of the above bond at 10%, assuming it matures in eight years.

Solution

This bond will pay its coupon for the next eight years and then be redeemed. Its value will, therefore, be as follows.

Time	Cash Flow (£)	DF (10%)	Present Value (£)
1-8	9.00	$\dfrac{1}{0.10}\left(1-\dfrac{1}{1.10^8}\right)$	48.01
8	100.00	$\dfrac{1}{1.10^8}$	46.65
			94.66

Semi-annual coupon redeemables

When we have a semi-annual coupon (e.g. gilts), we should discount the semi-annual cash flows at the semi-annual rate. **NB:** the market convention for gilts is to quote the annual yield by simply doubling the semi-annual figure.

Example

Evaluate a five-year 10% gilt on a quoted GRY of 8%.

Solution

This bond will pay a £5 coupon every six months for the next five years and then be redeemed at par. The appropriate rate for discounting these semi-annual flows is 4% (the semi-annual rate based on the above market convention). Its value will therefore be

Time (½ years)	Cash Flow (£)	DF (4%)	Present Value (£)
1-10	5.00	$\frac{1}{0.04}\left(1-\frac{1}{1.04^{10}}\right)$	40.55
10	100.00	$\frac{1}{1.04^{10}}$	67.56
			108.11

Irredeemables

When we have an irredeemable bond, we are evaluating a perpetuity stream of cash flows.

Example

Evaluate a 9% irredeemable, assuming interest rates are 10%.

Solution

Time (½ years)	Cash Flow (£)	DF (4%)	Present Value (£)
1-∞	9.00	$\frac{1}{0.10}$	90.00
			90.00

Strips

The price of a strip is calculated using the above ideas (adjusted to reflect the semi-annual convention in the gilts market) as for a zero-coupon bond.

Formula to learn

$$\text{Price} = \frac{£100}{(1+r)^n}$$

10: BOND DERIVATIVES

where

r = semi-annual GRY
n = number of ½ years to redemption

2.2.2 Floating rate note (FRN)

With a floating rate bond, the coupon rate is reset at each payment date (or possibly even more regularly) to prevailing interest rates. The implication of this is that at a reset date the bond will be valued at par based on the relationship that we established above. In addition, the cash value of the next coupon has now been set. Though all subsequent coupons will still be reset at the next reset date if interest rates move, the next coupon will not be.

This resetting of the coupon at each payment date ensures that the clean price of an FRN is always close to par.

FRNs therefore safeguard the par value of the investment rather than showing great swings in value as interest rates fluctuate (as is demonstrated by normal bonds).

To evaluate a FRN, we have a choice of methods, specifically

- First principles.
- A more practical alternative.

First principles

From first principles, we can evaluate the FRN using the relationship

$$\text{Price} = \frac{C_1}{(1+r)} + \frac{C_2}{(1+r)^2} + \frac{C_3}{(1+r)^3} + \cdots + \frac{C_n + R}{(1+r)^n}$$

The difficulty with this approach is that we do not know what the future coupons will be.

Example

The current interest rate is at 10% and expected to remain at that level for the foreseeable future. A floating rate note (FRN) has just paid its most recent annual coupon, and future coupons have been reset to 10%. Calculate the current market value of the FRN.

Solution

$$\text{Price} = \frac{10}{1.10} + \frac{10}{1.10^2} + \frac{10}{1.10^3} + \cdots + \frac{110}{1.10^n} = £100.00$$

Practical alternative

A more flexible alternative is to imagine that the bond may be sold at the next reset date at its par value. Though it is not necessary that the holder intends to sell at this date, it is always an option open to him and hence can validly be used to determine the current price. Based on this idea, we could establish the market value of this FRN as follows.

Formula to learn

$$\text{FRN Price} = \frac{\text{Next coupon} + \text{Par value}}{(1+r)^n}$$

Example

Calculate the current market value of the above FRN, if

- Interest rates stay at 10%.
- Interest rates suddenly leap to 11% and are expected to remain at that level.

Solution

Interest at 10%

$$\text{Price} = \frac{10 + 100}{1.10} = £100.00$$

Interest at 11%

In this situation, the next coupon in one year's time will remain at £10, its value determined at the last reset date. All further coupons will, however, be reset to £11 at the next date (assuming no further interest rate changes), giving rise to a par value at that time. The current market value is therefore

$$\text{Price} = \frac{10 + 100}{1.11} = £99.10$$

As we indicated above, however, the advantage of this method comes when we are evaluating the FRN between coupon payment dates. This can be easily achieved by a simple modification to the formula to give the general expression

Formula to learn

$$\text{FRN price} = \frac{\text{Next coupon} + \text{Par value}}{(1+r)^n}$$

where

n = time to the next coupon

Example

Calculate the market value of the above FRN if we are three months into the annual coupon payment period and interest rates have moved to 11%.

Solution

$$\text{Price} = \frac{10 + 100}{1.11^{3/4}} = £101.75$$

You will note that the bond is valued above par even though the interest rate exceeds the value of the next coupon. That is as a result of the three months' accrued interest in this FRN at that date (see clean and dirty pricing later).

Conclusion

FRN prices vary with

- Accrued interest.
- Interest rates.

10: BOND DERIVATIVES

Although the resetting of the coupon at each repayment date ensures that the clean price is always close to par.

As we noted above, FRNs safeguard the par value of the investment rather than showing great swings in value as interest rates fluctuate (as is demonstrated by normal bonds). What they do not do, however, is safeguard against any loss of real value due to the effects of inflation.

2.3 Clean and dirty prices

Exam tip | The ideas here of dirty pricing and accrued interest are directly relevant to derivatives pricing and need to be clearly understood.

2.3.1 Introduction

A further pricing aspect is clean and dirty pricing, the distinction being made for tax purposes as income and capital gains may be taxed differently on bonds.

The value of a bond has two elements, the underlying capital value of the bond itself (the **clean price** which is quoted) and the coupon that it is accruing over time (**accrued interest**). Periodically, this coupon is distributed as income to the holders or, more specifically, the individual who was the registered holder on the ex-div date (which for gilts is normally, **seven business days** prior to payment date).

The **dirty price** calculated above using DCF is the price that is paid for a bond, which combines these two elements. Consequently, ignoring all other factors that might affect the price, a dirty price will rise gradually as the coupon builds up and then falls back as the stock is either marked ex-div or pays the dividend.

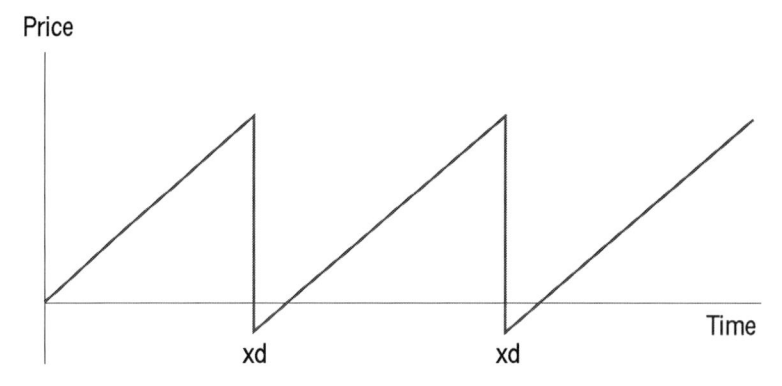

The advantage that this offered investors in the past was that rather than claiming the dividend, they could sell the bond at the high price just prior to the payment of the dividend, and this gain would be free of tax. This process was known as **bond washing**. In February 1986, the UK moved to a system of clean pricing that separates the two elements.

Under clean pricing, whenever an investor purchases a bond, they pay the quoted price (the **clean price**), which represents the capital value of the underlying bond with an allowance made for the interest element, allowing the two elements (income and gain) to be taxed separately.

2.3.2 Cum dividend bargains

A purchase made before the ex-div date is referred to as a cum div bargain. In this situation, the buyer of the bond will be the holder on the next ex-div date and will, therefore, receive the full coupon for the period. The seller, however, has held the bond for part of this period and is therefore entitled to a part of that coupon. To account for this, the purchaser of the bond must compensate the seller for the dividend which he has earned.

Example

```
Last coupon                              Next coupon
    |―――――――――――――●―――――――――――――|
                Purchase
```

As a result, the purchaser will pay the clean price plus the interest from the last payment date up to the purchase. On the next payment date, the holder will receive the whole of the interest for the six months. However, on a net basis, they will only have received the interest for the period of ownership.

The formula used by the Debt Management Office in the gilts market is

$$\text{Dirty price} = \text{Clean price} + \text{Periods coupon} \times \frac{\text{Days}}{\text{Days in period}}$$

where

Days = number of days from the last coupon payment date up to and including the calendar day before the settlement day (next business day following the trade)

Days in period = number of days from the last coupon payment date up to and including the calendar day before the next coupon

Thus, the periods coupon is spread over the number of days in the period, giving a coupon per day, then allocated to the relevant holder on a daily basis.

Example

Coupons are paid on 1 April and 1 October. On 10 July, an investor buys £10,000 nominal of Treasury 8% @ 101.50 for settlement on 11 July. How much is paid?

Solution

		(£)
Clean Price	£10,000 @ 101.50	10,150.00
Accrued Interest	(£10,000 × 4% = £400) × $\frac{101}{183}$	220.77
Dirty Price		10,370.77

The number of days having been calculated as follows.

Month		Days	Days in Period
April	**From last coupon (inclusive)**	30	30
May		31	31
June		30	30
July	**To day before settlement**	10	31
August			31
September			30
		101	183

10: BOND DERIVATIVES

2.3.3 Ex-dividend bargains

An ex-div bargain is one occurring after the ex-div date, but before the coupon is paid. Gilt-edged stocks, for example, are usually marked ex-div seven business days prior to the payment day in order to allow the DMO to ensure that the dividend is paid to the appropriate party. Any person buying the stock after it has been marked Ex will not, therefore, be entitled to the interest. Consequently, the pricing must reflect this.

Example

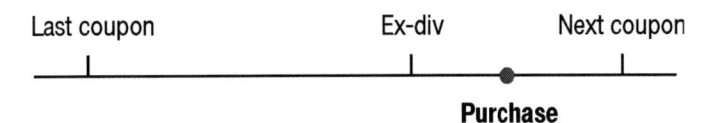

```
Last coupon              Ex-div         Next coupon
     |_____|_____●_____|
                            Purchase
```

In this situation, the buyer of the bond will be entitled to the coupon for the last few days of the period, but will receive nothing, as this will all go to the seller who held at the ex-div date. He will, therefore, require this to be adjusted in the price.

Accordingly, he pays the clean price as determined by the market less the number of days worth of interest that he is not receiving.

The formula used in this situation by the Debt Management Office in the gilts market is

Formula to learn

$$\text{Dirty price} = \text{Clean price} - \text{Periods coupon} \times \frac{\text{Days}}{\text{Days in period}}$$

where

Days = number of days from the settlement day (next business day) to the calendar day before the next coupon payment date (inclusive)

Days in period = number of days from the last coupon payment date up to and including the calendar day before the next coupon

3 RETURNS MEASURES – THE YIELD

Exam tip

You are unlikely to be asked to undertake yield calculations but you are expected to know what they represent

The value of any investment will depend on the return that it generates and the risks inherent in those returns. In bond markets, the single most important measure of return is the bond yield. There are, however, several different yield measures which we may wish to calculate, each having its own uses and limitations. For each of these measures, we need to know

- How it is calculated.
- Its uses.
- Its limitations.

3.1 The Flat Yield

3.1.1 Calculation

The simplest measure of the return used in the market is the flat (interest or running) yield. This measure looks at the annual cash return (coupon) generated by an investment as a percentage of the cash price. In simple terms, what is the regular annual return that you generate on the money that you invest?

Formula to learn

$$\text{Flat yield} = \frac{\text{Annual coupon rate}}{\text{Market price}}$$

Example

We hold 10% Loan stock (annual coupon) redeemable at par in four years. The current market price is £97.25. Calculate the flat yield.

Solution

The flat yield for the above would be

$$\text{Flat Yield} = \frac{10.00}{97.25} = 0.10283 \text{ or } 10.283\%$$

3.1.2 Uses

This measure assesses the annual income return only and is most appropriate when either

- We are dealing with irredeemables, which pay no return other than a coupon into perpetuity; or
- Our priority is the short-term cash returns that the investment will generate.

3.1.3 Limitations

This measure, while of some limited use (particularly in the short term), has three important drawbacks for the investment markets.

- In addition to the coupon flows, bonds may have returns in the form of the redemption moneys. Where the bond has been purchased at a price away from par, this will give rise to potential gains and losses, which are excluded from the calculation.

- The calculation completely ignores the timing of any cash flows and the time value of money.

- With some bonds (floating rate notes or FRNs), the return in any one period will vary with interest rates. If the coupon is not constant, then this measure is only of historic value unless the predicted return is used.

These limitations combine to make the flat yield of only marginal use.

3.2 The Japanese Gross Redemption Yield

3.2.1 Calculation

The idea behind the Japanese Gross Redemption Yield (GRY) calculation is to overcome the first of the limitations of the flat yield noted above, specifically that any gains or losses to redemption are ignored. This measure recognises that the total return in any period is a combination of both income and capital components, i.e. the coupon received plus any gain (minus any loss) for the period.

The Japanese method for calculating the GRY is to take the flat yield and then add the average annual capital gain (or deduct the average annual loss) to redemption, stated as a percentage of the current market price. Thus, we can state the Japanese GRY as follows.

Formula to learn

$$\text{Japanese GRY} = \frac{\text{Annual coupon rate}}{\text{Market price}} + \frac{\text{Average annual capital gain to redemption}}{\text{Market price}}$$

Or

$$\text{Japanese GRY} = \frac{\text{Annual coupon rate}}{\text{Market price}} + \frac{\frac{\text{Redemption price} - \text{Market price}}{\text{Years to redemption}}}{\text{Market price}}$$

Example

We hold 10% Loan stock (annual coupon) redeemable at par in four years. The current market price is £97.25. Calculate the Japanese GRY.

Solution

The Japanese GRY for the above would be

$$\text{Japanese GRY} = \frac{10.00}{97.25} + \frac{\frac{100.00 - 97.25}{4}}{97.25}$$

$$= \frac{10.00}{97.25} + \frac{0.6875}{97.25}$$

$$= 0.10283 + 0.00707 = 0.10990 \text{ or } 10.99\%$$

3.2.2 Uses

The main use of this method is to provide a quick and easy way of assessing the GRY that takes into account all of the returns, income and capital.

It should be noted that it is not an absolutely accurate measure of return, since it assumes linear capital growth rather than the more realistic compound growth. As a result, it is liable to overstate the effects of any capital gain or loss. Furthermore, this inaccuracy increases the further away a bond is from maturity.

It does, however, serve as a useful tool in determining the true GRY as we illustrate below.

3.2.3 Limitations

Whilst this method does overcome the first limitation of the flat yield, i.e. its failure to account for any capital gains or losses to redemption, it does not overcome the other noted drawbacks, specifically

- The calculation completely ignores the timing of any cash flows and the time value of money.
- With some bonds (FRNs), the return in any one period will vary with interest rates. If the coupon is not constant, then this measure is only of historic value unless the predicted return is used.

The first of these limitations can only be overcome through the use of discounted cash flow techniques as illustrated below. The second is a valid limitation of all yield measures.

3.3 Gross redemption yield

3.3.1 Calculation

Introduction

The gross redemption yield (GRY) resolves the issue of the redemption values **and** the time value of money by using discounted cash flow techniques.

The gross redemption yield is the internal rate of return (IRR) of

- The dirty price paid to buy the bond.
- The gross coupons received **to redemption**.
- The final redemption proceeds.

Mathematical formulation

This could be expressed mathematically as follows.

When GRY = r, then

Formula to learn

$$\text{Price} = \sum \frac{C_t}{(1+r)^t} + \frac{R}{(1+r)^n}$$

Alternatively, this may be expressed as

Formula to learn

$$\text{Price} = \frac{C_1}{(1+r)} + \frac{C_2}{(1+r)^2} + \frac{C_3}{(1+r)^3} + \cdots + \frac{C_n + R}{(1+r)^n}$$

It should be noted that these formulae **cannot** be algebraically solved (except in very rare circumstances) and that the process of interpolation described below represents the only practical method.

Interpolation approach

The interpolation approach is based on the fact that there is an inverse relationship between yields and bond prices, i.e. as yields rise, bond prices fall, and vice versa.

In order to calculate the GRY, we select two interest rates and calculate the net present value of the bond cash flows at each of these two rates. These calculations establish two reference points in terms of values and rates, which can be used to determine a linear relationship between changes in the bond price and changes in interest rates. We can then interpolate between the two, i.e. use this relationship to establish what rate gives rise to a zero NPV, giving the GRY (IRR).

The true relationship between bond prices and interest rates is **not** linear, hence this calculation is only an approximation.

This process is graphically illustrated below for our 10% four-year Loan stock, where 5% and 15% have been used as reference rates.

10: BOND DERIVATIVES

— Actual relationship between prices and yields
--- Interpolated linear relationship using 5% and 15%

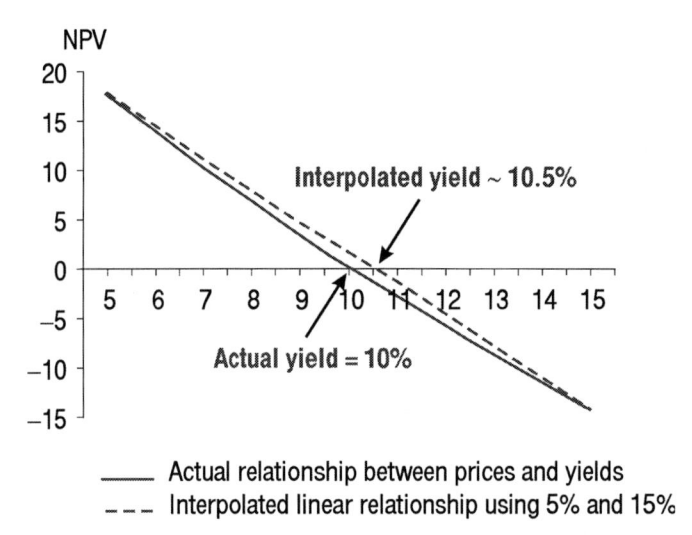

As this diagram illustrates, the process of interpolation is not absolutely accurate since, as we have already noted, the relationship between prices and interest rates is **not** linear. Furthermore, this inaccuracy increases if the two reference points are widely dispersed. It is therefore essential that our two selected rates are close to the actual GRY in order to produce an accurate result.

To get an indication of which rates are suitable, we should use either

- The conclusions established above regarding coupon rates, interest rates and bond prices; or
- The flat yield or Japanese GRY assessments.

Example

We hold 10% Loan stock (annual coupon) redeemable at par in four years. The current market price is £97.25. Calculate the GRY.

Solution

Assessing the rates to try based on current market value

Since the current market value is below par, it must be that the coupon rate is below prevailing interest rates or the yield. As a result, we should select some higher rates for our GRY computation. We could perhaps try 11% as our first reference point, then select something slightly higher or lower for the second, depending on what results were obtained from the first.

Assessing the rates to try based on flat yield and Japanese GRY

The flat yield completely ignores any gain (or loss) to redemption and hence will understate (overstate) the GRY. We established above that the flat yield (coupon return) on this bond is 10.283%.

The Japanese GRY overstates the effect of any gain or loss to redemption as we noted above, hence it will overstate the GRY if there is a gain, and understate it if there is a loss. We established above that the Japanese GRY on this bond is 10.99%.

The flat yield and Japanese GRY therefore represent two rates, one of which is normally higher than the GRY, and one of which is normally lower, though both may well be close to it. As such, they may well represent two good reference rates to try in our interpolation process.

Note that we said **normally** higher/lower, not always. There is one circumstance where this is not the case and this is when a bond is valued at par. In this situation, there will be no gain or loss to redemption and hence, all three measures will produce the same return.

The relationship between these three measures could be summarised as follows.

Bond Value	Relationship
Above par (loss to redemption)	Flat yield > GRY > Japanese GRY
At par	Flat yield = GRY = Japanese GRY
Below par (gain to redemption)	Flat yield < GRY < Japanese GRY

Conclusion

Whichever method we use to establish reference rates, we need to try rates above 10% for this example. The approach would be to select and try one rate, say 11%, and see if this gives a positive or negative NPV. If the NPV is positive, then our second selected rate needs to be even higher to try to establish a negative NPV, on the basis of the inverse relationship between prices and interest rates. Conversely, if the NPV is negative, then the second selected rate needs to be lower.

In this example, a rate of 11% was tried first, giving a negative NPV. A second (lower) rate of 10.5% was then selected, giving a positive figure.

Using the annuity formula

Time	Cash Flow (£)	DF (10.5%)	Present Value (£)	DF (11%)	Present Value (£)
0	(97.25)	1	(97.25)	1	(97.25)
1-4	10.00	$\frac{1}{0.105}\left(1-\frac{1}{1.105^4}\right)$	31.36	$\frac{1}{0.11}\left(1-\frac{1}{1.11^4}\right)$	31.03
4	100.00	$\frac{1}{1.105^4}$	67.07	$\frac{1}{1.11^4}$	65.87
Net present value			1.18		(0.35)

Yield assessment

We have found that the rate of 10.5% is too low and 11% is too high, hence the GRY lies between these two points.

The total range of values covered as a result of this 0.5% (11% − 10.5%) yield difference is a value of £1.53 (£1.18 + £0.35). We need to move so far from 10.5% towards 11% that we eradicate £1.18 of this £1.53. The GRY is, therefore

$$\text{GRY} = 10.5 + \frac{118}{153} \times (11.0 - 10.5) = 10.886\%$$

NB: The actual GRY is 10.8842%, hence this calculation has proved accurate to better than one basis point. If we required any greater accuracy, we could reassess the GRY taking 10.886% as a starting reference rate and continuing through a process of iteration with closer reference rates until we achieve the level of accuracy required.

3.3.2 Uses

This measure overcomes the major deficiencies highlighted in relation to the flat yield and the Japanese GRY. It considers all cash returns and exactly when they occur.

As a result, the GRY represents a realistic measure of the expected overall return from a bond at any point in time.

3.3.3 Limitations

As a measure of predicted return, the yield is limited, since it **assumes that interest rates remain constant throughout the period and hence, that any coupon receipts may be reinvested at the same rate as the yield**. If this is the case, then the GRY does represent the return achieved. If rates vary, however, the return achieved will differ from the GRY.

If the bond is not held to redemption, but sold at some earlier date, then the return achieved will be a function of the price of the bond (hence, interest rates) at the disposal date.

Even if the bond is held to redemption, the terminal value will differ, as the reinvested coupons will grow at a different rate, altering the ultimate return achieved.

4 THE RISKS OF HOLDING A BOND

Exam tip

> Once again, it is unlikely that you will be required to calculate the following sensitivity measures, however it is essential that you understand what effects bond prices and what these sensitivity measures show.

4.1 Introduction

An investor in a fixed income security is exposed to a number of different risks, and any complete assessment of a bond must include consideration of these factors. These bond risks include the following.

4.1.1 Interest rate risk

This is probably the most important risk because of the powerful relationship between interest rates and bond prices. Duration and modified duration (volatility) are the means of measuring this risk. Convexity is the measure that is used to explain the variation away from the predicted return.

4.1.2 Credit and default risk

Credit and default risk is the risk of the issuer defaulting on its obligations to pay coupons and repay the principal. The ratings by commercial rating companies can be used to help assess this risk.

4.1.3 Inflation risk

Inflation risk is linked to interest rate risk, as interest rates rise to compensate bondholders for inflation.

4.1.4 Liquidity and marketability risk

This has to do with the ease with which an issue can be sold in the market. Smaller issues especially are subject to this risk. In certain markets, the volume of trading tends to concentrate into the 'benchmark' stocks, thereby rendering most other issues illiquid. Other bonds become subject to 'seasoning' as the initial liquidity dries up and the bonds are purchased by investors who wish to hold them to maturity.

4.1.5 Issue specific risk

There may be factors specific to the issue, which tend to either increase or decrease the risk, e.g. issuer options such as the right to call for early redemption or possibly, holder options.

4.1.6 Fiscal risk

Fiscal risk represents risk that withholding taxes will be increased. For foreign bonds, there would also be the risk of the imposition of capital controls locking your money into the market.

4.1.7 Currency risk

For any investor purchasing overseas or international bonds, there is obviously also the risk of currency movements.

4.2 Interest rate risk

4.2.1 Introduction

The most predictable of these risks is the interest rate risk. Within bond markets, this is sometimes referred to, somewhat confusingly, as the **volatility**. The sensitivity of any bond to movements in the interest rate will be determined by a number of factors.

Sensitivity to maturity

Longer dated bonds will be more sensitive to changes in the interest rate than shorter dated stocks as illustrated by these prices for three 12% bonds of differing maturity subject to differing GRYs.

Coupon %	Maturity (Years)	Price for a GRY of 8%	Price for a GRY of 10%	Price for a GRY of 12%
12	4	£113.24	£106.34	£100.00
12	7	£120.83	£109.74	£100.00
12	26	£143.23	£118.32	£100.00

In this example, it is the price of the 26-year bond which exhibits the greatest range as the yield alters (moving from £143.23 to par). The logic behind this is that the longer dated bond is more exposed to the movements of the yield, since it has longer to go to maturity.

Sensitivity to coupon

With regard to the level of coupon, it is the lower coupon stocks that demonstrate the greatest level of sensitivity to the yield.

Coupon %	Maturity (Years)	Price for a GRY of 9%	Price for a GRY of 10%	Price for a GRY of 11%
5	15	£67.75	£61.97	£56.85
10	15	£108.06	£100.00	£92.81
15	15	£148.30	£138.03	£128.76

In this example, the price of the 5% bond moves from £61.97 when the GRY is 10% to £67.75 if GRY drops to 9% (a fall of 9%) to £56.85 if GRY rises to 11% (a fall of 8.2%). The other bonds whilst exhibiting the same overall relationship are not as responsive to the alteration in the GRY. The 10% bond rises by 8% and falls by 7.1%.

It should be noted that the relationship between the coupon and maturity and the price are not symmetrical (equal for both a rise or a fall in GRY). This is a relationship that we will return to later and is known as **convexity**.

The logic behind this relationship is that the lower coupon bonds have more of their value tied up in the terminal value. The ultimate low-coupon bond is, after all, the zero-coupon bond where the entire value is in the final payment.

The Impact of the yield

If yields are particularly high, then the flows in the future are worth relatively little and the sensitivity is diminished. Conversely, if the yield is low, then the present value of flows in the future is enhanced and the bond is more sensitive to the changing GRY.

Summary

Long dated > Short dated
Low coupon > High coupon
Low yields > High yields

Whilst these simple maxims are good indicators of the likely sensitivity to fluctuations in the rate of interest, they do not allow for two bonds to be compared.

For example, which of the following is likely to be the most sensitive to a rise in interest rates – a high-coupon long-dated stock or a low-coupon short-dated stock? It was for this reason that in the 1930s, a composite measure of interest rate risk was devised –the **duration**.

4.2.2 Macaulay duration

Introduction

As we have just seen, cash flows at different points in time have different sensitivities to rate movements (different risks). A bond may be thought of as an amalgamation of differently timed cash flows each with their own sensitivity. Hence, the sensitivity of a bond to changes in rates must be a weighted average of the sensitivities of the individual cash flows. This is a bond's duration.

Definition

Duration is the weighted average length of time to the receipt of a bond's benefits (coupon and redemption value), the weightings being the present value of the benefits involved.

This concept can be shown diagrammatically

Duration

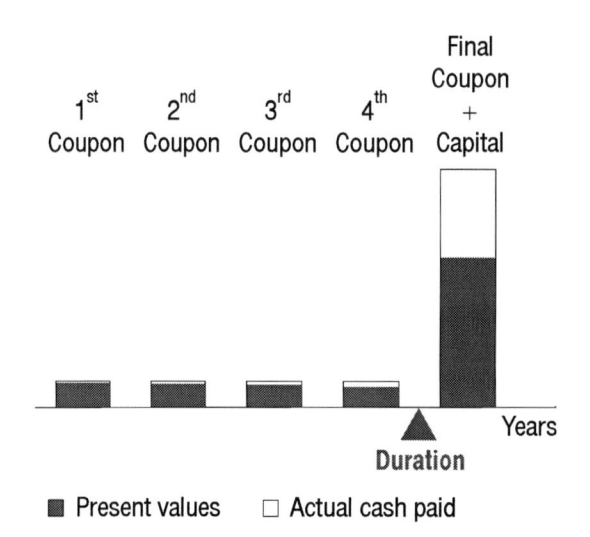

[Diagram showing 1st Coupon, 2nd Coupon, 3rd Coupon, 4th Coupon, Final Coupon + Capital across Years, with Duration marked as fulcrum. Legend: ■ Present values □ Actual cash paid]

where the fulcrum or point of balance represents the duration of the bond.

Calculation

Mathematically, duration can be expressed using the following formula.

Formula to learn

$$\text{Macaulay duration (D)} = \frac{\sum(t \times PV_t)}{\text{Price}}$$

Or

Formula to learn

$$\text{Macaulay duration (D)} = \frac{(1 \times PV_1) + (2 \times PV_2) + (3 \times PV_3) + \cdots + (n \times PV_n)}{\text{Price}}$$

where

PV_t = present value of cash flow in period t (discounted using the redemption yield)
n = number of periods to maturity

This may look difficult, but can be easily calculated in a table that simply adds one column to the one used for evaluation.

Example

What would be the duration of a three-year 9% annual coupon bond trading with a GRY of 8%?

Solution

Time	Cash Flow (£)	Discount Factor	Present Value (£)	Weighted (t × PVt)
1	9.00	$\frac{1}{1.08}$	8.33	8.33
2	9.00	$\frac{1}{1.08^2}$	7.72	15.44
3	109.00	$\frac{1}{1.08^3}$	86.53	259.59
			102.58	283.36

Using the above, the duration is

$$\text{Duration} = \frac{283.36}{102.58} = 2.7623 \text{ years}$$

Use

The uses of duration are

- As a measure of relative risk for a bond in a similar fashion to the standard deviation or the beta for a share. The higher the duration of the bond, the higher its risk or interest rate sensitivity.
- To calculate modified duration (discussed below).
- In the determination of the portfolio holdings necessary to establish a bond fund management strategy called immunisation. This is not covered in this section, but dealt with in the fund management section later.

Properties of duration

The basic features of sensitivity to interest rate risk are all mirrored in the duration calculation.

- **Longer dated bonds** will have longer durations. (**NB: The duration of an irredeemable** = $1 + \frac{1}{\text{Yield}}$).

10: BOND DERIVATIVES

- **Lower coupon bonds** will have longer durations. The ultimate low-coupon bond is a zero-coupon bond where the duration will be the maturity.
- **Lower yields** will give higher durations. In this case, the present value of flows in the future will fall if the yield increases, moving the point of balance towards the present day, therefore shortening the duration.

The duration of a bond will shorten as the lifespan of the bond decays. However, the rate of their decay will not be the same. In our example above, a three-year bond has a duration of 2.7623 years. In one year's time, the bond will have a remaining life of two years, and a duration based on the same GRY of 1.9182 years. The lifespan has decayed by a full year, but the duration by only 0.8441 of a year.

4.2.3 Modified duration/volatility

Introduction

At the same time as the Macaulay duration was being promoted as a means of expressing the sensitivity of a bond to movements in the interest rate, Hicks was developing a formula to explain the impact of yield changes on price. Not surprisingly, the two measures are linked.

Hick's basic proposition was that the change in yield multiplied by this sensitivity measure would give the resultant percentage change in the bond's price, i.e. the volatility gives the percentage change in price per unit change in yield.

Definition

Modified duration is the percentage change in the price of a bond arising from a 1% change in yields.

Calculation

The modified duration formula may be derived through the use of calculus, specifically differentiation of the price equation with respect to yields. Fortunately, there is an easier definition, specifically

Formula to learn

$$\text{Modified Duration/Volatility} = -\frac{\text{Macaulay duration}}{1+\text{GRY}}$$

Some texts do not include the minus sign in the calculation of modified duration but insert it on use. We have included it here to emphasise the inverse relationship between prices and yields, i.e. as yields rise, prices fall.

Exam tip

The examiner usually ignores the sign when giving information in questions

Use

The use of modified duration is to provide a first estimate of the change in the price of a bond that will result from a given change in yields.

Example

Using the example from above

$$\text{Modified duration} = -\frac{2.7623}{1.08} = -2.5577$$

This is negative, hence we can state that the price will **fall** by 2.5577% or £2.62 (102.58 × 2.5577%) for every one percentage point **increase** in the yield – we must bear in mind the inverse relationship.

Based on this, calculate the change in price and the new resulting price, if yields

- Fall 0.5%.
- Rise 1.0%.

Solution

Yields fall 0.5%

Alternative 1 – First principles

Bearing in mind the inverse relationship, if yields **fall** 0.5%, then prices will **rise** by £1.31 (£2.62 × 0.5) to £103.89 (£102.58 + £1.31).

Alternative 2 – Mathematical relationship

This relationship may be expressed mathematically as

Formula to learn

> Proportionate change in price = MD × ΔY

where

MD = modified duration
ΔY = percentage change in the gross redemption yield (expressed as a decimal)

Applying this relationship gives

Proportionate change in price = MD × ΔY = –2.5577 × (–0.005) = 0.01279 or 1.279%

This is a positive figure, hence prices will rise by 1.279% or £1.31 (£102.58 × 1.279%) as calculated above in Alternative 1 above.

The first principles approach is certainly easier and more intuitive when we are only considering modified duration. The second mathematical relationship approach comes in to its own, however, when we try to incorporate the effects of convexity below.

Yields rise 1.0%

Alternative 1 – First principles

Bearing in mind the inverse relationship, if yields **rise** 1.0%, then prices will **fall** by £2.62 (£2.62 × 1.0) to £99.96 (£102.58 – £2.62).

Alternative 2 – Mathematical relationship

Proportionate change in price = MD × ΔY = –2.5577 × (+0.010) = –0.025577 or –2.5577%

This is a negative figure, hence prices will fall by 2.5577% or £2.62 (£102.58 × 2.5577%) as calculated above in Alternative 1 above.

Comments

If a full DCF pricing exercise is carried out, we would find that the prices would become £103.90 if yields fell 0.5% to 7.5%, and £100 if yields rose 1.0% to 9.0%. The modified duration calculation produces a quite accurate result for small changes in yields, however it becomes increasingly inaccurate for larger shifts.

Properties of modified duration

As the modified duration is derived from the Macaulay duration, it shares the same properties.

- **Longer dated bonds will have higher modified durations (NB: The modified duration of an irredeemable = $-\dfrac{1}{\text{Yield}}$).**
- **Lower coupon bonds will have higher modified durations.**
- **Lower yields will give higher modified durations.**

The higher the modified duration value, the greater the sensitivity of that bond to a change in the yield.

4.2.4 Convexity

Introduction

Modified duration predicts a linear relationship between yields and prices. If the modified duration is 2, then if yields rise by 1%, the price will fall by 2%. If the rise in yields had been 3%, then the fall in price would have been 6%.

**The Price/Yield Relationship
Given by the Modified Duration**

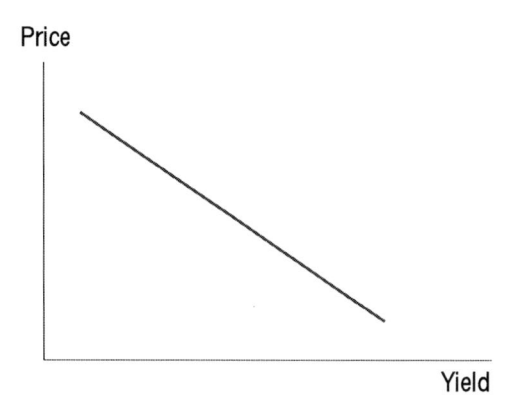

The slope of the line is the modified duration.

However, as the yield changes, so will the duration and consequently, the modified duration. It is this that gives rise to the concept of convexity.

**The Impact of Changing Yields
on the Modified Duration**

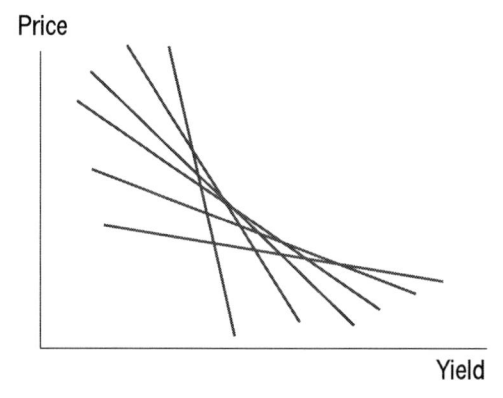

As the yield falls, the duration will increase and therefore, so will the modified duration. As modified duration increases, the line will steepen.

The actual relationship between the yield and price is given by the convex function that these individual linear relationships describe. We are after all aware that the relationship between bond prices and interest rates is not linear. The actual relationship between prices and yields is curved, with increases in yields resulting in prices falling, but at a reducing rate, as illustrated by the example at the start of this session.

The actual convex relationship and the linear one predicted by the modified duration formula are illustrated below.

Convexity

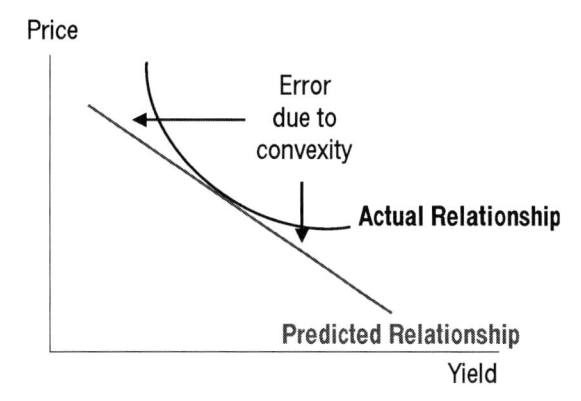

Price

Error due to convexity

Actual Relationship

Predicted Relationship

Yield

The impact of convexity will be that the modified duration will tend to **overstate the fall in a bond's price and understate the rise**. However, for relatively small movements in the yield, the modified duration will be a good estimate; the problem of convexity only becomes an issue with more substantial fluctuations in the yield.

Definition

Convexity is the change in the modified duration with respect to yields.

Calculation

The convexity formula may be derived once again through calculus, being a function of the second derivative of the price equation with respect to yields.

Formula to learn

$$\text{Convexity} = \frac{\sum t(t+1)PV_t}{\text{Price}(1+GRY)^2}$$

NB: Some texts include a ½ in this formula, others include the ½ when it is used within further calculations. How and when this ½ is included is of no relevance to its use as long as all calculations are done consistently.

Once again, this does not look like a very pleasant formula. However, it may easily be dealt with by extending our tabular duration calculation.

Example

Based on the previous duration calculation, calculate convexity (C).

Solution

Time	Cash Flow (£)	Discount Factor	PVt (£)	t × PVt (£)	t(t + 1)PVt (£)
1	9.00	$\frac{1}{1.08}$	8.33	8.33	16.66
2	9.00	$\frac{1}{1.08^2}$	7.72	15.44	46.32
3	109.00	$\frac{1}{1.08^3}$	86.53	259.59	1,038.36
			102.58	283.36	1,101.34

Hence

$$\text{Convexity} = \frac{\sum t(t+1)PV_t}{\text{Price}(1+\text{GRY})^2}$$

$$\text{Convexity} = \frac{1,101.34}{102.58 \times 1.08^2} = 9.2048$$

Use

The use of convexity is to

- Give a more accurate assessment of the change in the price of a bond that will result from a given change in yields.

- Indicate the risk of a bond fund immunisation strategy by comparing the convexity of the alternatives. Note, the relative convexity is unaffected by the consistent inclusion or exclusion of the ½ in the calculations. Once again, this is not covered in this section, but dealt with in the fund management section later.

Example

Using our ongoing example, calculate the change in the price of the bond, and the new resulting price, if yields

- Fall 0.5%.
- Rise 1.0%.

Solution

Yields fall 0.5%

Alternative 1 – Using an average modified duration

As we noted above, modified duration changes as yields change, hence using it to forecast price movements will lead to inaccuracies. To overcome this, we could use the convexity information to calculate the average modified duration over the given range of yields and use this to more accurately assess the change in prices as follows.

Modified duration at 8% GRY		−2.5577
Change due to convexity if yields fall 0.5% (−0.005)	9.2048 × (−0.005)	−0.0460
Modified duration at 7.5% GRY		−2.6037
Average modified duration	(−2.5577 − 2.6037) ÷ 2	−2.5807

Giving

Proportionate change in price = Average MD × ΔY = −2.5807 × (−0.005) = 0.01290 or 1.290%

Hence, prices will rise by £1.32 (£102.58 × 1.290%) to £103.90 (£102.58 + £1.32).

Alternative 2 – Mathematical relationship

Note, we could calculate the above average modified duration from the originally calculated modified duration (MD) as

$$\begin{aligned}\text{Average MD} &= \text{MD} + \tfrac{1}{2}\text{C} \times \Delta Y \\ &= -2.5577 + \tfrac{1}{2} \times 9.2048 \times (-0.005) \\ &= -2.5807\end{aligned}$$

Substituting this into the above price change formula would give

$$\text{Proportionate change in price} = \text{Average MD} \times \Delta Y$$
$$= (\text{MD} + \tfrac{1}{2}\text{C} \times \Delta Y) \times \Delta Y$$
$$= \text{MD} \times \Delta Y + \tfrac{1}{2}\text{C} \times \Delta Y^2$$

That is, this whole average modified duration approach may be combined into a single formula to speed the calculation and expressed mathematically as

Formula to learn

$$\text{Proportionate change in price} = \text{MD} \times \Delta Y + \tfrac{1}{2}\text{C} \times \Delta Y^2$$

where

- MD = modified duration at the original GRY
- C = convexity at the original GRY
- ΔY = percentage change in the gross redemption yield (expressed as a decimal)

Applying this relationship gives

$$\text{Proportionate change in price} = \text{MD} \times \Delta Y + \tfrac{1}{2}\text{C} \times \Delta Y^2$$
$$= -2.5577 \times (-0.005) + \tfrac{1}{2} \times 9.2048 \times (-0.005)^2$$
$$= 0.01290 \text{ or } 1.290\%$$

This is a positive figure, hence prices will rise by 1.290% or £1.32 (£102.58 × 1.290%) as calculated above in Alternative 1.

Yields rise 1.0%

Applying the formula gives

$$\text{Proportionate change in price} = \text{MD} \times \Delta Y + \tfrac{1}{2}\text{C} \times \Delta Y^2$$
$$= -2.5577 \times (+0.010) + \tfrac{1}{2} \times 9.2048 \times (+0.010)^2$$
$$= -0.02512 \text{ or } -2.512\%$$

This is negative, hence prices will fall by £2.58 (£102.58 × 2.512%) to £100.00, which we know to be correct.

Properties of convexity

Not all bonds have the same degree of convexity. The general rule is that bonds with a higher duration will exhibit the greatest degree of convexity.

For bonds with the same duration, it will be the higher coupon bonds that will be the most convex. The reason for this is that the lower coupon bonds, for example 0% bonds, will have durations that will change little with the alteration in yield. In the most extreme form, the 0% bond will have a duration equal to its maturity and this will not alter as yields move.

Investors may be prepared to pay for convexity. In a volatile market, the convex bonds at any particular maturity interval will outperform the bonds with lesser convexity.

4.3 Portfolio yields and sensitivities

Exam tip | Questions frequently require you to consider the position of a bond portfolio.

If we know the yields/sensitivities of a number of bonds that we have in a portfolio, how can we determine the yield/sensitivity of the portfolio. The answer proves to be quite simple. Any measure for a bond portfolio can be calculated as the weighted average of the measures for the individual bonds (weighting by market values).

Example

A gilt portfolio consists of £10m nominal of a two-year gilt with an annual coupon of 12% on which interest has just been paid, and £5m nominal of a five-year zero-coupon bond. The interest rate is 10% and the yield curve is flat.

(a) What is the price of each gilt and the value of the portfolio?
(b) What is the duration of each gilt and of the portfolio?
(c) What is the modified duration of each gilt and of the portfolio?

Solution

(a) To price each bond, we discount the cash flows back to their present value using the interest rate of 10%.

    (i) Two-year gilt cash flows

1 year	2 year
£12 coupon	£12 coupon + £100 redemption

$$PV = \frac{£12}{1.1} + \frac{£112}{1.1^2}$$

$$= 10.91 + 92.56$$

$$= 103.47 \text{ per £100 nominal or £10.347m in total}$$

    (ii) Zero-coupon bond

$$PV = \frac{100}{1.1^5}$$

$$= 62.09 \text{ per £100 nominal or £3.104m in total}$$

    (iii) Value of the portfolio = £10.347m + £3.104m = £13.451m

(b) Duration of coupon bond

$$= \frac{(10.91 \times 1) + (92.56 \times 2)}{103.47}$$

$$= 1.89 \text{ years}$$

Duration of zero

$$= \frac{(62.09 \times 5)}{62.09}$$

$$= 5 \text{ years}$$

As can be seen, the duration of a zero-coupon bond is its maturity.

Portfolio duration requires the weighted duration of two bonds

$$= \left(\frac{£10.347m}{£13.457m} \times 1.89\right) + \left(\frac{£3.104m}{£13.457m} \times 5\right)$$

$$= 2.61 \text{ years}$$

(c) Modified duration of coupon bond

$$= \frac{1.89}{1.1} = 1.72$$

Modified duration of zero

$$= \frac{5}{1.1} = 4.55$$

Modified duration of portfolio

$$= \left(\frac{£10.347m}{£13.451m} \times 1.72\right) + \left(\frac{£3.104m}{£13.451m} \times 4.55\right)$$

$$= 2.37$$

5 Bond Derivatives

In the UK, Euronext.LIFFE is the centre of bond derivative trading.

5.1 Summary of Euronext.LIFFE bond products

Futures	Options on Future
Long Gilt (£100,000)	✓
Japanese Bond (JGB) (¥100,000,000)	
2/5/10-year € Swapnote® (€100,000)	✓
2-year $ Swapnote® ($200,000)	
5/10-year $ Swapnote® ($100,000)	

Information correct at December 2006.

The JGB and swap notes are cash settled. The Gilt is physically settled. The options are American style.

5.1.1 Basis trading facility

A basis trade is the simultaneous exchange of a cash bond together with an appropriate number of futures contracts.

Euronext.LIFFE's Basis Trading Facility allows the necessary number of futures contracts to be traded at the required single price and removes the execution risk associated with trading the futures leg.

The details of the trade must be registered within 30 minutes of origination and the price should be in the high-low trading range of the contract during that period. All the above future contracts can be basis traded against either cash bonds (government and non-government), OTC interest rate swap contracts or OTC options.

5.1.2 Block Trading Facility

This facility allows members and wholesale clients to transact business of significant size as bilaterally agreed transactions on exchange with certainty of price and execution.

This facility is available on all Euronext.LIFFE's financial and index products, but excludes commodities.

5.1.3 Other exchanges

A couple of other important traded bond futures are

Exchange	Product	Size	Tick	Tick Value
Eurex	Euro-Bund	€100,000	0.0001	€10
CBOT	T-Bond	$100,000	$\frac{1}{32}$	$31.25

Contract details correct at January 2005.

5.2 Quotation

Below is the contract specification of Euronext.LIFFE's Long Gilt Future.

Contract details correct at December 2006.

5.2.1 Long Gilt Future

Unit of Trading	£100,000 nominal value notional Gilt with 6% coupon
Delivery Months	March, June, September, December, such that the nearest three delivery months are available for trading
Last Notice Day	First business day after the last trading day
Delivery Day	Any business day in delivery month (at seller's choice)
Last Trading Day	11:00 Two business days prior to the last business day in the delivery month
Quotation	Per £100 nominal
Minimum Price Movement (Tick Size & Value)	0.01 (£10)
Trading Hours	08:00-18:00

Trading platform

LIFFE CONNECT®.

Contract standard

Delivery may be made of any gilts on the List of Deliverable Gilts in respect of a delivery month, as published by the Exchange on or before the tenth business day prior to the First Notice Day of such delivery month. Holders of long positions on any day within the Notice Period may be delivered against during the delivery month. All gilt issues included in the List will have the following characteristics.

- Having terms as to redemption which provide for redemption of the entire gilt issue in a single instalment, on the maturity date, falling not earlier than 8.75 years from, and not later than 13 years from, the first day of the relevant delivery month.
- Having no terms permitting or requiring early redemption.
- Bearing interest at a single fixed rate throughout the term of the issue payable in arrears semi-annually (except in the case of the first interest payment period which may be more or less than six months).
- Being denominated and payable as to the principal and interest only in pounds and pence.
- Being fully paid or, in the event that the gilt issue is in its first period and is partly paid, being anticipated by the Board to be fully paid on or before the Last Notice Day of the relevant delivery month.
- Not being convertible.
- Not being in bearer form.
- Having being admitted to the Official List of the London Stock Exchange.
- Being anticipated by the Board to have (on one or more days in the delivery month) an aggregate principal amount outstanding of not less than £1.5bn which, by its terms and conditions (if issued in more than one tranche or tap or issue), is fungible.

Exchange Delivery Settlement Price (EDSP)

The LIFFE market price at 11:00 on the second business day prior to Settlement Day. The invoicing amount in respect of each Deliverable Gilt is to be calculated by the price factor system. Adjustment will be made for full coupon interest accruing as at Settlement Day.

5.3 Pricing bond futures

Bond futures are commitments to buy or sell bonds at a fixed future date at a price agreed today.

Sellers of bond futures are under an obligation to deliver bonds to the buyers of bond futures on delivery day.

The exchange will publish in advance which bonds are eligible for delivery in accordance with the contract specification.

In all this, bond futures are like the other futures products we consider in this manual. However, it is important to realise that bond futures are based upon 'notional' bonds, i.e. bonds that do not exist. This is a complicated idea that needs some explanation.

If bond futures were based on a 'real' bond, it could be that futures activity would be so great that there would not be enough of that particular bond available for the sellers to make delivery. This would be dangerous as the market could become subject to manipulation. To avoid these dangers of undersupply, the exchange allows a large range of bonds with different coupons and redemption dates to be delivered in satisfaction of the contract. When you look at the quote of a bond future, you are looking, in effect, at an index price of all deliverable bonds.

5.3.1 Fair value of bond futures

The fair value of a bond future will represent a price at which an investor would be indifferent as to whether he buys a bond today or acquires it via the futures contract. As briefly referred to in a previous chapter, account needs to be taken not only of the holding costs (especially the cost of finance), but also the yield from the underlying asset, i.e. the interest paid on the bond.

Formula to learn

Fair value = Cash price + Cost of carry

Becomes

Formula to learn

Fair value = Dirty price of bond
+ Cost of financing over holding period
− Coupon received over holding period and accrued to delivery

Example

Cash price = £100 (interest has just been paid)
Short-term interest rate = 6%
Long-term bond flat yield = 8%
Days to delivery = 95

	£
Cash price	100.00
+ Cost of carry $\left[£100.00 \times (6\% - 8\%) \times \dfrac{95}{365} \right]$	(0.52)
Fair Value	**99.48**

If a future was trading at a price that was theoretically incorrect then, subject to supply and demand considerations, the difference would be eliminated via a cash and carry (or reverse cash and carry) arbitrage.

5.3.2 Price factors

Of course, when it comes to delivery, sellers may be delivering bonds with a variety of coupons and redemption dates from the list published by the exchange. Different bonds have different market prices because of coupon and maturity. It is therefore necessary for the exchange to introduce, into the calculation of the invoice amount, a method of treating sellers who are delivering high coupon (and therefore high value bonds) fairly. This is done through what are known as price factors and their purpose is to bring all deliverable bonds onto a common basis. That common basis is to price them so that they would yield the notional coupon. In the case of the Long Gilt Future, this is currently 6%.

The use of the price factor thus ensures that sellers delivering bonds with a higher coupon than the notional are paid more, whilst sellers of lower coupon bonds are paid less.

The invoice amount formula for a bond future is

Formula to learn

Invoice amount = EDSP × Price Factor × Scaling Factor × No. of contracts + Accrued interest

The scaling factor here is 1,000 to reflect the fact that prices are quoted per £100 nominal but one contract is for £100,000 nominal.

Price factors are calculated by the exchange well before delivery. For December 2006, the following gilts, with their respective price factors, are available for delivery into the Long Gilt future.

Stock	Coupon	Redemption	Price Factor
Treasury	4.75%	07 Sept 15	0.9156637
Treasury	8.00%	07 Dec 15	1.1377447
Treasury	4.00%	7 Sept 16	0.8537314
Treasury	8.75%	25 Aug 17	1.2151760

You will notice that the high-coupon bonds have the highest price factors. This should make sense, as those delivering high-coupon bonds should expect to receive more money than those delivering cheaper low-coupon bonds. The notional coupon of the Euronext.LIFFE gilt future is 6%. Bonds with coupons greater than the notional coupon have price factors greater than one and vice versa.

As the amount received on delivery will be adjusted by the price factor and as the price of the future must converge with the cash price, the following relationship must hold *at delivery*.

Formula to learn

Gilt price = Futures price × Price factor

Or

Formula to learn

$$\text{Futures price} = \frac{\text{Gilt price}}{\text{Price factor}}$$

5.3.3 Basis

Basis, as we know, is the difference between the cash price (clean price) and the future price. For a bond future this will be

Formula to learn

Basis = Cash price − (Future price × Price factor)

This is known as the **gross basis** and will be different for each of the bonds in the deliverable basket.

It is also possible to calculate the zero gross basis future price for each of the deliverable bonds in the basket. This is the price the future would have to trade at so that the gross basis is zero.

The zero gross basis future price is thus calculated as

Formula to learn

$$\text{Zero gross basis future price} = \frac{\text{Bond price}}{\text{Price factor}}$$

5.3.4 Value basis or net basis

Value basis is the difference between the fair value of the future and the actual value of the future (future price × price factor). It can also be calculated as

Formula to learn

$$\text{Price of CTD} \times \left(\text{Actual repo rate} - \text{Implied repo rate} \times \frac{\text{Days}}{360 \text{ or } 365^*} \right)$$

*365 for Sterling denominated products, 360 for Dollar and Euro products.

5.3.5 Cheapest to deliver

Although the use of price factors seeks to bring all bonds onto a similar basis for delivery, they are, for a number of technical reasons discussed below, not entirely accurate. This means that the seller of the future needs to calculate which bond is best for him to deliver. Any seller will clearly want to select the bond that generates either the greatest profit or least loss. This bond is known as the cheapest to deliver (CTD).

The cheapest to deliver is discovered by calculating the returns from a cash and carry arbitrage for all the different deliverable bonds.

The bond that generates the greatest profit or the least loss from a cash and carry arbitrage is the cheapest to deliver. The importance of correctly identifying the CTD is obvious for the seller. For other market users, it is also important in the pricing of the future and in the creation of correct hedges.

Combining these comments with out earlier discussion of price factors, we must have *at delivery*.

Formula to learn

> CTD price = Futures price × Price factor

Or

Formula to learn

> Futures price = $\dfrac{\text{CTD price}}{\text{Price factor}}$

5.3.6 Seller's options

Although arbitrage goes some way to explain why futures are priced as they are, it is rare for a bond future to trade at precisely its theoretical value other than at delivery. This is due to there being a number of 'options' within the seller's control.

The first of these is the **quality option**. The seller retains the right to deliver any of the different deliverable bonds. As a rational seller, he will always seek to deliver the CTD. If the CTD changes, the seller can adjust the bond he delivers. This ability to switch can be priced as an option, the premium of which varies with market volatility and the likelihood of the CTD changing. The consequence of this option is that the theoretical futures price as derived by arbitrage should be reduced by the value of the option's premium. In other words, the long should be compensated for the granting of this option.

For US T-bond futures and UK Gilt futures, there is also a **timing option**. This is because, in both these products, the seller has the choice of making delivery on any business day in the delivery month. This enables the short to select the most advantageous moment for delivery. When might this be? Again assuming that the seller is rational, if short-term rates are lower than the yield on the bond, it will be best to deliver at the month end. Conversely, if short-term rates exceed the yield, delivery will take place at the beginning of the month. In this way, the short maximises his return.

When calculating cash and carry returns for either the US T-bond or UK Gilt, a vital first step is to compare the flat yield on the bond with short-term interest rates in order to determine when delivery will be made. From this analysis, the correct number of days involved in the carrying and coupon calculations can be derived.

The third option held by the short is called the **wild card option**. This relates to the ability of the short to decide which bond to deliver in the interval between the close of the market and the deadline for delivery notifications. For example, the US T-bond future traded on the CBOT closes at 14:00, but has a notification deadline of 20:00. During this time, the long will be unable to extinguish his position while the short will be able to watch the markets and select the best bond to deliver.

5.3.7 Calculating the cheapest to deliver

The conversion, or price factor, of the bond is calculated by the exchange well in advance of deliveries taking place. The method used is that the bond's future cash flows are discounted by the notional coupon of the future.

Whilst this would work perfectly if all deliverable bonds yielded the notional coupon, if the yields were all the same (but different to the notional coupon) one bond would become the CTD. This is because the durations of the deliverable bonds are different.

All other things remaining equal, when yields are high, high-duration bonds (long maturities, low coupons) become the CTD. If yields are low, low-duration bonds (short maturities, high coupons) tend to become the CTD.

The cash and carry arbitrage calculation to discover the CTD will be familiar from our earlier discussion of pricing. There are, however, a few adjustments that are necessary to take account of accrued interest. The basic formula prior to delivery is

Formula to learn

> CTD price + Finance cost − Bond income* = Futures price × Price factor

Or

Formula to learn

> $$\text{Futures price} = \frac{\text{CTD price} + \text{Finance cost} - \text{Bond income*}}{\text{Price factor}}$$

*Paid and accrued

Exam tip

> Questions involving pricing bond futures occur frequently.

Alternatively this may be laid out as follows

CTD cash price	C	= Dirty price
Cost of carry		
− Interest	X	$= C \times r \times \text{Days}/365$
− Coupon	(X)	= Coupon paid and accrued to maturity
CTD future price	X	
Price factor	÷PF	
Futures price	F	

where

Days = number of days to maturity

r = annual interest rate

This expresses the fact that there should be an equality between the attractiveness of the future and the alternative cost of buying the bond, and carrying it through until delivery. In buying the bond, money will need to be borrowed (or interest foregone); this cost will be offset in whole or in part by the amount of interest paid and accruing on the bond. If the future is bought, neither finance costs are incurred nor coupon payments received.

One method of calculating the CTD is to work out the theoretical futures price for each of the different deliverable bonds. The bond with the lowest theoretical futures price is the CTD.

10: BOND DERIVATIVES

Example 1

It is 12 June and you are considering a futures trade in the September gilt contract. The cheapest-to-deliver bond is the 9.5%, maturing 25 May 2015 paying coupons on 25 May and 25 November each year, which is currently trading at a clean price of 104.50. Interest rates are 5.125% and the price factor of the bond is 1.03419.

(a) When would you expect delivery to be made?
(b) What is the fair price of the futures contract?

Solution 1

(a) Delivery will be made at the seller's option. If the seller is rational, this will be made at the end of the month as the flat yield (the income from the gilt) exceeds interest rates.

$$\text{Flat yield} = \frac{9.5}{104.50} = 0.0909 \text{ or } 9.09\%$$

Delivery will take place at month end, i.e. 30 September.

(b) **Determine dirty price of bond on 12 June**

Month		Days	Days in period	12/6 to 30/9
May	From last coupon (inclusive)	7	7	
June	To day before settlement (tomorrow)	12	30	19
July			31	31
August			31	31
September	To day before 30/9		30	29
October			31	
November	To day before next coupon		24	
		19	184	108

The 9.5% gilt pays a semi-annual coupon of £4.75 (£9 ÷ 2), giving

	£
Clean price	104.50
Accrued interest $4.75 \times \frac{19}{184}$	0.49
Dirty price	104.99

Determine futures price

CTD cash price	104.99
Cost of carry	
– Interest $104.99 \times 5.125\% \times \frac{108}{184}$	3.16
– Coupon $4.75 \times \frac{108}{184}$	(2.79)
CTD future price	105.36
Price factor	÷ 1.03419
Futures value	£101.88

Example 2

On 1 January, the cheapest-to-deliver T-bond for June has a 12% coupon and a price factor of 1.5. Coupons are paid at the end of February and August. The bond price is $110 and the rate of interest 8% per annum.

Calculate the fair price for the June T-bond futures contract implied by this data.

Solution 2

1. Determine when delivery will take place.

    $$\text{Flat yield} = \frac{12}{110} \times 100 = 10.91\%$$

    Therefore, delivery will take place at *end* of June, i.e. in six months.

2. Determine the 1 January dirty price.

    The 12% T-bond pays $6 every six months, giving

	$
Clean price	110
Accrued $6 × $\frac{4}{6}$	4
Dirty price	114

3. Determine the bond income.

	$
Coupon paid at end of February	6.00
Interest on coupon received to 30/6 = $6 × 8% × $\frac{4}{12}$	0.16
Accrued interest from 1/3 to 30/6 = $6 × $\frac{4}{6}$	4.00
Interest paid and accrued	10.16

4. Determine the futures price

	$
CTD cash price	114.00
Cost of carry	
– Interest 114 × 8% × $\frac{6}{12}$	4.56
– Coupon	(10.16)
CTD future price	108.40
Price factor	÷1.50
Futures price	72.27

The cash bond that yields the lowest theoretical futures price is the CTD. Although computationally exhausting, such analysis is easily undertaken in practice by using programmed quote vendors such as Bloomberg.

5.3.8 Implied repo rates

Another method is to calculate the implied repo rate. The implied repo rate shows the annualised percentage return from a cash and carry arbitrage and the CTD is the bond with the highest implied repo rate.

The following formula is used.

Formula to learn

$$\text{Implied repo rate} = \frac{\text{Invoice amount} - \text{Initial cost}}{\text{Initial cost} \times \frac{\text{Days in holding period}}{365}}$$

Remember

  Invoice amount = Price of future × PF + Accrued interest

  Initial cost = Dirty price

Example

What is the implied repo rate if the cash price of a bond is £100, the future trades at 95, the price factor is 1.1 and delivery takes place in 180 days? [Ignore accrued interest.]

Solution

Initial cost = £100

Invoice amount = £95 × 1.1 (per £100 nominal)

$$\text{Implied repo rate} = \frac{(95 \times 1.1) - 100}{100 \times \frac{180}{365}}$$

= 0.09125 or 9.125%

In reality, the calculations will require a consideration of accrued interest. A more realistic calculation might therefore be as follows.

Example

Date: 10 December
March Gilt future = 99.88
Treasury 13.5% clean price = 131.46
Price factor = 1.3115201
Coupons paid 1/12 and 1/6
Delivery 31 March

What is the implied repo rate?

Solution

| Initial Cost | = 131.46 plus accrued interest |

$$= 131.46 + \left(100 \times \frac{1}{2} \times 13.5\% \times \frac{10}{182}\right)$$

= 131.46 + 0.3709

$$= 131.8309$$

Invoice Amount $= 99.88 \times 1.311520 +$ Accrued at delivery

$$= 99.88 \times 1.311520 + \left(100 \times \frac{1}{2} \times 13.5\% \times \frac{121}{182}\right)$$

$$= 130.9946 + 4.4876$$

$$= 135.4822$$

Implied Repo Rate $= \dfrac{135.4822 - 131.8309}{131.8309 \times \dfrac{111}{365}}$

$$= \dfrac{3.6513}{131.8309 \times \dfrac{111}{365}}$$

$$= 9.11\%$$

Also, if the holding period straddles a coupon payment date, then the coupon received will effectively reduce the cost. It will therefore be necessary to also adjust for this as shown in the following example.

Example

Date: 15 September
December future = 105.34 (assuming delivery is 31 December)
Treasury 8% 2008 = 113.75
Price factor = 1.0738215
Coupon paid: 4 April and 4 October

Solution

The formula to use is now

Formula to learn

$$\text{Implied repo rate} = \dfrac{\text{Invoice amount} - \text{Initial cost} + \text{Interest received}}{\text{Initial cost} \times \dfrac{\text{Days in holding period}}{365}}$$

What is the implied repo rate?

Initial cost $= 113.75$ plus accrued interest

$$= 113.75 + \left(100 \times \frac{1}{2} \times 8\% \times \frac{165}{183}\right)$$

$$= 117.3566$$

Interest paid on 4 October $= 100 \times 8\% \times \frac{1}{2}$

$$= 4.00$$

Invoice amount $= 105.34 \times 1.0738215 +$ Accrued interest

$$= 105.34 \times 1.0738215 + \left(100 \times \frac{1}{2} \times 8\% \times \frac{89}{183}\right)$$

$$= 115.0724$$

10: BOND DERIVATIVES

$$\text{Implied repo rate} = \frac{115.0724 - 117.3566 + 4.00}{117.3566 \times \frac{107}{365}}$$

$$= 4.99\%$$

If this were the highest implied repo across all deliverable bonds, this bond would be the cheapest to deliver.

The above approach can be made even more complex if we wish to include the interest that could be earned on the dividend received. The formula now becomes

Formula to learn

$$\text{Implied repo rate} = \frac{\text{Invoice amount} - \text{Initial cost} + \text{Interest received}}{\left(\text{Initial cost} \times \frac{\text{Days in holding period}}{365}\right) - \left(\text{Interest received} \times \frac{\text{Days between receipt of interest and delivery date of future}}{365}\right)}$$

5.4 Hedging with futures

5.4.1 Hedging the CTD

Through the process of arbitrage, the bond future moves in a highly predictable way against the cheapest-to-deliver bond. The relative volatility between the two products is in fact the CTD's price factor. So, if an exposure to the CTD is to be hedged, the formula used to calculate the correct number of contracts is

Formula to learn

$$\text{Number of contracts} = \frac{\text{Nominal value of CTD}}{\text{Face value of future}} \times \text{Price factor of CTD}$$

The price factor works in a similar fashion to the beta of an equity portfolio.

Example

A gilt fund manager fears that UK interest rates will rise and wishes to protect his holding of £100m nominal of the CTD. The future has a face value of £100,000 and the CTD has a price factor of 1.0654428.

$$\text{Number of contracts} = \frac{100,000,000}{100,000} \times 1.0654428$$

= Sell 1,065 contracts*

*Sell to protect against a fall – short hedge

When hedging issues other than the CTD, consideration needs to be given to the relative volatility of the future and the bond(s) to be hedged.

5.4.2 Hedging non-CTD bonds

When hedging bonds other than the cheapest to deliver, a further term needs to be used in determining the appropriate hedge ratio, namely the relative volatility of the bond to be hedged versus the cheapest to deliver.

The object of any futures hedge is to produce an offsetting position that will precisely compensate for any losses that arise in the cash market. To ensure this, the relative sensitivities of the bonds need to be identified. The most common method involves basis point hedging.

5.4.3 Basis point hedging

Modified duration (MD) expresses the sensitivity of a bond's price to a change in yield. Thus, if a bond has a modified duration of 8.62, this would imply that for a one basis point change in yield, the bond would change in price by 0.0862%. To convert this sensitivity into a price change, we would simply multiply by the current dirty price.

Thus, for a bond with a modified duration of 3.7537 and a price of £100, the change in price for a one basis point movement would be £0.037537.

The present value of a basis point (PVBP) or basis point value (BPV) measures the absolute change in price of **£100 nominal of a bond** for a one basis point (0.01% or 0.0001) change in yield (sometimes referred to as PV01).

To find the BPV, one undertakes the following calculation.

Formula to learn

> BPV = Modified duration × Dirty price of bond × 0.0001

Thus, for a bond with a modified duration of 3.5 and a dirty price of 98.

BPV = 3.5 × 98 × 0.0001 = 0.0343

Often, the BPV will be written as the number of ticks, in this example, 3.43 (on the assumption that a tick is 1bp).

To calculate a hedge ratio when hedging with futures, you work out the BPV of the bond to be hedged and the BPV of the cheapest to deliver. This then provides you with a ratio that describes the relative sensitivity of the bond to be hedged versus the CTD.

Example 1

The cheapest to deliver gilt trades at a dirty price of £108.04, with a modified duration of 7.12 and has a price factor of 1.17124.

The bond to be hedged trades at a dirty price of £102.10 and has a modified duration of 5.37. You are long £2,000,000 nominal of this bond. How many futures should be sold to hedge this position?

Solution 1

Step 1

Calculate the BPV of bond and CTD.

$$\text{Bond BPV} = 5.37 \times £102.10 \times \frac{0.01}{100} = 0.05483$$

$$\text{CTD BPV} = 7.12 \times £108.04 \times \frac{0.01}{100} = 0.07692$$

Step 2

Insert values into formula.

$$\text{Number of contracts} = \frac{\text{Nominal value of portfolio}}{\text{Nominal value of future}} \times \text{Price factor of CTD} \times \frac{\text{BPV portfolio}}{\text{BPV CTD}}$$

10: BOND DERIVATIVES

$$\frac{£2,000,000}{£100,000} \times 1.17124 \times \frac{0.05483}{0.07692} = 16.69 \text{ contracts}$$

Example 2

A portfolio of £15m nominal of gilts has a dirty price of £89.67 and a modified duration of 2.61.

The CTD has a dirty price, price factor and modified duration of £120, 1.15 and 8 respectively. How many futures should be sold to hedge the portfolio?

Solution 2

Step 1

Calculate the BPV of portfolio and CTD.

$$\text{Portfolio} = 2.61 \times £89.67 \times \frac{0.01}{100} = 0.02340$$

$$\text{CTD} = 8 \times £120 \times \frac{0.01}{100} = 0.096$$

Step 2

Insert values into formula.

$$\text{Number of contracts} = \frac{\text{Nominal value of portfolio}}{\text{Nominal value of future}} \times \text{Price factor of CTD} \times \frac{\text{BPV portfolio}}{\text{BPV CTD}}$$

$$\frac{£15m}{£0.1m} \times 1.15 \times \frac{0.02340}{0.0960}$$

$$= 42 \text{ contracts}$$

Example 3

The cheapest-to-deliver gilt has a modified duration of 8, a price factor of 1.15 and is priced at £120. The yield curve is flat at 10%. An investor holds a portfolio of £1m nominal of two-year zero-coupon bonds and £1m nominal of six-year zero-coupon bonds.

(a) What is the price of each bond, the value of the portfolio and the price of £100 nominal?
(b) What is the duration and modified duration of the portfolio?
(c) How many gilt futures are required to hedge it?

Solution 3

(a)

		£m
Two year zero coupon bond	$\frac{£1m}{1.10^2}$ =	0.8264
Six year zero	$\frac{£1m}{1.10^6}$ =	0.5645
Portfolio value		1.3909

$$\text{Price of £100 nominal} = \frac{£1.3909\text{m}}{2\text{m}} \times 100 = £69.545$$

(b) Duration of each zero is equal to each bond's maturity, i.e. 2 and 6. These are weighted by their market values to determine the duration of the portfolio.

$$\text{Portfolio duration} = \left(\frac{0.8264}{1.3909} \times 2\right) + \left(\frac{0.5645}{1.3909} \times 6\right)$$

$$= 1.188 + 2.435$$
$$= 3.623 \text{ years}$$

The modified duration is then

$$\text{MD} = -\frac{3.623}{1.10} = -3.294$$

(c) To find the number of futures to hedge with, determine the BPV of portfolio and CTD.

Portfolio = 3.294 × £69.545* × 0.0001 = 0.0229

* Price of £100 nominal of bond

Future = 8 × £120 × 0.0001 = 0.096

$$\text{Number of contracts} = \frac{2\text{m}}{0.1\text{m}} \times 1.15 \times \frac{0.0229}{0.096} = 5.48 \text{ contracts (5 rounded)}$$

Exam tip

> In the past, the examiner has sometimes only given the duration and not the modified duration. If it is not possible to calculate the modified duration then the duration will have to be used, even though it is not technically correct.

Example 4

A pension fund manager wishes to lock in long-term dollar interest rates in anticipation of receiving dollar investment funds in three months' time. The 11¼ bond is priced at $124.20 with a yield of 8.78% and a modified duration of 9.8. The CTD has a price of $139, a modified duration of 8.5 and a price factor of 1.474.

Calculate the number of futures to be bought to hedge $19m nominal of the bond.

Calculate BPV of bond and future.

Solution 4

Bond = 9.8 × $124.2 × 0.0001 = 0.1217

Future = 8.5 × $139 × 0.0001 = 0.1182

Therefore

$$\frac{19\text{m}}{0.1\text{m}} \times 1.474 \times \frac{0.1217}{0.1182} = 288 \text{ futures}$$

10: BOND DERIVATIVES

The above examples have included in the calculations the relative volatility of the bonds being hedged and the relative volatility of the future contract, i.e.

$$\text{Number of contracts} = \frac{\text{Nominal value of portfolio}}{\text{Nominal value of future}} \times PF_{CTD} \times \frac{\text{BPV of portfolio}}{\text{BPV of CTD}}$$

and

$$BVP = \text{Modified duration} \times \text{Dirty price} \times 0.0001$$

Therefore, the hedge calculation could alternatively be written as

Formula to learn

$$\text{Number of contracts} = \frac{\text{Nominal value of portfolio}}{\text{Nominal value of future}} \times PF_{CTD} \times \frac{\text{MD bond}}{\text{MD CTD}} \times \frac{\text{Dirty price of bond}}{\text{Dirty price of CTD}}$$

(The 0.0001's can be omitted as these would cancel each other out.)

Going one step further we remember that

$$MD = -\frac{\text{Duration}}{1+GRY}$$

therefore

Number of conracts =
$$\frac{\text{Nominal value of portfolio}}{\text{Nominal value of future}} \times PF_{CTD} \times \frac{\text{Duration of bond}}{\text{Duration of CTD}} \times \frac{\text{Dirty price of portfolio}}{\text{Dirty price of CTD}} \times \frac{1+GRY_{CTD}}{1+GRY_{Portfolio}}$$

which becomes

Formula to learn

$$\text{Number of contracts} = \frac{\text{Market value of portfolio}}{\text{Nominal future}} \times \frac{PF_{CTD}}{\text{Price}_{CTD}} \times \frac{\text{Duration of portfolio}}{\text{Duration of CTD}} \times \frac{1+GRY_{CTD}}{1+GRY_{Portfolio}}$$

Which equation to use will depend upon the way the information is presented. As should be obvious, they are all saying the same thing!

The logic behind the formula is quite straightforward. The ratio formed by the two BPVs simply provides a measure of the relative sensitivity of the bonds to a yield change.

Other methods of measuring relative volatility can be used, such as regression analysis. This approach models the historic price behaviour between the target bond and the CTD and calculates a correlation coefficient. Such an approach can be particularly useful for non-sovereign bonds where credit risks are high.

Despite the apparent sophistication of these methods, there are a number of potential shortcomings.

First, the CTD can change. CTD changes occur when either yields or the slope of the yield curve changes. Another connected problem is that as yields change over the lifespan of the hedge, so too will the relative sensitivities of the bonds. Not all bonds will be equally sensitive – a property known as convexity.

The final problem is that the hedge ratios rely on there being parallel changes in the yield curve to be effective. If there is a change in the slope, the hedge will not be efficient. This problem can be particularly acute when the CTD and the target bond have significantly different maturities.

5.4.4 Hedging non-matching dates

With only a limited number of delivery dates for bond futures, it is to be expected that the date the hedge is to be lifted will not coincide with a future delivery date. This will introduce basis risk and will impact on the appropriate number of futures to use in the hedge. An example of this is shown below.

Now

A fund manager intends to buy £10m (nominal) of the CTD bond in eight months' time and wishes to protect against an increase in price. Current price of the CTD is £100. The one-year interest rate is 6% and the coupon on the bond is 4%. The price factor on a one year future is 1.1.

Firstly, we will ignore the date we want to lift the hedge and just consider the two extreme possibilities of lifting the hedge immediately and running the hedge to maturity.

To do these assessments we will need to know the futures price now (before any price rise) after an immediate 10% price rise and the price after a 10% price rise in one year.

	Before price rise £	Now After 10% price rise £	Maturity After 10% price rise £
Cash price	100.00	110.00	110.00
Cost of carry			
– Interest 6%	6.00	6.60	–
– Coupon £4 fixed p.a.	(4.00)	(4.00)	–
Future CTD price	102.00	112.60	110.00
Price factor	÷1.10	÷1.10	÷1.10
Futures price	92.73	102.36	100.00

Giving the following futures price movements

	Immediate £	Maturity £
Closing price	102.36	100.00
Opening price	92.73	92.73
Profit	9.63	7.27
	or 963 ticks	or 727 ticks

Basic hedge

$$\text{Number of contracts} = \frac{£10,000,000}{£100,000} \times 1.1 = 110$$

Immediate 10% price rise

If hedge was to be lifted immediately following a 10% increase in the cash price of the bond, the result would be

	£
Bond cost (£10,000,000 × 110%)	11,000,000
Profit from future = 963 × £10 × 110	(1,059,300)
Net cost	9,940,700

Here the profit on the future has exceeded the increase in the cost of the asset leading to a net gain. If prices rose further this gain would get larger We have overhedged this position.

10% price rise by maturity

If hedge lifted at delivery day assuming a 10% increase in cash price by that day

10: BOND DERIVATIVES

	£
Bond cost (£10,000,000 × 110%)	11,000,000
Profit from future = 727 × £10 × 110	(800,000)
Net cost	10,200,000

What we see here is that we have locked in to the Future CTD price of £102 from the opening position. This would be the net portfolio value irrespective of how prices moved – a fully hedged position.

From above, it can be seen that the basic hedge calculates the correct number of contracts if the hedge is held to delivery, but overhedges if the hedge is not taken to delivery. For hedges **not going** to the delivery date, the number of contracts needs to be scaled down. To understand how we need to scale down the number of contracts we need to know why the overhedging occurs.

Looking at the futures pricing calculations above in respect of an immediate price rise, we can see that when the CTD cash price rises by £10.00 the Future CTD price rises by £10.60 due to the increase in the interest cost of carry. As a result, every £10.00 gain on the asset is more than cancelled by a £10.60 loss on the future. The future price movement is 6% more than required to achieve a hedge, hence we need to scale down the number of contracts accordingly.

In this example, the interest rate for the period is 6%. If the hedge was to be lifted immediately, the number of futures should be reduced as follows.

$$\text{Number of contracts} = \frac{£10,000,000}{£100,000} \times 1.1 \times \frac{1}{1.06} = 103.77 \text{ or } 104 \text{ (rounded)}$$

If the hedge was immediately lifted following a 10% increase in the cash price of the bond, the result would be

	£
Bond cost (£10,000,000 × 110%)	11,000,000
Profit from future: £963 × £10 × 104	(1,001,520)
Net cost	9,998,480

A perfect hedge except for a very small difference due to the rounding of prices and contract numbers.

Period of hedge

The scaling down is a function of the cost of carry interest rate and the time between putting on the hedge, taking off the hedge and the delivery date of the future being used. If, as the original example requires, the hedge is to be lifted two thirds of the way to delivery, the appropriate number of futures would be

$$\text{Number of contracts} = \frac{£10,000,000}{£100,000} \times 1.1 \times \frac{1}{1+(0.06 \times \frac{1}{3})} = 107.84 \text{ or } 108 \text{ (rounded)}$$

Futures price in eight months following a 10% price rise

	£
Cash price	110.00
Cost of carry	
– Interest 6% p.a.	2.20
– Coupon £4 p.a. fixed	(1.33)
Future CTD price	110.87
Price factor	÷1.10
Futures price	100.79

Giving the following futures price movement

	£
Closing price	100.79
Opening price	92.73
Profit	8.06
	or 806 ticks

	£
Bond cost (clean price)	11,000,000
Profit on futures: 806 × £10 × 107.84	(869,190)
Net cost	10,130,810

This is much closer to the expected eight-month forward price when the hedge was put on of £10,133,333 (two thirds of the way from the current £10m value to the £10.2m maturity value).

By scaling the number of contracts down in this way based on the interest cost of carry to delivery, we have achieved a better hedge.

5.4.5 Hedging with futures summary

Exam tip: Hedging bond futures is very regularly examined.

Pulling together the last two ideas of basis point hedging and non-matching dates we have that to hedge with futures

$$\text{Number of contracts} = \frac{\text{Nominal value of portfolio}}{\text{Nominal value of future}} \times PF_{CTD} \times \frac{\text{BPV portfolio}}{\text{BPV CTD}} \times \frac{1}{1 + r \times \text{Days}/365}$$

Where

    r = interest rate
    days = number of days from the date the hedge is to be released to the maturity date of the future.

    BVP = Modified duration × Dirty price × 0.0001

$$MD = -\frac{\text{Duration}}{1 + GRY}$$

5.5 Protecting and hedging with options

5.5.1 Protecting

The aim of protecting a bond/bond portfolio with options is to

- Place a minimum value on an existing portfolio – protective put.
- Place a maximum price on a future purchase – long call.

The number of contracts for either purpose is the number calculated above for the gilt futures contract, the options being on the futures contract. On exercise

- A long call settles into a long futures position.
- A long put settles into a short futures position.

5.5.2 Hedging

When hedging with options rather than with futures we have one more factor to contend with, the option delta. Futures effectively have a delta of one, and the formulae established above are based on this. As we saw with equity derivatives, when using options with deltas less than one we will need to scale up the number of contracts accordingly in order to get the correct offsetting effect, giving

$$\text{Number of option contracts} = \text{Number of futures contracts} \times \frac{1}{\text{Option delta}}$$

The issue that arises once again with options (that is not an issue with futures) is that the option delta changes as the bond price changes. Therefore if an investor wishes to maintain a delta neutral position he will need to constantly monitor and adjust the position. In doing this he will need to consider the cost and benefit of the continuous rebalancing. On balance, it may well be best to hedge with in-the-money options where the changes in delta will be low and the options are reasonably sensitive to price movements in the underlying bond.

5.6 Using futures to change interest rate risk exposure

A fund manager may wish to alter the fund's exposure to interest rate movements. If, for example, the manager believes that there will be an increase in interest rates, which will lead to a fall in the value of the fund's bonds, the manager may temporarily wish to reduce the fund's duration.

Example

Consider a gilt portfolio with a nominal value of £50m and a BPV of 4.8. The fund manager wishes to keep the nominal value of the portfolio the same, but reduce the BPV to 3.6. This could be achieved by selling low-coupon bonds and buying high-coupon bonds **or** by altering the interest rate sensitivity of the portfolio through the use of futures. We will examine the latter method.

As the fund manager wishes to reduce interest rate sensitivity, he must calculate the number of futures contracts he needs to sell.

As the nominal value will not change, the required number of contracts is calculated as

$$\text{Number of contracts} = \frac{\text{Nominal value of portfolio}}{\text{Nominal value of future}} \times \frac{\text{Change in BPV required}}{\text{BPV of future}}$$

Assuming the BPV of the future is 3.9, the required number of contracts will be

$$\frac{£50,000,000}{£100,000} \times \frac{4.8 - 3.6}{3.9} = 154 \text{ (rounded)}$$

NB: BPV of future = $\dfrac{\text{BPV}_{CTD}}{\text{PF}_{CTD}}$

The above approach can be complicated, however, when the nominal value of the portfolio changes. It must be remembered that the BPV reflects the change in price of £100 nominal for a change in yield of 1bp. Therefore, if the nominal value of the portfolio changes, this must be taken into account when calculating the total change in price that will be observed.

Example

Assume a fund manager wishes to change the asset allocation, but maintain the portfolio's existing duration.

The manager intends selling £20,000,000 nominal of Treasury 6% 2014 and investing the proceeds into Treasury 8% 2011. This switch would presumably reduce the duration of the portfolio and, therefore, the manager will need to buy futures to eliminate the fall. The following information is available.

CTD Bond : BPV = 5.1
PF = 1.0986357

Tr 6% 2014 : BPV = 5.3
Price = 106

Tr 8% 2011 : BPV = 4.8
Price = 108

The sale of £20m nominal of Treasury 6% 2014 would buy

$$\frac{£20,000,000 \times 106}{108} = £19,629,930 \text{ nominal of Treasury 8\% 2011}$$

Change in value of Treasury 6% 2014 for a 1bp change in yield

$$\frac{£20,000,000}{£100} \times \frac{5.3}{100} = £10,600$$

Change in value of Treasury 8% 2011 for a 1bp change in yield

$$\frac{£19,629,630}{£100} \times \frac{4.8}{100} = £9,422$$

Change in value of one gilt future for a 1bp change in yield

$$\frac{£100,000}{£100} \times \frac{5.1 \times 0.01}{1.0986352} = £46.42$$

Therefore, number of contracts needed to buy to offset fall in portfolio duration

$$\frac{£10,600 - £9,422}{£46.42} = 25$$

5.7 Bills and T-bill futures

Unlike coupon-bearing bonds, bills pay no coupon and trade at a discount, e.g. a 31-day UK bill is trading at a 12% discount. As with interest rates, discount rates are quoted on an annual basis. A 12% annual discount for a 31-day period represents an actual discount of 12% × $^{31}/_{365}$ = 1.019%. The price of this bill would, therefore, be 100 − 1.019 = 98.981. At a price of 98.981, this would represent an annual yield of

$$\left(\frac{100}{98.981} - 1\right) \times {}^{365}/_{31} = 12.1\%$$

Note that the yield is greater than the discount. This is because the yield is calculated on the price whilst the discount is calculated with reference to the nominal value.

Derivatives on bills like the IMM's T-bill future are quoted as 100 − T-bill discount rate. A price quoted of 94.80 represents a T-bill discount of 5.20%. On delivery (ideally of 90-day T-bills), the settlement value will be 100 minus the average discount rate on 91-day US T-bills.

10: BOND DERIVATIVES

By buying a T-bill future, it is possible to lock into the buying price and hence, the discount and yield of subsequent T-bills. If a T-bill future is trading at $94.80, the actual value locked into (per $1,000,000 – which is the contract size) will be $100 – (5.2 × $\frac{91}{360}$ *) × $1,000,000 = $986,856.

* Assuming 91 days from first delivery date up to and including the day prior to maturity date of the T-bill. In practice, this is allowed to be 90, 91 or 92.

Chapter Roundup

- You need to be familiar with the various
    - Bond products available (especially the UK Gilt future and option)
    - Exchanges they are traded on

- Futures pricing

CTD cash price	C	= Dirty price
Cost of Carry		
– Interest	X	$= C \times r \times \dfrac{t}{365}$
– Coupon	X	= Coupon paid and accrued
CTD future price	X	
Price factor	÷PF	= Price factor
Futures price	F	

    where

    r = interest rate p.a.
    t = days to maturity from the opening position.

- Implied repo rate

    $$\text{Implied repo rate} = \dfrac{\text{Invoice amount} - \text{Initial cost} + \text{Interest received}}{\text{Initial cost} \times \dfrac{\text{Days in holding period}}{365}}$$

- CTD can be established by determining which bond gives the
    - Lowest theoretical futures price
    - Highest implied repo rate

- Hedging with future/Protecting with options

    $$\text{Number of contracts} = \dfrac{\text{Nominal value of portfolio}}{\text{Nominal value of future}} \times PF_{CTD} \times \dfrac{\text{BPV portfolio}}{\text{BPV CTD}} \times \dfrac{1}{1 + r \times \text{Days}/365}$$

    where
    - r = interest rate
    - days = number of days from the date the hedge is to be released to the maturity date of the future.
    - BVP = Modified duration × Dirty price × 0.0001
    - $MD = \dfrac{\text{Duration}}{1 + GRY}$

- Hedging with options

    $$\text{Number of option contracts} = \text{Number of futures contracts} \times \dfrac{1}{\text{Option delta}}$$

10: BOND DERIVATIVES

Test Your Knowledge

Check your knowledge of the Chapter here, without referring back to the text.

1. On 14 February you enter a position in the September gilt futures contract. The CTD is a 4.75% Treasury which is quoted at £98.47 and pays coupons on 7 March and 7 September each year. The current interest rate is 5.25% and the price factor on the contract is 0.9263487. It is not a leap year.

    (a) Calculate the price of the future.

    (b) We wish to use this future to hedge a portfolio of £10,000,000 nominal value, £10,263,000 market value, out to maturity of the contract. The modified durations of the portfolio and the CTD are 10.2 and 8.3 respectively. Calculate the number of contracts required.

    (c) How would the number of contracts be altered if we intended to release the hedge after 100 days.

    (d) If we wished to hedge to maturity with options contracts with a delta of 0.76, how many contracts would be needed.

2. You hold the following portfolio

Bond	Holding (Nominal)	Dirty price	Duration	GRY	Price factor
4.5% Treasury	12,000,000	99.03	8.26	5.13%	0.9750382
7.5% Treasury	11,000,000	105.46	16.85	5.27%	1.0301679
6.0% Treasury	9,000,000	103.21	12.37	5.20%	1.0163275

Assuming the 4.5% Treasury is the CTD calculate the number of futures contracts needed to hedge the portfolio.

TEST YOUR KNOWLEDGE: ANSWERS

1. (a) **Futures price**

    Delivery date

    $$\text{Flat yield} = \frac{\text{Annual coupon}}{\text{Clean price}} = \frac{4.75}{98.47} = 4.82\%$$

    Current interest rate $\quad = 5.25\%$

    The return from holding cash is better than the return from holding the bond so deliver at the *start* of September i.e. 1st September.

    Dirty price

    The quoted price of £98.47 is the clean price, we need to determine the accrued interest. The accrued interest on the CTD and dirty price at that date can be calculated as follows

Month		Days	Days in period
September	From last coupon	24	24
October		31	31
November		30	30
December		31	31
January		31	31
February	To day before settlement	14	28
March	To day before next coupon		6
		161	181

    The semi-annual coupon is £2.375 (£4.75 ÷ 2) hence

	(£)
Clean price	98.47
Accrued interest £2.375 × $\frac{161}{181}$	2.11
Dirty price	100.58

    Bond income from 14 February

    Bond income is the coupon perceived and accrued to maturity date of 1st September, i.e.

		(£)
Received on 7 March		2.375
Interset on this coupon to maturity	£2.375 × 5.25% × $\frac{178}{365}$	0.061
Accrued interest to maturity from 7 March	£2.375 × $\frac{178}{184}$	2.298
		4.734

Month		Days From 14 February	Days From 7 March	Days in period From 7 March
February	From opening date	15	–	–
March	From last coupon	31	25	25
April		30	30	30
May		31	31	31
June		30	30	30
July		31	31	31
August	To day before settlement	31	31	31
September	To day before next coupon			6
		199	178	184

Futures price at 14 February

	(£)
CTD Cash price (dirty)	100.58
Cost of carry	
– Interest $100.58 \times 5.25\% \times \frac{199}{365}$	2.88
– Coupon (above)	(4.73)
CTD future price	98.73
Futures price	÷0.9263487
	106.58

(b) **Futures hedge to maturity**

BPVs

Portfolio dirty price = £102.63 $\left(\frac{10,263,000}{10,000,000} \times 100\right)$, hence

$BPV_{Portfolio} = 10.2 \times 102.63 \times 0.0001 = 0.1047$

$BPV_{CTD} = 8.3 \times 100.58 \times 0.0001 = 0.0835$

Number of contracts

Number of contracts = $\frac{10,000,000}{100,000} \times 0.9263487 \times \frac{0.1047}{0.0835}$ = 116.15 i.e. 116

(c) **Futures hedge released before maturity**

If we release the hedge after 100 days there are still a further 99 days to delivery. With interest rates at 5.25% p.a. we would have

Number of option contracts = $116.15 \times \frac{1}{1 + 0.0525 \times \frac{99}{365}}$ = 114.52 i.e. 115

(d) **Options hedge**

Number of option contracts = $116.15 \times \frac{1}{0.76}$ = 152.8 i.e. 153

2.

Bond	Nominal	Price	Value	Duration	GRY	Modified Duration	BPV
4.5%	12,000,000	99.03	11,883,600	8.26	5.13%	7.86	0.0778
7.5%	11,000,000	105.46	11,600,600	16.85	5.27%	16.00	0.1687
6.0%	9,000,000	103.21	9,288,900	12.37	5.20%	11.76	0.1214
	32,000,000		32,773,100				

Number

Hedging the 4.5% Treasury

$$\text{Number of contracts} = \frac{12{,}000{,}000}{100{,}000} \times 0.9750382 \times \frac{0.0778}{0.0778} = 117.0$$

Hedging the 7.5% Treasury

$$\text{Number of contracts} = \frac{11{,}000{,}000}{100{,}000} \times 1.0301679 \times \frac{0.1687}{0.0778} = 245.7$$

Hedging the 6% Treasury

$$\text{Number of contracts} = \frac{9{,}000{,}000}{100{,}000} \times 1.0163275 \times \frac{0.1214}{0.0778} = 142.7$$

505.4   i.e. 505 contracts

11 Interest Rate Derivatives

INTRODUCTION

Many businesses raise finance through borrowing. Many funds choose to gear up by borrowing and investing these borrowed funds. Many wealthy investors have significant sums on deposit. All of these individuals are exposed to interest rate fluctuations and may wish to hedge this exposure. We examine in this section the specific products available for gaining or hedging exposure to interest rate movements.

CHAPTER CONTENTS

	Page
1 The Cash Market	334
2 Interest Rate Derivatives	340
Chapter Roundup	363
Test Your Knowledge	365

11: INTEREST RATE DERIVATIVES

CHAPTER LEARNING OBJECTIVES

The syllabus areas covered by this section are

- **Uses of futures**

    Types of futures contracts

    – Money market, bond, currencies and stock indices.

    Hedging

    Students are required to display an understanding of the methodology of creating a hedge including:

    – Evaluation of exposure and setting objectives – choice of vehicle construction of a hedge ratio

    – Management of hedge programme

- **Uses of options**

    Types of options contract

    – Short-term interest rates

    Primary international exchanges where options are traded.

1 THE CASH MARKET

1.1 Introduction

The money markets are the focus for trading in short-dated (conventionally, with maturities of under one year) interest-bearing products and hedging instruments. The market itself is a complex intermeshed structure with a wide variety of instruments.

1.2 The instruments

As mentioned above, the normal definition of money market instruments encompasses any instrument with a maturity of under one year. However, in reality, longer dated instruments can come under the aegis of the market. Given the short maturities of the instruments, there is a tendency for them to be discount securities, issued at a discount to par, rather than carrying a coupon. However, some securities with a maturity of over one year pay annual coupons.

Whilst it is possible for some of the securities to be in registered form, the conventional approach is for these securities to be in bearer form. The security problems that this raises are now normally dealt with through the use of computerised book entry systems.

1.2.1 Deposits

The simplest of all money market instruments is cash itself. In the deposits market, banks simply take and lay off deposits from each other.

The market is liquid over a wide range of maturities, although primarily less than one year.

Interest is computed on a simple basis, i.e. no compounding. For example, for a £1m deposit for three months (91 days), the interest @ 10% would be

$$£1,000,000 \times \frac{10}{100} \times \frac{91}{365} = £24,931.51$$

In the UK, the day count convention is actual/365. This is a convention that is shared with Australia and South Africa. Most other markets use the convention of actual/360. Note this is often at variance with the accrued interest convention used in the bond markets.

1.2.2 Eurosterling

The historical development of the Euromarkets

In the immediate post-war period, the dollar became established as a quasi-international currency, due to its central position within the Bretton Woods system. Investors were keen to hold the dollar, and large overseas holdings of dollars started to build up outside the US. This process was accelerated by the start of the 'cold war' when the Eastern European countries repatriated their dollar assets.

The international or 'euro' dollar market gradually evolved from these deposits. London, by virtue of its position as an international banking centre between the two time zones, became the natural home for this market.

Whilst it is possible that there will be a discrepancy between the domestic and the euro rates due to differences in supply and demand conditions in the markets, normally, a process of arbitrage should alleviate relative surpluses and shortages.

With regard to sterling, and most other major currencies, the existence of tight exchange controls preventing currency from leaving the UK, hindered the development of a eurosterling market.

The removal of exchange controls in 1979 has meant that there is no real difference between domestic and international sterling and, consequently, the eurosterling market remains small.

1.2.3 Treasury bills

A Treasury bill is a promise to repay (**a promissory note**) a set sum of money by the Treasury (via the Bank of England) at a specified date in the future, normally not longer than 91 days.

T-bills are issued by way of a weekly auction and trade at a discount to their face value. Unlike gilts, they are not part of the government's funding programme per se, but are much more an instrument of monetary policy. The principal use of T-bills is to drain liquidity from the market, thereby making it easier for the authorities to conduct their open-market operations pursuant to establishing the interest rate.

The principal measures used to evaluate T-bills are

Formula to learn

$$\text{Discount rate} = \frac{100 - \text{Discounted value}}{100 \times \text{Days}/365}$$

$$\text{Yield} = \frac{100 - \text{Discounted value}}{\text{Discounted value} \times \text{Days}/365}$$

The yield can also be arrived at through the discount rate.

Formula to learn

$$\text{Yield} = \frac{\text{Discount rate}}{1 - \left\{\text{Discount rate} \times \text{Days}/365\right\}}$$

Example

91-day Treasury bill issued at 98.

The discount rate

$$\frac{100-98}{100 \times 91/365} = 0.0802 \text{ or } 8.02\%$$

The interest rate or yield

$$\frac{100-98}{98 \times 91/365} = 0.0818 \text{ or } 8.18\%$$

Alternatively, using the discount rate.

$$\frac{0.0802}{1-\{0.0802 \times 91/365\}} \times 0.0818 \text{ or } 8.18\%$$

It is conventional for bills to trade on the discount rate and this requires the holder to convert to the yield in order to compare with other investments.

1.2.4 Bills of exchange

A bill of exchange is an instrument that is drawn and issued by the seller of goods to the buyer, specifying an amount to be paid, either immediately, or at some particular date in the future. Once the bill has been accepted by the buyer (by stamping and signing the reverse), i.e. the buyer formally acknowledges the obligation to pay the amount stated, the bearer of the bill is entitled to the proceeds at maturity. The accepted bill may then be discounted, provided the purchaser is willing to take on the credit risk of the bill's acceptor, which is the promise of repayment.

During the 18th century, banks began adding their own acceptance to a bill, particularly for foreign trade, effectively providing the holder with a guarantee of repayment. As this was being done for merchants, the banks in this line of business, e.g. Rothschild, Schroder, Hambros, etc., became known as merchant banks and later formed a group known as the Accepting House Committee, which has evolved into today's London Investment Banks Association. These guaranteed bills are referred to as 'bank bills' or **'bankers' acceptances'**.

If the accepting bank is one of a list of approximately 168 'eligible' banks, maintained by the Bank of England, then it becomes an **eligible bill**.

Whilst it is possible to trade non-eligible bills, the market is limited by the fact that the Bank of England will only trade in eligible bills. This therefore restricts the bills that the discount houses can repo with the bank.

The other prime conditions required by the Bank of England for eligibility are

- That it be drawn in sterling.
- Has a maximum maturity of 187 days.
- Is payable within the UK.
- May not be accepted by a bank that has a direct link with the drawer.

1.2.5 Commercial paper

Many companies began to appreciate that their name was strong enough to enable them to issue discount securities without the need for a bank guarantee. This led to the emergence of the commercial paper market. Commercial paper is simply a promissory note issued at a discount to the face value with maturities normally up to 12 months.

It may be issued via the auspices of a bank-guaranteed programme or directly into the market.

1.2.6 Medium-term notes

Medmium-term notes (MTNs) are not strictly a type of security, but rather a facility enabling the issuer to issue a range of stock from one global facility. In the US, the facility can cover maturities of between one-year and 30-year debt. Until recently, the Bank of England imposed a five-year limit on the range of instruments available within a facility – this has now been removed.

The convenience to the issuer is that through one piece of documentation, it is able to issue a variety of paper, thereby saving on issuance costs and enhancing flexibility.

1.2.7 Certificates of deposit

A certificate of deposit is in effect a securitised bank deposit. Ideally, banks would like to be able to take deposits from customers on the understanding that these deposits would not be repayable within the short-term. However, investors are either unwilling to commit their funds for specified time periods (time deposits) or demand too high a premium.

The resolution to this dilemma came in the 1960s with the creation of certificates of a bank deposit (CD), committed for a period of time. Such certificates carry a fixed coupon rate and have a maturity of up to five years, more usually one year or less. Like any other security, the certificate can be traded enabling the deposit holder to realise the deposit through the sales proceeds and not by withdrawal.

Conventionally, CDs are issued by highly rated banks and therefore carry a limited credit risk. Unlike the other money market instruments, they carry a coupon but this is only paid on maturity. The exception to this is that any CD with a maturity of over one year will pay an annual coupon out to the holder.

Once issued, CDs trade on a yield basis. That is to say the amount that is to be paid for the CD means that given the fixed coupon, the new purchaser will generate the yield at which it is trading.

1.2.8 Short gilts

With their status as a relatively risk-free investment, the money market also trades short-term gilts (normally in market terms, with less than five years to go to redemption). The discount houses are deemed to be market makers in short-term gilts.

In particular, the banks, who are obliged to hold a proportion of their assets in the form of liquid investments, are active in the short gilts market. This is because, whilst offering a competitive return, the gilts are also highly liquid, enabling the banks to swiftly realise their positions if so required.

1.2.9 Other debt

As with the short gilts, other forms of 'low risk' debt will also be traded through the money markets, including local authority issues and highly rated corporate issues. In particular, FRNs, which are linked to the short-term, money market rates, are widely traded. The market will tend to prefer those issued by banks and building societies, since these will obviously carry very limited credit risk.

1.3 The participants in the market

1.3.1 The Bank of England

The Bank of England is a key player in the market. It is through the money markets that the Bank is able to dictate the direction of interest rates and monetary policy.

It also has a role in the market as the 'Lender of the Last Resort', whereby the Bank ensures that the market will not fail to meet its obligations. As the Barings crisis showed, this is not a blank cheque to the industry. The Bank will, however, step in where there is a 'systemic' risk to the market.

1.3.2 The banks

The principal users of the market are the banks who use the market to trade their own liquidity positions. Banks are faced with a dilemma with regard to liquidity. A bank takes deposits from its customers and then wishes to lend the money on to borrowers. In simple terms, the bank makes its profits from the difference between the deposit and lending rates.

The banks, in order to maximise their potential profit, would like to be able to lend the entire deposit out. However, they are constrained pragmatically by the need to maintain a proportion of liquid assets to satisfy the needs of their customers and, more importantly, by the prudential supervision of the Bank of England and the Financial Services Authority. The Bank dictates that each bank shall retain a proportion of its deposits in the form of liquid assets. These liquid assets partly comprise physical cash, but also certain liquid assets.

There are also many foreign and merchant banks that do not have access to a branch network in the UK and therefore need to obtain deposits via the wholesale, rather than retail, markets. Hence, the frequently used term for the money markets – the interbank market. From this market, come two very important reference interest rates that will be used to price many derivatives: LIBOR (the London Interbank Offered Rate), and LIBID (the London Interbank Bid Rate).

1.3.3 Companies

In addition to the banks (and financial institutions), larger corporates are also involved in the market, partly obtaining short-term flexible finance, but also using the derivative instruments to hedge their interest rate exposure.

1.3.4 Institutional investors

All portfolios will maintain a portion of the fund in the form of cash and near-cash instruments. The money markets provide an obvious and safe channel through which these liquid assets can be made to generate return.

1.4 Yield curves

The yield curve demonstrates the relationship between bond yields or money market instruments and their maturities.

Why are short-term rates different from long-term rates?

If you were to glance at the window of your local building society, you would be likely to see a notice board depicting available interest rates. You might see that the rates available to depositors seeking instant access to their money is 10%, whilst the rate offered to those willing to wait 90 days before a withdrawal is 10.5%.

Not all interest rates are the same because investors make judgements about risk and reward. In the example above, investors will need some encouragement to lock away their money for a 90-day period, hence the 0.5% premium for such deposits. If this premium was not offered, no rational person would make a 90-day deposit.

Interest rates therefore vary according to maturity. The relationship between return and maturity is often shown in graphs known as **yield curves**.

The Normal Yield Curve

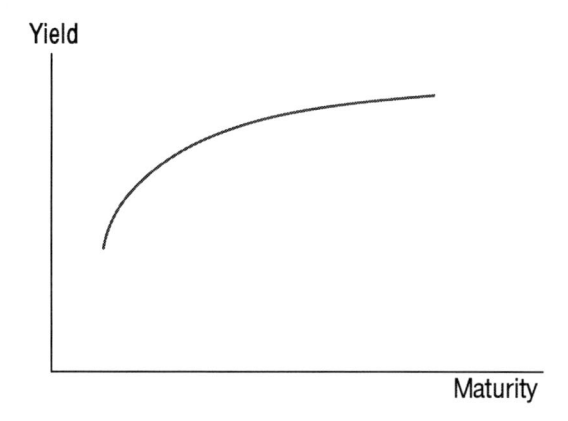

[Graph showing an upward sloping curve with Yield on y-axis and Maturity on x-axis]

1.4.1 The shape of the curve

Liquidity preference

The idea of liquidity preference is that if an investor's money is invested in longer term (and therefore riskier) stocks, then he will require a greater return – **risk premia**. Short-term liquid stocks carry a lower risk and therefore require a lower return. This gives rise to the normal upward sloping yield curve.

Expectations theory

Expectations theory states that the yield curve is a reflection of the market's expectation of future interest rates. If the market believes that the yield at the long end of the yield curve is high and is likely to fall, then in order to profit from the increase in prices that this will create, it will buy long-dated stocks. As a result, the demand for these stocks will rise and this demand pressure will force the price to rise. As a consequence, the yield will fall, reflecting the expectation of a fall.

On the other hand, if the market believes that rates will have to rise, then the forces will work in the opposite direction and this will lead to a fall in the price and a rise in the yield.

The expectations of the market can clearly be seen in an inverted yield curve.

The Inverted Yield Curve

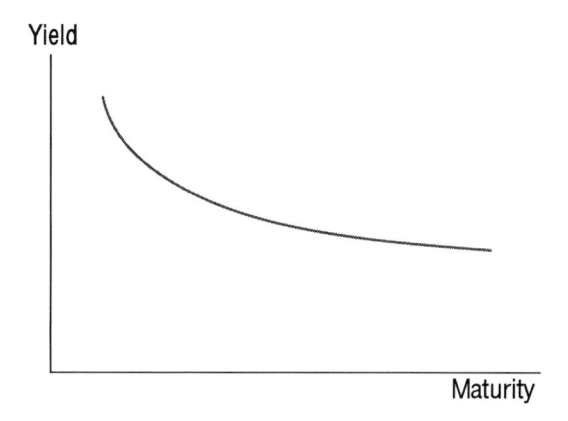

[Graph showing a downward sloping curve with Yield on y-axis and Maturity on x-axis]

Here, the short-term rates are high, but the market anticipates that this cannot last for long and the longer end of the market has anticipated this change by forcing yields down. This can lead to the anomalous situation where the long end of the market, because it has anticipated change, remains constant and the short end (which is technically the least volatile) exhibits all the movement.

Another key element of the market's expectations will be the **expectations of inflation**. If the market believes that inflation will rise in the future, then the yields on the longer dated stocks will have to rise in

11: INTEREST RATE DERIVATIVES

order to compensate investors for the fall in the real value of their money. The expectation of inflation is much more of a problem with the long rather than the short end.

Preferred habitat and market segmentation

Certain maturity ranges are appropriate to particular types of investors –they have a preferred habitat. In the UK, the short end of the market is dominated by the financial sector maintaining a proportion of its assets in liquid investments, whereas the long end is dominated by institutional investors such as pension funds. In effect, this gives rise to two markets and may be reflected in a discontinuity or hump in the yield curve.

Supply-side factors

The availability of stocks in certain maturity ranges may lead to either an excess or shortage of stock and consequently, an anomalous yield on some stocks.

2 INTEREST RATE DERIVATIVES

In the UK, Euronext.liffe is the centre of exchange-traded interest rate derivatives trading.

2.1 Summary of Euronext.liffe short-term interest rate products

Futures	Options	One-Year Mid-Curve Options
3-Month Sterling (£500,000)	3-Month Sterling	3-Month Sterling
3-Month Eurodollar ($1,000,000)	3-Month Eurodollar	3-Month Eurodollar
3-Month Euribor (€1,000,000)	3-Month Euribor	3-Month Euribor
3-Month Euroswiss (SFr1,000,000)	3-Month Euroswiss	
3-Month Euroyen (TIBOR) (¥100,000,000)		
1-Month EONIA-Indexed (€3,000,000)		

All the futures are cash-settled. The options are options on the futures and are American style.

2.1.1 Other exchange traded interest rate futures

Exchange	Product	Size	Tick	Tick Value
Eurex	3-Month Euribor	€1,000,000	0.00005	€12.50
CME	3-Month Eurodollar	$1,000,000	0.0001	$25.00

Contract details are correct at December 2006.

2.2 Quotation

The price of a futures contract is always stated as 100 minus the forward interest rate. For instance, if the forward rate is 6%, the future would equal 94.00 (100 – 6).

This method of quotation means that as interest rates rise, futures prices fall, and vice versa. This is done so that short-term interest rate futures follow the normal inverse relationship that is found in bond markets.

When investors buy or sell short-term interest rate futures, they are trading an index. The index measures the impact of interest rate changes on a **notional** borrowing or lending. On Euronext.liffe's short-sterling contract, the notional amount is £500,000 over a specific three-month period, e.g. the June future measures the period between June and September. The word notional is very important – the notional amount does not change hands at delivery. All that is delivered is the impact of an interest rate change. What one contract does is allow you to gain or hedge exposure to interest rates on a capital value of £500,000.

The tick size of short-term interest rates is 0.01 or 0.005 depending on the contract. This is one **basis point** or a half of one basis point.

As the amount of money and the period of time are fixed, it is possible to attribute a monetary value to each tick.

For the Euronext.liffe short-sterling future, this is

Contract size × Time period × Tick
£500,000 × $\frac{3}{12}$ × 0.01%
= **£12.50**

Below is the contract specification of Euronext.liffe's three-month sterling (short sterling) interest rate futures.

Unit of Trading	£500,000
Delivery Months	March, June, September, December, and two serial months, such that 22 delivery months are available for trading, with the nearest three delivery months being consecutive calendar months
Delivery Day	First business day after the last trading day
Last Trading Day	11:00 Third Wednesday of the delivery month
Quotation	100.00 minus rate of interest
Minimum Price Movement (Tick Size & Value)	0.01 (£12.50)
Trading Hours	07:30-18:00

Trading Platforms – LIFFE CONNECT™; central order book applies a pro rata algorithm with priority to the first order at the best price; Block Trading, Basis Trading and Asset Allocation facilities.

Contract standard – Cash settlement based on the Exchange Delivery Settlement Price.

Exchange Delivery Settlement Price (EDSP) – Based on the British Bankers' Association London Interbank Offered Rate (BBA LIBOR) for three-month sterling deposits at 11:00 on the last trading day. The settlement price will be 100.00 minus the BBA LIBOR rounded to three decimal places. Where the EDSP Rate is not an exact multiple of 0.01, it will be rounded to the nearest 0.01 or, where the EDSP rate is an exact uneven multiple of 0.005, to the nearest lower 0.01 (e.g. a BBA LIBOR of 5.43750 becomes 5.437).

11: INTEREST RATE DERIVATIVES

2.3 Pricing short-term interest rate futures (STIR)

Exam tip | The calculation of short-term interest rate futures prices is regularly examined.

Interest rate futures are not priced on the basis of cash and carry arbitrage, since deposits cannot be bought and sold. Nonetheless, they are priced with reference to other available rates so as to prevent arbitrage. As already noted, short-term interest rate futures prices are quoted as 100.00 minus a rate of interest. That rate of interest is the 3-month forward rate commencing at the expiry date of the future (or 1-month forward rate for the 1-month contract).

To illustrate this, consider the following rates.

3-month $ LIBOR = 6.50%
6-month $ LIBOR = 7.00%

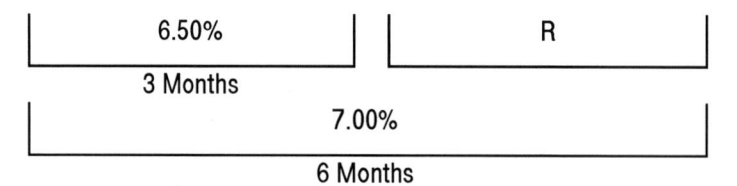

6.50%	R
3 Months	
7.00%	
6 Months	

What should be the rate for three months starting in three months' time?

To prevent arbitrage, an investor should feel indifferent to his investment choices. Either he could simply deposit for six months at 7.00% or alternatively, he could deposit for three months now and simultaneously buy a futures contract to lock in the deposit rate for three months in three months' time. The returns made from either route should be equivalent.

From our diagram above, we could guess that the deposit rate for 90 days (three months) in 90 days' time should be about 7.5%. This will not, however, be quite the right number, as it takes no account of compounding.

The formula using the rates mentioned above would be

$$\left(1+7.0\% \times \frac{180}{360}\right) = \left(1+6.5\% \times \frac{90}{360}\right)\left(1+R \times \frac{90}{360}\right)$$

Rearranging the equation to solve for R we get

$$R = \left(\frac{1+7.0\% \times {180}/{360}}{1+6.5\% \times {90}/{360}} - 1\right) \times \frac{360}{90}$$

$$= 7.38\%$$

Does this work?

   Deposit $100 for 6 months at 7.0% simple interest = $3.5 interest
or Deposit $100 for 3 months at 6.5% and then reinvest $100 plus interest at 7.38%
   Deposit $100 for 3 months at 6.5% = $1.625 interest
   Now deposit $101.625 for 3 months at 7.38% = 1.875 interest
   Total interest = $3.5

As can be seen, the results are equivalent and 7.38% is the rate required to prevent arbitrage. R in this calculation is known as the forward/forward rate or simply the forward rate and in this example, as it is a 3-month rate starting in three months and ending in six months, it may be written as $_3f_6$.

Example

What is the 3-month forward rate in 6 months if the 6-month rate is 6% and the 9-month rate is 6.5%?

$$_6f_9 = \left(\frac{1+6.5\% \times 270/360}{1+6.0\% \times 180/360} - 1\right) \times \frac{360}{90}$$

$$= 7.28\%$$

The general formula for determining implied forward (or forward/forward rates) is

Formula to learn

$$\text{Forward Rate} = \left(\frac{1+r_L \times t_L/360}{1+r_s \times t_s/360} - 1\right) \times \frac{360}{90}$$

where

r_L = interest rate for long period in decimal
r_s = interest rate for short period in decimal
t_L = number of days in long period
t_s = number of days in short period

NB: Use actual/360 days for all contracts except three-month sterling. The sterling money market uses an actual/365-day count.

2.3.1 Bid/Offer spreads

The examples shown above are simplistic in that they take no account of the difference between the LIBOR and LIBID rates, which is normally 1/8% (0.125%).

In calculating forward bid or forward offer rates, the following conventions should be applied.

	Long Period	Short Period
Forward Bid	LIBID	LIBOR
Forward Offer	LIBOR	LIBID

The rationale behind this is that to be able to exploit the arbitrage we would need to, for example, be able to borrow at a cheap rate (LIBOR) and deposit at a better rate (LIBID).

Example

Find the 3-month future price (LIBOR) for a three-month period starting in two months' time.

60-day deposit rates =   LIBID 6.6875%
                         LIBOR 6.8125%

150-day deposit rates = LIBID 6.5%
                        LIBOR 6.625%

To achieve this 3 month borrowing in 2 months time we could borrow now for 5 months at 150 day LIBOR and deposit these funds for the next 2 months at the 60 day LIBID rate giving

$$\text{Forward rate} = \left(\frac{1+6.625\% \times 150/360}{1+6.6875\% \times 60/360} - 1\right) \times \frac{360}{90}$$

$$= 6.51\%$$

In this way, the forward bid and forward offer prices can be determined.

Arbitrage will become possible between the futures and forward markets when an implied deposit rate in one market exceeds the implied borrowing rate in the other.

	Futures Implied LIBOR	<	Forward LIBID
i.e.	100 – Futures Price	<	Forward LIBID
i.e.	100 – Forward LIBID	<	Futures Price

or

	Futures Implied LIBID	>	Forward LIBOR
i.e.	100 – Futures – 0.125%	>	Forward LIBOR
i.e.	100 – Forward LIBOR – 0.125%	>	Futures Price

Assuming a bid/offer spread of 1/8%.

To prevent arbitrage, the futures should trade between 100 – forward LIBID and 100 – forward LIBOR. If it does not trade in this range, an arbitrage would be possible.

To illustrate this, contemplate the following example that assumes no bid/offer spread between the borrowing and deposit rates.

3-month rate	= 7.00%
6-month rate	= 7.50%
Futures (for period of 90 days in 90 days' time)	= 92.00

Calculate the forward rate

$$\text{Forward rate} = \left(\frac{1 + 7.50\% \times 180/360}{1 + 7.00\% \times 90/360} - 1 \right) \times \frac{360}{90}$$

= 7.86% (against an implied rate of 8% from the futures quote)

How could the inefficiency be exploited?

Based on this calculation the future is cheap and should be priced at 92.14 (100 – 7.86). Therefore

Borrow $100 for 180 days at 7.50%.

Deposit for 90 days at 7.00% and simultaneously lock in a deposit rate for subsequent 90-day period by buying future at 92.00.

In this case, a riskless profit of 14 basis points would be achieved.

Convergence

The price of the future will converge to 3-month LIBOR.

2.4 Using short-term interest rate derivatives

2.4.1 Speculation

An investor believes the government will lower short-term interest rates and seeks to speculate on this view.

Action: Buy one future at 94.01

Government reduces rates. Investor sells future to close position.

Action: Sell one future at 94.88

$$\text{Tick movement} = \frac{94.88 - 94.01}{0.01} = 87 \text{ ticks}$$

Ticks × Tick value × Contracts

87 × £12.50 × 1

= £1,087.50 Profit

2.4.2 Hedging

Although short-term interest rate futures are intangible products and as a result more difficult to visualise, the way in which they are used for hedging is similar to the products already discussed.

In constructing the hedge, you need to create an equal and opposite exposure to that which exists in the real or cash market.

A borrower of money at a variable rate (such as most house owners) gains if rates fall, but loses if rates rise. Whilst the futures contract cannot **directly** change the amount of money to be paid to a lender, the future can be used to lock in or fix the overall interest rate payable by generating compensating losses or gains.

To fix his borrowing costs, the lender would establish a short position in the futures contract. He sells futures to establish a position that will generate profits if rates rise, and losses if rates fall – the mirror image of his cash market position.

To demonstrate this, imagine that an investor sells one contract at 94.00 (implied rate 6%). If interest rates rise to 7%, the future will theoretically trade at 100 – 7 or 93.00. The move from 94.00 to 93.00 gives rise to a profit. If rates had fallen from 6% (94.00) to 5% (95.00), a loss would have arisen.

Borrowers sell futures to hedge.

Lenders or depositors of money suffer if rates fall, but gain if rates rise. Thus, to fix their deposit rates, they buy futures.

Depositors buy futures to hedge.

Let us work through an example of hedging a borrowing requirement.

Basic hedge

In order to correctly hedge we need to determine the correct number of contracts. To understand this we need to recall that one contract allows you to hedge £500,000 of capital against interest rate movements. So for a basic hedge

$$\text{Number of contracts} = \frac{\text{Principal risk exposure}}{\text{Notional principal of future}}$$

Example

10 April

A company treasurer fears that interest rates will rise. He will need to borrow £10m for a three-month period, beginning in two months' time on 15 June, when the June future expires. Current 3-month LIBOR = 5.7%.

Action: Sell 20 June short-sterling futures at 94.10

Contract size is £500,000

$$\text{Number of contracts} = \frac{£10m}{£500,000} = 20 \text{ contracts}$$

15 June

Action: Borrow £10m at interest rate of 6.5%, fixed for 3 months
Close futures position by buying 20 June futures at 93.50

	£
Cost of borrowing = £10m × 6.5% × 3/12 =	162,500
Profit from futures = $\frac{94.10 - 93.50}{0.01}$ = 60 ticks	
Ticks × Tick value × Contracts	
60 × £12.50 × 20 =	(15,000)
	147,500

$$\text{Effective rate} = \frac{£147,500}{10,000,000} \times \frac{12}{3} = 0.059 \text{ or } 5.9\%$$

As can be seen, the profit from the futures trade compensates the corporate treasurer for the increased cost of borrowing, leaving the net cost of borrowing at 5.90% – the rate implied (100 – 94.10) is the price of the future when it was sold.

2.4.3 Effective rates

What rate do you hope to achieve?

When putting on a hedge, it is possible to calculate the effective rate you should obtain, as the following will demonstrate.

Example

Date: 15 October

3-month LIBOR = 6%

December future @ 93.00 (expires 15/12) – implied rate of 7%

Assume no change in the yield curve over the period from 15 October to 15 December.

Scenario 1

Hedge a 3-month borrowing of £500,000 starting on 15 December.

Hedging action	
15/10 Sell to open	93.00
15/12 Buy to close (100 – 6)	94.00
Loss	1.00
	or 100 ticks

Hence, net cost of borrowing (15/12) – LIBOR still 6%

	£
Actual interest paid = £500,000m × 6% × 1/4 =	7,500
Loss on future = 100 × £12.50 × 1 =	1,250
Net borrowing cost	8,750

$$\text{Effective rate} = \frac{£8,750}{£500,000} \times 4 = 7\%$$

Conclusion

By holding the hedge to the expiry date of the future, the future rate of 7% has been obtained, i.e. cash 3-month LIBOR + **100% of basis**.

Scenario 2

Hedge a 3-month borrowing of £500,000 starting on 15 November.

Hedging action	
15/10 Sell to open	93.00
15/12 Buy to close (assuming steady convergence)	93.50
Loss	0.50
	or 50 ticks

Hence

Cost of borrowing (15/11) – LIBOR still 6%

	£
Actual interest paid = £500,000m × 6% × ¼ =	7,500
Loss on future = 50 × £12.50 × 1 =	625
Net borrowing cost	8,125

$$\text{Effective rate} = \frac{£8,125}{£500,000} \times 4 = 6.5\%$$

Conclusion

By holding the hedge half way to the expiry date, an effective rate of 6.5% has been obtained, i.e. 3-month LIBOR + **50% of basis**.

Scenario 3

Hedge a 3-month borrowing of £500,000 starting on 6 November, i.e. 22 days' time.

Anticipated effective rate = $6 + (1 \times {}^{22}\!/_{61}) = 6.36\%$

(61 days between 15 October and 15 December)

The above calculations assume that any movement in the yield curve is a parallel one and that basis erodes in a linear fashion.

2.4.4 Other considerations

Two very important factors that must be considered are how long the period being hedged is and what to do if the commencement of the exposure period does not match the expiry date of a futures contract. These two points will be considered next.

2.4.5 Period of risk

Exam tip | Hedging loan exposure is an area frequently covered in the exam.

11: INTEREST RATE DERIVATIVES

This is a simple adjustment to make.

Multiply the basic number of contracts by the factor $\dfrac{\text{Period of risk}}{\text{Period covered by future}}$, giving

Formula to learn

$$\text{Number of contracts} = \dfrac{\text{Principal risk exposure}}{\text{Notional principal of future}} \times \dfrac{\text{Period of risk}}{\text{Period covered by future}}$$

Example

A company needs to hedge a 6-month borrowing of £50m starting at the expiry of the June three-month sterling future. How many contracts should be sold?

Solution

$$\text{No. of contracts sold} = \dfrac{£50,000,000}{£500,000} \times \dfrac{6}{3} = 200$$

But which hich contracts should be sold? There are two possibilities.

- Sell 200 June contracts; **or**
- Sell 100 June contracts and sell 100 Sept contracts.

The first possibility is known as a **stack** hedge, the second is known as a **strip** hedge.

A stack hedge would look like

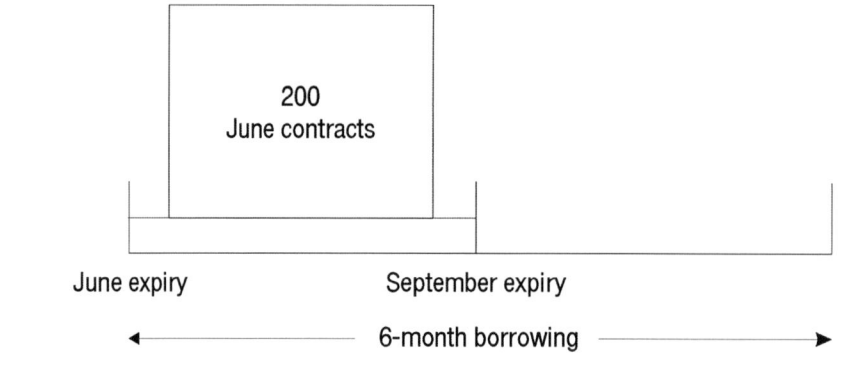

```
                    ┌──────────────────┐
                    │                  │
                    │      200         │
                    │  June contracts  │
                    │                  │
         ┌──────────┴──────────────────┴──────────┐
         │                                        │
      June expiry                          September expiry
         ◄─────────── 6-month borrowing ──────────►
```

A strip hedge would look like

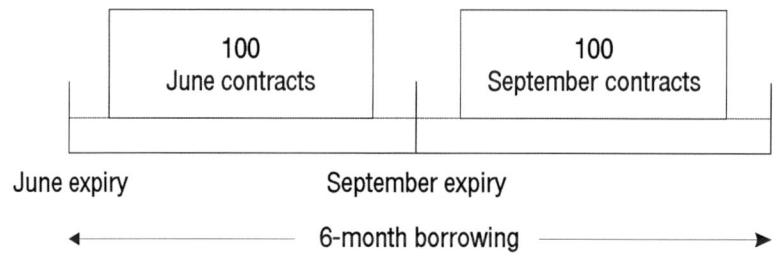

```
              ┌──────────────────┐  ┌──────────────────┐
              │       100        │  │       100        │
              │  June contracts  │  │September contracts│
              └──────────────────┘  └──────────────────┘
           June expiry            September expiry
              ◄─────────── 6-month borrowing ──────────►
```

Which is better?

The major risk of the stack hedge is that the three-month forward rate between September and December should move in an adverse, unanticipated and different way to the June-September forward rate. In short, the danger is of a non-parallel shift in the yield curve. If the yield curve were to exhibit a parallel shift (say, go up by 25bp), the stack hedge would work equally as well as the strip. However, if liquidity allows, the strip should be viewed as preferable, as it can more fully compensate for non-parallel moves.

A further point relates to the floating rate benchmark. In our example, the borrowing is for a six-month term, i.e. based on the six-month LIBOR rate. The strip hedge accommodates this in trading two three-month futures and thereby synthesizing the six-month forward rate (see explanation below).

The stack hedge seeks to hedge against movements in six-month rates by using three-month futures, obviously exposing the user to adverse movements in the three versus six-month rates, i.e. a non-parallel shift in the yield curve as mentioned above.

2.4.6 Strip rates

When a strip of futures contracts is used to hedge an exposure, e.g. selling contracts in consecutive periods to hedge a borrowing, the expected forward rate can be obtained using the following formula, solving for r.

Formula to learn

$$1 + \left(r \times \frac{\text{Days in period}}{360^*} \right) = \left[1 + \left(\text{Implied rate}_1 \times \frac{\text{Days in period}_1}{360^*} \right) \right] \times \left[1 + \left(\text{Implied rate}_2 \times \frac{\text{Days in period}_2}{360^*} \right) \right]$$

* Use 365 if a contract is denominated in sterling.

Example

A treasurer hedges a six-month borrowing of €10m, matching Euronext.liffe dates by selling 10 September and 10 December 3-month euro futures.

What is the expected forward borrowing rate if futures prices are

September = 96.00, December = 95.00

Calculate the strip rate – r.

Solution

$$1 + \left(r \times \frac{180}{360} \right) = \left[1 + \left(0.04 \times \frac{90}{360} \right) \right] \times \left[1 + \left(0.05 \times \frac{90}{360} \right) \right]$$

$$1 + \left(r \times \frac{180}{360} \right) = 1.01 \times 1.0125$$

$$1 + \left(r \times \frac{180}{360} \right) = 1.022625$$

r = 4.525%

In September, when the hedge is lifted, the following rates apply.

3-month LIBOR	4.25
6-month LIBOR	4.50
December Future price	95.30

11: INTEREST RATE DERIVATIVES

Interest paid on borrowings

	€
Actual interest paid €10m × 4.5% × $\frac{180}{360}$ =	225,000
Profit on September future = 10 × (96.00 − 95.75) × €25 =	(6,250)
Loss on December future = 10 × (96.30 − 95.00) × €25 =	7,500
	226,250

Giving an effective rate of

$$\frac{€226{,}250}{€10{,}000{,}000} \times \frac{360}{180} = 4.525\%$$

The hedge has obtained the strip rate.

2.4.7 Non-matching dates

Introduction

If a futures hedge is held to maturity, then basis, i.e. the simple differential between cash and futures prices, will be zero. Consequently, the price at which the future was either bought or sold will represent the actual borrowing/lending rate achieved.

However, if a hedge is not held until delivery, there is the possibility that the basis may be different from that anticipated.

Example

To illustrate this, imagine the date is mid-August and that a corporate treasurer intends borrowing £10m for a 3-month period commencing 22 November. The futures market offers liquidity in the September, December and March futures (assume all have a delivery date of the 22nd of the respective month).

This situation can be represented as follows.

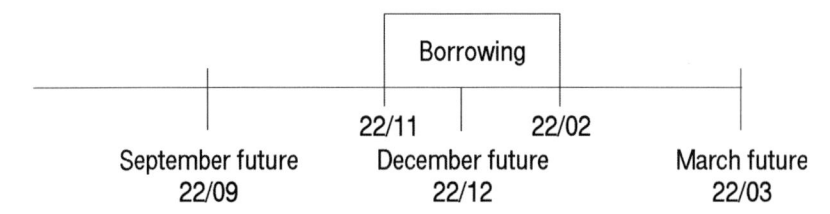

```
                              ┌── Borrowing ──┐
        |                     |               |              |
                            22/11           22/02
   September future       December future              March future
        22/09                 22/12                       22/03
```

The basic number of contracts will be

$$\text{Number of contracts} = \frac{£10{,}000{,}000}{£500{,}000} = 20$$

Unfortunately no contract covers the exact borrowing period. The September contract covers the first month but not the last two, whereas the December contract covers the last two but not the first. So which should we use? As we will see, the answer is either but the choice of the basic hedging instrument effects how we deal with the uncovered period.

Solution – Using December futures

The corporate treasurer could sell 20 December futures.

11: INTEREST RATE DERIVATIVES

This would hedge the treasurer against a parallel shift in the yield curve, but because of the mismatch in dates, i.e. borrowing commencing on 22 November but December futures maturing on 22 December, the treasurer will be exposed to a non-parallel shift in the yield curve.

In this scenario, where the futures are being sold and a later dated future is being used, the hedger is exposed to a **flattening** of the yield curve. To demonstrate this, imagine that it is just before 22 November and the hedge has not yet been lifted. There is a sudden reduction in longer term rates, but no change to the 3-month spot rate that will represent the treasurer's actual borrowing rate.

A fall in longer term rates, i.e. a flattening of the yield curve, will see a fall in forward rates and hence, an increase in the price of the future. This increase in the price of the future will represent an unexpected loss to the hedger. This is the risk of a non-parallel shift in the yield curve.

Intramarket spread

Exam tip | Exam questions in this area invariably involve non-matching dates and intra-market spreads.

To overcome this potential loss, the hedger can, **in addition to the basic hedge**, do an intramarket spread, i.e. sell futures for one month and buy for another (this is sometimes referred to as a futures straddle). As the basic hedge will suffer a loss if the yield curve flattens, what is needed is a short spread, i.e. the sale of near-dated futures and the purchase of later dated futures. A short spread will generate a profit if the yield curve flattens as the following demonstrates.

Near-dated future price 95 (implied rate = 5%).
Later dated future price 94 (implied rate = 6%).

If the yield curve flattens, the longer dated rate will fall by more than the near-dated rate, so that the price of the longer dated future will rise by more than the short-dated.

Assume

Near-dated future price becomes 95.50 (fall in rate of 0.5%).
Later dated future price becomes 95.00 (fall in rate of 1.0%).

	Today	Later	Profit/(Loss)
Near-dated	Sell @ 95.00	Buy @ 95.50	(0.50)
Later dated	Buy @ 94.00	Sell @ 95.00	1.00
		Profit	0.50

This demonstrates that if the yield curve flattens, a short spread will generate a profit. The next question is how many spreads? The formula used to determine the number is as follows.

Formula to learn | No. of short spreads = No. of basic × $\dfrac{\text{Time between start of exposure and futures maturity date}}{\text{Basic futures contract length}}$

For this example

No. of spreads $= 20 \times \dfrac{1 \text{ month}}{3 \text{ months}}$

$= 6.67$

$= 7$ (rounded) as only whole contracts can be traded

So, in addition to the basic hedge, the treasurer should sell seven near-dated futures and buy seven later dated futures. This could be achieved by

(i) Selling 7 December and buying 7 March; or
(ii) Selling 7 September and buying 7 December.

11: INTEREST RATE DERIVATIVES

However, as the hedge still needs to be in place when the September contract expires, if the second method is chosen, the September/December spread will have to be rolled forward into a December/March spread. It will, therefore, subject to liquidity and the futures trading at a fair price, be more sensible to do a December/March spread in the first place.

Overall hedge

	September	December	March
Basic hedge	–	–20	–
December/March short spread	–	–7	+7
	–	–27	+7

or

	September	December	March
Basic hedge	–	–20	–
September/December short spread	–7	+7	–
	–7	–13	–

but, at expiry of September futures

	September	December	March
	+7	–7	–
	–	–7	+7
	–	–27	+7

NB: Using a September/December spread and rolling forward will end up the same as if the December/March spread is used in the first place.

Solution – Using September futures

What if the treasurer had decided to do a basic hedge comprising the sale of 20 September futures? The treasurer, by using an earlier dated future in a short hedge, is now exposed to a **steepening** of the yield curve. If this happened, the cost of borrowing would go up, but without the offsetting gain in the future. To compensate for a steepening of the yield curve, it follows that a **long** spread should be employed.

Formula to learn

$$\text{No. of long spreads} = \text{No. of basic} \times \frac{\text{Time between start of futures maturity date and start of exposure}}{\text{Basic futures contract length}}$$

$$= 20 \times \frac{2 \text{ months}}{3 \text{ months}}$$

$$= 13.33$$

$$= 13 \text{ (rounded)}$$

Overall hedge

	September	December	March
Basic hedge	–20	–	–
September/December long spread	+13	–13	–
	–7	–13*	–
but, at expiry of September futures	+7	–7	–
	–	–7	+7
	–	–27	+7

* This may be called an interpolated hedge and could quickly be calculated by realising that 1/3 of the exposure is covered by September future and 2/3 by December futures.

11: INTEREST RATE DERIVATIVES

We see that trading a basic futures hedge in either delivery month, and then adjusting with an appropriate spread trade, will result in the same final hedge allocation of contracts between the two delivery dates.

We have been looking so far at a hedger doing a short hedge, i.e. a borrower. If a long hedge was to be employed by a depositor, logic would dictate that the necessary spreads would be the opposite to those outlined above.

Summary	Using Later Dated Futures	Using Earlier Dated Futures
Short hedge	Short spread to protect against a flattening of the yield curve	Long spread to protect against a steepening of the yield curve
Long hedge	Long spread to protect against a steepening of the yield curve	Short spread to protect against a flattening of the yield curve

2.4.8 Non-matching dates and non-three-month exposure

To illustrate this, imagine a corporate treasurer needs to borrow £10m on 1 August for six months. How can he hedge against movements in both the level and the shape of the yield curve? Using the relationship we established earlier for an extended period of risk

$$\text{Number of contracts} = \frac{\text{Principal risk exposure}}{\text{Notional principal of future}} \times \frac{\text{Period of risk}}{\text{Period covered by future}}$$

Gives

$$\text{Number of contracts} = \frac{£10m}{£0.5m} \times \frac{6}{3} = \text{Sell 40 contracts}$$

If liquidity allowed, the basic hedge would be undertaken as a strip hedge, i.e. sell 20 September and 20 December contracts.

This would hedge the treasurer against the level of the yield curve, but leaves a residual exposure to a change in its shape. This can be hedged by doing the appropriate number of spreads.

The easiest way of analysing the situation is to consider the 6-month exposure as consisting of two 3-month exposures. The first 3-month period runs from 1 August to 31 October and the second period runs from 1 November to 31 January.

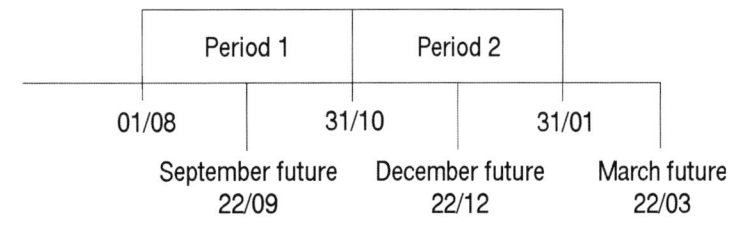

```
            |    Period 1    |    Period 2    |
            |                |                |
           01/08           31/10            31/01
                  
          September future  December future  March future
             22/09              22/12           22/03
```

Thinking of these as three-month periods allows us to apply our previous approach. Firstly, to Period 1, then to Period 2.

Period 1 – 1 August to 31 October

Basic hedge is to sell 20 September futures. A short hedge using later dated futures will require a short spread to protect against a flattening of the yield curve.

The basic contract for this hedge would be the September future, giving

- Time from start of exposure to futures maturity (1/8 – 22/9)   = 53 days
- Basic futures contract length (22/9 – 22/12)   = 91 days

Giving

$$\text{No. of short spreads} = 20 \times \frac{53 \text{ days}}{91 \text{ days}}$$

$$= 11.6$$

$$= 12 \text{ (rounded)}$$

Period 2 – 1 November to 31 January

Basic hedge is to sell 20 December futures. A short hedge using later dated futures will require a short spread to protect against a flattening of the yield curve.

The basic contract for this hedge would be the December contract giving

- Time from start of exposure to futures maturity (1/11 – 22/12) = 52 days
- Basic futures contract length (22/12 – 22/3) = 90 days

Giving

$$\text{No. of short spreads} = 20 \times \frac{52 \text{ days}}{90 \text{ days}}$$

$$= 11.55$$

$$= 12 \text{ (rounded)}$$

Summary

		September	December	March
Period 1	– Basic	−20	–	–
	– September/December Spreads	−12	+12	–
Period 2	– Basic	–	−20	–
	– December/March Spreads	–	−12	+12
Overall		−32	−20	+12

If there was insufficient liquidity for the March contracts, then Period 2 would be protected against a non-parallel shift in the yield curve by doing a further short spread with September and December contracts. The overall result would be

		September	December
Period 1	– Basic	−20	–
	– September/December Spreads	−12	+12
Period 2	– Basic	–	−20
	– December/March Spreads	−12	+12
Overall		−44	+4

Even this spread will not prevent all the difficulties presented by non-parallel shifts, but will certainly enhance hedge efficiency.

2.4.9 Calculating the strip rate for non-matching dates

The date is 15 August. What is the expected rate a hedger would anticipate for the 6-month period 15 November to 15 May? The prices of relevant interest rate futures are

Sept	95.50
Dec	95.00
Mar	94.80

The current 3-month rate is 4.1%.

Once more a linear representation will make it easier.

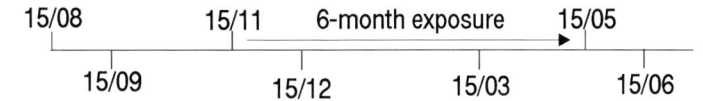

```
15/08        15/11    6-month exposure    15/05
 |    15/09   |    15/12        15/03     |   15/06
```

We will interpolate the yields implied from each futures price to calculate the relevant rate.

		%
15/11-15/12:	$\frac{1}{12} \times 4.5\%$ =	0.3750
15/12-15/03:	$\frac{3}{12} \times 5.0\%$ =	1.2500
15/03-15/05:	$\frac{2}{12} \times 5.2\%$ =	0.8667

Compounding these gives the rate for six months

$(1 + r_b) = 1.00375 \times 1.0125 \times 1.008667 = 1.0251$

r_b = 0.0251 or 2.51% for 6 months

Expressed annually = $2.51 \times \frac{12}{6}$ = 5.02%

A more accurate approach would have been to do the calculations using day counts rather than months. The above, although simplified, shows the approach that should be taken.

2.4.10 When should the hedge be lifted?

The hedge should be lifted, i.e. closed out, when it is no longer needed, that is at the **commencement** of the exposure period to which it relates, when the actual borrowing or lending rate will be fixed. In the last spread example, a six-month borrowing exposure starting 1 August could be hedged by selling 32 September contracts, selling 20 December contracts and buying 12 March contracts. On 1 August, when the hedger would fix the actual six-month borrowing rate, the hedge would no longer be required and therefore, the hedger should now buy 32 September contracts, buy 20 December contracts and sell 12 March contracts, thereby lifting the hedge completely.

If instead of being a single six-month exposure, the borrower was facing two three-month exposure periods, i.e. setting the rate on 1 August for the three-month period to 31 October, and separately having to set the rate on 1 November for the three-month period to 31 January.

The first 3-month period may be hedged by selling 32 September futures and buying 12 December futures, whilst the second three-month period may be hedged by selling 32 December futures and buying 12 March futures.

When the three-month rate for the period 1 August to 31 October is set, i.e. at 1 August, the futures hedging this period are no longer required, necessitating the purchase of 32 September futures and the sale of 12 December futures. It is important to realise that the futures hedging the period 1 November to 31 January should be left in place until they are no longer needed, which is until 1 November.

2.4.11 Further complexities

Exposure basis

Almost all short-term interest rate futures are 3-month LIBOR based, however, the customers' exposure may be to another money market benchmark, such as prime rates or commercial paper. Using regression analysis, a historic measure of the relationship between, for example, prime rates and 3-month LIBOR can

11: INTEREST RATE DERIVATIVES

be calculated and the hedge ratio adjusted. This antidote will only be effective if the relationship remains the same throughout the hedge.

Settlement sum

Interest rate futures are settled gross (via accumulated variation margin) by the beginning of the contract period with no such adjustment. This contrasts with the settlement sum for an FRA (see the chapter on other OTC derivative products) which is discounted to take account of the fact that it is paid at the beginning of the contract period rather than at the end.

To illustrate this, imagine that a corporate treasurer is looking to borrow £50m for three months in three months' time, a period that matches Euronext.liffe dates. Fearing an interest rate rise, he sells 100 contracts at 94.00. Three months later, he borrows from the bank at 8% for the subsequent three-month period and closes his futures position. The futures position will yield a 200-tick profit per contract.

In money terms, this will be

$$200 \times £12.50 \times 100 = £250,000$$

This money will be received at the beginning of the borrowing term, but will not be 'needed' until three months later, when the loan and interest must be repaid. The money could be placed on deposit to earn the risk-free rate for three months. This feature introduces a virtuous (at least in this case) imbalance into the hedge.

Additional Cost of Borrowing	Futures Profit
$2\% \times £50m \times \dfrac{3}{12}$	$£250,000 + \left(£250,000 \times \dfrac{8}{100} \times \dfrac{3}{12} \right)$
$= £250,000$	$= £255,000$

When trading a small number of lots, it is impossible to adjust for this defect. For larger exposures, the following hedge ratio may be used.

Formula to learn

$$\text{Settlement hedge ratio} = \dfrac{1}{t\left(\dfrac{\text{Basis}}{\text{Days}} + 1 - \dfrac{\text{FP}}{100}\right)}$$

where

- t = nominal length of the futures contract in years
- Basis = the day count convention, e.g. 360 for dollars or Euro, 365 Sterling
- Days = actual number of days in futures period (usually 91)
- FP = current futures price

If we had applied this to our hedging example and if we assumed we could trade in fractions of a contract, the number of futures would become

$$100 \times \dfrac{1}{0.25\left(\dfrac{365}{91} + 1 - \dfrac{94}{100}\right)}$$

= 98.255 contracts

Therefore, futures profit would have been

$200 \times 12.50 \times 98.255$
$= £245,637$

If this sum was now invested for three months at 8%, it would become

245,637 + 4,912.74 = 250,549.74

Very much nearer the required £250,000.

Margin flows

As we know, futures positions are marked-to-market each day and profits/losses are realised each day through variation margin. These flows, aside from being administratively irksome, can also affect the outcome of the hedge, as credit variation margins will earn interest whilst debits will incur funding costs. The effect of this will be to magnify profits or losses in the hedge. To overcome this, another hedge ratio can be devised. In this formula, it is assumed that futures move in a linear fashion.

Formula to learn

$$\text{Margin hedge ratio} = \frac{1}{1+\left(\frac{i}{2} \times \frac{D_H - 1}{\text{Basis}}\right)}$$

where

i = short-term interest rate at start of hedge
D_H = the number of days in hedging period

To illustrate this, imagine that $i = 8\%$ and D_H is 91 days for a sterling investor.

$$\text{Margin hedge ratio} = \frac{1}{1+\left(\frac{0.08}{2} \times \frac{90}{365}\right)}$$

$$= \frac{1}{1.01}$$

$$= 0.99 \text{ (implying that 99\% of the number of futures should be bought/sold)}$$

This adjustment is known as 'tailing the hedge' or as 'variation margin leverage' and should also be applied for large positions in bond, equity or currency futures.

2.4.12 Summary

The determination of the appropriate number of interest rate futures to buy or sell can become quite sophisticated if users are sensitive to the cash flow consequences of variation margin and the settlement date.

In calculating the correct number of contracts, it is suggested that a progressive approach is adopted as follows.

Formula to learn

$$\text{Number of contracts} = \frac{\text{Principal risk exposure}}{\text{Notional principal of future}} \times \frac{\text{Period of risk}}{\text{Period covered by future}} \times \text{Exposure hedge ratio} \times \text{Settlement hedge ratio} \times \text{Margin hedge ratio}$$

Example

A corporate treasurer wishes to hedge a 12-month borrowing of US$200m, with 3-month rollovers. The dates match CME dates. The borrowing will be made at the prime rate, which from regression analysis has a beta of 1.1213. The settlement and margin hedge ratios are both 0.97.

Therefore

$$\frac{\$200m}{\$1m^*} \times \frac{12}{3} \times 1.1213 \times 0.97 \times 0.97 = 844 \text{ contracts}$$

* The Eurodollar future has a notional principal of $1m.

As the borrowing matches CME dates, the number of contracts would be spread evenly across the delivery dates, i.e. March, June, September and December.

2.4.13 Interest rate sensitivity of a STIR

We have considered in the bond chapter how bonds and therefore bond futures exhibit a sensitivity to interest rate changes. This sensitivity has been measured as duration, modified duration and BPV. It has also been mentioned that a change in yield will affect a bond's interest rate sensitivity, therefore introducing the idea of convexity.

Does a change in interest rates affect the sensitivity of an interest rate future? Put another way: does an interest rate future exhibit convexity?

The answer to this question is no! This is because the tick value (£12.50 for the short-term £ future) does not change as interest rates change. Irrespective of where interest rates are, a 1bp change will have the same impact on the price of the future – £12.50. This means that there is a linear relationship between interest rates and prices of interest rate futures.

2.4.14 Protecting and hedging with STIR options

Introduction

STIR options are options on futures, i.e.

- A long call settles into a long futures position.
- A long put settles into a short futures position.

Depositors buy STIR futures to hedge against a future fall in interest rates since as interest rates fall, futures prices rise. However, if futures prices are rising then the price of STIR call options must also be rising, hence calls offer an alternative for depositors.

If we are a depositor and we are worried that rates may fall we may either

- Buy STIR futures in order to hedge.
- Buy STIR call options in order to either
    - Protect by establishing on interest rate floor.
    - Hedge completely if we account for the option delta.

Correspondingly, if we are a borrower and we are worried that rates may rise we may either

- Sell STIR futures in order to hedge.
- Buy STIR put options in order to either
    - Protect by establishing an interest rate cap.
    - Hedge completely by also taking account of the delta.

Protection

To protect a borrowing/deposit by establishing an interest rate cap/floor we will need to buy futures/options, and the number of contracts will be

$$\text{Number of contracts} = \frac{\text{Principal risk exposure}}{\text{Notional principal of future}} \times \frac{\text{Period of risk}}{\text{Period covered by future}}$$

Hedging

In order to use options to completely hedge our interest rate exposure we would need to take account of the options delta as we did with both equities and bonds earlier. That is

Formula to learn

$$\text{Number of options contracts} = \text{Number of futures contracts} \times \frac{1}{\text{Option delta}}$$

Hedging/Protection summary

Individual	Concern	Futures	Options
Depositor	Rates may fall	Buy	Long call
Borrower	Rates may rise	Sell	Long put

2.5 Intermarket spread trades

Exam tip — Intermarket spread trades are regularly examined.

A trader may wish to do a spread trade between the short end and the long end of the yield curve in one particular currency, or perhaps a spread trade between the interest rates of different currency. This can be achieved by an intermarket spread.

2.5.1 Single currency yield curve spreads

If the trader believes the yield curve will steepen, he could, as we have already seen, profit from that by doing a long spread, i.e. buy the near month and sell the later month.

Alternatively, the trader could buy short-sterling futures and sell long-gilt futures. This yield curve spread trade would benefit from a steepening of the yield curve.

In order to make the trade neutral to a parallel shift, the exposure of the long-gilt future must be matched to the exposure of the short sterling future. It is, therefore, vital to take into account the different sensitivities that the contracts will have to a change in yields, i.e. their basis point values BPVs.

The BPV for the short sterling future, by definition, is the tick value, i.e. £12.50 for a 1bp change, but what is the BPV for a gilt futures contract?

The basic relationship we saw in the bond derivations section was

$$\text{CTD price} = \text{Futures price} \times \text{PF}$$

$$\text{Futures price} = \frac{\text{CTD Price}}{\text{PF}}$$

To get the value of one gilt futures contract (£100,000 nominal) we need to scale up for the nominal value difference as follows

$$\text{Gilt futures contract value} = \frac{\text{CTD Price}}{\text{PF}} \times \frac{100,000}{100}$$

Since the price factor (PF) is fixed it follows that the sensitivity of the Gilt future to change in rates is a function of the sensitivity of the CTD, specifically

$$\text{BPV}_{\text{Future}} = \frac{\text{BPV}_{\text{CTD}}}{\text{PF}} \times \frac{100,000}{100}$$

or more generally,

11: INTEREST RATE DERIVATIVES

Formula to learn

$$BPV_{Bond\ Future} = \frac{BPV_{CTD}}{PF} \times \frac{\text{Nominal of future}}{\text{Nominal of CTD}}$$

Example

A trader wishes to initiate a spread trade that involved selling 100 long-gilt futures – how many short-sterling futures must be bought given

BPV of CTD = 5.9p

Price factor of CTD = 0.986352

Solution

$$BPV_{Gilt\ Future} = \frac{£0.059}{0.986352} \times \frac{100,000}{100} = £59.82$$

Therefore, to hedge the sale of 100 gilt futures, requires the purchase of

$$\text{Number of contracts} = 100 \times \frac{£59.82}{£12.50} = 479 \text{ short-sterling futures}$$

This position, i.e. long 479 short sterling futures and short 100 long gilt futures, will leave the trader immune to a parallel shift in the yield curve, but exposed to a non-parallel shift, which is exactly what the trader wants.

This can be shown by considering a parallel increase in the yield curve of 5bp.

Profit on short position in gilt futures.

Change in value of gilt future, for a 1bp change in yield = £59.82

Profit = 5 × £59.82 × 100
= £29,910

Loss on long position in short sterling futures

Loss = 5 × £12.50 × 479
= £29,938

The slight difference is due to rounding the number of short sterling futures.

This relationship could be generalised as

$$\text{Number of STIR contracts} = \text{Number of bond contracts} \times \frac{BPV_{Bond}}{BPV_{STIR}}$$

or perhaps more conveniently as

Formula to learn

Number of STIR contracts × BPV_{STIR} = Number of bond contracts × $BPV_{Bond\ future}$

Example

A trader believes that the yield spread on the euro will narrow (the yield spread is often quoted as the yield of the longer term instrument less the yield from the shorter term instrument). This suggests that the yield curve is flattening and it is therefore appropriate to sell the shorter term instrument and buy the longer term instrument in order to profit from this belief. The contract size of the Euribor future is €1,000,000 and each basis point change is worth €25, i.e. BPV_{STIR} = €25.

The contract size of the 10-year Bund future is €100,000 nominal. The trader wishes to have a €1,000 exposure per basis point change, i.e. a change in the yield relationship of one basis point will produce a profit of €1,000. If the BPV of the Bund future = €0.055 (per €100 nominal), calculate the number of Euribor futures.

Solution

Number of Euribor contracts required to gain an exposure of €1,000 per basis point is

$$\text{Number of contracts} = \frac{€1,000}{€25} = 40 \text{ contracts}$$

The basis point value of the Bund contract will be

$$BPV_{Bund\ future} = BPV_{Future} \times \frac{100,000}{100} = €0.055 \times \frac{100,000}{100} = €55$$

and so applying the above

40 × €25 = Number of Bund contracts × €55

giving

$$\text{Number of Bund contracts} = \frac{40 \times €25}{€55} = 18.18 \text{ or } 18 \text{ contracts}$$

The trader should sell 40 Euribor futures and buy 18 Bund futures.

Does this work?

For a parallel shift, e.g. an increase of 10bp

    Profit from euro futures = 10 × €25 × 40 = €10,000

    Loss on Bund futures = 10 × €55 × 18 = €9,900
    (difference due to rounding the number of Bund futures)

For the non-parallel shift that the trader is anticipating.

(i)   Long-term yields fall by 1bp – no change to short-term yield

    Profit from Bund futures = 1 × €55 × 18 = €990

(ii)   Short-term yields increase by 1bp – no change to long-term yields

    Profit from euro future = 1 × €25 × 40 = €1,000

Subject to restrictions imposed by having to trade in a round number of contracts, the trader has the required exposure to a change in the relative yields, but is protected against a parallel shift in the yield curve.

2.5.2 Cross-currency yield spreads

Exam tip | Cross-currency yield spreads are frequently covered in the exam.

When considering single-currency spreads, we have to take into account the relative price sensitivity of the two futures contracts (using BPV) and the size of the contracts. With cross-currency yield spread, we must still do this but in addition, we must also consider the exchange rate between the two currencies in

11: INTEREST RATE DERIVATIVES

which the contracts are denominated. The quickest way of determining the correct hedge ratio is to use the following approach.

Formula to learn

$$\text{Hedge ratio}^* = \frac{BPV_A}{BPV_B} \times \frac{\text{Contract size}_A}{\text{Contract size}_B} \times \text{FX Rate (B to one A)}$$

* No. of B to one A

These first two terms could be used to calculate the hedge ratio for a single-currency spread

Example

BPV of Bund future = 5.7916p or £0.057916
BPV of gilt future = 6.3012c or €0.063012
Contract size of Bund future = €100,000
Contract size of gilt future = £100,000
Exchange rate = £0.67 to €1

Solution

Based on the exchange rate, we have £0.67 to €1, i.e. the euro is the base currency (A) and the sterling is the variable currency (B) and so

A = Bund contract
B = gilt contract

$$\text{Hedge ratio} = \frac{5.7916}{6.3012} \times \frac{100,000}{100,000} \times 0.67 = 0.616$$

This means that for every 100 Bund futures bought or sold, 62 gilt futures would be sold or bought.

Chapter Roundup

- You need to be familiar with the various
    - Interest rate products available (especially short sterling)
    - Exchange they are traded on.
- STIR price = 100 − LIBOR

    where LIBOR is the 3 month forward rate from the delivery date.

    $$\text{Forward Rate} = \left(\frac{1 + r_L \times t_L/360}{1 + r_s \times t_s/360} - 1\right) \times \frac{360}{90} \quad \text{NB: 365 for sterling}$$

- Derivative use

Individual	Concern	Futures	Options
Depositor	Rates may fall	Buy	Long call
Borrower	Rates may rise	Sell	Long put

- Hedging with futures/protecting with options
    - Basic relationship (Matching dates).

        $$\text{Number of contracts} = \frac{\text{Principal risk exposure}}{\text{Notional principal of future}} \times \frac{\text{Period of risk}}{\text{Period covered by future}}$$

    - More complex applications (Matching dates)

        $$\text{Number of contracts} = \text{Basic number (above)} \times \text{Exposure hedge ratio} \times \text{Settlement hedge ratio} \times \text{Margin hedge ratio}$$

        where
        - Exposure hedge ratio must be given (assume 1 if not)
        - Settlement hedge ratio = $\dfrac{1}{t\left(\dfrac{\text{Basis}}{\text{Days}} + 1 - \dfrac{\text{FP}}{100}\right)}$

            where

            t = nominal length of the futures contract in years
            Basis = the day count convention, e.g. 360 for dollars or Euro, 365 Sterling
            Days = actual number of days in futures period (usually 91)
            FP = current futures price

        - Margin hedge ratio = $\dfrac{1}{1 + \left(\dfrac{i}{2} \times \dfrac{D_H - 1}{\text{Basis}}\right)}$

            where

            i = short-term interest rate at start of hedge
            D_H = the number of days in hedging period

11: INTEREST RATE DERIVATIVES

- Non-matching dates and intra market spreads

Summary	Using Later Dated Futures	Using Earlier Dated Futures
Short hedge	Short spread to protect against a flattening of the yield curve	Long spread to protect against a steepening of the yield curve
Long hedge	Long spread to protect against a steepening of the yield curve	Short spread to protect against a flattening of the yield curve

where

$$\text{No. of short spreads} = \text{No. of basic} \times \frac{\text{Time between start of exposure and futures maturity date}}{\text{Basic futures contract length}}$$

$$\text{No. of long spreads} = \text{No. of basic} \times \frac{\text{Time between start of futures maturity date and start of exposure}}{\text{Basic futures contract length}}$$

- Hedging with options

$$\text{Number of options contracts} = \text{Number of futures contracts} \times \frac{1}{\text{Option delta}}$$

- Intermarket spreads

$$BPV_{\text{Bond Future}} = \frac{BPV_{CTD}}{PF} \times \frac{\text{Nominal of future}}{\text{Nominal of CTD}}$$

$$\text{Number of STIR contracts} \times BPV_{STIR} = \text{Number of bond contracts} \times BPV_{\text{Bond future}}$$

$$\text{Hedge ratio} = \frac{BPV_A}{BPV_B} \times \frac{\text{Contract size}_A}{\text{Contract size}_B} \times \text{FX Rate (B to one A)}$$

Test Your Knowledge

Check your knowledge of the Chapter here, without referring back to the text.

1. In the UK, 3 month (91 day) LIBOR is 5.25% and 6 month (183 day) LIBOR is 5.5%. Calculate the price of a short sterling future for delivery in 3 months.

2. It is currently 18 December and a borrower wishes to hedge a £40,000,000 six month loan. Three month LIBOR is currently 4.5% and you are given the following information about the three month sterling contract.

Delivery month	Price	Delivery date
March	95.42	18/3
June	95.67	17/6
September	95.82	16/9
December	96.03	16/12

   (a) Determine the optimal hedge and effective lending rate if the loan commences on 18 March.

   (b) Determine the optimal hedge and effective lending rate if the loan commences on 20 February (not a leap year).

3. An investor believes that the spread between short term UK rates and UK long bond yields will widen and wishes to establish a position that will provide a positive payoff in that event but is immune from a parallel shift in the yield curve. He also expects a narrowing of yields between sterling bonds and euro bonds and wishes to establish a position to benefit from this that is immune to parallel shifts in yields in the two countries.

   You are provided with the following information in respect of the CTD on the UK gilt future and the Eurex Euro-bund future.

	Gilt	Euro-bund
Quoted price	104.62	105.60
Accrued interest	2.14	1.37
Yield to maturity	5.08	4.23
Macaulay duration	8.63	9.44
Price factor	1.0368195	0.9865913

   The exchange rate is GBP/EUR = 1.4986

   (a) Explain how to establish a position to benefit from a widening of UK yields to gain £10,000 for a 1 basis point widening.

   (b) Explain how to establish a position to benefit from a narrowing of yields between sterling and the euro bond on 12,000,000 nominal of gilts.

11: INTEREST RATE DERIVATIVES

TEST YOUR KNOWLEDGE: ANSWERS

1. Forward Rate $= \left(\dfrac{1+0.055 \times {}^{183}\!/_{365}}{1+0.0525 \times {}^{91}\!/_{365}} - 1 \right) \times \dfrac{365}{92} = 0.0567$ or 5.67%

   Short sterling quote = 100 − 5.67 = 94.33

2. (a) **Loan commences 18 March**

   Optimal hedge

   $$\text{Number of contracts} = \dfrac{\text{Principal risk exposure}}{\text{Notional principal of future}} \times \dfrac{\text{Period of risk}}{\text{Period covered by future}}$$

   $$= \dfrac{40,000,000}{500,0003} \times \dfrac{6}{3} = 160 \text{ contracts}$$

   The optimal hedge would be a strip hedge, selling 80 March contracts and 80 June contacts.

   Effective rates

Contract	Quote	Rate	Period (3 months from)	Days in a period	Time weighted rate
March	95.42	4.58	18/3	91	1.142 $(4.58 \times {}^{91}\!/_{365})$
June	95.67	4.33	17/6	91	1.080 $(4.33 \times {}^{91}\!/_{365})$
				162	

   Compounding these rates gives

   $(1 + r_b) = 1.01142 \times 1.01080 = 1.02234$

   $r_b \quad = 0.02234$ or 2.234% for the 182 day period

   Annualised this would be 4.48% $\left(2.234 \times {}^{365}\!/_{182}\right)$

   (b) **Loan commences 20 February**

   Optimal hedge – Three months from 20/2

   - Period 1 (89 days)

     – Basic hedge = Sell March contracts

     $$\text{Number of contracts} = \dfrac{40,000,000}{500,000} \times \dfrac{89}{91} = 78.2 \text{ or } 78 \text{ contracts}$$

     – Spread

       The basic trade is a short hedge using a later date future. Therefore we need to set-up a short spread to cover the period from the start of the exposure (20/2) to the futures maturity date (18/3), a period of 26 days, using the March and June contracts, hence

       $$\text{Number of short spreads} = 78 \times \dfrac{26}{91} = 22.3 \text{ or } 22 \text{ contracts}$$

- Period 2 (92 days)
  - Basic hedge = Sell June contracts

  $$\text{Number of contracts} = \frac{40{,}000{,}000}{500{,}000} \times \frac{92}{91} = 80.9 \text{ or } 81 \text{ contracts}$$

  - Spread

    Again we need a short spread to cover the period from 20/5 to 18/6, i.e. 29 days, this time using the June and September contracts, hence

    $$\text{Number of short spreads} = 81 \times \frac{29}{91} = 25.8 \text{ or } 26 \text{ contracts}$$

- Summary

	March	June	September
Period 20/2–19/5 – Basic	(78)		
– Spread	(22)	22	
Period 20/5–19/8 – Basic		(81)	
– Spread		(26)	26
Net long/(short) position	(100)	(85)	26

Sell 100 March contracts, sell 85 contracts, buy 26 September contracts.

Effective lending rate

The total exposure from 20/2 to 20/8 is 181 days

From	Rate	Period	Days Exposure		Rate for Exposure
18/12	4.50	90	26	From period 1 spread	0.321
18/3	4.58	91	91	March future	1.142
17/6	4.33	91	64	Balance	0.759
			181	Total	

Compounding these gives

$(1 + r_b) = 1.00321 \times 1.01142 \times 1.00759 = 1.02237$

$r_b = 2.237\%$ for 181 days

Annualising this gives 4.51% $\left(2.237 \times \frac{365}{181}\right)$

3. (a) **Intermarket spread**

$\text{BPV}_{\text{Bond}} = \text{Modified duration} \times \text{Dirty price} \times 0.0001$

$\text{BPV}_{\text{Bond}} = \dfrac{\text{Duration}}{1+\text{GRY}} \times (\text{Clean price} + \text{Accrual}) \times 0.0001$

So for the Gilt CTD

$\text{BPV}_{\text{CTD}} = \dfrac{8.63}{1.0508} \times (104.62 + 2.14) \times 0.0001 = £0.08768$

Now

$\text{BPV}_{\text{Bond Future}} = \dfrac{\text{BPV}_{\text{CTD}}}{\text{PF}} \times \dfrac{\text{Nominal of future}}{\text{Nominal of CTD}}$

So

$$BPV_{Gilt\ Future} = \frac{0.08768}{1.0368195} \times \frac{100,000}{100} = £84.57$$

Now

$BPV_{Short\ Sterling} = £12.50$ (tick value as tick size is one basis point)

To gain £10,000 from a one basis point move in short rates would need

$$\text{Number of contracts} = \frac{£10,000}{£12.50} = 800 \text{ contracts}$$

And to hedge against a parallel movement in rates we need

Number of STIR contracts × BPV_{STIR} = Number of bond contracts × $BPV_{Bond\ Future}$

i.e.

800×12.50 = Number gilt futures × 84.57

giving

$$\text{Number of gilt futures} = \frac{800 \times 12.50}{84.57} = 118.2 \text{ or } 118 \text{ contracts}$$

To benefit from a widening spread (falling short rates/rising high rates) we should go:

– long 800 short sterling contracts

– short 118 gilt futures contracts

(b) For the Euro-bund

$$BPV_{CTD} = \frac{9.44}{1.0423} \times (105.60 + 1.37) \times 0.0001 = €0.09688$$

So

$$BPV_{Bond\ Future} = \frac{0.09688}{0.9865913} \times \frac{100,000}{100} = €98.70$$

The hedge ratio is therefore

$$\text{Hedge ratio} = \frac{84.57}{98.70} \times \frac{100,000}{100,000} \times 1.4986 = 1.2906$$

So for every gilt futures contract we will need 1.2906 Euro-bund contracts

To gain the required exposure we need 120 gilt futures ($\frac{12,000,000}{100,000}$) hence we will need 155 (120 × 1.2906, rounded) Euro-bund futures.

Currently the sterling CTD is yielding more than the Euro CTD so a narrowing of this spread suggests

– falling UK yields, hence rising UK prices therefore long gilt futures

– rising Euro yields, hence falling Euro prices therefore short Euro-bond futures

Conclusion

Sell 155 Euro-bund futures, buy 120 UK gilt futures.

12 Currency Derivatives

INTRODUCTION

Many businesses are exposed to exchange rate fluctuations, especially importers and exporters. For importers, a weakening of sterling will make imported goods more expensive, damaging corporate profits. For exporters, a strengthening of sterling will make UK goods appear expensive overseas, possibly leading to reduced demand. In truth there are very few UK companies that do not face an exposure to exchange rate movements. An ability to hedge this risk is, therefore, very important and we examine in this section the specific products available for this purpose.

CHAPTER CONTENTS

	Page
1 The Cash Market	370
2 Currency Derivatives	375
Chapter Roundup	385
Test Your Knowledge	387

12: CURRENCY DERIVATIVES

CHAPTER LEARNING OBJECTIVES

The syllabus areas covered by this section are

- **Uses of futures**

  Types of futures contracts

  – Money market, bond, currencies and stock indices.

  Hedging

  Students are required to display understanding of the methodology of creating a hedge including:

  – evaluation of exposure and the setting of objectives – choice of vehicle construction of a hedge ratio

  – management of the hedge programme

- **Uses of Options**

  Types of options contract

  – currencies

  Primary international exchanges where options are traded.

- **Over-the-Counter Derivatives**

  Types of contract

  – Forwards

1 THE CASH MARKET

The foreign exchange market provides one of the largest and deepest financial markets in the world. Today, foreign exchange dealing is estimated to exceed $2,600bn a day. Of this turnover, no more than 20% is concerned with trade and portfolio investment. The remaining 80% is made up of dealings between banks and other financial operators.

The market place is worldwide, with London being the most important centre, accounting for more than 30% of turnover. Dealing takes place via telephones and screen trading systems such as Reuters.

1.1 Currency rates

In order to be able to analyse foreign currency risk in more detail, it is important to be able to perform basic foreign currency calculations.

1.1.1 Spot rates

The spot market is the market for immediate currency trades. Delivery will take place two business days after the deal is made (t+2). The market has no formal market place and trading takes place via telephones with prices being quoted on screen services.

Most corporates will access this market via clearing banks. Individuals, unless they have very significant net worth, will not have the necessary credit standing to trade in the professional market and will therefore be doomed to trade with bureaux de change at excessive spreads and commissions. The discussion that follows relates to the professional markets.

1.1.2 How spot rates are quoted

Most spot rates are quoted as bid/offer prices per US$1. The two main exceptions to this are when the € or £ is involved. In these cases, the price of the €1 or £1 is stated in $s.

1.1.3 £/$ Spot rate

1.4275 - 1.4285	
The market maker's BID rate. He will buy £1 from you and pay (sell you) $1.4275.	The market maker's OFFER rate. He will sell £1 to you in exchange for (he buys) $1.4285.

To assist in remembering which rate to use, remember that the bank always gives you the worst side. For example, if you want to buy dollars with £1, the bank will give you the least dollars it can, i.e. $1.4275 rather than $1.4285 in return. Alternatively, if you have dollars and want to buy £1, then the bank will charge you the most it can, i.e. $1.4285 rather than $1.4275.

1.2 Direct and indirect quotes

A direct quote is when the number of domestic currency units is expressed as one unit of the foreign currency.

An indirect quote is when the number of foreign currency units is expressed as one unit of the domestic currency.

1.3 Cross rates

Most foreign exchange rates are quoted against the US dollar. If we were seeking to calculate a rate between, for example yen and Swiss francs, the following cross rate method would be used.

1.3.1 Indirect quotes

$/SFr: 1.7119-1.7129
$/¥: 133.75-133.95

Let us imagine that a customer wishes to buy SFr5m against yen. What is the rate? The transactions might be as follows.

The bank will need to buy SFr against US$ at a rate of 1.7119.

To produce the requisite dollars, the bank would sell yen, which it receives from its customer. The rate at which the yen are sold for dollars is 133.95.

Thus, the cross rate would be

$$\frac{133.95}{1.7119} = 78.25$$

1.3.2 Calculating for both bid and offer rates

$/SFr: 1.7119-1.7129

$/¥: 133.75-133.95

SFr/¥: $\dfrac{133.75}{1.7129}$ $\dfrac{133.95}{1.7119}$

78.08   78.25

1.3.3 Indirect/Direct

To calculate the cross rate between an indirect and a direct currency, the same sides are multiplied, e.g.

$/SFr: 1.7119-1.7129

£/$:   1.4230-1.4240

1.7119×1.4230 1.7129×1.4240

£/SFr: 2.4360-2.4392

1.4 Forward rates

The forward market is a market in currencies for delivery at an agreed date in the future. The exchange rate at which delivery will take place is agreed now.

1.4.1 How forward rates are quoted

Forward rates are quoted as premiums (pm) or discounts (dis) to the spot rate. It is possible for rates to be quoted at par where the spot and forward are the same.

Example

Spot £/$	1.4275-1.4385
One-month forward	0.37-0.35
Three-month forward	1.00-0.97

Calculate the three-month forward rate.

Solution

It is important to note that the forward points adjustments are **quoted in cents** whereas the spot rate is quoted in dollars.

A premium implies that the currency is becoming more valuable, i.e. £1 will buy more dollars.

Based on the above figures, the three-month forward rate

Spot rate	1.4275	-1.4385
	(0.0100)	-(0.0097)
	1.4175	-1.4288

1.4.2 How forward rates are calculated by the bank

One important factor to remember about this market is that it does not necessarily reflect an expectation of what the spot rate will be in three, six or nine months' time. It is simply a mathematical result of the difference in interest rates in the two countries.

Example

In the above example, 3-month sterling interest rates were 10%, meaning the interest rate for the 3-month period is 2.5% (10 × 3/12). Three-month dollar rates were 6%, meaning the interest rate for the 3-month period is 1.5% (6 × 3/12).

Now Spot Rate				Three Months' Time Forward Rate
£1,000	→	@ 3-month £ rates at 2.5%	→	£1,025
↓				↓
@ 1.4275				**Therefore, @ 1.4136**
↓				↑
$1,427.50	→	@ 3-month $ rates at 1.5%	→	$1,448.91

The forward rate is simply calculated on the basis that the money is invested at the current rate of interest in the two countries. At the end of the period, the relationship between the value of the two deposits gives the forward rate.

$$\frac{1,448.91}{1,025} = 1.4136$$

If this relationship were not the case, it would be possible to make an arbitrage profit by borrowing in one currency, converting it at today's spot rate into the other currency and placing this on deposit for, say, three months. At the same time, a forward contract could be taken out to reverse the original spot transaction, locking in a profit.

1.4.3 Interest rate parity formula

Exam tip | This is a key relationship for any currency questions

The link between exchange rates and interest rates can be worked through using first principles as above. Alternatively, the link can be summarised by the **interest rate parity** formula, which says that

Formula to learn | Forward rate = Spot rate $\times \dfrac{1+r_V}{1+r_F}$

where

r_V = interest rate for the relevant period in the variable currency
r_F = interest rate for the relevant period in the fixed or base currency

12: CURRENCY DERIVATIVES

In the above example

$$\text{Forward rate} = 1.4275 \times \frac{1.015}{1.025} = 1.4136$$

It is worth noting the specific way in which r_V and r_F are calculated. They should be based on the number of days in the period and the relevant money market convention. For example, if dollar interest rates for a 3-month (91-day) period are 8%, the relevant value for r_V is (8% × 91/360) 2.02%. If sterling interest rates for a 3-month (91-day) period are 10%, then the relevant value for r_F is (10% × 91/365) 2.49%.

The use of a 365-day year for sterling interest rates and a 360-day year for dollar, Euro, Yen and most others are market conventions. When banks work out the yield they wish to pay or receive, they take this into account in their quote.

As an alternative to being given interest rates in each currency you may be given discount factors $\left(\frac{1}{1+r}\right)$ for each currency. In this situation, the easiest formulation of interest rate parity is

Formula to learn

$$\text{Forward rate} = \text{Spot rate} \times \frac{DF_F}{DF_V}$$

Where

- DF_F = discount factor for the fixed currency
- DF_V = discount factor for the variable currency

Example

If the 3-month money market rate in the UK is 10% and in the US is 6% and the spot rate is $1.4275:£1, calculate

- UK and US 3-month discount factors
- 3 month forward rate using these discount factors

Solution

Discount Factors

- Fixed rate is sterling

    3-month rate = 2.5% (10% × 3/12)

    $$DF_F = \frac{1}{1.025} = 0.9756098$$

- Variable rate is dollar

    3 month rate = 1.5% (6% × 3/12)

    $$DF_V = \frac{1}{1.015} = 0.9852217$$

Forward rate

$$\text{Forward rate} = \text{Spot rate} \times \frac{DF_F}{DF_V} = 1.4275 \times \frac{0.9756098}{0.9852217} = 1.4136 \text{ (as before)}$$

12: CURRENCT DERIVATIVES

1.4.4 Market quotes

Details of exchange rates are included in the *Financial Times* every day.

2 CURRENCY DERIVATIVES

Surprisingly, no currency futures or options are traded on the London exchanges. This is because the banks themselves provide a market place in these products. When derivative products are not traded on an exchange, they are said to trade over-the-counter (OTC). The major difference between exchange-traded and OTC products is the degree of standardisation. Exchange-traded products are governed by contract specifications that fix contract sizes and delivery dates. OTC products are not standardised, with the contract size and delivery date being mutually agreed at the time of trade.

Despite London's lack of exchange-traded currency products, there are two US exchanges that do trade them: the Chicago Mercantile Exchange (CME) and the Philadelphia Stock Exchange (PHLX).

Both the CME and PHLX trade by open outcry. However, after US trading hours, CME currency products are available on GLOBEX.

Some of the Exchange-Traded Currency Futures and options on these exchanges are as follows.

Exchange	Product	Size	Tick	Tick Value
CME options and futures	British Pound	£62,500	0.0001	$6.25
	Euro	€125,000	0.0001	$12.50
	Japanese Yen	¥12,500,000	0.000001	$12.50
PLX options	British Pound	£31,250	0.0001	$3.125
	Euro	€62,500	0.0001	$6.25
	Japanese Yen	¥6,250,000	0.000001	$6.25

The CME options are deliverable into the relevant futures contract, the futures themselves all being physically settled.

The PHLX options are physically settled.

Contract details correct at December 2006.

2.1 Quotation

The quotation of all the US currency products is in **American terms**.

Thus, a quote of 1.4108 for the sterling future means that it costs $1.4108 to buy £1. American term quotes state how many dollars it costs to buy 1 unit of a foreign currency.

The total dollar value of one sterling future would be

$1.4108 \times 62,500 = \$88,175$

The next concept to master is who delivers what in a currency futures contract.

If you **buy** a currency future, you enter into an obligation to buy the foreign currency, e.g. sterling, yen, and thus sell US dollars.

If you **sell** a currency future, you enter into an obligation to sell the foreign currency and thus buy US dollars.

12: CURRENCY DERIVATIVES

2.2 Pricing currency futures

Similar to the other futures we have studied, currency futures have a cash and carry relationship with spot exchange rates. The theoretical currency futures price is the price at which a profitable cash and carry or reverse cash and carry arbitrage does not exist.

If we take the sterling future traded on the Chicago Mercantile Exchange as an example, we can identify the stages in the arbitrage.

The arbitrage would involve borrowing dollars to buy sterling and simultaneously selling the future to lock in a sale price for sterling. The financing costs of this position will depend on short-term dollar interest rates, while the benefits will depend on short-term interest rates in the foreign currency.

The financing costs are a function of the spot price of sterling in dollars, the US short-term interest rates and the number of days until delivery, whilst the benefits are the sterling interest rate and the days until delivery converted back into dollars.

Example

Spot rate: 1.4100 ($1.4100 = £1)
$ interest rates: 6.5%
£ interest rates: 5.0%
Days until delivery: 90

Today: Borrow $88,125 and buy £62,500

Finance cost: $= \$88{,}125 \times 6.5\% \times \dfrac{90}{360} = \$1{,}432$

Benefit: $= £62{,}500 \times 5\% \times \dfrac{90}{365} = £771$

To prevent arbitrage the sterling principal plus interest must equal the sum required to repay the dollar loan plus interest.

Total dollars required = $88,125 + $1,432 = $89,557

Total sterling available = £62,500 + £771 = £63,271

Required rate to prevent arbitrage.

$$\dfrac{\$89{,}557}{£63{,}271} = 1.4155$$

More elegantly, we could use the interest rate parity formula introduced earlier as the forward rate is the theoretical futures price.

Example

Spot $ = 1.4100
Dollar interest rate = 6.5%
Sterling interest rate = 5.0%
Days = 90

What is the theoretical futures price?

Solution

Theoretical futures price = $1.4100 \times \left[\dfrac{(1+0.065 \times 90/360)}{(1+0.05 \times 90/365)}\right] = 1.4155$ (as before)

2.2.1 Pricing currency future/Forwards including bid offer spreads

Example

Spot euro	1.1000-1.1500 ($ to €1)
Dollar interest rate	6%-6¼%
Euro interest rate	5%-5¼%

Forward Euro buying rate (from bank's point of view)

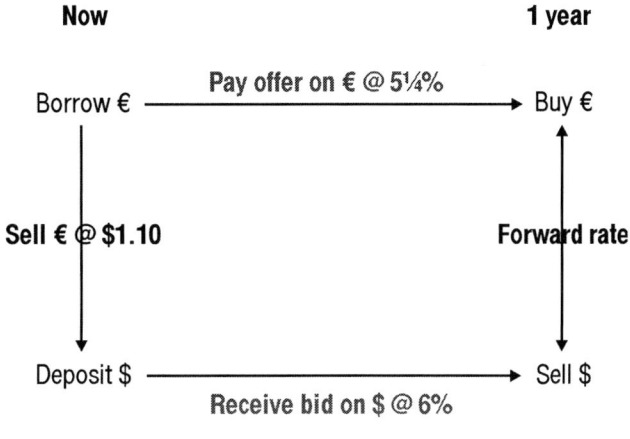

```
         Now                                    1 year
                   Pay offer on € @ 5¼%
    Borrow €  ─────────────────────────────→  Buy €
        │                                        ↑
        │                                        │
    Sell € @ $1.10                          Forward rate
        │                                        │
        ↓                                        │
    Deposit $ ───────────────────────────────→ Sell $
                   Receive bid on $ @ 6%
```

Forward rate = $1.10 \times \left(\dfrac{1.06}{1.0525}\right) = 1.1078$

This is the forward bid rate.

Forward Euro selling rate (from bank's point of view)

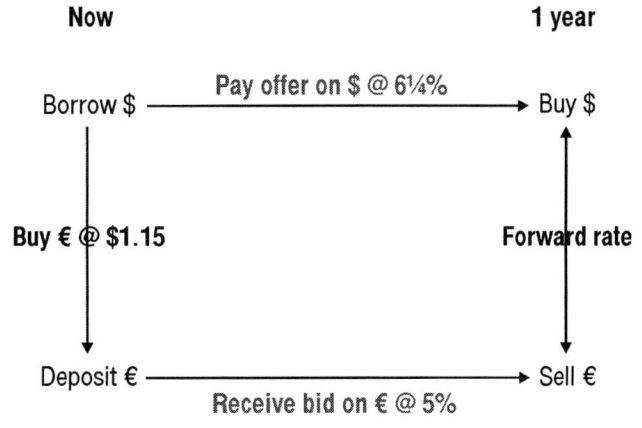

```
         Now                                    1 year
                   Pay offer on $ @ 6¼%
    Borrow $  ─────────────────────────────→  Buy $
        │                                        ↑
        │                                        │
    Buy € @ $1.15                           Forward rate
        │                                        │
        ↓                                        │
    Deposit € ───────────────────────────────→ Sell €
                   Receive bid on € @ 5%
```

Forward rate = $1.15 \times \dfrac{1.0625}{1.05} = 1.1637$

This is the forward offer rate.

12: CURRENCT DERIVATIVES

Summary

	Bid	Offer	Spread
Spot	1.1000	1.1500	0.0500
1 year forward	1.1078	1.1637	0.0559

The forward spread will always be greater than the spot spread. This is compensation for increased risk.

2.3 Using currency derivatives

2.3.1 How prices change

What would happen to a sterling futures quote of 1.4200 if the dollar strengthens?

If the dollar 'strengthens', it means that the dollar has more value and purchasing power. The strengthening of the dollar will mean that it will cost fewer dollars to buy each £ sterling. The quote might move to 1.4150.

Conversely, if the dollar weakened and sterling strengthened, it would take more dollars to buy each £ sterling, so the quote might change to 1.4250.

2.3.2 Calculating profits and losses

The tick size of currency products varies from market to market. If we look at the CME's euro future, we would find that the size is $0.0001, indicating that the smallest permitted price movement is $1/10,000$ of a dollar, i.e. $1/100$ of a cent.

The contract size is €125,000 and therefore, the value of each tick is

$125,000 \times 0.0001 = \$12.50$

Example

A speculator feels that the dollar will strengthen against the euro.

The current exchange rate USD/EUR = 0.8550 (ie $0.855 = €1). Interest rates in the US are 7.04% p.a. and in the Eurozone are 4.20% p.a.

(a) Calculate the 3 month currency futures price

(b) What action should the investor take to benefit from any strengthening of the dollar

(c) If the spot rate moves to 0.8500 in three months calculate the gain made on 10 contracts

Solution

(a) 3 month interest rates   – US $r_v = 1.76\% (7.04 \times 3/12)$

                             – Eurozone $r_F = 1.05\% (4.20 \times 3/12)$

$$\text{Futures price} = \text{spot price} \times \frac{1+r_v}{1+r_F} = 0.8550 \times \frac{1.0176}{1.0105} = 0.8610$$

(b) A strengthening dollar means there will be more Euros per dollars or less dollars per Euro. Given how the futures are quoted (dollars per euro) we would expect the price to fall. Our action shoud be to sell futures.

(c)

Action	Quote	
Now – sell to open	0.8610	
5 days – Buy to close	0.8500	
Profit	$0.0110	or 110 ticks

The profit or loss is found by

Profit = Ticks × Tick value × Contracts

Profit = 110 × $12.50 × 10 = $13,750

Summarising use of currency futures

Exam tip

> The most common mistake with currency futures is getting the action wrong

We drew an important conclusion in part (b) above regarding the action to take when either speculating or hedging. In that example we believed that the dollar (the variable currency) would strengthen or appreciate, which may alternatively be expressed as the Euro (the fixed currency has weakened or depreciated). These terms are relative in that if one currency appreciates, then relatively the other has depreciated. Our action with the strengthening dollar was to sell futures. More generally we could summarise the use of currency futures as

Fixed currency	Variable currency	Action
Appreciate/Strengthen	Depreciate/Weaken	Long
Depreciate/Weaken	Appreciate/Strengthen	Short

2.3.3 Using currency futures

Matching dates

Example

Using the interest rate and exchange rate information from the last example, imagine a US company exports aeroplanes to Germany and raises an invoice for €200m in March.

The terms of the invoice are that the German airline will pay for the planes in September. This creates a foreign exchange risk for the US company – between March and September, the euro could weaken, meaning that the €200m will be worth less in dollar terms.

If the date in September coincides with the expiry of the September contract and the contract size is €125,000.

(a) What action should the US exporter take?

(b) What would be the exporters position in September if the exchange rate has moved to $0.8450?

Solution

(a) *March*

Amount to hedge = €200m

Futures contract size = €125,000

The number of contracts could be calculated as

Formula to learn

$$\text{Number of contracts} = \frac{\text{Amount to be hedged}}{\text{Nominal value of future}}$$

giving

$$\text{Number of contracts} = \frac{200{,}000{,}000}{125{,}000} = \text{contracts}$$

The exporter is concerned that the Euro (fixed currency in FX quote) will weaken, therefore his action in March is sell to 1,600 Euro futures.

(b) *September*

In September the exporter will buy to close the futures position, hence the futures trades have been

Action	Quote
March – Sell to open	0.8610
September – Buy to close	0.8450
Profit	0.0160

or 160 ticks

And so we have

Net position

	$
Euro value at spot = €200,000,000 × 0.8450 =	169,000,000
Profit on future = 160 × $12.50 × 1,600 =	3,200,000
Net Receipt	$172,200,000

$$\text{Effective exchange rate} = \frac{\$172{,}200{,}000}{\$200{,}000{,}000} = 0.8610$$

Note that as the hedge was held to the delivery date of the future, the rate obtained was the rate implied in the future. If the hedge was to be lifted before the delivery date, then the number of contracts would have to be recalculated.

Non-matching dates

Imagine that the hedge was protecting against an immediate change. For reasons similar to those we have seen with equity and bond futures, the number of futures required would have to be reduced, otherwise the position would be overhedged.

The number of contracts now could be calculated as

Formula to learn

$$\text{Number of contracts} = \frac{\text{Amount to be hedged}}{\text{Nominal value of future}} \times \frac{\text{Spot rate}}{\text{Forward rate}}$$

Example

Based on our example above

(a) Calculate the number of contracts needed to hedge a receipt due almost immediately

(b) Calculate the net position and effective exchange rate on receipt if the spot rate moves immediately to 0.845

Solution

(a) If the hedge was to be lifted immediately, the number of contracts would be

$$\text{Number of contracts} = \frac{€200,000,000}{€125,000} \times \frac{0.8550 \text{ (spot rate)}}{0.8610 \text{ (forward rate)}} = 1,588.85$$

(b) If the spot rate moves to 0.845 then the futures price becomes

$$\text{Futures price} = 0.845 \times \frac{1.0176}{1.0105} = 0.8509$$

Action	Quote $
Now Sell to open	0.8610
Later Buy to close	0.8509
Profit to dollar investor	$0.0101

or 101 ticks

So we have

Profit = 101 × $12.50 × 1,588.85 = $2,005,923

Net position	$
Euro value at spot €200,000,000 × 0.8450	169,000,000
Futures profit	2,005,923
Net receipt	171,005,923

Effective exchange rate is

$$\frac{\$171,005,923}{€200,000,000} = 0.8550$$

This is the current spot rate, which is what the anticipated rate would be. Thus, by factoring the number of contracts down in this way, a better hedge has been achieved.

If the hedge is to be released between now and expiry then the spot rate in the above calculation needs to be replaced by anticipated forward rate at the date the hedge is to be released.

Anticipated Forward Rate

The anticipated forward rate can be established by interpolating between the spot rate and the futures (maturity) rate as follows

Formula to learn

Anticipated forward rate = Spot rate × P_2 + forward rate × P_1

Where

- P_1 = Proportion of the contract maturity period arising before the hedge is lifted
- P_2 = Proportion of the contract maturity period arising after the hedge is lifted

Example

Based on the above example, what is the number of contracts if the future matures in three months and the hedge is to be lifted in two months

12: CURRENCT DERIVATIVES

Solution

Anticipated forward rate = $0.8550 \times \frac{1}{3} + 0.8610 \times \frac{2}{3} = 0.8590$

And so now

Number of contracts = $\frac{200,000,000}{125,000} \times \frac{0.8590}{0.8610} = 1596.28$ or 1596 contracts

---

The required number of contracts now becomes

Formula to learn

$$\text{Number of contracts} = \frac{\text{Amount to be hedged}}{\text{Nominal value of future}} \times \frac{\text{Anticipated forward rate}}{\text{Forward rate}}$$

In the previous example, we were hedging a known amount of Euros, and number of contracts was simply the euro amount divided by the size of the contract in euro.

What if we need to hedge a given amount of dollars? We need to estimate what the foreign currency value of the dollars will be and then divide by the contract size.

Estimating the foreign currency value is best done by simply dividing the dollar amount by the forward rate.

Example

On the 15 December, the spot rate is $1.5000 to £1.0000. The CME March sterling future is $1.5300 (expires 15th). A manufacturer needs to hedge the $5,163,750 that have to be bought on 15 February to pay a US supplier and the company is concerned that the dollar may strengthen.

(a) How many contracts should he trade and what actual position should he take

(b) What is the net position and effective rate if the spot rate on 15 February is then 1.5500 and the March future is at 1.5603

Solution

(a) Anticipated forward rate = $1.5000 \times \frac{1}{3} + 1.5300 \times \frac{2}{3} = 1.5200$

Anticipated sterling payment = $\frac{5,163,750}{1.5200} = £3,397,204$

So now

Number of contracts = $\frac{3,397,204}{62,500} \times \frac{1.52}{1.53} = 54$ contracts

Since he is concerned about a strengthening of the dollar (variable currency in the FX quote) the manufacturer should sell 54 contracts.

(b) He lifts the hedge on 15 February when spot rate is $1.5500 and the March future is $1.5603.

The futures position has been

Action	Quote
	$
15/12 Sell to open	1.5300
15/2 Buy to close	1.5603
Loss	$0.0303

or 303 ticks

So the net position to the sterling investor/manufacturer is

		£
Cash cost	$5,163,750 ÷ 1.55	3,331,452
Future loss =	303 × $6.25 × 54 ÷ 1.55	65,976
Total cost		£3,397,428

Effective rate = $\dfrac{\$5,163,750}{£3,397,428}$ = 1.5199, or 1.52 – the anticipated forward rate.

2.3.4 Currency options

PHLX currency options are quoted in cents per foreign currency unit. Thus, a quote of '1.00' means one cent, not one dollar.

Another peculiarity of currency option markets is that a £ call (the right, but not the obligation, to buy sterling) is the same thing as a dollar put.

£ Call = $ PUT
£ Put = $ CALL

Many questions will require a calculation of the number of contracts needed. A possible complication in calculating this may be a requirement to hedge a given amount of dollars rather than a given amount of foreign currency.

We can, therefore, use currency options to

- Establish a cap (maximum exchange rate) or floor (minimum exchange rate) that we may face.
- Provide a hedge against exchange rates by accounting for the delta.

Protection

As with equities, bonds and interest rate products, the number of contracts needed to protect a position can be calculated in the same way as the number needed to hedge with futures.

Example

A US exporter is due to receive £2m in 3 months and is concerned that sterling may weaken, reducing the dollar value of this future receipt. What action should he take using CME options or futures

Solution

Number of contracts = $\dfrac{£2,000,000}{£62,500}$ = 32

Since the exporter wishes to sell sterling and buy dollars in three months he will buy 32 sterling puts (dollar calls)

Alternatively he would go short futures since the fixed currency in the futures price quote (sterling) is weakening.

Example

A UK exporter is to pay $2m in 3 months and is concerned that the dollar may weaken, reducing the sterling value of this future receipt. What action should he take with CME options or futures based on an exchange rate USD/GBP = 1.72

Solution

Number of contracts = $\dfrac{\$2{,}000{,}000}{62{,}500} \div 1.72 = 18.6$ i.e. 19 contracts

The exporter needs to buy sterling/sell dollars in three months, hence he should buy 19 sterling calls (dollar puts)

If hedging with futures, since the variable currency in the futures quote (dollar) is weakening he should go long futures

Hedging

As with all previous options hedging, we need to establish a delta neutral position, hence

Number of options contracts = Number of futures contracts $\times \dfrac{1}{\text{option delta}}$

Currency Option Quotes

In the traded options markets, options quotes tend to be in points of currency. For example if for sterling/dollar the premium on a 1.7650 CME sterling call was 5.23 this means a 5.23c or $0.0523 premium on a $1.7650 strike price. With a standard contract size of £62,500, the premium on the contract would be $3,268.75 (62,500 × $0.0523) and the dollar cost of buying this sterling would be $110,312.50 (62,500 × $1.7650). The premium is paid up front.

With OTC currency options the premium tends to be quoted as a percentage of the currency value.

Chapter Roundup

- You need to be familiar with the various
  - currency products available
  - exchanges they are traded on
- Forward/futures price
  - Using interest rates

    Forward rate = Spot rate $\times \dfrac{1+r_V}{1+r_F}$

    Where
    - r_V = interest rate for the relevant period in the variable currency
    - r_F = interest rate for the relevant period in the fixed or base currency
  - Using discount factors

    Forward rate = spot rate $\times \dfrac{DF_F}{DF_V}$

    Where
    - DF_F = discount factor for the fixed currency
    - DF_V = discount factor for the variable currency
- Futures use

Fixed currency	Variable currency	Action
Appreciate/Strengthen	Depreciate/Weaken	Long
Depreciate/Weaken	Appreciate/Strengthen	Short

- Hedging with futures/protecting with options
  - Basic Hedge – Matching Dates

    Number of contracts = $\dfrac{\text{Amount to be hedged}}{\text{Nominal value of future}}$
  - Non-Matching Dates

    Anticipated forward rate = Spot rate $\times P_2$ + forward rate $\times P_1$

    Where

    P_1 = Proportion of the contract maturity period arising before the hedge is lifted
    P_2 = Proportion of the contract maturity period arising after the hedge has been lifted

    Number of contracts = $\dfrac{\text{Amount to be hedged}}{\text{Nominal value of future}} \times \dfrac{\text{Anticipated forward rate}}{\text{Forward rate}}$
- Hedging with options

    Number of options contracts = Number of futures contracts $\times \dfrac{1}{\text{option delta}}$

12: CURRENCT DERIVATIVES

Test Your Knowledge

Check your knowledge of the Chapter here, without referring back to the text.

1. The current sterling dollar exchange rate USD/GBP = 1.6836

   Interest rates in the UK and US are

	UK	US
3 months (91 day)	4.75%	3.96%
6 moths (183 day)	4.82%	4.04%

   Calculate the price of 3 and 6 month currency futures

2. A European manufacturer is importing goods from the US. Goods to the value of $12,000,000 already received need to be paid for in the near future, and a further order for $10,000,000 is considered likely but as yet not confirmed. The spot rate is 1.7635 but the manufacturer believes the dollar is strengthening

CME Euro futures prices	
March	1.7526
June	1.7413
September	1.7297

CME Euro options				
	Call Options		Put options	
Strike	March	June	March	June
1.7250	3.86	5.36	3.51	6.03
1.7500	2.86	4.48	5.67	8.34
1.7750	2.03	3.41	6.78	9.37

   Suggest how the manufacturer may best be able to hedge his position if

   (a) The $12m payment coincides with the March delivery date and the $10m possible order coincides with the June delivery date

   (b) If the $12m payment is due to be paid three weeks before the March future delivery date and we are currently eight weeks from delivery, calculate the number of contracts needed to hedge, the net position at the payment date and the effective exchange rate achieved if the spot rate is then 1.7300 and the March future is trading at 1.7260.

3. Based on the price information in the previous question, suggest three trading strategies that could be used by a speculator who believes exchange rates will remain stable until March. Calculate the maximum profit achieved by each strategy and the exchange rate at which it is achieved.

TEST YOUR KNOWLEDGE: ANSWERS

1. Interest rates for the periods

	UK	US
3 month (91 day)	$4.75 \times \frac{91}{365} = 1.1842\%$	$3.96 \times \frac{91}{360} = 1.0010\%$
6 month (183 day)	$4.82 \times \frac{183}{365} = 2.4166\%$	$4.04 \times \frac{183}{360} = 2.0537\%$

    Based on the quote of $1.6836:£1, the dollar is the variable currency and sterling is fixed so

    3 month future = $1.6836 \times \frac{1.010010}{1.011842} = 1.6806$

    6 month future = $1.6836 \times \frac{1.020537}{1.024116} = 1.6777$

2. (a) *$12m definite payment*

    The $12m definite payment is best hedged with the March future

    The hedged Euro value of this receipt will be

    Euro value = $\frac{12,000,000}{1.7526}$ = €6,846,970

    And the number of contracts required is

    Number of contracts = $\frac{6,846,970}{125,000}$ = 54.77 i.e. 55 contracts

    The manufacturer is concerned that the dollar (the variable currency in the contract quote) is strengthening, therefore he should sell 55 contracts

    $10m possible payment

    Non-contracted payments are best protected with options. In six months the months the manufacturer will wish to be able to buy dollars (sell Euros) in order to pay this figure – he needs to buy June Euro puts.

    Considering the available options we have

Strike	Cost of $10m	Number of contracts	Premium @ Spot	Total cost
	€		€	€
1.7250	5,797,101	46.4 or 46	196,612	5,993,713
1.7500	5,714,285	45.7 or 46	271,931	5,986,216
1.7750	5,633,803	45.1 or 45	298,873	5,932,676

    Here

    - The € cost has been calculated as $\frac{10,000,000}{\text{Strike}}$

    - The number of contracts is $\frac{\text{€ Cost}}{125,000}$

- Premium = $\dfrac{\text{No. contracts} \times 125{,}000 \times \text{Premium}}{1.7635 \text{ (spot rate)}}$

- Total cost = € Cost + Premium

The 1.7750 option offers the lowest total cost but at the highest up front premium. Which contract is optimal will, therefore, be heavily dependent on the likelihood that the purchase will be made.

(b) Anticipated forward rate = $1.7635 \times \dfrac{3}{8} + 1.7526 \times \dfrac{5}{8} = 1.7567$

Sterling value of $12m payment = $\dfrac{12{,}000{,}000}{1.7567}$ = £6,830,990

Number of contracts = $\dfrac{6{,}830{,}990}{125{,}000} \times \dfrac{1.7567}{1.7526}$ = 54.78 i.e. 55 contracts

Futures trades

Sell to open	1.7526
Buy to close	1.7260
Profit	0.0266

or 266 ticks

Net position

	€
Cash paid 12,000,000 ÷ 1.73	6,936,416
Futures profit 226 × $12.50 × 54 ÷ 1.73	(88,179)
Net cost	€6,848,237

Effective rate = $\dfrac{12{,}000{,}000}{6{,}848{,}237}$ = 1.7523

3. *Short Straddle*

Say on the 1.75 options

	c
Sell March 1.75 call	2.86
Sell March 1.75 put	5.67
Maximum profit	8.53c

We have a maximum profit of 8.53c or $0.0853 per €1 which would arise at the 1.75 common strike price.

Short Strangle

	c
Sell March 1.775 call	2.03
Sell March 1.725 put	3.51
Maximum profit	5.54c

We have a maximum profit of 5.54c or $0.0554 per €1 which would arise between the two strike prices of 1.725 and 1.775.

12: CURRENCT DERIVATIVES

Long Butterfly

There are several ways of achieving this, however, perhaps the easiest here is

	c
Sell March Straddle above	8.53
Buy March Strangle above	(5.54)
Maximum profit	2.99c

We have a maximum profit of 2.99c or $0.0299 per €1 which would arise at the 1.75 straddle peak.

13 Swaps

INTRODUCTION

Futures and options on bonds, equities, interest rates and currencies enable us to speculate or hedge on price/rate movements, though only short term to the maturity of the contract. If we wish to hedge exposure longer term then we need to consider swaps which are available for substantially longer maturities. The analysis and valuation of any swap position inherently involves the scheduling and discounting of the relevant swap cash flows.

CHAPTER CONTENTS

		Page
1	Introduction to OTC	392
2	Swaps	393
3	Interest Rate Swaps	394
4	Short-Term Currency Swaps/Foreign Exchange Swaps	414
5	Long-Term Currency Swaps	417
6	Equity Swaps	421
7	Commodity Swaps	427
8	Non-Generic Swaps	429
9	Asset Swaps	432
10	Cross-Currency Asset Swaps	434
	Chapter Roundup	436
	Test Your Knowledge	437

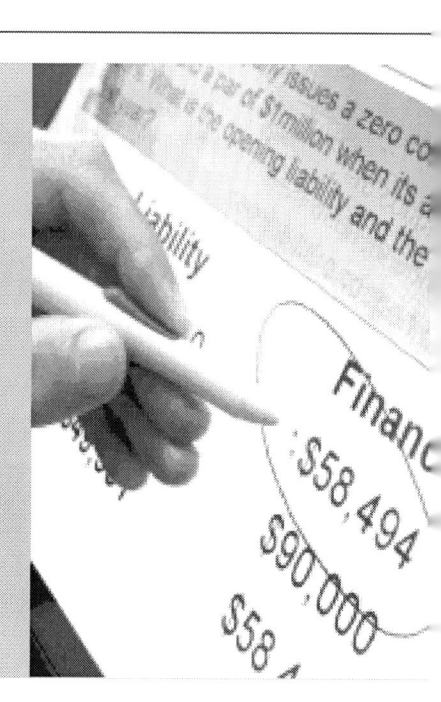

13: SWAPS

CHAPTER LEARNING OBJECTIVES

The syllabus areas covered by this section are

- **Over-the-Counter-Derivatives**

    Swaps and Related Derivatives

    – Interest rate Swaps
    – Currency Swaps
    – Asset and Basis Swaps
    – Equity Swaps
    – Caps, Floors and Collars

1 INTRODUCTION TO OTC

Alongside the exponential growth of exchange-traded derivatives over the past decade, there has been a similar, if less visible, growth in so-called 'over-the-counter' (OTC) products, particularly swaps. Before discussing the various products that have driven this growth, it is important to understand some of the reasons behind the appeal of the OTC markets.

1.1 Flexibility

While exchange-traded structures, by dint of their standardisation, liquidity and visibility, have provided the investment community with much needed risk management tools, some attributes of these markets are particularly irksome. The limited availability of products, fixed delivery dates, standardised contract sizes, limited exercise prices and expiry dates and the strictures of exchange-margining rules have all conspired to make the bespoke OTC markets particularly attractive.

Although exchanges are now seeking to satisfy customer demand by offering variable strike prices and maturities in their 'Flex' options and a number of other longer dated products, there is a real limit to this initiative. OTC products, because they are bilaterally negotiated, will always be better placed to satisfy customer needs. This, in part, explains their popularity.

1.2 Profit margins

As the world's derivative exchanges have become busier, they have also become more competitive. The profit margins for all exchange members, from brokers to principal traders, have thus been squeezed. Investment banks have seen the more sophisticated and more opaque OTC market as providing an opportunity to maximise profits from their derivative skills. Over time, it can be expected that the OTC market will itself become crowded, but it should be remembered that as OTC market contracts are undertaken on a bilateral basis, rather than via a clearing house, only institutions with good credit ratings can hope to be large players.

1.3 Acceptance

As investors become familiar with the attributes and payoffs of exchange-traded products, they become more likely to see the advantages of OTC products. This acceptance, coupled with improvements in regulations and taxation, may further stimulate growth.

1.4 Risk in the OTC markets

Whilst all derivative products present participants with exposures to market risks, OTC products present further specialised difficulties. These risks are examined in more detail in a subsequent chapter.

1.4.1 Credit risk

Unlike exchange-traded products, in which there are no counterparty risks, at least for clearing members, OTC products present considerable counterparty risk exposure.

To minimise this risk, participants normally undertake a lengthy due diligence investigation of their counterparty to avoid entering into contracts that may be the subject of a default.

There is also a growing use of central counterparty clearing services provided by the London Clearing House (LCH.Clearnet), which accepts certain OTC trades as intermediary, protected by a margining system.

Credit risks are also minimised through the netting of cash flows in products such as interest rate swaps and, more broadly, by favouring products that are settled on a difference rather than by delivering the physical underlying.

1.4.2 Legal and documentation risk

Counterparties to an OTC product are at risk if either the paperwork does not operate as envisaged in the case of a default, or if one party is acting in a capacity for which it is not authorised.

The documentary risk is less intense than before as the International Swaps & Derivatives Association (ISDA) has produced a standard master agreement to cover most bilateral OTC derivatives transactions. It has also published suggested contract confirmation documentation and a 'dictionary' of definitions. The standardisation of documentation should help rebut legal challenges as to its validity.

1.4.3 Capital adequacy

For banks and other financial institutions contemplating entry into the OTC markets, consideration needs to be given to the impact of OTC exposures to their capital adequacy.

In the UK, the Financial Services Authority regulates the activities of financial institutions, monitoring their risk exposures.

Considerable amounts of capital need to be allocated to meet both the market risks and credit risks that emerge in the OTC markets.

1.4.4 Valuation

Although many institutions may see merit in using OTC products, one difficulty is in the valuation of such positions. Whilst exchange-traded markets provide daily mark to markets against authoritative settlement prices, many OTC products are valued by the issuing bank. This may not provide the objectivity required by many trustees and custodians.

2 SWAPS

Swaps are agreements under which counterparties agree to exchange (swap) specific future cash flows. For example, in an interest rate swap, the counterparties agree to exchange future interest payments.

Historically, these arrangements were first developed as corporate-to-corporate deals with any financial intermediary simply acting as a broker. Now, the financial intermediaries act as market makers. They execute swaps where there is no counterparty as yet, holding one side of the deal on their own account (warehousing one leg) until a counterparty can be found. In this way, they face the true risk of an intermediary. The market makers build a book of transactions that offset each other overall, if not on a deal-by-deal basis.

3 INTEREST RATE SWAPS

3.1 Definition

An interest rate swap is a contract that commits two counterparties to exchange, over an agreed period, two streams of interest payments, each calculated using a different interest rate index, but applied to a common notional principal amount.

3.1.1 Key points

Only interest payments are exchanged in the swap – there is no exchange of principal. Interest rate swaps do not, therefore, impact on the balance sheet, only on the profit and loss account. Hence, they are classed as 'off-balance sheet instruments'.

Movements in the interest cash flow streams take place at intervals during the swap's life and are normally netted. For example, in a swap in which one side is paying a fixed rate and the other a floating rate, such as 6-month LIBOR, only the cash difference is exchanged. This reduces credit risks between the counterparties.

3.1.2 A basic interest rate swap

The cash flows in a basic interest rate swap could be pictured as follows.

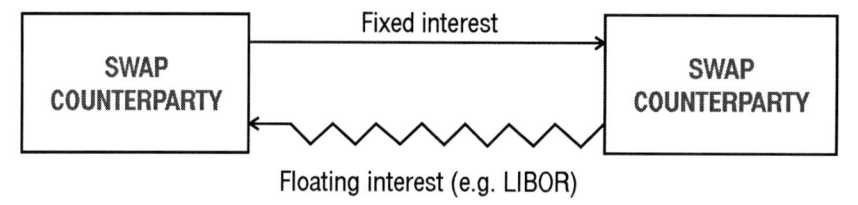

3.2 The anatomy of a swap

An example of a coupon swap might look like this.

Notional Principal Amount	$10m
Type of Swap	Coupon
Maturity	2 years
Fixed Rate	8.50% per annum
Floating Rate	6-Month LIBOR
Day Count	Fixed Actual/360 Floating Actual/360
First Floating Rate	7.87%
Payments	Semi-annual. 19/12 and 19/06 in each year or modified following business day.
Reset	19/12 and 19/06 in each year or modified following business day.

Note that the floating rate for the first six-month period is known at the outset of the swap. Subsequent rates will be determined on the relevant reset dates.

3.3 Terminology

3.3.1 Coupon swap

Definition

A coupon swap involves the exchange of a fixed interest rate (analogous to the coupon payment on a bond) for the floating rate as measured by an index such as LIBOR. These are sometimes called fixed against floating or generic swaps.

Counterparties to a coupon swap

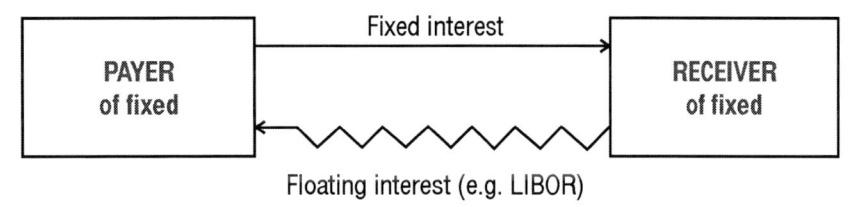

```
                    Fixed interest
    PAYER      ───────────────────▶    RECEIVER
    of fixed   ◀~~~~~~~~~~~~~~~~~~    of fixed
              Floating interest (e.g. LIBOR)
```

Counterparties – Alternative terminology

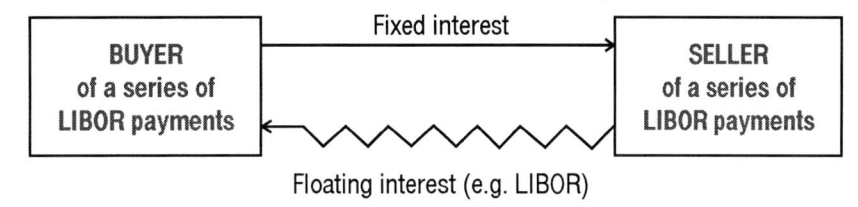

```
                      Fixed interest
    BUYER         ───────────────────▶    SELLER
    of a series of                        of a series of
    LIBOR payments ◀~~~~~~~~~~~~~~~~~~    LIBOR payments
                  Floating interest (e.g. LIBOR)
```

3.3.2 Basis swap

Definition

It is possible to swap two interest streams that are both calculated using floating interest rates, e.g. 3-month LIBOR vs. 6-month LIBOR.

Counterparties to a basis swap

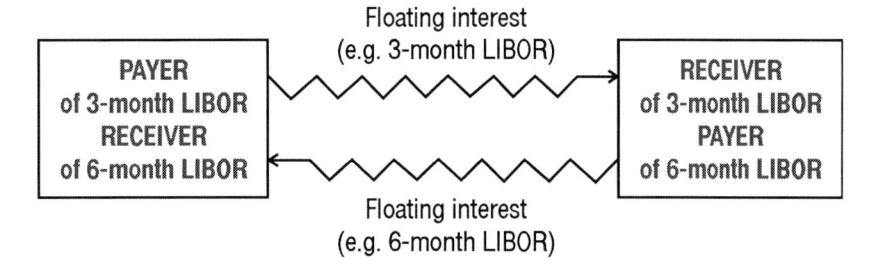

```
                       Floating interest
                       (e.g. 3-month LIBOR)
    PAYER              ~~~~~~~~~~▶    RECEIVER
    of 3-month LIBOR                  of 3-month LIBOR
    RECEIVER                          PAYER
    of 6-month LIBOR   ◀~~~~~~~~~~    of 6-month LIBOR
                       Floating interest
                       (e.g. 6-month LIBOR)
```

3.3.3 Asset swap

When the interest streams being exchanged through an interest rate swap are funded with interest received on specific assets, the swap is called an asset swap. Asset swaps may also be coupon or basis swaps.

3.3.4 Term swap

A term swap is a swap with a lifespan of more than two years.

3.3.5 Money market swap

A money market swap is a swap with up to two years of life when originally negotiated.

3.4 Dealing

3.4.1 Inception

The market in interest rate swaps is an over-the-counter (OTC) market. Trading is conducted over the telephone (or, since October 2002, SwapsWire) and price information is disseminated through quote vendor systems such as Reuters and Telerate.

In interest rate swaps, the floating rate in a coupon swap (the most common type of swap) is assumed to be 6-month LIBOR. Negotiation therefore concentrates on the fixed rate, sometimes called the swap rate.

There are two methods of quoting the fixed rate – the all-in price, or as a swap spread on a benchmark rate.

All-in prices

A quote for a one-year swap may be given as an all-in price of 7.85% – 8.00%. This is a two-way price in which the dealer would pay a fixed rate of 7.85% (in exchange for receiving LIBOR payments) and would look to receive 8.00% fixed (in exchange for paying LIBOR payments). The dealing spread of 15 basis points represents the dealer's profit if he could do both transactions.

Swap spreads

In the US, the use of all-in terms for quoting the fixed rates in coupon swaps has been replaced by the convention of quoting in two parts – swap spread and a benchmark interest rate.

The benchmark interest rate is usually the yield on the 'on the run' (OTR) i.e. most actively traded Government bond, with a remaining life similar to the swap. When the swap is agreed, the spread and the benchmark are fixed, and the all-in rate is set.

Example

	Swap Spread	Annual Interest	All-in Rate
2 years	22/26	6.70-6.75	6.92-7.01

The dealing in interest rate swaps is governed by the Bank of England's 'London Code of Conduct'. The pattern of these dealings has evolved as the market has become bigger and more liquid.

Originally, investment banks and merchant banks sought only to arrange swap deals rather than to become principals in the transaction. However, as the market grew, customers increasingly sought anonymity and the comfort of a bank rather than a corporate as their counterparties. Thus, the banks, including commercial banks, were required to become principals rather than agents in the transactions.

Principal intermediaries initially limited themselves to running matched books (books in which they had offsetting swap positions with different counterparties). However, as hedging techniques and tools developed and customer demands grew, the larger banks have moved to making markets in swaps. Whilst most will seek to run matched books, they will be more willing to temporarily 'warehouse' or hedge individual swaps.

The warehousing of an interest rate swap is examined below.

Imagine a customer transacts a three-year swap with a notional principal amount of $1m in which it receives fixed interest at 50 basis points over the yield of the on-the-run US Treasury bond.

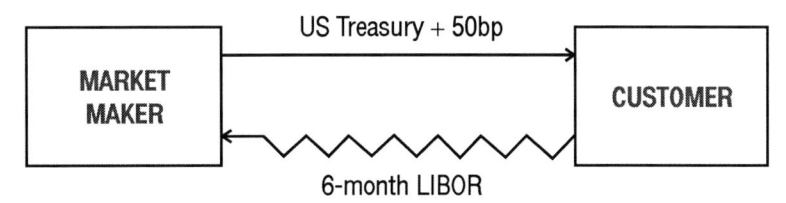

```
                    US Treasury + 50bp
   ┌─────────┐ ─────────────────────→ ┌──────────┐
   │ MARKET  │                         │          │
   │ MAKER   │                         │ CUSTOMER │
   └─────────┘ ←∿∿∿∿∿∿∿∿∿∿∿∿∿∿∿∿∿∿∿─── └──────────┘
                    6-month LIBOR
```

If the market maker is unable to find a matching swap, he is exposed to a fall in US interest rates. What he needs to do is synthesise offsetting cash flows to immunise his exposure.

The way in which the market maker could hedge himself would involve

(a) The purchase of $1m of the on-the-run US Treasury bond.

(b) Financing the purchase of the note by repoing out the bonds, receiving cash and paying the repo interest rate.

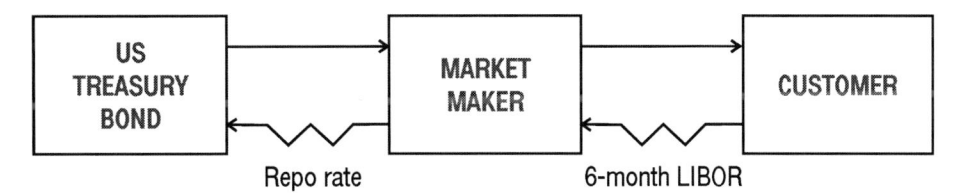

```
   ┌──────────┐      ┌─────────┐      ┌──────────┐
   │   US     │ ───→ │ MARKET  │ ───→ │          │
   │ TREASURY │      │ MAKER   │      │ CUSTOMER │
   │  BOND    │ ←∿∿─ └─────────┘ ←∿∿─ └──────────┘
   └──────────┘
      Repo rate          6-month LIBOR
```

Whilst the majority of the risk is overcome, there remains a residual risk, namely to the basis between the repo rate and 6-month LIBOR.

The repo rate used will normally be the overnight rate which, in a positive yield curve environment, will be lower than 6-month LIBOR. In addition, the payment dates for the interest flows under the swap may be different from those of the underlying bond – consequently, there may also be a reinvestment risk. Notwithstanding these shortcomings, the market maker has a reasonably resilient hedge.

Instead of using cash bonds, the fixed interest stream in a coupon swap can be hedged using bond futures, and the floating interest stream can be hedged using short-term interest rate futures. Even this structure can produce problems, as bond futures are typically related to bonds with long terms, e.g. in the UK, 10-15 years, whilst swap maturities are rarely greater than ten years. In addition, short-term interest rate futures are linked to three-month rates whilst swaps are related to six-month rates, again leaving residual basis risk.

A further residual risk relates to swap-spread risk, i.e. the spread over Treasuries at which the swap is negotiated. In the period during which the swap is being warehoused and before a matching swap can be found, there is the risk that swap spreads may change. Neither the futures nor bond hedges discussed above deal with this problem.

Swap spreads reflect supply and demand for swaps, but the benchmark yield is unlikely to be affected by the supply/demand for swaps. In a swap market in which rates are expected to go higher, customers looking to pay fixed predominate, therefore the spread will widen. Conversely, when rates are expected to fall, customers wishing to receive fixed dominate, therefore spreads will narrow. Aside from supply/demand, credit perceptions are also influential. If the credit ratings of market-making banks are downgraded, those receiving fixed from such banks will require a premium for the additional risks being run.

3.4.2 Termination and assignment

Termination and assignment are two methods by which counterparties can exit their swap positions. A third route, the reversal, in which an equal and opposite position is taken is also available.

Termination is simply the mutual cancellation of the swap. Assignment is the process through which existing swaps are sold to new counterparties.

When a swap is terminated or assigned, it is valued and a cash compensation paid to the party that is in-the-money.

13: SWAPS

The termination value will be the NPV of the cash flows (see valuation below). Assignment values are calculated in the same way, although the pricing can be complicated by credit issues.

3.5 Uses of interest rate swaps

As with futures and options, there are three basic motivations – speculation, hedging and arbitrage.

3.5.1 Speculation

Interest rate swaps can be used to take risky positions independent of any underlying instruments. In a coupon swap

- **The payer of fixed interest** is exposed to the risk of an interest rate fall, but will benefit if rates rise, since he is in the same commercial position as an issuer of a fixed coupon bond or fixed rate mortgage borrower.

- **The receiver of fixed interest** is exposed to the risk of an interest rate rise, but will benefit if rates fall, since he is in the same commercial position as an investor in a fixed coupon bond.

3.5.2 Hedging

Swap hedges work in a very similar way to futures hedges, in that swaps are used to establish an equal and opposite position. For example, assume a bank has invested its assets in fixed rate bonds, but has liabilities (depositors) to whom it has to pay floating rates. The bank is exposed to rising rates that will increase its payments without the benefit of increased returns on its bonds.

This position could be hedged using swaps and the cash flows for the hedged arrangement are illustrated below.

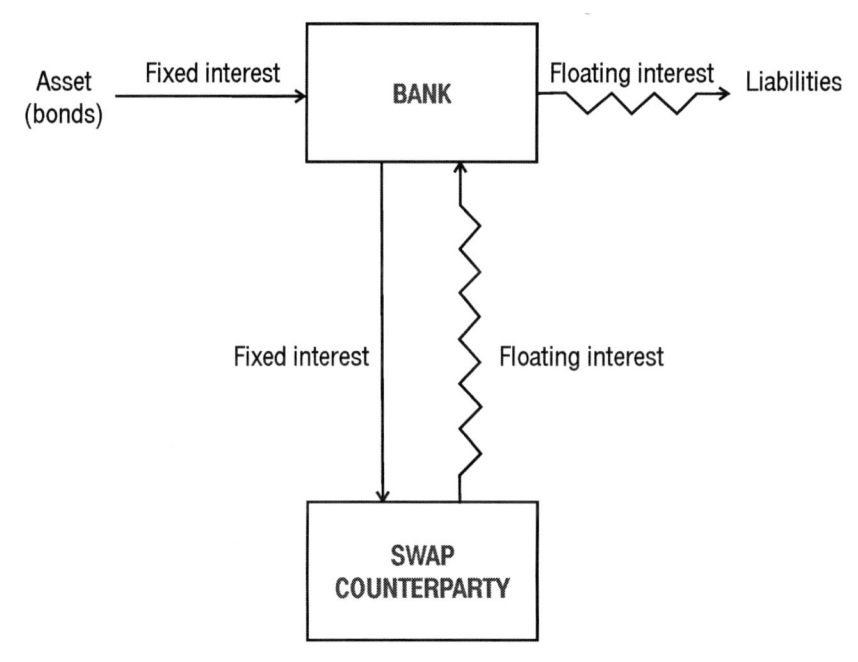

Asset (bonds) → Fixed interest → BANK → Floating interest → Liabilities

BANK → Fixed interest → SWAP COUNTERPARTY
SWAP COUNTERPARTY → Floating interest → BANK

In this hedge, the bank

Receives	Fixed interest from the bonds
	Floating interest from the swap counterparty
Pays	Floating interest to depositors
	Fixed interest to the swap counterparty

In this way, the mismatch between the asset and liability cash flows is overcome.

Example

An institution raises money by issuing a five-year bond at a yield of 8.75%, but would prefer floating rate funding. Five-year swaps are quoted at all-in rates of 8.95 – 9.075. How could the institution change its interest rate exposure to floating rates and what would be the all-in cost of its borrowing after swapping?

Solution

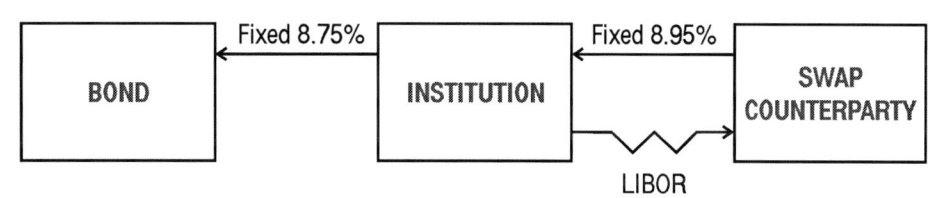

```
           Fixed 8.75%              Fixed 8.95%
  ┌──────┐ ←──────────── ┌───────────┐ ←──────────── ┌──────────────┐
  │ BOND │               │INSTITUTION│               │     SWAP     │
  │      │               │           │               │ COUNTERPARTY │
  └──────┘               └───────────┘ ~~~~~~~~~~~→  └──────────────┘
                                          LIBOR
```

Summary of cash flows

Cost of bonds	–8.75%
Fixed receipts via swaps	+8.95%
Floating payments via swaps	LIBOR
Net cost of borrowing	**LIBOR – 20 basis points**

3.5.3 Arbitrage

Another important use of interest rate swaps is arbitrage. Indeed, it was the driver behind the early development of the market. The arbitrage occurs when the fixed rate bond market and the floating rate banking markets have differing perceptions of an institution's credit risk.

The result of a collaboration between two institutions, which are viewed differently by the markets, can result in an interesting example of financial alchemy.

Example

Let us take two companies who have a borrowing need for $100m for six years.

Company A   AAA rating   Requires floating funds
Company B   BBB rating   Requires fixed funds

Available rates

	Bond Market	Bank Market
Company A	8.20%	LIBOR + 35bp
Company B	10.10%	LIBOR + 125bp
Advantage of A over B	1.90%	0.90%

Whilst A can raise cheaper finance in both markets, Company B has a comparative advantage in the floating market. This is because it only pays 0.9% more in the bank market as opposed to 1.9% in the bond market.

This difference is known as the market arbitrage and is the result of differing perceptions by lenders in the two markets.

This arbitrage is 1% (1.9 – 0.9) and can be exploited by companies A and B working in collaboration.

13: SWAPS

Swap structure

Exam tip

> You are often required to establish the swap structure and associated arbitrage gain within questions, though usually it does not involve an intermediary

Each company raises money in its market of comparative advantage (A fixed, B floating) and they, say, share the arbitrage equally (50bp each). The arrangement could be viewed as follows.

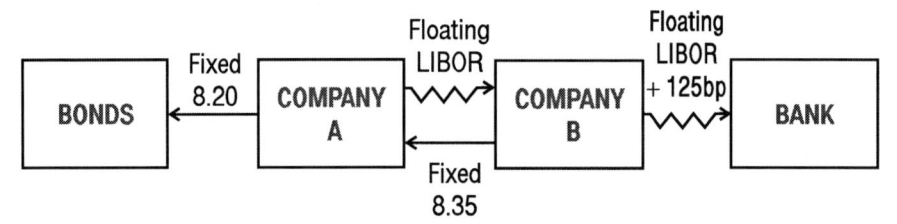

```
                      Floating              Floating
         Fixed        LIBOR                 LIBOR
         8.20                                + 125bp
BONDS <──────── COMPANY ────── COMPANY ────────────── BANK
                   A    ~~~~~~~    B     ~~~~~~~
                        ←──────
                         Fixed
                         8.35
```

	Company A		**Company B**
Pays	Fixed 8.20%	**Pays**	Fixed 8.35%
	Floating LIBOR		Floating LIBOR + 125bp
Receives	Fixed 8.35%	**Receives**	Floating LIBOR
Net	LIBOR – 15bp	**Net**	Fixed 9.60%

Each company ends up 50bp better off: Company A at LIBOR – 15bp (rather than LIBOR + 35bp) and Company B with fixed funds at 9.60% (rather than 10.10%).

The above example illustrates an important feature of the swap market: swaps enable borrowers to raise funds in the market to which they have best access, but to make interest and principal payments in a preferred form or currency. This separation of the funding decision and the choice of servicing debt enables borrowers to exploit their comparative advantages.

A more likely arrangement would involve an intermediary, perhaps a bank, who would also take a share of this arbitrage benefit. However, the idea is the same. Perhaps, the arrangement would be as follows.

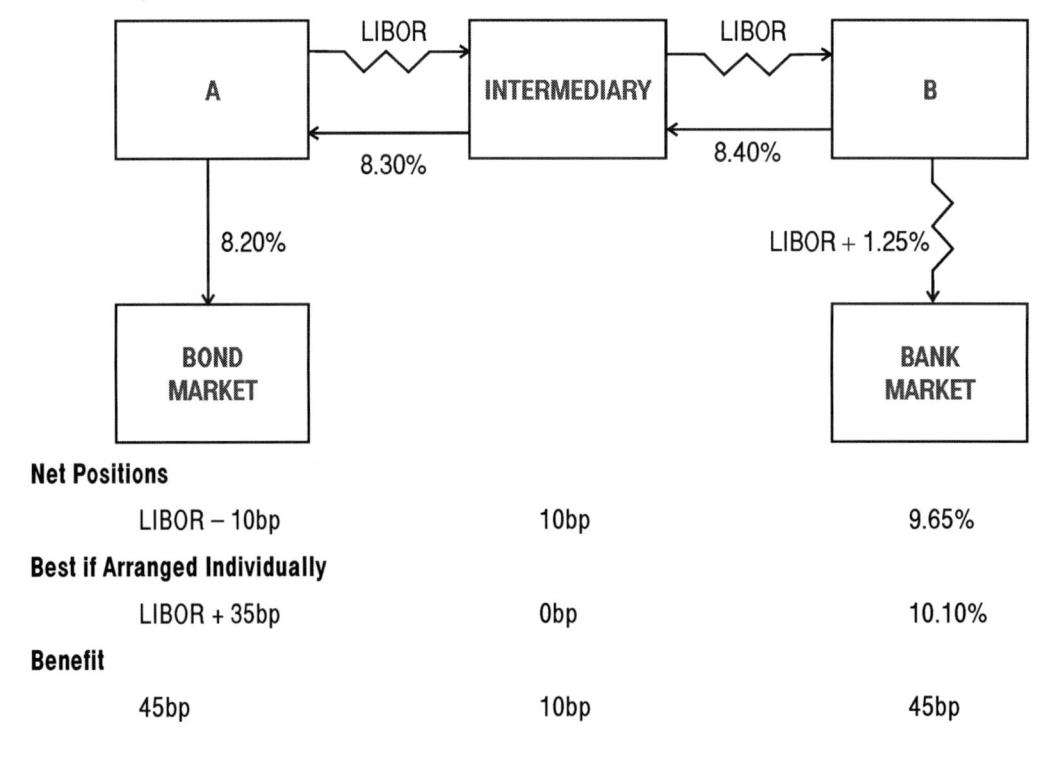

```
              LIBOR                    LIBOR
      A ~~~~~~~~~~~~~→ INTERMEDIARY ~~~~~~~~~~~~~→ B
        ←──────────                    ←──────────
           8.30%                          8.40%

      │                                              │
      │ 8.20%                            LIBOR +1.25%│
      ↓                                              ↓
   BOND                                           BANK
   MARKET                                         MARKET
```

Net Positions

    LIBOR – 10bp   10bp   9.65%

Best if Arranged Individually

    LIBOR + 35bp   0bp   10.10%

Benefit

    45bp   10bp   45bp

3.6 Valuation

3.6.1 Spot rates and forward rates

Before we look at the valuation of swaps, it is essential to understand what spot rates are and their relationship to forward rates.

A spot rate is the interest rate for a specific length of time. If you deposited money for a two-year period, you would earn the two-year spot rate. If you borrowed money for a fixed period of three years, you would pay the three-year spot rate. A spot rate can be for any length of time, but it is always for a period starting now. This can be shown easily as follows.

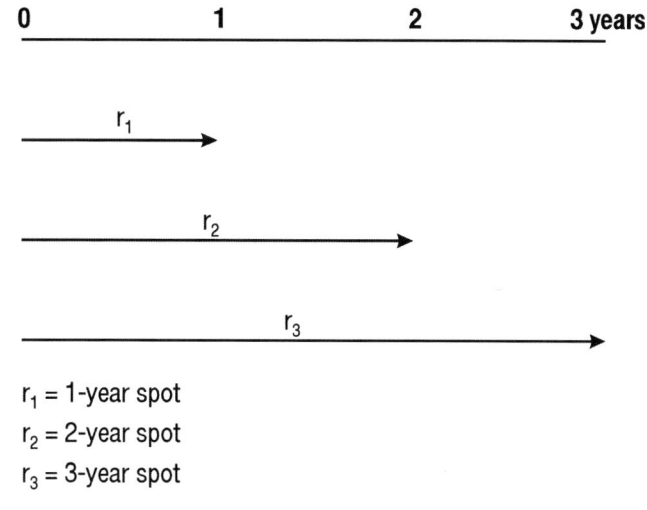

r_1 = 1-year spot
r_2 = 2-year spot
r_3 = 3-year spot

If spot rates are known, then it is possible to calculate what a forward rate should be. A forward rate is an interest rates for a period starting in the future.

If r_1 = 6% and r_2 = 7%, what should the one-year rate in one year's time be? We will call this $_1f_2$.

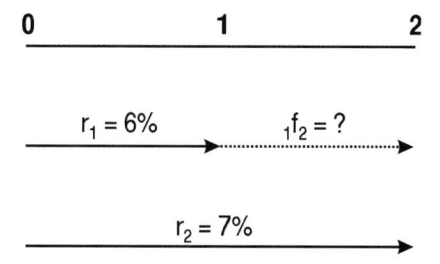

The logic of the calculations is to assume that one year at 6% followed by one year at the forward rate must equal two years at the two-year rate. If this relationship did not hold, there would be arbitrage opportunities.

$$(1.06)(1 + {_1f_2}) = 1.07^2$$

$$_1f_2 = \frac{1.07^2}{1.06} - 1$$

$$_1f_2 = 8.01\%$$

This logic can be extended. If the three-year spot rate is 7.5%, what is the one-year rate starting in two years' time, i.e. $_2f_3$?

$$(1.07^2)(1 + {_2f_3}) = 1.075^3$$

$$_2f_3 = \frac{1.075^3}{1.07^2} - 1$$

$$_2f_3 = 8.51\%$$

13: SWAPS

What is the two-year rate starting in one year's time, $_1f_3$?

$$1.06(1 + {}_1f_3)^2 = 1.075^3$$

$$_1f_3 = \sqrt{\frac{1.075^3}{1.06}} - 1$$

$$_1f_3 = 8.26\%$$

We can now see the following relationship.

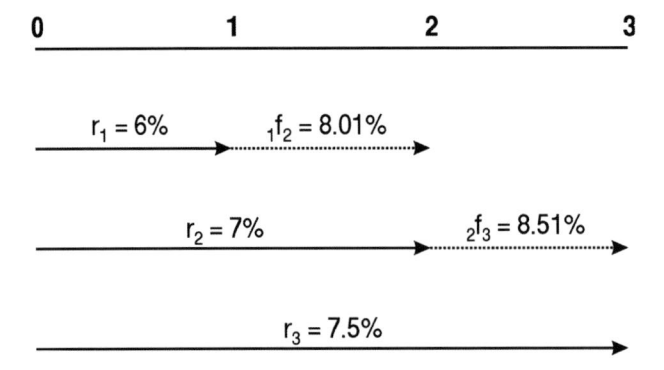

```
0                1                2                3
|----------------|----------------|----------------|
         r₁ = 6%        ₁f₂ = 8.01%
         ------------->-------------->
                  r₂ = 7%              ₂f₃ = 8.51%
                  -------------------->-------------->
                          r₃ = 7.5%
                  -------------------------------->
```

Having spot rates and forward rates allows us to calculate the present value of future flows, from a bond perhaps.

What is the fair price of a three-year zero-coupon bond, given the previous spot rates?

$$\text{Price} = \frac{100}{(1+r_3)^3}$$

where r_3 is the three-year spot rate.

$$\text{Price} = \frac{100}{1.075^3}$$

$$= 80.50$$

Alternatively, but more time consuming, the forward rates could have been used.

$$\text{Price} = \frac{100}{1.06 \times 1.0801 \times 1.0851}$$

$$= 80.50$$

This approach can also be used to value coupon paying bonds. Given the above spot rates, what is the price of a three-year bond paying an annual coupon of 8%?

$$\text{Price} = \frac{8}{1.06} + \frac{8}{1.07^2} + \frac{1.08}{1.075^3}$$

$$= 101.47$$

We have just introduced the idea that the price of a bond is the present value of the future bond cash flows discounted by the relevant **spot rates**. In the earlier chapter on bonds, we saw that you could also value a bond by discounting the bond cash flows by the yield. These two approaches will give the same bond price, therefore discounting all future cash flows by the yield or discounting each cash flow by the relevant spot rate are alternative pricing methods. For a three-year annual coupon bond, we could say

$$\frac{C_1}{1+r} + \frac{C_2}{(1+r)^2} + \frac{C_3+R}{(1+r)^3} = \frac{C_1}{1+r_1} + \frac{C_2}{(1+r_2)^2} + \frac{C_3+R}{(1+r_3)^3}$$

where

r = three-year yield
r_1 = one-year spot rate
r_2 = two-year spot rate
r_3 = three-year spot rate

The yield can be thought of as a complex average of the spot rates.

Using the previous example, where we calculated the price of a three-year coupon paying bond to be 101.47 by discounting the future flows at the spot rates, we could now calculate what the yield on this bond is, by solving for r in the following.

$$101.47 = \frac{8}{1+r} + \frac{8}{(1+r)^2} + \frac{108}{(1+r)^3}$$

We can determine that r = 7.44%.

Note that the three-year spot rate is 7.5%, whereas the three-year yield is 7.44%. In an upward-sloping yield curve environment, the yield for a certain maturity will be less than the spot rate for the same maturity, as has been demonstrated above.

3.6.2 Introduction to swap valuation

In all swaps, there must be an equality between the value of the two legs at the inception date. The value of the swap at its start date is zero, with the net present value of one leg equalling the net present value of the other. If this were not the case, one party would be unable to rationalise entering into the swap, as they would immediately suffer a loss.

At any later date, the present value of the two legs may vary as spot rates change and the swap may have a value being the difference between the present values of the two legs.

The value of the swap to either counterparty at any time will be given by

Formula to learn

Swap value = Difference between PV of cash flows swapped

Swap value = PV of cash flows acquired – PV of cash flows sold

3.6.3 Approach

The neatest approach to valuing an interest rate swap is to use bond pricing ideas along with the ideas of arbitrage. Arbitrage ensures that if there are two different ways of achieving the same end result, then they must have the same value, and when it comes to swap cash flows, it is quite easy to replicate them with fairly simple instruments.

The cash flows that the payer of fixed interest (receiver of floating) would experience are identical to those that would be experienced if he borrowed with a fixed rate bond and invested the proceeds raised in a floating rate note (FRN). That is, throughout the term of the swap, he would pay fixed and receive floating. At the termination date, the capital flows cancel, with the capital received on the maturity of the FRN repaying the fixed borrowing.

As such, the value of a swap could be established as the difference between the value of a FRN and a fixed rate bond as follows.

13: SWAPS

Value of swap

Value to Payer of Fixed	£
Value of FRN asset	X
Value of fixed coupon bond liability	(Y)
Value of swap	Z

And we can use the bond valuation ideas.

FRN Price

Formula to learn

$$\text{FRN Price} = \frac{\text{Next coupon} + \text{Par value}}{1 + \frac{r}{n}}$$

where n represents the number of payments per annum and r is the annualised spot rate to the next coupon payment date.

Fixed coupon bond price

Formula to learn

$$\text{Fixed coupon bond price} = \frac{C_1}{(1+r_1)} + \frac{C_2}{(1+r_2)^2} + \frac{C_3}{(1+r_3)^3} + \cdots + \frac{C_n + R}{(1+r_n)^n}$$

where $r_1, r_2, r_3, \ldots r_n$ are the relevant spot rates given the timing of the interest cash flows.

3.6.4 Value at inception

The pricing of interest rate swaps is concerned with the determination of the rate for the fixed interest leg, as traditionally, the floating rate leg is simply an agreed benchmark such as 6-month LIBOR.

If we remember that in the generic interest rate swap, no money passes between the payer and receiver at the initiation of the swap, this must mean that the net present value of the fixed leg equals the net present value of the floating leg at inception. Using this gives

Value to Payer of Fixed	£
Value of FRN asset	X
Value of fixed coupon bond liability	(Y)
Value of swap	0

When issued, an FRN is always valued at par and therefore the problem is identifying the coupon to price the bond at par, the par yield.

Example

What is the required swap rate for a five-year swap with annual payments on a notional principal of £100? Twelve-month LIBOR is 10% and the following spot rates are observed.

1 year	10%
2 years	11%
3 years	12%
4 years	13%
5 years	14%

Solution

Value of FRN

This calculation is not strictly required, but included here for illustration.

$$\text{FRN Price} = \frac{\text{Next coupon} + \text{Par value}}{1 + \frac{r}{n}} = \frac{110}{1.10} = 100$$

Value of swap and fixed rate bond

Value to Payer of Fixed	£
Value of FRN asset	100
Value of fixed coupon bond liability	(100)
Value of swap	0

Coupon on fixed rate bond

Exam tip

> Interest rate swap questions invariably require the determination of the fixed rate

We now need to find the fixed rate necessary to result in a par value on the 'bond'.

$$\text{Fixed coupon bond price} = \frac{C}{1.10^1} + \frac{C}{1.11^2} + \frac{C}{1.12^3} + \frac{C}{1.13^4} + \frac{C+R}{1.14^5}$$

$$= \frac{C}{1.10^1} + \frac{C}{1.11^2} + \frac{C}{1.12^3} + \frac{C}{1.13^4} + \frac{C}{1.14^5} + \frac{100}{1.14^5}$$

Gives

$$100.00 = 0.9091C + 0.8116C + 0.7118C + 0.6133C + 0.5194C + 51.94$$
$$100.00 = 3.5651C + 51.94$$
$$48.06 = 3.5651C$$

Hence, the fixed interest cash value is

$$C = \frac{48.06}{3.5651} = 13.48$$

Which, on a £100 nominal value, corresponds to a coupon rate of 13.48%.

This approach, where the values of inception are equal, is also called a par swap.

3.6.5 Later valuation

As we have noted, the value of a generic interest rate swap at its start date will be zero. At any later date, the present value of the two legs may vary as spot rates change and the swap may have a value being the difference between the present values of the two legs, which can again be established using the above idea.

We can see that as interest rates rise and the market value of bonds fall, the buyer's position (payer of fixed) will be showing a gain and the seller a loss. This is what we would expect. When interest rates rise, fixed rate payers gain and floating rate payers lose.

Example

The above swap is to be valued one year later, when the spot rates have fallen to

1 year	9%
2 years	10%
3 years	11%
4 years	12%

Solution

Approach 1

Value of original swap using prevailing spot rates

Value of FRN

$$\text{FRN Price} = \frac{\text{Next coupon} + \text{Par value}}{1 + \frac{r}{n}} = \frac{109}{1.09} = 100$$

Value of Bond

Time	Cash Flow	DF	PV
1	13.48	$\frac{1}{1.09^1}$	12.37
2	13.48	$\frac{1}{1.10^2}$	11.14
3	13.48	$\frac{1}{1.11^3}$	9.86
4	113.48	$\frac{1}{1.12^4}$	72.11
			105.48

Value of Swap and Fixed Rate Bond

Value to Payer of Fixed	£
Value of FRN asset	100.00
Value of fixed coupon bond liability	(105.48)
Value of swap	(5.48)

Hence

Swap value to buyer (payer of fixed) = –5.48
Swap value to seller (payer of floating) = +5.48

i.e. locking in to a fixed rate (the buyer) loses money when we experience generally declining interest rates, whereas paying variable rates (the seller) results in a gain.

Approach 2

Step 1 New swap rate

Par yield calculation

$$100.00 = \frac{C}{1.09^1} + \frac{C}{1.10^2} + \frac{C}{1.11^3} + \frac{C}{1.12^4} + \frac{100}{1.12^4}$$

$$100.00 = 0.9174C + 0.8264C + 0.7312C + 0.6355C + 63.55$$

$$36.45 = 0.9174C + 0.8264C + 0.7312C + 0.6355C$$

$$36.45 = 3.1105C$$

Hence, the fixed interest cash value is

$$C = \frac{36.45}{3.1105} = 11.72$$

Which, on a £100 nominal value, corresponds to a coupon rate or swap rate of 11.72%.

Step 2 Value of Original Swap Using New Swap Rate

Value of FRN

$$\text{FRN Price} = \frac{109}{1.09} = 100$$

Value of bond

Time	Cash Flow	DF (11.72%)	PV
1	13.48	$\frac{1}{1.1172^1}$	12.07
2	13.48	$\frac{1}{1.1172^2}$	10.80
3	13.48	$\frac{1}{1.1172^3}$	9.67
4	113.48	$\frac{1}{1.1172^4}$	72.85
			105.39

You will note that this value is marginally different as to Approach 1, as we are using one average rate of 11.72% as representative for all four years, which could never be 100% accurate. It does, however, represent a quick method when spot rates are not immediately available but swap rates are.

Value of swap and fixed rate bond

Value to Payer of Fixed	£
Value of FRN asset	100.00
Value of fixed coupon bond liability	(105.39)
Value of swap	(5.39)

13: SWAPS

Hence

Swap value to buyer (payer of fixed)	= –5.39
Swap value to seller (payer of floating)	= +5.39

3.6.6 Other picing apects

Non-LIBOR floating rate flows

The previous discussion on swap pricing took the floating rate flows to be LIBOR. This will have the effect, as noted, of valuing the floating rate flows at par, i.e. £100. But what if the floating rate is **not** going to be LIBOR?

The following example considers this.

Example

Year	Spot rate
1	10%
2	11%
3	12%

Calculate

One-year rate forward one year, i.e. $_1f_2$

$$(1.1)(1 + {_1f_2}) = 1.11^2$$

$$_1f_2 = 12.01\%$$

One-year rate forward two years, i.e. $_2f_3$

$$(1.11)^2(1 + {_2f_3}) = 1.12^3$$

$$_2f_3 = 14.03\%$$

If floating rate bond was based on LIBOR

$$\text{FRN price} = \frac{10}{1.1} + \frac{12.01}{1.11^2} + \frac{14.03}{1.12^3} + \frac{100}{1.12^3}$$

FRN price = 100

But now assume it is based on **LIBOR + 20bp**

$$\text{FRN price} = \frac{10.2}{1.1} + \frac{12.21}{1.11^2} + \frac{14.23}{1.12^3} + \frac{100}{1.12^3}$$

FRN price = 100.49

If using LIBOR, what would be fair price of fixed leg

$$100 = \frac{C}{1.1} + \frac{C}{1.11^2} + \frac{C}{1.12^3} + \frac{100}{1.12^3}$$

C = 11.85%

If using **LIBOR + 20bp**, what would be fair price of fixed leg

$$100.49 = \frac{C}{1.1} + \frac{C}{1.11^2} + \frac{C}{1.12^3} + \frac{100}{1.12^3}$$

C = 12.05%

From above, it can be seen that the effect of increasing/decreasing the floating rate by above/below LIBOR is to increase/decrease the fixed rate by the same amount.

Exam tip

> If presented with a floating rate that is not LIBOR, the easiest approach is to calculate the fixed rate **based on a floating rate of LIBOR (therefore, FRN price = £100)** and simply add or subtract the difference to/from the fixed rate thus calculated.

In the above example based on LIBOR, the fixed rate was calculated as 11.85% (the advantage of doing it this way is that it is not necessary to calculate the actual MV of a FRN based on a rate that is not LIBOR). The fixed rate based on LIBOR + 20bp is therefore 11.85% + 0.2% = 12.05% (as previously shown).

The approach detailed above is appropriate when the cash flows on both sides of the swap occur **at the same time**, e.g. pay floating or fixed every 12 months.

A further problem arises when the flows occur at different times, because now the difference of 20bp (as used in the previous example) will not have the same present value on both sides of the swap.

The following example considers this.

Example

Year	Spot rate
½	10%
1	11%
1½	12%
2	13%

Value a two-year fixed vs floating swap, where floating is LIBOR + 20bp paid **semi-annually** against fixed paid **annually**.

Calculate

Present value of 10bp received/paid semi-annually.

$$= \frac{0.1}{1.05} + \frac{0.1}{1.11} + \frac{0.1}{1.12^{1\frac{1}{2}}} + \frac{0.1}{1.13^2}$$

$$= 0.3480$$

Therefore, present value of floating = 100 + 0.3480

$$= 100.3480$$

Therefore, fixed rate will be

$$100.3480 = \frac{C}{1.11} + \frac{C}{1.13^2} + \frac{100}{1.13^2}$$

C = 13.08%

NB: If floating had been paid at same time as fixed, i.e. annually, the present value of the extra 20bp would have been

$$\frac{0.2}{1.11} + \frac{0.2}{1.13^2} = 0.3368$$

13: SWAPS

and fair price of fixed leg would have been

$$100.3368 = \frac{C}{1.11} + \frac{C}{1.13^2} + \frac{100}{1.13^2}$$

C = 13.0769 (which is 20bp greater than the rate it would have been if priced off LIBOR)

This example shows that only if the cash flows (fixed and floating) occur at the same time in the swap, can the difference in LIBOR simply be added/taken off the fixed. If they occur at different times, then the approach is firstly to calculate the impact on the value of the floating flows and then equate these to the fixed flows.

Deferred start swaps

A customer may ask for the price of a swap that does not commence now, i.e. a deferred start swap. The approach is the same as we have previously seen, i.e. equating the value of the floating rate flows to the value of the fixed rate flows.

Previously, we have taken the price of the floating rate flows to be £100 assuming LIBOR. This, however, assumes the swap is entered into immediately. If, for example, the swap will be entered into in one year's time, the value of the floating rate flows will be £100 **in one year**. To obtain the value **today**, this needs to be discounted back by the one-year spot rate. The fixed-rate side will be the same, except that for a swap entered into in one year's time, the first flow will be in two years, i.e. there will be **no** flow in one year's time.

Example 1

What is the rate for a four-year swap paying annually, deferred start one year, assuming the following spot rates.

Year	%
1	10
2	11
3	12
4	13
5	14

FRN Price = fixed bond price

$$\frac{100}{1.1} = \frac{C}{1.11^2} + \frac{C}{1.12^3} + \frac{C}{1.13^4} + \frac{C}{1.14^5} + \frac{100}{1.14^5}$$

C = 14.67%

Example 2

What is the rate for a three-year swap, deferred two years using the same spot rate as the previous example?

$$\frac{100}{1.11^2} = \frac{C}{1.12^3} + \frac{C}{1.13^4} + \frac{C}{1.14^5} + \frac{100}{1.14^5}$$

C = 15.84%

3.6.7 Swap rates, spot rates and bootstrapping

Remember that the fixed side of an interest rate swap is equivalent, in cash flow terms, to a fixed coupon bond. Also, if a bond is priced at par, then the yield will be equal to the coupon. Therefore, the fixed rate in a par value swap is equivalent to the yield.

It might be necessary in the exam to determine spot rates, having been given the swap rates for different maturities. This can be done by a process known as bootstrapping.

Example

You are given the following swap rates and need to calculate the appropriate spot rates.

Maturity	Swap Rate
1	6%
2	6.5%
3	7.2%
4	8.0%
5	9.0%

Consider the swap as a fixed coupon bond, valued at par paying a coupon equal to the swap rate. For simplicity, assume the swaps settle annually.

One-year spot rate (r_1)

$$100 = \frac{106}{1+r_1}$$

$r_1 = 6\%$

Having calculated the one-year spot rate from the one-year maturity swap, we can now calculate the two-year spot rate, using the two-year swap. The important thing is to discount the one-year flow at the one-year spot rate, thus leaving the two-year spot rate as the only unknown.

Two-year spot rate (r_2)

$$100 = \frac{6.5}{1.06} + \frac{106.5}{(1+r_2)^2}$$

$r_2 = 6.52\%$

Having calculated the two-year spot rate, move on to the three-year swap and calculate the three-year spot rate. Continue in this way until all the required spot rates have been calculated. This process is called bootstrapping.

13: SWAPS

Three-year spot rate (r_3)

$$100 = \frac{7.2}{1.06} + \frac{7.2}{1.0652^2} + \frac{107.2}{(1+r_3)^3}$$

$r_3 = 7.26\%$

Four-year spot rate (r_4)

$$100 = \frac{8}{1.06} + \frac{8}{1.0652^2} + \frac{8}{1.0726^3} + \frac{108}{(1+r_4)^4}$$

$r_4 = 8.16\%$

Five-year spot rate (r_5)

$$100 = \frac{9}{1.06} + \frac{9}{1.0652^2} + \frac{9}{1.0726^3} + \frac{9}{1.0816^4} + \frac{109}{(1+r_5)^5}$$

$r_5 = 9.35\%$

We can now see the following.

Maturity/Term	Swap Rate	Spot Rate	Spot Discount Factor
1	6%	6%	0.9434
2	6.5%	6.52%	0.8813
3	7.2%	7.26%	0.8104
4	8.0%	8.16%	0.7307
5	9.0%	9.35%	0.6396

3.7 Pricing an interest rate swap as a series of FRAs

NB: FRAs are covered in the next chapter. You may wish to read up on that subject before continuing.

It is possible to price a swap by thinking of it as a series of forward rate agreements (FRA).

From the following spot rate, calculate the 1-year forward rates starting in one year and two years.

Year	Spot rate
1	10%
2	11%
3	12%

One-year rate starting in one year ($_1f_2$)

$(1.1)(1 + {_1f_2}) = 1.11^2$

$_1f_2 = 12.01\%$

One-year rate starting in two years ($_2f_3$)

$$1.11^2(1 + {_2f_3}) = 1.12^3$$

$$_2f_3 = 14.03\%$$

These forward rates could be locked in by buying FRAs. We will borrow for the first year at 10% (the 1-year spot rate), for the second year at 12.01% (buy a $_1f_2$ FRA) and for the third year at 14.03% (buy a $_2f_3$ FRA). The interest paid on £100 for each of the three years and the present value of these flows can be calculated as follows.

$$\text{Present value} = \frac{10}{1.10} + \frac{12.01}{1.11^2} + \frac{14.03}{1.12^3}$$

$$= 28.82$$

We can now calculate what fixed rate for the three years would equate to the same present value.

$$28.82 = \frac{C}{1.10} + \frac{C}{1.11^2} + \frac{C}{1.12^3}$$

$$C = 11.85\%$$

What has been demonstrated above is that buying the series of FRAs is the same as locking in a fixed rate of 11.85% for three years.

As an alternative to buying the FRAs, we could lock in a three-year rate by paying fixed in a plain vanilla interest rate swap. What would be the fixed rate in a three-year swap?

$$100 = \frac{C}{1.10} + \frac{C}{1.11^2} + \frac{C}{1.12^3} + \frac{100}{1.12^3}$$

$$C = 11.85\%$$

We have shown that the fixed rate in an interest rate swap is equivalent to a series of FRAs.

This is not a surprising conclusion as we have already seen that the discounted value of the forward rates is 100 – the basis of pricing a par value swap.

3.7.1 The swap spread

As we have seen, the swap rate is closely related to the general term structure of interest rates. This linkage is most noticeable when, in certain markets (such as the US), the swap rate is quoted as a swap spread over the yield of the on-the-run bond.

Several influences can be identified in the difference between the yield and the swap rate. First is pure supply and demand. When market expectations are that rates are currently low and likely to rise, the demand to pay fixed and receive floating will rise and spreads will rise. If rates are expected to fall, swap spreads will also fall.

Aside from supply/demand, the spread will also take account of transaction costs – such costs normally only occur if the swap is connected with a new issue.

The final factor is credit risk. To protect the bank, in part for the risk of default, the spread will move to accommodate this.

3.7.2 Euronext.liffe's Swapnote future

The Swapnote future contract is essentially a forward starting swap contract that cash settles on the start/effective date of the underlying swap, which operates on the usual March, June, September, December cycle. Contracts are available for two, five and ten-year swaps in both euros (€100,000 nominal) and US dollars ($200,000 nominal). Notional coupons of 6% apply for both currencies, but assume annual flows for euros and semi-annual flows for dollars, in line with the underlying swap and bond markets.

13: SWAPS

The EDSP of the Swapnote future will be the sum of the discounted cash flows, each of which has been given a present value using zero coupon discount factors derived from the ISDA Benchmark Swap Rates at 10.00 hrs (London time) on the last trading day. For these purposes, the zero coupon discount factors are calculated using a standard bootstrapping technique.

Up to expiry, the price will of course vary according to supply and demand, and price sensitivity is highly correlated to the swap markets rather than the government bond markets, thus mitigating basis risk between the two.

4 Short-Term Currency Swaps/Foreign Exchange Swaps

Exam tip

> This is regularly examined

4.1 Definition

A short-term currency swap is a contract that commits two parties to exchange pre-agreed foreign currency amounts now and re-exchange them back at a given future date (the maturity date). The flows are capital only. There is no direct interest payment involved.

4.2 Terminology

4.2.1 Primary and secondary currencies

Primary currency

One currency is defined as the primary currency and most deals are structured such that the nominal value of the primary currency exchanged on the two dates is equal.

Secondary currency

The other currency is the secondary currency and the nominal value of this exchanged on the two dates is a function of the spot rate and the swap market forward rate.

4.2.2 Buyer and seller

Terms

The terms buyer and seller are a little awkward in relation to FX swap dealing, since in both legs each party is giving (selling) one currency and receiving (buying) the other.

The terms buyer and seller relate to these swap arrangements from the point of view of the primary currency cash flows at inception. The **buyer** is the person who, at inception, purchases the primary currency (sells the secondary currency); the seller is the individual who, at inception, sells the primary currency (buys the secondary currency). The definition of the primary currency is agreed by the counterparties. It will usually be the one where the amount is the same in both legs.

Cash flows

Buyer		Seller
At Inception	←—— Buy $1.5m (primary currency) —— ——— Sell £1m (secondary currency) ——→	At Inception
At Maturity	——— Sell $1.5m (primary currency) ——→ ←—— Buy £0.95m (secondary currency) ——	At Maturity

4.2.3 Synthetic Agreement for Forward Exchange (SAFE)

A SAFE is a variation on the short-term currency swap. It is a collective term for FXAs (Forward Exchange Agreements) and ERAs (Exchange Rate Agreements) that are both a means of trading FX swaps for the future. There is no actual exchange of principal at inception or at maturity, the arrangement being a contract for differences based on notional cash sums.

When the two parties agree to execute a SAFE, they agree the exchange rates at which the notional deals will be executed at inception and maturity. At maturity, one party pays the other the difference in the value of the secondary currency between the rate originally contracted and the rate actually prevailing.

This is an example of a non-deliverable forward (NDF).

4.3 Dealing

The market in short-term currency swaps, as for interest rate swaps, is an OTC market. Trading is conducted over the telephone or through the Reuters Dealing system, and price information is disseminated through quote vendor systems such as Reuters and Telerate.

The quotes are given as a swap spread on the current spot rate.

4.4 Using short-term currency swaps

4.4.1 Hedging

Short-term currency swaps provide an alternative to forward exchange rate agreements through simultaneously entering spot forward deals. The arrangement may result in a better forward exchange rate being achieved as a result of differences between interest rates in swap and money markets.

The swap deal is chosen to achieve the correct cash flows at the maturity date, as could be achieved through the use of a forward exchange contract. The spot deal is undertaken to cancel the initiation leg of the swap so that the net position is that the only cash flow occurs at maturity. This is most easily seen with an example.

Example

$3m is to be received in three months from a US customer. The current spot rate is $1.733:£1 and three-month market interest rates are 10% in the UK and 4% in the US. How can a swap arrangement be structured to translate this amount into sterling, and what will be the sterling receipt in three months?

Solution

The swap arrangement needs to be selling US dollars in three months, hence buying US dollars now. If the US dollar is the primary currency, we need to be the buyer of the swap.

Based on the information provided, the relevant exchange rates and corresponding secondary currency (sterling) values are

Now: Spot rate = 1.7330 $\Rightarrow$ £1,731,102

3 months: Forward rate = $1.7330 \times \dfrac{1.01}{1.025}$ = 1.7076 $\Rightarrow$ £1,756,812

The whole deal can, therefore, be structured as

Spot Market	Swap Market	
	Now	**3 months**
Sell $3,000,000	Buy $3,000,000	Sell $3,000,000
Buy £1,731,102	Sell £1,731,102	Buy £1,756,812

These cancel out resulting in a net zero cash flow at inception

Leaving the second leg as the only actual commercial cash flow

4.4.2 Speculation

Since short-term currency swaps reflect forward exchange rates and respond to interest rate differentials, a speculator may use them to speculate on future

- Forward exchange rate spreads.
- Changes in interest rate differentials.

If, for example, a speculator believed that US rates were going to rise relative to UK rates in the near future, then the forward exchange rate on the US dollar would move to a lower premium, resulting in fewer pounds sterling being received per US dollar for forward exchange deals at that future date.

Entering a swap as in the above hedging example would, therefore, result in a gain to the speculator.

A buyer gains and a seller loses when the primary currency interest rate increases in relative terms.

Example

A speculator enters the above swap transaction, buying $3m in the belief that US interest rates will increase in the near future relative to UK rates. Next day, US rates move up to 5% to support the dollar, keeping the spot rate at 1.733, but UK rates are unaltered. What will be the speculator's gain or loss?

Solution

With US rates at 5%, the three-month forward exchange rate, and sterling value corresponding to $3m, will be

$$\text{Forward rate} = 1.7330 \times \frac{1.0125}{1.025} = 1.7119 \Rightarrow £1,752,439$$

The speculator can now close out his swap position with a forward exchange contract buying $3m in three months for £1,752,439, hence realising a sterling profit of £4,373 (£1,756,812 – £1,752,439) at maturity.

4.5 Valuation

At inception, as for all swaps, the two legs will have the same value and hence, the swap has zero value. Later, as interest rate differentials move, the swap position may give rise to a gain or loss at maturity as we illustrated above.

This gain or loss at maturity is established as the changes in the value of the maturity cash flow in relation to the **secondary currency**, the primary currency cash flow being fixed. The value of the swap position will then be the present value of this maturity gain or loss.

5 LONG-TERM CURRENCY SWAPS

5.1 Definition

A standard long-term currency swap is a contract that commits two counterparties to exchange, over an agreed period, two streams of interest payments in different currencies and, at the end of the period, to exchange the corresponding principal amounts at an exchange rate agreed at the start of the contract (there may or may not be an exchange of principal amounts at the start of the contract).

5.1.1 Key Elements

Thus, broken down into its constituent parts, we might see

- A UK corporate contracted to pay a US bank the interest payments on $15m at a rate agreed when the swap is negotiated.
- A US bank contracted to pay the UK corporate the interest payments on £10m at a rate agreed when the swap was negotiated.
- At the end of the, say, 3-year term of the swap, the principal amounts involved would be exchanged, with the UK corporate paying the US bank $15m and receiving £10m.

You will immediately notice two important differences between currency swaps and interest rate swaps.

- The cash flows involved take place in two currencies.
- There is an exchange of principal amounts.

As a result of these differences, the currency swap can help reduce, or increase, exposure to both currencies and interest rates.

5.2 Terminology

As with interest rate swaps, there are many different structures that have developed from the simple currency swap outlined above. Some of the more important ones are listed below.

5.2.1 The currency swap

As with so much of the jargon of the financial industry, different practitioners often use the same term to mean different things but, strictly speaking, a currency swap is a swap involving the exchange of two fixed interest streams in different currencies with an exchange of principal at maturity.

This could be represented diagrammatically as follows.

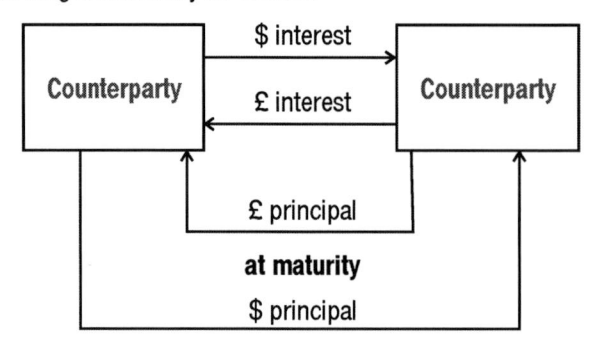

```
                $ interest
   Counterparty ─────────────► Counterparty
                ◄─────────────
                £ interest

                £ principal
                     ▲
                at maturity
                $ principal
```

Some currency swaps may involve exchange of principals, both at the beginning and end of the term. These are undertaken when the swap is associated with new borrowings by either or both of the counterparties. This form of currency swap was, in fact, the first manifestation of the product and was used to overcome some of the difficulties of back-to-back or parallel loans. These products are sometimes called cash swaps.

5.2.2 Cross-currency swaps

Cross-currency swaps involve an exchange of interest streams in different currencies of which at least one is at a floating rate of interest.

These swaps could therefore include.

Cross-currency coupon swaps	In which a fixed rate is exchanged for a floating rate in a different currency; or
Cross-currency basis swaps	In which two floating rates in different currencies are exchanged.

5.2.3 Circus swaps

A circus swap is a swap made up of a cross-currency coupon swap (fixed against floating) and a single-currency coupon swap. The purpose is to synthesize either a pure fixed-against-fixed currency swap or a cross-currency basis swap.

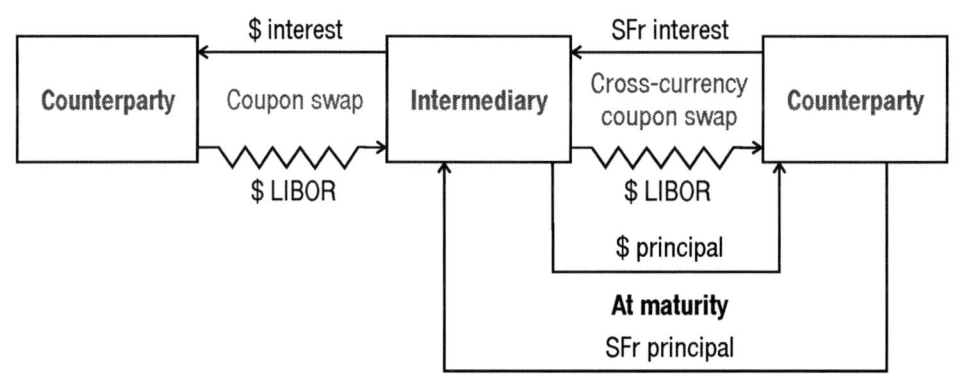

```
             $ interest                    SFr interest
Counterparty ◄──────── Intermediary ◄──────────── Counterparty
             Coupon swap            Cross-currency
                                    coupon swap
             $ LIBOR                 $ LIBOR
                                     $ principal
                                     At maturity
                                     SFr principal
```

5.3 Dealing

It is conventional with interest rate coupon swaps to use 6-month LIBOR as the standard index for the floating rate, thus leaving the fixed rate to be agreed. With currency swaps where a currency is also involved, the standard is to use 6-month US dollar LIBOR.

Cross currency basis swaps also use 6-month US dollar LIBOR as the reference point, with the other floating rate being quoted as a margin over or under LIBOR in the non-dollar currency.

For example, a £/$ cross-currency basis swap might be quoted at +10, meaning the swap is between US dollar LIBOR on one hand and sterling LIBOR plus 10 basis points on the other.

Conventionally, currency swaps are quoted in terms of all-in prices, i.e. as absolute interest rates as two-way prices, e.g.

7.15%	7.25%
Receive 7.15% fixed	Pay 7.25% fixed

5.4 Uses of currency swaps

5.4.1 Speculating

Although currency swaps create exposures to both fluctuations in interest rates and exchange rates, they are not used as trading vehicles in the same way as futures. This is because of the credit risks involved in exchanging principals. Currency swaps are therefore used mostly for hedging and arbitrage.

5.4.2 Hedging

Imagine a British pharmaceutical company that has issued a dollar bond to finance development. The company expects the dollar to appreciate and sterling interest rates to fall.

If this happens, the foreign currency liability (the bond) will increase in sterling terms and the cost of servicing the bond begins to look increasingly unattractive. Which swap structure could be used to achieve the required end of accessing lower UK rates and fixing the sterling value of the liability?

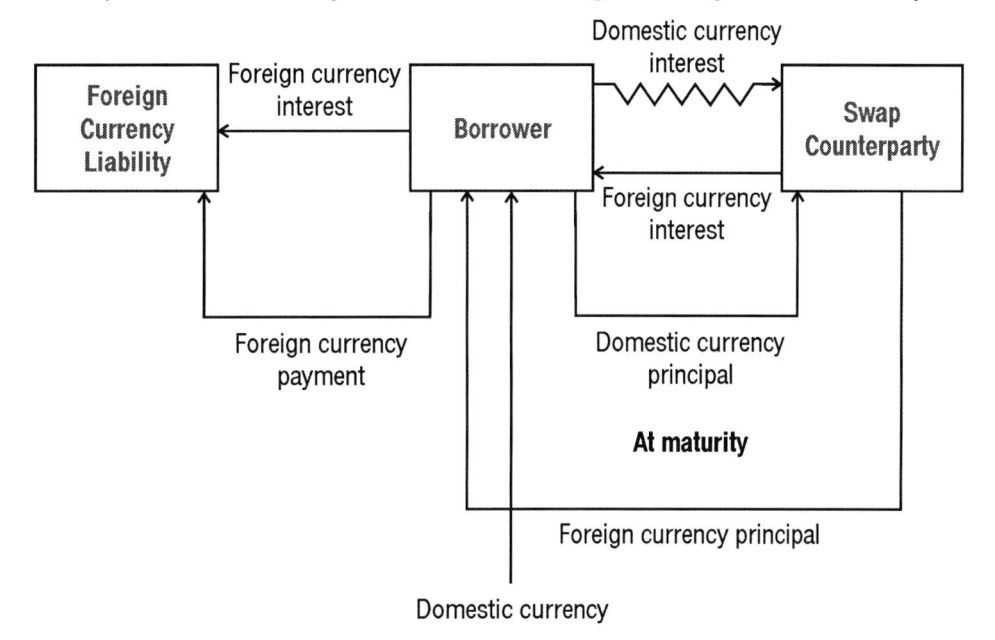

13: SWAPS

In the previous example, it was assumed that the British company could access the US bond market. In reality, the UK company might have a comparative advantage in its domestic corporate bond market and therefore raise funds there and swap the sterling into dollars at the start of the swap.

These are just two simple examples of swap hedges – there are, of course, many other potential uses.

5.4.3 Arbitrage

Currency swaps can be used in a similar way to interest rate swaps in order to arbitrage comparative advantage in different markets. It is also possible to arbitrage absolute advantage. For example, a Swiss company may be able to borrow dollars more cheaply than Swiss francs (perhaps because the domestic Swiss market is already saturated with its paper) and a US company may be able to borrow Swiss francs more cheaply than dollars for the same reasons.

The appeal of new issue arbitrage using currency swaps is that borrowers can separate their funding decisions from risk management decisions about currency and interest rate risk.

5.5 Valuation

Exam tip

> This area is regularly examined requiring the scheduling and discounting of cash flows

Once again, in order to initially conclude the swap deal, the present value of the swapped future cash flows must be identical, hence the value of the swap is zero. The swap will attract a value if these present values change as a result of interest and foreign exchange rate movements.

The valuation of a long-term currency swap (as for all swaps), requires us to evaluate the present values of the two legs and determine the difference. Once again, however, the cash flows involved are identical to those for two bonds, this time in two different currencies. The bonds may be either fixed or floating rate. However, the approach to both of these was discussed above under interest rate swaps and the problem, once again, amounts to that of bond valuation.

If, for example, we have entered into a swap under which we pay sterling and receive dollars, then the cash flows are identical to those of borrowing in sterling and investing in dollars. Hence, the value of the swap to us could be calculated as

Value to Payer of Sterling	£
Value of dollar bond asset	X
Value of sterling bond liability	(Y)
Value of swap	Z

The approach is to evaluate each bond separately in its own currency based on the relevant currency cash flows and spot rates. These present values can then be translated into the same currency using the prevailing spot exchange rate and hence, the swap value, being the difference between these two values, can be determined in that currency.

Example

Two years ago, a UK company and a US company entered into a six-year currency swap under which the UK company agreed to pay 6% on a notional borrowing of $8.5m in exchange for the US company paying 9% on a notional borrowing of £5m, with an exchange of these capital amounts at maturity.

The current term structure of interest rates is flat in both countries – at 5% in the US and 10% in the UK. The exchange rate is $1.50:£1. What is the value of the swap to the UK corporate?

Solution

Sterling bond value

Time	Cash Flow (£)	DF 10%	PV (£)
1	450,000	$\frac{1}{1.10^1}$	409,091
2	450,000	$\frac{1}{1.10^2}$	371,901
3	450,000	$\frac{1}{1.10^3}$	338,092
4	5,450,000	$\frac{1}{1.10^4}$	3,722,423
			4,841,507

Dollar bond value

Time	Cash Flow ($)	DF 5%	PV ($)
1	510,000	$\frac{1}{1.05^1}$	485,714
2	510,000	$\frac{1}{1.05^2}$	462,585
3	510,000	$\frac{1}{1.05^3}$	440,557
4	9,010,000	$\frac{1}{1.05^4}$	7,412,549
			8,801,405

Swap value

Value to Payer of Dollars	£
Value of dollar bond liability ($8,801,405 ÷ 1.50)	(5,867,603)
Value of sterling bond asset	4,841,507
Value of swap	(1,026,096)

6 EQUITY SWAPS

6.1 Definition

Equity swaps are similar in concept to interest rate swaps. The buyer pays the return on a money market deposit (e.g. LIBOR) and in exchange receives the total return on an equity investment (capital gains plus dividends). The two payments are usually netted and are generally exchanged between two and four times annually. As with interest rate swaps, no exchange of principal is involved.

Example

A fund manager has £20m to invest. He places the cash on deposit and enters into a one-year FTSE 100 index swap with a notional principal amount (NPA) of £20m and quarterly reset dates.

13: SWAPS

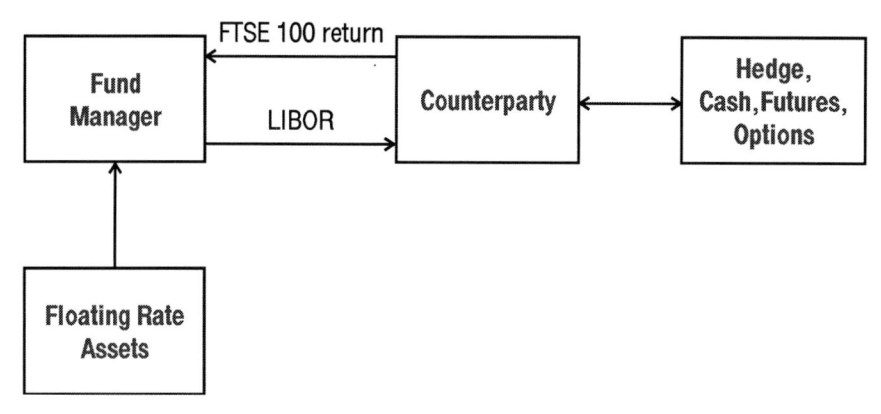

```
                    FTSE 100 return
        ┌─────────┐ ←──────────── ┌──────────────┐        ┌───────────────┐
        │  Fund   │                │              │  ←→    │    Hedge,     │
        │ Manager │                │ Counterparty │        │ Cash, Futures,│
        │         │ ────────────→ │              │        │    Options    │
        └─────────┘     LIBOR      └──────────────┘        └───────────────┘
             ↑
        ┌─────────┐
        │Floating │
        │  Rate   │
        │ Assets  │
        └─────────┘
```

What will be the cash flows at the first reset date, given the following information?

	FTSE 100	Yield	3m LIBOR
Start date of Swap **1 January 2001**	6000		5%
1st Reset **31 March 2001**	6600	$1\frac{1}{3}$%	5.25%

Solution

Three calculations are required in order to undertake the valuation of an equity swap.

- The capital performance of the index (a swap benefit to the fund manager).
- The dividend income (another swap benefit to the fund manager).
- The floating rate payment (a swap cost to the fund manager).

Capital performance

As can be seen from the table, the market has moved sharply higher over the first quarter and thus, the swap counterparty will need to pay the fund manager. It should be noted that had the market fallen, the fund manager would have to pay both LIBOR and the capital depreciation.

The sum due to the fund manager as a result of capital appreciation is calculated as

$$\text{Value of position at 31 March} = \text{Opening NPA} \times \frac{\text{31 March index value}}{\text{1 January index value}}$$

$$= £20\text{m} \times \frac{6600}{6000} = £22\text{m}$$

Payment required = Reset value − Opening NPA

= £22m − £20m = £2m

Dividends

As the swap relates to total return, the dividends earned on the FTSE 100 Index also need to be exchanged. Of course, UK dividends accrue unevenly throughout the year and the terms of the swap would need to specify whether interest is earned on dividends paid within the quarter.

The dividend yield through the first quarter has been $1\frac{1}{3}$%, corresponding to a level of dividend payments due to the fund manager of

$$£20\text{m} \times 1\frac{1}{3}\% = £266,667$$

Floating rate payments

The fund manager is required under the terms of the swap to pay interest which, for the first quarter, amounted to

$$\text{Interest} = \text{Initial NPA} \times \text{Initial LIBOR} \times \frac{\text{Days}}{365}$$

$$= £20m \times 5\% \times \frac{90}{365} = £246,575$$

The floating rate payment made by the fund manager would normally be financed by the return from his own floating rate deposits. If these floating rate assets earn only LIBOR flat, then the receipts and payments wash each other out.

If, however, the fund manager is willing to take some credit risk on his floating rate assets, there is the opportunity for the assets to yield better than LIBOR, thus introducing some yield enhancement into the fund manager's strategy.

Summary of swap cash flows at the 1st reset

	(£)
Benefit of Swap Arrangement to Fund Manager	
Capital Appreciation	2,000,000
Dividend Income	266,667
Cost of Swap Arrangement to Fund Manager	
Floating Rate Interest	(246,575)
Value of Swap Arrangement to Fund Manager at 31 March	2,020,092

When this amount is added to the receipts from the fund manager's interest bearing deposits of £246,575 (assumed to be LIBOR), the total receipt on 31 March amounts to £2,266,667. Thus, it can be seen that the fund manager receives the total return just as if he had invested directly in the stocks themselves.

6.2 Uses of equity swaps

6.2.1 Indexation

As a route to indexation, the equity swap may hold certain advantages over either a physically constructed fund or one synthesized using futures. The table below highlights the differences.

13: SWAPS

Index funds – The alternatives

	Physical	**Futures**	**Swaps**
Settlement	Physical	Cash difference + Initial margin	Cash difference. No margin
Lifespan	Perpetual	Normally quarterly rollovers	Normally up to five years
Tracking Risk	Unless fully replicated, fund may not track	Subject to fair pricing of future	Guaranteed
Mark-to-Market	No	Yes, daily (Thus, cash float must be maintained)	Yes, quarterly
Currency Risk	Yes, if not in base currency	Yes, but only variation margin flows	Payments can take place in any negotiated currency
Yield Enhancement	Stock Lending	Low costs and tight bid/offer spreads. May also be possible to buy future below fair value	Cash asset may yield better than LIBOR flat
Credit Risk	None once settled	None, at least for clearing members	Yes
Liquidity	Good	Best	Worst

6.2.2 Speculating and hedging

Counterparties can use swaps to either gain or hedge their own exposure to physical equities.

The opportunities for swap counterparties to run a matched book in equity swaps are limited, as whilst the index funds are naturally receivers of index returns, there are fewer people who would wish to pay equity returns other than over a short period of time (as they would for short futures).

Therefore, there is a fundamental disequilibrium that may limit further growth.

6.2.3 Arbitrage

There are opportunities for arbitrage profits where offsetting equity swaps and futures positions are taken and futures trade away from their fair value.

6.3 Valuation

Exam tip

This area is frequently examined

Imagine an equity swap with a notional principal amount of £10m, swapping LIBOR for FTSE 100 total returns.

At inception, the value of the swap will be zero. This will entail exchanging LIBOR on £10m for the total return on £10m of FTSE 100 stock. It might sound as if these two flows cannot have equal present value, but they do. We have already seen that the LIBOR flows, using the idea of valuing an FRN, will have a par value. Using discounted cash flow principles, the value of equity today is the present value of the future expected receipts (dividend and growth). Therefore, £10m invested at LIBOR is worth £10m. £10m invested in equities is worth £10m. Therefore, at inception, both flows have equal present values of £10m.

Further proof of this can be had by considering the following.

Two parties enter a one-year swap to exchange (in one year) LIBOR for the FTSE 100 total return on £1m principal. One-year LIBOR = 5% and the anticipated annual dividend yield is 3%. We will consider the anticipated cash flows in one year but first, we need to calculate the current forward price of equity. Assume the cash index is 5000.

$$\text{Forward price} = 5000 \times [1 + (5\% - 3\%)] = 5100$$

Assume the one-year equity future is trading at this fair value, and that the counterparty will hedge its position by going long a synthetic equity fund, i.e. buying 20 FTSE 100 futures and investing £1m in a risk-free asset (assumed to be 5%).

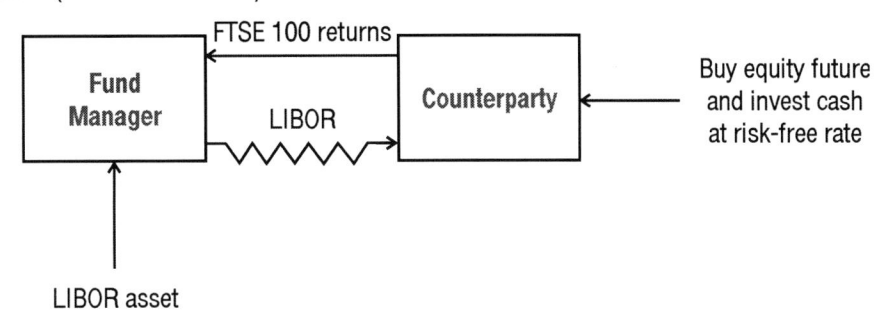

```
                    FTSE 100 returns
              ┌─────────────────────┐
   ┌────────┐                         ┌──────────────┐     Buy equity future
   │ Fund   │ ←─────────────────────  │ Counterparty │ ←── and invest cash
   │Manager │ ────LIBOR────────────→  │              │     at risk-free rate
   └────────┘                         └──────────────┘
        ↑
        │
    LIBOR asset
```

Consider the flows to the counterparty in one year on the assumption that the value of equity in one year's time is £1.02m, i.e. the value of equity grew as the forward price suggested it would (2%).

Receipt:	LIBOR flow = £1m × 5% =	£50,000
Payout:	Dividend flow = £1m × 3% =	(£30,000) } These flows have been generated
Payout:	Capital gain (£1m × 2%)	(£20,000) } from the hedge that the counterparty
		0 established

	£
Profit/Loss from futures	Zero
Interest in cash deposit	50,000
(£1m × 5%)	50,000

What has been demonstrated above is that at inception, the anticipated cash flows net off against each other, therefore the value is zero.

The above has shown that the hedge 'worked' when the value of equity at the end of the year was the same as that predicted by the forward price at the start of the year. The total return on equity was £50,000 and the cash generated from the hedge was £50,000.

Would the hedge have worked if the value of equity in the future was not the same as that predicted by the current future price?

Example

Current forward price = 5100 (as before)

Assume in one year, the index had risen to 5200, i.e. the capital gain was twice that anticipated at the start of the swap. The counterparty would have to give the fund manager

	£	
Dividends (as before)	30,000	
Capital gains	40,000	(previously £20,000)
	70,000	

For the hedge to 'work', it must generate income to the counterparty of £70,000 (as this is what the counterparty must give the fund manager). What income will the synthetic fund generate?

	£
Interest on cash deposit	50,000
Capital gains on future	
(5200 – 5100) × £10 × 20	20,000
	70,000

The hedge works!

Note that the above example assumed that at inception, the future was trading at its fair value. If it was trading above fair value (for example), then the counterparty would lose on the futures component of its synthetic fund hedge. Anticipating the loss, the counterparty will charge a spread above LIBOR on the floating leg. Note that anticipations at that time are factored into the pricing calculation of the swap.

This is demonstrated below.

Example

Fair value forward price = 5100
Actual future price = 5125 (i.e. 25 points above fair value)

The counterparty will anticipate a loss on its long future leg (assuming the value of the index in one year is 5100, i.e. its current fair value) of (5125 – 5100) × £10 × 20 = £5,000.

As the counterparty anticipates this loss, it will add this amount into the floating flows. On a notional principal of £1,000,000, the additional amount of £5,000 represents an additional 0.50%. The floating rate will therefore be LIBOR + 50bp.

Another way the spread above LIBOR could have been determined was by looking at the implied financing rate in the actual future price of 5125. If the dividend yield is still anticipated to be 3%, then a future price of 5125 when the cash index is 5000 implies a finance rate of

$$\left(\frac{5125}{5000} - 1\right) + 0.03 = 0.055 = 5.5\%$$

As this is 50bp above the actual finance rate of 5%, this is the spread above LIBOR that must be paid.

After initiation, its value will be affected by changes in LIBOR, dividend yield and gains/losses on the underlying equity. Any subsequent value will be the difference between the value of the floating flows (valued as a FRN) and the value of the equity.

NB: The value of equity always represents the present value of future expected receipts.

6.4 Price return swap

A variation on the above is a price return swap. This is a swap when only the capital gain/loss is paid, but not the dividends. If we assume the future is trading at fair value, then the floating flows, as shown above, would be LIBOR if the total return were to be paid. If the counterparty is not going to pay the dividend flows, then the fund manager will pay (on assumption future is at fair value) LIBOR **less** dividend yield.

7 COMMODITY SWAPS

7.1 Introduction

The most recent addition to the stable of swap products is the commodity swap. These products are available on a wide variety of crude oils, refined products, non-ferrous metals and foodstuffs.

Commodity swaps overcome some of the limitations of exchange-traded futures in that they can be long dated and tailored to particular delivery points and grades.

7.2 Definition

In a commodity swap, the counterparty offers a series of cash-settled futures contracts to the hedger. The hedger is offered a single fixed price at which he will notionally buy or sell on an agreed date. Cash settlement is calculated on the difference between the fixed price and the price of an agreed index for a stated notional amount of the underlying asset.

Commodity swaps enable users to immunise their price risk to a particular commodity for periods of up to ten years. Unlike interest rate swaps, they are predominantly hedging vehicles.

Once again, this idea is best illustrated with an example.

Example

Notional Principal	One million barrels of Brent Crude
Start Date	1 January 2001
Reset Dates	31 March, 30 June, 30 September, 31 December
Index	IPE Brent Index
Fixed Rate	$20.45 per barrel

Calculate the cash flows at the first reset date.

Swap structure

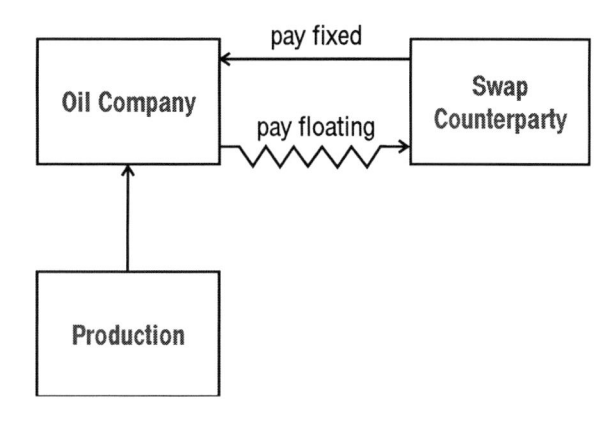

Solution

IPE Index = $18.50

Oil Company			$m
Receives	$20.45 × 1m	=	20.45
Pays	$18.50 × 1m	=	(18.50)
Net			1.95

In this way, the oil producer has a fixed sale price of $20.45 per barrel for a production of one million barrels each quarter.

This simple structure could be refined to take account of differing production levels by adjusting the notional principal for each period.

7.3 Uses of commodity swaps

7.3.1 Speculating and Hedging

Counterparties can use swaps to either gain or hedge their own exposure to commodities by dealing as illustrated above.

7.3.2 Arbitrage

There are opportunities for arbitrage profits where offsetting commodity swaps and futures positions are taken and futures trade away from their fair value, as with equity swaps.

7.4 Valuation

In common with other swap structures, the swap counterparty will price the commodity swap by calculating the present value of a strip of futures contracts. However, the pricing of (for example) energy futures, is not quite as straightforward as financial futures.

Whilst financial futures are priced in accordance with arbitrage conditions that take account of the cost of carry, energy futures' prices are less amenable to arbitrage, as reverse cash and carries cannot be undertaken. In addition, energy futures prices may also include, particularly in near months, a convenience premium (i.e. a premium to fair value that consumers are willing to pay in order to guarantee supply).

As a consequence of this, commodity futures prices are more difficult to model, as their term structure is considerably less visible than that of the interest rate markets.

Notwithstanding such problems, commodity swaps do offer a long-term hedging mechanism for both consumers and producers that avoids basis risk, rollover risks and the margin administration of exchange-traded futures.

8 NON-GENERIC SWAPS

8.1 Introduction

One of the features of OTC instruments is the proliferation of different structures.

Non-generic or exotic swaps are those that differ from straight or plain vanilla swaps. These plain vanilla swaps have seven attributes.

- Constant principal amount.
- Exchange of fixed for floating interest (fixed from fixed or currency swaps).
- Constant fixed rate.
- Flat floating rate (i.e. no premium over the floating rate index).
- Regular interest payments.
- Immediate start date (two business days after the transaction is agreed).
- No other special features (e.g. attached options).

To cope with customer requirements and sometimes to please the egos of the financial engineers, a large number of exotic structures have been created, the most important of which are reviewed below.

8.1.1 Margin swaps

A margin swap is simply a coupon swap in which the floating leg is not flat LIBOR, but LIBOR +/– a margin, e.g. LIBOR + 50bp.

8.1.2 Forward start swaps

Generic swaps normally start a number of days after the trade date. Forward start swaps allow hedgers to lock in rates for exposures that will emerge in months or even years.

8.1.3 Off-market swaps

Most swaps are priced so that payer and receiver cash flows have the same net present value at inception. As a consequence, no payments are made on entering the swap. With an off-market swap, the fixed rate differs from the market rate and therefore, a payment should be made to compensate one party. One reason for doing this is that when a company wishes to cover the issuing costs of a bond, by setting the fixed rate to the apparent advantage of the swap bank, they will receive compensation with which to cover the issue costs.

8.1.4 Zero-coupon swaps

As with a zero-coupon bond, no coupon payments are made under a zero-coupon swap until the end of the swap's life.

8.1.5 Amortising/Accreting/Rollercoaster swaps

Swaps within which the notional principal reduces (amortising swap), increases (accreting swap) or fluctuates (rollercoaster swap).

An Amortising Swap

An Accreting Swap

A Rollercoaster Swap

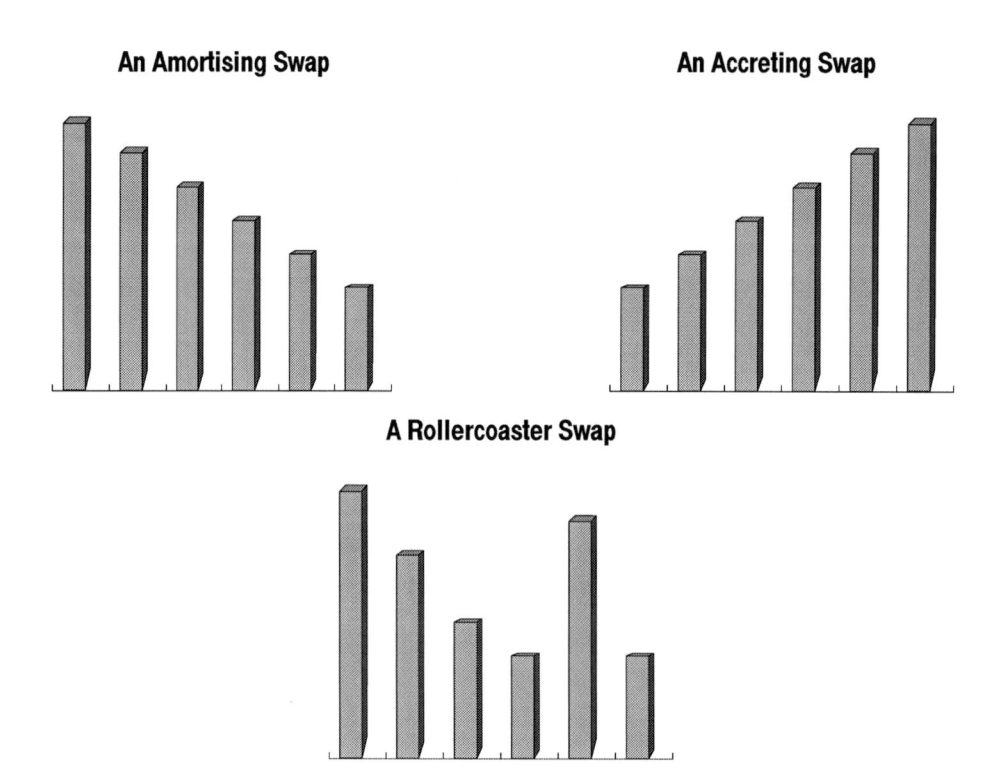

8.1.6 Differential swaps

Differential swaps (also known as a quanto swap, currency protected swap (CUP) or a cross-index basis swap (CRIB)), first appeared in the early 1990s.

In essence, a diff swap is a variation on the basis swap theme. In a normal basis swap, one floating rate is exchanged for another, for example, 3-month versus 6-month US dollar LIBOR. Although the bases may be different, the currencies are the same. In a diff swap, however, one of the floating rates is indexed to the LIBOR of a foreign currency, but all payments are made in a single currency.

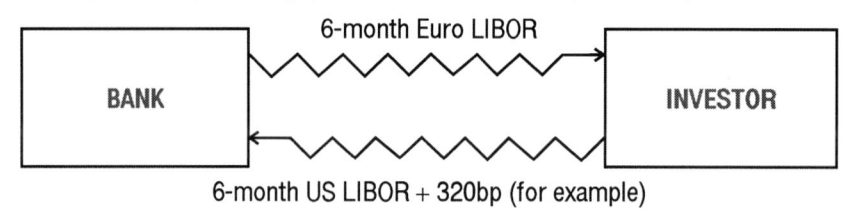

```
                 6-month Euro LIBOR
   ┌──────┐  ──────────────────────→  ┌──────────┐
   │ BANK │                            │ INVESTOR │
   └──────┘  ←──────────────────────   └──────────┘
              6-month US LIBOR + 320bp (for example)
```

All settlements are made in dollars.

Most of the early diff swaps emerged when US short-term rates were extremely low, but with a steeply positive yield curve. Deutschemark (DM) rates on the other hand were sharply inverted.

The following rates might have been observed in January 1992.

Period	$ (%)	DM (%)
3 months	4.25	9.5000
6 months	4.3125	9.4375
1 year	4.6250	9.2500
2 years	5.4700	8.7500

Keen to capture the high short-term DM rates, and confident that the Bundesbank would not ease short-term rates, the investor could have entered a two-year swap. In this swap, 6-month DM LIBOR is paid in dollars, based on a dollar principal. Six-month $ LIBOR plus 320 basis points constitutes the other leg of the trade.

The diff swap is particularly appealing in that the investor remains immunised from exchange rate risk. The higher DM rates are earned without foreign exchange exposures emerging.

At the first reset date, the following rates prevail.

July 1992		
Period	$ (%)	DM (%)
3 months	3.4375	9.8125
6 months	3.6250	9.8750
1 year	3.8125	9.7500
2 years	4.4300	9.4000

During the six-month period, there have been two dollar rate cuts whilst money supply growth has kept Bundesbank policy tight.

The cash flows on a semi-annual $10m notional would therefore be

US$ LIBOR + 320bp

$$3.6250 + 3.20 = \frac{6.8250\%}{2} \times 10m = \$341,250$$

DM LIBOR

$$\frac{9.8750\%}{2} \times 10m = \$493,750$$

A pick-up of 3.05%.

In this example, the investor guessed right, that the forward yield curve was inaccurately expressing the DM/$ interest rate differentials.

Aside from speculation, the diff can be used to convert dollar-denominated floating rate securities into higher yielding euro-linked floating rate assets with no foreign exchange exposure.

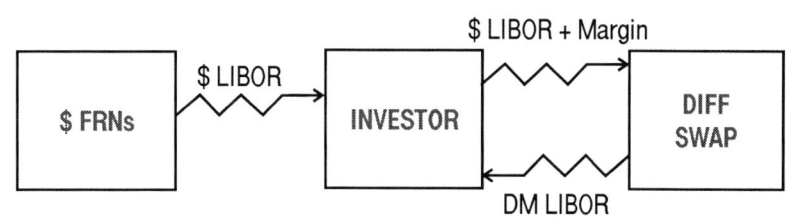

Diff swaps can also be used by borrowers. For example, in countries where short-term rates are high, diff swaps can be used to access lower cost overseas rates at no exchange rate risk. For example, a UK company could issue a normal sterling denominated floating rate note linked to LIBOR and then enter into a diff swap receiving sterling LIBOR but deliver $ LIBOR plus margin, paid in sterling. As long as the spread remains above the agreed margin, low cost borrowing will be achieved.

In using the diff swap, the user is second guessing the market and the expectations represented in the forward yield curve. Whilst the diff swap has obvious appeal to the user, it presents considerable hedging problems for the swap bank. These problems lie in hedging the relationship between two interest rates **and** two exchange rates at the same time. This difficulty became very apparent during the ERM crisis of September 1992. Connected with the inter-relationship between interest rates and exchange rates is the liquidity risk evident during market turmoil – some markets stopped trading in September 1992.

8.1.7 Diff caps/Floors

In addition to diff swaps, there are also diff caps and floors. An alternative term for these products is cross-currency caps/floors.

Like normal caps/floors, these are option products. However, they become in-the-money only when the differential between the two interest rates breaches a certain margin. For example, a diff cap might pay out if $ LIBOR – € LIBOR exceeds 200 basis points. These products become necessary to protect users against the risks inherent in leveraged diff products (discussed below).

A further variation on this theme is the spread cap, which also limits the differential between two floating rates, but with the payment being made in a third currency.

9 ASSET SWAPS

Exam tip

> An asset swap is an interest rate swap plus a bond. Full analysis needs you to schedule the cash flows individual and then deal with them. Don't let the terminology frighten you, take it step-by-step

An asset swap is a package that consists of the fixed cash flows of a bond and an agreement to swap these fixed cash flows for a series of floating payments. The reference rate from the floating payments is normally LIBOR.

Consider the following example that demonstrates the motivation and use of an asset swap. A company is borrowing at LIBOR and wishes to invest in a floating rate note. However, because the FRN market is small compared to the fixed coupon bond market the company is going to achieve its aim by investing in a fixed coupon bond and then swapping the fixed coupon for a floating rate of interest.

The fixed coupon bond can be a fairly illiquid Eurobond (for example) that pays a coupon above the current swap rate. In exchange for paying this coupon to its swap counterparty, the company will receive a floating rate that is at premium over LIBOR. These flows can be shown below.

1. Company is borrowing at LIBOR.

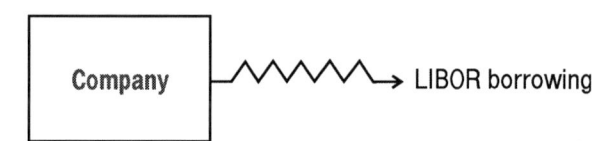

   Company ⟶ LIBOR borrowing

2. Company Invests in a Fixed Coupon Bond, e.g. a Eurobond Paying 8% Coupon.

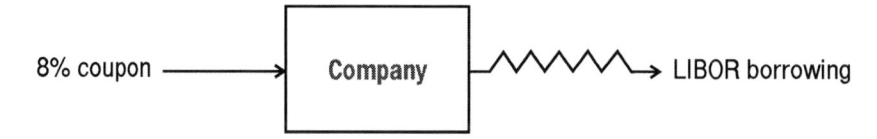

   8% coupon ⟶ Company ⟶ LIBOR borrowing

3. Company Swaps Fixed Coupon for Floating.

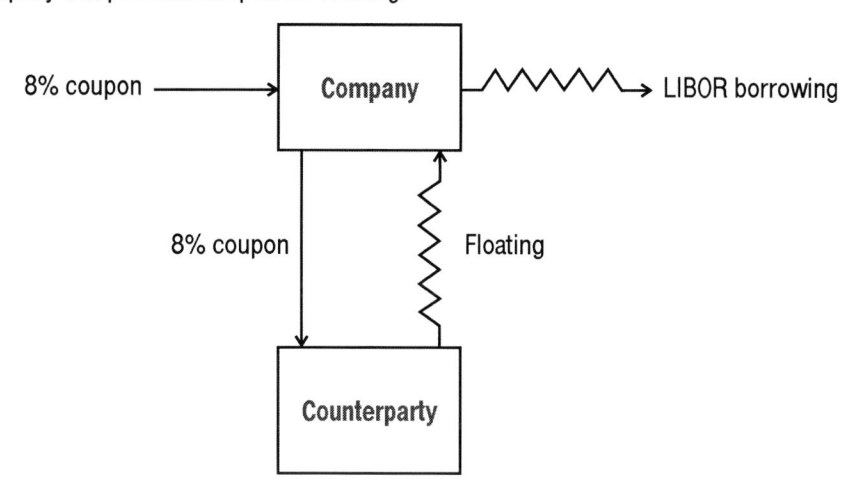

```
8% coupon ──────► ┌─────────┐ ～～～► LIBOR borrowing
                  │ Company │
                  └────┬────┘
                       │        ▲
                  8% coupon    Floating
                       │        │
                       ▼        │
                  ┌──────────────┐
                  │ Counterparty │
                  └──────────────┘
```

4. If the coupon is above the par swap rate and the swap is going to be priced at par, then the floating rate will be a spread over LIBOR relating to the difference between the coupon and the par swap rate. If, for example, the par swap rate was $7\frac{1}{2}\%$, the asset swap would look as follows.

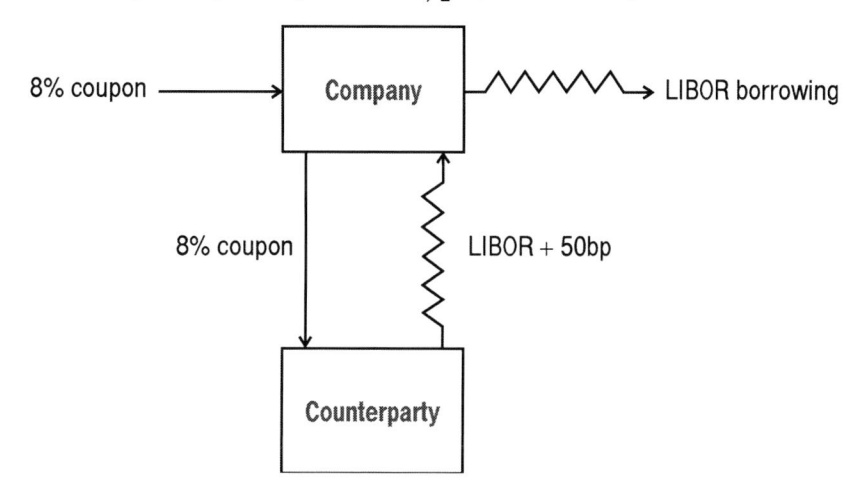

```
8% coupon ──────► ┌─────────┐ ～～～► LIBOR borrowing
                  │ Company │
                  └────┬────┘
                       │        ▲
                  8% coupon    LIBOR + 50bp
                       │        │
                       ▼        │
                  ┌──────────────┐
                  │ Counterparty │
                  └──────────────┘
```

It can be seen from the above that the company can achieve sub-LIBOR funding (L – 50bp) and thereby enhance its returns.

The above calculations are somewhat simplified, as they have assumed that the underlying fixed coupon bond was trading at par. If this is not the case, the floating rate will have to be adjusted to reflect the difference between the par value of the bond and the market value of the bond.

The reasoning behind this is that asset swaps are typically sold as a package. In the above example, the company would buy the bond, typically at par, from the counterparty and then swap the cash flows from the bond for floating. If the market value of the bond is greater than par, the counterparty must be compensated for the fact that they are receiving less than the market value. The way this compensation works is for the counterparty to pay a lower floating rate, over the life of the swap, to the company. This reduction to LIBOR will have the same PV as the difference between the par value and the market value of the bond.

In the above example, let us say that the market price of the 8% coupon bond was £105, but the company and counterparty entered into a three-year par value asset swap.

We must calculate what adjustment to LIBOR over the next three years has a present value of £5. To do this, we need the spot rates.

13: SWAPS

Year	%
1	6
2	6½
3	7

$$£5 = \frac{C}{1.06} + \frac{C}{1.065^2} + \frac{C}{1.07^3}$$

C = £1.89

The difference of £5 in the price today is the same in present value terms as £1.89 per £100 for each of the next three years.

The resulting floating rate would be

LIBOR + 50bp − 189bp = LIBOR − 139bp

An alternative to a spread over/under LIBOR could be a one-off payment at the start of the swap equal to the PV of the difference.

It is usual to trade asset swaps by quoting the asset swap spread. This is the spread referred to above that is necessary to price the swap at par. Obviously, this spread will be different for different underlying fixed coupon bonds.

The above example had the fixed rate in the swap equal to the coupon on the bond. If the fixed rate in the swap was the current swap rate, then the company could make a profit equal to the difference between the coupon and the swap rate. This is shown below.

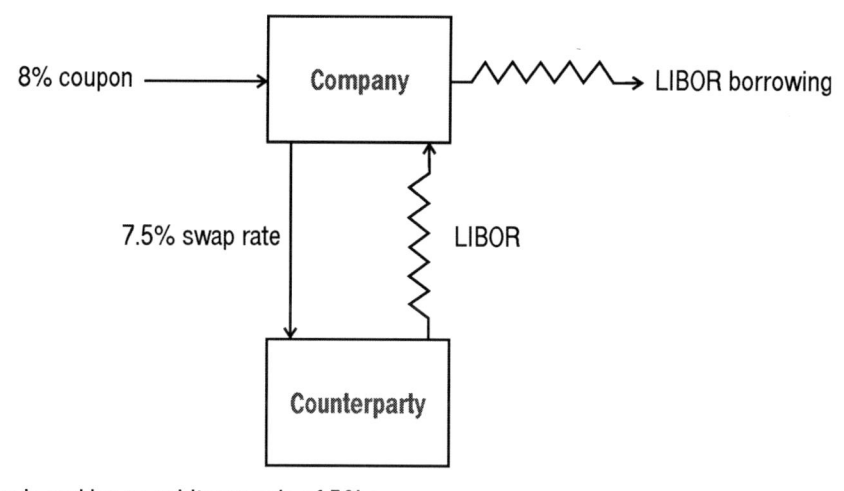

```
8% coupon ──→ [Company] ~~~→ LIBOR borrowing
                 ↑ ↓
      7.5% swap rate   LIBOR
                 ↓ ↑
              [Counterparty]
```

The company is making an arbitrage gain of 50bp.

10 CROSS-CURRENCY ASSET SWAPS

The basic asset swap has all its cash flows in one currency. It is possible to combine an asset swap with a cross-currency basis swap to gain an exposure to a second currency.

1. Company enters into a £ asset swap.

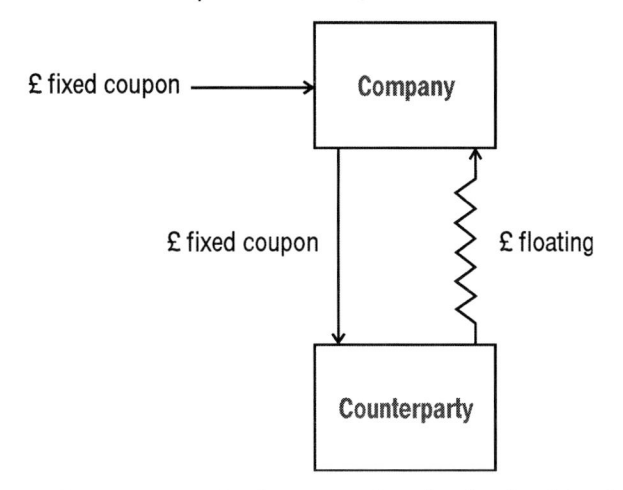

```
£ fixed coupon ─────► Company
                         │  ▲
                         │  │
                  £ fixed coupon   £ floating
                         ▼  │
                      Counterparty
```

2. Company also enters into a currency basis swap exchanging floating £ for floating $.

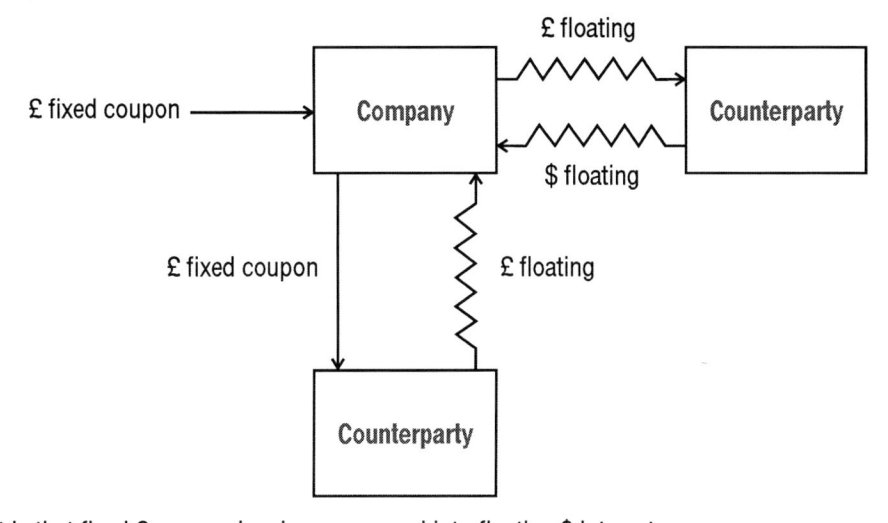

```
                              £ floating
                         ┌──────────────►
£ fixed coupon ─────► Company            Counterparty
                         │  ▲  ◄──────────
                         │  │   $ floating
                  £ fixed coupon   £ floating
                         ▼  │
                      Counterparty
```

Net result is that fixed £ coupon has been swapped into floating $ interest.

Chapter Roundup

- Spot rates, forward rates and swap rates
    - Spot rate is a rate from now to a given future date
    - Forward rate is a rate agreed today covering a future period of time
    - Swap rate is a fixed rate on a swap agreed for a specific term

    You need to be able to calculate and use these measures

- Swap value (all swaps)
    - At inception = 0 (swap is fair to both counterparties)
    - Later maybe < > 0 (One counterparty has gained, the other has lost)

- Interest rate swap value

Value FRN asset	X
Value fixed bond liability	(X)
Interest rate swap value	X

- Long-term currency swap

Value of currency A bond asset	X	} Both valued in the
Value of currency B bond liability	(X)	} same currency
Currency swap value	X	

- Equity swap

Capital gain on index	X
Dividend income earned for period	X
Interest due for period	(X)
Equity swap value	X

13: SWAPS

TEST YOUR KNOWLEDGE

Check your knowledge of the Chapter here, without referring back to the text.

1. You are given the following spot rates

1 year	5.0%
2 year	5.2%
3 year	5.3%

   (a) Calculate all the possible forward rates
   (b) Determine the one year, two year and three year swap rates for an annual swap

2. The current discount factors for euros are

1 year	0.963855
2 years	0.925446
3 years	0.885416
4 years	0.845336
5 years	0.805144

   A 5 year 4.5% AA bond paying annual interest is available at a price of €99.82. The quote for a credit default swap on this bond for 5 years is 36-38 bp per annum.

   (a) Determine the 5 year swap rate
   (b) Determine the spread over LIBOR from an asset swap using this bond.
   (c) Compare this to the position of selling credit protection on the bond and buying a AAA FRN paying LIBOR –20bp

3. Following on from the information in question 2, you are now given the following dollar discount rates

1 year	0.954198
2 years	0.908413
3 years	0.863344
4 years	0.819264
5 years	0.776106

   The current exchange rate is $1.2953:€1

   (a) Assuming a German corporation wishes to enter into a 5 year currency swap receiving Euros at 4.25% fixed per annum, calculate the dollar rate payable and the annual cash payable on a principle sum of €100m.

   (b) Two years later the exchange rate has moved to $1.3237:€1 and discount rates are

	Euro	Dollar
1 year	0.961538	0.956938
2 years	0.920127	0.913543
3 years	0.876297	0.870137

   Determine the mark-to-market profit or loss to the German corporation

13: SWAPS

4. We are three months before delivery of the September FTSE 100 futures contract and are provided with the following information

   3 month (91 days) LIBOR = 4.75%
   6 month (182 days) LIBOR = 4.86%
   Current 100 index level = 6,200
   FTSE dividend yield = 3.2%

   (a) Calculate the fair value of 3 month and 6 month FTSE 100 futures contract

   (b) Calculate the necessary payment at the end of six months on a notional principal of £40m if the index has fallen to 6,100

TEST YOUR KNOWLEDGE: ANSWERS

1. *Forward rates*

    - $(1 + r_1)(1 + {}_1f_2) = (1 + r_2)^2$

      $1.05 \times (1 + {}_1f_2) = 1.052^2$

      $(1 + {}_1f_2) = \dfrac{1.052^2}{1.05} = 1.0540$

      ${}_1f_2 = 0.054$ or 5.4%

    - $(1 + r_2)^2(1 + {}_2f_3) = (1 + r_3)^3$

      $1.05^2 \times (1 + {}_2f_3) = 1.052^3 = 1.1676$

      $(1 + {}_2f_3) = \dfrac{1.052^3}{1.052^2} = 1.0550$

      ${}_2f_3 = 0.055$ or 5.5%

    - $(1 + r_1)(1 + {}_1f_3)^2 = (1 + r_3)^3$

      $1.05 \times (1 + {}_1f_3)^2 = 1.053^3$

      $(1 + {}_1f_3)^2 = \dfrac{1.053^3}{1.05} = 1.1120$

      $(1 + {}_1f_3) = \sqrt{1.1120} = 1.0545$

      ${}_1f_3 = 0.0545$ or 5.45%

    Swap rates

    - 1 year swap rate

      $100 = \dfrac{C + 100}{1.05}$

      $C = 5.00\%$

    - 2 year swap rate

      $100 = \dfrac{C}{1.05} + \dfrac{C}{1.052^2} + \dfrac{100}{1.052^2}$

      $100 = C\left(\dfrac{1}{1.05} + \dfrac{1}{1.052^2}\right) + 90.358$

      $9.642 = 1.8560C$

      $C = 5.195\%$

13: SWAPS

- 3 year swap rate

$$100 = \frac{C}{1.05} + \frac{C}{1.052^2} + \frac{C}{1.053^3} + \frac{100}{1.053^3}$$

$$100 = C\left(\frac{1}{1.05} + \frac{1}{1.052^2} + \frac{1}{1.053^3}\right) + 85.648$$

14.352 = 2.7124C

C = 5.291%

- Summary

3 year swap rates

1   5.000%
2   5.195%
3   5.291%

2. *5 Year swap rate*

100 = C(0.963855 + 0.925446 + 0.885416 + 0.845336 + 0.805114) + 100 × 0.805114

100 = 4.425197C + 80.5114

19.489 = 4.425197C

C = 4.4033 ie 4.40%

Spread

There are two components to consider

- Coupon difference

Coupon received from bond	4.500
Coupon paid on swap	4.403
Gain from coupon (p.a)	0.097

- Cost difference

'Cost' of fixed coupon leg of swap	100.00	(par value)
Cost of bond	99.82	
Gain from lower cost (PV)	0.18	

This PV corresponds to an annuity of 0.041 (0.18 ÷ 4.425197)

- Spread achieved

Coupon difference	0.097
Cost difference annuity	0.041
	0.138

i.e. a gain of 0.14% or 14bp

Alternatively

- Valuing the bond using swap rates gives

Bond value = 4.5 × (0.963855 + 0.925446 + 0.885416 + 0.845336 + 0.805114) + 100 × 0.805144
= 100.43

Bond value using swap rates	100.43
Actual bond value	99.82
Gain from lower cost	0.61

This corresponds to the PV of an annuity of 0.138 (0.61 ÷ 4.425197), i.e. a gain of 0.14% or 14bp.

FRN alternative

	bp
Premium to LIBOR	
FRN receipt	(20)
Premium from credit protection	36
	16bp

This is better than the asset swap.

3. *Fair Value of Dollar Rate*

At inception we must have

PV of $ payments = PV of € receipts

Based on the exchange rate the principal sum must be

- Euro = €100.00m
- Dollar = $129.53m (100 × 1.2953)

Now

PV € receipts = 4.25 × (0.963855 + 0.925446 + 0.885416 + 0.845336 + 0.805144) + 100 × 0.805144
= €99.3215

To balance this we need the dollar 'bond' value to be $99.3215, hence for the dollar rate

99.3215 = C × (0.954198 + 0.908413 + 0.863344 + 0.819264 + 0.776106) + 100 × 0.776106
21.7109 = 4.321325 C
C = 5.024%

So the swap is €100.00m @ 4.25% against $129.53m @ 5.024%

2 years later

€ 'bond' value = 4.25 × (0.961538 + 0.920127 + 0.876297) + 100 × 0.876297 = €99.3510
$ 'bond' value = 5.024 × (0.956938 + 0.913543 + 0.870137) + 100 × 0.870137 = $100.7826

	€m
Euro value of € bond asset $\left(100m \times \dfrac{99.3510}{100}\right)$	99.3510
Euro value of $ bond liability $\left(129.53m \times \dfrac{100.7826}{100} \div 1.3237\right)$	(98.6203)
	€0.7307m

4. *Futures prices*

	3 month		6 month
Cash price	6200.0		6200.0
Cost of carry			
– Interest $\left(6{,}200 \times 4.75\% \times \dfrac{91}{365}\right)$	73.5	$\left(6{,}200 \times 4.86\% \times \dfrac{182}{365}\right)$	146.8
– Dividends $\left(6{,}200 \times 3.2\% \times \dfrac{91}{365}\right)$	(49.5)	$\left(6{,}200 \times 3.2\% \times \dfrac{182}{365}\right)$	(98.9)
Fair futures value	6,223.9		6,247.9
Quote (nearest 0.5)	6,223.0		6,248.0

13: SWAPS

Gain/loss

	£
Capital loss on index £40m × $\frac{6,100}{6,200}$ − £40m	(645,161)
Dividend income £40m × 3.2% × $\frac{6}{12}$	640,000
Floating rate payment £40m × 4.86% × $\frac{182}{365}$	(969,337)
Loss	(£974,498)

14 Other OTC Derivative Products

INTRODUCTION

We have examined in previous sections the standardised exchange traded products and the main OTC product, swaps. This section provides an overview of other available OTC products, including interest rate products, credit derivatives, structured products and exotic options.

CHAPTER CONTENTS

	Page
1 The Forward Rate Agreement	444
2 Caps, Floors and Collars	450
3 Credit Derivatives	454
4 Other Structured Finance Products	457
5 Exotic Options	463
Chapter Roundup	470
Test Your Knowledge	471

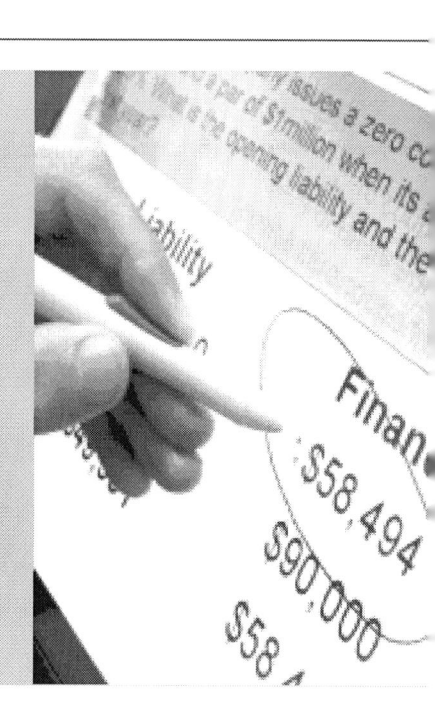

14: OTHER OTC DERIVATIVE PRODUCTS

CHAPTER LEARNING OBJECTIVES

The syllabus areas covered by this section are

Over-the-Counter-Derivatives

- Forwards
- FRAs
- Exotic Derivatives
    - Special Profiles
    - Path Dependent Derivatives
    - Multi- Asset Derivatives
    - Applications of Exotics
- Credit Derivatives
    - Nature of Credit Derivatives
    - Total Return Swaps
    - Credit Default Swaps
    - Spread Options
    - Applications of Credit Derivatives

Derivatives Risk Management

Individual derivatives

– Risks of Exotics

1 THE FORWARD RATE AGREEMENT

Exam tip | FRAs are the most important products in this section and are frequently examined, other areas tend to be optional discussions

1.1 Definition

A forward rate agreement is a contract between two parties who fix an agreed interest rate for a specified future period on an agreed notional amount.

An FRA fixes an interest rate for a period of time which commences in the future. It can be looked upon as an OTC short-term interest rate future, although the mechanics of settlement are different.

14: OTHER OTC DERIVATIVE PRODUCTS

FRAs relate solely to interest rates and do not involve the lending or borrowing of cash. Thus, like a short-term interest rate future, there is no exchange of the principal. They are used in much the same way as futures to protect borrowers or depositors from interest rate fluctuations. Unlike futures, however, there are no margin requirements or brokerage costs involved (if transacted directly with a bank).

1.2 Terminology

Term	Meaning
Agreement/deal/transaction date	The date on which the FRA is agreed.
Contract rate	The rate agreed at the outset upon which settlement will be based, e.g. 3-month LIBOR, 6-month LIBOR.
Settlement value date	The day when settlement between the parties takes place. On the settlement date, the contract rate is compared to the underlying reference rate, e.g. 3-month LIBOR. This is the start of the contract period.
Contract period	The interest rate period covered, i.e. the term of the actual borrowings.
Settlement amount	The amount paid between the two parties in settlement of the FRA.
Maturity date	The end of the contract period.

The gross settlement amount on the settlement date would be calculated as follows.

Formula to learn

$$\text{Gross settlement amount} = \text{Principal} \times (\text{Actual rate} - \text{Contract rate}) \times \frac{\text{Days}}{365}$$

* The denominator used depends upon the money market convention in the currency used, e.g. £ = 365, $/€ = 360.

Since the settlement amount is made at the start of the contract period, it is discounted at the actual market rate of interest. Thus, the actual settlement amount becomes

Formula to learn

$$\text{Actual settlement amount} = \frac{\text{Principal} \times (\text{Actual rate} - \text{Contract rate}) \times \frac{\text{Days}}{365}}{1 + \text{Actual rate} \times \frac{\text{Days}}{365}}$$

Example

Actual rate = 5.25%
Contract rate = 6.00%
Days in contract period = 90
Principal amount = £5m

$$\text{Actual Settlement amount} = \frac{£5m \times (0.06 - 0.0525) \times \frac{90}{365}}{1 + 5.25 \times \frac{90}{365}} = £9,128.41$$

14: OTHER OTC DERIVATIVE PRODUCTS

FRAs are quoted as an explicit interest rate rather than as 100 – rate of interest (which is the convention within short-term interest rate futures). In FRA market terminology, users

BUY an FRA to protect against a rise in rates

SELL an FRA to protect against a fall in rates

An FRA buyer is effectively agreeing to pay fixed over the contract period and receive floating.

An FRA seller is effectively agreeing to pay floating over the contract period and receive fixed.

1.3 Contract periods

As FRAs are OTC products, the contract periods are negotiable. However, the normal maximum maturity is two years.

FRA contracts have developed their own shorthand to describe their contract periods. These are expressed with reference to their settlement or value date and maturity date.

Example

Assume today is 30 June.

An FRA is agreed with a contract period of 31 October (settlement date) to 30 April (maturity date).

This would be described as '4s against/to 10s' or 4 vs 10.

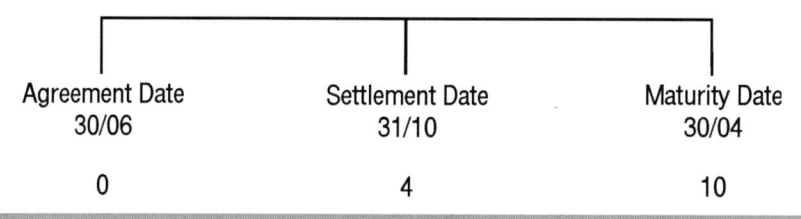

```
        Agreement Date       Settlement Date       Maturity Date
           30/06                31/10                 30/04

             0                    4                    10
```

The most usual contract periods are 1, 3, 6 and 12 months, although non-standard periods are available, albeit at less attractive prices.

1.4 Pricing an FRA

FRAs are priced in a similar way to pricing interest rate futures, i.e. calculating a forward rate. Theoretically, there is the same bid/offer spread but, as with interest rate futures, the market will trade around a central value, effectively priced off LIBOR.

With forward rates, if

- r_1 = time apportioned rate to the start of the contract period
- r_2 = time apportioned rate to the end of the contract period

Then we can calculate the forward rate using

$$(1+r_1)(1+{_1f_2}) = (1+r_2)$$

Which could be expressed as

$$(1+{_1f_2}) = \frac{(1+r_2)}{(1+r_1)}$$

As an alternative to being given spot rates, we may be given discount factors for the relevant period. If

- DF_1 = discount factor for the period to the start of the contract period
- DF_2 = discount factor for the period to the end of the contract period

Then an alternative calculation is

$$(1+{}_1f_2) = \frac{DF_1}{DF_2}$$

Example

   6 month LIBOR = 4.6%

   9 month LIBOR = 4.8%

a) Calculate the 6v9 FRA rate based on the interest rates

b) Calculate the discount factors from these rates and the FRA rate from these discount factors

Soultion

a) $r_1 = 4.6\% \times \dfrac{6}{12} = 2.3\%$

   $r_2 = 4.8\% \times \dfrac{9}{12} = 3.6\%$

   $(1+{}_1f_2) = \dfrac{1.036}{1.023} = 1.0127$

   ${}_1f_2 = 0.0127$ or 1.27% for 3 months

   FRA rate $= 1.27 \times 4 = 5.08\%$

b) $DF_1 = \dfrac{1}{1.023} = 0.977517$

   $DF_2 = \dfrac{1}{1.036} = 0.9652251$

   $(1+{}_1f_2) = \dfrac{DF_1}{DF_2} = \dfrac{0.977517}{0.965251} = 1.0127$

   ${}_1f_2 = 0.0127$ or 1.27% for 3 months

   FRA rate $= 1.27 \times 4 = 5.08\%$ as before

1.5 Trading system

The FRA market is global, though London is generally regarded as its centre.

It is a telephone market, and indicative prices are shown on information services such as Reuters, Telerate and Bloomberg.

A quote for 3 vs 6 might look like this

   5.22 – 5.27

Thus, you could buy the FRA at 5.27 or sell it at 5.22. The bid/offer spreads are typically 4-5 basis points, as opposed to the futures market where the spread is 1 tick/basis point.

Example

A corporate treasurer will need to borrow £5m for a period of six months in three months' time. He fears that between now and then, rates may rise.

Action

Buy a 3 vs 9 FRA at 5.27%.

Three months later, rates have risen so that 6-month LIBOR stands at 6%.

Calculate the settlement amount

$$\frac{(0.06 - 0.0527) \times {}^{182}\!/\!_{365} \times £5m}{1 + (0.06 \times {}^{182}\!/\!_{365})} = £17{,}671$$

This amount is the net present value of the increased cost of borrowing £5m for 182 days at an increase of 0.73%.

$$£5m \times 0.73\% \times \frac{182}{365} = £18{,}200$$

Thus, a locked-in rate of 5.27% is achieved.

1.5.1 Interest rate sensitivity of a FRA

Earlier, we discussed the interest rate sensitivity of bonds by calculating how a change in yield affected the present value of the bond flows. It was also noted that the relationship between price and yield was not linear. This non-linearity was called convexity.

If a hedger is using a FRA, then he will have to be given to the interest rate sensitivity and convexity of the FRA.

How does the value of a FRA change with a change in interest rate?

To answer this, we need to consider the cash flows that would represent a FRA. We will consider the situation from the FRA's buyer's perspective. These can be presented as follows.

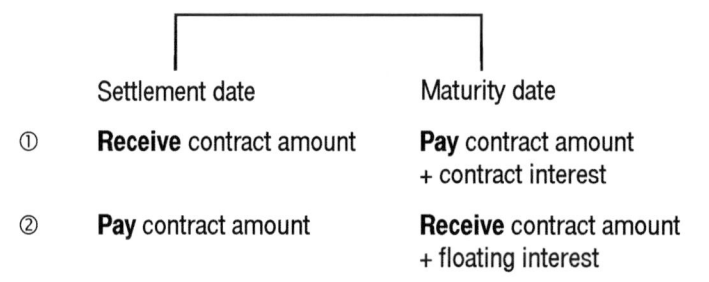

	Settlement date	Maturity date
①	**Receive** contract amount	**Pay** contract amount + contract interest
②	**Pay** contract amount	**Receive** contract amount + floating interest

Please note these cash flows do not actually occur with a FRA, but the net of the cash flows discounted back to the settlement date are the same as the FRA payoff. It can be seen that the value of the FRA at the settlement date is the difference between the contract rate and the actual rate over the contract period, discounted at the actual rate to the start of the borrowing (or contract) period.

How will a change in the actual rate affect the value of the FRA at the settlement date?

Consider a FRA with a notional principal of £100,000, a contract period of one year and a contract rate of 8%. If we calculate the PV of the difference between the contract rate and a range at the start of the contract period, we get the following.

14: OTHER OTC DERIVATIVE PRODUCTS

Settlement Rate	PV at Maturity	Discount Rate[#]	PV at Settlement Date
6%	(2,000)	$\frac{1}{1.06}$	(1,887)
7%	(1,000)	$\frac{1}{1.07}$	(934)
8%	0	$\frac{1}{1.08}$	0
9%	1,000*	$\frac{1}{1.09}$	917
10%	2,000**	$\frac{1}{1.10}$	1,818

* (9% – 8%) × £100,000 payable to the buyer of the FRA, therefore shown as a positive value.
** (10% – 8%) × £100,000 payable to the buyer of the FRA, therefore shown as a positive value.
\# Contract period is one year.

This shows that the change in value of the FRA, the PV at settlement date, changes as the actual settlement rate changes, but in a **non-linear way**. If the settlement date is still in the future, then the PV of the settlement value, discounted back to the correct date will still exhibit the same convexity.

This value can be shown graphically.

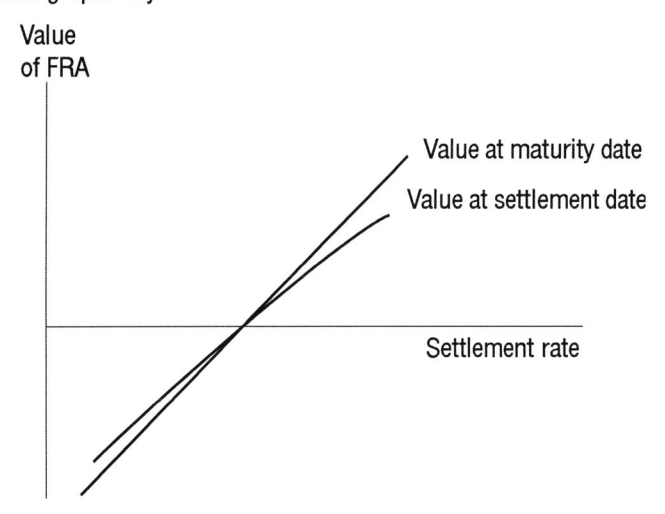

Thus, the relationship between the value of a FRA and interest rates exhibits convexity. FRAs become less sensitive as rates fall, and more sensitive as rates rise.

Having just highlighted the convexity of a FRA, it is appropriate to compose the interest rate sensitivity of a FRA with the interest rate sensitivity of an alternative hedging instrument: a short-term interest rate (STIR) future.

What effect does a change of interest rates have on the value of a STIR future? Is it linear or convex?

It is linear! This is because the tick value is fixed and does not change with changing interest rates. For the short sterling future, every 1% change (100bp) changes the value by £1,250 (£12.50 × 100), thus giving a linear relationship between value and interest rates. STIRs do not exhibit convexity.

1.6 Futures vs FRAs

	Futures	FRAs
Market	Exchange	OTC
Maturities	Fixed	Negotiable
Contract Size	Fixed	Negotiable
Reference Rate	LIBOR	LIBOR
Settlement	IR Diff	Net Present Value (IR Diff)
Bid/Ask Spread	1 to 2 ticks	4 to 5 ticks

1.7 Reversals

It is possible to cancel FRAs by either approaching the counterparty to the transaction and asking for a cancellation price, or undertaking equal and opposite trades as shown below.

> XYZ Co buys a 3 vs 6 FRA at 5.25%.
> One month later, it sells a 2 vs 5 FRA at 5.5%.

A profit of 25 basis points has been locked in.

2 CAPS, FLOORS AND COLLARS

There are three basic structures – the cap, floor and collar. In common with other OTC structures, they offer considerably more flexibility than their exchange-traded cousins, especially options on short-term interest rate futures.

2.1 The cap

The cap gives the buyer the right, but not the obligation, to fix the cost of borrowing.

Caps are most commonly used by variable rate borrowers to fix the maximum they will pay.

Example

A corporate treasurer buys a 6% cap on a notional amount of £10m.

At the rollover date, the cap strike rate is compared with an agreed benchmark, usually 3-month LIBOR. If the strike is below the benchmark, the option is exercised for that particular period and the cash difference is delivered.

If the benchmark were 7% and the period three months, the settlement amount would be

$$1\% \times £10m \times \frac{3}{12} = £25,000$$

If, however, the strike is above the market rate, the option is simply not used.

The table below shows the structure of a two-year cap, with quarterly rollovers.

Month	Period
March	3 months
June	6 months
September	9 months
December	12 months
March	15 months
June	18 months
September	21 months
December	24 months

Caps (and floors) are available in all the major currencies. The normal dealing size is $5-$50m and maturities are usually between one and five years. The premiums are quoted in basis points.

Caps offer an OTC alternative to a strip of put options on short-term interest rate futures, or they could be viewed as a strip of call options on FRAs.

2.2 Cap valuation

The valuation of a cap is similar to the pricing of other options and can be undertaken using a slight modification of the Black Scholes model.

The more important difference relates to the anatomy of a cap, specifically in that it is in fact a packaged product composed of a number of separate options or caplets. The value of the cap is therefore the sum of the value of these caplets.

One further point is that the first caplet is normally set out-of-the-money, and since its expiry date is the same date as the cap start date, it will have zero value.

The most commonly used caplet valuation formula is

Formula to learn

$$\text{Caplet} = \frac{Te^{-rt}}{(1+fT)}\left[fN(d_1) - XN(d_2)\right]$$

And

Formula to learn

$$d_1 = \frac{\ln\left(\frac{f}{X}\right) + \left(r + 0.5\sigma^2\right)t}{\sigma\sqrt{t}}$$

$$d_2 = d_1 - \sigma\sqrt{t}$$

where

- X = the cap strike
- f = the forward rate for the period protected by the cap
- σ = the volatility of the forward interest rate
- T = the period protected by the caplet
- t = the period between the start date of the cap and the start of the period protected by the caplet
- $N(.)$ = the Normal distribution function
- r = the spot rate for the exposure period

The caplet value is expressed as a percentage of the principal amount.

Care must be taken when using these models, as the data could be given in one of two ways.

Thinking of a cap as a series of interest rate puts it must be remembered that puts on interest rate futures are quoted with a strike of 100 minus the interest rate. Therefore, to be consistent, the actual rate at expiry of each of the caplets must also be expressed as 100 minus the rate and, very importantly, the volatility must be the volatility of the future.

Alternatively, if actual rates are going to be used (rather than 100 minus the rate), then the appropriate formula for a call must be used with the volatility reflecting the interest rate volatility.

2.3 The floor

The OTC equivalent to a strip of call options on a short-term interest rate future. The floor enables the buyer (usually a depositor) to obtain protection against falling interest rates. As with the cap, it is a cash-settled European style option in which, usually, quarterly settlements are made against a benchmark index. Settlement is usually made against the offer rate, e.g. LIBOR, although LIBID is the rate more likely to be achieved.

Liquidity and availability are somewhat more restricted than in the cap market.

2.4 The collar

The collar is the combination of both a cap and a floor in the same product at different strikes, and is comparable to options 'cylinders' and 'fences'.

Two main varieties are available.

2.4.1 Borrower's collar

A cap is purchased to protect against rises. This purchase price is offset in whole or in part by the sale of a floor. The sale of the floor limits the borrower's ability to take advantage of falls in interest rates.

Interest rate collar

Buy 10% cap.

Sell 5% floor.

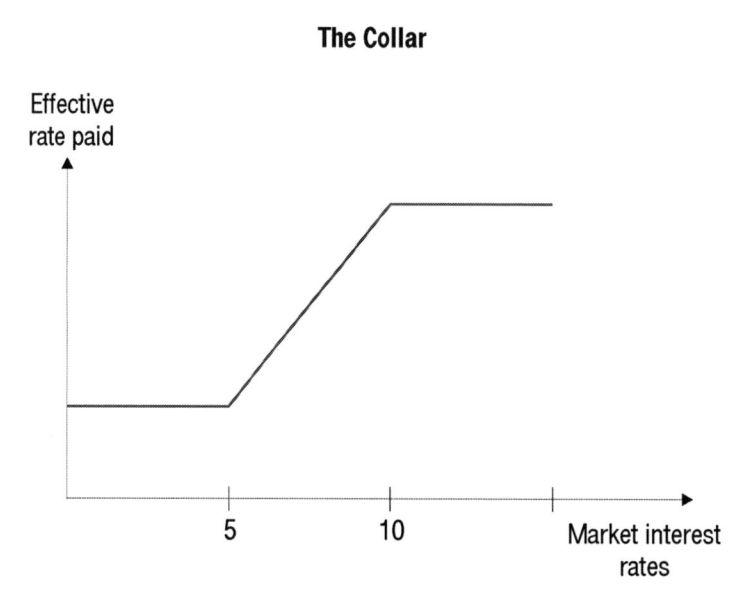

The Collar

As can be seen, a synthetic bull spread is created.

2.4.2 Investor's collar

This is constructed in a reverse style, e.g. the cap is sold and the floor is purchased. The investor knows he will earn at least a minimum return, but sacrifices some benefit of higher rates.

2.5 Interest rate guarantees

These are simply options on FRAs or one-period caps/floors.

They work in exactly the same way as caps and floors, but simply relate to one period.

2.6 Captions and floptions

These are options on either caps (captions) or floors (floptions or floortions).

Although these sound complicated, they do have important applications for hedgers who face a contingent interest rate risk, but are uncertain as to whether or not an interest rate exposure may occur.

The pricing of such options on options (sometimes called compound options) is more complex. A model was devised by Geske to price these products and is a variation on the Black Scholes model. In the Geske model, the value of the underlying asset is substituted by the strike of the underlying cap/floor.

2.7 Swaptions

Swaptions are options, normally on coupon swaps. They come in two varieties.

2.7.1 Receiver swaptions

The buyer has the right, but not the obligation, to receive fixed and pay floating.

2.7.2 Payer swaptions

The buyer has the right, but not the obligation, to pay fixed and receive floating.

Swaptions are usually European style and are comparable to interest rate caps. There are, of course, some differences.

The swaption allows the holder the right to pay (or receive) a specific fixed rate and receive (or pay) a floating rate for an agreed term. The swaption can only be exercised into the underlying interest rate swap **once**. A cap agreement gives the right to fix a series of individual interest payments. Thus, the cap tends to be more expensive because the holder has multiple exercise dates, can benefit if rates fall during the life of the agreement, and can limit his loss potential if interest rates have risen at any point.

2.8 Rate spread options

These products offer a basis play between two benchmark rates. For example, an investor may think the spread between US dollar LIBOR and Euribor is expected to widen. To receive the anticipated increase, the investor would buy the call spread and upon exercise, receive the increased differential multiplied by the notional amount and the number of days.

2.9 Better performance bond options

Better performance options pay the greater of two assets' returns over the period to exercise, if both are positive. These may have important applications for money managers who are uncertain as to which of two assets to invest in.

3 CREDIT DERIVATIVES

Credit derivatives allow users to manage their exposure to credit risk. They are bilateral contracts whereby one party agrees to make a payment to the other following a credit event by one or more third parties. The event refers to some observable change in the credit quality of the third party (the Reference Credit) such as default, credit-rating downgrade or a change in credit spread.

3.1 Credit default swap

A credit default swap enables the transfer of default risk. A bank may agree to receive a premium, usually expressed as a number of basis points per annum on the nominal of the contract, in exchange for agreeing to pay an amount if there is a credit event by a third party.

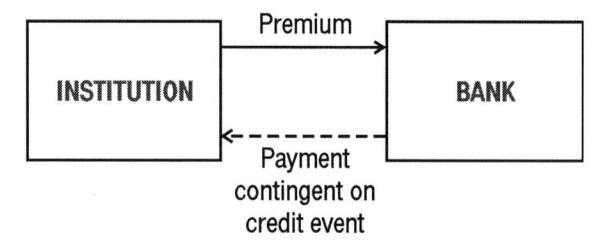

```
                    Premium
                    ───────►
   ┌───────────┐              ┌──────┐
   │INSTITUTION│              │ BANK │
   └───────────┘              └──────┘
                    ◄ ─ ─ ─ ─
                    Payment
                    contingent on
                    credit event
```

In a credit default swap, the protection buyer is basically buying insurance, for a fee, against a possible credit event on a reference asset they (usually) own.

The reference asset could be a bond, line of credit or loan, or possibly a swap. The premium fee is usually expressed as a number of annual basis points but paid quarterly. If during the term of the agreement, the credit event has not occurred, then the seller of the protection will keep the premium and make no payments. This will represent profit to them.

If the credit event takes place, then the protection buyer will either have the right to sell the underlying asset to the counterparty or, alternatively, the swap might be cash settled. If the reference asset is a bond, then selling it at a pre-determined price (possibly its value before the credit event or par value) is a possibility – assuming the bond is tradable.

If the reference asset is a line of credit or loan, then physical delivery is not an option and cash settlement would be the result. The cash would represent the difference in value between the asset before the credit event (or par) and its value after it.

It was stated above that the swap will be priced as a number of basis points. The institution making the market in these swaps will quote them on a bid/offer basis. An example would look as follows.

> 1 year: 0.60% p.a. – 0.65% p.a.
> on $5m of XYZ 8% 2010

The market maker will sell protection at the higher rate, typically receiving a quarter of the quoted rate each quarter. A money market convention will apply – taking into account the actual number of days in the quarter. If default occurs, then these payments cease and the market maker will either buy the underlying asset or will pay a cash sum in settlement.

Buyers of swaps are looking to reduce their exposure to a major customer or reducing their capital requirements. They might also be using the swaps to lend synthetically to a good quality credit by investing in a risky asset and buying a credit default swap to reduce the risk.

3.1.1 Pricing a credit default swap

There is no universally accepted pricing model for this type of derivative. However, as with other derivative instruments, a no-arbitrage approach is a suitable starting point. This approach can be shown below. The bank buys a risky bond that is yielding over LIBOR, funding it by borrowing at LIBOR. The no-arbitrage price for the credit default swap would be the excess yield over LIBOR.

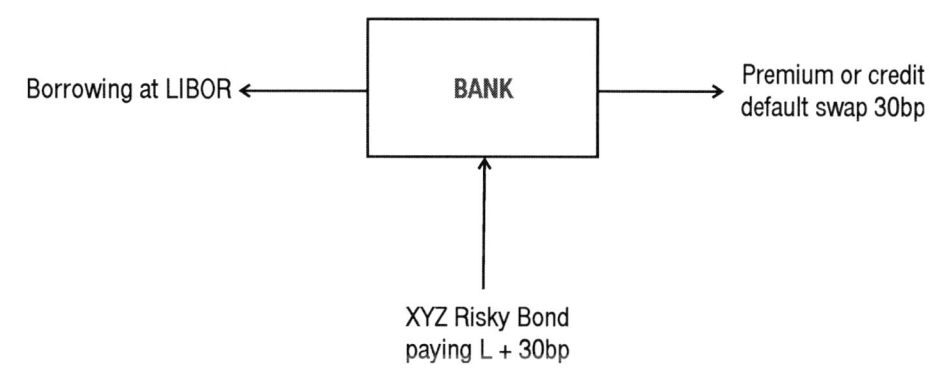

```
Borrowing at LIBOR  ←  [ BANK ]  →  Premium or credit
                                     default swap 30bp
                          ↑
                    XYZ Risky Bond
                    paying L + 30bp
```

3.1.2 Credit-linked note

A credit-linked note (CLN) is a debt instrument that has a credit derivative embedded in it. The most common form is when the derivative is a credit default swap. This gives the holder of the note an exposure to the credit of the issuer, another reference entity or indeed to a portfolio of companies. In exchange for taking on this risk, the investor in the rate enjoys an enhanced return.

A typical structure would be that an issuer of a CLN issues an asset-backed security, for example, backed by a AAA rated bond, and sells a credit default swap on a separate security, called the reference security.

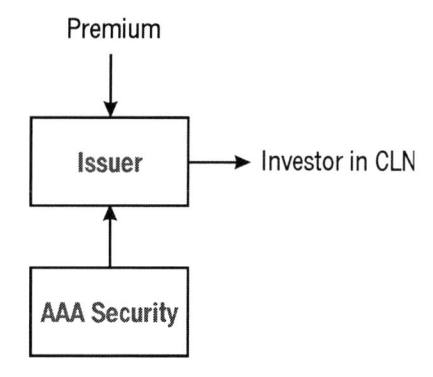

```
            Premium
              ↓
          [ Issuer ]  →  Investor in CLN
              ↑
        [ AAA Security ]
```

Assume in the above structure that the AAA security pay a coupon of LIBOR + 10bp, and that the premium received from selling the credit default swap is 15bp per annum. The investor in the CLN can receive LIBOR + 25bp. The premium therefore provides an enhanced return to the investors in the CLN.

But what of the downside? If the reference security defaults, then the issuer who sold the swap would typically buy the reference security at par and receive the recovery price. This 'loss' is then passed on to the investors in the CLN, who rather than receive the par value of their investment back, receive the recovery value of the reference security.

3.2 Total return swap

A total return swap is a swap whereby one party agrees to pay the other the total return (interest plus price appreciation, less price depreciation) of an asset, e.g. a bond in exchange for receiving LIBOR plus a spread. The buyer of the swap will receive the money market rate and pay out the total return on the asset. The buyer is locking in a return on a reference asset, irrespective of subsequent credit events.

14: OTHER OTC DERIVATIVE PRODUCTS

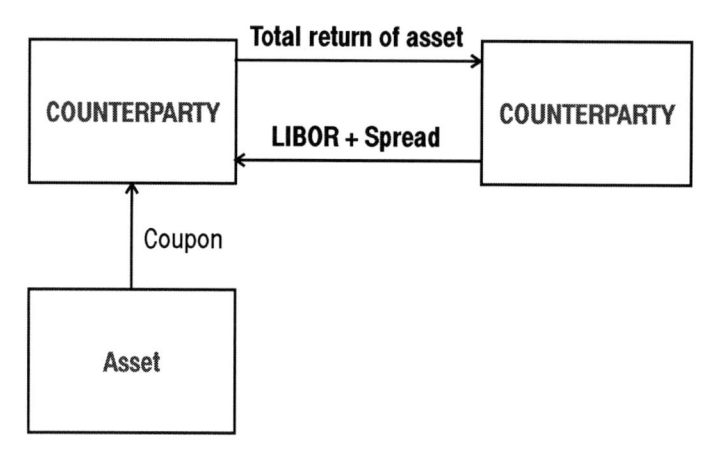

```
                    Total return of asset
    ┌──────────────┐ ──────────────────> ┌──────────────┐
    │ COUNTERPARTY │                     │ COUNTERPARTY │
    │              │ <────────────────── │              │
    └──────────────┘    LIBOR + Spread   └──────────────┘
           ▲
           │ Coupon
           │
    ┌──────────────┐
    │              │
    │    Asset     │
    │              │
    └──────────────┘
```

With this type of swap, there is no credit event and no contingent payment. There is an exchange of payment at the end of each period, unless default occurs, in which case the next payment is brought forward to the time of default and the contract is terminated.

The payer of the total returns has hedged the economic risk of the asset, whilst the receiver has the exposure of the asset without having the operational complications of buying it. It is possible to introduce variations on a plain vanilla structure by incorporating puts and calls to establish caps or floors on the returns of the underlying assets. The finance leg can similarly incorporate caps and floors to control financing costs. These types of swaps will always be cash settled and will be marked-to-market periodically.

What the counterparty on the left has done is to remove from its portfolio the credit risk of holding the bond. It should be noted that the receipts to this counterparty are LIBOR and spread. Clearly, LIBOR can still go up or down and so, this participant to the swap still forms a variable receipt. This could, of course, be turned into a fixed return via an interest rate swap or even the return on an equity index in an equity swap. By fixing the spread above LIBOR, the left counterparty has protected itself against events that could lead to a change in the spread, such as credit events.

If during the term of the swap the reference asset defaults, the buyer of the swap, who owns the asset, will receive from the swap seller an amount in cash equal to the difference between the last mark-to-market price and the market value after the default.

3.3 Credit spread swap

A credit spread swap allows firms to trade smaller shifts in a borrower's credit rating short of outright default. One party makes payments based on the yield to maturity of a specific issuer's debt and the other makes payments based on comparable sovereigns' bond yield plus a spread reflecting the difference in credit rating.

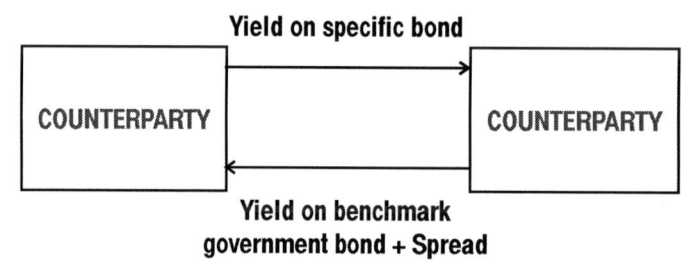

```
                     Yield on specific bond
    ┌──────────────┐ ──────────────────> ┌──────────────┐
    │ COUNTERPARTY │                     │ COUNTERPARTY │
    │              │ <────────────────── │              │
    └──────────────┘                     └──────────────┘
                      Yield on benchmark
                    government bond + Spread
```

If the above two flows are equal at inception of the swap, any change in credit rating of the specified bond relative to the benchmark will result in a payment being made from one party to the other.

This, like the total return swap, allows an investor to lock in a specific spread above a benchmark yield. Naturally, one of the prime causes of the spread is the difference in credit rating between the corporate bond and the government bond.

Variations on the above could see a swap between yields on a specific bond above a benchmark and the yield between two other bonds, or swap the spread on one security above a benchmark with a spread on another security above a benchmark.

3.4 Credit spread options

The most popular form of credit spread option is a put on an asset swap. Typically, a bank will pay an investor a premium for the right to deliver an asset swap package at expiry of the option, e.g. one year's time. The strike will be expressed as a yield, e.g. LIBOR + 40, rather than as a particular price. If the option is exercised, the bank will sell the bond and receive a price that will give the strike yield. Therefore, this type of option would be bought if the bank thought the spread would widen. If the yield on the bond was above the strike, e.g. LIBOR + 60, the bank would sell the bond for more than the bond was worth. Remember, a lower yield means a higher price.

3.4.1 Bank buys credit spread option

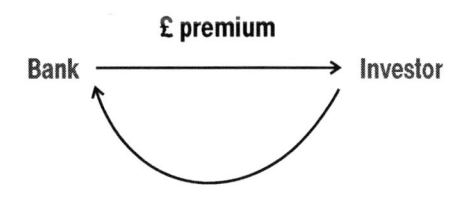

£ premium

Bank ────────────► Investor

Put option : Strike @ LIBOR + 40
Expiry in 1 year

3.4.2 Bank exercise options in one year as spread has widened to LIBOR + 60

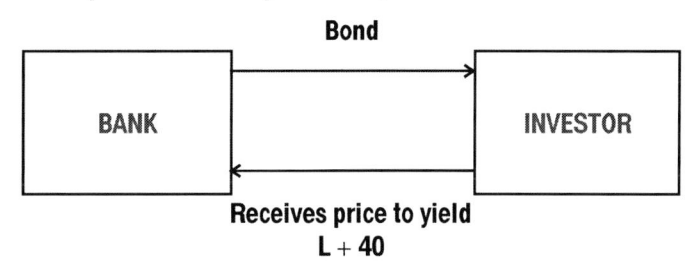

Bond

| BANK | → | INVESTOR |

Receives price to yield
L + 40

Note that as the spread is now L + 60, the value of the bond the bank sells will be less than the amount the bank receives.

In this example, the bank has gone long spread volatility, i.e. assume the spread will widen.

4 OTHER STRUCTURED FINANCE PRODUCTS

4.1 Equity-linked, high-income bonds

With an equity linked high income bond, a bank will sell a bond to investors and, to increase what it can pay out to these investors, will additionally sell a put option (not to the original investors) on an equity index. The receipt from the put option will enhance the coupon that can be paid on the original bond.

If the equity index increases, the put will not be exercised and the investors will have enjoyed the higher return. The risk is that the index will fall and that the holders of the put will exercise against the bank. The bank will suffer a loss, which will be recovered from the investors in the initial bond by them giving up some of their capital.

14: OTHER OTC DERIVATIVE PRODUCTS

To summarise, the investor in the high-income bond will experience above-average reward, but at the risk of capital loss.

It has already been stated that the sale of the put provides the bank with the means of increasing the coupon paid to the investors. It will be necessary to determine what increase in coupon is achievable – which would depend upon the value of the premium received from the sale of the put option.

Example

A bank sells £1m now of a 5-year equity-linked, high-income bond, and sells a 5-year put on the same value of the FTSE 100 index for a premium of £30,000.

What enhanced coupon can the bank pay over the next five years? The answer to this is the 5-year annuity that equates to £30,000. Assume the spot rates are

$1/r$	%
1	4.0
2	4.5
3	5.0
4	5.5
5	6.0

$$£30,000 = \frac{F}{1.04} + \frac{F}{1.045^2} + \frac{F}{1.05^3} + \frac{F}{1.055^4} + \frac{F}{1.06^5}$$

F = £6,984

This equates to an increased coupon (£6,984 ÷ £1,000,000) 70bp per annum.

4.2 Range notes

Range notes are instruments that pay out a fixed amount if an underlying asset (e.g. an equity index) is between a certain range at maturity. For example, a range note could pay out LIBOR + 50 if the FTSE 100 was between 4200 and 4400, and nothing if it is outside this range.

These products will normally be constructed using binary options. This can be shown if the payoff of the product is examined.

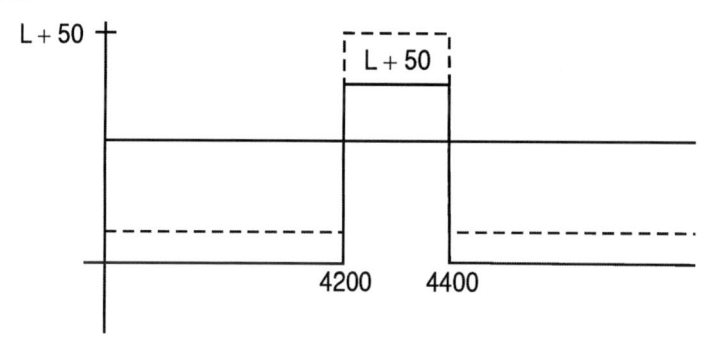

This structure could be created by buying a 4200 binary call option and selling a 4400 binary call. These would be priced so that the issuer could afford to pay out the stated amount within the stated range.

4.3 Callable/Putable bonds

A callable bond gives the **issuer** the right, but not the obligation, to redeem bonds early. This feature can be used to advantage if the cost of financing debt decreases over the lifespan of the bond. If cheaper finance becomes available, the issuer will call the existing bond and reissue at lower rates. Such bonds will be more expensive for the issuer, as the investor needs to be compensated for the option he is granting.

A putable bond gives the **investor** the right, but not the obligation, to put the bond back to the issuer if rates rise.

4.4 Swap-linked notes

As we know, when yields fall, bond prices rise. However, this relationship varies in its effect. Bonds with greater duration will rise more for a given fall in yields. Another feature of the bond markets is that long-term bond yields are typically less volatile than short-term yields. Investors looking to capture gains from yield changes have to make a compromise between long-duration bonds and the volatility of short-dated bonds.

The swap-linked note provides a solution to this problem. Short-term notes could be issued with a redemption value linked to five-year swap rates. An example of this is a two-year € note whose redemption value equals

$$100\% + [15 \times (6.39\% - r)]$$

where r is the five-year swap rate at maturity.

Thus, if swap rates fall by 1%, the redemption value will increase by 15%. This transforms the duration of the note which, although it has a life of only two years, has a duration of a longer dated bond.

4.5 Deleveraged floating rate notes

When the yield curve is positive, investors may wish to benefit from higher long-term yields, but with a short-dated instrument. A method of achieving this is the deleveraged floating rate note, in which coupons are linked to long-term yields.

For example, a note could be issued in which coupons are linked to the yield on ten-year Treasuries, less a margin related to the initial shape of the yield curve. If the slope becomes more positive, the investor will derive profits. However, if the slope becomes less positive then, as implied by the forward curve at the start date, losses will occur.

4.6 Index amortisation swaps

An important part of the US debt market is mortgage-backed securities. These securities, issued by a number of Federal Agencies (Fannie Maes, Ginnie Maes) are fixed income products with an important additional feature.

As we will know from personal experience, mortgage payments to banks and building societies incorporate two things – interest payments and principal payments. In the US, where mortgages have traditionally been fixed rate, a drop in interest rates means existing mortgages tend to be repaid early, a tendency known as prepayment.

The income stream to a holder of this debt is therefore unpredictable. While you could start by holding a 20-year mortgage-backed security, you may find that the debt is fully paid after ten years, should interest rates fall. This feature makes the bonds behave strangely. As rates fall, mortgage-backed securities will also fall, as debt is prepaid at par and the interest income stream is foregone.

To enable people to hedge this prepayment risk, the index amortisation swap, i.e. the speed at which the underlying notional amount is reduced, is related to an index. For example, the percentage amortised at each fixing date might be

$$25 \times (8 - i\%)$$

where

i = 3-month LIBOR

and

Maximum amortisation = 100%
Minimum amortisation = 0%

Thus, if LIBOR were 6%, the amortisation would be 50% [(8 − 6) × 25]. Amortisation would be complete if rates fell to 4% or lower.

4.7 Delayed reset floaters

Normal floating rate notes fix the floating rate at the start of each interest period and pay interest at the end. In a delayed reset floater, the floating rate index is determined only a couple of days before the coupon payment is made. Clearly, in a rising interest rate environment, this can be advantageous to the investor. The structure is available in the FRN market and is also available in the interest rate swap market, where it is described as either a delayed reset swap or a LIBOR in arrears swap.

In a rising interest rate environment, such a swap will have a higher fixed rate price, as it will be arrived at by using higher forward rates.

4.8 Reverse floating rate notes

If rates are expected to fall, an investor might choose to lock in using a coupon swap (pay floating, receive fixed), but an alternative is to invest in a reverse floating rate note – a note whose coupon will rise if LIBOR falls.

The mechanics of this structure are quite simple. For example, an issuer could issue a note that would pay a coupon equal to 17% − LIBOR. If LIBOR stands at 6%, the payout is 11% (17% − 6%). Should LIBOR drop to 4%, the coupon would become 13% (17% − 4%).

4.9 Capped floaters

Capped floaters are FRNs in which the payout to the investor is limited once LIBOR reaches a certain level. For the investor, such a product clearly limits the yield potential; to compensate for this lost opportunity, the investor should receive an enhanced return equivalent to the premium of the cap.

These products will be appropriate for investors who feel interest rates are unlikely to rise above the cap level.

An example might be a capped floater that pays LIBOR + 30bp, subject to a maximum coupon of 7%.

4.10 Collared floaters

A collared floater is simply an FRN that caps the maximum coupon and limits the minimum coupon.

For example, a collared FRN might be issued that pays LIBOR flat, capped at 7% with a floor at 4%. Subject to a positive shape of the yield curve, it is possible to sell an out-of-the-money cap to finance a cheap floor purchase and possibly lock in the floor level at above prevailing market rates.

4.11 Leveraged capped floaters

This is a capped floater in which the cap sold is for more than the principal of the note. The advantage is that if market rates remain at or below the cap level, the yield is significantly enhanced by the premium income. However, should market rates rise, returns will not be capped but rather will decline.

For example, an FRN might be structured to include a cap sold on 2× the principal. The normal floating rate will be LIBOR + 50bp. However, if the LIBOR rate exceeds 6%, the cap will activate. The cash flows could be visualised as follows.

4.11.1 Cash flows when LIBOR is less than 6%

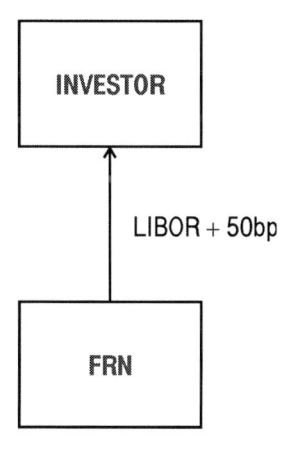

```
      INVESTOR
         ↑
    LIBOR + 50bp
         |
        FRN
```

4.11.2 Cash flows when LIBOR exceeds 6%

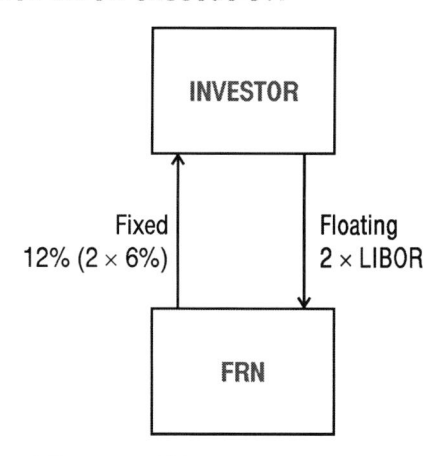

```
          INVESTOR
         ↑       ↓
    Fixed      Floating
   12% (2 × 6%)  2 × LIBOR
         |       |
            FRN
```

If LIBOR were at 8%, the cash flows would be

RECEIVE	Fixed	2 × 6%	**12%**
PAY	Floating	2 × 8%	**16%**

If LIBOR were at 10%, the cash flows would be

RECEIVE	Fixed	2 × 6%	**12%**
PAY	Floating	2 × 10%	**20%**

As can be seen, the gearing works rapidly against the investor. To avoid the danger of a negative payout when structured in a note, the FRN would normally incorporate a levered collar to prevent this happening.

4.12 Leveraged diff floater

Earlier, we saw how a diff swap could provide a single-currency return generated from the differential between two floating rate bases.

The leveraged diff floater embellishes this theme by providing a return linked to a multiple of the interest rate differential. These swaps can be incorporated in a floating rate note. To prevent negative returns from the debt, a leveraged diff floor would be used as protection.

Example

$$2 \times (€ \text{ LIBOR} - \$ \text{ LIBOR}) + 70\text{bp}$$

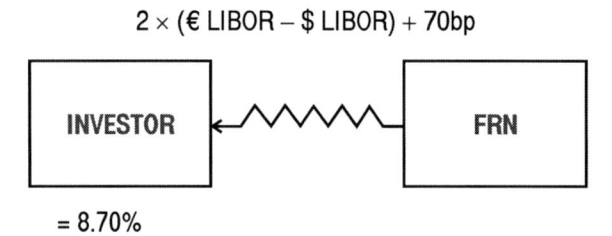

INVESTOR ←∿∿∿— FRN

Thus if   € LIBOR   = 8.70%
          US$ LIBOR = 4.00%

the payment would be

　　　Differential of 4.40% + 70bp = 5.10%

However, should € rates fall further than 70bp below $ rates, the return would be negative.

If € LIBOR   = 5%
    % LIBOR   = 7%
    2 × (5 − 7) + 70bp = Payment of −3.30%

To avoid this, a leveraged diff floor is bought. The floor will pay out if the spread falls below 35 basis points. The cash flow from the floor will net out against the negative cash flows that emerge if the euro rates exceed dollar rates by 70 basis points.

4.13 Reverse diff floater

A reverse diff floater is another hybrid debt instrument that increases coupon payments on the note if the differential between two bases (one fixed, the other floating) falls.

Example

A note pays a coupon of 11% − € LIBOR, payable in dollars.

　　　If € rates are 8%, the coupon is 3%.
　　　If € rates are 6%, the coupon becomes 5%.

Such an investment could be useful for a dollar investor with an expectation that € rates will fall fast.

5 EXOTIC OPTIONS

Also called 'second generation' options, exotic options are diverse in nature and can be grouped into three main headings: variations, path-dependent and multi-factor. Some answer a genuine need and are important risk management tools, others are innovative and have niche applications, whilst others seem to have been invented for no apparent purpose. The more common ones are described below using the general headings listed above.

5.1 Variations on standard terms

5.1.1 Semi-American or Bermudan options

Halfway between American and European style exercise (hence the name), a Bermudan allows the holder to exercise on specified dates during the option's life.

Useful if, for example, an investor has entered into a swap that they may wish to cancel on pre-set dates. Having a Bermudan style option on a swap might, therefore, be a good idea.

5.1.2 Digital or binary options

These pay a pre-determined fixed amount upon exercise, **not**, as is usual, the difference between the strike and the underlying. They are sometimes referred to as bet options or gap options. The payoff profile of a digital or binary call (excluding premium) will look as follows.

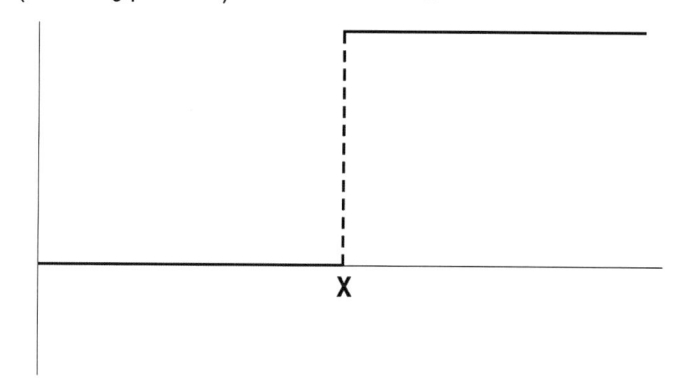

These can be 'all-or-nothing' or 'one-touch'. An all-or-nothing will pay the fixed amount only if the option is in-the-money at expiry. A one-touch will pay the fixed amount if the option has been in-the-money at **any** stage during its life. A one-touch may pay out either when the option becomes in-the-money or may delay the payout until the expiry date. A one-touch may be thought of as an American bet option.

To demonstrate the usefulness of a binary option, consider a UK firm committed to buying machinery from the US. The firm will be concerned about a strengthening of the dollar (or a weakening of sterling). This could be hedged in the normal way by buying a sterling put, i.e. a dollar call. Alternatively, the firm could buy a binary put in sterling that paid out a fixed amount if the dollar strengthened beyond a certain price. Although the payoff will be different to a standard option, one of the attractions is that the binary will be cheaper.

Hedging the sale of a binary option will necessitate considering the delta of the option. As the profit/loss profile of a binary option shows, the value of the option increases rapidly as the underlying asset rises to the strike price, but will then fall off drastically as the underlying continues to rise, as there are no further gains to be made from the option. For a call, this can be shown diagrammatically as follows.

14: OTHER OTC DERIVATIVE PRODUCTS

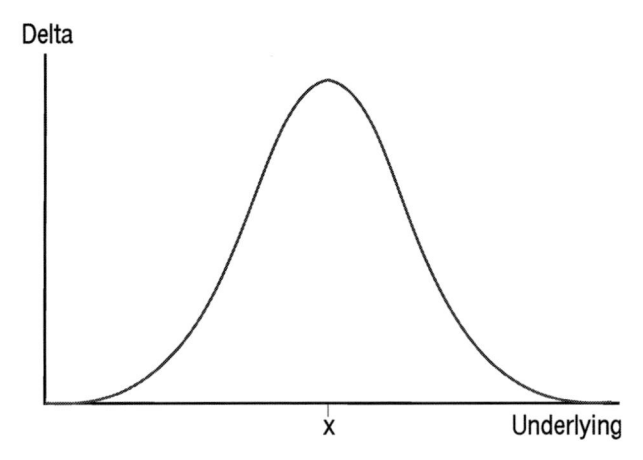

[Graph: Delta curve — bell-shaped curve peaking at strike X, plotted against Underlying]

From the above diagram, it is apparent that below the strike when the option is out-of-the-money, a binary will have a positive gamma, whilst above the strike when it is out-of-the-money, it will be gamma negative. This is shown below.

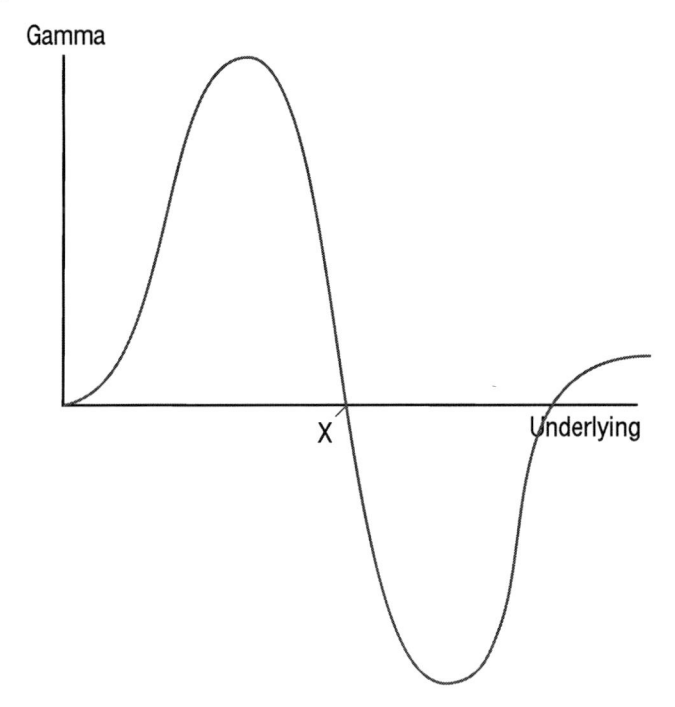

[Graph: Gamma curve — positive hump below strike X, negative trough above strike X, plotted against Underlying]

A possible way of hedging these particular dynamics would be to use two ordinary call options with strike prices either side of the binary strike. If the binary had been sold, the lower strike call would be bought and the higher strike call would be sold. This will be recognised as a bull call spread. The closer the strikes the better.

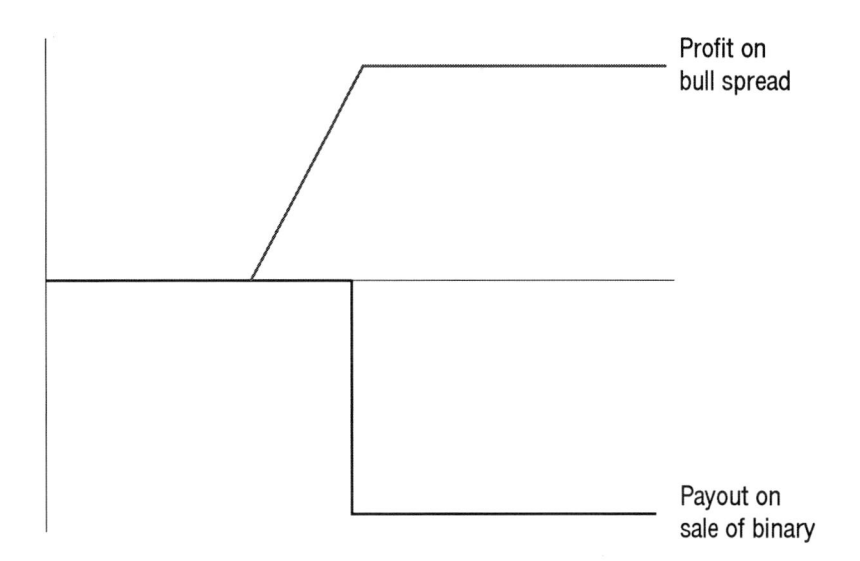

14: OTHER OTC DERIVATIVE PRODUCTS

[Diagram showing profit on bull spread combined with payout on sale of binary]

5.1.3 Pay later or contingent options

As its name suggests, the premium on a pay later or contingent option is only paid if the option is exercised. However, if it is in-the-money at expiry, it **must** be exercised even if it is in-the-money by less than the premium. Pay later options can be calls on puts.

These options, which have been available on foreign currencies, stock indices and commodities, allow the buyer to safeguard against large one-way price movements at zero initial cost.

The payoff profile of a pay-later call will look as follows.

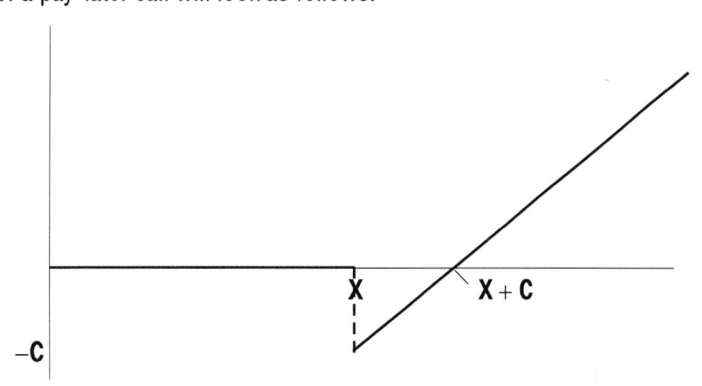

[Payoff diagram for a pay-later call showing exercise price X, X+C on horizontal axis, and –C level]

where

X = exercise price
C = call premium

Although there is an advantage to not paying the premium upfront, a major disadvantage is that these will be more expensive than a standard option, hence the attraction to protect against large movements.

Looking at the payoff diagram, it can be seen that being long a pay-later call is the same as being long an ordinary call and being short a digital call (the ratio need not be 1:1). Hedging such an option will, therefore, involve a combination of previously discussed hedging approaches.

5.1.4 Chooser option

With a chooser option, the holder can choose at a later date whether the option is a call or put. Similar to a straddle but cheaper, as only buying one option.

Consider a UK company that is having to pay dollars in 50 days' time and is, therefore, exposed to a weakening of sterling. The company also expects to be having a dollar receipt in 70 days' time and is, therefore, exposed to a strengthening of sterling. Due to economic events over the next couple of weeks, the company believes there will be an impact on exchange rates, but does not know whether it will result in a strengthening or weakening of sterling. The company can buy a chooser option with a maturity of 0 days. In 20 days, the company can decide whether they will have a sterling put with a maturity of 30 days or a sterling call with a maturity of 40 days.

Valuing a chooser option is effectively valuing a call on a call and a call on a put, each with a zero strike. If the date when the holder can choose is equal to the expiry date, then it would be valued as a straddle. If, however, the 'choosing' date is very near (but not at expiry), it would be priced as the higher of the call or put. A chooser option is half way between a plain vanilla call and a straddle.

5.1.5 Delayed option

With a delayed option, the holder has the right to receive in the future another option with a strike price set according to the price of the underlying on that date.

5.2 Path-dependent

5.2.1 Average rate or average price or Asian options

The payout on Asian options is not calculated as the difference between the strike and the underlying at exercise, it is instead calculated as the difference between the strike and the average price of the underlying. The averaging period can vary and could be a week, a month, the entire life of the option – the average itself could be arithmetic or geometric.

These options are valuable when an investor has a series of exposures over a period of time rather than just on one date. Most beneficial in interest rate or currency hedging.

5.2.2 Average-strike option

In an average-strike option, the strike price is set to the average price and the payout is the difference between the strike and the asset price at maturity.

5.2.3 Lookback options

With a lookback option, the holder can, at expiry, look back over the life of the option and set the strike price at the highest (for a lookback put) or the lowest (for a lookback call) price the underlying asset achieved. These may be called no-regret options. These options will be much more expensive than a standard option, as they are much more likely to expire in-the-money.

With this type of option, the principal risk is gamma risk. It has an 'own-sided' gamma. Consider a lookback that has reached a maximum and then dropped below it. The only additional gamma risk is if the market was to go above the maximum, i.e. one-sided.

5.2.4 Barrier or knock-out or knock-in options

In a barrier option, two prices are established at the outset – the strike price and the barrier (or trigger) price. The option will either be triggered or extinguished when the barrier level is touched or the price moves through it.

The barrier price on a call is normally set below both the strike and the current underlying price. The barrier price of a put is normally set above both the strike and the current underlying price. This means that they are activated or extinguished when they are out-of-the-money. These might be known as 'regular' barrier options. It is possible to set the barrier so that they are triggered when they are in-the-money. These may be called 'reverse' barrier options.

This gives rise to

> Down and in calls (option activated)
> Down and out calls (option extinguished)
> Up and in puts (option activated)
> Up and out puts (option extinguished)

As these may be extinguished or indeed, never activated, they tend to be cheaper than the conventional options.

A further twist is to have a double barrier – one above and one below the current asset price. In a 'double out', the option becomes worthless if either barrier is reached. A 'double in' – one of the barriers must be reached, otherwise it will expire worthless. Finally, one could be in and the other out.

Consider a US company having to make a € payment in 30 days. Instead of buying a € call, it could instead buy a down and out call. If the € strengthens, the company will have a € call and will, therefore, have fixed the purchase price of €. If, however, € weakens below a certain rate, the call will be extinguished, as it will no longer be needed. There is, however, an obvious risk and that is that once extinguished, € then strengthens, but the company no longer has a call option.

Hedging these types of options will once again necessitate a study of delta and gamma. As may be imagined, the delta of a barrier option shows discontinuity at the barrier price. Imagine a knock-out call at 98, the delta would look as follows.

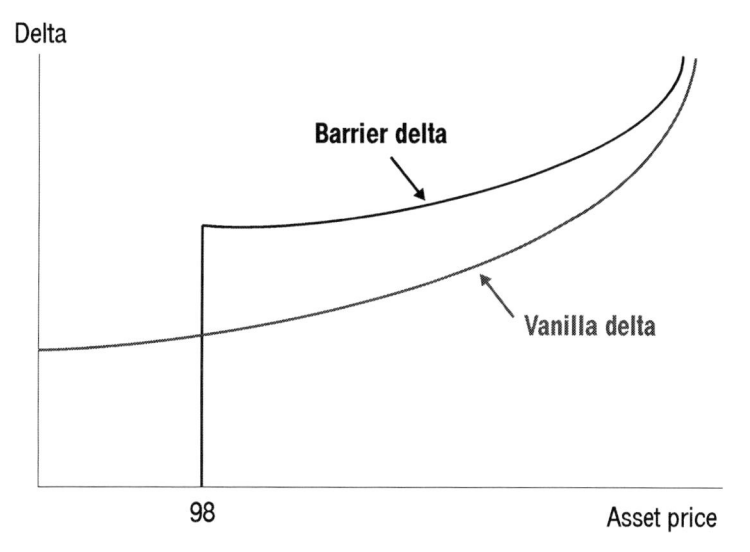

A trader selling a regular barrier will hedge in a similar way as a vanilla, but will have a different hedge ratio due to the difference in delta. When the knock-out occurs, the hedge will have to be unwound quickly – this can often lead to larger than expected losses to the trader, a fact that should be considered when pricing it.

The delta of a knock-in call, however, will look quite different to the knock-out, as shown below.

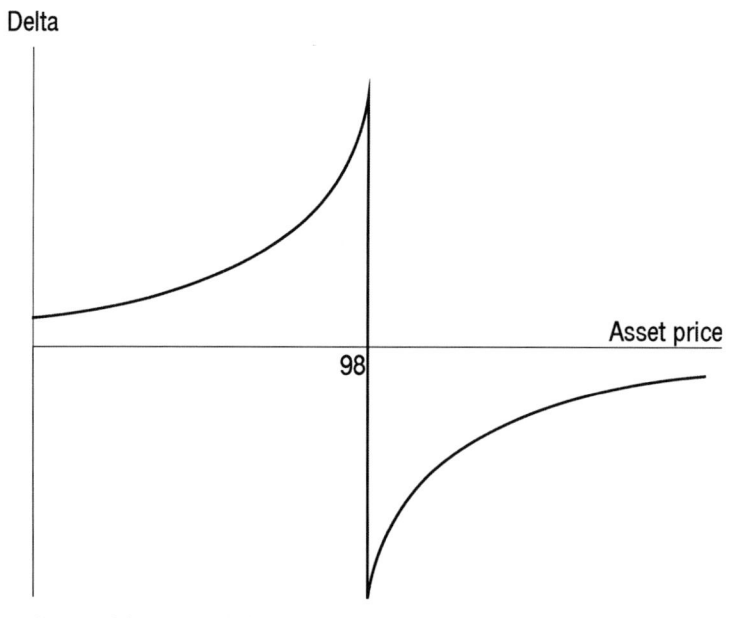

[Graph showing Delta on y-axis and Asset price on x-axis, with a value of 98 marked on the x-axis. The curve shows delta increasing sharply to a peak at 98, then dropping to negative values and gradually returning toward zero.]

The above can be understood by appreciating that if you are long a knock-in call, you benefit as the asset price falls to the barrier (delta negative), but when it is activated, it shows the delta characteristic of a vanilla call below the barrier.

Other features of barrier style options could include

- Early exercise.
- Instalment premiums. This is when monthly premiums have to be paid to keep the option alive.
- Intermittent premiums. The position of the barrier can be time-dependent. An extreme example is when the barrier disappears completely for certain specific time periods.
- Repeated hitting of the barrier. A double-barrier option where both barriers must be hit before the option is triggered.
- Resetting of barriers. When the barrier is hit, the option turns into another barrier option with a different barrier.

5.2.5 Cliquet or ratchet options

The strike price of a ratchet option is reset to match the prevailing asset price at pre-determined dates. Any intrinsic value at this date is thus 'locked in'.

5.2.6 Ladder option

Like a cliquet option, the strike price of a ladder option is reset when the price of the underlying asset reaches pre-determined levels (rather than pre-determined dates).

5.2.7 Shout option

Like a cliquet or ladder, the intrinsic value of a shout option is locked in and the strike reset when the holder 'shouts', thus it is not set according to pre-determined dates or asset values.

5.3 Multi-factor

5.3.1 Rainbow or outperformance option

The payoff is the difference between the strike and the best (call) or worse (put) prices at expiry, from a number of underlying assets.

5.3.2 Basket option

Similar to a rainbow, but now the payout is the difference in strike and the average price (or total basket value) of the underlying assets.

5.3.3 Spread option

In a spread option the payout is the difference between a pair of asset prices.

5.3.4 Quanto option

A quanto option is also known as quarterly adjusted options. The payout depends on one underlying price, but the actual value is determined with reference to another, e.g. pay the difference in the FTSE 100 out in US dollars.

5.4 Exchange options

Exchange options allow the holder the right to exchange one asset for another. These are more common in foreign exchange markets, stock markets and bond markets. It is like having a call option on one asset and a put option on another.

Imagine that an option allows the holder to exchange Asset 2 (current price S_2, dividend yield y_2) for Asset 1 (current price S_1, dividend yield y_1). This is equivalent to a call on Asset 1, where the strike price is the value of Asset 2. Within the Black Scholes framework, this would look like

$$\text{Price of exchange option} = S_1 e^{-y_1 t} N(d_1) - S_2 e^{-y_2 t} N(d_2)$$

$$\text{where } d_1 = \frac{\ln\left(\frac{S_1}{S_2}\right) + \left(y_2 - y_2 + \sigma^2/2\right)t}{\sigma\sqrt{t}}$$

$$d_2 = d_1 - \sigma\sqrt{t}$$

All of this looks pretty familiar. One question to ask however is: what is the volatility measure that goes into the d_1 calculation? This must represent not only the volatility of the two assets involved, but also the correlation between them. It is important to realise that unlike a basket equity option where negative correlation between the asset returns reduces the volatility and hence value of the option, negative correlation will increase the value of an exchange option, as it will increase the price difference of the two assets as they move in opposite directions. The appropriate formula for the combined volatility for an exchange option is

Formula to learn

$$\sigma = \sqrt{\sigma_a^2 + \sigma_b^2 - 2\sigma_a \sigma_b \text{cor}_{ab}}$$

14: OTHER OTC DERIVATIVE PRODUCTS

Chapter Roundup

- You need to be familiar with and be able to describe the characteristics of all the products discussed in this section

- FRAs

$$\text{Gross settlement amount} = \text{Principal} \times (\text{Actual rate} - \text{Contract rate}) \times \frac{\text{Days}}{365}$$

$$\text{Actual settlement amount} = \frac{\text{Principal} \times (\text{Actual rate} - \text{Contract rate}) \times \frac{\text{Days}}{365}}{1 + \text{Actual rate} \times \frac{\text{Days}}{365}}$$

    BUY an FRA to protect against a rise in rates

    SELL an FRA to protect against a fall in rates.

- FRA rate

    With forward rates, if

    r_1 = time apportioned rate to the start of the contract period

    r_2 = time apportioned rate to the end of the contract period

    $$(1 + {}_1f_2) = \frac{(1 + r_2)}{(1 + r_1)}$$

    DF_1 = discount factor for the period to the start of the contract period

    DF_2 = discount factor for the period to the end of the contract period

    $$(1 + {}_1f_2) = \frac{DF_1}{DF_2}$$

TEST YOUR KNOWLEDGE

Check your knowledge of the Chapter here, without referring back to the text.

1. You have entered into an FRA to fix the borrowing rate on a £55m borrowing for a period of six months (182 days) starting in three months. The FRA quote is 5.20-5.25. What cash flow would you expect to arise at of the settlement date if rates at that time are

    a) 5.0%

    b) 5.5%

2. You are given the following discount factors

6 month	0.971365
12 month	0.941635
18 month	0.912032

    Calculate the actual settlement sum on a 12v18 FRA on a principal sum of £25,000,000 if six month LIBOR in 12 months time is 6.6%

Test Your Knowledge: Answers

1. **5% Rate**

    Gross settlement amount $= £55\text{m} \times (0.050 - 0.0525) \times \dfrac{182}{365} = -£68,562$

    Actual settlement amount $= \dfrac{-68,562}{1 + 0.05 \times \dfrac{182}{365}} = -£66,894$

    i.e. a payment of £66,894

    5.5% Rate

    Gross settlement amount $= £55\text{m} \times (0.055 - 0.0525) \times \dfrac{182}{365} = £68,562$

    Actual settlement amount $= \dfrac{68,562}{1 + 0.055 \times \dfrac{182}{365}} = £66,732$

    i.e. a receipt of £66,732

2. **FRA rate**

    $(1 + {}_{12}f_{18}) = \dfrac{0.941635}{0.912032} = 1.03246$

    ${}_{12}f_{18} = 0.03246$ or 3.246%

    FRA rate = (3.246 × 2) = 6.491%

    Settlement Amount

    Gross settlement amount $= £25\text{m} \times (0.066 - 0.0649) \times \dfrac{6}{12} = £13,570$

    Actual settlement amount $= \dfrac{13,750}{1 + 0.0649 \times \dfrac{6}{12}} = £13,318$

15 Hybrid Securities

INTRODUCTION

This section considers a range of hybrid securities, i.e. securities with the characteristics of two or more other securities, such as convertible bonds. Such securities can invariably be viewed as a straight bond plus an embedded option. This section considers the characteristics and valuation of such hybrid securities

CHAPTER CONTENTS

		Page
1	Convertible bonds, callable bonds and putable bonds	474
2	Dual Currency Bonds	487
3	Mortgage Derivatives	487
4	Asset-Backed Securities	490
5	Option-Adjusted Spread	490
6	Warrants	492
	Chapter Roundup	494
	Test Your Knowledge	495

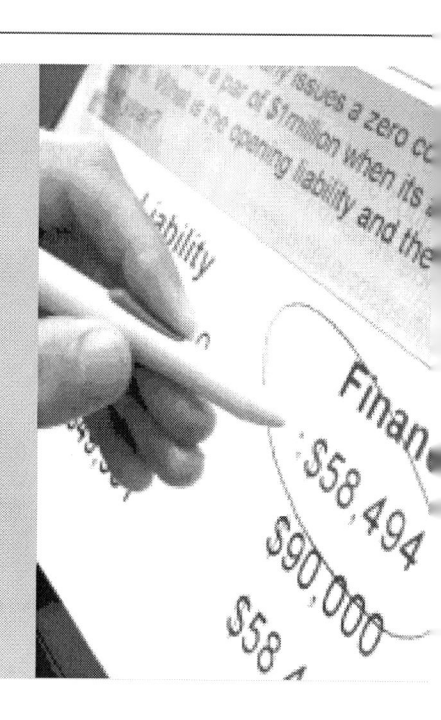

15: HYBRID SECURITIES

CHAPTER LEARNING OBJECTIVES

The syllabus areas covered by this section are

Over the counter Derivatives

Types of contracts

- Warrants
    - Equity
    - Currency
    - Interest Rate
    - Baskets
- Hybrid securities
    - Convertible Bonds
    - Callable and Puttable Bonds
    - Dual Currency Bonds
    - Mortgages
    - Option – Adjusted Spread Analysis

Exam tip

> This area is not regularly examined in detail

1 CONVERTIBLE BONDS, CALLABLE BONDS AND PUTABLE BONDS

1.1 Convertible bonds

1.1.1 Introduction

A convertible bond gives the bondholder the right at a specified date or dates in the future to convert their bond into shares of the issuing company. The rate of conversion will be fixed at the time of issue and represents an option to purchase the shares at a given price. Depending on the movement in the underlying share price, this conversion right or option may be very valuable indeed. The trade-off in this sort of issue is that the coupon will often be much lower than the market would otherwise expect on a bond from that particular company.

1.1.2 Valuation

When a company is considering the issue of a convertible, an investor will need to ensure that it is fairly priced. If the price is too expensive, then investors will not buy the convertible and the issue will flop. If the price is very cheap, then the company will be obtaining finance on disadvantageous terms and value for existing shareholders will fall.

The conversion right can be expressed in a number of ways. By convention, the right is normally to convert the debt into the ordinary shares of the company at a given **conversion ratio**, e.g. £100 nominal is converted into 25 shares (a conversion ratio of 25). The conversion right may exist for a period of time during the bond's life (the conversion window) or may only be available on maturity.

Additional terms may include

- Different conversion ratios at different maturities of the bond.
- The holder of the bond may also be obliged to contribute additional capital on the conversion, e.g. £100 nominal of the debt converts into 20 shares and the bondholder is obliged to contribute an additional £2.50 per share. Therefore, each share has an effective cost (assuming the bond is trading at par) of £100/20 = £5 + £2.50 = £7.50.
- Put rights enabling the holder of the bond to force an early redemption of the bond, normally at a premium to the par value.

When establishing the terms of the convertible, the issuer will normally avoid unduly complicated terms, since this will confuse, and thereby dissuade, potential purchasers of the bond.

Valuation of convertibles is very difficult to do in practice, but various models have been developed. Three common methods are the dividend valuation model, the crossover method and the option pricing method. We will discuss the option pricing method first, as it is the most appropriate.

1.1.3 Option pricing method

Convertibles contain an option to acquire equity

The most appropriate method of valuing a convertible is to use option pricing theory. A bond with a conversion right attached is basically a combination of two separate instruments: a low-coupon bond and an option into the underlying equity.

Factors affecting option values

The value of the option will be determined by a number of factors as we have already seen, specifically

- The exercise price of the option.
- The actual price of the underlying share.
- Expected volatility in the price of the underlying share.
- The time to expiry of the option.
- Interest rates.
- Whether a dividend is due to be paid on the share or not in the option period.

Value of a convertible at its expiry date

A simple example of this technique would be to consider a convertible on its date of expiry. It can either be converted into shares with a value of £120 or redeemed for cash of £100. Clearly, the total value of the convertible is £120. This is made up of its value as straight debt (£100) plus the value of the option to convert into equity, which must be worth an additional £20.

Since the option is at its expiry date, there is no time value and the whole of the £20 is intrinsic value. Remember that intrinsic value is the difference between the market price of the shares (£120) and the exercise price of the option. In the case of a convertible, the exercise price of the option is the lost proceeds from redeeming the instrument as straight debt – in other words, £100.

Value of a convertible before its expiry stock

Intrinsic value of conversion option

The minimum intrinsic value of the convertible prior to conversion will be the higher of

- The value of the plain vanilla bond (ignoring the conversion right); or
- The value of the bond in terms of the number of shares that could be created at their current market price.

15: HYBRID SECURITIES

Example 1

A 4% convertible 2008 contains the right to convert £100 nominal value into 35 shares or redeem at par. At present, the shares are trading in the market at £1.25 and 4% non-convertible redeemable 2008 bonds are trading at £88. What is the floor value of this convertible?

Solution 1

The value of a non-convertible 4% bond redeeming in 2008 is £88. This bond could be converted into 35 shares, each with a value of £1.25, that is 35 × £1.25 = £43.75. At this point, the conversion right is of no value and it is best to regard the bond as a 'straight', i.e. the conversion option has no intrinsic value.

Example 2

Assume that debt has one year to maturity and will be redeemed for £108 cash. Alternatively, the investor can convert into shares at any time over the next year. The current value of the shares is £120. The debt holder's required rate of return is 10%.

Solution 2

The value of the instrument now as straight debt is the present value of the proceeds as debt of £98.18 $\left(£108 \times \frac{1}{1.1}\right)$. The value in terms of the shares that could be created is £120. The minimum value of the convertible will therefore be £120, being the value of the straight debt of £98.18 plus the intrinsic value of the option of £21.82.

Time value of conversion option

Whilst the above calculation establishes a minimum value, the market value of the convertible will obviously be affected by the potential increase in the price of the underlying share i.e. the time value. It is likely that the total value of the convertible will be higher than this, due to time value of the option. Option-pricing models will allow us to calculate this.

The bond investors position is as follows

Long convertible = Long straight bond and long call option

The value of this is given by

Formula to learn

> Convertible value = Straight bond value + Call option value

Example 3

A convertible bond with one year to maturity pays an annual coupon of 8%. At maturity, it can be redeemed at par or converted into 25 ordinary shares. These shares have a current price of £3.80 per share. Volatility of the shares is 20% p.a. and risk-free interest rates are currently 7% p.a. Debt holders require a return of 10%. Calculate the fair value of the convertible.

Solution 3

Step 1

Value of bond ignoring the conversion rights

$$= £108 \times \frac{1}{1.1} = £98.18$$

Step 2

Value of option using Black Scholes model

$$C = SN(d_1) - Xe^{-rt}N(d_2)$$

$$S = 25 \times £3.80 = £95$$

$$d_1 = \frac{\ln\left(\frac{S}{X}\right) + \left(r + 0.5\sigma^2\right)t}{\sigma\sqrt{t}}$$

$$d_2 = d_1 - \sigma\sqrt{t}$$

$$d_1 = \frac{\ln\left(\frac{95}{100}\right) + \left(0.07 + 0.5 \times 0.2^2\right)1}{0.2\sqrt{t}}$$

$$d_1 = 0.19$$

$$d_2 = 0.19 - 0.2\sqrt{t}$$

$$d_2 = 0.01$$

from tables: $N(d_1) = 0.57535$

$N(d_2) = 0.49601$

$$C = 95 \times 0.57535 - 100e^{-0.07 \times 1} \times 0.49601$$

$$C = £8.41$$

Value of Convertible Bond

= Value of bond ignoring conversion rights + Value of option
= £98.18 + £8.41
= **£106.59**

Conclusion

If the value of the shares is significantly less than the cash redemption option, then the value of the convertible is likely to be its value as straight debt. The option is significantly out-of-the-money and is almost worthless.

If, however, the value of the shares exceeds the cash redemption price, then the conversion option will have some intrinsic value.

In both cases, however, it is likely that the conversion option will have some time value and we could use our option pricing theory to evaluate it.

This pricing approach, using the Black Scholes model, does not allow for changes in the interest rate structure over the bond's life. As interest rates are so important in bond valuation, we will next consider a binomial approach, which can allow for interest rate volatility. This will be demonstrated in the next section which considers pricing a callable bond.

1.2 Callable Bonds

1.2.1 Components in a callable bond

Non-Callable Bond Plus an Option

A callable bond could be viewed as a straight bond with an embedded option. The company has sold a straight bond to investors but at the same time, has bought an option from the investors, enabling the company to buy back the straight bond at the agreed call price.

This explains why the proceeds on the issue of a callable bond are less than those for an equivalent straight bond. The company receives the proceeds from the straight bond, but then uses part of those proceeds to buy a call option from the bond investors. The net proceeds received are therefore lower.

Value of a Callable Bond

The bond investor's position is as follows.

Long callable bond = Long straight bond and Short call option

The value of this is given by

Formula to learn

> Callable bond value = Straight bond value − Call option value

If the value of the call option increases, then the value of the callable bond will decrease. For example, an increase in the price of the straight bond (caused by a decrease in interest rates) will increase the intrinsic value of the call option. Although the straight bond will increase in value, the call option also increases in value, meaning that the callable bond value may hardly change at all. The relationship depends on whether interest rates are high or low.

Low interest rates

If interest rates are low, the value of the straight bond will be high, meaning that the right to call it at a price close to par of, say, 102 will be in-the-money and very valuable. In this case, a fall in interest rates will cause a rise in the price of the straight bond, but a rise in the value of the option of almost equal value. The net change in the callable bond value is minor.

High interest rates

If interest rates are very high, then the price of the bond will be very low and the call option will be deeply out-of-the-money. This means that the value of the option will change by very little for a small change in interest rates. Therefore, the price behaviour of the callable bond mimics the behaviour of the straight bond.

Volatility of interest rates

An increase in expected volatility of interest rates will increase the value of the option, since it makes the bond price more volatile. This will reduce the value of the callable bond.

1.3 Putable bond

A putable bond is where the investor has the right to redeem the bond early, by putting it back to the issuer. In this case, it is the investor who has the right to exercise the option, not the company. The investor will wish to do this if interest rates rise significantly, since he will be able to recover his money and reinvest it at higher rates.

The position of an investor with a putable bond is as follows.

Long putable bond = Long straight bond and Long put option

The value of this is given by

Formula to learn

> Putable bond value = Straight bond value + Put option value

The price of the putable bond is therefore higher than for a comparable straight bond.

1.4 Volatility of interest rates and the binomial tree

Whether we are dealing with convertible bonds, callable bonds or putable bonds, the key factor is going to be the value of the option. The value of the option will depend on interest rates and interest rate volatility. This is allowed for in the valuation process by constructing a **binomial tree** of future interest rates.

We will first look at how the concept of interest rate volatility and a binomial tree can be applied in the context of an option-free bond. We will then move on to look at their application in the valuation of bonds with embedded options.

1.4.1 Valuing a straight bond with a binomial tree

Basic principles when valuing option-free bonds

Valuation using spot rates

The basic principle behind option-free bond valuation, as shown in the convertible pricing example, is to discount each individual flow using the appropriate spot rate. For example, assume a two-year bond is priced at 98.40 and has an annual 8% coupon. Spot rates (calculated on an effective annual basis) are 7% for the first year and 9% for the second year. The price of the bond is equal to the present value of the future cash flows as the following calculation demonstrates.

$$\text{Price} = \frac{8}{1.07} + \frac{108}{1.09^2}$$

Price = 98.40

Using forward rates instead of spot rates

Note that this could also have been done using forward rates. The one-year forward rate for the second year can be calculated as the value of r in the following equation.

$$(1.07)(1+r) = 1.09^2$$
$$r = 0.11 \text{ or } 11\%$$

The value of the bond could have then calculated using forward rates, as follows.

$$\text{Price} = \frac{8}{10.7} + \frac{108}{(1.07)(1.11)}$$

Price = 98.40

It is inevitable that this will come back to the same answer, since we know that $1.09^2 = 1.07 \times 1.11$.

However, it demonstrates a different conceptual view of the valuation process. We are firstly taking the proceeds in two years' time and discounting them back for one year using the relevant interest rate for the second year, i.e. the forward rate. We are then discounting them back for another year to bring them to a present value, using the one-year interest rate applicable for the first year.

15: HYBRID SECURITIES

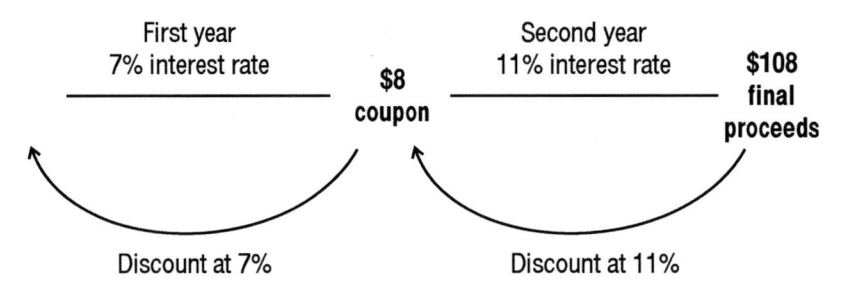

```
First year              Second year           $108
7% interest rate        11% interest rate     final
                $8                            proceeds
              coupon

Discount at 7%          Discount at 11%
```

Using the above idea, the calculation could have been broken down as follows.

$$\text{Value of \$108 discounted for one year} = \frac{108}{1.11} = \$97.30$$

$$\text{Value of \$97.30 discounted for one year} = \frac{97.30}{1.07} = \$90.93$$

$$\text{Value of \$8 discounted for one year} = \frac{8}{1.07} = \$7.47$$

Value of bond = $90.93 + $7.47 = $98.40

Extending this to introduce interest rate volatility

The above valuation using forward rates assumed just one value for the forward rate in the second year. However, it would be possible to factor in different possible values for interest rates in the second year and ascribe a probability to each arising. An expected value for the flows at the end of the first year could then be calculated.

This would be done by calculating the value of the $108 by discounting at each of the possible interest rates selected. These separate values would then be combined using their probability weightings to give an expected value.

Example

If there were two possible interest rates for the second year, being 10.5% and 11.5%, each with a 0.5 probability of arising, what would be the expected value in one year's time of the $108 received at the end of the second year?

Solution

Value assuming 10.5% interest rate

$$\text{Value} = \frac{108}{1.105} = \$97.74$$

Value assuming 11.5% interest rate

$$\text{Value} = \frac{108}{1.115} = \$96.86$$

Expected value

$$\text{Value} = \frac{97.74 + 96.86}{2} = \$97.30$$

The present value for this could then be identified by discounting it back for one more year, using the current one-year interest rate of 7%.

$$\text{Present value} = \frac{97.30}{1.07} = \$90.93$$

It can be seen that this is the same as the value calculated above for the flow, assuming just the one forward rate of 11%. Using this approach, the present value of the bond once again equals its price, i.e. $90.93 + $7.48 = $98.40.

The binomial interest rate tree

The binomial interest rate tree builds in interest rate volatility by assuming that there are two possible interest rates for each period of time – a high interest rate and a low interest rate.

The interest rate for the first year is already known (r_0). The interest rate for the second year is assumed to be a high or low rate. The higher rate for year two is r_H, the lower rate is r_L.

In the third year, the interest rate that arises depends on whether the rate was high or low in Year 2. If the rate was high in Year 2, then the rate for the third year could be even higher (r_{HH}) or lower (r_{HL}). If the rate in Year 2 was low, then the rate for the third year could be higher than this (r_{LH} assumed to be the same as r_{HL}) or lower (r_{LL}).

This process can be represented on a binomial probability tree, as follows.

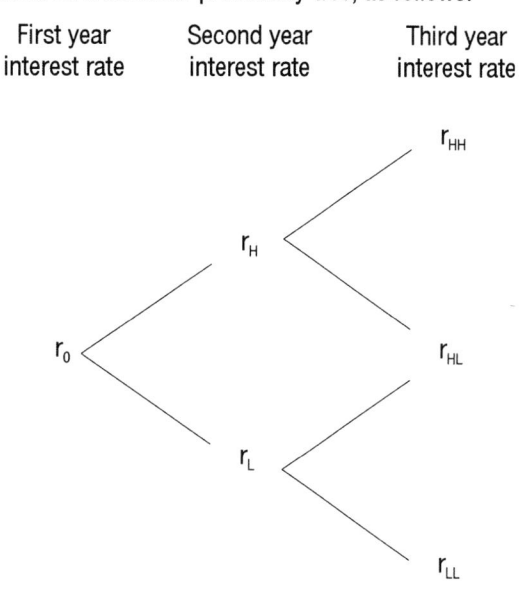

	First year interest rate	Second year interest rate	Third year interest rate

$$
\begin{array}{c}
r_0 \to r_H \to r_{HH} \\
r_0 \to r_H \to r_{HL} \\
r_0 \to r_L \to r_{HL} \\
r_0 \to r_L \to r_{LL}
\end{array}
$$

This tree could be extended out for any desired number of years.

In order to use this idea, we now need to be able to identify the high and the low rates for each year. In order to do this, various assumptions are possible. A typical assumption would be that the one-year forward rate follows a **lognormal random walk** through time. This means that it is equally likely that the rate will be high or low, meaning that there is a 0.5 probability of the high or low rate arising. It also means that if we now **assume a level of volatility** for the interest rate, as measured by σ, we can predict a relationship between the higher and lower interest rates. Having identified the lower interest rate, we know the higher interest rate with which it would be associated.

1.4.2 Constructing a binomial tree

Trial and error approach

The above example was contrived so that all the interest rates and numbers fitted together such that the value of our two-year bond was the same as its current price of $98.40. How would we identify the relevant interest rates to put into the binomial tree in practice? It is done by a trial and error approach.

15: HYBRID SECURITIES

Exam tip | In the exam you will be given all relevant rates, the following discussion is to help you deal with discussion questions

The approach is to identify a straight bond with its current market price and estimate expected volatility for interest rates. A low rate for the first forward period is then selected arbitrarily. Since we have established a level of interest rate volatility and assumed a lognormal random walk for interest rates, it is possible from this to also establish the high interest rate. From this, the binomial tree can be built up in the same way as above. The present value of the bond using this arbitrarily constructed tree is calculated. If it equals the price of the bond, we have the binomial tree.

What is more likely is that the calculated present value will not equal the price of the bond. We then select a different low rate for the first forward period and continue the process until, by trial and error, we identify the appropriate binomial tree.

Example

Assume that we had taken an interest rate of 10% as the low rate for the second year in the above example. From this, assume that we had estimated that the high rate of interest is 10.95%. We could then calculate the bond's present value based on these two interest rates. Remember, the bond has a two-year maturity and an 8% annual coupon.

Value of $108 in one year's time assuming 10.0% interest rate

$$\text{Value} = \frac{\$108}{1.10} = \$98.18$$

Value of $108 in one year's time assuming 10.95% interest rate

$$\text{Value} = \frac{\$108}{1.1095} = \$97.34$$

Expected value of $108 in one year's time

$$\text{Value} = \frac{\$98.18 + \$97.34}{2} = \$97.76$$

Present value of the $108

$$\text{Present value} = \frac{\$97.76}{1.07} = \$91.36$$

Total present value of the bond

This is given by the above present value plus the $8 received in one year's time, discounted at 7% for the first year.

$$\text{Present value of bond} = \frac{\$97.76}{1.07} + \frac{\$8}{1.07} = \$98.84$$

Compare this to the actual price of the bond

The actual bond price is $98.40, indicating that the assumption of 10% for the low rate was incorrect. We would now need to repeat the process using a higher rate (since the present value above exceeds the actual price of the bond), until we identify the correct lower rate, which we actually know in this case to be 10.5%.

Extending the tree to include a third and further periods

Having identified the binomial tree for two periods out in the future using a two-period bond, we can now move on to the third period. We would select a bond with payments at Times 1, 2 and 3. We know the appropriate interest rates for valuing the first two flows, since we have already constructed a two-period binomial tree. In order to identify the interest rates for the third period, we would now use a process of trial and error, until we have identified the rates that give a present value equal to the actual price of the bond.

Having identified the three-period binomial tree, we could move on to a four-period tree by using a four-period bond, etc.

Arbitrage-free binomial tree

When we have correctly identified the binomial tree, we refer to it as the **arbitrage-free tree**, since it correctly prices on-the-run issues. This tree could be used to value any bond whether it is option free or has an embedded option.

1.4.3 Valuing bonds with embedded options

Use of the arbitrage-free binomial tree

Having identified the arbitrage-free tree, it can be used to establish the option embedded bond value and there are two alternative approaches we could adopt.

Alternative 1

The valuation of a convertible, callable, or putable bond can be done in exactly the same way as valuing the option free bond. The only difference is that at each stage of the tree, the investor will have to consider whether the option is going to be exercised (assuming it can be exercised at any time). If the option is exercised, the value of the future flows of the bond along that path is replaced by the alternative value available, ie

- intrinsic value of the conversion option for a convertible
- exercise price of the call or put option for callable or putable bonds

In this context

- A convertible bond call option will be exercised by the investor if the bond value is less than the intrinsic value of the conversion option.

- A callable bond will be exercised by the issuer if the call exercise price is less than the bond price at that point.

- A putable bond will be exercised by the investor if the put option exercise price is greater than the bond price at that point.

Note, the above assumes that the embedded option can be exercised at any time. While this may be the case, it may also be the case that the option can be exercised over a specific term or at a specific time only.

If there is a specific period during which the option can be exercised, then we only do the above replacing of values during this period.

If, as is frequently the case for convertibles, the embedded option can only be exercised at expiry/maturity then a simple European binomial or Black Scholes calculation could be undertaken to evaluate the embedded option.

15: HYBRID SECURITIES

Alternative 2

A second alternative is to

- Value the bond separately in its own binomial tree
- Obtain option intrinsic values by comparing the bond value to the
  - conversion intrinsic value
  - call/put exercise price
- Evaluate option separately
- Combine bond and option value appropriately.

Example

Assume that a bond is paying a 12% annual coupon and is redeemable in two years' time. The bond is callable at a price of $101 in one year's time. The binomial interest rate tree to be used is the same as the one above, i.e. the current one year interest rate is 7% and there rate two equally likely rates for year 2 of 10.5% and 11.5%.

Calculate the value of the bond.

Solution

Alternative 1

The first stage is to calculate the value of the cash flow in two years' time ($112), given the above interest rates for the second year.

Value of $112 in one year's time assuming 10.5% interest rate

$$\text{Value} = \frac{\$112}{1.105} = \$101.36$$

Value of $112 in one year's time assuming 11.5% interest rate

$$\text{Value} = \frac{\$112}{1.115} = \$100.45$$

The second stage is to determine whether the call option will be exercised or not. In the case of the low interest rate, it can be seen that the value of the bond is $101.36. It is therefore worthwhile for the company to call the bond, paying only $101. The value along this path is therefore $101 in one year's time.

In the case of the high interest rate, the value of the bond is only $100.45. Therefore, it would not be worthwhile calling the bond at $101. The value along this path is therefore $100.45.

The expected value of the bond in one year's time can now be calculated.

Expected value of bond in one year's time, excluding the first year's coupon

$$\text{Value} = \frac{\$101 + \$100.45}{2} = \$100.725$$

Value of the bond in one year's time, including the first year's coupon

$$\text{Value} = \$100.725 + \$12 = \$112.725$$

Present value of the bond

$$\text{Present value of bond} = \frac{\$112.725}{1.07} = \$105.35$$

This could be laid out in a table as follows

Callable bond binomial tree

Year 2		10.5%		11.5%	
End of year	– Ex div	100.00		100.00	
	– Coupon	12.00		12.00	
	– Cum div	112.00		112.00	
	– Discount factor	$\frac{1}{1.105}$		$\frac{1}{1.115}$	
Start of year	– Straight bond value	101.36		100.45	
	– Callable bond value	101.00	(Exercised)	100.45	(not exercised)

Year 1		$[0.5 \times 101.00 + 0.5 \times 100.45]$
End of year	– Ex div	100.75
	– Coupon	12.00
	– Cum div	112.75
	– Discount factor	$\frac{1}{1.07}$
Start of year	– Callable bond value	105.35

This is simply a binomial table laid out vertically rather than horizontally for the convenience of incorporating all coupons, exercise choices etc. All the values in this table are those described above.

Alternative 2

Deal with the straight bond and the embedded option separately

Straight bond binomial tree

Year 2		10.5%	11.5%
End of year	– Ex div	100.00	100.00
	– Coupon	12.00	12.00
	– Cum div	112.00	112.00
	– Discount factor	$\frac{1}{1.105}$	$\frac{1}{1.115}$
Start of year	– Straight bond value	101.36	100.45

Year 1		$[0.5 \times 101.36 + 0.5 \times 100.45]$
End of year	– Ex div	100.91
	– Coupon	12.00
	– Cum div	112.91
	– Discount factor	$\frac{1}{1.07}$
Start of year	– Bond value	105.52

15: HYBRID SECURITIES

Option Binomial Tree

Year 2			10.5%		11.5%	
End of year	– Time 2 option value		0.00		00.00	
	– Discount factor		$\dfrac{1}{1.105}$		$\dfrac{1}{1.115}$	
Start of year	– Time 2 option value		0.00		0.00	
	– Time 1 option value		0.36	(Exercised)	0.00	(Not exercised)
Year 1			$[0.5 \times 0.36 + 0.5 \times 0.00]$			
End of year	– Time 1 option value		0.18			
	– Discount factor		$\dfrac{1}{1.07}$			
Start of year	– Time 1 option value		0.17			

Combined

Callable bond = Straight bond – call option value
= 105.52 – 0.17
= 105.35 (as before)

This second alternative is probably the most flexible as it enables you to evaluate both the bond (convertible, callable, putable) and the embedded option.

1.4.4 Calculating the value of the call option embedded in the bond

We know the formula for valuing the call option, from above.

Callable bond value = Straight bond value – Call option value

This can be rearranged as follows.

Formula to learn

> Call option value = Straight bond value – Callable bond value

Hence, if we now also work out the value of the bond if there were no call option, we can identify the value of the call option.

The value of the bond, assuming there were no call option, is as follows.

Expected value of bond in one year's time, excluding the first year's coupon.

$$\text{Value} = \frac{\$101.36 + \$100.45}{2} = \$100.905$$

Value of the bond in one year's time, including the first year's coupon.

Value = $100.905 + $12 = $112.905

Present value of the bond

$$\text{Present value of bond} = \frac{\$112.905}{1.07} = \$105.52$$

The value of the option is as follows.

Call option value = $105.52 – $105.35 = $0.17

This approach can be used to value bonds and embedded options, regardless of the nature of the option, be it a call or a put.

2 DUAL CURRENCY BONDS

Dual currency bonds pay interest in one currency, but are redeemed in another. The most common variety recently has been a bond that pays interest in yen and is redeemed in US dollars. These can be structured in many different ways. For example, the issuer could redeem at an exchange rate fixed at the issue date, the exchange rate prevailing at redemption or an average exchange rate. These possibilities clearly give option-like characteristics to these dual (or multi) currency bonds.

3 MORTGAGE DERIVATIVES

3.1 Introduction

Mortgage passthrough certificates are securities which enable an investor to receive a pro rata share of the cash flows coming from a pool of mortgages. As such, they are fairly simple instruments. It is possible to create more complex derivative structures for pools of mortgages, such that an investor need not receive a pro rata share of the cash flows. The benefit of this is that each mortgage derivative security can be more precisely tailored to individual investor requirements.

Two forms of mortgage derivatives are as follows.

- Collateralised Mortgage Obligations (CMOs).
- Stripped Mortgage-Backed Securities.

3.2 Collateralised mortgage obligations

3.2.1 The purpose of CMOs

Collateralised mortgage obligations are designed to redistribute the risk and return from a pool of mortgages to meet investors' needs. As a result, CMOs are not one form of security, as is the case with simple mortgage passthroughs, but a range of different securities.

3.2.2 Sequential pay tranches

The original CMOs were fairly simple in structure and took the form of sequential pay tranches or bonds. The CMO is split into several tranches, identified as A, B, C, etc. Interest from the mortgages is paid to all tranches in proportion to their principal investment. However, principal repayments are first used to repay Tranche A. When all of Tranche A has been repaid, the next principal repayments are used to repay Tranche B and so on.

Although the priority for repayment of principal is known, the timing of principal repayments is not, although it can be forecast with a prepayment speed assumption (PSA).

The sequential order of repayment means that the first tranches will have average lives shorter than the underlying mortgage collateral, while the later tranches will have average lives longer than the underlying collateral.

However, the volatility of the average life for each tranche is still significantly affected by the prepayment speed.

The simple sequential pay CMOs are sometimes referred to as plain vanilla CMOs.

3.2.3 Accrual bonds

Accrual bonds are sometimes referred to as Z bonds. They are so called because they are similar to zero-coupon bonds. In addition to the usual tranches in a sequential pay CMO, a Z bond may be added. The Z bond does not receive any cash interest in the early years, receiving instead additional Z bonds. The cash interest so released is then used to pay down the principal balances on the other tranches.

Effectively, the Z bond investors are using their interest to buy principal from investors in the other tranches.

Some bonds are partial accrual bonds, which receive part accrual of interest and part cash interest.

The impact of Z bonds is to shorten the average life of the other tranches, while the Z bonds have a very long average life.

Investors who wish to avoid reinvestment risk will find Z bonds attractive, since they receive no intermediate cash flows.

3.2.4 Planned Amortisation Class tranches

A planned amortisation class (PAC) tranche is one that is expected to amortise at a rate fixed in advance. If the actual prepayment speed lies within a particular range, the amortisation rate will be achieved. However, if the prepayment speed is significantly different from that expected, the amortisation rate may be faster or slower than expected. Hence, it is not guaranteed.

If the actual prepayment speed is uncertain but one tranche is given a planned amortisation rate within a particular range of prepayment speeds, the amortisation of another tranche must become more uncertain as a result. This is known as the **companion bond**. Other names for it are 'non-PAC' or 'support'.

3.2.5 Targeted Amortisation Class (TAC)

A targeted amortisation class (TAC) is similar to a PAC, except that its targeted amortisation schedule will only be met at one prepayment speed. If the actual prepayment speed is higher than expected, then the TAC will be repaid earlier than targeted. If the actual prepayment speed is lower than expected, the TAC will be repaid later than targeted.

The certainty of cash flows for a TAC is less than for a PAC and it has a more volatile average life. As a result, yields on TACs will exceed yields on PACs.

The cash flow certainty of a TAC depends to some extent on the other tranches within the CMO pool. If there are also PAC tranches in issue, it is effectively subordinated to these and therefore has less cash flow certainty. If there are only companion bonds, there is more protection against prepayments.

3.2.6 Companion bonds

As noted above, whenever one tranche is given priority in some way, another tranche has to absorb extra risk. It is the companion bond that takes on the extra risk.

Due to their high average life volatility and uncertain cash flows, companion bonds offer a high spread over Treasury bonds.

If interest rates increase substantially, the level of prepayments will fall, meaning that the companion bond's average life will increase. Since interest rates have risen, this will give large falls in price for the companion bond as it is locked into lower returns for a longer period of time.

If interest rates fall, prepayment rates will increase, meaning that the companion bond will be repaid more quickly and its average life will fall. Again, the companion will suffer because of early repayment and the need to reinvest at the lower rates of interest. The companion bond will do best when interest rates are fairly stable and prepayments do not vary significantly from the expected rate. In this case, their higher yield will give a superior return to other tranches.

3.2.7 Floaters

Even though the mortgage collateral for a CMO may be fixed rate, it is still possible to construct floating rate tranches. However, it is necessary to have a cap on the floating rate to ensure that there is sufficient cash to pay the floating rate interest.

If market rates of interest increase substantially, this will activate the rate cap. It will also reduce prepayments. This will cause the value of the floating tranche to fall, since its average life will increase and the interest rate being paid has effectively been fixed at the cap.

If interest rates do not fluctuate beyond the cap, the price of the floating tranche will not be affected by the prepayment speed, but will remain around par.

If prepayments are high, then even the existence of the rate cap does not affect the price of the floating tranche significantly, since the principal value declines rapidly due to the prepayments.

3.2.8 Super floaters

A super floater has interest rate payments that are leveraged compared to changes in the underlying index rate. For example, the coupon rate might be set at 2 × LIBOR – 10%. If LIBOR increases, the coupon will increase substantially. If LIBOR falls, the coupon will decrease dramatically.

This structure would appeal to an investor who believes interest rates are going to rise.

3.2.9 Inverse floaters

Inverse floaters are also known as reverse floaters. The coupon paid moves in the opposite direction to the index rate and often has a leverage factor. These bonds will do better when interest rates fall.

3.2.10 Residuals

There may be a final class of bond referred to as the residual. This is designed to receive any payments not attributable to another class. These are also called excess bonds. The flows that they receive will be due to over-collateralisation of the mortgage pool, interest payments on the mortgages exceeding interest payments on the CMO tranches and reinvestment income where mortgage interest is paid monthly but payments to CMO tranches are made quarterly or semi-annually.

When interest rates rise, prepayments will decrease and interest payments received from the mortgages are reinvested at higher interest rates. As a result, the value of the residual class will increase. When interest rates fall, the opposite is true.

3.3 Stripped mortgage-backed securities

3.3.1 Principal-Only (PO) securities

Principal-only securities do not receive any payments of interest from the mortgage collateral. Instead, they only receive payments of principal. Like all zero-coupon securities, they are priced at a discount to par. As a result, their final yield is heavily dependent on the prepayment speed. The faster prepayments are made, the greater the yield on the PO securities.

Declining mortgage interest rates will cause the price of the PO to rise for two reasons. Firstly, the discount rate used to value the PO will be lower, increasing price. Secondly, the cash flow is now expected to be received more quickly, increasing price.

Conversely, increasing mortgage rates will reduce the price of the PO significantly.

15: HYBRID SECURITIES

3.3.2 Super PO securities

Super POs are a companion bond to POs. The impact of having a companion bond is to make the cash flow predictability of the PO greater. If the prepayment speed is greater than expected, it will not be used to repay the PO, but the super PO. As a result, the super PO gains even more when interest rates fall and prepayment rates increase.

3.3.3 Interest-Only (IO) securities

Interest-only securities receive only the interest payments from the mortgage collateral and are not entitled to any principal payments. They have a notional principal amount on which interest payments are calculated. As the actual principal is repaid to the PO securities, the notional principal on the IO securities declines, meaning that the interest payments decline. Once all the principal is repaid, the IO securities receive no further interest.

If prepayment speeds are very high, IO securities will suffer because the amount of interest received will be less than expected. In extreme circumstances, it is possible that they could receive back less interest than the original sum paid to buy the IO.

As a result, when interest rates fall and prepayment speeds rise, the price of the IO will fall. When prepayment rates fall (possibly due to interest rate rises), the price of IO securities will rise, reflecting the greater interest payments that they will receive. This is in contrast to PO securities.

The price of an IO will always be at a deep discount to its notional principal value.

4 ASSET-BACKED SECURITIES

Asset-backed securities are similar to mortgage-backed securities above. Essentially, a pool of assets, such as automobile loans or credit card receivables, are pooled together. The cash flow from these assets is then used to service securities issued, which participate in the pool.

5 OPTION-ADJUSTED SPREAD

5.1 Basic features of option-adjusted spread

5.1.1 Option-adjusted spread and static spread

The option-adjusted spread is the spread over the Treasury spot rates which, when used in a valuation model, sets the theoretical price of the bond equal to its market price. The difference from the static spread is that it is **option adjusted**.

The static spread assumes that the cash flows of the bond are not affected by changes in interest rates. Whereas the option-adjusted spread recognises that they may be.

5.1.2 OAS with a binomial interest rate tree

In the context of the binomial model considered above for callable bonds, OAS is the constant spread over the interest rates given in the binomial tree, which equates the present value of the future cash flows along each interest rate path with the price of the bond.

15: HYBRID SECURITIES

5.1.3 Impact of interest rate volatility on OAS

OAS will be affected by interest rate volatility. The higher the interest rate volatility, the lower the OAS will be. This is because greater interest rate volatility implies greater likelihood of the call option being exercised, worsening the expected cash flow to the investor and reducing the return on the bond.

5.1.4 Expressing option value as a yield spread

The value of the embedded option in a callable bond was previously expressed in dollars. It can also be expressed as a number of basis points, as follows.

Formula to learn

> Option cost = Static spread – OAS

The static spread is calculated on the basis of the cash flows for the bond assuming zero interest rate volatility. It is done in the usual way, taking the forward rates implied by the current yield curve as the basis for the spot rates to be used in the discounting process.

The OAS is calculated on the basis of an assumed level of interest rate volatility. The greater the volatility of interest rates, the lower the OAS will become, as noted above. As a result of this, the OAS will be less than the static spread. The lower the OAS, the higher the cost of the option to the investor in the bond. This ties in with what we already know, i.e. the greater the volatility of interest rates, the higher the cost (or value) of the option.

For a given level of interest rate volatility, the option cost should be roughly constant, regardless of the value of the static spread. As a result, once the option cost has been estimated, OAS is often subsequently calculated by taking the current static spread and deducting from this the option cost already calculated. Static spread is quicker and easier to calculate than OAS. This approach therefore avoids the expense and time of recalculating OAS on an ongoing basis.

5.2 Uses of Option-Adjusted Spread

5.2.1 Evaluating richness or cheapness

The OAS is a spread over a benchmark set of interest rates. If the benchmark rates are based on Treasury securities, then the spread for a non-Treasury bond will reflect the credit and other risks associated with the particular issuer. In addition, it may reflect an element of richness (overvaluation) or cheapness (undervaluation) in the bond relative to Treasury securities.

If the benchmark interest rates have been derived from the spot rate curve of the issuer of the bond being evaluated, then credit risk will not be a reason for the OAS. This is because the spot rates used already reflect the issuer's credit risk. In this case, the OAS will reflect the richness or cheapness of the bond.

If the OAS is excessively high, it indicates that the bond is cheap. If the OAS is excessively low, it indicates that the bond is overvalued.

Since the binomial tree could have been constructed using different benchmarks, it is important to know how it was constructed prior to evaluating any OAS for a particular bond.

5.2.2 Using OAS to derive a theoretical value

Given a specified OAS for a security, it is possible to identify the theoretical value for that security by calculating the present value of the future cash flows based on the benchmark rate plus the OAS.

5.3 Benefits and problems of OAS

5.3.1 Benefits of OAS

The OAS approach has several theoretical benefits.

- It looks at securities and their cash flows over a number of interest rate paths. If these paths are a good representation of the possible future outcomes for interest rates, then the OAS represents a summary of virtually all likely outcomes.

- The interest rate paths selected are based on the current yield curve, avoiding biases that might occur in more judgmental methods of analysing interest rate volatility, such as simple scenario analysis.

- The approach looks at the likelihood of the option to repay being exercised along each path, reflecting the variability in cash flow due to the embedded option.

- It is possible to incorporate various levels of complexity into the modelling process. For example, interest rate volatility can be kept constant through time or changed.

5.3.2 Problems and caveats with OAS

OAS does not represent a guaranteed yield

The OAS does not represent a guaranteed yield spread over Treasury securities. It is simply the spread calculated based on an average of a number of different interest rate paths. It is not a given outcome, but a summary measure of a number of different outcomes.

If interest rates follow a path that adversely affects the value of the bond, then the actual yield achieved could be well below the predicted yield based on OAS. If interest rates fall dramatically, the actual path could produce a very low present value for the security compared to the average price based on all the interest rate paths.

This means that any analysis based on OAS should give details of the distribution of interest rate paths, to enable an investor to assess potential downside risk. However, it is often the case that these details are not provided.

Analysing OAS correctly is difficult

It is difficult to interpret OAS to make investment decisions. OAS is typically used to determine the impact of the optionality of the cash flows in the security on its yield. The difference between the static spread on the security and its OAS is referred to as the option value or option cost.

It is difficult to compare OAS across securities, since different securities will have different credit risk and different durations. With regard to the second point, if there is a term structure to OAS, then such different securities would have different OAS.

It may be that the bond with the highest OAS is not the bond that is most underpriced.

6 WARRANTS

6.1 Definition

A company warrant is a tradable security that gives the holder the right to buy shares from the company that issued the warrant at a specified price on or before a specified date.

It can be seen that a warrant is essentially the same as a call option, giving the right to buy a share. The major difference is that warrants are issued by and exercisable on the company, which will issue new shares on exercise. Traded and traditional options are issued by investors and relate to shares already in issue. They are not exercised on the company, which will not issue any new shares.

A covered warrant is issued by a third party (typically an investment bank) and no new shares in the underlying company will be issued. Covered warrants may be puts or calls, and may have any asset type or index as the underlying, not just equities.

Warrants have all the characteristics of options, such as volatility, risk and valuation factors.

6.2 Why Issue warrants?

The benefits to a company of issuing warrants include the following.

- Raising immediate cash without the need to finance dividend payments to new shares. The problem is that when the warrants are exercised, the dividend payments in total may increase dramatically.

- Increasing the attraction of a debt issue. Many warrants are attached to a debt issue, giving debt investors the added attraction of an 'equity kicker'. This will translate into lower required yields on the debt, meaning that the initial financial burden on the company is lower. After the debt is issued, the warrants are usually detached from the debt and traded separately in the market place.

- Capitalising on an overvalued share price. If the company believes that its share price will fall, then any warrants issued are unlikely to be exercised. This means that the company will receive the money on issue of the warrants, but anticipates that it will not have to issue any new shares.

6.3 The attractions of warrants for investors

An investor will find warrants attractive for various reasons.

- A geared investment in a company's shares, being a cheaper alternative to buying the share itself, in much in the same way as for a call option.

- A way of securing an income yield while keeping open the possibility of high equity performance, through buying debt plus warrants from the company. This is similar to the principle of buying a convertible debt issue.

Additional factors to consider include

- The marketability of the warrant.

- The period to expiry, exercise price and current share price (i.e. basic valuation factors).

- The likelihood that the company's share price will perform adequately.

- The gearing risk implicit in the warrant.

- The risk of a takeover. If a company is taken over, it is often the case that the exercise date of the warrants will be accelerated to the takeover date. This will destroy any time value in the warrant, meaning that an investor could suffer a serious loss. If the warrant is out-of-the-money, having just been issued for example, then it may become worthless.

A warrant holder will not be affected by bonus issues or rights issues because the terms of the warrant will adjust in the same way as the terms of options contracts, outlined above.

15: HYBRID SECURITIES

Chapter Roundup

- Convertible value = Straight bond value + Call option value
- Callable bond value = Straight bond value − Call option value
- Callable bond value = Straight bond value + Put option value
- In this context
    - A convertible bond call option will be exercised by the investor if the bond value is less than the intrinsic value of the conversion option.
    - A callable bond will be exercised by the issuer if the call exercise price is less than the bond price at that point.
    - A putable bond will be exercised by the investor if the put option exercise price is greater than the bond price at that point.

Test Your Knowledge

Check your knowledge of the Chapter here, without referring back to the text.

1 A convertible bond is in issue paying a 4% coupon, maturing in 4 years and able to be converted at any coupon payment date after the coupon has been paid. The conversion ratio is 20, the current share price is £4.00 and the volatility of the shares is 8%. If the yield curve is flat at 6% calculate the value of the convertible using discrete discounting throughout

2 A 3 year putable bond is in issue giving the holder the right to sell the bond back to the company at £99.00 following the payment of the second annual coupon. The coupon on the bond is 4%, the current interest rate is 5% (continuously compounded) and interest rate volatility is 8%. Calculate the value of the bond.

15: HYBRID SECURITIES

TEST YOUR KNOWLEDGE: ANSWERS

1. *Bond value each year*

		£
Time 4	– Ex div value	100.00
	– Coupon	4.00
	– Cum div value	104.00
		$\times \dfrac{1}{1.06}$
Time 3	– Ex div value	98.11
	– Coupon	4.00
	– Cum div value	102.11
		$\times \dfrac{1}{1.06}$
Time 2	– Ex div value	96.33
	– Coupon	4.00
	– Cum div value	100.33
		$\times \dfrac{1}{1.06}$
Time 1	– Ex div value	94.65
	– Coupon	4.00
	– Cum div value	98.65
		$\times \dfrac{1}{1.06}$
Current value		£93.07

Straight bond price = £93.07

Asset price each year

Current share value = 20 × £4 = £80

From the volatility figure we have

- Expected percentage up-move

$$u = e^{\sigma\sqrt{t}} = e^{0.08} = 1.083287$$

$$d = \dfrac{1}{u} = 0.923116$$

- Probability of an upmove

$$p = \dfrac{e^{rt} - d}{u - d} = 0.866077$$

So we can construct the following asset price matrix

Time 0	Time 1	Time 2	Time 3	Time 4
				110.17
			101.70	
		93.88		93.88
	86.66		86.66	
80.00		80.00		80.00
	75.85		75.85	
		68.17		68.17
			62.93	
				58.09

Option Intrinsic Value

Comparing these asset prices to the ex-div bond values for the relevant times as calculated above gives us the following option intrinsic value matrix

Time 0	Time 1	Time 2	Time 3	Time 4
				10.17
			3.59(C_a)	
		0.00(C_b)		0.00
	0.00(C_c)		0.00	
0.00(C_d)		0.00		0.00
	0.00		0.00	
		0.00		0.00
			0.00	
				0.00

And so using discrete discounting

$$C_a = \frac{0.866077 \times 10.17 + 0.133023 \times 0.00}{1.06} = 8.309 > 3.59 \text{ so use } 8.309 \text{ to evaluate } C_b$$

$$C_b = \frac{0.866077 \times 8.309 + 0.133023 \times 0.00}{1.06} = 6.789 > 0.00 \text{ so use } 6.789 \text{ to evaluate } C_c$$

$$C_c = \frac{0.866077 \times 6.789 + 0.133023 \times 0.00}{1.06} = 5.547 > 0.00 \text{ so use } 5.547 \text{ to evaluate } C_d$$

$$C_d = \frac{0.866077 \times 5.547 + 0.133023 \times 0.00}{1.06} = 4.53$$

Combining

Convertible value = Straight bond value + Call option value

Convertible value = 93.07 + 4.53 = £97.60

2. Current interest rate = 5% (continuously compounded)

Interest rate volatility = 8%

Expected percentage upmove $u = e^{\sigma\sqrt{t}} = e^{0.08} = 1.083287$

Expected percentage downmove $d = \frac{1}{u} = 0.923116$

15: HYBRID SECURITIES

Interest rate matrix

Year 1	Year 2	Year 3
		5.8676%
	5.4164%	
5%		5.0000%
	4.6156%	
		4.2607%

Bond binomial tree

Probability of an upmove

$$p = \frac{e^{rt} - d}{u - d} = \frac{e^{0.05} - 0.923116}{1.083287 - 0.923116} = 0.800113$$

$1 - p = 1 - 0.800113 = 0.199887$

Year 3	UU	UD	DD
Year end – Ex-div value	100.0000	100.0000	100.0000
– Coupon	4.0000	4.0000	4.0000
– Cum div value	104.0000	104.0000	104.0000
	$\times e^{-0.058676}$	$\times e^{-0.05}$	$\times e^{-0.042607}$
Start of year value	98.0733	98.9279	99.6619

Year 2		$[p \times 98.0733 + (1-p) \times 98.9272]$	$[p \times 98.9279 + (1-p) \times 99.6619]$
Year end – Ex-div value		**98.2441** (Exercise)	99.0746
– Coupon		4.0000	4.0000
– Cum div value		102.2441	102.0746
		$\times e^{-0.054164}$	$\times e^{-0.046156}$
Start of year value		96.8535	98.4252

Year 1		$[p \times 96.8535 + (1-p) \times 98.4252]$
Year end – Ex-div value		97.1676
– Coupon		4.0000
– Cum div value		101.1676
		$\times e^{-0.05}$
Straight bond value		96.2336

Option binomial tree

	U	D
Year 2 – End of year	0.7559	0.0000
	$\times e^{-0.058676}$	$\times e^{-0.046156}$
– Start of year	0.7160	0.0000

Year 1 – End of year	$[p \times 0.7160 + (1-p) \times 0.0000]$
	0.5729
	$\times e^{-0.05}$
Put option value	0.5450

Combining

Putable bond value = Straight bond value + Put option value
Putable bond value = 96.2386 + 0.5450 = £96.7786

16 Risk Management

INTRODUCTION

In this section we consider the types of risks that financial institutions and commercial entities may be exposed to. One of the primary purposes of derivatives is to control or hedge financial risk (exposure to interest rates, currencies etc.) However trying to achieve this with derivatives frequently opens the business up to operational risk – the risk that their use was incorrect or not as the business intended.

We need to be fully aware of the types of risk a company/individual may be exposed to and how this exposure maybe managed.

CHAPTER CONTENTS

		Page
1	Introduction	500
2	Market Risk	501
3	Credit Risk	506
4	Liquidity Risk	507
5	Operational Risks	508
6	Controlling Risk – Limits	509
7	Value At Risk	512
	Chapter Roundup	524
	Test Your Knowledge	525

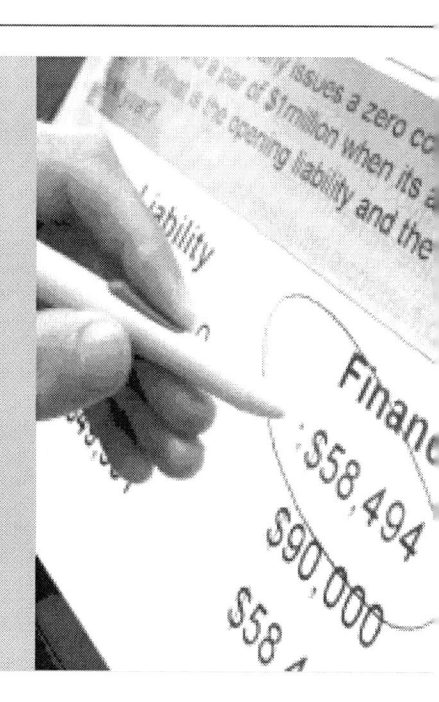

16: RISK MANAGEMENT

CHAPTER LEARNING OBJECTIVES

The syllabus areas covered by this section are

Derivatives risk management

- Types of risk
    - Market Risk
    - Credit Risk
    - Liquidity Risk
    - Operational Risk
- Derivatives Portfolios
    - Value at Risk Approaches
    - Average and Worse Case Risk Analysis
    - Regulatory Capital
    - Gamma and Vega Mapping
    - Correlation Risks

Exam tip | Other than VAR, questions in this area are discussions, perhaps based on a specific scenario

1 INTRODUCTION

Banks take financial risks in order to earn a return. The risks, however, must be kept under control. This calls for a system of setting limits to risk and measuring/monitoring positions continually to ensure that the limits are not exceeded.

This chapter is concerned with different types of financial risk and methods used to control these risks. It is essential to remember, however, that unless certain basic operational controls are in place, systems for monitoring and controlling financial risk will not work properly. Several banking 'scandals' in recent years illustrate this.

In particular, basic operational controls should ensure that

- Individuals responsible for dealing do not have responsibility for confirmations.
- Individuals responsible for dealing do not have responsibility for settlements.

In other words, the roles of the front and back office should be strictly segregated (although a good working relationship between dealers and confirmations/settlement staff will promote operational efficiency).

1.1 Types of risk

Risk can, therefore be divided into two broad categories

- Financial risk
- Operational risk

And we need to examine each one of these

Financial risk itself can be classified in a variety of different ways, and by a variety of different names. Financial risk arises when a transaction or a position will result in a loss if there is an adverse change in financial conditions or circumstances.

Commonly used categories of financial risk include the following.

- *Market risk* or price risk, which can be sub-divided into other, more specific, types of risk, such as currency risk and interest rate risk.
- *Credit risk*, which includes the sub-categories of counterparty risk and delivery risk or settlement risk.
- *Liquidity risk*, i.e. the risk of having insufficient cash to meet payment obligations.

The types of risk shown in the diagram below might give you some idea of how risks can be categorised. The diagram is for illustration only – it does not give a comprehensive analysis of risk types.

1.1.1 Types of financial risk

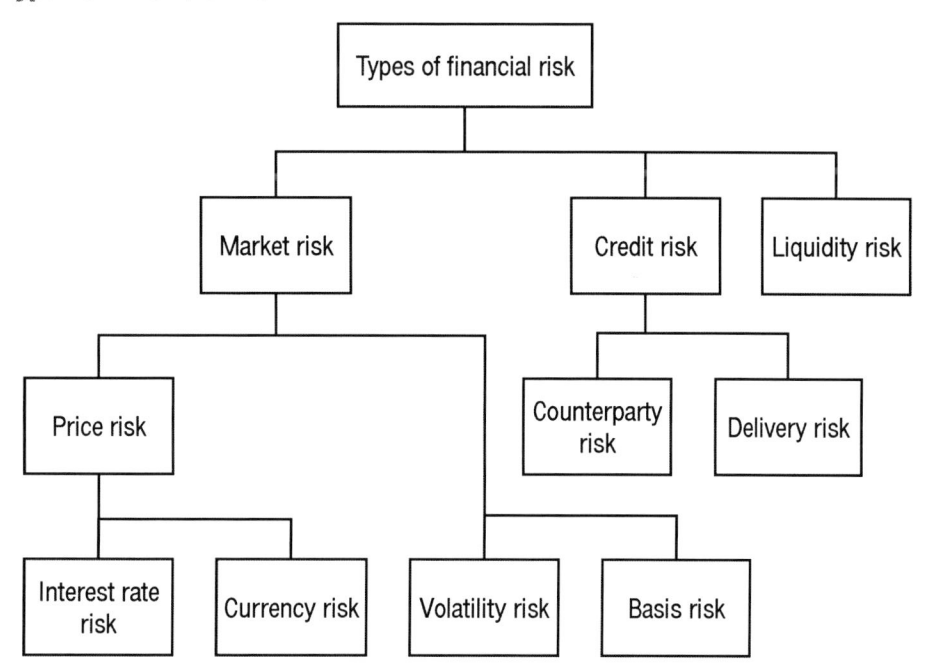

```
                    ┌─────────────────────┐
                    │ Types of financial  │
                    │        risk         │
                    └──────────┬──────────┘
           ┌───────────────────┼───────────────────┐
     ┌─────┴─────┐       ┌─────┴─────┐       ┌─────┴─────┐
     │  Market   │       │  Credit   │       │ Liquidity │
     │   risk    │       │   risk    │       │   risk    │
     └─────┬─────┘       └─────┬─────┘       └───────────┘
           │                   │
     ┌─────┴─────┐       ┌─────┴─────┐
     │   Price   │       │Counterparty│    ┌──────────┐
     │   risk    │       │   risk    │     │ Delivery │
     └─────┬─────┘       └───────────┘     │   risk   │
           │                               └──────────┘
  ┌────────┼────────┬──────────┐
┌─┴──┐ ┌───┴───┐ ┌──┴───┐ ┌────┴───┐
│Int.│ │Currency│ │Volat.│ │ Basis  │
│rate│ │  risk  │ │ risk │ │  risk  │
│risk│ └────────┘ └──────┘ └────────┘
└────┘
```

Some types of risk are 'one way', meaning that the situation might turn out badly, and there will be a loss, but the situation cannot turn out better than 'normal', for example credit risk. This is the risk of non-payment of a debt by a customer, such as the risk of failure by a borrower to repay a loan at maturity. The risk is 'one way', since the customer is expected to pay what he owes on time and in full. The customer will not pay more than what he owes. The risk, however, is that he will not pay, so that a loss will be incurred.

Other risks are 'two way', in the sense that the financial situation could change for the better as well as for the worse, for example currency risk. If a dealer buys € in exchange for dollars, the €/$ rate might move substantially in the dealer's favour (€ strengthens against $), but it might move adversely (€ weakens). A profit or loss will be incurred when the dealer's position is marked-to-market, according to how the rate has moved.

2 MARKET RISK

Market risk is the risk of losses arising on positions taken in the market, due to adverse changes in market conditions, i.e. it is the risk of a change in the prices of items traded. The scale of risk depends on the size of the position, long or short, and the volatility of the item's price, as well as on the liquidity of the market in which the position can be closed.

Market risk can be sub-divided into the following categories.

- Price risk.
- Volatility risk.
- Basis risk.

A significant aspect of market risk is price risk, i.e. the risk that market prices of certain items will move adversely.

For example, a bank that trades in equities is exposed to the risk of losses on its holdings of equities, which would arise if prices fell.

Other types of price risk include

- Currency risk (also called exchange rate risk and foreign exchange risk). This is the risk of losses from an adverse movement in an exchange rate.
- Interest risk (also called interest rate risk). This is the risk of losses from an adverse movement in an interest rate.

Volatility risk is the risk arising from changes in the volatility of price movements in an item, e.g. volatility in interest rates, exchange rates or equity prices. For example, volatility risk is high for a currency whose exchange value is subject to frequent and fairly large movements. This type of risk is of particular significance to options traders.

Basis risk arises from exposure to losses caused by a mismatch in the maturities of assets and liabilities. Such losses would arise, for example, if there were a shift or change in the shape of the yield curve.

2.1 Currency risk

Currency risk arises whenever an organisation has an excess of assets/income over liabilities/expenditures, or an excess of liabilities/expenditures over assets/income, in a currency that is not its domestic currency.

Non-bank corporates can analyse their exposures to currency risk within three broad categories.

- Transaction exposures.
- Translation exposures.
- Economic exposures.

2.1.1 Transaction exposures

Transaction exposures relate to current transactions that will result in a currency cash flow in the future. They are largely connected with buying and selling goods or services between countries, but transaction exposures can also arise from financing transactions (interest and capital payments) and intra-group dividends from a foreign subsidiary to another group company. Transaction exposures can affect the cash flows as well as profits of corporates, and can have fairly immediate consequences for both.

Exposure to transaction risk arises when there is a specific arrangement to make payment in a foreign currency or receive a payment in a foreign currency at some future time. The exposure lasts from the time the transaction is arranged (e.g. a sales contract is signed) until the payment is made or received. If exchange rates move adversely before the payment is made or received (unless the exposure is hedged), the company will have to do one of the following.

- Pay more in its own currency to make a foreign currency payment.
- Receive less in its own currency from a foreign currency receipt.

Therefore, cash inflows will be lower, or outflows higher, than expected.

2.1.2 Translation exposures

Translation exposure is an oddity of financial accounting. It differs from transaction exposure in that it does not relate to cash flows and the payments or receipts of money. It is a risk of losses, or lower profits, arising from the preparation of the consolidated financial accounts of a company with foreign subsidiaries.

When a multinational prepares its consolidated accounts, the assets, liabilities and profits of foreign subsidiaries are translated from their local currency into the reporting currency of the group. For example, UK-based multinationals must translate everything into sterling in order to present their accounts (although accounts in € are also permitted). Such companies face a gain or loss on translation of the financial results of their non-UK subsidiaries, because exchange rates alter between the start and the end of the financial year. Translation exposures affect both of the following.

- The consolidated balance sheet of the group.
- The consolidated profit and loss account of the group.

A consolidated balance sheet for a group of companies shows the combined value of the assets and liabilities of all the companies in the group, in the group's reporting currency. The assets and liabilities of each foreign subsidiary in the group must therefore be translated into the reporting currency.

The net investment in a foreign subsidiary is the balance sheet value of what the parent company owns, and is the difference between the subsidiary's total assets and its external liabilities. (External liabilities are amounts owed by the subsidiary, excluding debts to the parent company and other companies in the group.) The value of the net investment, translated into the parent company's domestic currency, will rise or fall with movements in the exchange rate.

The profits of a foreign subsidiary are consolidated into the group financial accounts by translating them at an appropriate rate (or rates) of exchange into the reporting currency of the parent company. Commonly, the rate used is either the average rate for the year or the year-end rate.

The profits of a subsidiary, translated into the parent company's currency, could decline from one year to the next because of a fall in the value of the subsidiary's domestic currency, even though its reported profits in that currency are stable or have even increased year-on-year.

2.1.3 Economic exposures

In the context of currency risk, economic exposure refers to the implications of exchange rate movements for any future contracts and transactions that might occur in a company's business.

Economic exposures are longer term and are potentially the most damaging manifestation of currency risk. They can have profound implications for the strategy of global companies.

There are two main consequences of economic exposures.

- Exchange rates have an impact on the revenues or costs of future production. If exchange rates move adversely, a company will suffer a reduction in profits due to lower income or higher costs (imported materials) from future transactions. These economic exposures are **direct**.

- If exchange rates move adversely, a company will also forfeit a degree of price competitiveness to foreign producers. These economic exposures are **indirect**.

Direct economic exposures are currency exposures that will arise in the future from a company's trading transactions. For example, suppose that a Paris-based jewellery maker has an ongoing need for gold, a commodity denominated in US dollars. A strengthening of the dollar will raise the price of gold in euros, affecting the French jeweller's prices, or profit margins, on future output. So long as the jeweller continues to produce in France and incur expenditures in euros, direct economic exposures will always exist.

Direct economic exposures will eventually become transaction exposures, when future production and sales become 'current' transactions, and the amount of an exposure is known exactly as a contracted amount to be received or paid.

Indirect economic exposures, sometimes called 'strategic exposures', refer to the implications for cost and price-competitiveness of exchange rate changes. A significant change in the €/£ rate, for example, will affect the relative competitiveness of Continental and UK producers.

Changes in exchange rates affect the relative costs of producers in different countries. If a UK producer, for example, paying its costs in sterling competes in world markets with a German producer, whose expenses are in euros, their comparative costs of production will be affected by changes in the €/£ exchange rate. Any such changes will affect the ability of either the UK or the German producer (depending on which way the exchange rate moves) to compete effectively.

Currency risk: Possible consequences

- Transaction exposure
    - Risk of lower cash income or higher cash spending.
    - Risk of lower profits and lower earnings per share.
- Translation exposure
    - **Group balance sheet risks**

        Reduction in the reported value of overseas assets or increase in the cost of foreign currency liabilities, leading to a lower net worth.
    - **Group profit and loss account risks**

        Risk of lower reported profits and lower earnings per share.
- Economic exposure
    - Risk of erosion of competitive advantage.
    - Risk of lower market share.
    - Risk to longer term profitability.

2.1.4 Hedging currency exposures

Hedging transaction exposures

Avoiding risks from transaction exposures will involve measures that eliminate the uncertainty about the actual rate of exchange, between the time the transaction is made and the time when the currency is bought or sold. These measures include

- Refusing to buy or sell in foreign currency. This avoids all need for converting one currency into another.
- Matching income and expenditure in the same currency. This avoids currency risk, since income in the currency is used to pay for the expenditures, and there is no requirement to convert foreign income into domestic currency.

For example, a Japanese company that earns $500,000 and spends $500,000 can use the income to make the payment, without having to convert dollars into yen or yen into dollars. Matching income and expenditures in the same currencies is called **structural hedging**. It can only be done by companies with income and expenditure streams in the same currency. Furthermore, it is often difficult to match income and expenditure exactly.

- Preventing variations in the future exchange rate by fixing now the rate for future transactions, for example using outright forward exchange contracts.

- Preventing adverse variations in the future exchange rate, without avoiding exposures to **favourable** variations that would result in currency gains. This is achievable with currency options.

In practice, many companies

- Hedge all their net exposures from trading transactions, for which firm sales or purchased orders have been made.
- Take hedging measures for a proportion (say 50%-75%) of export sales that are expected to happen over the next 6 to 12 months or so, but have not yet become firm orders.

Hedging translation exposures

Translation exposures are unavoidable for companies with foreign subsidiaries. The size of the exposure can be controlled by choosing to finance expansion, where possible, with loans in the domestic currency of the subsidiary, i.e. by matching the currency of external liabilities with the currency of the subsidiary's assets.

2.2 Interest rate risk

Interest rate risk has been defined as the risk to profits from adverse changes in interest rates, adding to interest costs or reducing investment and lending income.

Interest rates can change in various ways.

- The general level of interest rates for all maturities and instruments rises and falls over time.
- Interest rates on some financial instruments could change in relation to interest rates on other financial instruments. For example, the rate on a three-month bank deposit could rise by a quarter of a percent when the rate on a three-month corporate loan note might rise, say, by just 3/16 of a percent.

There could be a change in the **yield curve** (term structure of interest rates) so that short-term interest rates change in relation to long-term interest rates. For example, short-term rates could fall while long-term interest rates rise. Alternatively, short-term rates could rise by, say, 2% per annum and long-term rates by just 1%.

There are three aspects of risk arising from such rate changes.

- The risk of higher interest charges or lower investment income than anticipated, because of a movement up or down in the general level of interest rates.
- The risk that a borrowing decision will not achieve the lowest possible interest costs because of the way that interest rates move after the decision has been made.
- The risk that a lending/investment decision might be made that in retrospect will not have yielded the greatest income, because of the way in which interest rates have moved since the decision was taken.

Judgement is important in deciding **how, when** and for **how long** to borrow or invest.

2.2.1 Changes in the general level of interest rates

Companies that borrow, lend or invest are exposed to any adverse movements in the general level of interest rates. A rise in interest rates would mean higher charges for variable rate borrowers. Lower interest rates would reduce the income from variable rate investments. Since most medium-sized and smaller companies can only borrow at a variable rate of interest, these borrowers will be exposed to the risk of higher interest rates. Their interest rate exposure is the full amount of their borrowed funds.

A distinction can be made between the risk from higher interest rates for borrowers and the broader risks (including interest rate risk) that arise from high financial gearing in a company's capital structure.

2.2.2 Interest rate risk and credit standing

A company borrowing from a bank is at risk not only to higher interest rates, but also to a change in the bank's perception of the company as a credit risk.

When interest rates generally are falling, companies are often surprised and annoyed that interest rates on their bank loans do not fall by the same amount. It is suggested that the banks keep the benefits of lower market rates to themselves instead of passing them on to customers. However, a period of falling interest rates is associated with the need to stimulate a weak economy. At such times, the creditworthiness of corporate customers will be reassessed, and some will be charged interest on their loans at a higher margin above the base rates than before. Thus, a company might have paid 4% over base when the base rate was 12%, but 6% over base when the rate fell to 10%, with the result that the interest on its loan would have stayed the same at 16%, despite the general fall in market rates.

2.2.3 Other types of interest rate exposure

In addition to the risk from a change in the general level of interest rates, three other types of interest rate exposure can be identified.

Exposure	Nature of the Risk
Fixed rate or floating rate interest	There is a risk of higher interest charges by borrowing on a fixed basis when a floating rate basis would have been cheaper; or borrowing on a floating rate basis when a fixed rate would have been cheaper.
Term of funding: the yield curve	There is a risk that a change in the yield curve will make it more expensive to have borrowed short term rather than longer term; or long term rather than shorter term.
Currency of funding	There is a risk that borrowing in one currency will be more expensive than borrowing in a different currency. Interest rate risk and foreign currency risk are both involved, since movements in the exchange rate during the term of the loan will add to or reduce the overall cost of borrowing in that currency, by increasing the value of the loan in the borrower's domestic currency.

3 CREDIT RISK

Lending always carries some risk that the borrower will be unable to repay either in full or on time. The lending bank must assess the probability of this event, and charge higher interest rates in proportion to the likelihood of default. Compensation for this credit risk may also be charged in the form of fees and commissions so that the interest rate appears more competitive. This method has the additional advantage that the fees are payable at the beginning of the loan period.

Credit risk is also taken when a bank guarantees performance by a customer. If called upon to make payment under this guarantee, the bank then faces the risks that the funds will not be recovered from the customer.

3.1 Counterparty risk

Counterparty risk, a form of credit risk, is the risk that the counterparty to a transaction will fail to carry out his side of the agreement.

In the case of a loan, for example, counterparty risk arises from the possibility that the borrower will fail to pay the interest or repay the loan principal in full and on time.

In the case of an FX deal, counterparty risk arises from the possibility that the counterparty to the deal will fail to deliver the expected amount of currency.

3.2 Delivery risk (Settlement risk)

Delivery (or settlement) risk is the risk that a deal will not be completed, forcing the bank to make a substitute transaction, perhaps at a higher cost. A greater loss will be incurred if the bank settles its part of the bargain, but does not receive the countervalue. This occurs because it is often not possible to complete both sides of the deal simultaneously.

Delivery risk arises from the possibility that the counterparty to a transaction will fail to deliver currency or funds on the value/settlement date for a transaction, or that delivery fails to occur for other reasons, e.g. incorrect settlement instructions might have been given.

For example, if a bank agrees a spot transaction to buy dollars in exchange for euros, delivery risk arises from the possibility that the counterparty will fail to deliver the dollars at the value/settlement date.

Settlement office staff should check that counterparties do make delivery as agreed. The risk is greater, however, when one counterparty has to settle at an earlier time in the day than the other, due to differences in time zones. For example, with a €/$ foreign exchange transaction, the payer of € will settle in Europe several hours before the payer of dollars settles in the US. There is a risk for the payer of euro that, having paid the euro to settle his side of the deal, the counterparty will fail to settle in the US.

In contrast, the payer of dollars will be able to check that the euro have been delivered before having to settle in the US.

Settlement risk is inherent in every transaction involving an exchange of payments where the exchange cannot be guaranteed. In their report published in 1996, the Committee on Payment and Settlement Systems of the Group of Ten countries defined foreign exchange settlement risk as follows.

> "A bank's actual exposure – the amount at risk – when settling a foreign exchange trade equals the full amount of the currency purchased and lasts from the time a payment instruction for the currency sold can no longer be cancelled unilaterally, until the time the currency purchased is received with finality."

The number of days at risk varies, according to the settlement systems being used in different countries and the bank's own systems for identifying receipts.

4 LIQUIDITY RISK

Banks normally 'borrow short and lend long'. This is the key to the role of banks in the economy, namely to provide long-term funding for commerce and industry, obtaining the funds from short-term investors.

Current account balances form a float of low-cost funds in the banking system. If demand for withdrawals exceeds liquid assets, the bank must raise deposits more expensively in the money markets, or must sell assets in a forced manner.

A bank therefore needs to maintain an adequate level of liquid assets and have standby facilities in place for unforeseen peaks in demand.

Liquidity risk is increased if confidence in the banking system, or in the bank itself, falters. Concentration of liabilities (deposits) makes demand for cash less predictable.

This risk can therefore be reduced by maintaining a diversified deposit base, and good management of the maturity structure of the bank's assets and liabilities. Government deposit insurance serves mainly to bolster confidence in the system and prevent a run on the banks in periods of uncertainty.

5 OPERATIONAL RISKS

Operational risk is the risk that a business may suffer as a result of some internal errors or failures.

5.1 Systems

Banks are heavily dependent on their operating systems. Plans must exist to deal with system failure, and development must be carefully controlled. The implementation of new or revised systems can lead to losses caused by delays, underestimation of required capacity, or failure to address the issues of training, security and user needs.

5.2 Fraud

Banks are obvious targets for fraud and theft, as their product is money. Clearly, the control systems employed must be designed to prevent misappropriation of the bank's assets.

5.3 Breaches of fiduciary or statutory duty

Errors within the bank may lead to compensation claims for loss by customers, or may result in a breach of the law. Security of confidential information must be assured.

5.4 Errors

Undetected errors in general may easily lead to financial loss for the bank. Incorrect calculation of the bank's exposures and failure to make correct settlement of transactions increase the level of market risk. A high level of errors increases the overall cost of the bank's operations. Adherence to well-structured and supervised procedures minimises this risk.

5.5 Legal risk

The application of the law to banking may sometimes be unclear, especially where new products and markets are being developed. The bank must be sure it has obtained the best possible advice, but the risk of legal action cannot be eliminated.

5.6 Environment

Legislation on pollution and waste disposal becomes ever more stringent. A bank can be liable for the cost of repairing environmental damage caused by a borrower. Lending to, or association with, companies with a poor environmental record can lead to financial loss due to the bank's reputation being negatively impacted.

5.7 Cost control

Profits can be eroded just as easily by poor cost control as by mistaken strategic or lending decisions.

5.8 Reputation risk

It is essential to maintain customer confidence in the bank. It must be clearly visible that the bank has adequate capital and that it is profitable. Strategic errors, the perception of management weakness and scandals will all damage the bank's reputation and consequently perceived creditworthiness.

6 CONTROLLING RISK – LIMITS

Banks control their risks in various ways, for example by setting up suitable operating procedures and systems for reporting and monitoring positions. A structure for controlling risk is to set various limits on exposures or transaction volumes.

The structuring of limits depends partly on regulation, e.g. the capital adequacy requirements, and partly on management judgement. A limit structure should be aimed at setting maximum permissible exposures to each type of risk.

The broad outline of a limit structure is set out below.

- Country limits.
- Counterparty limits.
- Nostro limits.
- Maturity limits.
- Instrument limits.
- Regulatory limits.
- Dealer limits/position limits.

6.1 Country limits

The risk to which a bank is exposed when dealing with a counterparty is partly dependent on the political and economic environment of the country where the counterparty is located.

A country limit restricts the amount of transactions awaiting settlement (loans, FX deals, etc.) with counterparties in that country. The size of the limit for each country will depend on the bank's assessment of the country's political and economic stability.

If there is a sudden change in the political regime, or in the policies of an existing regime, or in economic circumstances in the country, a resident bank or corporation in that country might be prevented from meeting its obligations to foreign banks, e.g. because foreign exchange controls are introduced. It is not unknown for the assets of branches of foreign banks to be frozen after a political upheaval.

It is therefore wise for banks to limit their exposure to counterparties in countries where they consider these risks to be especially great. A bank dealing in foreign exchange must consider how much it can afford to lose if all its deals with a particular country cannot be settled.

6.2 Counterparty limits

A bank will set a limit on the total value of outstanding transactions with another organisation/counterparty.

Before agreeing to deal with any counterparty, the bank must examine the financial position and profitability of that organisation.

On the basis of this analysis, the bank will decide what the likelihood is that this counterparty will fail, and how great the maximum exposure should be.

It is important that dealers should understand that the limit is there for good reason. It may be tempting to break a counterparty limit if the counterparty is providing a lot of profitable business for the bank, but if the counterparty's balance sheet is not strong, the business may not be worth the risk.

Each counterparty will have an overall limit for all transaction types. Within that, there should be

- A daily settlement limit, i.e. the amount that a counterparty can have outstanding for settlement on any one day.
- Limits for each type of instrument, e.g. foreign exchange, money market.

16: RISK MANAGEMENT

6.2.1 Monitoring counterparty limits

The client will not be informed of the size of their line, although in practice, they may well find this out.

A counterparty dealing line can be withdrawn or revised at any time. Dealing lines should be reviewed on receipt of any news about the counterparty – including financial statements, press cuttings, etc. – at least once a year. (The most important source of information is the people in the market!)

6.2.2 Maturity limits

A bank is exposed to greater risk when entering into deals for settlement a long time in the future than for spot deals. There is a greater possibility that the deal will fail to settle for some reason. There should therefore be a limit on how far ahead a bank will deal in each type of instrument. For example, a bank might refuse to deal forward more than one to two years in any currency.

This may sometimes mean that a dealer will be unable to meet all the requirements of his customers. However, the bank has made a decision about the degree of risk it is prepared to accept, based partly on its own size and financial position. No individual dealer is in a position to see the whole picture.

6.3 Liquidity limits

The bank must ensure that it has sufficient cash and liquid assets to meet the likely demands at any time. Demand for cash by depositors may vary according to a pattern from day to day. The bank will set a minimum liquidity level that must be maintained, a liquidity limit, and will adjust the amount of liquid assets it holds as appropriate. This may mean that dealers have to dispose of positions in less liquid instruments simply to ensure that the bank has sufficient cash to meet demand (and potential demand).

The required levels of liquidity will be, to some extent, dictated by the regulatory authorities. Liquid assets have a lower risk weighting in the calculation of capital adequacy.

6.4 Regulatory limits

The operations of commercial banks are governed by a regulatory authority, usually the central bank. This authority may place regulatory limits or restrictions on the amount or type of business the bank can carry on, based on its size or management experience. These must be strictly adhered to, otherwise the bank risks losing its licence to trade.

Regulatory authorities will not normally set quantitative limits on the size of foreign exchange deals or positions. However, if the risks attached to these exposures put the bank in a position where it fails to meet the requirements for capital adequacy, then the situation must be immediately rectified or action will be taken against the bank.

6.5 Instrument limits

The amount of risk to which a bank is exposed varies according to the financial instrument. Some instruments are more volatile in price than others, and some are traded in an illiquid market where it can be impossible to unwind positions quickly.

Instrument limits are limits that are set for trading in particular instruments will be part of an overall strategy on the part of the bank to spread and manage risk over the complete range of financial instruments that it trades. This will take into account the potential loss to the bank in the event of, say, a 1% change in interest rates, and the limit will reflect how much the bank could afford to lose if that were to happen.

6.6 Dealer limits/Position limits

Dealers have the capability to commit very large amounts of their bank's capital to transactions with counterparties. There is usually a greater risk for a bank to entrust this authority to young or inexperienced dealers. It is therefore sensible for a bank to restrict the size of trades and positions that each dealer is permitted, until he/she has gained more experience or demonstrated his capability.

The size of such dealer limits will also depend on what type of instrument he is trading. The setting of these limits should be based on a 'worst case scenario', in other words, how much he is prepared to lose.

The size of acceptable loss is related to profit levels and capital. For example, a bank may decide that it is acceptable to lose one average month's profit on a particular instrument for every 1% movement in interest rates, or a 5% change in the exchange rate. If such an event occurs, it is likely that large losses on some instruments or currencies will be offset, at least to some extent, by profits on other desks.

6.6.1 Position limit

Each **dealer** or **book** should have a position limit set. This usually applies to **overnight positions**, although a dealer may be instructed to reduce the size of his position during the day at the manager's discretion (intra-day position limit). It is not always possible to square a position immediately in less liquid markets.

For example, a spot market making desk of three traders might be required to have a square overnight position, i.e. zero limit, but each of the three traders may have a different intraday position limit, depending on the market and his experience and abilities.

The size in which a dealer is allowed to quote may also be restricted, e.g. the **dollar-euro** dealer may be allowed to make prices for up to $10 million, but no larger.

Other position limits for a dealer or a book to control market risk might be

- A stop-loss limit. If a position runs up losses beyond a certain limit, the position must be unwound immediately. The bank will accept the losses incurred, but will not keep the position open and run the risk of further losses.
- A forward-gap limit. A limit might be set on the size of the gap or mismatch between assets/liabilities or inflows/outflows in each currency for each forward value date.

6.7 Limit maintenance and control

It is the responsibility of the support staff to ensure that limits are monitored, kept up to date, and adhered to. There should be a regular process for the review of existing limits. This applies to all the different types of limit.

Any information received by the bank that may be relevant should be channelled to the appropriate department, and a decision must be taken as to whether it warrants a revision of the limit. This will include news of political developments in other countries as well as news about counterparty organisations.

When a counterparty publishes financial results, these should be used to ensure that the limit is still in line with the company's financial position and profitability.

It is essential to have a system that will show when a limit is exceeded. A report that lists any limits that have been broken should be generated daily. Each item must be investigated promptly, and the appropriate action must be taken.

7 Value At Risk

7.1 Overview

Value at risk (VAR) is the amount by which the value of an investment or portfolio may fall over a given period of time at a given level of probability.

For example, if VAR is $1m at a probability level of 5% for one week, this indicates that there is a 5% probability that the value of a portfolio will fall by more than $1m over the next week.

It therefore gives investors an idea of the amount of potential loss and the probability of that loss arising.

7.1.1 Inputs required

The following are needed to calculate VAR.

- A common unit of measurement, such as US dollars.
- A specified time period. This is usually taken to be one day, one week or two weeks. It will depend on the liquidity of the assets concerned and the frequency of their trading.
- A specified probability. This is usually between 1% and 5%.

7.1.2 Approved VAR models

Two types of VAR models have been approved by the Basle agreement, relating to banks and their capital adequacy.

- Standardised models, developed for general public use.
- Internal models, developed by the bank specifically for their own use.

Internal models must meet the following standards to qualify.

- Qualitative standards.
    - Independent validation of the model by a third party.
    - Internal controls over inputs, data and changes to the model.
    - Separation of risk management from business lines.
    - Integration of the model into risk management.
    - Senior management oversight for risk management.
- Quantitative standards.
    - 1% probability level or 99% confidence level.
    - Two-week holding period.
    - The VAR identified should be multiplied by three, allowing for potential weaknesses in the model and its inputs.

These standards are often viewed as being excessively restricted. A two-week holding period is fairly long and will give a higher VAR. Banks will often trade investments over a far shorter period. In addition, combining a two-week period with a 1% probability means that the VAR is likely to be breached only once in four years.

16: RISK MANAGEMENT

7.2 Approaches to VAR measurement

7.2.1 Introduction

There are three main approaches to measuring VAR.

- Parametric.
- Historical simulation.
- Stochastic simulation.

7.2.2 Parametric VAR

Exam tip | Calculations have arisen in this area

The parametric approach is also known as the correlation method, variance/covariance method or analytical method. It is the most popular of the various methods.

It assumes that the distribution of investment returns is normal, meaning that it can be described by the variances and covariances of the investments concerned.

It estimates the standard deviations of investments and their correlations with other investments, using historical data. It then prepares a variance-correlation matrix of investment returns. Given this information, it is possible to calculate the variance/standard deviation of the overall portfolio. The formula for this, based on just two investments (a and b), would be as follows.

Formula to learn

$$\sigma_{a+b} = \sqrt{p_a^2 \sigma_a^2 + p_b^2 \sigma_b^2 + 2 p_a p_b \sigma_a \sigma_b cor_{ab}}$$

σ = standard deviation

cor = correlation coefficient

p = proportion of portfolio invested in each investment

The same principles apply for a portfolio with more investments, with the calculations just becoming more involved.

The impact of correlation coefficients being included is that unless all the investments are perfectly positively correlated, the portfolio risk will be less than the weighted average of the risks of the individual investments.

When analysing portfolios in this way, the constituents of the portfolio are 'mapped' in a way such that each instrument in the portfolio is exposed to a minimum number of factors. For example, a long-term government bond could be stripped into its component flows, each flow representing a single instrument subject to one risk factor, the spot rate for its maturity. If the bond was in foreign currency, a second relevant factor would be exchange rates.

Such a mapping technique is quite detailed. There are alternatives available that are less accurate, but involve more approximations.

Assessing Parametric VAR

If an asset with a price S returns r p.a. then after a particular time (t) we expect its value to rise by

$$\Delta S = S \times r \times t \text{ or } Srt$$

If it has a volatility or standard deviation of σ, then if there is a downmove the average downmove will be

$$\text{Downmove} = S \times \sigma \times \sqrt{t} \text{ or } S\sigma\sqrt{t}$$

16: RISK MANAGEMENT

So combining these two effects for a volatile security, if there is a downmove then the average change in price will be

$$\Delta S = Srt - S\sigma\sqrt{t}$$

Note: we are only considering downmoves because with VAR we are only concerned by losses.

Now the above considers the average downmove whereas VAR considers extremes – downmoves we may experience only 5% or 1% or 0.5% of the time.

If we look to the normal distribution table appendix in the probability section we can see that a value of 1.645 corresponds to a probability of 0.05 or 5%. What this means is there is a 5% chance of observing a movement in one direction that is greater than 1.645 standard derivations. It therefore follows that there is a 5% chance of observing a downward change in value of more than

$$\Delta S = Srt - S \times 1.645 \times \sqrt{t}$$

This may be referred to as a 95% one-sided confidence interval and gives us our VAR at a 5% confidence level.

Picking some other important points from the normal distribution table, a value of

- 1.645 corresponds to a probability of 0.05 or 5%
- 2.055 corresponds to a probability of 0.02 or 2%
- 2.325 corresponds to a probability of 0.01 or 1%
- 2.575 corresponds to a probability of 0.005 or 0.5%

If we use ϕ to represent the relevant value for the appropriate probability we can express the VAR as

Formula to learn

$$VAR_s = Srt - S\phi\sigma\sqrt{t}$$

Example 1

Assume that we have a T-bond future, with a price of 105 based on the $100,000 face value of bonds. The mean of the daily returns on the future is 0.01%. The standard deviation of the daily returns is 0.5%. We wish to calculate VAR at a probability level of 1% and for a time period of one day.

Solution 1

Alternative 1

$$S = \$100,000 \times \frac{105}{100} = \$105,000$$

$$VAR = Srt - S\phi\sigma\sqrt{t}$$

$$= 105,000 \times 0.01\% \times 1 - 105,000 \times 2.325 \times 0.5\% \times \sqrt{1} = -\$1,210$$

Note: It is normal to ignore the sign and just give the value, i.e. VAR = $1,210

Alternative 2

$$\%\Delta S = rt - \phi\sigma\sqrt{t}$$

$$= 0.01\% \times 1 - 2.325 \times 0.5\% \times \sqrt{1} = -1.1525\%$$

Now $S = \$100,000 \times \frac{105}{100} = \$105,000$, so

VAR = 105,000 × −1.1525% = −$1,210, i.e. VAR = $1,210

This indicates that the value of the future is likely to fall by more than $1,210 once every hundred days.

If we had wanted to use a time period different from one day (say, one week, i.e. five business days) and assume that there is no serial correlation in the returns from day to day, we can calculate the five-day VAR as follows.

Alternative 1

$$\text{VAR} = Srt - S\phi\sigma\sqrt{t}$$
$$= 105,000 \times 0.01\% \times 5 - 105,000 \times 2.325 \times 0.5\% \times \sqrt{5} = -\$2,677$$

i.e. VAR = $2,677

Alternative 2

$$\%\Delta S = rt - \sigma\sqrt{t}$$
$$= 0.01\% \times 5 - 2.325 \times 0.5\% \times \sqrt{5} = -2,5494\%$$

so VAR = 105,000 × − $2.5494% = −$2,677, i.e. VAR = $2,677

This indicates that the value of the future is likely to fall by more than $2,677 only one week in a hundred.

Example 2

VAR – Single asset

For a single asset

$$\text{VAR} = Srt + S\phi\sigma\sqrt{t}$$

where

σ = annual volatility
t = time horizon as a fraction of a year
S = value of asset

VAR – Asset portfolio

Calculate the combined volatility, taking into account the correlation between the two assets.

$$\sigma_{a+b} = \sqrt{p_a^2\sigma_a^2 + p_b^2\sigma_b^2 + 2p_a p_b \sigma_a \sigma_b cor_{ab}}$$

$$\text{VAR} = Srt + S\phi\sigma_{a+b}\sqrt{t}$$

where now

S = value of portfolio

Example

- Stock A: σ = 8%, price = 100p, holding = 10,000 shares
- Stock B: σ = 10%, price = 150p, holding = 8,000 shares

Assume r = 0% and the correlation of these securities is +0.5, calculate VAR for one week at the 99% confidence level for

(i) Stock A on its own.
(ii) Stock B on its own.
(iii) The portfolio containing Stock A and Stock B.

16: RISK MANAGEMENT

Solution

Stock A

$S = 10{,}000 \times 100p = £10{,}000$

$VAR = 10{,}000 \times 2.325 \times 8\% \times \sqrt{1/52} = £257.94$

Stock B

$S = 8{,}000 \times 150p = £12{,}000$

$VAR = 12{,}000 \times 2.325 \times 10\% \times \sqrt{1/52} = £386.90$

Alternative 1

Portfolio

Calculate combined volatility, if $cor_{ab} = 0.5$.

$$\sigma_{a+b} = \sqrt{p_a^2 \sigma_a^2 + p_b^2 \sigma_b^2 + 2 p_a p_b \sigma_a \sigma_b cor_{ab}}$$

$$p_a = \frac{£10{,}000}{£22{,}000} = 0.4545$$

$$p_b = \frac{£12{,}000}{£22{,}000} = 0.5455$$

$$\sigma_{a+b} = \sqrt{0.4545^2 \times 8^2 + 0.5455^2 \times 10^2 + 2 \times 0.4545 \times 0.5455 \times 8 \times 10 \times 0.5}$$

$$= 7.925$$

$VAR = 22{,}000 \times 2.325 \times 7.925\% \times \sqrt{1/52} = £562.14$

Note this is less than the two individual VARs added together. This is because of the diversification of risk caused by the correlation between the two assets.

Alternative 2

An alternative approach to calculating the VAR for the portfolio is

Formula to learn

$$VAR_p = \sqrt{VAR_a^2 + VAR_b^2 + 2 \times VAR_a \times VAR_b \times cor_{ab}}$$

$VAR_p = \sqrt{257.94^2 + 386.90^2 + 2 \times 257.94 \times 386.90 \times 0.5} = £562.16$ (minor rounding difference)

The impact of changing volatilities through time

The approach is sensitive to the estimate of volatility used. This could vary substantially, depending on the historical time period on which it is based, since historical volatilities can vary substantially.

In order to allow for changing volatility over time, it is possible to base the estimate on a longer period of time, say one year, but to weight the calculation towards the more recent observations. The calculation of the weighted average volatility is redone on a daily basis. The weighting can vary. A rapid **decay factor** means that there is a greater weighting towards more recent observations.

Strengths of the parametric approach

- Easy to calculate.
- Easily available market data for inputs.
- No need for powerful computer systems.

Problems of the parametric approach

- Assumption of constant volatility and correlations across time. This is particularly inappropriate in times of market crises.
- Becomes cumbersome with an excessive number of risk factors, meaning that more computing power is needed.
- Requires cash flow mapping, as noted above.
- Less suitable for portfolios with non-linear risk, such as those with option-based products.

7.2.3 Correlation risks

The parametric approach to VAR relies on statistical data such as standard deviations and correlation coefficients. This is fine if the variables being assessed are believed to be correlated with each other. But what if they are not? If mapping different risk components separately, such as credit risk, is it reasonable to assume that the risk factor is at all correlated between investments, market sectors, or indeed with other risk factors? Work has been done to suggest it **is** possible to calculate correlations between credit risk in different industry sectors – this can then be used when assessing the credit risk of a portfolio. However, many authors have suggested that calculating and using correlation measures in this way suggests relationships that do not exist.

7.2.4 VAR and derivatives

A key point about VAR and derivatives is that although the underlying asset may follow a Normal distribution, the derivatives may exhibit a distinct non-linear function, e.g. options. Using the above technique (which relies on a Normal distribution) is therefore potentially unrealistic for certain derivatives. However, if we are just considering very small movements over short periods of time, we could approximate the sensitivity of the option price to a change in the value of the underlying by considering the option's delta. We have already seen, in an earlier chapter, how the delta of a portfolio consisting of various options on a single underlying asset can be calculated. It is therefore a small step to multiply the volatility of the underlying asset by the delta of the option to give an estimate of the likely change in value of the option. This is the **Delta Normal** Approach.

Example 3

Assume that we now have a portfolio consisting of call options on the two stocks used in Example 2.

The delta of the option on Stock A is 0.6.

The delta of the option on Stock B is 0.5.

Now delta gives the change in the price of an option for one unit change in the price of the asset, hence

$$VAR_{option} = \delta \times VAR_{share} = \delta\left(Srt - S\phi\sigma\sqrt{t}\right)$$

Therefore

$$VAR_{optionA} = 0.6 \times £257.94 = 154.76$$

Similar logic will suggest that the option on Stock B will move by 50% of the value of Stock B.

16: RISK MANAGEMENT

Therefore

$$VAR_{optionB} = 0.5 \times £386.90 = £193.45$$

Having calculated the VAR on the individual options, we will now calculate the VAR for the portfolio containing both options. Remember the correlation between Stock A and Stock B is 0.5. We firstly need to calculate the weighted portfolio delta or £ value of delta of the portfolio i.e.

$$£ \text{ value of delta} = 0.6 \times £10,000 + 0.5 \times £12,000 = £12,000$$

i.e. $\delta S = £12,000$

Then we can calculate the combined volatility of the two options portfolio.

Alternative 1

$$\sigma_{a+b} = \sqrt{p_a^2 \sigma_a^2 + p_b^2 \sigma_b^2 + 2 p_a p_b \sigma_a \sigma_b cor_{ab}}$$

where

$$p_a = \frac{£ \text{ value of delta of option A}}{£ \text{ value of delta of portfolio}} = \frac{£10,000 \times 0.6}{£10,000 \times 0.6 + £12,000 \times 0.5} = 0.5$$

$$p_b = \frac{£ \text{ value of delta of option B}}{£ \text{ value of delta of portfolio}} = \frac{£12,000 \times 0.5}{£10,000 \times 0.6 + £12,000 \times 0.5} = 0.5$$

$$\sigma_{a+b} = \sqrt{0.5^2 \times 8^2 + 0.5^2 \times 10^2 + 2 \times 0.5 \times 0.5 \times 8 \times 10 \times 0.5}$$

$$= 7.81\%$$

$$VAR_{option\ portfolio} = 12,000 \times 2.325 \times 7.81\% \sqrt{1/52} = £302.11$$

Alternative 2

$$VAR_p = \sqrt{VAR_a^2 + VAR_b^2 + 2 \times VAR_a \times VAR_b \times cor_{ab}}$$

$$VAR_p = \sqrt{154.76^2 + 193.45^2 + 2 \times 154.76 \times 193.45 \times 0.5} = £302.17$$

But, we also know that the delta of an option changes, which is why we stated above that the delta could be an approximation for small movements in the underlying over a short period of time. Remember, an option's delta is sensitive to changes in value of the underlying and time. We can extend our approximation by also considering the gamma of the option, which introduces a non-linear relationship into our thinking. (Remember, the delta is the slope of the value line, whereas the gamma is the curve of the value line.)

The delta-gamma approximation

The delta normal approach ignores gamma. We will now include the gamma impact.

From our knowledge of the Greeks, we can calculate the change in value of an option as

$$\Delta 0 = \delta \times \Delta S + \tfrac{1}{2} \gamma \times \Delta S^2 + \theta \times \Delta T + \kappa \times \Delta\sigma + \rho \times \Delta r$$

where

$\Delta 0$ = change in the value of the option
ΔS = change in value of underlying asset
δ = option delta
γ = option gamma
θ = option theta
κ = option kappa
ρ = option rho

16: RISK MANAGEMENT

And so it follows that

Formula to learn
$$VAR_{option} = \delta VAR_s + \tfrac{1}{2}\gamma VAR_s^2 \times \theta \times \Delta T + \kappa \times \Delta\sigma + \rho \times \Delta r$$

Where VAR_s = VAR of underlying asset
i.e. $VAR_s = Srt - S\phi\sigma\sqrt{t}$

This gamma effect will cause the distribution of the option's value to be far from normal. Is this gamma effect big enough to consider the use of the Normal distribution inappropriate?

Consider the following diagram.

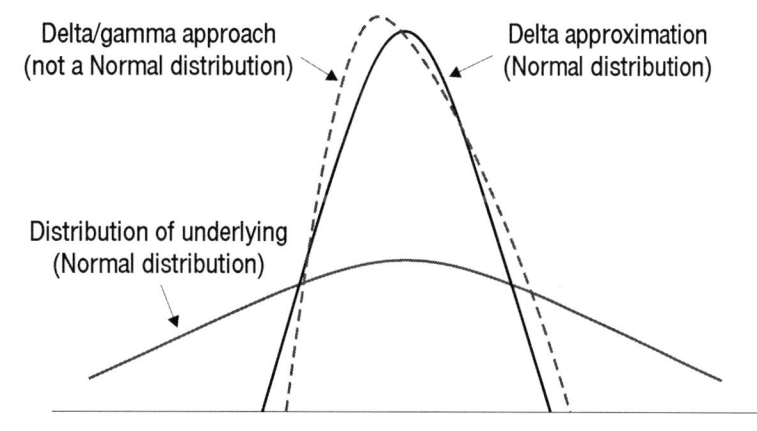

Delta/gamma approach (not a Normal distribution)
Delta approximation (Normal distribution)
Distribution of underlying (Normal distribution)

It would appear that mapping delta and gamma in this way allows us to question the stochastic approach and its validity, based as it is on a Normal distribution. If the delta/gamma approach renders this approach to VAR unsuitable, other approaches such as simulations (discussed later) will have to be used.

7.2.5 Historical approach

The problem with the parametric approach is that it assumes a Normal distribution, when there is plenty of evidence to suggest that investment returns do not follow a Normal distribution.

- Generally, investment returns are more peaked towards the mean than a Normal distribution and have fatter tails, i.e. they are leptokurtic.

- There may be a negative skew, meaning that greater losses are possible than a Normal distribution would imply.

It is possible to overcome this problem by constructing a distribution of historical returns and establishing its actual shape. The bottom percentile point can then be identified. Returns less than this represent the bottom 1% of returns on a daily basis. If the bottom percentile point is, for instance −1.5%, this would give a daily VAR for our future calculated as follows.

$$VAR = 1.5\% \times \frac{105}{100} \times \$100{,}000 = \$1{,}575$$

With this approach, it is not possible to do a quick calculation of the VAR for another time period by assuming no serial correlation. It is necessary to recalculate historical returns for the desired time period.

Comparing the historical and parametric methods

- The historical method makes no specific assumptions about the shape of the distribution and linearity. This makes it more suitable for portfolios containing option products.

- The historical method makes no specific assumptions about variances and covariances.

- The historical method is not very flexible, e.g. it cannot be easily manipulated to give different VARs, unlike the parametric method.
- The historical method involves manipulation of large amounts of historical data.

Another possible problem with the historical approach is that the portfolio held in the past, for which historical data is available, might not be the same as the current portfolio, for which you want to calculate VAR.

To overcome this, it is necessary to try and reflect differences between the current portfolio and the historic portfolio, and what the historic returns would have been on the current portfolio. When a company uses a different portfolio to the one it actually had in the past to calculate historical data, this might be called historical simulation.

7.2.6 Stochastic simulation

This is also referred to as the Monte Carlo simulation. It is an alternative to historical simulation. Its benefit is additional flexibility. It entails constructing distributions and specifying parameters for each of the factors and then running a Monte Carlo simulation based on these distributions.

The stages are illustrated as follows, using an option on an index as an example. We will be working out VAR for a probability level of 1% and a time period of one day.

- Calculate returns for the index over time and prepare a distribution of returns.
- Simulate returns for the index over a day, using random numbers based on the above distribution. Complete a large number of simulations.
- Calculate the price of the index, using the simulated return.
- Use the price of the index to value the option on the index, using an option-pricing model such as the Black Scholes model.
- Calculate the daily return on the option, using the simulated option price.
- Lay out the distribution for the option's daily returns.
- Identify the bottom percentile.

Strengths of Stochastic simulation

- Greater flexibility.
- Ability to generate a large number of random simulations. This makes it more comprehensive than using one historical path.
- No need to assume Normal distributions or linearity.
- Not constrained by assumptions about asset returns.
- Suitable for portfolios based on option products.

Problems of Stochastic simulation

- Needs substantial computing power.
- Needs sophisticated mathematic modelling.
- Highly dependent on assumptions input into the model.
- If there are a lot of risk characteristics in the portfolio, a greater number of scenarios will need to be generated.

7.2.7 Stress testing of VAR results

In order to allow for the weaknesses in each of the methods of calculating VAR, it is important to stress test any results.

Stress testing involves testing the VAR for different market assumptions. Ways of doing stress testing are as follows.

- The impact on portfolio value of large shifts in the yield curve, changes in commodity prices, changes in exchange rates, etc., can be calculated.

- The impact on the portfolio of a market crisis could be considered, such as the impact of a stock market crash or a currency crisis.

This allows the exposure of the portfolio to abnormal market circumstances to be established.

7.3 Benefits and problems of VAR

7.3.1 Benefits

- Accepted measure of risk for banks.
- Easy to understand.
- Provides one measure of risk for a portfolio.
- Easy to apply for frequently traded securities.

7.3.2 Problems

- Focuses on a single arbitrary point rather than looking at the whole distribution of returns.
- Does not measure risk in extreme circumstances. In market crises, normal relationships fail, correlations change, liquidity falls and price data may be unavailable.
- Harder to apply for less frequently traded securities, since less reliable pricing information.
- Dependent on assumptions used in the VAR model, data inputs and methodology adopted.
- Not necessarily appropriate for asset liability management. For example, pension funds have long-term liabilities, thus looking at short-term fluctuations in asset values may be less relevant.

7.3.3 Risks for which it is a valid measure

Risks where it may be used appropriately are those that can be quantified, as follows.

- **Credit risk**, i.e. losses arising on default.
- **Liquidity risk**, i.e. inability to fund illiquid assets.
- **Market risk**, i.e. price movements due to market factors such as interest rates and currencies. **Interest rate risk** is particularly important for banks and can be analysed into yield curve shifts, twists and basis risk. Basis risk is where instruments of the same maturity but linked to a different index, e.g. LIBOR versus a T-bill rate, have different price movements.

7.3.4 Risks for which it is not a useful measure

Risks that cannot be quantified cannot be measured effectively by VAR.

- **Operational risk**, i.e. losses due to errors in payment instructions, etc.
- **Legal risk**, i.e. losses when a contract cannot be enforced.

7.4 Uses of VAR for an asset manager

7.4.1 Portfolio management

Common basis for risk measurement

VAR provides a common framework for risk measurement across assets, portfolios and products. Although VAR was originally geared towards fixed income analysis, it provides a measure of risk that can be compared across different types of securities, such as equities and bonds.

Although it is more difficult to model the risk of assets such as venture capital, it is possible to create proxies that replicate the risk of these assets.

The ability to provide a common measurement enables risk to be measured across asset classes and consequently gives useful information on the overall portfolio characteristics. Although the final VAR is a single number for the portfolio, it can be disaggregated to establish the contribution of different risk factors to the VAR. As a result, the investment manager can identify the key risks and, if desired, take actions to reduce those risks.

When calculating VAR, a portfolio manager would probably use a longer time period than a trader, reflecting his less frequent trading. The time period could link to the period over which the manager is assessed.

Construction of efficient portfolios

VAR can be used to help in the construction of efficient portfolios. It enables the manager to quantify the impact of adding or removing an asset class or an individual security from the portfolio. In addition, volatilities and correlations used in the parametric model can be revised to reflect expected changes in market conditions.

In the construction of efficient portfolios, it is often using the VAR methodology that is most helpful to the manager, rather than the results of the VAR analysis itself.

Setting risk limits

VAR can be used to control the risk limits of a portfolio. Limits may be expressed as an absolute VAR for the portfolio or a relative VAR compared to a benchmark.

Such limits should be fairly wide for active managers to enable them to make the bets necessary to beat the benchmark.

Potential risks

It is important to ensure that senior management understands the VAR methodology so that it can understand the techniques being used by the manager.

The VAR model results will depend on the historic market conditions used to represent the future. Hence, it does not provide a guaranteed result and is heavily reliant on the data and assumptions input into the model.

7.4.2 Performance measurement

Traditionally, performance measurement has been focused on total return achieved. VAR enables risk to be brought into the assessment in considering how the returns were achieved. There are various issues to be considered in this respect.

- Combining use of the standard deviation with VAR.
- Peer group measurement.
- Performance versus an index.

Use of the standard deviation and VAR

Although the problems with the standard deviation have been highlighted above, the benefits of the standard deviation are as follows.

- The calculation is consistent across managers, giving comparable results.
- The calculation is coincident with the timeframe for the returns. This enables measures such as the Sharpe ratio to be calculated.

VAR does not have these attributes. Since VAR is calculated using different methodologies and assumptions, it is not comparable across managers.

VAR produces a measure of the current risk of the portfolio, whereas standard deviation provides a measure of risk for the changing historical portfolio. If the portfolio composition has changed significantly over the period, the two risk measures are looking at totally different things. In order to achieve measures of risk that are measuring the same thing, an average VAR over the period would be needed.

Even then, it would not be totally comparable, since standard deviation is a measure of actual volatility, whereas the VARs calculated through the period to give the average would each have been an estimate of future volatility.

Peer group measurement

It is possible to use VAR to compare risk across a set of portfolios for peer group managers. However, it is difficult to compare returns and risk (as measured by VAR) for different portfolios. Which is better, a return of 20% with a VAR of 15% or a return of 15% with a VAR of 7%?

In addition, VAR is not calculated on a consistent basis across different managers, with different models and assumptions being used. Either there will need to be a standardised form of VAR calculation or the composition of the portfolio will need to be known to enable VAR to be calculated in the desired fashion. Both of these possibilities are unlikely to be achievable.

Comparison with an index

When comparing performance with an index, it is possible to calculate the VAR of the index in the desired way, since the exact composition of the index will be known. Hence, VAR can be used as a relative measure of risk.

The relative risk of the portfolio compared to the index can be found by dividing the VAR of the portfolio by that of the index.

7.5 Worst Case Risk

Worse case risk is a variation of VAR in which, for example, rather than assuming a seven day volatility for a seven day VAR we may take a three month volatility as representative of the worst case possibility over a seven day period. The calculations would be as above but substituting the three month volatility in place of the more normal seven day in this situation.

Chapter Roundup

- You need to be familiar with and discuss in the context of a scenario
    - Financial risks, i.e.
        - Market risk
        - Credit Risk
        - Liquidity risk
    - Operational risk
    - Controlling risk
- VAR
    - Parametric VAR

    $$VAR_s = Srt - S\phi\sigma\sqrt{t}$$

    $$VAR_{option} = \delta VAR_s + \tfrac{1}{2}\gamma VAR_s^2 \times \theta \times \Delta T + \kappa \times \Delta\sigma + \rho \times \Delta r$$

    $$VAR_p = \sqrt{VAR_a^2 + VAR_b^2 + 2 \times VAR_a \times VAR_b \times cor_{ab}}$$

Test Your Knowledge

Check your knowledge of the Chapter here, without referring back to the text.

1. A portfolio contains two shares and you are given the following

Share	Price	Quantity	Return p.a.	Volatility
A	100	7,000	8%	18%
B	160	5,000	8%	20%

   Calculate the VAR at the 1% level over a week of

   a) Share A holding

   b) Share B holding

   c) Entire portfolio assuming that the correlation coefficient of A and B of 0.37

2. A currency option book runs in $/£ and $/€. You observe the following dollar risk sensitivities for the positions for one cent movement in the spot rate

	Delta	Gamma	Theta	Rho
$/£	4,800,000	13,000	12,000	40,000
$/€	5,200,000	15,000	16,000	50,000

   If the spot rates exchange are 1.82 for sterling and 1.21 for euro, the volatilities are 12% and 10% respectively and the correlation between the two currencies is 0.41 calculate the VAR at the 0.5% level over one week

   a) Of each currency position

   b) Of the combined position

16: RISK MANAGEMENT

TEST YOUR KNOWLEDGE: ANSWERS

1. (a) *Share A holding*

    $VAR_s = Srt - S\phi\sigma\sqrt{t}$

    $VAR_a = £7,000 \times 8\% \sqrt{1/52} - £7,000 \times 2.325 \times 18\% \times \sqrt{1/52} = -£395.48$

    $VAR_a = 395.48$

    (b) *Share B holding*

    $VAR_b = £8,000 \times 8\% \sqrt{1/52} - £8,000 \times 2.325 \times 20\% \times \sqrt{1/52} = -£503.56$

    $VAR_b = 503.56$

    (c) *Portfolio VAR*

    $VAR_p = \sqrt{VAR_a^2 + VAR_b^2 + 2 \times VAR_a \times VAR_b \times cor_{ab}}$

    $= \sqrt{395.48^2 + 503.56^2 + 2 \times 395.48 \times 503.65 \times 0.37} = 746.56$

2. (a) $VAR_{option} = \delta VAR_s + \frac{1}{2}\gamma VAR_s^2 + \theta \Delta T + \rho \Delta r$

    Sterling

    $VAR_s = Srt - S\phi\sigma\sqrt{t}$

    At the 0.5% level $\phi = 2.575$, giving

    $VAR_£ = 182 \times 0 \times \sqrt{1/52} - 182 \times 2.575 \times 12\% \times \sqrt{1/52} = -7.7988$

    i.e. $VAR_£ = 7.7988$

    $VAR_{option} = 4,800,000 \times -7.7988 + \frac{1}{2} \times 13,000 \times (-7.7988)^2 + 12,000 \times 7 + 40,000 \times 0$

    $= \$36,954,902$

    Euro

    $VAR_€ = 121 \times 0 \times \sqrt{1/52} - 121 \times 2.575 \times 10\% \times \sqrt{1/52} = -4.3208$

    $VAR_€ = 4.3208$

    $VAR_{option} = 5,200,000 \times -4.3208 + \frac{1}{2} \times 15,000 \times (-4.3208)^2 + 16,000 \times 7 + 50,000 \times 0$

    $= \$22,216,140$

    (b) *Portfolio*

    $VAR_p = \sqrt{VAR_a^2 + VAR_b^2 + 2 \times VAR_a \times VAR_b \times cor_{ab}}$

    $= \sqrt{36.955^2 + 22.216^2 + 2 \times 36.955 \times 22.216 \times 0.41} = \$50.323$ million

17

The Regulatory Environment

INTRODUCTION

Just as it is importantant to understand the different derivatives available to an invetor or fund manager, it is equally essential to be familiar with the rules and regulations that apply to their use as investment vehicles. This section studies the major regulatory aspects that apply to the derivatives industry and that participants in the industry must be aware of.

CHAPTER CONTENTS

		Page
1	Overview	528
2	Background to the UK Regulatory System	528
3	European Initiatives	529
4	The Financial Services and Markets Act	531
5	The Objectives	532
6	Rights of Private Persons	532
7	The General Prohibition	532
8	Obtaining Authorisation	536
9	The FSA Handbook	538
10	Financial Services Ombudsman	550
11	Financial Services Compensation Scheme	551
12	US Regulation	551
13	The Commodity Futures Trading Commission (CFTC)	552
14	OTC regulation	555
15	Litigation	558
16	Taxation	563
	Chapter Roundup	566
	Test Your Knowledge	567

17: THE REGULATORY ENVIRONMENT

CHAPTER LEARNING OBJECTIVES

- **Knowledge of the regulatory bodies governing or controlling the markets/exchanges in the UK and of the requirements for authorisation and registration.**
- **Knowledge of the legislative rules and guideline laid down by the Government/FSA including G30 and ISDA which affect an institution's ability to deal in traded options or futures.**

Exam tip | Questions may arise from anywhere in this session as basic definitions in Section A, through these are quite rare. Regulations tend to only be examined in times of regulatory change.

1 OVERVIEW

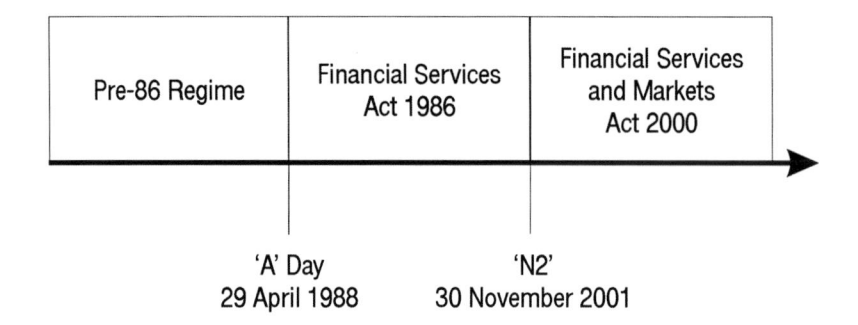

| Pre-86 Regime | Financial Services Act 1986 | Financial Services and Markets Act 2000 |

'A' Day
29 April 1988

'N2'
30 November 2001

2 BACKGROUND TO THE UK REGULATORY SYSTEM

The regulation of the UK financial services industry continues to evolve.

Prior to the advent of the 1986 Financial Services Act, the industry was completely self-regulating. Whilst there were some statutory provisions (such as the Prevention of Fraud Act 1958), these were limited in scope and largely unenforceable. Standards were maintained by an assurance that those in the financial services industry had a common set of values and were able and willing to ostracise those who violated them.

However, the advent of the Conservative Government in 1979 saw big changes to the industry. The late Professor Gower was appointed to report on the appropriate structure of regulation. Initially, it was felt that he would have a simple choice between either a statutory system, similar to that operated in the US by the SEC, or to continue to rely upon practitioner self-regulation. Instead, Gower chose to recommend a hybrid between the two, a system that became known as self-regulation within a statutory framework. A key element of the system was the Financial Services Act 1986, which contained the basic premise that those conducting investment business in the UK obtain authorisation. Once authorised, firms and individuals would be regulated by self-regulating organisations such as IMRO, SFA or PIA. It should be noted that the Financial Services Act 1986 only covered investment activities. Retail banking, general insurance, Lloyd's of London and mortgages were all covered by separate Acts and Codes.

The system was created in the belief that it could combine both the flexibility and understanding of practitioner self-regulation, with the enforceability of statute and consequently deliver the appropriate level of protection. Additionally, this was felt to be the only style of regulation that would be appropriate and acceptable to the UK markets.

In 1997, Labour won a landslide majority. One of the first statements made by the new Chancellor was that there would be radical reform of the financial services system. The Chancellor's statement to the House of Commons on 20 May came as a shock, not so much because of its general thrust, but due to its timing and effect on the status of the Bank of England.

In summary, his announcement indicated the government's intention of unifying most aspects of financial services regulation within a single statutory regulator. The process would take place in two phases: first, the Bank's responsibility for banking supervision would be transferred to the FSA as part of the Bank of England Act 1998. The second phase would consist of a reformed Financial Services Act, which would repeal the main provisions of the Financial Services Act 1986, the Insurance Companies Act 1982 and the Banking Act 1987. The 'patchwork quilt' of regulation would, therefore, be swept away and the Financial Services Authority would regulate investment business, insurance business, banking, building societies, Friendly Societies and Lloyd's. Prior to new legislation, the Chancellor expected the FSA, the Bank and the SROs to co-operate and embark on the transition.

The Chancellor further announced that Howard Davies, a Deputy Governor at the Bank, would succeed Sir Andrew Large and head up the new agency.

On 30 November 2001, the Financial Services and Markets Act 2000 (FSMA) came into force, moving from the hybrid that Gower created to statutory regulation. Whilst practitioners and consumers are actively consulted, it is the Financial Services Authority, a public authority, that co-ordinates the regulation of the industry.

The new regime seeks to learn from many of the regulatory failures that occurred during the 80s and 90s. Undoubtedly, the most important has been that of pensions mis-selling, whereby salesmen encouraged some 2.2 million people to move out of their employers' schemes into personal pension plans. These transfers were often unsuitable and have given rise to some major compensation claims. This has led to the increased importance, in the new regime, on educating investors to ensure that they understand the risks of transactions.

BCCI was an important international bank with many UK offices and customers, which was the subject of an £8bn fraud. The subsequent insolvency of the bank caused great harm to many creditors. This has led to the FSA taking on regulatory responsibility for banks and increased regulation to prevent money laundering.

The Barings crisis was caused by the actions of a single rogue trader, Nick Leeson, whose unauthorised trading, coupled with the inadequacy of controls, lead to the collapse of the bank. This has led to a big drive towards ensuring that senior management take their responsibilities seriously and ensure that systems and controls are adequate.

Finally, world copper prices were manipulated by the unauthorised trading of Mr Hamanaka of Sumitomo. As much of his trading took place on the London Metal Exchange, there was cause for UK regulatory concern. Ultimately, the unauthorised trading cost Sumitomo $2.7bn. As a result, the new regime introduced more stringent rules to deal with market abuse.

3 European Initiatives

The UK's regulatory structure is determined by both UK and European law. Much European law seeks to support the creation of a single, competitive and efficient European market. Indeed, one of the key objectives of the European Union is to create a common market that allows for free and unencumbered trade. To this end, a large number of directives have been agreed amongst the member states and have subsequently entered into domestic legislation. These directives seek to 'harmonise' regulations in order to create a fair market place. Differences in regulation between states need to be justified so that their impact is not unduly anti-competitive.

Over the last few decades, a number of directives related to financial services have been implemented. Amongst them are the following.

17: THE REGULATORY ENVIRONMENT

Directive	Implementation Date	Scope
UCITS Directive	1989	Undertakings in Collective Investments in Transferable Securities; created the ability to sell certain unit trust style products freely throughout Europe
Second Banking Co-Ordination Directive (2BCD)	1993	Created a single market for banks and their associated investment business
Insurance Directive	1994	Created single market for insurance
Investment Services Directive (ISD)	1996	Created single market for investment firms
Capital Adequacy Directive (CAD)	1996	Created harmonised set of financial regulations for banks and investment firms

Of greatest importance to our discussion are the ISD and 2BCD. These two directives allow investment firms and credit institutions (banks) to carry out securities and banking business throughout the European Economic Area (EEA: EU states plus Norway, Iceland and Liechtenstein).

3.1 Investment Services Directive

The Investment Services Directive, which was passed by the European Commission and Parliament in 1992, became effective on 1 January 1996. The directive gives a **'common passport'** to all securities firms within the community. This allows a firm authorised in an EEA state to passport that authorisation into another EEA state.

Therefore, a firm may obtain authorisation in its home state, for example, Germany, and then wish to open a branch or cross-border sell in the UK. Subject to the scope of the ISD (which will be dealt with later in this chapter), the firm is not required to seek authorisation from the UK regulator. Their authorisation to conduct business in this jurisdiction will, instead, stem from the fact that the German regulator has already deemed them to be fit and proper.

Whilst the firm will follow UK conduct of business rules with respect to its activities in the UK, it will always be subject to its home state rules regarding authorisation, fitness and propriety, capital adequacy and client assets. The table below summarises the basic split of responsibilities.

Home	Host
Authorisation	Conduct of Business (when in host state)
Fitness and Propriety	
Capital Adequacy	
Client Assets	
Conduct of Business (when in home state)	

It should be remembered that client assets will be governed by home state regulation. Therefore, in looking at the FSA Conduct of Business Rules, we will find that the sections relating to client assets are disapplied to inwardly passporting firms.

One worry was that firms might set up in the easiest jurisdiction within the EEA and then outwardly passport. This worry prompted the EC to require implementation of the Capital Adequacy Directive, which harmonises financial resource rules for all firms authorised to passport their services.

A further concern relates to the ability to discipline passported business. At present, the ultimate sanction is the withdrawal of authorisation, thereby removing the ability of the firm to trade. Whilst the situation would appear to be that UK regulators are able to use the full range of disciplinary powers open to them, there is a conflict here. If the UK expels a 'passported' firm, then it is implicitly questioning the fitness and propriety of the firm. This would mean that the UK regulator is contradicting the home state regulator. If this is not possible, then the UK regulator would only have fines as a sanction, which does not create a 'level playing field' between UK and non-UK firms.

3.2 The Second Banking Co-ordination Directive (2BCD)

The Second Banking Co-Ordination Directive (2BCD) is similar to the ISD, but relates to banking activity. Once again, the concept is that the home state authority may grant a passport to the firm to operate throughout the EEA.

The directive is based on the German model of the 'universal bank' and therefore extends to cover more than straightforward banking activities. The passport covers the following.

- Trading in securities.
- Participation in securities issues.
- Advice with regard to corporate finance activities such as takeovers and mergers.
- Portfolio management.

This passport is only available to **credit institutions** and **financial institutions** as defined in the directive. The limitations on the definitions in the directive led in part to the ISD, since many firms in direct competition with the passported banks would not themselves fall within the definition of credit or financial institutions and would therefore not be able to obtain the passport. With the introduction of the ISD, investment firms are now able to compete on the same basis as the banks.

The 2BCD came into effect on 1 January 1993 and since that date, a number of overseas banks have been allowed to trade on the basis of their home state authorisation, subject only to the local rules of the UK.

4 THE FINANCIAL SERVICES AND MARKETS ACT

4.1 Primary and secondary legislation

Before looking further at the detail of FSMA, it is important to understand the legislative structure that exists. FSMA itself only provides the skeleton of the regulatory system, with much of the detail being provided by secondary legislation. The secondary legislation links into various sections of FSMA, fleshing out the requirements and thus, requiring the two to be read in conjunction. An example of this is with regard to the authorisation requirement. FSMA requires that any firm undertaking a regulated activity must be authorised or exempt. Whilst ways that a firm may obtain authorisation are contained in FSMA, the meaning of the term 'regulated activity' and the exemptions are found in secondary legislation – namely the Regulated Activities Order.

```
         FSMA
           │
           ▼
  Secondary Legislation

e.g. Regulated Activities Order
     Financial Promotions Order
```

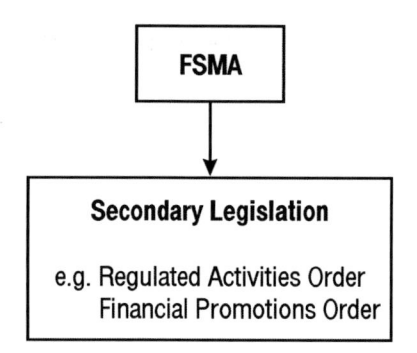

5 THE OBJECTIVES

Section 3 of FSMA spells out the purpose of regulation by specifying four regulatory objectives. The emphasis that is placed on these objectives makes FSMA unusual compared to the Acts that it supersedes – none of which clearly articulated their objectives. FSMA is seeking to inject much needed clarity into what the regulatory regime is trying to achieve and, perhaps more importantly, seeking to manage expectations regarding what it cannot achieve. These objectives are summarised below.

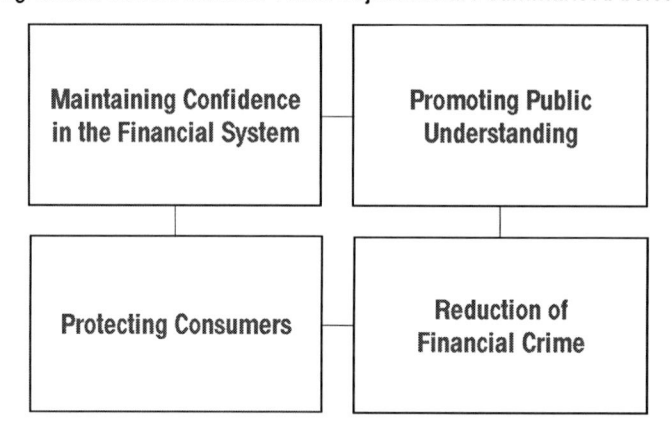

```
┌──────────────────────┐ ┌──────────────────────┐
│ Maintaining Confidence│ │   Promoting Public   │
│ in the Financial System│ │    Understanding    │
└──────────────────────┘ └──────────────────────┘
┌──────────────────────┐ ┌──────────────────────┐
│                      │ │    Reduction of      │
│  Protecting Consumers│ │   Financial Crime    │
└──────────────────────┘ └──────────────────────┘
```

6 RIGHTS OF PRIVATE PERSONS

Section 150 creates a right of action in damages for a 'private person' (meaning individuals not doing a regulated activity and businesses not acting in the course of business of any kind) who suffers loss as a result of a contravention of a rule by an authorised person. This exists in addition to common law actions such as negligence or misrepresentation. However, S150 provides a privileged right of action, as there is no need to prove negligence – it is simply enough that there has been a rule breach leading to loss.

7 THE GENERAL PROHIBITION

Section 19 contains what is known as the general prohibition. This states that no person may carry on a regulated activity in the UK or purport to do so unless they are authorised or exempt.

The sanctions for breaching S19 are fairly severe, namely criminal sanctions and unenforceability of agreements, compensation and actions by the FSA or DTI to restrain such activity.

- **Criminal sanctions** – Breach of the general prohibition is an offence punishable by two years in jail and/or an unlimited fine. It is a defence if it can be shown that all reasonable precautions were taken and all due diligence exercised to avoid committing the offence.

- **Unenforceable agreements** – Any agreement made by an unauthorised person will be unenforceable against the other party. FSMA makes it clear that agreements are not illegal or invalid as a result of a contravention of the general prohibition. This ensures that the innocent party to the agreement will still be able to enforce the agreement against the other party, notwithstanding the fact that performance may be a criminal offence.
- **Compensation** – The innocent party will be entitled to recover compensation for any loss sustained if the agreement is made unenforceable.
- The FSA and DTI may seek injunctions and restitution orders to restrain the contravention of the general prohibition and seek to disgorge profits from perpetrators.

We shall now look at the circumstances in which a firm must seek authorisation.

Do I Need Authorisation?

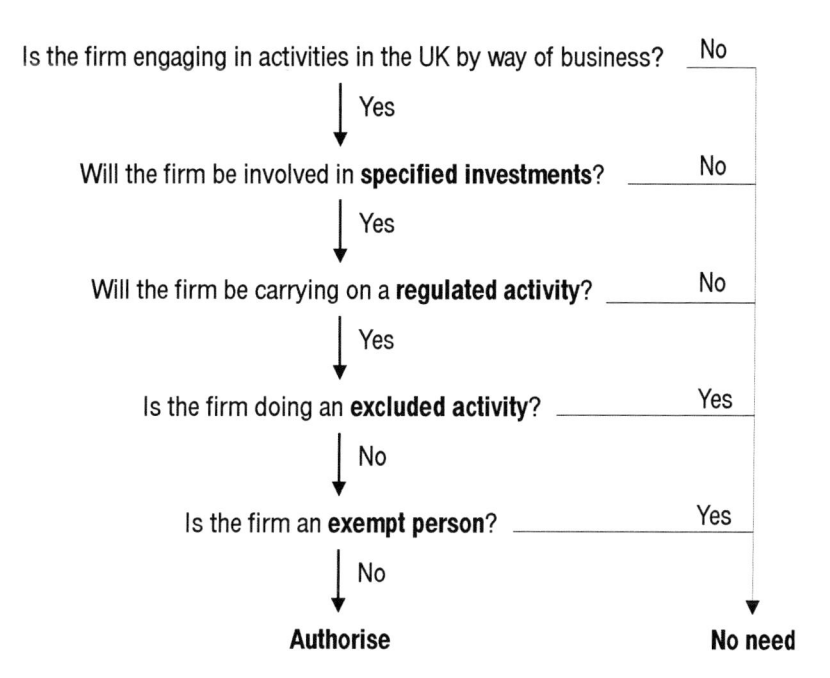

Is the firm engaging in activities in the UK by way of business? — No → No need
↓ Yes
Will the firm be involved in **specified investments**? — No → No need
↓ Yes
Will the firm be carrying on a **regulated activity**? — No → No need
↓ Yes
Is the firm doing an **excluded activity**? — Yes → No need
↓ No
Is the firm an **exempt person**? — Yes → No need
↓ No
Authorise

7.1 Activities carried on in the UK by way of business

For an activity to be covered by FSMA, it must be carried on in the UK by way of business. Whilst this phrase is not defined, most commentators have distilled it down to two factors: continuity and profit. Therefore, a firm doing isolated activities or members of the public buying shares for themselves will not require authorisation, as it will not be done by way of business.

Treasury are given the power to specify circumstances in which an activity is not carried on by way of business. Activities specified by Treasury are discussed in detail when we look at the exceptions.

In terms of territorial scope, broadly speaking, a person will be covered by FSMA if he carries on the activity

- In the UK.
- Into the UK (subject to certain exclusions for overseas persons).
- In another EEA state if his registered office is in the UK and he is passporting services into that state under one of the single-market directives.
- In another EEA state if his registered office is in the UK and the day-to-day management of the activity is the responsibility of that office.

7.2 Specified investments

Only activities with regard to specified investments are covered by FSMA. Specified investments are defined in the Regulated Activities Order 2000. In general terms, these are as follows.

- **Deposits.** Simply defined, this is a sum of money paid by one person to another on terms that it will be repaid on a specified event, e.g. demand.

- **Rights under contracts of insurance.** Included in this category are general insurance contracts (such as motor insurance, accident or sickness), long-term insurance contracts (such as life and annuity) and other insurance contracts (such as funeral expense contracts).

- **Shares** or stock in the capital of a company **wherever the company is based**.

- **Debentures**, loan stock and similar instruments, **e.g. certificate of deposit, bills of exchange**.

- **Government and public securities**, e.g. gilts, US Treasury Bonds.

- **Warrants.**

- **Certificates representing certain securities**, e.g. American Depository Receipts.

- **Units in collective schemes**, including shares in or securities of an open-ended investment company (OEIC).

- **Options** to acquire or dispose of any specified investment or currencies, gold, silver, platinum or palladium.

- **Futures** on anything for investment purposes. This differs from the treatment of options, as it will cover all futures regardless of the underlying investment, so long as it is for investment purposes. The definition of 'investment purposes' is complex. However, in general terms, any futures contract traded either on an exchange or in an over-the-counter market or form similar to that traded on an exchange will constitute an investment. The type of future in effect excluded by this definition would be a short-term contract between a producer and a consumer of a good to purchase that good in the future, e.g. a wheat buyer buying from a farmer.

- **Contracts for differences.** A contract for a difference is a contract in a product that in itself has no physical basis, which essentially means cash-settled derivatives such as interest rate swaps and stock index futures as well as spread betting and forward rate agreements.

- **Lloyd's.** Detailed coverage of the regulation of Lloyd's is beyond the scope of this document. Suffice to say that Lloyd's is an insurance institution specialising in aviation and marine insurance.

- **Regulated mortgages.** This is a significant departure from the 1986 regime, which left the regulation of mortgages to a voluntary code.

7.3 Regulated activities

- Accepting deposits.
- Effecting or carrying out contracts of insurance.
- Dealing as principal or agent in investments.
- Arranging deals in investments.
- Managing investments.
- Advising on investments.
- Safeguarding and administering investments.
- Establishing or operating a collective investment scheme.
- Lloyd's.
- Entering into a regulated mortgage contract as lender.

The activities that are to be regulated by FSMA are also set out in the Regulated Activities Order 2000. As can be seen, the activities cover the investment industry, banking, insurance, mortgage lending and Lloyd's.

7.4 Excluded activities

- **Trustees.** Trustees who do not hold themselves out to the general public as providing this service and are not separately remunerated for the activity are excluded from the need to seek authorisation. This exception is principally designed to cover those who undertake trustee activities not by way of business, e.g. a vicar collecting money for a community project.

- **Activities carried on in the course of a profession or non-investment business.** This exception covers those who carry on a regulated activity as a necessary part of their profession or other business. This exception is principally designed for lawyers, accountants or actuaries who may give investment advice in the course of their activities, e.g. a lawyer who wishes to advise a client to invest money received as a result of litigation. As with trustees, the exception would not apply if the person was remunerated separately for the advice.

- **Groups and joint enterprises.** This allows an exemption for companies who exclusively provide services for other group companies.

- **Newspapers.** Most newspapers give investment advice. However, provided this is not the primary purpose of the newspaper then, once again, under the exceptions granted within the act, they need not seek formal authorisation. On the other hand, the publication of **'tip sheets'** (written recommendations of investments) will require authorisation.

There are a number of other technical excluded activities such as activities relating to an employee share scheme.

7.5 Exempt persons

There are a number of persons who are exempt from the requirement to seek authorisation under FSMA. Section 39 contains the **Appointed Representative** exemption. In markets such as life assurance, the bulk of sales take place through self-employed individuals who act on behalf of the companies. As the companies do not employ them, if this exemption was not in place, such persons would need separate authorisation. The exemption removes them from the scope of authorisation so long as they act solely on behalf of one firm and that firm takes complete responsibility for their actions.

Section 38 of FSMA permits HM Treasury to specify other exempt persons, which was done via the Financial Services and Markets Act (Exemption) Order 2001. Amongst those included are the following.

- The Bank of England.
- Local Authority.
- The central bank of any EEA state.
- The European Central Bank.
- The International Monetary Fund.

Although the running of an exchange is, *prima facie*, a regulated activity, S285 of FSMA states that Recognised Investment Exchanges (RIE) and Recognised Clearing Houses (RCH) are exempt from the requirement to seek authorisation. These are considered in more detail below.

7.5.1 Recognised Investment Exchanges (RIE)

The act of running an investment exchange is, in itself, a regulated activity (arranging deals in investments) and therefore requires regulatory approval. It is, however, exempt from the requirement if it has been given **Recognised Investment Exchange** status. This status assures any parties using the exchange that there are reasonable rules protecting them.

Many firms are members of both a Recognised Investment Exchange (RIE) and regulated by the FSA. It is important to note that firms are obliged to seek authorisation from the FSA. Membership of an RIE merely gives the member privileges of membership associated with the exchange, such as the ability to use the exchange's systems. **Membership of an RIE does not confer authorisation to conduct regulated activities.**

The following are UK exchanges that have been given Recognised Investment Exchange status.

- London Stock Exchange.
- London International Financial Futures and Options Exchange (Euronext.liffe, formerly known as LIFFE).
- London Metal Exchange (LME).
- International Petroleum Exchange (IPE).
- OM London Exchange.
- virt-x.
- EDX.

In addition to the UK exchanges that are permitted to operate under the RIE status above, certain overseas exchanges are also permitted to operate in the UK. Examples of these include

- NASDAQ.
- Chicago Mercantile Exchange.
- Globex.

7.5.2 Designated Investment Exchanges

In addition to those recognised investment exchanges in the UK and overseas that the FSA or the Treasury recognises as being effectively run, there are also overseas exchanges that have been given a form of approval, yet are unable to conduct regulated activities in the UK. Designated Investment Exchange (DIE) status assures any UK user of that overseas market that the FSA believes there are appropriate forms of local regulation guaranteeing the investor's rights.

Examples of DIEs include

- The Tokyo Stock Exchange.
- The New York Stock Exchange.

8 OBTAINING AUTHORISATION

FSMA creates a single authorisation regime for the regulated activities within its scope. This contrasts with the previous financial services regime, which contained a patchwork quilt of regulatory regimes. The FSA has set out the way in which it will exercise its statutory power in The Authorisation Manual. This covers four main areas, namely how it will grant permissions, how it will grant individual approval, authorisation of passporting firms and refusals to grant authorisation or individual approval.

If a firm requires authorisation, it may obtain it by one of three main routes.

- Authorisation by the FSA.
- Passporting.
- Treaty rights.

8.1 Authorisation by the FSA

By far the most common way to obtain authorisation is obtaining permission from the FSA to do one or more regulated activity. The 'permission' that a firm receives will play a crucial role in defining the firm's business scope.

To obtain permission, the FSA must be satisfied that the firm is fit and proper. The firm must therefore meet the 'threshold conditions' for the activity concerned. These link closely with the statutory objective of protecting consumers in that they all go towards ensuring that the business will be run and supervised by the FSA effectively. The threshold conditions are set out in Schedule 6 of FSMA.

- **Legal status.** This is relevant for insurance business and deposit taking where, in order to be authorised, the applicant must be a corporate body, a registered friendly society or a member of Lloyd's.

- **Location of offices.** A UK incorporated company must have its head office and its registered office in the UK. This was inserted to deal with a problem that has caused difficulties in the implementation of single-market directives.

- **Close links.** If the applicant has close links with another company, the FSA must be satisfied that those links will not hinder effective supervision by the FSA. This is designed to deal with situations like that of BCCI where, due to the size of the organisation, the supervision of the whole entity became very difficult indeed.

- **Adequate resource.** In terms of delivering against this condition, applicants should construe the term resource in a broad way, encompassing both financial resource (e.g. capital) and human resources.

- **Suitability.** Applicants must be fit and proper to conduct a regulated activity. Specific reference is made to the fact that an applicant's affairs must be conducted soundly and prudently. One would therefore expect the FSA to consider the management structure of the business to ensure that it is competent, effective and ethical.

It is not a criminal offence for a firm to go beyond its permission, but it may give rise to claims from consumers and the FSA will be able to use the full range of disciplinary sanctions, such as cancelling or varying permission.

The firm itself may vary its permission by applying to the FSA to add or remove a regulated activity. The FSA will consider the interests of consumers of financial services when deciding to allow such an application.

Certain individuals within the firm will require **approval** from the FSA. This is considered in more detail in Chapter 3.

8.2 ISD/2BCD Passport

As detailed earlier, these Directives allow a firm authorised in an EEA state to passport that authorisation into another EEA state.

We must now look at the specific mechanics of passporting in more detail. In particular, we must focus on some of the practical limitations placed on the use of this route.

Firstly, scope of the ISD is slightly different to that of FMSA. Therefore, certain activities that are covered by FSMA (in particular, pure commodities business) are not covered by the ISD. Such activities may not, therefore, be passported and if a firm wishes to do them in another EEA state, it must seek authorisation from the regulator of that state if required by local law to do so.

Secondly, ISD divides the types of business that it covers into core and non-core business. Core business may always be passported, whilst non-core business may only be passported if coupled with a core activity.

These are summarised in the table below.

ISD	ISD	Non-ISD
Core	**Non-Core**	
These will benefit from the passport enabling firms to conduct business across the EEA.	These may be passported providing the firm also conducts a core activity. However, if conducted on their own, they will not be able to seek the passport.	Services not covered within the ISD may not be passported into other member states.
<ul><li>Firms dealing in investments.</li><li>Firms arranging deals in investments.</li><li>Firms managing investments.</li></ul>	<ul><li>Corporate finance advice.</li><li>Safe custody services.</li><li>Investment advice.</li></ul>	<ul><li>All pure commodity business.</li></ul>

As time has passed, the rationale for the split between core and non-core activities (and indeed, the exclusion of commodity business from the scope of ISD) has become more and more unhelpful. Therefore, as part of the drive towards a single market, there are proposals to update the ISD.

8.3 Treaty rights

As we have seen above, single-market directives do not cover the full range of authorisable activities. Therefore, in the absence of passporting rights, FSMA provides a mechanism for EEA firms to conduct regulated activities in other EEA states without the need for separate licensing. Treaty rights are not defined by FSMA – this is something that is the subject of developing case law in the EU. The proviso that FSMA lays down is that the home state must provide equivalent protection or meet harmonised EU minimum standards (this may be confirmed by a certificate from HM Treasury). The FSA must then receive confirmation from the home state regulator that the firm has authorisation in that jurisdiction.

9 THE FSA HANDBOOK

Earlier, we highlighted the link between FSMA and the Secondary Legislation. However, both of these will have a very limited effect on the day-to-day running of a firm. The rules and regulations that a firm must adhere to when running a business are generally found in the *FSA Handbook*. Indeed, even where standards are imposed by FSMA itself, such as in the case of market abuse and financial promotion, the Handbook is used to provide additional requirements.

17: THE REGULATORY ENVIRONMENT

```
    FSMA
      |
      v
Secondary Legislation
e.g. Regulated Activities Order
     Financial Promotions Order
      |
      v
  FSA Handbook
```

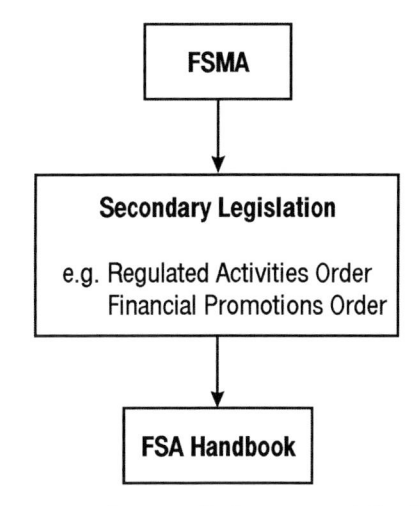

Since 1997, when the move to the new regime was first announced, the FSA has undergone a massive consultation exercise. Indeed, over 100 consultation papers have been released dealing with all aspects of the new regulatory regime. One of the main functions of the consultation process was to alleviate concerns regarding accountability of the FSA and practitioner involvement under FSMA.

The consultation papers have resulted in the *FSA Handbook* – a final set of rules, principles and guidance that a firm must adhere to. Therefore, it includes Principles for Business, Conduct of Business Rules and Money Laundering Rules. It is hardly surprising, therefore, that the Handbook is a lengthy document.

The Handbook is split into a number of blocks. Within each block there are a number of sourcebooks. The full text of the FSA Handbook is available at the FSA's website www.fsa.gov.uk.

High Level Standards

Principles for Businesses (PRIN)	Fit and Proper Test for Approved Persons (FIT)	Threshold Conditions (COND)	Fees Manual (FEES)
Statements of Principle and Code of Practice for Approved Persons (APER)	Senior Management Arrangements, Systems and Controls (SYSC)	General Provisions (GEN)	

Prudential Standards

General Prudential Sourcebook (GENPRU)		Prudential Sourcebook for UCITS Firms (UPRU)	Prudential Sourcebook for Mortgage and Home Finance Firms and Insurance Intermediaries (MIPRU)
Prudential Sourcebook for Banks, Building Societies and Investment Firms (BIPRU)	Prudential Sourcebook for Insurers (INSPRU)		

Interim Prudential Sourcebooks (IPRU):
- Banks
- Building Societies
- Friendly Societies
- Insurers
- Investment Businesses

Business Standards

Conduct of Business (COB)	Insurance: Conduct of Business (ICOB)	Mortgages: Conduct of Business (MCOB)
Client Assets (CASS)	Training and Competence (TC)	Market Conduct (MAR)

Regulatory Processes

Authorisation Manual (AUTH)	Supervision Manual (SUP)	Enforcement Manual (ENF)	Decision Making Manual (DEC)

Redress		
Dispute Resolution: Complaints (DISP)	Complaints Against the FSA (COAF)	Compensation (COMP)

Specialist Sourcebooks		
Collective Investment Schemes (CIS) – *until 13 February 2007 only*	New Collective Investment Schemes (COLL)	Lloyd's (LLD)
Professional Firms (PROF)	Credit Unions (CRED)	Recognised Investment Exchanges/ Clearing Houses (REC)
Electronic Money (ELM)		Electronic Commerce Directive (ECO)

Listing Prospectus and Disclosure		
Listing Rules (LR)	Prospectus Rules (PR)	Disclosure and Transparency Rules (DTR)

9.1 The High Level Standards

The main focus of the High Level Standards of the *FSA Handbook* is with over-arching principles that provide ethics codes for the business and its approved persons. In this chapter, we shall look at these principles in detail.

9.1.1 Principles for Businesses

The Principles for Businesses form the bedrock of the regulatory system. Whilst it is easy to criticise them as being little more than "statements of the blindingly obvious", they are useful in that they help to clarify our thoughts about what may constitute unethical behaviour.

The principles for business apply to every **authorised firm**, which is carrying on a regulated activity (approved persons are not covered by these principles, but are instead subject to a separate set of principles that we shall look at later). However, for an EEA firm that is passporting into the UK, the principles only apply insofar as the matter is the responsibility of the host state regulator. For example, the principle regarding client assets will not apply to an EEA firm passporting into the UK, as this is dealt with by home state regulation.

Note that the consequence of breaching a principle makes the firm liable to enforcement or disciplinary sanctions. A private person may not sue a firm under S150 for breach of a principle.

Below are listed the 11 Principles for Businesses with a brief description of the activity to which each one relates.

1	**Integrity**
	A firm must conduct its business with integrity.
2	**Skill, Care and Diligence**
	A firm must conduct its business with due skill, care and diligence.
3	**Management and Control**
	A firm must take reasonable care to organise and control its affairs responsibly and effectively, with adequate risk management systems.
4	**Financial Prudence**
	A firm must maintain adequate financial resources.
5	**Market Conduct**
	A firm must observe proper standards of market conduct.
6	**Customers' Interests**
	A firm must pay due regard to the interests of its customers and treat them fairly.
7	**Communications with Clients**
	A firm must pay due regard to the information needs of its customers, and communicate information to them in a way that is clear, fair and not misleading.
8	**Conflicts of Interest**
	A firm must manage conflicts of interest fairly, both between itself and its customers and between one customer and another.
9	**Customers: Relationships of Trust**
	A firm must take reasonable care to ensure the suitability of its advice and discretionary decisions for any customer who is entitled to rely upon its judgement.
10	**Clients' Assets**
	A firm must arrange adequate protection for customers' assets when it is responsible for them.
11	**Relations with Regulators**
	A firm must deal with its regulators in an open and co-operative way, and must tell the FSA promptly anything relating to the firm of which the FSA would reasonably expect prompt notice.

It should be noted that some principles refer to clients (such as Principle 10) whilst others refer to customers (such as Principle 9). This affects the scope of the principle. Client is an all-encompassing term that includes everyone from the smallest retail customer through to the largest investment firm. It therefore includes market counterparties, intermediate and private customers. Customer is a more restricted term that excludes 'market counterparties'.

9.1.2 Systems and controls

The FSA has drafted a large amount of guidance on Principle 3. This emphasis comes from a desire to avoid a repetition of Barings, where it was clear that management methods and the control environment were deficient.

Clearly, the extent of the systems and controls within a firm is dependent on a number of factors including

- The nature, scale and complexity of the business.
- The diversity of its operations.

- The volume and size of its transactions.
- The degree of risk associated with each area of its operation.

FSA guidance suggests that in order to comply with its obligation to maintain appropriate systems, a firm should carry out a regular review of the above factors.

The main issues that a firm is expected to consider in establishing compliance with Principle 3 are as follows.

Organisation

The emphasis here is on clear and appropriate reporting lines. Furthermore, where duties are delegated, clear limits should be set out, the firm should assess whether the recipient is suitable to carry out the task and there should be adequate monitoring and supervision of the delegation. Where appropriate, firms should also have clear business strategy plans documented and updated on a regular basis and business continuity plans, which are tested and updated to ensure their effectiveness.

Compliance

Depending on the size of the business, it may be appropriate for the firm to have a separate compliance function. The organisation and responsibilities of compliance should be documented and the department should be staffed by an appropriate number of competent staff who are sufficiently resourced and who have unrestricted access to the firm's records and governing body.

The firm must allocate responsibility for the oversight of compliance and reporting to the governing body in respect of each responsibility to a director or senior manager.

Risk assessment

Where appropriate, a firm should have a separate risk assessment function responsible for assessing the risks the firm faces.

Management information

The firm's arrangements should be such as to furnish the governing body with adequate information to measure, manage and control the risks of regulatory concern.

Employees and agents

A firm should have adequate systems to ensure the suitability of anyone who acts for it.

Audit committee

Where appropriate, a firm should have an audit committee to examine arrangements made by management to ensure compliance with the requirements and standards under the regulatory system. It may also be appropriate to have an internal audit function for the day-to-day monitoring of systems and controls.

Remuneration policies

If a firm's remuneration policies will, from time to time, lead to tensions between the ability of the firm to meet the requirements and standards under the regulatory system and the personal advantage of those who act for it, those tensions must be managed appropriately.

9.1.3 Approved persons

Section 59 of FSMA states that a person cannot carry out a Controlled Function in a firm unless that individual has been approved by the FSA. FSMA sets out three broad categories of persons who will require FSA approval.

- Individuals exerting a significant influence on the conduct of the firm's affairs.
- Individuals dealing directly with customers.
- Individuals dealing with the property of clients.

The *FSA Handbook* (specifically, the *Supervision Manual*) then identifies 27 specific Controlled Functions that can be split into the following groups.

- 1-7 relate to governing functions, e.g. a director, chief executive or partner.
- 8-12 relate to required functions, e.g. compliance officer or money laundering reporting officer.
- 13-15 relate to systems and control functions, e.g. finance officer or head of risk.
- 16-20 relate to significant management functions, e.g. head of settlement or head of claims.
- 21-27 relate to customer functions, e.g. dealers, advisers or investment managers.

Individuals who fall within all of the above categories **except** customer functions would be considered to be exerting a significant influence on the conduct of the firm's affairs. The relevance of this fact is that those who are exerting a significant influence over the firm will have to comply with all seven Statements of Principles, whereas individuals undertaking customer functions will only have to comply with the first four. This is discussed in more detail below.

To obtain approval, a person must satisfy the FSA that they are fit and proper to do the controlled function. The most important considerations are

- Honesty, integrity and reputation.
- Competency and capability.
- Financial soundness.

The person will apply to the FSA using its standard application form.

9.1.4 Statements of Principle

The Statements of Principle apply to all **approved persons** when they are performing a controlled function.

There are seven Statements of Principle. The first four apply to all approved persons, whilst the final three only apply to approved persons exerting a significant influence over the firm.

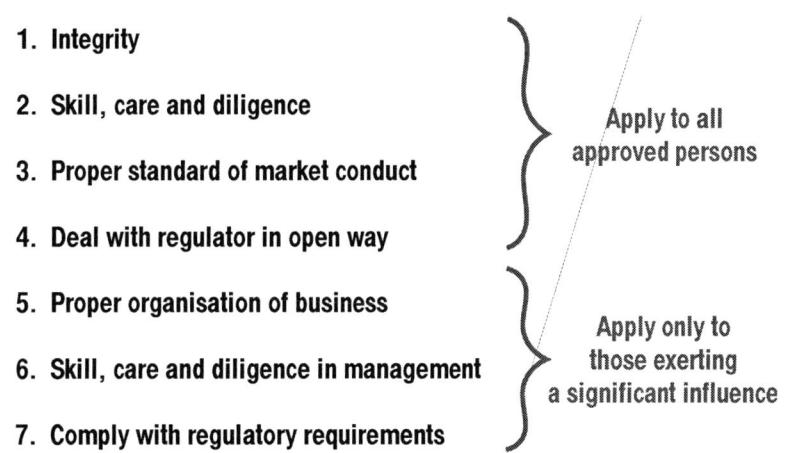

1. **Integrity**
2. **Skill, care and diligence**
3. **Proper standard of market conduct**
4. **Deal with regulator in open way**

} Apply to all approved persons

5. **Proper organisation of business**
6. **Skill, care and diligence in management**
7. **Comply with regulatory requirements**

} Apply only to those exerting a significant influence

Section 62(2) of FSMA requires the FSA to issue a code of practice to help approved persons to determine whether or not their conduct complies with the Statements of Principle. The FSA has complied with this obligation by issuing The Code of Practice for Approved Persons. This sets out descriptions of conduct which, in the FSA's opinion, does not comply with a Statement of Principle and factors that will be taken into account in determining whether or not an approved person's conduct does comply with a Statement of Principle.

The Code is not conclusive – it is only evidential towards indicating that a Statement of Principle has been breached. Account will be taken of the context in which the course of conduct was undertaken. In determining whether there has been a breach of Principles 5-7, account will be taken of the nature and complexity of the business, the role and responsibilities of the approved person and the knowledge that the approved person had (or should have had) of the regulatory concerns arising in the business under his control.

We shall now look at the seven Statements of Principle in detail, taking into account the treatment of each by the Code.

Statement of Principle 1 – An approved person must act with integrity in carrying out his controlled function.

The Code provides examples of behaviour that would not comply with this Statement of Principle. These include **deliberately** misleading people, falsifying documents, other improper actions such as theft, fraud, insider dealing or front running client orders.

Statement of Principle 2 – An approved person must act with skill, care and diligence in carrying out his controlled function.

Examples of non-compliant behaviour under Statement of Principle 2 include failing to inform persons of material information, failing to disclose risks, charges or personal account dealings or other acts falling below a reasonable standard of conduct such as recommending unsuitable transactions or failing to control client assets.

The coverage of Statement of Principle 2 is similar to Principle 1. The difference is that Principle 1 states that each act needs to be deliberate. Principle 2 may be breached by acts which, whilst not deliberate wrongdoing, are negligent.

Statement of Principle 3 – An approved person must observe proper standards of market conduct in carrying out his controlled functions.

Examples of non-compliant behaviour under Statement of Principle 3 include

- Breach of market codes and exchange rules.
- Breach of Inter-Professional Conduct or the Code of Market Conduct.

The FSA expects all approved persons to meet proper standards whether they are participating in organised markets such as exchanges, or trading in less formal over-the-counter markets.

Statement of Principle 4 – An approved person must deal with the FSA and with other regulators in an open and co-operative way and must disclose appropriately any information of which the FSA would reasonably expect notice.

This Statement of Principle concerns the requirement to co-operate, not only with the FSA, but also with other bodies such as an overseas regulator or an exchange.

Approved persons do not have a duty to report concerns directly to the FSA unless they are responsible for such reports. The obligation on most approved persons is to report concerns of 'material significance' in accordance with the firm's internal procedures. If no such procedures exits, the report should be made direct to the FSA.

Statement of Principle 5 – An approved person performing a significant influence function must take reasonable steps to ensure that the business of the firm for which he is responsible in his controlled function is organised so that it can be controlled effectively.

As stated above, Principles 5-7 related only to those performing a significant influence function. This Principle requires those performing a significant influence function to delegate responsibilities sensibly and effectively. Paramount to this is the requirement that they should delegate only where it is to a suitable person. In addition, they must provide those persons with proper reporting lines, authorisation levels and job descriptions. Clearly, all of these factors (and in particular the suitability requirement) should be regularly reviewed.

Statement of Principle 6 – An approved person performing a significant influence function must exercise due skill, care and diligence in managing the business of the firm for which he is responsible in his controlled function.

This principle requires those performing a significant influence function to inform themselves about the affairs of the business for which they are responsible. They should not permit transactions or an expansion of the business unless they fully understand the risks involved. They must also take care when monitoring highly profitable or unusual transactions and in these (or other cases) must never accept implausible or unsatisfactory explanations from subordinates.

This principle links to Principle 5, as it makes it clear that delegation is not an abdication of responsibility. Therefore, where delegation has been made, a person must still monitor and control that part of the business and, therefore, should require progress reports and question those reports where appropriate.

Statement of Principle 7 – An approved person performing a significant influence function must take reasonable steps to ensure that the business of the firm for which he is responsible in his controlled function complies with the regulatory requirements imposed on that business.

This has a clear link to Principle 3. Those exerting a significant influence on the firm must take reasonable steps to ensure that the requirements set out therein are implemented within their firm. They should also review the improvement of such systems and controls, especially where there has been a breach of the regulatory requirements.

9.2 The Financial Services Authority (FSA)

Prior to FSMA, a patchwork quilt of legislation existed. There were a number of different regulators.

- Within the investment industry, a firm would be regulated by any or all of SFA, IMRO and PIA depending upon what activities it was undertaking.

- Insurance companies were regulated by the DTI under the Insurance Companies Act 1982.

- Banks were regulated by the Bank of England (supervision of retail banks was in fact passed to the FSA in June 1998 (a date known as N1) via the Bank of England Act 1998.

- Finally, the role of the Listing Authority was held by the London Stock Exchange.

- There were also specialist bodies regulating building societies, friendly societies and Lloyd's.

Under FSMA and its related legislation, all of these functions are undertaken by a single statutory regulator – the Financial Services Authority.

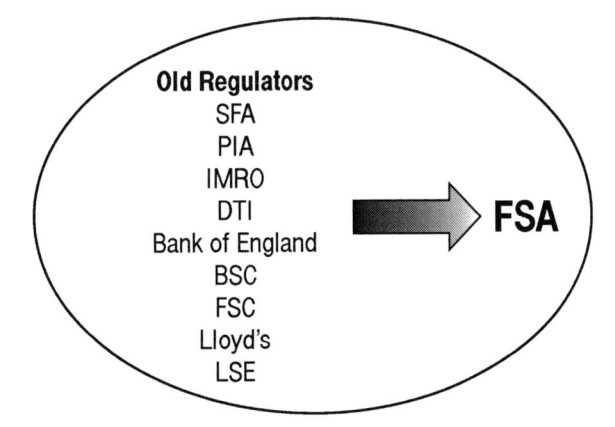

Old Regulators
SFA
PIA
IMRO
DTI
Bank of England
BSC
FSC
Lloyd's
LSE
→ **FSA**

9.2.1 Functions of the FSA

The FSA is an unusually large and powerful regulator. It regulates investment banking and insurance businesses and is the sole authorising body. The FSA is not, however, regarded as acting on behalf of the

17: THE REGULATORY ENVIRONMENT

crown. Its members, officers and staff are therefore not crown servants. In fact, the FSA is a private company given powers by FSMA. Its principal powers include the following.

- Granting authorisation and permission to firms to undertake regulated activities.
- Approving individuals to perform controlled functions.
- The right to issue
    - General rules (such as conduct of business rules or money laundering rules) subject to S155 of FSMA that requires the FSA to consult and undertake a cost-benefit analysis when it increases the regulatory burden.
    - Principles (such as the Principles for Businesses).
    - Codes of conduct (such as the Code of Conduct for Approved Persons).
    - Guidance.
- The right to investigate authorised firms or approved persons.
- The right to take enforcement action against authorised firms and approved persons.
- The right to discipline authorised firms and approved persons.
- The power to take action against any person for market abuse.
- The power to recognise investment exchanges and clearing houses.

9.2.2 Accountability of the FSA

During the passage of the Act through Parliament, much was made of the need to ensure that the FSA used its considerable powers in a responsible and accountable manner. However, it was also acknowledged that accountability must be balanced with the need to ensure that the regulator is independent and effective. As we have already seen, FSMA sets out four statutory objectives that the FSA must consider when performing its regulatory role. In addition, a number of other accountability measures are included.

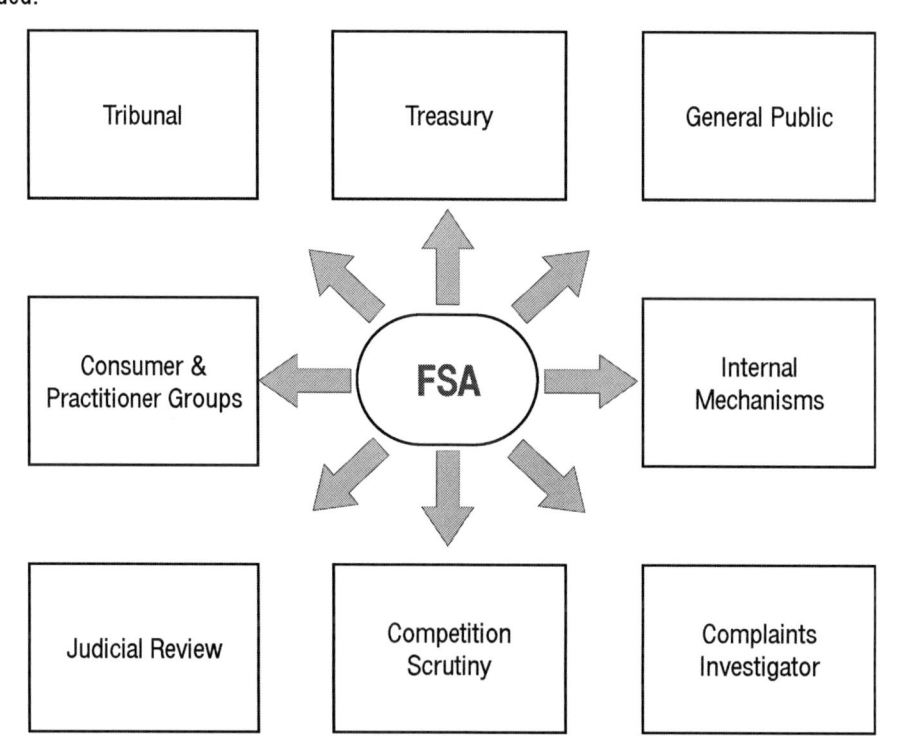

Diagram: FSA at centre with arrows pointing to: Tribunal, Treasury, General Public, Consumer & Practitioner Groups, Internal Mechanisms, Judicial Review, Competition Scrutiny, Complaints Investigator.

HM Treasury

The FSA's main line of accountability is to HM Treasury, which appoints the Board and Chairman. HM Treasury will judge the FSA against the requirements laid down in S2 of FSMA, which include a requirement to ensure that the burdens imposed on the regulated community are proportionate to the benefits they provide. In delivering against this, the FSA does a cost-benefit analysis whenever it increases the burden of a rule.

Treasury also requires that the FSA submit an annual report covering such matters as the discharge of its functions and the extent to which the four statutory objectives have been met. Treasury also has powers to commission and publish an independent review of FSA's use of resources and commission official enquiries into serious regulatory failures.

General public

Within three months of submitting its annual report to HM Treasury, the FSA must hold a public meeting to facilitate open discussion of the contents of the report. This forum also allows the general public to probe the FSA about any of its acts or omissions in the discharge of its functions.

Internal mechanisms

The FSA must have clear corporate governance structures. Therefore, the board that HM Treasury appoints must have a majority of non-executive directors to ensure balanced debate. A committee consisting solely of non-executive board members must also be set up with the role of ensuring the economic and efficient use of resources and setting the pay of the executive directors.

Complaints investigator

The FSA is required to set up a complaints scheme for dealing with complaints arising from the discharge of its functions. This is manned by an independent investigator who is able to report publicly and recommend compensation payments. Whilst this may seem significant, serious doubts have been expressed about the adequacy of the arrangements. Certainly, when the issue was discussed in Parliament, the circumstances in which it was envisaged that the FSA may be required to make a compensatory award were limited to nominal compensation for administrative errors.

Competition scrutiny

The FSA's rules and practices are subject to competition vetting by the Director General of Fair Trading and the Competition Commission. The FSA has therefore been very careful to ensure that it does not draft rules or act in a way that is anti-competitive. Indeed, the FSA is currently reviewing the rules on polarisation after the Director General of Fair Trading concluded that they were anti-competitive.

Judicial review

Whilst the the FSA is a private company, it is clearly performing a public function and is empowered to do so by statute. Therefore, the FSA will be subject to administrative law, in particular, judicial review. Judicial review is a process by which public bodies' actions can be scrutinised in court if they have acted outside the scope of their powers. Unfortunately, many provisions in FSMA, such as the regulatory objectives, give the FSA broad discretion on how they use their powers. The effect of this may be to limit the availability of judicial review.

Consumer and practitioner groups

The FSA's accountability is further advanced by two statutory bodies – the practitioner and consumer panels that must be consulted on general policies and practices. FSMA requires that the FSA "has regard" to representations made by these panels. The practitioner panel is designed to advise the FSA on the interests and concerns of the businesses that the FSA regulates. The consumer panel is designed to advise on the interests and concerns of consumers. The membership of both panels is determined by the FSA, although HM Treasury's approval is required for the appointment and dismissal of chairmen.

Financial Services and Markets Tribunal

The final significant check on accountability is the Financial Services and Markets Tribunal. The FSMA makes provision for an independent body run by the Lord Chancellor's Department, which will provide for a complete rehearing of the FSA's enforcement and authorisation cases where the firm or individual and the FSA have not been able to agree the outcome.

9.3 Authorisation

As we have already seen, if a firm wishes to do a regulated activity by way of business in the UK, it must be authorised or exempt. Previously, we considered the scope of the exemptions (e.g. Appointed Representatives and RIE/RCHs). We also considered the process of receiving authorisation (from the FSA, Passporting or Treaty Rights). As part of the *FSA Handbook*, the FSA has published The Authorisation Manual, detailing the conditions that must be satisfied when seeking authorisation and how applications will be determined.

Where a firm wishes to obtain permission from the FSA to do a regulated activity, it will be sent an application pack requiring detailed information from the firm. The amount of detailed information that the applicant will have to submit will be related to the risks posed to the four statutory objectives. Therefore, although some applicants will have to complete all sections of the pack, other sections are specific to certain types of business.

In order to get permission, the applicant must show that it is fit and proper. This means a number of things.

- Firstly, the applicant must satisfy the threshold conditions that we saw previously.
- Secondly, the FSA will operate a risk assessment process. This allows the FSA to be proportional in terms of the information required and the allocation of the FSA resources.

In order to assess the above, the applicant will need to detail such matters as the precise scope of the permission it wishes to apply for, the impact of the Handbook on its activities, systems and controls needed, and prepare a full business plan setting out its resources (human, systems and capital). The FSA may require applicants to attend meetings to discuss the application before the application documents are submitted. This will be required in cases where the applicant's plans are complex, high risk or innovative.

The initial determination of the application is taken by FSA staff. When the firm is given permission to do a regulated activity, it will be recorded on the public register of authorised persons maintained by the FSA.

If the FSA staff decide to refuse the application or impose a limit on it, they must give this recommendation to the Regulatory Decisions Committee (RDC) who will consider the facts and decide whether to proceed with the staff recommendation or grant the application.

Where an application is refused or limited by the RDC, the applicant may appeal to the Financial Services and Markets Tribunal.

9.4 Disciplinary powers

9.4.1 Information gathering and investigatory powers

The FSA has the power to require an authorised firm (or any person connected with it), appointed representatives or certain other persons, e.g. RIEs, to provide it with information, reports or other documents it needs to carry out its duties.

If the FSA has good reason, it may launch a general investigation into the affairs, ownership or control of any authorised firm or appointed representative (see Chapter 1 for a discussion of the meaning of this

17: THE REGULATORY ENVIRONMENT

term). An investigation need not be limited to the regulated activities of the firm. Furthermore, if it is relevant to the main investigation, the FSA may investigate any member of the firm's group.

Where it appears that a specific contravention or offence has occurred, the FSA may appoint investigators. This power covers authorised firms, approved persons, appointed representatives and, indeed, in some cases such as market abuse, all persons. In some cases, such as money laundering and insider dealing, the FSA will share investigatory powers with the DTI.

The FSA can require a person under investigation, or connected person, to attend questioning by an investigator and can require a person to produce documents and answer questions. This effectively removes the right to silence. In order to ensure that the regime is compliant with human rights legislation, such answers will not be admissible in market abuse proceedings.

The FSA will not normally make public the fact that it is or is not investigating a particular matter, or the outcome of any investigation.

9.4.2 Reports by skilled persons

The FSA has the power to require a firm to appoint accountants, actuaries and other professionals to do a one-off investigation into the firm's activities and report back to the FSA.

9.4.3 Varying permission

The FSA has a general power to vary or cancel a firm's permission to undertake a regulated activity. Cancellation of a firm's permission will take place where the FSA has serious concerns regarding the firm's business activities. More commonly, the FSA will vary a firm's permission by placing tailored requirements on the firm. For example, the FSA may use the power to stop the firm seeking a particular class of client or selling particular investments. Such action is normally taken to protect consumers, but the FSA may vary permission for other reasons such as the fact that a firm has changed its controller or stops using its permission.

9.4.4 Redress powers

There are two types of redress powers available to the FSA – those that require a court order and those that the FSA can impose itself.

The FSA will be able to apply to the court to require any person who has breached a rule or other requirement of FSMA to provide compensation or restitution to those who have suffered loss as a result. This will be particularly important where the FSA seeks to enforce rules such as market abuse against non-authorised persons.

Where an authorised firm has breached a rule or other requirement of FSMA, the FSA may require the firm to provide compensation or restitution without a court order.

Where there is evidence of industry-wide rule breaches (such as that seen in the pensions misselling scandal), the FSA may ask Treasury to make an order authorising an industry-wide review.

The FSA may also apply to a court for an injunction to restrain or prohibit persons from breaking a rule or other requirement of FSMA.

9.4.5 Disciplinary powers

The FSA may discipline firms or approved persons for acts of misconduct. Disciplinary measures available are private warnings, public statements of misconduct, fines, variation or cancellation of permission.

The disciplinary process has been designed to ensure that it is compliant with human rights legislation. Therefore, whilst FSA staff will investigate the matter and decide whether they feel enforcement action is appropriate, they will not take the final decision on this. Instead, they pass the case to the Regulatory

Decisions Committee (RDC), which will look at the case and decide whether or not to take action. If they decide to take action, a warning notice will be sent, containing details of the proposed action. The person concerned then has access to the material that the FSA is relying on and may make oral or written representations to the RDC. The RDC will then issue a decision notice detailing the reasons for the decision, proposed sanction and a notice of the right to refer the matter to the Financial Services and Markets Tribunal, which undertakes a complete rehearing of the case. This is summarised as follows.

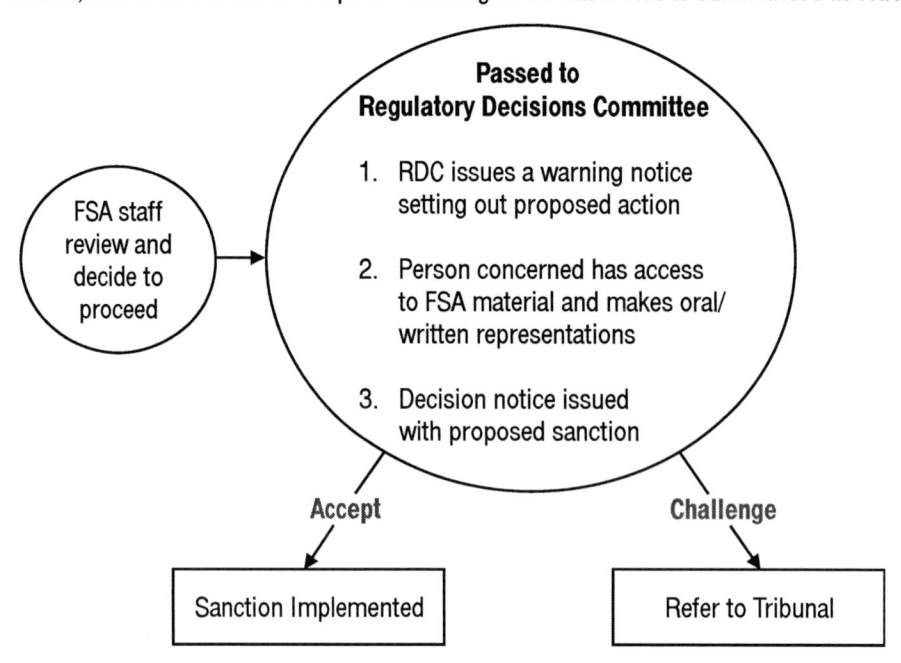

```
FSA staff          Passed to
review and   →   Regulatory Decisions Committee
decide to
proceed      1. RDC issues a warning notice
                setting out proposed action

             2. Person concerned has access
                to FSA material and makes oral/
                written representations

             3. Decision notice issued
                with proposed sanction

        Accept                    Challenge
          ↓                           ↓
    Sanction Implemented        Refer to Tribunal
```

Market abuse

The FSA may take sanctions against any person who has engaged in market abuse. Or has required or encouraged another to engage in market abuse by taking or refraining from action. The FSA may issue a public statement stating that someone has engaged in market abuse or issue an unlimited fine.

The Enforcement Manual is designed to protect the interests of the general public by providing powers that the FSA may exercise swiftly and conclusively to remedy or prevent wrongs. However, the processes set out by the Enforcement Manual show that the FSA is also keen to ensure that the process is fair and that it does not exercise its powers without any accountability. This provides the rationale for the Financial Services and Markets Tribunal, which will provide a complete rehearing of cases that are not settled. Furthermore, any financial penalties received by the FSA must be used for the benefit of authorised firms.

10 FINANCIAL SERVICES OMBUDSMAN

The Financial Services Ombudsman offers a cheap and informal method of independent adjudication of disputes between a firm and its customers. This is used as an alternative to courts, but is as binding upon the parties as a court's decision.

Only eligible complainants may use the Ombudsman system. Eligible complainants are defined as private individuals and small businesses (other than those who are properly classified as intermediate customers) who are customers or potential customers of the firm.

Where an eligible complainant refers a matter to the Ombudsman, a firm has no definitive right to block the matter being referred, but may dispute the eligibility of the complaint or the complainant. In such circumstances, the Ombudsman will seek representations from the parties.

The Ombudsman may investigate the merits of the case and may also convene a hearing if necessary. Where the Ombudsman finds in favour of the complainant, it can force the firm to pay up to £100,000 and reasonable costs (although awards of costs are not common).

11 FINANCIAL SERVICES COMPENSATION SCHEME

The compensation scheme is designed to compensate eligible claimants where a relevant firm is unable or likely to be unable to meet claims against it. Generally speaking, therefore, the scheme will only apply where the firm is declared insolvent or bankrupt.

A relevant firm means the following.

- An authorised firm, except an EEA firm, passporting into the UK (customers who lose as a result of default by an EEA firm must seek compensation from the firm's home state system).
- A UK branch of an EEA firm.
- An appointed representative of one of the above.

Only eligible claimants may seek compensation from the scheme. An eligible claimant is defined as

- Private customers
    - But not customers with connection to the firm, e.g. directors.
    - Not large company or large partnership.
- Intermediate customers and market counterparties (for long-term insurance only).

The maximum awards per claim are summarised in the table below.

	Limit
Deposits	£31,700 (100% of £2,000 and 90% of the next £33,000)
Investments	£48,000 (100% of £30,000 and 90% of the next £20,000)
Long-Term Insurance	At least 90% of value attributed to the policy
General Insurance	Compulsory: 100% of valid claim Non-compulsory: 100% of £2,000 and 90% of the remainder

The scheme is funded by levies on the authorised community.

12 US REGULATION

The existing UK regulatory structure for financial services stems from two key definitions: those of 'investments' and 'investment business'. If engaged in 'investment business', unless exempted in some way, it is necessary to become authorised.

US regulation is somewhat differently organised, as within it, there are three distinct and separate regimes.

One for the banking industry, another for the securities industry and yet a third for most exchange-traded derivatives.

17: THE REGULATORY ENVIRONMENT

	Function		
	Banking	**Securities**	**Futures**
Regulatory Agency	Federal Reserve Board (FED) / Federal Deposit Insurance Corp (FDIC) / Office of the Comptroller of the Currency (OCC)	Securities and Exchange Commission (SEC)	Commodity Futures Trading Commission (CFTC)
Primary Statute	Array of State and Federal statutes	Securities and Exchange Act	Commodity Exchange Act

As can be seen, the focus in each case is on the category of participants. It is also necessary to mention the Glass Steagal Act, a federal law which, until 1999, prohibited banks from engaging in securities dealing.

The existing US structure of regulation has evolved over the past century or so to deal with the creation of a single US currency, the Wall Street crash and the development of the futures industry.

As financial product development continues, the traditional distinctions between banking, securities and derivatives business have become increasingly blurred, giving rise to jurisdictional disputes or 'turf battles' over which agency has responsibility for a particular product.

Beyond the regulatory agencies so far mentioned are other agencies such as

Savings and Loans	Office of Thrift Supervision
Insurance Companies	Regulated at the state level
Pension Funds	Pension funds are regulated under the Employment Retirement Income Security Act (ERISA) by the Department of Labour

13 THE COMMODITY FUTURES TRADING COMMISSION (CFTC)

The CFTC was created by Congress in 1974 with a mandate to regulate commodity futures and options markets. This agency replaced the Commodity Exchange Commission that had emerged in the 1920s.

Through the Commodity Exchange Act, Congress sought to stamp out 'bucket shops' or companies that used the prices of the exchanges without trading their products. In short, a key objective of the act was to bring futures trading on exchange and then to ensure the activities of those connected with exchange-traded products were themselves well regulated.

The act therefore states that a futures contract, unless specifically exempted by the CFTC, is illegal unless it is traded on an organised commodity exchange. The term 'futures contract' is not explicitly defined. The act was revised in 1974 in part to take account of the development of financial futures and consequently, the term 'commodity' was defined more broadly to incorporate not just traditional commodities, but a range of financial instruments as well.

There have been ongoing disputes between the CFTC and the SEC as to who regulates what. With respect to derivatives products the division is as follows.

- CFTC regulates futures and options on futures based on traditional commodities, government securities and stock indices.
- SEC regulates options on securities and options on stock indices (but not options on stock index futures).
- OTC products in commodities, currencies and interest rates (but not equities or credit) are excluded from the principal regulatory regime.

13.1 Organisation

The CFTC has delegated much of its direct regulatory responsibilities to self-regulatory organisations, which are overseen by the CFTC.

These organisations are the National Futures Association and the ten US exchanges on which commodity futures and commodity options are traded, the so-called "contract markets".

13.1.1 National Futures Association

The NFA is responsible for some 3,800 firms and has 45,000 individuals registered in a variety of categories. The NFA sets qualification standards for these individuals (generally, the National Commodity Futures Examination – Series 3). The registration process also involves the checking of fingerprints against FBI files as well as applicants' records against files maintained by the regulatory agencies to gauge that they are fit and proper.

The NFA also undertakes member visits and reviews and has a range of enforcement powers varying from fines to expulsion.

13.2 Membership categories

Membership of the NFA is open to any person registered with CFTC, all futures exchanges, and any other person engaged in the futures business, provided the applicant meets the NFA's membership qualification standards.

Membership in the NFA and registration are required by the Commodity Exchange Act for firms and individuals who conduct futures-related business with the public. NFA bylaws further stipulate that no NFA member may do business with any firm or individual who is not an NFA member, other than a direct customer.

13.2.1 Associated Person (AP)

An AP is an individual who solicits orders, customers or customer funds, or who supervises other individuals who do so on behalf of a Commodity Pool Operator, Commodity Trading Advisor, Futures Commission Merchant or Introducing Broker. In other words, an AP is anyone who is a salesperson or who supervises salespersons in any of our Member categories. Registration requirements apply to every individual in the supervisory chain of command, not just to individuals who have direct supervisory responsibilities.

13.2.2 Commodity Pool Operator (CPO)

A CPO is an individual or organisation that operates or solicits funds for a commodity pool. A commodity pool is a collective investment vehicle in which funds contributed by a number of persons are combined for the purpose of trading futures contracts or commodity options, or for the purpose of investing in another commodity pool.

13.2.3 Commodity Trading Advisor (CTA)

A CTA is an individual or organisation that, for compensation or profit, directly or indirectly advises others as to the value of, or the advisability of, buying or selling futures contracts or commodity options. Providing advice indirectly includes exercising trading authority over a customer's account as well as giving advice through written publications or other media.

13.2.4 Futures Commission Merchant (FCM)

An FCM is an individual or organisation that solicits or accepts orders to buy or sell futures contracts or commodity options and accepts money or other assets from customers to support such orders. Registration is required in all cases. **There are no exemptions.**

13.2.5 Introducing Broker (IB)

An IB is an individual or organisation that solicits or accepts orders to buy or sell futures contracts or commodity options, but does not accept money or other assets from customers to support such orders.

13.2.6 Floor Brokers (FB)

An FB is a contract market member who executes futures trades for the account of another on the floor of a contract market.

13.2.7 Floor Trader (FT)

An FT is a contract market member who trades for his own account on the floor of a contract market.

13.3 Exchanges

The US futures exchanges also act as self-regulating organisations for their members. To avoid regulatory overlap, each market professional has a primary self-regulatory organisation referred to as a Designated Self-Regulatory Organisation or DSRO.

NFA is the DSRO for CTAs, CPOs and for FCMs and IBs who are not members of a contract market.

The contract market is the DSRO for its members, including FBs, FTs, FCMs and IBs.

13.4 Impact of US Regulation on UK Firms

The most direct impact of the rules of the CFTC on UK-based and authorised firms is through the provisions of CFTC Part 30.

Historically, the US authorities have been anxious to ensure that US persons are adequately protected when trading futures.

Domestically, this has been achieved in two ways: firstly, through the CFTC's approval of US products and exchanges and secondly, by their insistence on participants being registered with the CFTC and the various SROs.

The regime worked well whilst the futures industry was dominated by the American exchanges and their products. More recently, US investors have increasingly wished to trade non-US products often through non-US firms. The Part 30 rules seek to provide the opportunity for such trading without compromising the protections afforded.

In common with the CEA itself, Part 30 outlines requirements both for products and intermediaries.

14 OTC REGULATION

The regulation of OTC derivatives is complex and controversial. It lacks the rigour and prescription of the exchange-traded world and, because of the pace of product innovation, the regulators are constantly engaged in a game of catch up.

In this section, the legal background of the principal centres of OTC trading are reviewed for the US and UK. The work of the leading trade association, the International Swaps and Derivatives Association (ISDA) is examined and, finally, there is a summary of certain key issues and cases affecting the industry.

14.1 ISDA

The International Swaps and Derivatives Association (ISDA) is the global trade association representing participants in the OTC derivatives industry, a business that includes interest rate, currency, commodity and equity swaps, as well as related products such as caps, collars, floors and swaptions. ISDA was chartered in 1985, and today numbers over 300 members from around the world. These members include most of the world's major institutions who deal in, as well as leading end-users of, OTC derivatives.

The International Swaps and Derivatives Association was established to

- Promote practices conducive to the efficient conduct of the business of its members in swaps and other derivatives (collectively 'derivatives'), including the development and maintenance of standard documentation for derivatives, and to foster high standards of commercial honour and business conduct among its members.

- Create a forum for the discussion of issues of relevance to participants in derivatives transactions and to co-operate with other organisations on issues of mutual concern in order to promote common interests.

- Advance international public understanding of derivatives.

- Inform its members of legislative and administrative developments affecting participants in derivatives transactions; to provide a forum for its members to examine and review such developments; and to represent effectively the common interests of its members before legislative and administrative bodies and international quasi-public institutes, boards and other bodies; and

- Encourage the development and maintenance of an efficient and productive market for derivatives through action in furtherance of the foregoing purposes.

ISDA's Board of Directors, which consists of 18 directors drawn from and elected annually by its Members, manages the Association's activities and sets its policies. The International Swaps and Derivatives Association maintains its principal offices in New York and also has offices in London and Tokyo.

The most important aspects of ISDA's day-to-day work focus on three areas.

14.1.1 Regulation

ISDA acts as a lobbyist on all areas concerned with OTC regulation and frequently makes submissions to the SFA, the Bank of England, Congress and other federal US agencies to ensure appropriate regulation. A recent focus of this lobbying has been with respect to Capital Adequacy rules.

14.1.2 Documentation

ISDA has created a range of standardised documentation that is used throughout the industry to establish the contractual relationship between the parties to OTC transactions. Key amongst these documents is the 1992 ISDA Master Agreement that is exchanged between participants at the start of their OTC trading. The document is designed to clarify default procedures, netting arrangements, etc. and may be used to document a variety of derivative transactions.

In addition, ISDA also produces many other standard documents for commodity and equity trades, confirmations and definitions.

The effect of the documentation is to serve a role analogous to contract specifications and procedures in the exchange-traded world.

14.1.3 Netting

A key concern in the exchange and OTC world is to minimise credit risk.

To understand ISDA's work in this area, it is worth outlining the potential problem. Imagine that a bank has two outstanding interest rate swaps with a counterparty. Under Swap A, the bank has a marked-to-market profit of $1m, whilst in Swap B, the bank has a loss of $400,000. In aggregate, therefore, the exposure to the counterparty would intuitively appear to be the sum of the positives and negatives, i.e. the net amount, $600,000.

However, whether the exposure is actually $600,000 is a function of whether it is appropriate to aggregate the exposure and view the position as essentially a single contract. The appropriateness of the aggregation will depend on how bankruptcy/insolvency is treated in a particular jurisdiction.

In certain jurisdictions, if a firm goes bankrupt, the receiver will be allowed to cherry pick – in other words, honour contracts profitable to the firm in receivership and dishonour those that would require the receiver to pay out funds. In such a jurisdiction, netting plainly does not work.

ISDA's 1992 Master Agreement incorporates clauses in which the counterparties recognise 'close out' netting if the swaps or other contracts were to be terminated because of, for example, one party's bankruptcy. To support these provisions, ISDA has obtained legal opinions on the enforceability of such clauses. ISDA also lobbies 'debtor-friendly' countries to introduce revised legislation.

ISDA's initiative mirrors that of the Futures and Options Association (FOA) in the exchange-traded world. Aside from the importance of ensuring enforceability to minimise actual credit risk, netting also has ramifications with respect to regulatory capital. If netting arrangements are not supported by robust legal opinions, the regulated entity will find itself having to provide more capital to cover its counterparty role requirements.

14.2 Master agreements

In the early days of the OTC market, banks typically used their own bespoke documentation for swap transactions. The absence of uniform definitions and terminology made the whole business time consuming, so much so that documents were often exchanged long after the actual trade, thus heightening credit and legal risks.

Nowadays, in a typical OTC trade, the bank will supply its preferred type of master agreement (normally ISDA) as part of the account opening process. The ISDA master in fact normally incorporates three documents: the master agreement itself, a schedule (in which the parties can signify their agreements to modifications of the standard terms) and a form of confirmation (in which the details of the trade are outlined). In addition, various other documents might be exchanged, for example, credit support documents.

Once agreed, the master agreement and schedule form the basis of all subsequent trades and need not be renegotiated.

ISDA has developed a range of master agreements to deal with different products. Nonetheless, they follow the model of the most widely used, the 1992 ISDA Master Agreement (Multicurrency - Cross Border), the main clauses of which are discussed below.

14.2.1 Interpretation

The first section states that the master and all transactions under it form a single agreement.

Aside from avoiding lengthy renegotiations for each trade, the clause seeks to reduce credit risks by portraying the relationship as the net sum of its parts.

14.2.2 Obligations

Most importantly, this section addresses payment netting (not to be confused with close-out netting). Payment netting refers to the practice of only settling the net amount on each payment date. For example, in a fixed/floating interest rate swap, A may be due to pay 7% fixed whilst B may be due to pay six-month LIBOR, currently 8%. Under payment netting, B will simply pay A 1% × notional principal × time.

The effect of payment netting minimises administration and credit risk.

14.2.3 Representations

Within this section, the parties make representations to each other with respect to their authority to enter into transactions. Each party also indicates that it is not in default and there is no outstanding litigation that is likely to affect the performance of the contract. These representations are to be supported by opinions from auditors and lawyers.

14.2.4 Agreements

This clause provides for the parties to conduct ongoing risk assessment of each other. In the schedule, for example, one party may agree to supply financial statements at particular intervals.

14.2.5 Default and termination

This section outlines what would constitute default and give rise to the end of the entire agreement. The clause also outlines what would cause the termination of a particular transaction or set of transactions.

It is possible for the parties to include in the schedule other events that might precipitate default, e.g. a credit downgrade.

The four key events of default are

- Failure by a party to make a payment or delivery.
- Failure by a party to perform an obligation.
- Misrepresentation.
- Bankruptcy.

14.2.6 Early termination

In this section, the procedural issues arising from a default are discussed. Most importantly, the clauses on close-out netting appear here.

14.2.7 Miscellaneous

The document includes various other clauses on the transfer of positions and contractual currency.

There is also a clause in which the parties agree that the contract is a principal-to-principal transaction.

Following litigation surrounding the issue of suitability and other fiduciary duties (discussed below), ISDA has released new wording to be included in the master agreement for counterparties to document the nature of their relationship.

The clauses state that each party agrees it is acting for its own account and has made its own decision on the merits of the transaction and is not relying on the other party's advice.

ISDA suggests that such wording be included in the schedule or as a new schedule.

15 Litigation

Any discussion of OTC regulation would not be complete without mentioning some important US and UK court cases.

15.1 Court cases

15.1.1 Hazell vs Hammersmith and Fulham LBC

Arguably the most famous of all, these were cases that confirmed that local authorities did not have the legal power to enter into interest rate swap transactions. It is from this and a string of similar cases that the industry's preoccupation with the authority of the parties to enter into trades has stemmed.

In the wake of the House of Lords' decision in Hazell vs Hammersmith and Fulham, a large number of cases were brought by banks to try and recover payments made under these void contracts.

15.1.2 Westdeutsche Landesbank vs Islington LBC

In this case, the bank had made an upfront payment at the inception of the swap and sought recovery of this amount following the decision that the contracts were void.

The bank's case ended in the House of Lords, which held that where money is paid over under a contract that is subsequently found to be *ultra vires* and therefore void, restitution should be made.

15.1.3 Bankers Trust International plc vs Dharmala

This UK case is mirrored by a number of US cases against Bankers Trust. They involve two key issues – misrepresentation and whether Bankers Trust owed Dharmala a duty of care.

The case involved transactions in a range of barrier swaps and like the US cases, difficulties arose from the unanticipated rise of US interest rates in early 1994.

The following swap exemplifies the structure.

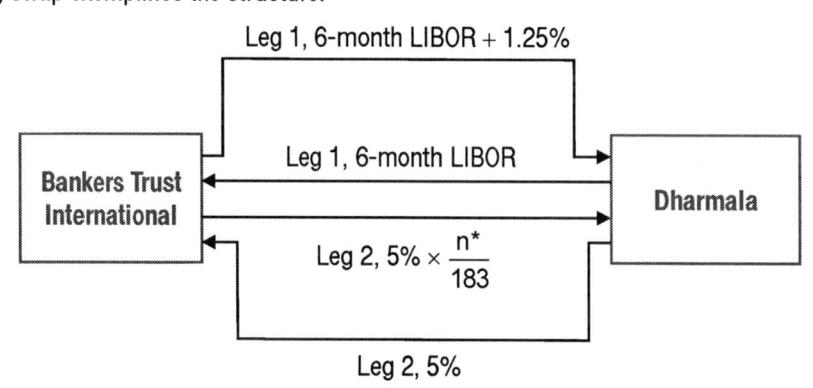

```
                    Leg 1, 6-month LIBOR + 1.25%
         ┌──────────────────────────────────────┐
         │                                      │
    ┌─────────────┐   Leg 1, 6-month LIBOR   ┌──────────┐
    │  Bankers    │◄─────────────────────────│          │
    │   Trust     │──────────────────────────►│ Dharmala │
    │International│◄──────────────────────────│          │
    └─────────────┘   Leg 2, 5% × n*/183     └──────────┘
         │                                      │
         └──────────────────────────────────────┘
                         Leg 2, 5%
```

* Where n = number of days in six-month period, where US six-month LIBOR was less than 4.125%.

Under this swap, there were two legs. Leg 1 provided that if US interest rates remained low, Dharmala would make 1.25%. However, under the second leg of the trade, if US six-month LIBOR rates were to rise above 4.125% for an entire six-month period (as happened), Dharmala would end up paying Bankers Trust a net 3.75% interest [5% less the 1.25% gained on Leg 1].

Dharmala defaulted on the swap and Bankers Trust initiated proceedings to try and recover some $64m.

In the case, Dharmala alleged that Bankers Trust had misrepresented the swap, highlighting the rewards and not the risk. Dharmala also claimed that Bankers Trust owed it a very significant duty of care, including a duty to advise of the risks and to ensure that the swaps were safe and suitable products for the company.

Ultimately, the court ruled in Bankers Trusts' favour, finding that the facts had not been misrepresented and that no duty of suitability was owed to Dharmala, whom the court deemed more than capable of understanding the transaction.

The case is important in that it shows the court's willingness to hold counterparties to their contracts.

As would be expected, there are a far greater number of US cases involving OTC derivatives. Many of these involve jurisdictional questions concerned with interpretations of the CEA and Securities Act. Others deal with the enforceability of contracts and *ultra vires* claims. However, the most recent cases, involving Procter and Gamble and Orange Country have, like the Dharmala case in the UK, revolved around misrepresentation and suitability.

The Procter and Gamble case was ultimately settled out of court, but it is likely that New York courts will take some convincing about fiduciary duties emerging in principal-to-principal contracts.

> "New York law is quite clear.....that a conventional business relationship does not become a judiciary relationship by mere allegation. Indeed [the Courts] have concluded that where parties deal at arm's length in a commercial transaction no relation of confidence or trust sufficient to find the existence of a fiduciary relationship will arise absent extraordinary circumstances."
>
> Sud-Americana de Vapores vs IBJ Schroder Bank & Trust Co.

As a footnote, it is interesting to note that despite the actions of Bankers Trust being upheld by the courts, the reputational damage sustained was enormous and necessitated a restructuring and refocusing of all the bank's activities.

15.2 Global Derivatives Study Group (G30) Report Recommendations for Dealers and End-Users

General Policies
Recommendation 1: The Role of Senior Management Dealers and end-users should use derivatives in a manner consistent with the overall risk management and capital policies approved by their boards of directors. These policies should be reviewed as business and market circumstances change. Policies governing derivatives use should be clearly defined, including the purposes for which these transactions are to be undertaken. Senior management should approve procedures and controls to implement these policies, and management at all levels should enforce them.
Valuation and Market Risk Management
Recommendation 2: Marking-to-Market Dealers should mark their derivatives positions to market on, at least, a daily basis for risk management purposes.
Recommendation 3: Market Valuation Methods Derivatives portfolios of dealers should be valued based on mid-market levels less specific adjustments, or on appropriate bid or offer levels. Mid-market valuation adjustments should allow for expected future costs such as unearned credit spread, close-out costs, investing and funding costs, and administrative costs.

17: THE REGULATORY ENVIRONMENT

Recommendation 4: Identifying Revenue Sources

Dealers should measure the components of revenue regularly and in sufficient detail to understand the sources of risk.

Recommendation 5: Measuring Market Risk

Dealers should use a consistent measure to calculate daily the market risk of their derivatives positions and compare it to market risk limits.

Market risk is best measured as 'value at risk', using probability analysis based upon a common confidence interval (e.g. two standard deviations) and time horizon (e.g. a one-day exposure).

Components of market risk that should be considered across the term structure include absolute price or rate change (delta), convexity (gamma), volatility (vega), time decay (theta), basis or correlation, and discount rate (rho).

Recommendation 6: Stress Simulations

Dealers should regularly perform simulations to determine how their portfolios would perform under stress conditions.

Recommendation 7: Investing and Funding Forecasts

Dealers should periodically forecast the cash investing and funding requirements arising from their derivatives portfolios.

Recommendation 8: Independent Market Risk Management

Dealers should have a market risk management function, with clear independence and authority, to ensure that the following responsibilities are carried out.

- The development of risk limit policies and the monitoring of transactions and positions for adherence to these policies. (See Recommendation 5.)
- The design of stress scenarios to measure the impact of market conditions, however improbable, that might cause market gaps, volatility swings, or disruptions of major relationships, or might reduce liquidity in the face of unfavourable market linkages, concentrated market making, or credit exhaustion. (See Recommendation 6.)
- The design of revenue reports quantifying the contribution of various risk components, and of market risk measures such as value at risk. (See Recommendations 4 and 5).
- The monitoring of variance between the actual volatility of portfolio value and that predicted by the measure of market risk.
- The review and approval of pricing models and valuation systems used by front and back office personnel, and the development of reconciliation procedures if different systems are used.

Recommendation 9: Practices by End-Users

As appropriate to the nature, size and complexity of their derivatives activities, end-users should adopt the same valuation and market risk management practices that are recommended for dealers. Specifically, they should consider regularly marking-to-market their derivatives transactions for risk management purposes, periodically forecasting the cash investing and funding requirements arising from their derivatives transactions, and establishing a clearly independent and authoritative function to design and assure adherence to prudent risk limits.

Credit Risk Measurement and Management

Recommendation 10: Measuring Credit Exposure

- Dealers and end-users should measure credit exposure on derivatives in two ways.
- Current exposure, which is the replacement cost of derivatives transactions, that is, their market value and
- Potential exposure, which is an estimate of the future replacement cost of derivatives transactions. It should be calculated using probability analysis based upon broad confidence intervals (e.g. two standard deviations) over the remaining terms of the transactions.

Recommendation 11: Aggregating Credit Exposures

Credit exposures on derivatives, and all other credit exposures to a counterparty, should be aggregated taking into consideration enforceable netting arrangements. Credit exposures should be calculated regularly and compared to credit limits.

Recommendation 12: Independent Credit Risk Management

Dealers and end-users should have a credit risk management function with clear independence and authority, and with analytical capabilities in derivatives, responsible for

- Approving credit exposure measurement standards.
- Setting credit limits and monitoring their use.
- Reviewing credits and concentrations of credit risk.
- Reviewing and monitoring risk reduction arrangements.

Recommendation 13: Master Agreements

Dealers and end-users are encouraged to use one master agreement as widely as possible with each counterparty to document existing and future derivatives transactions, including foreign-exchange forwards and options. Master agreements should provide for payments netting and close-out netting, using a full two-way payments approach.

Recommendation 14: Credit Enhancement

Dealers and end-users should assess both the benefits and costs of credit enhancement and related risk reduction arrangements. Where it is proposed that credit downgrades would trigger early termination or collateral requirements, participants should carefully consider their own capacity and that of their counterparties to meet the potentially substantial funding needs that might result.

Enforceability

Recommendation 15: Promoting Enforceability

Dealers and end-users should work together on a continuing basis to identify and recommend solutions for issues of legal enforceability, both within and across jurisdictions, as activities evolve and new types of transactions are developed.

Systems, Operations and Controls

Recommendation 16: Professional Expertise

Dealers and end-users must ensure that their derivatives activities are undertaken by professionals in sufficient number and with the appropriate experience, skill levels, and degrees of specialisation. These professionals include specialists who transact and manage the risks involved, their supervisors, and those responsible for processing, reporting, controlling and auditing the activities.

Recommendation 17: Systems

Dealers and end-users must ensure that adequate systems for data capture, processing, settlement, and management reporting are in place so that derivatives transactions are conducted in an orderly and efficient manner in compliance with management policies. Dealers should have risk management systems that measure the risks incurred in their derivatives activities, including market and credit risks.

End-users should have risk management systems that measure the risks incurred in their derivatives based upon their nature, size and complexity.

Recommendation 18: Authority

Management of dealers and end-users should designate who is authorised to commit their institutions to derivatives transactions.

Accounting and Disclosure

Recommendation 19: Accounting Practices

International harmonisation of accounting standards for derivatives is desirable. Pending the adoption of harmonised standards, the following accounting practices are recommended.

- Dealers should account for derivatives transactions by marking them to market, taking changes in value to income each period.

- End-users should account for derivatives used to manage risks so as to achieve a consistency of income recognition treatment between those instruments and the risks being managed. Thus, if the risk being managed is accounted for at cost (or, in the case of an anticipatory hedge, not yet recognised), changes in the value of a qualifying risk management instrument should be deferred until a gain or loss is recognised on the risk being managed. Or, if the risk being managed is marked to market with changes in value being taken to income, qualifying risk management instrument should be treated in a comparable fashion.

- End-users should account for derivatives not qualifying for risk management treatment on a mark-to-market basis.

- Amounts due to and from counterparties should only be offset when there is a legal right to set off or when enforceable netting arrangements are in place.

Where local regulations prevent adoption of these practices, disclosure along these lines is nevertheless recommended.

Recommendation 20: Disclosures

Financial statements of dealers and end-users should contain sufficient information about their use of derivatives to provide an understanding of the purposes for which transactions are undertaken, the extent of the transactions, the degree of risk involved, and how the transactions have been accounted for. Pending the adoption of harmonised accounting standards, the following disclosures are recommended.

- Information about management's attitude to financial risks, how instruments are used, and how risks are monitored and controlled.

- Accounting policies.

- Analysis of positions at the balance sheet date.

- Analysis of the credit risk inherent in those positions.

- For dealers only, additional information about the extent of their activities in financial instruments.

17: THE REGULATORY ENVIRONMENT

Recommendations for Legislators, Regulators and Supervisors
Recommendation 21: Recognising Netting Regulators and supervisors should recognise the benefits of netting arrangements where and to the full extent that they are enforceable, and encourage their use by reflecting these arrangements in capital adequacy standards. Specifically, they should promptly implement the recognition of the effectiveness of bilateral close-out netting in bank capital regulations.
Recommendation 22: Legal and Regulatory Uncertainties Legislators, regulators and supervisors, including central banks, should work in collaboration with dealers and end-users to identify and remove any remaining legal and regulatory uncertainties with respect to - The form of documentation required to create legally enforceable agreements (statute of frauds). - The capacity of parties, such as governmental entities, insurance companies, pension funds and building societies, to enter into transactions (ultra vires). - The enforceability of bilateral close-out netting and collateral arrangements in bankruptcy. - The enforceability of multibranch netting arrangements in bankruptcy. - The legality/enforceability of derivatives transactions.
Recommendation 23: Tax Treatment Legislators and tax authorities are encouraged to review and, where appropriate, amend tax laws and regulations that disadvantage the use of derivatives in risk management strategies. Tax impediments include the inconsistent or uncertain tax treatment of gains and losses on the derivatives, in comparison with the gains and losses that arise from the risks being managed.
Recommendation 24: Accounting Standards Accounting standards-setting bodies in each country should, as a matter of priority, provide comprehensive guidance on accounting and reporting of transactions in financial instruments, including derivatives, and should work toward international harmonisation of standards on this subject. Also, the International Accounting Standards Committee should finalise its accounting standard on financial instruments.

Source: *Derivatives: Practices and Principles*, The Group of Thirty, 1993

16 TAXATION

Below is a summary of the tax treatment of financial futures and options transactions by different types of institution.

16.1 Pension funds

Profits from transactions in futures and options are exempt from tax whether they arise from capital or trading transactions. This tax exemption applies regardless of the frequency of transactions.

16.2 Authorised unit trusts

As with pension funds, all dealings in futures and options by authorised unit trusts are exempt from tax, whether they are capital or trading transactions.

16.3 Investment trusts

Profits from capital transactions are exempt from tax, whilst other profits are taxed as income.

If a transaction in futures and options is to reduce the economic risk of a portfolio, then this is regarded as a capital transaction and therefore exempt of tax. Other transactions clearly ancillary to this aim are also exempt, but if the aim is not clear, it will be a question of fact as to whether it will be treated as a capital transaction. Clear documentation is therefore essential to help determine the use to which futures and options are being made.

16.4 Charities

The use of futures and options by charities will not attract tax. Any profits will generally be classified as capital and are exempt of tax.

16.5 Banks and building societies

Profits from futures and options will be treated as trading profits and therefore taxed as income.

16.6 Insurance companies

Profit will be treated as trading and taxed as income, or capital and taxed under Capital Gains Tax rules.

For all of the above, there are exceptions. The above should be regarded as the general rules.

16.7 Private investors

The taxation of futures and options for a private investor comes under Capital Gains Tax rules. More specifically, the rules are as follows.

16.7.1 Options

For private investors, quoted and traded options are subject to Capital Gains Tax. Purchase of an option is acquisition of an asset, the premium being the cost.

Buying options

If the option is allowed to expire worthless, the abandonment is treated as a disposal for CGT purposes, giving a capital loss on the date of expiry.

If a call option is exercised, the purchase price of the shares will be treated as being the total cost of purchase, i.e. the exercise price plus the original premium. If a put option is exercised, the proceeds will be the exercise price and the premium cost will be treated as part of allowable deductions.

Writing options

Writing an option is initially treated as disposing of an asset where the allowable deductions are zero. The capital gain is therefore given by the premium received. If the option expires worthless, this is the end of the story.

If the option is subsequently exercised, the writing and exercise of the option will be treated as part of the same transaction. For a call option, the total proceeds to the writer will be the premium plus the exercise price of the option, and the allowable deductions will be the cost of buying the relevant shares. For a put option, the purchase price of the shares (being the exercise price of the option) will be reduced by the premium received.

Where an option writer closes out his position by buying an option himself, the two options are dealt with separately for tax purposes.

16.7.2 Futures

Upon closing out a futures position, any money received is treated as consideration for the disposal of the futures contract, and any money paid is treated as an incidental cost of disposal.

If the futures contract is not closed out, then each party is treated as having disposed of an asset consisting of that entitlement or liability. Any payment made or received is treated as consideration for, or incidental cost of, the disposal respectively.

Chapter Roundup

- The Financial Services and Markets Act 2000 (FSMA 2000) created the Financial Services Authority (FSA) as the overall statutory regulator of the UK financial services industry.

- The current regulatory regime has grown out of the experience of a number of regulatory failures.

- FSMA 2000 is supported by detailed secondary legislation.

- No person may carry on a regulated activity in or into the UK unless authorised or exempt (the 'general prohibition').

- Regulated activities and the specified investments covered by regulation are defined in the Regulated Activities Order 2001, as amended.

- Activities excluded from the Regulated Activities Order include dealing as principal, trustees and personal representatives and overseas persons.

- Exempt persons include appointed representatives, members of designated professional bodies and members of the Lloyd's insurance market.

- Authorisation is usually by obtaining 'Part IV' permission from the FSA. The applicant firm must show that it is 'fit and proper' and must meet the Threshold Conditions.

- As well as being the regulator of the banking system and the investment and insurance industries, the FSA acts as the UK Listing Authority.

- The FSA has wide powers and has statutory immunity from prosecution unless it acts in bad faith or in breach of human rights legislation.

- The FSA's four statutory objectives are: maintaining confidence in the financial system, promoting public understanding, protecting consumers, reduction of financial crime.

- The FSA is accountable to HM Treasury, which appoints the Board and Chairman.

- The FSA has functions in supervising authorised firms and approved persons, enforcement of rules and decision-making.

- A risk-based approach is taken to supervision of firms, based on an impact and probability assessment of each firm.

- The FSA has extensive enforcement rights, covering information gathering, investigation, varying permission and withdrawing authorisation.

- The FSA may take sanctions and issue public statements when any person has engaged in market abuse. It may prosecute authorised firms committing money laundering or certain other criminal offences.

- The Decision Making Manual sets out procedures to ensure that powers are exercised fairly.

- Under s150 FSMA 2000, a private person has a privileged right of action in damages if they suffer a loss resulting from an authorised person breaking a regulation.

- Hedge funds present special problems for regulators and further consultations are expected during 2007.

17: THE REGULATORY ENVIRONMENT

TEST YOUR KNOWLEDGE

Check your knowledge of the Chapter here, without referring back to the text.

1 When was 'N2'?

2 Identify three of the areas of regulatory failure which encouraged the establishment of the statutory post-'N2' system of regulation of the UK financial services industry.

3 A firm carrying on regulated activities which involve specified investments is required to be authorised by the FSA unless either the activity is .... or the firm is .... *Fill in the blanks.*

4 Which of the following is *not* exempt from the authorisation requirement?

　A　An independent financial adviser
　B　An appointed representative
　C　A local authority
　D　A Recognised Investment Exchange

5 The FSA's four objectives have been laid down by:

　A　The FSA Board
　B　The Financial Services and Markets Tribunal
　C　The European Commission
　D　Parliament

6 Complaints against the FSA are handled by:

　A　The Financial Ombudsman Service
　B　The Financial Services and Markets Tribunal
　C　The Complaints Commissioner
　D　The Practitioner Panel

7 What does the acronym **ARROW** stand for, as applied to the FSA's approach to supervision?

8 In cases of market abuse, the FSA is empowered to take action against:

　A　Any approved person or authorised firm only
　B　Any approved person only
　C　Any authorised firm only
　D　Any person

9 S150 FSMA 2000 gives a right of action in damages against an authorised person who has contravened FSA rules. This right of action can be exercised by:

　A　The FSA only
　B　Any approved person or authorised firm only
　C　Any private person only
　D　Any person

17: THE REGULATORY ENVIRONMENT

Test Your Knowledge: Answers

1. The date known as N2 was 30 November 2001. (See 1.1.)

2. You could have mentioned any three of: pensions mis-selling, BCCI, Barings Bank, Sumitomo. (See 1.2.)

3. A firm carrying on regulated activities which involve specified investments is required to be authorised by the FSA unless either the activity is *an excluded activity* or the firm is *exempt*. (See 2.2.)

4. You should have chosen Option A. An IFA is not exempt from authorisation. (See 2.7.)

5. The objectives are statutory and are set out in FSMA 2000. Therefore D is the correct answer. (See 4.2.)

6. The Complaints Commissioner has this responsibility – Option C. (See 4.5.4.)

7. **A**djusted **R**isk **R**eturn **O**peration frame**W**ork. (See 5.2.1.)

8. D is the correct choice. The FSA can take action against any person. (See 5.3.12.)

9. C is the correct choice. A 'private person' is an individual not carrying out a regulated activity and businesses not acting in the course of business. (See 6.)

INDEX

Asset swap, 432
Asset-backed securities, 490
Assumptions of DCF, 80

Bank of England, 337
   Expectations theory, 339
   Liquidity preference, 339
   Preferred habitat, 340
   Yield curve, 338
Binomial distribution, 103, 105
   Binomial expression, 103
   Negatively skewed, 106
   Positively skewed, 105
   Symmetrical, 105
   Use of the binomial expression, 104
Binomial model, 194
   American style options, 205
   Continuous compounding, 195
   Currency options, 208
   Discrete compounding, 196
   Equity index option, 207
   Expected percentage downmove, 195
   Expected percentage upmove, 195
   Hedge ratio, 201
   Multi-period binomial, 197
   Non-annual interest rate, 199
   Non-annual volatility, 200
   Probability of an upmove, 195
   Single period binomial, 194
Black Scholes, 208
   American style, 217
   Assumptions underlying the Black Scholes option pricing model, 215
   Basic Black Scholes, 208
   Black Model, 219
   Currency options, 217
   Dividends paid before expiry, 217
   Equity index, 217
   European options, 208
   Garman-Kohlhagen, 219
   Heath-Jarrow-Morton model, 219
   Implied volatilities, 220
   Known Dividend Model, 219
   Options on futures, 218
   Pseudo-American model, 219
   Roll-Geshe-Whaley model, 219
Bond, 276
   Bond coupon, 278
   Maturity, 277
   Nominal value, 277
Bond pricing, 280
   Clean and dirty pricing, 286
   Cum div bargain, 286
   DCF evaluation, 280
   Ex-div bargain, 288
   Floating rate bond, 284
   Semi-annual coupon, 283
Bond risks, 294
   Duration, 296
Bond yield, 288
   Flat yield, 289
   Gross redemption yield, 291
   Japanese GRY, 290

Callable bond, 459, 478
   Callable bond value, 478
Cap, floor and collar
   Cap, 450
   Captions, 453
   Swaptions, 453
Cap, floor and collar, 450
   Collar, 452
   Floor, 452
   Floptions, 453
Capped floaters, 460
Clearing and settlement, 39
   Independent guarantee, 40, 56
   London Clearing House, 40
   Mutual guarantee, 40
   Recognised Clearing House, 40
   Registrar and guarantor, 40
Clients orders, 28
   Closing settlement prices, 29
   Cross transactions, 28
   Dispute, 29
   Fast market, 29
   Improper Trades, 29
   Trading cards, 29
Collared floater, 460
Commodity swap, 427
Contracts for differences, 53
Controlling risk, 509
   Counterparty limit, 509
   Country limit, 509
   Dealer limits, 511
   Instrument limits, 510
   Liquidity limit, 510
   Regulatory limits, 510

INDEX

Convertible bond, 474
   Conversion ratio, 474
   Intrinsic value, 475
   Time value, 476
   Valuation of convertibles, 475
Convexity, 300
   Convexity formula, 301
   Use of convexity, 302
Credit derivatives, 454
   A credit spread swap, 456
   Credit default swap, 454
   Credit spread option, 457
   Total return swap, 455
Credit risk, 506
   Counterparty risk, 506
   Delivery (or settlement) risk, 507

Delayed reset swap, 460
Deleveraged floating rate note, 459
Delivery, 47
   Cash settled, 49
   Closing a long position, 52
   EDSP, 48
   Exercise options before expiry, 50
   Scaling factor, 48
   Sellers choices, 47
Dual currency bonds, 487
Duration, 296
   Macaulay duration, 297
   Uses of duration, 297

Equities hedging, 262
   Equities hedge with index futures, 262
   Locked in value, 264, 265
   Period of the hedge, 264
   Protecting equities with options, 266
Equity linked high income bond, 457
Equity options, 256
Equity swaps, 421
   Valuation of an equity swap, 422
Euronext.LIFFE, 24, 254, 305
   Euronext.LIFFE's Basis Trading, 305
Euronext.LIFFE membership, 26
   London Clearing House, 26
   Public Order Members, 27
Euronext.LIFFE trading rules, 28
   Basis trading, 28
   Standard contract specifications, 28
   Trading times, 28
Exotic options
   Digital, 463
Exotic options, 463
   An average-strike option, 466

Asian options, 466
Barrier option, 466
Bermudan, 463
Binary, 463
Chooser option, 465
Delayed option, 466
Exchange options, 469
Ladder option, 468
Lookback option, 466
Pay later or contingent option, 465
Quanto option, 469
Ratchet option, 468
Shout option, 468
Spread option, 469

Foreign exchange, 370
   Anticipated forward rate, 381
   Cross rate, 371
   Currency options, 383
   Forward rates, 372
   Interest rate parity, 373
   Spot rate, 371
   Use of currency futures, 379
Forward rate agreement, 444
   Actual settlement amount, 445, 470
   Contract periods, 446
   Gross settlement amount, 445, 470
Forward rate agreements
   Interest rate sensitivity, 448
FSA, 25
   Proper market, 25
   Proper trades, 25
FTSE 100 future, 255
FTSE 100 option, 257
Future, 3
   Hedgers, 7
   Long futures position, 5
   Long hedge, 9
   Obligations, 3
   Short futures position, 6
   Short hedge, 7
   Users of futures, 4
Futures price, 122
   Arbitrage, 125
   Arbitrage channel, 126
   Backwardation, 123
   Basis, 122
   Basis risk, 124
   Contango, 123
   Convergence, 126
   Cost of carry, 125
   Fair value, 124

Futures strategy, 186
    Basis trades, 187
    Intermarket spreads, 187
    Intramarket spreads, 186
    Stack hedge, 187
    Strip hedge, 187

Gilts, 279
Guarantee fund, 268

Hedging bonds, 316
    Basis point value, 317
    Hedging with futures, 317
    Hedging with options, 324
    Modified duration, 317

Index amortisation swap, 460
Interest rate derivatives, 340
    Cross-currency yield spread, 361
    Effective rate, 346
    Expected rate, 354
    Forward bid and forward offer prices, 344
    Hedging, 345
    Implied forward, 343
    Intermarket spread, 359
    Intramarket spread, 351
    Short-term interest rate futures prices, 342
    Stack hedge, 348
    Strip hedge, 348
    Three-month sterling, 341
    Yield curve spread, 359
Interest rate swap, 394
    All-in price, 396
    Asset swap, 395
    Bootstrapping, 411
    Coupon swap, 395
    Deferred start swap, 410
    Forward rates, 401
    Money market swap, 396
    Spot rates, 401
    Swap spread, 396
    Term swap, 395
    Termination and assignment, 397
    Valuing an interest rate swap, 403
Internal rate of return, 76
    Interpolation, 77

Leveraged diff floater, 462
Liquidity risk, 507
Lognormal distribution, 111
Long Gilt Future, 306
    Cheapest to deliver, 310
    Fair value of a bond future, 308
    Futures price, 311
    Gross basis, 309
    Implied repo rate, 314
Long-term currency swap, 417
    Circus swap, 418
    Cross-currency basis swaps, 418
    Cross-currency coupon swaps, 418
    Valuation of a long-term currency swap, 420

Margin, 41
    Automatic exercise, 53
    Collateral, 46
    Initial margin, 41
    Maintenance margin, 44
    Marking-to-market, 43
    SPAN, 45
    Variation margin, 43
Market risk, 501
    Currency risk, 502
    Economic exposures, 503
    Interest rate risk, 505
    Transaction exposures, 502
    Translation exposure, 503
Modified duration, 298
    Modified duration formula, 298
    Use of modified duration, 298
Money market instruments, 334
    Bill of exchange, 336
    Certificate of deposit, 337
    Commercial paper, 337
    Deposits, 334
    Medium-term notes, 337
    Short-term gilts, 337
    Treasury bill, 335
Money markets, 334
Mortgage derivative, 487
    Accrual bonds, 488
    Collateralised mortgage obligations, 487
    Companion bond, 488
    Floating rate tranches, 489
    Interest-only securities, 490
    Inverse floaters, 489
    Planned amortisation class, 488
    Principal-only securities, 489
    Residual, 489
    Reverse floaters, 489
    Sequential pay tranches, 487
    Super floater, 489
    Super POs, 490
    Targeted amortisation class, 488
    Z bonds, 488
    Zero-coupon bonds, 488

INDEX

Non-generic or exotic swaps, 429
    Accreting swap, 429
    Amortising swap, 429
    Generic swaps, 429
    Off-market swap, 429
    Rollercoaster swap, 429
    Zero-coupon swap, 429
Normal distribution, 106
    Calculate probabilities, 107
    Characteristics, 107

Operational risk, 508
    Breach of the law, 508
    Cost control, 508
    Environmental, 508
    Errors, 508
    Fraud, 508
    Legal, 508
    Reputation, 508
    System failure, 508
Option, 10, 22
    American style, 12
    Buying a call, 14
    Buying a put, 16
    Call option, 11
    Covered, 12
    European style, 12
    Exercise, 12
    Exercise price, 12
    Expiry date, 12
    Holder, 11
    Options gearing, 17
    Options on futures, 17
    Premium, 11, 13
    Put option, 11
    Selling a call, 15
    Selling a put, 16
    Strike price, 12
    Writer, 11
    Writing a call, 15
    Writing a put, 16
Option embedded bond value, 483
Option sensitivities, 222
    Delta, 222
    Delta of a call, 231
    Delta of a put, 231
    Gamma, 226
    Hedge ratio, 232
    Rho, 229
    Theta, 228
    Vega, 229
Option strategies, 152
    Arbitrage, 153
    Bear spread, 163
    Bearish, 153
    Box, 183, 184
    Bull spread, 162
    Bullish, 153
    Combinations, 153
    Conversions, 181
    Covered call/synthetic short put, 184
    Cylinder, 171
    Diagonal spread, 154, 170
    Directional, 153
    Horizontal spread, 154, 180
    Long butterfly, 177
    Long call, 158
    Long put, 159
    Long straddle, 172
    Long strangle, 174
    Options combinations, 156
    Options spread, 155
    Ratio back spread, 178
    Ratio spread, 179
    Reversals, 182
    Short butterfly, 176
    Short call, 161
    Short put, 160
    Short straddle, 173
    Short strangle, 175
    Spreads, 153
    Synthetic long, 164
    Synthetic long call, 166
    Synthetic long put, 169
    Synthetic short, 165
    Synthetic short call/covered put, 167
    Synthetic short put/covered call, 168
    Vertical spread, 154
    Volatility, 153
Option-adjusted spread, 490
    Option cost, 491
Option-free bond valuation, 479
    Arbitrage-free tree, 483
    Binomial, 481
    Binomial tree, 482
Options pricing, 128
    At-the-money, 129
    Convexity, 141
    Exercise price, 128
    Factors that affect the price of an option, 128
    Forecast volatility, 133
    Future volatility, 133
    Historic volatility, 133
    Implied volatility, 133
    Interest rates, 133
    In-the-money, 129
    Intrinsic value, 128
    Options price boundary conditions, 135

Out-of-the-money, 129
Put/call parity, 136
Time decay, 130
Time value, 129
Value of the underlying asset, 128
Volatility, 131
Order types, 30
Guarantee stops, 31
Limit order, 30
Market order, 30
Stop order, 31
Over-the-Counter, 19

Position limits, 30
Present value, 71
Annuity discount factor, 74
Discount factor, 72
Discount factor table, 75
Net present values, 73
Perpetuity discount factor, 74
Price limits, 30
Closing order, 32
Crossing, 33
Good till cancelled, 32
Limit order, 32
Market order on the close, 32
Market-if-touched orders, 31
Opening order, 32
Public limit orders, 32
Side orders, 32
Spread orders, 31
Stop limit order, 32
Time and sales, 33
Price return swap, 427
Pricing the FTSE 100 future, 258
Arbitrage channel, 259
Fair value, 259
Probability of an event, 96
Addition law, 102
Multiplication law, 101
NOT, 99
Sum of the probabilities, 98
Putable bond, 459, 478
Putable bond value, 479

Range notes, 458
Reverse diff floater, 462
Reverse floating rate note, 460

Short-term currency swap, 414
Swap-linked note, 459
Swaps, 392
Synthetic tracker fund, 267

Terminal/Future value, 68
Net terminal value, 70
Time value of money, 60
APR, 65
Compound interest, 62
Continuously compounded, 66
Simple interest, 61

Value at risk, 512
Historical returns, 519
Monte Carlo simulation, 520
Parametric, 513
Volatility, 81
Correlation, 83
Standard deviation, 81

Warrant, 492

INDEX